Teaching Secondary and Middle School Mathematics

RCF 8847

Daniel J. Brahier

Bowling Green State University

PEARSON

Boston   Columbus   Indianapolis   New York   San Francisco
Upper Saddle River   Amsterdam   Cape Town   Dubai   London   Madrid
Milan   Munich   Paris   Montreal   Toronto   Delhi   Mexico City   Sao Paulo
Sydney   Hong Kong   Seoul   Singapore   Taipei   Tokyo

Vice President and Editorial Director: Jeffery W. Johnston
Senior Acquisitions Editor: Kelly Villella Canton
Editorial Assistant: Annalea Manalili
Senior Marketing Manager: Darcy Betts
Production Manager: Susan Hannahs
Manager Central Design: Jayne Conte
Cover Designer: Bruce Kenselaar
Cover Art: Shutterstock
Full Service Project Manager: Rashmi Tickyani/Aptara®, Inc.
Composition: Aptara®, Inc.
Text Printer and Bindery: Edwards Brothers Malloy
Cover Printer: Lehigh-Phoenix Color
Text Font: Sabon

Photo Credits: Daniel Brahier: pp. 18, 35, 58, 89, 119, 143, 174, 224, 350, 374; © Thomas Imo/Alamy, p. 260; Layland Masuda/Shutterstock.com, p. 303; Michaeljung/Shutterstock.com, p. 326.

Common Core State Standards © Copyright 2010.

Credits and acknowledgments borrowed from other sources and reproduced, with permission, in this textbook appear on the appropriate page within the text.

Library of Congress Cataloging-in-Publication Data
Brahier, Daniel J.
  Teaching secondary and middle school mathematics / Daniel J. Brahier.—4th ed.
    p. cm.
  Includes bibliographical references and index.
  ISBN-13: 978-0-13-269811-5
  ISBN-10: 0-13-269811-0
  1. Mathematics—Study and teaching (Middle school)   2. Mathematics—Study and teaching (Secondary)   I. Title.
  QA11.2.B73 2013
  510.71'2—dc23   2012002676

10 9 8 7 6 5 4 3 2 1

ISBN 10:   0-13-269811-0
ISBN 13: 978-0-13-269811-5

This book is dedicated to my father, Frank, who has taught me the values of patience and persistence, and to the memory of my mother, Joyce, who was the author of the first book in the Brahier family and a source of support and love beyond imagination . . . "the finest of teachers I've ever known."

About the Author

Daniel Brahier is a professor of mathematics education at Bowling Green State University in Ohio and the Director of the Science and Math Education in ACTION scholarship program at BGSU. He also teaches junior high (Grades 7 and 8) mathematics at St. Rose School in Perrysburg, Ohio. He has worked in the field of education for more than 31 years, having served as a high school and middle school mathematics teacher, a science teacher, a guidance counselor, a high school principal, and a district curriculum coordinator before assuming a full-time position at the university level. He is a past president of the Ohio and the Greater Toledo Councils of Teachers of Mathematics and is the author of five books on teaching mathematics. He has written extensively for publications of the National Council of Teachers of Mathematics, and has served on the Editorial Panel for *Mathematics Teaching in the Middle School* journal. He has lectured on mathematics education in Canada, Mexico, Australia, Germany, and Singapore, in addition to school districts throughout the United States. The father of three sons, Dr. Brahier spends his free time writing and recording music, as well as hiking and camping with his wife and sons.

Contents

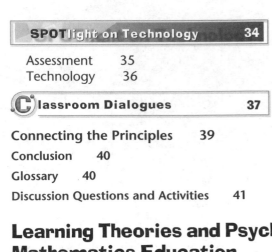

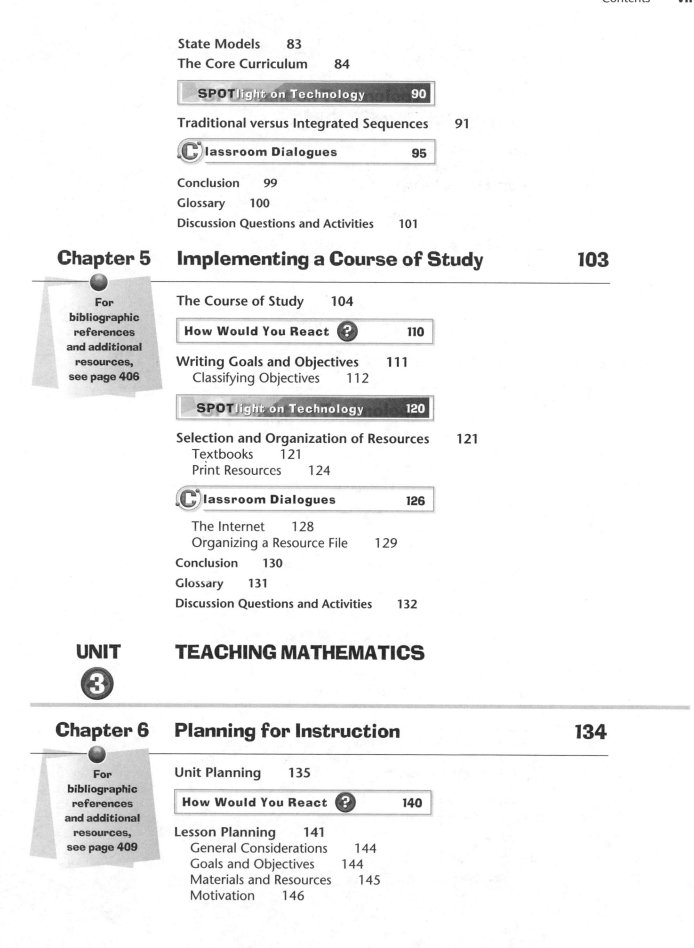

Chapter 7   Teaching Tools and Strategies   167

For bibliographic references and additional resources, see page 411

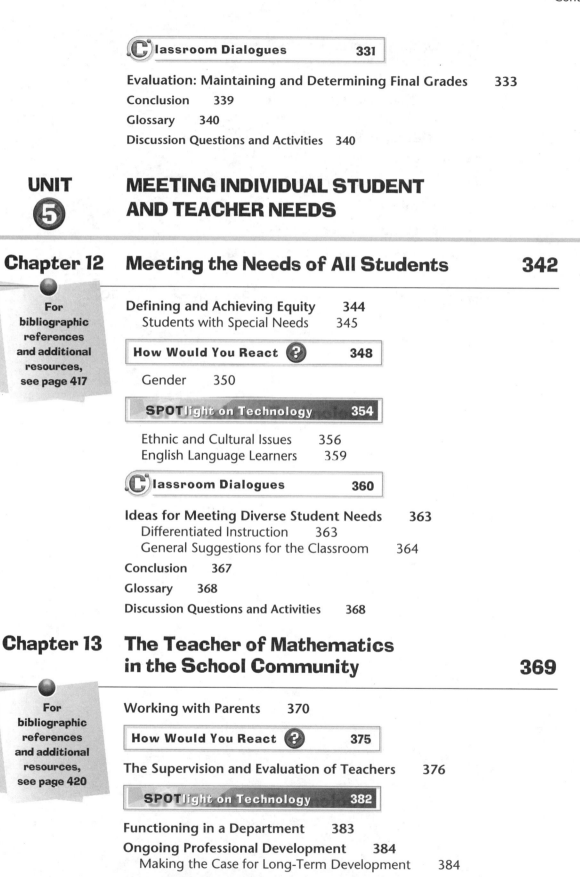

Preface

Teaching secondary and middle school mathematics has never been more exciting than it is today. The *Common Core State Standards*, released in 2010, as well as *Principles and Standards for School Mathematics* by the National Council of Teachers of Mathematics (NCTM) in 2000 both promoted a comprehensive mathematics curriculum for all students, rooted in significant research on how students learn mathematics and the role of technology in the teaching and learning process. In 2007, NCTM released the second edition of its teaching standards document, now entitled *Mathematics Teaching Today*. Meanwhile, the ongoing Trends in International Mathematics and Science Study has resulted in the most comprehensive international comparisons of mathematics education that have ever been conducted.

In the midst of all of the reform efforts that have been put in motion, it is important that teacher candidates and inservice teachers investigate the nature of the mathematics curriculum and reflect on research-based "best practices" as they define and sharpen their own personal styles. The format of the fourth edition of *Teaching Secondary and Middle School Mathematics* is designed to provide the reader with the total picture of the multifaceted art of teaching.

What Is New to the Fourth Edition?

The fourth edition of *Teaching Secondary and Middle School Mathematics* features a number of significant changes and enhancements:

- A brand-new chapter elaborates on the vision for teaching the major content strands in the secondary and middle school mathematics curriculum. The former Chapter 8 has been expanded into two chapters—Chapters 8 and 9—to provide a more in-depth look at reasoning and sense making in the classroom, as well as curriculum and teaching strategies for number sense, algebra, geometry, statistics and probability, and discrete mathematics—specific content areas. These two chapters provide the reader with several detailed lesson plans as well as 60 field-tested, practical teaching ideas that can readily be expanded into full lessons.
- Chapter 4, "Curricular Models," was completely revised to reflect the *Common Core State Standards* (CCSS), released in 2010 and used in more than 45 states and territories. At the same time, information on the NCTM Standards was maintained for users whose states may not be implementing the CCSS, as well as to provide background for where the CCSS has its roots. References to features of the CCSS are integrated throughout the

entire book. Chapter 4 also includes new information on integrated versus traditional curricular sequences and considerably more detail on how curricular models affect middle school classrooms. Similarly, Chapter 1 now includes a section on the mathematical practices outlined in the CCSS and how they parallel the five mathematical processes described in the NCTM Standards.

- Chapter 5, "Implementing a Course of Study" now addresses the idea of how to implement state and national standards, including a discussion of backward design and how to "unpack" a standard, as opposed to simply teaching to behavioral objectives.
- Chapter 7, "Teaching Tools and Strategies," now includes a discussion of how the mathematics teacher is also a literacy teacher and how students develop their reading skills in the mathematics classroom. Some reading and comprehension ideas are presented with examples of how they can be used in teaching mathematics.
- Chapter 12, "Meeting the Needs of All Students," was expanded to include a more in-depth discussion of how teachers' understanding (or misconceptions) about diversity affect the way that they run their classrooms. Also, a new section on English language learners addresses the issue of teaching mathematics to students who are not fluent in speaking English.
- Each chapter now includes three different features to spark classroom discussions, which have been revised, with features new to the fourth edition now appearing in Chapters 8 and 9. One of these is entitled "Classroom Dialogues," which begins with a conversation between a student (or group of students) and the teacher about some mathematical problem or idea, taking the reader directly into a classroom situation. Following the scenario, the reader is challenged with several questions regarding mathematics content, as well as a discussion of ideas for the reader to keep in mind when faced with a similar situation. "How Would You React?" describes a classroom situation—from students forgetting to bring a calculator to class to the teacher discovering that students have been cheating—and provides the reader with a variety of choices that a teacher can make, together with suggestions on how to handle the issue. Finally, "Spotlight on Technology" highlights a different form of current technology in each chapter, describing how technology can be used for teaching or professional development.

Every chapter in the book has been updated with the latest information, revised citations, and additional bibliographic resources.

How Is the Book Structured?

The book is divided into five units:

1. What Does It Mean to "Do," "Teach," and "Learn" Mathematics?
2. The Mathematics Curriculum
3. Teaching Mathematics
4. Assessment in Mathematics
5. Meeting Individual Student and Teacher Needs

Unit 1 consists of three chapters that prompt the reader to think about the nature of mathematics and the psychology of student learning. Chapter 1 introduces the reader to the notion of mathematics as a process—a verb—and describes the mathematical practices that underlie the Common Core State Standards. (The *Common Core State Standards for Mathematics* is abbreviated in some publications as CCSS-Math or CCSS-M. In this book, the simple abbreviation of CCSS is used, with the assumption that "mathematics" is the subject area.) Chapter 2 describes the six principles that are necessary for creating an effective mathematics program. Contemporary research on how students learn mathematics and develop dispositions toward the content area is presented through numerous classroom examples in Chapter 3. The two chapters comprising Unit 2 deal with the mathematics curriculum. Chapter 4 provides descriptions of current curricular issues, such as advantages and drawbacks to a school offering a "traditional" curriculum of Algebra, Geometry, and Algebra II versus an integrated sequence of courses. The issue of promoting a core curriculum for *all* students is also discussed in Chapter 4, whereas Chapter 5 describes the nature of a local course of study and how to write and classify objectives. The reader is also exposed to the philosophy of several reform curriculum projects funded by the National Science Foundation.

The four chapters of Unit 3 illustrate in detail the teacher's role in planning and teaching mathematics. Chapter 6 outlines the unit and lesson planning process; Chapter 7 examines the role of the teacher in the effective implementation of a lesson plan, including the use of various tools for the promotion of classroom discourse. Chapter 8 has been revised and expanded into Chapter 9, which is new to the fourth edition. These chapters feature descriptions of what it means to promote reasoning and sense making in the classroom as well as how to effectively teach number sense, algebra, geometry, statistics and probability, and discrete mathematics topics in secondary and middle school classrooms. The two chapters feature a total of 65 sample lesson plans and field-tested classroom activities that are "ready to use."

Unit 4 turns the reader's attention to the assessment process and begins in Chapter 10 with a detailed discussion on how to write a mathematics test and then expands the role of assessment to include alternative strategies that are available to teachers. Chapter 11 addresses the NCTM assessment standards, as well as practical matters such as assigning and checking homework, managing a grade book, and determining final grades in a course. The final unit focuses on meeting individual needs, both in terms of needs that students have in the classroom and that teachers have in their ongoing professional development. Chapter 12 has been significantly revised and addresses practical considerations of achieving equity in the mathematics classroom. This chapter focuses on special needs students, gender equity, ethnic and cultural diversity, English language learners, and general suggestions for differentiating instruction to meet the needs of all students. Finally, Chapter 13 discusses the role of the teacher in the school community and how the mathematics teacher interacts with students, parents, and administrators in a lifelong cycle of professional development.

The Appendix presents an annotated list of some of the best Web sites on the Internet for teacher and student use. These sites are organized by subject matter and cover a spectrum of topics from professional organizations to the Common Core State Standards and lesson plans. Each site is presented with its title, Internet address, and a short description of what can be found at the location. As Web sites often change addresses or content and are frequently added and deleted, the author has provided links at his site that will keep the Appendix updated and accurate. The reader should be aware that, while the author has made every effort to keep Web references in the Bibliography and throughout the text current, address changes are inevitable and beyond the author's control.

What Is the Best Way to Use the Book?

The book was written with both the instructor and the undergraduate or graduate methods student in mind. Given that some colleges and universities are on a quarter system, whereas others are on semesters, it is important to have a book that is realistic in terms of the number of chapters it contains. Therefore, the reading of approximately one chapter per week will enable a class to progress at a reasonable pace, because the chapters, by design, are roughly equal in length. The instructor may choose to follow the sequence of the book, which resulted from field-testing several alternatives. However, a class may have initial field experiences that require students to write lesson plans early in the course. Consequently, an instructor may choose to visit Unit 3 immediately after Chapters 1 and 2, which can serve as an introduction to Chapters 6 through 9 on lesson planning, teaching, and mathematics content issues. Later, a class may return to the psychological and curricular issues explored in Chapters 3 through 5. However, it is recommended that regardless of how Chapters 3 through 8 are sequenced, a class should generally begin with Chapters 1 and 2, which explore the nature of mathematics education, and finish with Chapter 13, which encourages the reader to view the process of professional development as a lifelong endeavor. Assessment and equity—the topics of Chapters 10, 11, and 12—can be addressed whenever the instructor sees it appropriate, although Chapter 10 is designed to precede Chapter 11. Some instructors emphasize the role of assessment in using a backward design approach to planning. In this case, an instructor may choose to address Unit IV on assessment prior to discussing curriculum and lesson planning.

Instructors may want to use the three features in each chapter—"How Would You React?," "Spotlight on Technology," and "Classroom Dialogues"—as catalysts for classroom discussions and debates on how to handle various content and discipline issues that arise when teaching mathematics. Methods students can write reflections on questions raised in these features or discuss the issues in small groups.

General topics, such as the appropriate use of manipulatives and effective classroom management techniques, are included in discussions throughout the book where the topics arise naturally in context. Each chapter begins with a list of anticipated outcomes and finishes with a "Conclusion" section that summarizes the chapter and sets up the reader for the next. Each chapter also includes a glossary of terms and discussion questions that provide the instructor with ideas for activities and classroom interaction points. Some instructors use the discussion questions as prompts for threaded debates on electronic discussion boards. An extensive bibliography with additional resources, including books, journal articles, Web sites, and other resource materials, for the reader and the instructor to consult for further information on the topics, is found at the end of the book. This resource list has been significantly expanded for the fourth edition.

The author's unique background as a secondary mathematics and science teacher, a middle school mathematics teacher, a guidance counselor, a high school principal, and a K–12 district curriculum consultant is evident as he explores the issues facing teachers of mathematics from many angles. The author is currently serving as a professor of mathematics education at the university level on a full-time basis but also teaches one section of a junior high (Grades 7 and 8) mathematics course in a local school every day. Also, the author has recently taken two sabbaticals from the university to immerse himself in different high schools as a full- and part-time teacher and department chair to reexamine the issues that teachers face every day in their jobs. Consequently, the examples used throughout the book are "real" and carefully described, based on more than 31 years of classroom teaching experience. Students in the author's mathematics methods courses have field-tested drafts of the book and its features and have provided detailed feedback to help in refining the book to its current form—one that is readable and interesting to a methods student. The fourth edition of *Teaching Secondary and Middle School Mathematics* features a mix of research-based theory, vignettes, and discussions of practical issues of teaching mathematics at the secondary and middle school levels. As such, the book can be used at both the undergraduate and graduate levels for secondary or middle school mathematics methods courses.

New! CourseSmart eTextbook Available

CourseSmart is an exciting new choice for students looking to save money. As an alternative to purchasing the printed textbook, students can purchase an electronic version of the same content. With a CourseSmart eTextbook, students can search the text, make notes online, print out reading assignments that incorporate lecture notes, and bookmark important passages for later review. For more information, or to purchase access to the CourseSmart eTextbook, visit www.coursesmart.com.

Supplements

Instructor's Resource Manual and Test Bank, prepared by Daniel Brahier, will help instructors design experiences and lead class discussions that challenge the thinking of methods students. This resource includes a **rationale** describing the purpose of each unit and an overview of how each unit fits into the course. The manual also includes the following for each chapter: an **overview** of the chapter, how it fits into the unit, and how it connects to the rest of the course; a list of **learning outcomes** from the book enhanced with additional descriptors for the instructor; field-tested **sample classroom activities**, including suggested problems, discussion questions, or other activities that complement the book discussions; blackline **reproducible masters** to assist the instructor in presenting major points and preparing PowerPoint slides; and **test bank items** for assessing student understanding of chapter contents, including approximately 50 multiple-choice questions, six essay questions, and three performance items that may be used as long-term student projects or explorations. Instructors should consult their Pearson representatives for guidance about downloading this manual from the Instructor Resource Center.

Acknowledgments

A book like this doesn't happen by itself; it takes a team of people surrounding the author to provide the research and support to see the project through to completion. First and foremost, I want to thank my family—my wife, Anne, our sons, John, Mark, and Luke, and our parents (Frank, Linda, Loretta, and James)—for their support and patience throughout the writing process over more than a decade. I am fortunate to be married to Anne, an outstanding secondary and middle school mathematics teacher and mother, who has consistently provided me with suggestions for making the book user friendly and accurate. I continue to be grateful to Bill Speer (University of Nevada–Las Vegas) and Jim Heddens (Professor Emeritus from Kent State University, Ohio) for their inspiration, wisdom, and advice in my writing career. I also wish to thank the reviewers for this edition: Barbara Hess, California University of Pennsylvania; Maribeth Juraska, Aurora University; and Anthony D. Thompson, East Carolina University. Thanks also to Kelly Villella Canton, Annalea Manalili, and Greg Erb at Pearson Education for believing in this project and for their guidance. Thanks as well to Rashmi Tickyani and Bret Workman for designing and copyediting the book. I particularly want to thank You-Mi Seo, my graduate student at Bowling Green State University (BGSU), who spent countless hours conducting research for updating references and the bibliography. I am also very grateful to Sarah Keane, Jenna Vermilya, and Rhonda Aguiton in the Mathematics Education Office at BGSU who have assisted in various stages of preparation of this fourth edition of the book and its instructor's manual, from reviewing drafts from a student perspective to conducting research. I wish to thank my students at St. Rose School in Perrysburg, as well as Notre Dame Academy and St. John's Jesuit High School in Toledo, who provided me with their reflections on many of the activities and teaching strategies described in the book. I am also grateful to the EDTL 3450, 3460, and 4740 students at BGSU who have used this book over the years and have given me extremely helpful input on how to improve its content. While my name is on the final product, this book and its revisions would not have been possible without the help and input of many people.

Mathematics as a Process

For a project in a Year I Integrated Mathematics class, Mr. James asked his students to think of an authentic example of a linear function that they have encountered in their lives. He asked his students to describe the function in words, to determine the independent and dependent variables, to generate a table of values, to write an equation based on the table, and to create a graph of the function. Finally, students were asked to present their functions to the class and were graded on their written papers and on the quality of their presentations. Mr. James listened to the presentations and read the papers enthusiastically because he was able to see his students applying their understanding of functions to their lives. However, the projects submitted by Francis and Joyce were different from those of the others in the class, and Mr. James immediately faced a decision about how to handle their examples. Francis's function was worded as follows:

The monthly fee for phone calls at my house is $10, which includes the first four outgoing calls. After that, every additional outgoing call costs another 50¢. The total cost for a month is a function of the number of outgoing calls.

Joyce's function problem was the following:

My family belongs to a fitness club. The club has a flat rate of $55.00 a month, but in order to reserve a racquetball court you have to pay an additional $8.00 per hour. If you want a court for a fraction of an hour, it always rounds up to the nearest hour (1.25 or 1.50 hours = 2 hours = $16). The total cost of membership for a month is a function of the number of hours of court time reserved.

After reading Chapter 1, you should be able to answer the following questions:

- What do the results of national and international mathematics examinations tell us about current practices in mathematics education?
- What are the five process skills and the eight mathematical practices often associated with doing mathematics? How are they developed in the secondary and middle school mathematics programs?
- What should be the role of problem solving in the mathematics classroom?
- Can you list and illustrate several problem-solving strategies that can be promoted in the secondary and middle school mathematics classroom?
- What does it mean to "do," to "teach," and to "learn" mathematics?

When Mr. James read these papers, he recognized a "teachable moment"—an opportunity to use the two examples generated by the students as tools to get the class to consider functions that appeared to be simple and linear on the surface but were actually much more complex. So, the following day, he handed out a sheet with the two problems retyped and asked teams of four students to carefully draw a graph of the functions and to think of other functions they have encountered that had the same characteristics or behavior.

On careful inspection, students realized that the shape of Francis's graph depended on whether the number of outgoing calls was less than or greater than four. They modeled the problem by drawing the graph in Figure 1.1.

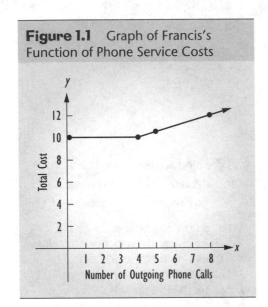

Figure 1.1 Graph of Francis's Function of Phone Service Costs

As students in the class presented their solutions, they shared similar examples, such as the cost of an on-line Internet service provider with a monthly access fee that includes a certain number of on-line hours, coupled with per-hour line charges after the number of free hours is exceeded. Mr. James recognized that, technically, the graph of Francis's function was not continuous; therefore, the individual points should not be connected to form a segment and a ray. He mentioned this point in passing but decided to save the discussion of "continuous" versus "discrete" for another day. More important, the students had discovered their first piecewise function with the rule:

$$f(x) = \begin{cases} 10 \text{ if } x \le 4 \\ 0.5x + 10 \text{ if } x > 4 \end{cases}$$

While exploring Joyce's function, students noticed that the monthly cost would be the same whether, for example, they reserved 2.25, 2.50, 2.75, or 3.0 hours of court time in a month. After some class discussion, they came up with the graph presented in Figure 1.2.

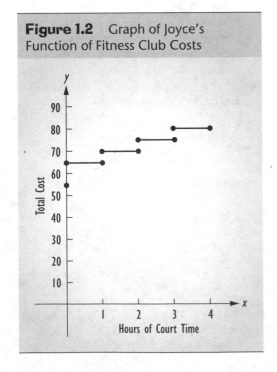

Figure 1.2 Graph of Joyce's Function of Fitness Club Costs

Toni then raised her hand and said, "That's not exactly right. If you rent the court for one hour, you pay a total of $63, but the graph has a point above both $63 and $71. Only one of those points can actually be there, or it doesn't make any sense." Mr. James validated Toni's statement by showing the class how an "open point" can be placed at the left end of each segment to avoid the confusion. He went on to define Joyce's example as a *step function* because of its unique nature. Meanwhile, the class offered additional examples of step functions, such as postage cost that remains the same until a weight limit is reached, and then the price "steps up" to the next level.

Mr. James's classroom is not unusual; almost every day students raise important issues and ask questions that a teacher can use as a springboard for further discussion. In this sense, the students have the potential to steer the class and not simply be passive "sponges" that attempt to absorb mathematical content. Mr. James values the exploration of student ideas, and entered the teaching profession not only because he enjoyed mathematics but also because he was excited about having the chance to work with adolescents at a critical time in their development as students and young adults.

There are various reasons why people choose careers in mathematics education. In many cases, they experienced effective teaching in their own school endeavors and so they want to pass that same level of enthusiasm on to the next generation. Others were simply good at mathematics in school and, as a result of their interest in the subject area, decided to try teaching young adolescents. Still others have had unfortunate experiences with teachers of mathematics in school and want to try to improve the situation for future students. It is important for educators to reflect on the reasons for making a career choice and to discern whether their primary interest was mathematics, working with young students, or a combination of both. Although there is no formula for being an effective mathematics teacher, successful teaching requires a caring individual who is interested in both the field of mathematics and the development of students. This chapter introduces the discussion of mathematics teaching as a profession by examining trends in mathematics education over time and by evaluating various national and international assessments of student achievement.

National and International Assessment Data

In 1995, the most comprehensive international comparison of mathematics education in history was conducted. The Third International Mathematics and Science Study (TIMSS) report compared achievement, curriculum, and teaching practices in more than 50 countries around the world at the fourth, eighth, and twelfth grade levels. One of the questions[†] asked of seventh and eighth grade students was

If $3(x + 5) = 30$, then $x =$

A. 2

B. 5

C. 10

D. 95

This equation, most would agree, should be fairly simple for a 13-year-old to answer. In fact, by placing a thumb over the $x + 5$ expression, even a fourth or fifth grader should be able to reason that 3 must be multiplied by 10 to get a result of 30. So, in the parentheses, x would have to be equal to 5. However, in the United States, only 63 percent of seventh graders and less than 75 percent of eighth graders were able to answer this question correctly. In Japan and Korea, more than 90 percent of the eighth graders obtained a correct answer.

[†]The International Association for the Evaluational Achievement (IEA) granted permission to reproduce exemplary items from A. E. Beaton et al. (1996), *Mathematics Achievement in the Middle School Years* (Chestnut Hill, MA: Center for the Study of Testing, Evaluation, and Educational Policy). Reprinted by permission.

On another item, students were given the sequence of triangles shown in Figure 1.3:

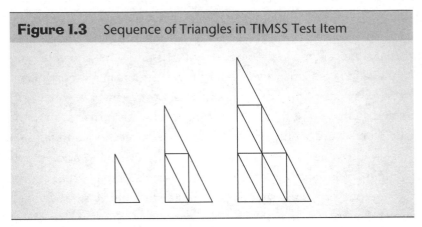

Figure 1.3 Sequence of Triangles in TIMSS Test Item

(Beaton et al., 1996. Reprinted with permission.)

The problem stated: "The sequence of similar triangles is extended to the eighth figure. How many small triangles would be needed for Figure 8?" An examination of the sequence reveals that the number of triangles required is always equal to the square of the figure number. Therefore, the eighth figure should need 64 (or 8^2) triangles. On this item, only 18 percent of the seventh graders and 25 percent of the eighth graders in the United States were able to give the correct answer. In Japan, the results were 43 percent and 52 percent, respectively.

On a geometry item for seventh and eighth graders, students were shown the diagram in Figure 1.4:

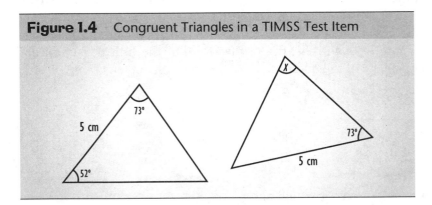

Figure 1.4 Congruent Triangles in a TIMSS Test Item

(Beaton et al., 1996. Reprinted with permission.)

The question read as follows: "These triangles are congruent. The measures of some of the sides and angles of the triangles are shown. What is the value of x?"

    A. 52
    B. 55
    C. 65
    D. 73
    E. 75

Fifteen percent of the seventh graders and 17 percent of the eighth graders in the United States answered this item correctly with choice B (55°). In Japan, 40 percent of the seventh graders and 69 percent of the eighth graders found the correct answer. In fact, students in 25 out of 26 countries outscored the United States on this geometry question that involves fairly typical middle school mathematical content.

The results of the 1996 TIMSS achievement test report not only placed eighth graders in the United States well below the international average, but also showed that the U.S. middle school and secondary curricula were less rigorous than those in most other countries, with an overemphasis on number skills and a deficiency in algebra and geometry. Reports from the study described the mathematics curriculum in the United States as "an inch deep and a mile wide," meaning that U.S. schools tend to address a great deal of content at a surface level that does not promote understanding of the underlying mathematics.

In 1999, the Third International Mathematics and Science Study–Repeat (TIMSS–R) was conducted. The major purpose of this study was to examine the performance of eighth graders on achievement tests 4 years after many of the same students were tested in the original TIMSS. Approximately one-third of the achievement test items used on the first TIMSS examination were repeated on the TIMSS–R. A total of 38 nations participated in the TIMSS–R study, 23 of which had also been involved in the first TIMSS.

The TIMSS–R achievement test placed U.S. eighth graders slightly above the average. While 27 of 40 nations (68 percent) outscored the United States at the eighth grade level in 1995, only 18 of 37 nations (49 percent) outscored the United States in 1999 (Gonzales et al., 2000). This result appears promising, except that one must also consider that when those same U.S. students were in the fourth grade (in 1995), they were outperformed by only 11 of 25 nations (44 percent). Statistically, the average score of eighth graders in 1999 was about the same as the scores of eighth graders in 1995. However, the performance levels of eighth graders in 1999, relative to the same nations tested in 1995 when they were fourth graders, declined. In other words, U.S. students' achievement levels dropped on an international scale as they progressed from fourth to eighth grade between 1995 and 1999. Also, the TIMSS–R results showed that students in the United States continued to have their greatest difficulty in the areas of geometry and measurement.

As the TIMSS–R data were being collected, a parallel Video Study was conducted (Hiebert et al., 2003). Eighth grade mathematics teachers from seven different countries were videotaped, and their lessons were analyzed. The results of this study showed that typical teaching strategies used in all of the countries included both small- and large-group work, review of previously studied content, and the use of textbooks and worksheets. However, major differences were identified when teachers' presentations of new content, difficulty level of mathematics problems posed by teachers, and teachers' handling of classwork and homework were considered. For example, whereas Japanese teachers spent approximately 60 percent of their class time introducing new mathematics content, only 23 percent of class time in the United States was used for this purpose, with more than half of the class time in the United States being spent on reviewing content. Similarly, when the complexity of problems posed to students was analyzed, only 17 percent of the Japanese problems were classified as "low-level" complexity, compared with 67 percent of the problems posed in the United States. Also, researchers noted that Japanese teachers were much more likely to make connections between a problem presented and another problem already explored than were teachers in any of the other six nations. Generally speaking, the

Figure 1.5 Eighth Grade TIMSS Item from 2003 Assessment

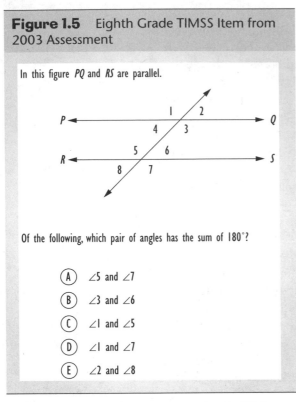

In this figure *PQ* and *RS* are parallel.

Of the following, which pair of angles has the sum of 180°?

(A) ∠5 and ∠7

(B) ∠3 and ∠6

(C) ∠1 and ∠5

(D) ∠1 and ∠7

(E) ∠2 and ∠8

(National Center for Education Statistics, 2005b.)

Figure 1.6 Eighth Grade TIMSS Item from 2007 Assessment

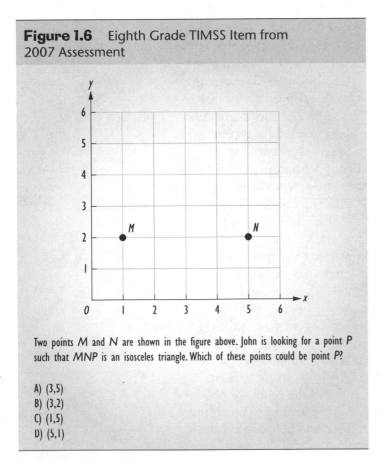

Two points *M* and *N* are shown in the figure above. John is looking for a point *P* such that *MNP* is an isosceles triangle. Which of these points could be point *P*?

A) (3,5)

B) (3,2)

C) (1,5)

D) (5,1)

(Gonzales et al., 2009)

authors of the report noted that teachers from nations with high-achieving students tend to use different teaching strategies than their counterparts.

By 2003, the project was renamed the Trends in International Mathematics and Science Study, maintaining the same acronym of TIMSS. A four-year cycle was established so that assessments could be compared from 1995 to 1999, 2003, 2007, 2011, and so on. In each instance, questionnaires were administered to students and teachers, and achievement tests were taken by students in the fourth, eighth, and/or twelfth grades. On the 2003 achievement test, 46 countries were involved at both the fourth and eighth grade levels (National Center for Education Statistics, 2005a). An example of a typical eighth grade geometry item on the 2003 test is shown in Figure 1.5.

On this item, the international average showed that 43 percent of the eighth graders answered the question correctly (choice B, which are same-side interior angles). In the United States, only 37 percent of the students got the item correct (significantly lower than the international average), whereas 83 percent of Japanese students answered it correctly. On the test as a whole, however, both fourth and eighth graders in the United States scored above the international average. The fourth graders performed lower than 11 countries but outperformed 13 of their peers. At the eighth grade level, students in the United States were outperformed by 9 countries but scored higher than 25 others (National Center for Education Statistics, 2005a).

On the 2007 TIMSS exam, eighth graders in the United States achieved a scaled score of 508, slightly above the international average of 500. Eighth graders in the United States outperformed 37 of 48 participating countries, with 5 Asian countries scoring significantly higher (Chinese Taipei, Korea, Singapore, Hong Kong, and Japan), and 5 countries scoring about the same (Hungary, England, Russia, Lithuania, and the Czech Republic) (International Association for the Evaluation of Educational Achievement, 2007). Interestingly, eighth graders in the United States in 2007 scored 16 scaled points higher than in 1995 when the average score was 492 (Gonzales, 2009). Still, on some items, students in the United States scored much lower than we might want or expect. Figure 1.6 illustrates a geometry item from the 2007 exam. On this question, only 45 percent of eighth graders in the United States correctly responded with choice A (showing their ability to create an isosceles triangle), while 81 percent of Japanese and 86 percent of Chinese students answered correctly.

Also, beginning in 2000, the Organization for Economic Co-operation and Development (OECD) began administering an international exam in mathematics, science, and reading literacy to 15-year-olds. The test is on a 3-year cycle, having also been given in 2003, 2006, 2009, and so on. The OECD is a collaborative of 34 countries whose main goal is to "foster prosperity and fight poverty through growth and financial stability" (OECD, 2011a). The test is called the Program for International Student Assessment (PISA). On the 2009 exam, students in the United States scored 487, whereas the international average was 496 (OECD, 2011b)—a performance that was statistically lower than that of 17 other countries and higher than that of only 5 other OECD countries (Greece, Israel, Turkey, Chile, and Mexico). While scores were higher in 2009 than in 2006, they were not significantly higher than in 2003 (Fleischman et al., 2010). So once again, in yet another assessment, we see the students in the United States scoring at or below the international average.

So, what does all of this international information tell us? In comparing performances over time, fourth graders in the United States scored higher in 2007 than in 1995 (fourth graders were not tested in 1999). Also, in 2007, there was a marked improvement at the eighth grade level over 1995, with the first test scoring 8 points below the scaled international average and the 2007 test being 8 points above the average (Gonzales et al., 2009). Twelfth graders were not tested on TIMSS after 1995 (National Center for Education Statistics, 2005a). Therefore, on an international scale, at middle school level (grades 4 and 8), we can detect an increase in mathematical content knowledge of students in the United States when compared with students in the rest of the world. Whether this trend will continue remains to be seen.

Results similar to those on TIMSS can be found when looking at reports from the National Assessment of Educational Progress (NAEP)—often called the Nation's Report Card—in the United States. Consider, for example, the following item that was featured on the 1996 NAEP for high school seniors (National Center for Education Statistics, 2007a):

This question requires you to show your work and explain your reasoning. You may use drawings, words, and numbers in your explanation. Your answer should be clear enough so that another person could read it and understand your thinking. It is important that you show all of your work.

The table below shows the daily attendance at two movie theaters for 5 days and the mean (average) and the median attendance.

	Theater A	Theater B
Day 1	100	72
Day 2	87	97
Day 3	90	70
Day 4	10	71
Day 5	91	100
Mean (Average)	75.6	82
Median	90	72

(a) *Which statistic, the mean or the median, would you use to describe the typical daily attendance for the 5 days at Theater A? Justify your answer.*

(b) *Which statistic, the mean or the median, would you use to describe the typical daily attendance for the 5 days at Theater B? Justify your answer.*

This item is particularly interesting because it does not ask students to compute the mean or the median but, instead, to consider the appropriate use of a statistic in a given situation. Twelfth graders are supposed to notice that the outlier of 10 people on Day 4 results in a mean that is lower than any of the other pieces of data, making the median the best measure of central tendency for Theater A. Likewise, the median for Theater B is an unrealistic "average," as it represents only one of the two clusters of data collected. At this point, you might want to ask yourself, "What percentage of high school seniors should be able to recognize the appropriate use of mean versus that of median?" Most people would agree that the vast majority of twelfth graders should be able to do that. After all, the concepts of mean and median are often introduced as early as the fourth or fifth grade.

This statistics item was scored on a **rubric**, a grading scale on which a student's response can fall into one of five categories—incorrect, minimal, partial, satisfactory, or extended. Papers were sorted into one of these five categories, depending on the correctness of the responses and the clarity of explanations. A satisfactory or an extended response is considered an acceptable answer. Only 4 percent of the twelfth graders tested in this national sample were able to perform at the top two levels. In fact, 56 percent of the students either left the item blank or wrote totally incorrect responses on their papers. It is possible that these students knew *how to calculate* a mean or a median but did not have the conceptual understanding of these statistics to know when to apply them. Moreover, although 27 percent of the white students left the item blank, 42 percent of African American and 48 percent of Hispanic students did not respond.

Likewise, results from NAEP tests between 2000 and 2009 showed that at all of the grade levels tested (grades 4, 8, and 12 in 2000, 2005, and 2009; grades 4 and 8 in 2003, 2005, and 2007), white students scored significantly higher than did African American, Hispanic, or Native American students (Braswell et al., 2001; Braswell, Daane, & Grigg, 2003; National Center for Education Statistics, 2007a, 2009, 2011). In addition, students at all grade levels who were at or near the poverty line in terms of family income tended to have, on average, lower scores than did their peers who came from wealthier families. Consequently, we perceive a wide gap between the performances of various socioeconomic groups—a trend that has been consistent throughout the NAEP reports. Such data prompted the National Council of Teachers of Mathematics (NCTM) to assert, "Expectations must be raised—mathematics can and must be learned by *all* students" (NCTM, 2000, p. 13). The optimistic news on the NAEP mathematics test is that between 1990 and 2009, the percentage of students who scored at or above the "basic" level increased from 50 to 82 percent for fourth graders and from 52 to 73 percent for eighth graders. Similarly, performance at or above the "proficient" level increased at both of these grade levels over the 19-year period as well (National Center for Education Statistics, 2007a, 2009). The percent of students at or above basic and proficient levels on the twelfth grade NAEP has shown an increase as well (National Center for Education Statistics, 2011). These results indicate a steady trend toward improvement in mathematics performance over time.

International assessment items explored in this chapter (involving a basic algebraic equation, a visual pattern, an angle measurement, a coordinate geometry question for eighth graders, and a straightforward statistics question for twelfth graders) should be fairly easy for most students to answer. Yet these items were missed by a large percentage of U.S. students who took these national and international exams. Why? What is it about the system that has made mathematics so inaccessible to so

How Would You React

S C E N A R I O

A senior comes to you during your planning period and asks for your signature on a form to drop your class. The student tells you it is because the class is too difficult and is not necessary, but the "word" in the halls is that the student, a starter on the basketball team, would rather drop your mathematics class than to jeopardize athletic eligibility. Your response is

a. Sign the slip and let the student go; it's probably not worth an argument.

b. Sign the slip but encourage the student to reconsider dropping the class because you are fairly certain that any college major will require some form of mathematics class.

c. Refuse to sign the slip and call the student's parents immediately.

d. Refuse to sign the slip, contact the student's guidance counselor, and arrange a meeting for the three of you to discuss the implications of this class change.

e. Other.

D I S C U S S I O N

When it comes to choosing mathematics courses, many students—as well as their parents and even their guidance counselors—often do not recognize the importance of having a significant background in mathematics. In a report from the Mathematical Sciences Education Board (1989), the authors pointed out that 75 percent of all jobs require at least some background in basic algebra and geometry. A decade later, the National Commission on Mathematics and Science Teaching for the Twenty-First Century (2000), headed by astronaut and senator John Glenn, reported that a firm background in mathematics and science is necessary to ensure that the workforce in the United States will continue to be able to compete globally, to "solve the unforeseen problems and dream the dreams that will define America's future" (p. 4). Similarly, the American Mathematical Society and the Mathematical Association of America jointly published a report entitled *The Mathematical Education of Teachers* (Kessel, Epstein, & Keynes, 2001) that emphasized that the nature of most jobs entails a background in mathematics. The authors described the influence of technology and noted that even those who work on a line in a factory are now expected to have a background in statistics to analyze their effectiveness.

The changing nature of our world and its workforce has made it more important today than ever for students to have a strong background in mathematics—a background that includes not only number sense but also a basic understanding of algebra, geometry, statistics, and probability. In many cases, secondary and middle school mathematics teachers are preparing students for professions that have yet to be created. Often students consider dropping (or not even enrolling in) mathematics classes, fearing that the courses will be too challenging as well as embracing a misconception that "my career area will never involve any math." But many students are mistaken, as mathematics will ultimately be necessary in most jobs, and one of the responsibilities of mathematics teachers is to encourage students to take—and to finish—courses that will give them the background they need to be successful in their careers.

many students over the years? Mathematics anxiety and a general fear of mathematics are quite common, but how did these fears evolve, and how are they perpetuated?

Perhaps one of the greatest myths about mathematics is that some people are natural "math people," and some are not. A common misconception is that mathematical ability is genetically inherited or predetermined. On the contrary, research does not support the idea of innate mathematical ability. Consequently, with the possible exception of individuals who are severely disabled, every student can become mathematically literate. Whether students will understand the content may depend not so much on the material itself but on the way in which teachers present it. Although a certain percentage of students will understand a mathematical concept despite a poor teacher, most students will thrive only in an atmosphere created by caring, knowledgeable teachers.

use in paper

The Need for Reform

In the 1960s, students and their teachers experienced a mathematics reform movement known as the New Math, which was sparked by the launching of *Sputnik* satellites by the USSR in 1957 and 1958. The success of the *Sputnik* program fueled a national fear of falling behind the rest of the world and motivated U.S. educators to reconsider the topics explored in the curriculum. In her book *A Parent's Guide to the New Mathematics* (1964), Evelyn Sharp discussed the need for an updated mathematics curriculum, noting that a seventeenth-century teacher could readily walk into a classroom in the 1960s and teach mathematics because "the content of the courses hadn't changed in 300 years" (p. 11). Recognizing the need for mathematicians and scientists to be able to compete on a global level, the New Math exposed high school students to topics such as set theory and non-Euclidean geometry, which had not historically been explored until the college level. Sharp noted that the New Math moved mathematical topics down to lower grade levels to ensure that "all students" visited content that required much more rigor than had previously been the case. In his famous book, *Why Johnny Can't Add* (1973), Morris Kline assailed the New Math, stating that

> The new mathematics is taught to elementary and high school students who will ultimately enter into the full variety of professions, businesses, technical jobs, and trades or become primarily wives and mothers [sic]. Of the elementary school children, not one in a thousand will be a mathematician; and of the academic high school students, not one in a hundred will be a mathematician. Clearly then, a curriculum that might be ideal for the training of mathematicians would still not be right for these levels of education. (pp. 21–22)

In its attempt to expose all students to higher mathematics, the New Math movement catered more to the top students than the marginal or average students of mathematics. Furthermore, the public was confused about its intent, and the movement eventually fell to the wayside, only to be replaced by a "back-to-basics" movement in the 1970s.

The mathematics reform effort that began in the 1980s, however, was very different. In 1980, the NCTM countered the "back-to-basics" movement in the famous book *An Agenda for Action* (1980) by suggesting that problem solving should be the focal point of the curriculum. Three years later, the U.S. Department of Education's National Commission on Excellence in Education released a landmark document entitled *A Nation at Risk*. Recognizing that the rest of the world was catching up with the United States, the authors of the book called for a dramatic reform of mathematics education, including requiring three years of mathematics in high school to graduate from high school. The report stated, "The teaching of mathematics in high school should equip graduates to: (a) understand geometric and algebraic concepts; (b) understand elementary probability and statistics; (c) apply mathematics in everyday situations; and (d) estimate, approximate, measure, and test the accuracy of their calculations. In addition to the traditional sequence of studies available for college-bound students, new, equally demanding mathematics curricula need to be developed for those who do not plan to continue their formal education immediately" (U.S. Department of Education, 1983). A logical "next step" for the NCTM was to develop and promote a national vision of mathematics education.

As a result, the NCTM released a series of three Standards documents: *Curriculum and Evaluation Standards for School Mathematics* (1989), *Professional Standards for Teaching Mathematics* (1991), and *Assessment Standards for School Mathematics* (1995). The contents of these documents were then updated and refined into one volume, *Principles and Standards for School Mathematics,* in 2000 to set the tone for mathematics education in the third millennium. A **standard** is a benchmark that can be used by a school, a district, a state, or a country to determine the degree to which the educational program meets a list of recommendations. The Standards documents from the NCTM emphasized that mathematics should be for *all* students—regardless of gender, race, socioeconomic status, or any other factor that may have caused inequities in the past. This way of thinking was an invitation to stronger and weaker students alike to develop their mathematical abilities and a challenge for teachers to discern how to make the teaching and learning of mathematics accessible to all. By 2010, a more detailed (in terms of content to be taught at each grade level) national vision was completed by the National Governors Association Center for Best Practices and the Council of Chief State School Officers and released as a set of *Common Core State Standards* to be used by all states that chose to adopt them (Common Core State Standards Initiative, 2010).

As we think of mathematics for all students, we will need to turn our attention to research on effective teaching practices. Within that body of research lies a great deal of evidence as to how to structure classrooms; how to pose meaningful, motivational problems; and how to use technology and teaching strategies, such as cooperative learning, to appeal to the vastly different learning styles and confidence levels of students in the classroom. We now assume, as a premise, that all of the students in our secondary and middle school classes are capable of learning mathematics, and we can begin to decide how to structure learning experiences for students that will appeal to their curiosity and intellect simultaneously. If students can be actively engaged in "doing" mathematics, they may be motivated enough to perform their best in the classroom and on assignments. Let's explore what it means to "do" mathematics.

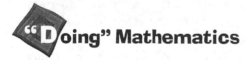oing" Mathematics

Problem Solving

Suppose that you were asked to find the circumference of a circle with a radius of 5 centimeters. Easy, right? Sure, you simply double the radius and multiply it by π to get an answer of about 31.4 centimeters. But what if you didn't already know that the circumference of a circle can be found by multiplying $2\pi r$ or πd? You might have to resort to drawing a sketch of the circle, laying a piece of string on the sketch, and stretching it out along a meter stick to estimate the length. Can you think of another way to determine the circumference without knowing the formula? Here is another option: Draw a line segment with a ruler on a piece of paper, cut out the circle, roll it along the segment until the circle has completed one revolution, and then measure the length of the path. Finding a circumference is a routine task—an **exercise**—if you already know a formula and have encountered that type of question before. However, if the situation is new to you and you have no such formula, the question becomes a problem to be solved. A **problem**, then, can be defined as a task for which there is no immediate solution. The situation is generally unfamiliar to the person attempting to find the answer. When confronted with a problem, we have no choice but to dig deeply into a bag of tricks—a list of strategies—to attempt to solve it. It is important to distinguish between routine exercises that students do for practice and problem solving in the classroom. Also, keep in mind that an exercise for one student may be a problem for another. For example, the circumference question may be a problem for a sixth grader but an exercise for a high school sophomore.

Problem solving can be defined as the process by which an individual attempts to find a solution to a nonroutine mathematical question. Probably the most famous book on this topic was published in 1945 by George Polya, then at Stanford. Polya described problem solving as a four-step process: (1) understanding the problem, (2) devising a plan for finding a solution, (3) implementing the plan, and (4) looking back at the answer to ensure that it makes sense and to determine if another plan might have been more effective (Polya, 1945). Although much additional research and writing on problem solving have been conducted since his book appeared, Polya's four steps are still cited as being fundamental in solving problems and in teaching problem-solving skills in the classroom. In 1980, the NCTM document *An Agenda for Action* called for the 1980s to be a problem-solving decade. The NCTM *Curriculum and Evaluation Standards* (1989) listed problem solving as the first Standard at all grade levels, K–12, and *Principles and Standards for School Mathematics* (2000) also lists problem solving as the sixth Standard at all grade levels. Furthermore, the *Common Core State Standards* state that the first mathematical practice for emphasis in the classroom is to have students "make sense of problems and persevere in solving them" (2010, p. 6). But the vision of problem solving embodied in these documents goes beyond simple, routine tasks. Instead, they suggest rich, meaningful experiences through which students develop and refine strategies that can be used to solve other problems.

Consider the following problem:

> *A certain farmer in Florida has an orange grove. In his grove are 120 trees. Each tree ordinarily produces 650 oranges. He is interested in raising his orange production and knows that because of lost space and sunlight, every additional tree that he plants will cause a reduction of 5 oranges from each tree. What is the maximum number of oranges that he will be able to produce in his grove, and how many trees will he need to reach this maximum?*

It is unlikely that you have ever thought about this situation, and the problem does not have an obvious answer; therefore, it is probable that the statement constitutes a problem for you. How would you begin to solve it? Generally, people reach back and try to apply a strategy that they have used for similar problems in the past. Take a minute with a piece of paper, and think about how you would solve it. Let's look at several ways the problem can be approached.

A middle school child might analyze the problem by *guessing-and-checking* in some orderly fashion. If 120 trees produce 650 oranges per tree, the current production must be 78,000 oranges. However, an increase of 1 tree will result in 121 trees but only 645 oranges per tree for a total of 78,045 oranges, an increase of 45 oranges altogether. Similar calculations can be organized into a *table*. See Table 1.1.

Table 1.1 Orange Grove Problem Data

Total Trees	Oranges per Tree	Total Oranges
120	650	78,000
121	645	78,045
122	640	78,080
123	635	78,105
124	630	78,120
125	625	78,125
126	620	78,120
127	615	78,105
128	610	78,080
129	605	78,045
130	600	78,000

From Table 1.1 it is apparent that the maximum orange production occurs at 125 trees—the addition of 5 trees to the orange grove. However, students may notice some other things as well. For example, some may recognize that the orange production increases by 45 with the addition of one tree, 35 with the next tree, then 25, 15, and 5, decreasing beyond that point. The identification of this type of *pattern* can eliminate the need to generate the entire table, either by hand or on a computer spreadsheet. A seventh grader began by "guessing" what would happen if 10 trees were planted. When she realized that orange production was the same as the original amount, she immediately yelled out, "I think it goes up and back down, so if it's back to normal at 10, then it must reach its maximum with 5 new trees planted!" Because of a clever first guess (some might call it lucky) and a careful analysis of its result, she solved the problem before most of the others in the class could even write it down.

Suppose that the same problem was raised in a first-year algebra course in which students had been exposed to the use of variables for problem solving. In this case, a student might *write a variable expression* $(650 - 5x)(120 + x)$, where x stands for the number of trees added, to find the total production. The first binomial determines the number of oranges per tree, and the second binomial represents the total number of trees in the grove. At this point, the student can *graph* the function $y = (650 - 5x)(120 + x)$ on a graphing calculator (see Figure 1.7) and TRACE (TRACE is a common command on a graphing calculator) the curve to its vertex, finding that the parabola peaks at $x = 5$.

The student might also choose to solve the quadratic equation $(650 - 5x)(120 + x) = 0$ by setting the two factors equal to zero and find that the solutions are $x = 130$ or $x = 120$; therefore, the maximum must be the input value halfway between the x-intercepts, or when $x = 5$.

Figure 1.7 Orange Grove Parabolic Curve on a Graphing Calculator

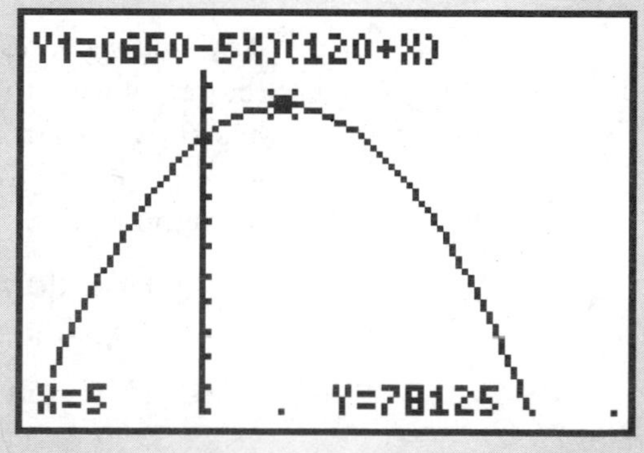

Finally, a student with calculus background might choose to solve the problem by taking a first derivative to determine the maximum:

$$y = (650 - 5x)(120 + x)$$
$$y = 78,000 + 50x - 5x^2$$
$$y' = 50 - 10x$$

Setting the first derivative equal to 0,

$$0 = 50 - 10x, \text{ therefore}$$
$$x = 5$$

The orange grove problem is said to be *rich* in that it is nonroutine and can be solved in a variety of ways, featuring a number of different entry points. Depending on the grade level and experiences of the student, several problem-solving strategies can be applied, such as guess and check, make a table, look for a pattern, write a variable expression or equation, or draw a graph. Once students have effectively used a problem-solving strategy, they can apply the same technique to future problems as well. Ideally, a teacher would assign a problem such as this one, allow students to solve it individually or in small groups, and encourage students to share solutions and strategies so that students can reflect on their approaches when compared to strategies used by others. Then, if some students use a guess-and-check strategy but observe others writing an equation, they may choose to use an equation the next time a problem of this kind is posed. Students should not only seek accurate solutions to problems but also examine their problem-solving strategies to find the one that is most efficient.

Various resource books and materials provide students with examples of problems that use different strategies. Some of these resources are listed at the end of this chapter, and others are cited throughout the text. Some of the other common problem-solving strategies developed in the secondary and middle school mathematics classroom include the following:

- Act out the problem.
- Make a drawing or diagram.
- Construct a physical model.
- Restate the problem in other words.
- Identify and verbalize the given, needed, and extraneous information.
- List all possibilities.
- Solve a simpler or similar problem.
- Work backwards.

Any single strategy or combination of these may be used for solving problems, and they constitute the "tool kit" that a student carries to a problem situation. Research has shown that in order for students to be effective problem solvers, they must have plenty of tools in their kits so that if one method is not working, they can move on to another one. There is an old joke that mathematicians tell:

Q. How do you kill a blue elephant?

A. With a blue elephant gun.

Q. How do you kill a white elephant?

A. With a white elephant gun?

No, you strangle it until it turns blue and then use the gun you already have!

Often, solving a problem boils down to nothing more than forcing it to look like a problem you've previously solved and using the same tools to find its solution. The *Common Core State Standards* call for the mathematical practice that students should "look for and express regularity in repeated reasoning" (Common Core State Standards Initiative, 2010, p. 8), which means that students should discover and use shortcuts and approaches that make them more effective problem solvers.

In *Principles and Standards for School Mathematics* (2000), the NCTM states that problem solving should enable all students to

- build new mathematical knowledge through problem solving;
- solve problems that arise in mathematics and in other contexts;
- apply and adapt a variety of appropriate strategies to solve problems;
- monitor and reflect on the process of mathematical problem solving. (p. 52)

Clearly, the emphasis of the Standards has been, and continues to be, on using problem solving both to develop strategies for solving future problems and as a context in which to learn or practice skills. Ideally, in the contemporary view of mathematics, every lesson should include some opportunity for students to refine their problem-solving skills. In addition, students should be required to reason mathematically—to think—in every lesson.

Reasoning and Proof

Try this trick on a friend: Write down the number of the month in which you were born (e.g., if you were born in October, write down a 10). Double this number. Add 6. Multiply this new number by 50. Then add on the day of your birth (e.g., if you were born on October 20, add 20). Finally, subtract 365. Now, ask your friend to give you the final number. On a calculator, secretly add 65 to that number. The result will tell you the day and month of your friend's birthday. This "trick" is particularly effective if you have several people do the calculation at once and ask for their answers, quickly telling each person the correct birthdate. But why does it work? Is it magic? No, it's mathematics.

Let m stand for the month in which the person is born and d for the day of the month. The steps of the problem for a person whose birthday is on October 20 are as follows, for that specific date and in general:

Instruction	Specific	General
Write down the month.	10	m
Double the number.	20	$2m$
Add 6.	26	$2m + 6$
Multiply by 50.	1300	$50(2m + 6) = 100m + 300$
Add the day of birth.	1320	$100m + 300 + d$
Subtract 365.	955	$100m - 65 + d$
Secretly add 65.	1020	$100m + d$

The answer 1020 represents the 10th month and 20th day, or October 20. Similarly, the final variable expression takes the birth month and moves it over two places to the left by multiplying by 100. When the day of birth is added, the result is a number from which the birthdate can be determined. With the power of algebra, this puzzle or trick can readily be analyzed.

In a mathematical situation, any time our students ask, "Why?" "How do we know that?" "What would happen if . . . ?" "Would it ever be true that . . . ?" they are asking questions that involve **reasoning** skills. In the orange grove problem, for example, the student might not be satisfied with seeing the production peak at five trees and might ask why this occurs. This can ignite a class discussion about how adding new trees may remove enough nutrients from the ground and shade enough sunlight from other trees so that eventually additional trees do more harm than good. Puzzles and other problems are generally worth exploring only if they engender discussions or discourse about why the problem works the way that it does. The pursuit of the question "why" in the mathematics classroom is critical. Students want to know, for example, why fractions are divided by inverting the last fraction and multiplying, why the formula for the area of a circle is $A = \pi r^2$, why the value of the constant e is irrational, and why the first derivative of the sine function is the cosine function. As they study mathematics, students should become inquisitive and inclined to seek proof and verification of conjectures raised in the classroom. And this is most likely to occur in classrooms in which mathematical reasoning is valued. Again, the mathematical practices in the *Common Core State Standards* call for helping all students to reason abstractly and to "construct viable arguments and critique the reasoning of others" (2010, p. 6).

Principles and Standards for School Mathematics (NCTM, 2000) lists reasoning and proof as Standard 7 and states that through emphasis on reasoning and proof in the classroom, all students will

- recognize reasoning and proof as fundamental aspects of mathematics;
- make and investigate mathematical conjectures;
- develop and evaluate mathematical arguments and proofs;
- select and use various types of reasoning and methods of proof. (p. 56)

Principles and Standards for School Mathematics states that "reasoning mathematically is a habit of mind, and like all habits, it must be developed through consistent use in many contexts" (p. 56). Every day that a child is in school, the student should be encouraged to reason mathematically by being challenged with "why" and "how" questions. In this way, students begin to recognize that it is not enough to be *able to* solve a problem; they must reason out the underlying mathematics, make conjectures or hypotheses, and communicate solutions and strategies to others.

Communication

Mrs. King teaches an Honors Geometry course in a small high school. In the spring, she divides her students into learning teams and assigns a famous mathematician to each team, such as Gauss, Newton, Pythagoras, Descartes, or Euclid. Each team is asked to research the life and contributions of its assigned mathematician. Then each student writes a term paper about the person, and the team creates a short skit about their mathematician and presents it to the class. The grade that students receive on the project is determined by a combination of individual written papers, self-assessments of how well the teams worked together, and the quality of their classroom presentations. (For details on this project, see the introductory chapter of the *Seventy-Third Yearbook of the National Council of Teachers of Mathematics* Brahier, 2011.)

SPOTlight on Technology

A common concern that teachers hear from parents and the community is that "when calculators are used in school, students become dependent on them"; parents and community members believe that calculators do more harm than good. This claim is certainly understandable because the parents of our secondary and middle school students often did not have access to calculators when they were in school. The first Texas Instruments graphing calculator was the TI-81, and it was released in 1990 at a cost of $110. So, the graphing calculator was not even invented until the parents of current secondary and middle school students were well out of high school. Consequently, many parents cannot relate to what it means for a student to learn mathematics using calculators. Research on calculator use, however, contradicts the general opinion that using technology hinders the learning of mathematics.

The most comprehensive meta-analysis (study of studies) on the use of basic, four-function calculators showed that regular use of calculators in the classroom improves student performance and attitudes in mathematics (Hembree & Dessart, 1992). In addition, the report from the 2000 National Assessment of Educational Progress (Braswell et al., 2001) showed that students at the eighth and twelfth grade levels who most frequently used calculators in their classes tended to outperform their peers who used calculators infrequently. The NAEP report also showed that 69 percent of eighth graders report that they use a calculator in class at least once a week. In fact, 44 percent of all eighth graders indicated that they use a calculator every day.

Another study synthesized the results of 43 other pieces of research on the use of graphing calculators. In this report, the authors noted that students who used graphing calculators in school have a better understanding of functions, their graphs, and the use of algebra in real-life contexts (Burrill et al., 2002). Interestingly, students who were taught with graphing calculators also showed no significant difference in their ability to do more traditional "paper-and-pencil" procedures than their peers. Finally, Dunham (2000),

in reviewing research on graphing calculator use, pointed out that students who use graphing calculators are better able to connect various representations of the same function—algebraic, graphical, and tabular.

Using graphing calculators, students have opportunities to compare different representations of a function with the stroke of a key. The ability to switch back and forth from one representation to another, in turn, helps the student to think more deeply about the function and its meaning. Consider, for example, the linear function $y = 2x - 5$. On a graphing calculator, students can view the representations shown in Figure 1.8 within seconds.

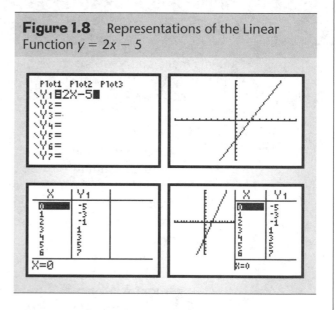

Figure 1.8 Representations of the Linear Function $y = 2x - 5$

The student enters the algebraic equation of the function in the calculator and, with a few keystrokes, can view the function as a graph, as a table, or as a combination of a graph and a table in a single screen. Then, by making simple changes to the equation, such as using $y = 2x + 5$ or $y = 2x - 5$, students can readily explore the effects of these parameter changes on the graphs and tables. These types of explorations eliminate the tedious process of repeatedly drawing graphs on paper and place the emphasis on the behavior and meaning of the functions, rather than simply the skill of drawing them.

Mr. Shirley teaches in a middle school and requires his students to keep a mathematics journal. Students are regularly provided with prompts for their journal entries. Prompts include statements such as, "Identify the most difficult problem we solved this week and explain what made it difficult for you" and "Write a letter to a friend, explaining how to add numbers that include decimals. Be sure to

Students make presentations to the class and are assessed on their ability to communicate mathematically.

include a diagram." By collecting the journals every 2 weeks, Mr. Shirley learns much more about how his students are thinking than he can gather during class time. Also, as students write responses to the prompts, they are pushed to clarify their thinking and to explain it to another person. The authors of the *Common Core State Standards* stated that students should "make conjectures and build a logical progression of statements to explore the truth of their conjectures . . . They justify their conclusions, communicate them to others, and respond to the arguments of others" (2010, pp. 6–7). In addition, the document includes the mathematical practice of attending to precision, noting, "Mathematically proficient students try to communicate precisely to others" (p. 7). Often, it is not until we are asked to explain something to someone else that we realize there are gaps in our own understanding.

How often have you heard someone say, "Well, I know how to do it, but I can't really explain it"? Or they simply say, "I just did it." Learning mathematics effectively should exceed the ability to demonstrate skills; students should be able to explain, describe, and clearly communicate solutions and strategies that lead to the answers. The ability to communicate mathematically is a major goal of current reform efforts. In order to validate our thinking or to convince another person that our thinking is accurate, we need to communicate verbally and in writing. Consequently, when we think of "doing" mathematics, we should include the process of communicating with others as a critical component. Projects, written papers, presentations, and journals are examples of classroom strategies that promote mathematical communication.

In *Principles and Standards for School Mathematics* (2000), the authors point out in Standard 8 that **communication** should be stressed so that students

- organize and consolidate their mathematical thinking through communication;
- communicate their mathematical thinking coherently and clearly to peers, teachers, and others;
- analyze and evaluate the mathematical thinking and strategies of others;
- use the language of mathematics to express mathematical ideas precisely. (p. 60)

Since the release of the Standards, we have seen considerably more emphasis on communication in the classroom. For example, many teachers have begun to use cooperative learning teams in which students have specific roles and depend on the input of others. We discuss cooperative learning strategies in some depth in Chapter 7. Also, teachers who consider communication an important goal frequently ask free-response questions, as in the example of the movie theater problem, in which the student is required to show work and to explain the thinking process in words or with diagrams. When a student provides a "correct answer" in the classroom, logical follow-up questions are "How do you know?" and "What were you thinking?" Whenever a teacher pushes students to explain their reasoning, the level of questioning is enhanced, and students are challenged to communicate mathematically.

Connections

Consider the following problem from an NCTM resource book (Phillips, Gardella, Kelly, & Stewart, 1991). The student is provided with the diagram shown in Figure 1.9:

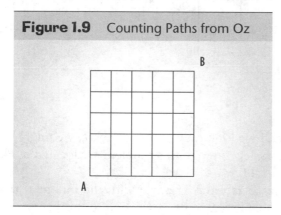

Figure 1.9   Counting Paths from Oz

The problem states that the city of Oz is located at point A and that a person wants to travel to point B, moving only right along horizontal lines or up along vertical lines. The question is to determine how many paths there are to move from point A to point B. Before reading on, take a few minutes with a piece of paper and a pencil, and think about how you would proceed to find a solution.

Often, students approach this problem by tracing possible routes on the grid while searching for a rule or pattern that can be generalized. They think about decisions that need to be made any time the pencil reaches an intersection point at which the "traveler" has a choice of directions to pursue. It is not unusual for students to struggle with solutions such as 5! or 2 raised to some power. These solutions, although incorrect, can help the students refine their thinking and lead them to a different way of viewing the problem. Often, a useful problem-solving strategy is to *solve a simpler problem* and then *look for a pattern,* and the teacher may choose to lead them in this direction. In Figure 1.10, there are three smaller grids that students might consider.

If the size of the map is 1 × 1, then there is exactly one way for the traveler to reach the vertices directly to the right and above A, the starting point. Consequently, there are two ways to reach the final destination. Using the same logic, students can construct a 2 × 2 grid and build on the previous map to find a total of six ways to get to the city. Can you trace all six possible paths in the second picture? Extending the idea to a 3 × 3 diagram, there are 20 paths that lead to the destination point. At this point, students might recognize the pattern and continue the process to find that there are 252 possible paths to get from point A to point B in the original problem. (Did you find this?) Turning the paper so that point A is at

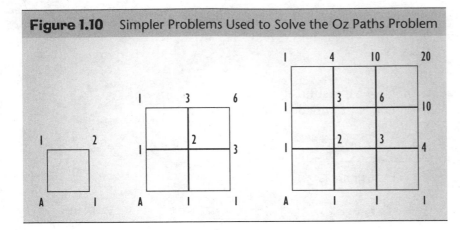

Figure 1.10 Simpler Problems Used to Solve the Oz Paths Problem

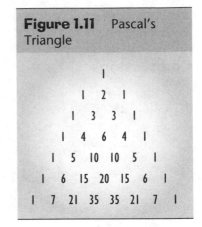

Figure 1.11 Pascal's Triangle

the top of the page, if we look only at the numbers, we might recognize a familiar pattern. The numbers generated in this problem are located in Pascal's Triangle, as illustrated in Figure 1.11.

Most students associate the Triangle with the binomial theorem or with the determination of probabilities, so its connection to this path-counting problem may not be intuitively "obvious." However, it is important for students to make this type of connection across topics in mathematics. It may also be difficult to categorize this problem, because it falls into content topics such as coordinate graphing, patterning, and discrete mathematics while making important connections to the study of advanced algebra and probability.

In other words, this problem unites several mathematical concepts within a single investigation. It emphasizes the mathematical **connections** between a variety of topics. In the classroom, students should be encouraged to think of mathematics as the connected whole that it is rather than see a course as a chapter of this and a chapter of that. As such, even the idea that one can take an algebra class one year and a geometry class the following year as if they are not inherently connected can be very misleading to the young learner. Recent reform efforts have called for teachers to use activities and examples that help students to see how the various areas of mathematics are related. For example, the *Common Core State Standards'* mathematical practices include looking for and using patterns and structure, as well as making use of repeated reasoning strategies (2010).

NCTM's *Principles and Standards for School Mathematics* (2000) states in Standard 9 that connections should be made in the mathematics classroom to help students

- recognize and use connections among mathematical ideas;
- understand how mathematical ideas interconnect and build on one another to produce a coherent whole;
- recognize and apply mathematics in contexts outside of mathematics. (p. 64)

In the Standards, the idea of connecting mathematical topics to one another is joined with the notion of helping students see applications of mathematics in other subject areas so that they come to appreciate the utility of mathematics across the curriculum. When studying genetics in a biology course, for example, the student can explore some practical implications of probability theory. Matrices can be used to model production costs and profits for a business, and a discussion of symmetry or ratio and proportion can be rooted in the analysis of a piece of art. Again, the very fact that students take an Algebra II class during first period and a Chemistry class during sixth period almost suggests that there is a wall between these courses; but in reality, each subject depends on the other, and unless teachers help students make these connections by virtue of the problems posed, many of the applications are lost. Recent trends in the development of the middle school concept have addressed the issue of connections by providing teachers with common planning time during which they can discuss and arrange for experiences that help students make connections across the disciplines.

Representation

The last mathematical process described in *Principles and Standards for School Mathematics* (2000) is **representation**. The mathematics classroom frequently involves students attempting to represent problem situations in a variety of ways, deciding on which representation is the most helpful and appropriate in a given situation. For example, if you wanted to explore the orange grove problem in some depth, you might want to use an equation, as it is helpful in finding x-intercepts and calculating function values. However, it might be more useful to view a graph in such a way that a comparison could be made to related real-world phenomena. Similarly, the following three equations describe the same function:

(a) $y = x^2 + 2x - 15$
(b) $y = (x - 3)(x + 5)$
(c) $y + 16 = (x + 1)^2$

Although the first version is in Standard Form and communicates a y-intercept at $(0, -15)$, equation (b) is factored to make it much easier to determine that the parabola intersects the x-axis at the points $(3, 0)$ and $(-5, 0)$. And although equation (b) is useful for finding the roots of the function, equation (c) may be much more helpful if one needs to know that the vertex is at the point $(-1, -16)$ and that the minimum y-value is at -16. Equation (c) masks the coordinates of the x-intercepts, while making it easy to determine the vertex. So, although all three of these equations are acceptable and reasonable, we choose a particular representation of the function depending on the context of the problem and what information we need. Likewise, although the fraction $\frac{3}{5}$ is considered "simplified" and, therefore, a desirable way to express a quantity, we may choose to represent it as $\frac{12}{20}$ if we have been asked to add $\frac{3}{5} + \frac{1}{4}$ or as 0.6 if the object is to find $\frac{3}{5}$ of 75.

Specifically, *Principles and Standards for School Mathematics* (2000) stated that instructional programs from prekindergarten through grade 12 should enable all students to

- create and use representations to organize, record, and communicate mathematical ideas;
- select, apply, and translate among mathematical representations to solve problems;
- use representations to model and interpret physical, social, and mathematical phenomena. (p. 67)

In the *Common Core State Standards*, one of the mathematical practices is to model with mathematics. The authors of the document asserted that students

Classroom Dialogues

The class in this scenario has been studying the formulas for finding the areas of various polygons. The diagram shown in Figure 1.12 is drawn on the whiteboard.

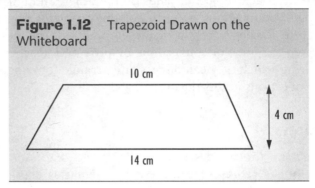

Figure 1.12 Trapezoid Drawn on the Whiteboard

10 cm

4 cm

14 cm

Teacher: Can anyone tell me what this figure appears to be?

Student 1: It looks like a trapezoid.

Teacher: How do you know?

Student 2: A trapezoid has two parallel sides, and the sides that are 10 and 14 are parallel.

Teacher: What if the other two opposite sides were parallel?

Student 2: Then it would be a parallelogram.

Teacher: Good. So, how can we find the area of this trapezoid?

Student 1: You take one-half of the height times the sum of the bases. So, it would be like this (student comes up and writes on the whiteboard):

$$A = \frac{1}{2}(4)(10 + 14) = 2(24) = 48$$

So, the answer is 48.

Teacher: Okay, 48 what?

Student 1: Just 48.

Teacher: What about the units?

Student 2: It's 48 centimeters, not just 48.

Teacher: Are you sure it's centimeters?

Student 2: Square centimeters?

Student 1: I'm thinking cubic centimeters, but I'm not sure.

Teacher: Why cubic centimeters?

Student 1: Because you actually used three different numbers from the trapezoid, so wouldn't that make it cubed units?

Student 2: But I thought that cubed units were only for volume.

The confusion in this classroom discussion is very common in secondary as well as middle school mathematics classrooms. Often students know and can apply a formula to determine perimeter, area, or volume, but they do not understand how to label the answer properly so that the dimensions make sense. On the 2003 National Assessment of Educational Progress, eighth graders were asked whether the measure of the area of a triangle could be represented as 2 cm, 3 m, 5 cm^2, or 8 cm^3. In the United States, only 47 percent of the students answered this question correctly (National Center for Education Statistics, 2005a)! What might you say to these students to help them place the correct label on the answer? Do you consider it a "major" issue in your class if one student writes "48," while others write "48 cm," "48 sq cm," or "48 cu cm" on their papers as the answer to this question?

Although unit labeling often does not appear to be an important issue—after all, the student did the correct calculation and found the answer of 48—the science community and others have serious concerns about these types of errors. In a physics class, for example, velocity is often written in $\frac{m}{sec}$ (meters per second) because it represents distance traveled in a given amount of time. However, acceleration is a measure of how rapidly velocity changes over time, so it is expressed in $\frac{m}{sec}$/sec (meters per second, per second) or $\frac{m}{sec^2}$. Although these units differ by "only" an exponent of 1 or 2 in the denominator, they represent two very different conceptual ideas. Particularly in the study of physics and chemistry, proper labeling of units is essential. So, the better students are prepared to think about the accuracy of units in a mathematics class, the more likely they will be to apply the ideas to science and other contexts.

The teacher in this scene needs to step back with the class and talk about how perimeter represents the distance around a region and is, therefore, measured in units such as feet or meters. However, area involves multiplying two dimensions—length times width, squaring a radius, and so on—so that a unit is multiplied by the same unit, resulting in a square unit. Students should be encouraged to think of area as the number of square units required to cover a region, so the answer to an area problem should be in "squares." Likewise, because volume involves determining the number of cubes required to fill a three-dimensional space, the answer to a volume problem should be expressed in cubic units.

The last question raised by Student 1 should not be taken lightly. The student recognizes that three dimensions were used in the area calculation and assumes, therefore, that the answer should be written in cubic units. However, what the student does not realize is that two of the dimensions were added together prior to multiplication, so that only two dimensions were actually multiplied (half of 4 cm is multiplied by 24 cm to result in an answer in square centimeters). It is important for teachers of mathematics to insist that students think carefully about the units they use to express answers to measurement problems, as the reasoning behind the units they choose can often reveal deeper misconceptions that can be addressed in the classroom.

should be able to "identify important quantities in a practical situation and map their relationships using tools such as diagrams, two-way tables, graphs, flow-charts and formulas" (2010, p. 7) as well as to use tools such as technology, rulers, or physical materials appropriately when solving a problem. Representation is an important part of the process of doing, teaching, and learning mathematics because students often find themselves trying to determine the best and the most appropriate way to model a problem situation.

In summary, the *Common Core State Standards* (2010) list eight **mathematical practices** that "mathematics educators at all levels should seek to develop in their students" (p. 6). These practices are as follows:

1. Make sense of problems and persevere in solving them.
2. Reason abstractly and quantitatively.
3. Construct viable arguments and critique the reasoning of others.
4. Model with mathematics.
5. Use appropriate tools strategically.
6. Attend to precision.
7. Look for and make use of structure.
8. Look for and express regularity in repeated reasoning. (pp. 6–8)

In *Principles and Standards for School Mathematics* (NCTM, 2000), there are five mathematical process skills that are described in detail. These skills are as follows:

1. Problem Solving
2. Reasoning and Proof
3. Connections
4. Communication
5. Representation

These two documents highlight many of the same skills, though they state them in different ways. A book, published by the NCTM and entitled *Making It Happen: A Guide to Interpreting and Implementing the Common Core State Standards for Mathematics* (NCTM, 2010), includes detailed comparisons of the "practices" of the Common Core and the "processes" of *Principles and Standards*.

Of course, leading a group of students through a problem-solving situation—as well as helping the students to reason, communicate, connect, and represent problems appropriately—requires a classroom teacher who is well-versed in mathematical content. The Conference Board of the Mathematical Sciences (2001) has called for deeper, higher-quality mathematics content backgrounds for prospective teachers. Likewise, in her book *Knowing and Teaching Elementary Mathematics* (1999), Liping Ma asserted the following:

> The teaching of a teacher with profound understanding of fundamental mathematics has connectedness, promotes multiple approaches to solving a given problem, revisits and reinforces basic ideas, and has longitudinal coherence. [Such a teacher] is able to reveal and represent connections among mathematical concepts and procedures to students. He or she appreciates different facets of an idea and various approaches to a solution, as well as their advantages and disadvantages—and is able to provide explanations for students of these various facets and approaches. [The teacher] is aware of the "simple but powerful" basic ideas of mathematics and tends to revisit and reinforce them. He or she has a fundamental understanding of the whole . . . curriculum, thus is ready to exploit an opportunity to review concepts that students have previously studied or to lay the groundwork for a concept to be studied later. (p. 124)

⬤ Conclusion

Think back to Mr. James's classroom as described in this chapter. His students were asked to select a real-life problem and find a function that modeled it. We can analyze the class project and student responses through the lens of the five mathematical processes described in this chapter. Students selected a function and were faced with the problem of expressing it in a variety of ways and determining how the function behaved so that they could explain it to others. As they explored the ways to write the function in a sentence, in a table, with an equation, and as a graph, they were faced with the task of representing their functions in a variety of ways and determining the strengths and weaknesses of each method of representation. When students made presentations to the class and submitted written papers about their functions, they were communicating the mathematics in written and oral form to their peers and teacher. Mr. James asked students to analyze two of the problems posed by others in the project; thus, he was promoting reasoning skills as students explored the question of "what about these functions makes them different?" Finally, the students were making connections among various representations of their functions as well as connecting algebra concepts to real-world phenomena in their daily lives.

Books have been written on the nature of mathematics and what it means to do mathematics. Although many people think of mathematics as a content area—algebra, geometry, number theory, and so on—the purpose of this chapter is to remind us that mathematics is also a process, something that one "does." NCTM has defined five **mathematical processes** that should permeate every lesson every day in the classroom—problem solving, reasoning and proof, communication, connections, and representation. These are often referred to as the *umbrella standards* because they constitute what students should be doing as they learn about specific content issues such as algebra or probability. Similarly, the *Common Core State Standards* include eight mathematical practices that parallel NCTM's process skills.

When a lesson is planned, mathematics teachers often consider the processes and practices and how they can be incorporated into the class period. The main intent of the class may be to learn to sketch a sine and cosine curve, but in the process, students are presented with problems and questions that develop their mathematical thinking skills along the way. As Mark Twain said, "Education is what's left over when you forget all the facts that your teachers made you memorize when you were in school." Students may forget how to factor a perfect cube six months after the method was taught, but if the lesson was effective, they will have learned to apply mathematical processes that will be useful long after the formulas have been forgotten. In addition, they should be able to reconstruct the method for themselves.

Surveys from industry consistently indicate that employers are looking for a workforce that has problem-solving and communication skills (see, for example, the famous *SCANS* [Secretary's Commission on Achieving Necessary Skills] *Report,* 1991). Businesses claim that they will undertake the necessary on-the-job training, but they need as their raw material employees who can think and work with others. Mathematics teachers can help produce reflective problem solvers by focusing lessons and activities on the mathematical processes and practices. In the next chapter, we examine six principles that underlie the teaching and learning of mathematics, as described by the NCTM, and how understanding these principles can be helpful to a teacher.

For bibliographic references and additional resources, see page 399.

● Glossary

Communication: Communication is the process by which students express their mathematical thinking to others in oral or written form. Students are encouraged to go beyond "being able to do" the mathematics and to communicate their thinking to others.

Connections: Making mathematical connections is the process by which students connect the mathematics they are studying to (1) other areas of the mathematics curriculum (such as knowing how Pascal's Triangle applies to the binomial theorem in algebra while it also is useful in determining sample spaces in the study of probability), (2) other areas of the curriculum, such as science or social studies, and to (3) the real world.

Exercise: An exercise is a task with which a person is already familiar, and doing an exercise is considered routine practice of a skill. This differs from a problem, in which there is no immediate solution.

Mathematical Practices: The *Common Core State Standards for Mathematics* describe eight practices that should be emphasized in the mathematics classroom at all grade levels, such as making sense of problems and persevering in solving them and reasoning abstractly and quantitatively.

Mathematical Processes: The National Council of Teachers of Mathematics has identified five processes that underlie the teaching and learning of mathematics.

These *umbrella* processes include problem solving, reasoning and proof, communication, connections, and representation.

Problem: A problem is a task that has no immediate solution, and the person solving it has to begin by defining the problem and identifying a strategy. This differs from an exercise, in which a person is already familiar with the task and merely needs to practice a skill.

Problem Solving: Problem solving is a mathematical process by which students attempt to identify what is needed, to set up a plan, to implement the plan, and to check the reasonableness of their answer (see Polya's 1945 book). As students engage in problem solving, they develop a set of problem-solving strategies that can be applied in other situations. Some of these strategies include writing an equation, making a physical model, working backward, drawing a graph, making a table, and using guess and check.

Reasoning: Reasoning is the mathematical process by which students seek to explain "why" something happens the way it does or "what would happen if . . ." something were different in a problem. Mathematical reasoning deals with constructing proof (either formally or informally) that conjectures are true or false.

Representation: Representation is the mathematical process by which students take a given problem situation and attempt to model it in a useful way that will enable them to solve the problem. Different representations of problems are appropriate at different times, depending on the context.

Rubric: A rubric is a grading scale that is often used for scoring open-ended (free-response) questions, essays, presentations, and projects within and outside of mathematics. Generally, each scale number in a rubric is attached to a description of student performance that is required to reach that particular level.

Standard: A standard is a benchmark that can be used by a school, a district, a state, or a country to determine the degree to which the educational program "measures up" to what is expected. The National Council of Teachers of Mathematics released three standards documents in the 1980s and 1990s and another comprehensive document entitled *Principles and Standards for School Mathematics* in 2000. The intent of these documents was to provide a direction and set of goals for those involved in planning mathematics curriculum, instruction, and assessment.

● Discussion Questions and Activities

1. Why did you choose to enter the teaching profession and teach mathematics? In what ways might your reasons for becoming a mathematics teacher influence your beliefs about education?

2. Take some time to explore a TIMSS Web site. What are the implications of the results of TIMSS? What do the data tell us about mathematics education in the United States, including its apparent strengths and weaknesses?

3. Visit the Web site for the National Assessment of Educational Progress (NAEP) test. Explore recent results of the test, including examining several sample items. Are you surprised by the questions asked or the results? Explain.

4. Obtain the *Curriculum and Evaluation Standards for School Mathematics* (1989) and *Principles and Standards for School Mathematics* (2000) in hard copy or by visiting www.nctm.org. Compare the philosophy and contents of these two standards documents. How did the philosophy of mathematics education change during the 10 years between these documents, and what appears to have remained the same?

5. In a small group, select one of the process standards or mathematical practices. Obtain a copy of one of the source documents—*Principles and Standards for School Mathematics* (2000) or the *Common Core State Standards for Mathematics* (2010)—and research the process or practice. Present any new insights gained from the narratives or examples presented in the source documents.

6. Observe a secondary or middle school mathematics lesson (or view one on a videotape) and outline what the teacher does in the lesson to promote any or all of the mathematical processes or practices.

7. What does it mean if someone suggests that you "place problem solving at the focal point" of your mathematics classroom? How is this different from what we have traditionally experienced in the teaching and learning of mathematics?

8. Identify a rich problem in a resource book, a textbook, or on the Internet, and explain how it can be used to promote and develop a number of different problem-solving strategies.

9. Identify a routine algorithm such as "adding up the total number of decimal places and counting that many to the left" when you multiply decimals, "inverting the second fraction and multiplying" when you divide fractions, or "adding the opposite" when you subtract integers. Then think about and discuss how one might teach a class how to use the algorithm while you are promoting mathematical processes or practices in a lesson.

10. Discuss the degree to which Chapter 1 changed your thinking on what it means to "do," to "teach," and to "learn" mathematics.

Principles of Mathematics Education

M r. Dussan walks into his mathematics classroom on a Tuesday morning. His students are seated and take out their homework assignments. As the bell rings to start the class period, Mr. Dussan takes out his teacher's manual and reads the answers to each of the 25 problems that had been assigned the day before. Several students have questions about the problems, so their teacher stands at the chalkboard and walks the class through each of the problems that gave the students difficulty on the homework. He then collects the assignments and instructs the students to take out their notebooks. For the next 20 minutes, he shows the class how to factor trinomials. In the process, he works through five factoring examples, from $x^2 + 5x + 4$ to $2x^2 - 5x - 3$, with each example becoming increasingly difficult. At the conclusion of his lecture, Mr. Dussan tells the students to take out a sheet of paper and a pencil and assigns 30 homework problems—the odd-numbered problems from 1 through 60 on page 117. The students are told to spend the last 10 minutes of class starting on the homework, although it is evident that most of them are wasting time and avoiding the work. The bell rings, students pack up their materials and leave, and Mr. Dussan prepares to repeat this lesson in the following class period.

Sound familiar? The previous paragraph describes a generalization of mathematics classrooms at the secondary and middle school levels all over the United States. The routine is familiar to most people; in fact, it is so typical that the average person believes that this is what mathematics teaching and learning are *supposed* to look like. The image is so heavily engrained in the minds of students that when those who are

After reading Chapter 2, you should be able to answer the following questions:

- What are the six principles of mathematics education, as outlined by the NCTM, and what does each mean?
- How can the principles be used to help mathematics teachers define an ideal mathematics education program?
- How does a traditional mathematics teaching model compare to one that embraces the six principles?
- What is the role of professional development in the improvement of classroom teaching practices?
- How do the six principles interact with one another—specifically, what is the relationship among curriculum, teaching, and assessment?

successful in school decide to become mathematics teachers, they run their classrooms in exactly the same manner, assuming that all students will benefit from this type of instruction. But, unfortunately, not everyone is so successful in mathematics. Teaching methods, curricular choices, and assessment strategies all too often are the downfall of students in mathematics classes, who rapidly decide that they are unsuccessful and give up on the subject. These students might have learned much in a different environment but simply never were exposed to the quality of mathematics education that was possible if basic principles had been followed. In this chapter, we will explore those principles of mathematics education, as outlined by the National Council of Teachers of Mathematics (NCTM).

The Six Principles

In 2000, the NCTM released an important document entitled *Principles and Standards for School Mathematics* (2000). While much of the book was devoted to building and improving on previous Standards publications that had been released between 1989 and 1995, a new section outlined six elements necessary to create an exemplary mathematics program for middle and high school students. These six elements, referred to as the **principles**, are equity, curriculum, teaching, learning, assessment, and technology. In the *Standards*, NCTM states that these six areas are "features of high-quality mathematics education" (p. 11). The following short descriptors are provided in the document:

- **Equity.** Excellence in mathematics education requires equity—high expectations and strong support for all students.
- **Curriculum.** A curriculum is more than a collection of activities; it must be coherent, focused on important mathematics, and well articulated across the grades.
- **Teaching.** Effective mathematics teaching requires understanding what students know and need to learn and then challenging and supporting them to learn it well.
- **Learning.** Students must learn mathematics with understanding, actively building new knowledge from experience and prior knowledge.
- **Assessment.** Assessment should support the learning of important mathematics and furnish useful information to both teachers and students.
- **Technology.** Technology is essential in teaching and learning mathematics; it influences the mathematics that is taught and enhances students' learning (NCTM, 2000, p. 11).

Let's take a closer look at each of these principles and the roles they play in the teaching and learning of school mathematics.

Equity

In many schools, an Algebra I course is used as a gatekeeper to higher levels of mathematics. Those who are unable to pass an algebra course are often relegated to a lower track of mathematics courses, which might include pre-algebra, a basic skills review, or some other general mathematics class. Consequently, the mathematical experiences of students in a school often greatly differ. Although some students are challenged by geometry and pre-calculus courses, others may never access these courses or topics at all because of lack of success at earlier levels. But if we believe, for example, that a background in geometry is important, then it follows that we would want geometry to be part of *every* student's background—not just a select few who survive a traditional algebra course.

Another common practice in many schools is that seniority (i.e., years of teaching experience in the district) is often the determining factor when selecting the teachers for various mathematics courses. As a result, the stronger, more experienced teachers tend to choose to teach the higher-level courses, leaving the weaker and less-experienced teachers in charge of classes that include primarily low-achieving students who have been unsuccessful in mathematics. And, as those students are placed in classes with others who have not performed acceptably in mathematics in the past, the result can be a downward spiral in which historically unsuccessful students never experience the finest of teachers and the interaction with peers who enjoy mathematics and contribute significantly to a positive classroom climate. **Equity** in mathematics, then, is defined as the assumption that all students have a right to equally access all areas of the curriculum as well as high-quality instructional materials and teaching.

Take a minute to think about your basic beliefs about the potential of your students to learn mathematics. Do you believe that *all* students are capable of learning mathematics? And, if so, then what kinds of experiences would be necessary in a school to ensure that even those who struggle with mathematics can become successful and have access to algebra, geometry, and statistics content? As much as anything, achieving equity depends on teachers operating under the assumption that all students can learn mathematics, given the appropriate conditions. So, the use of hands-on teaching strategies, computers, cooperative group work, individual tutoring, and other techniques can contribute to helping every student learn the mathematics needed to be an informed citizen. We will return to this issue in some depth, particularly in Chapter 12.

Curriculum

When most people hear the word *curriculum*, they immediately think of textbooks and, in fact, those terms are often used synonymously. A generally accepted definition of curriculum includes not only the textbooks used but also a program of studies or a series of courses that a student takes in a subject area. However, **curriculum** can be thought of as a much broader term still, as it includes all of the experiences that a student has throughout an educational career. In addition, Elliot Eisner, a curricular theorist, stated that students may learn as much by virtue of the way that teachers structure their classrooms as from the books that they use. Eisner (1994) refers to this as the **implicit curriculum** in that students learn about the nature of the content area by virtue of the way the classroom is arranged, the psychological environment established by the teacher, the way that lessons are arranged, the manner in which learning tools such as calculators are used, and so forth. Therefore, in this more comprehensive view of curriculum, we consider not only *what* is taught in the mathematics classroom but also *how* it is being taught.

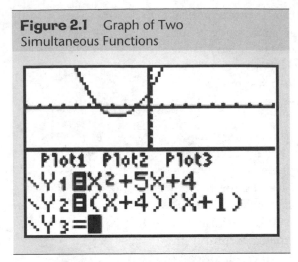

Figure 2.1 Graph of Two Simultaneous Functions

Figure 2.2 Functions Displayed in Tabular Form

Returning to Mr. Dussan's classroom, suppose that students are able to correctly factor the trinomial $x^2 + 5x + 4$ into the two binomials $(x + 4)(x + 1)$. Often, teachers will ask students to "check their answer" by multiplying the resulting binomials to determine whether the product matches the original expression. However, a richer approach to verifying this solution might be to use a graphing calculator and explore the graphs of the functions $y_1 = x^2 + 5x + 4$ and $y_2 = (x + 4)(x + 1)$. If both of these equations describe the same function, we would expect their graphs to be the same. The graphing calculator screen shot in Figure 2.1 shows the image that students would see if they graphed both functions simultaneously, using the setting that allows them to view the equations and the graphs at the same time.

In this situation, it would not be unusual for a student to ask whether one of the curves could be located off the viewing window, making the solution incorrect. In response, the teacher might invite students to switch their calculators to Table mode, as shown in Figure 2.2.

Students can readily see that when the same x-value is substituted into each equation, the resulting y-values are the same, since the Y_1 and Y_2 columns display identical function values. The visual approach of utilizing graphs and tables as well as the use of technology is much more appealing to students than using paper and pencil to remultiply the two binomials in the solution. Furthermore, this strategy promotes equity as it may make more sense to the visual learner who otherwise could have been excluded from the lesson.

In viewing this example, one might ask, "But what if the students don't already know what a parabola looks like? Would the image in Figure 2.1 make much sense to them?" These are good questions because this manner of viewing the solution is much more powerful if studied *after* a unit on graphing parabolas. Yet most textbooks and mathematics programs study manipulation of polynomials (including factoring trinomials) before graphing quadratics. So, it is up to the teacher and the local district to properly *sequence* the learning experiences in the most meaningful order possible. Therefore, curriculum not only is about *what* is taught and *how* it is taught but also is concerned with how big ideas of mathematics are emphasized and the *order* in which topics are introduced. There are far too many instances of middle school students, for example, beginning each school year with yet another unit on fractions. Consequently, students become frustrated (if they struggled with fractions last year and are experiencing the same topic again) or bored (if they have already mastered the skills) with the class within the few days of the school year. In designing the curriculum, it is important to consider a reasonable sequence of topics over the years—as well as within a single school year—to avoid duplication of topics and to meaningfully build on student knowledge. The curriculum is the focus of Unit 2, which includes Chapters 4 and 5.

How Would You React

SCENARIO

You have devised a series of lessons in which students are exploring the relationships between similar right triangles on the computer. The plan is for students to discover that the ratios of the lengths of sides in the triangles remain the same as long as the angles are equal. The goal is for the students to eventually discover the trigonometric ratios. After the first day's exploration, you assign some homework problems for students to try. The following day, a student in your class announces to everyone, "I showed this assignment to my sister, and she showed me something called trigonometry. By using three buttons on the calculator, you can get all of these answers without having to use the computer or anything!" Your response is to

a. Ignore the student's comment and move on with your lesson so that the "discovery" aspect of the lesson is not affected.

b. Praise the student for obtaining help but ask him or her not to share any further so that others can find a shortcut by themselves.

c. Ask the student to share what his or her sister has explained so that the whole class can benefit.

d. Speak individually with the student and remind him or her that the assignment was supposed to be completed without assistance.

e. Other.

DISCUSSION

The situation described in this scenario is very familiar to mathematics teachers who utilize discovery lessons that are intended for students to create their own generalizations. The use of this "inquiry" method of teaching can be a powerful way to get students *doing* and *inventing* mathematics rather than simply being given rules or shown procedures. However, if an investigation takes place over the course of multiple lessons, almost inevitably one or more students will seek assistance from a parent, sibling, or peer and be "told" something more than the teacher intended the student to know at this point in the process.

This is a situation in which "an ounce of prevention is worth a pound of cure." In other words, teachers who routinely use inquiry lessons need to discuss this teaching strategy, in advance, with the students

and their parents. When the school year begins, either at a parent–teacher meeting (such as Meet the Teacher Night at school) or by means of a printed or emailed newsletter, the teacher should explain to parents that discovery will be used as a common teaching tool throughout the year. Parents should be told that the goal of this technique is for the students to discover some of the mathematics on their own. As a result, though parents may feel that they are helping by "showing" or "giving" answers to their children, they can actually be of more assistance by allowing the students to struggle a bit. Parents are in an excellent position to encourage the students to try their best, as well as to ask them questions about what they know and what they are trying to figure out. But to give answers or explain shortcuts will undermine the teacher's strategy and, in the long run, may harm the instructional process. For most parents, this information is a relief, as they now know that they are not responsible for explaining the mathematics content themselves. Once they realize that the child will eventually learn the material, the parents will recognize that struggling is part of the learning process.

Likewise, students in the class deserve an explanation of this teaching process as well. A simple explanation can be given, such as, "When you go home tonight, I want you to attempt these five problems. They're not easy, but I know you can figure them out on your own. Over the next couple of days, you may discover a few shortcuts for solving them. But I want you to find those shortcuts yourself because, if you do, you'll understand why they work and will remember them longer. Please don't ask your friends, your parents, or your brothers and sisters for help tonight. It's really important that you try to solve the problems on your own, and we'll talk about what you came up with when you come back to class tomorrow." Generally, students are very good about respecting the teacher's wishes when this type of explanation is provided. Once they realize what the teacher is attempting to accomplish, they are likely to "play the game" and will not come in the next day eager to share what a brother, sister, or parent showed them. But if this groundwork is not laid in advance, you may very well get the response described in this scenario, and the manner in which you handle it will be up to you.

Teaching

Of course, the most important factor in the mathematical development of students lies in the skill of the teacher. An effective teacher needs not only a high level of competence in the content area but also considerable knowledge of how students learn, as well as a well-crafted set of teaching activities and strategies and the wisdom to know which technique will work best with a given class in a particular situation. An effective teacher constantly reflects on practice and obtains professional development to keep up with the latest in educational research and practice.

The classroom teacher makes numerous decisions every day. Examples of these decisions include selecting content and processes to emphasize, determining how long to spend on a given topic or student question, choosing appropriate activities and problems, deciding which problems to assign for homework, and selecting what content should be measured and how to measure it (e.g., through tests, projects, presentations, etc.). The mathematics teacher must also be successful at establishing a positive classroom environment. This environment includes both physical characteristics of the room and a positive psychological climate that welcomes risk taking and encourages participation by all students.

The process of becoming a teacher is a lifelong endeavor, as discussed in detail in Chapter 13. Most importantly, the teacher needs to seek out professional development to learn about and reflect on the latest instructional ideas for the classroom. Although many courses, conferences, and workshops are available, one way that teachers can conduct self-directed plans for improvement is through sites on the Internet. One such Web site is Learner.org, which is sponsored by Annenberg Media. At this Web site, hundreds of hours of streaming video are available for teachers to view, both for professional development and for use in the classroom. Figure 2.3 shows a screen shot of this Web site as it appears when "Mathematics" is chosen from a pull-down menu as the discipline of choice.

Most importantly, it is the teacher's responsibility to develop the skills required to motivate and engage the learner so that significant mathematics concepts can be made available to all students. The processes of writing good lesson plans and implementing helpful teaching strategies are the focus of Unit 3, which includes Chapters 6 through 9. A further discussion of professional development of teachers is presented in Chapter 13.

Learning

In thinking about the learning principle, consider a person who is taking lessons to play the guitar. Suppose that the teacher emphasizes playing scales, and week after week, the student spends endless hours practicing the C, G, and D scales. After some time, the student will be considerably skilled at playing two octaves of these scales, forward and backward. But then a friend comes over who plays the piano and wants to perform a song with the guitar student. The guitarist is confused and does not know what to do. Unless the piano player wants to play the C scale forward and backward, there is nothing else that the guitarist can do. In short, this student has been taught the basics of playing scales but was never taught how to play a song, so the skills are fairly worthless.

In a similar way, the focus in the mathematics classroom needs to be broader than "showing" students how to perform skill-based procedures. Just as the guitarist is taught the scales, many students sit endlessly in mathematics classrooms, with the teacher showing them how to compute the area of a trapezoid, add fractions

Figure 2.3 Learner.org Search Result

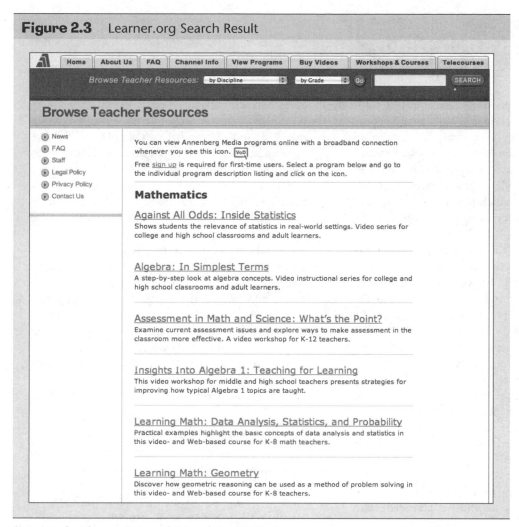

(Reprinted with permission of Annenberg Media.)

with unlike denominators, find a median, solve a linear equation, and construct a perpendicular bisector with a compass and straightedge. But these skills appear to the mathematics students to exist in a vacuum unless they are challenged with real-life problems and situations in which the skills are *applied* in a meaningful way. Problem solving is the "song" of mathematics—the opportunity to develop and put skills to use to explore real situations. Although no one will deny that developing skills is important (just as learning to play the scales is a fundamental component of learning to play an instrument), the learning process needs to involve more than acquiring procedural knowledge. NCTM stated that the learning process should involve "factual knowledge, procedural proficiency, and conceptual understanding" (2000, p. 21), and all three of these are necessary components in a rich mathematics classroom setting.

A simple example of this is the use of the distributive property. In algebra classes, students generally are taught how to expand an expression by using this property, such as determining that $3n(2n + 5) = 6n^2 + 15n$. However, the first time that this same algebra class encounters a problem that requires multiplying 17×8, we often see the students rushing to get their hands on a calculator to find the

SPOTlight on Technology

One of the most rapidly growing classroom technologies is the interactive whiteboard (IWB). Many educators refer to this technology as a Smart Board because Smart Technologies was the first company to produce such a board that could be used in a classroom. Although several companies now produce these devices, the name "Smart Board" has stuck, much like a copy machine is often referred to as a Xerox machine and tissues are often called Kleenex.

An IWB can be installed on a wall with a permanent projector mounted on the ceiling or can be placed on wheels as a portable unit. The IWB is connected to a computer that generally has Internet access, and the projector displays the computer's screen image on the whiteboard. Some models do not require a projector at all and are stand-alone devices that operate much like a flat screen television. What makes this technology unique is that the whiteboard is touch sensitive. Using either a finger or a stylus, the teacher can simply touch the screen to interact with it. So, notes can be written on the board by using a pallet of different colors. These notes, in turn, can be saved and then printed out, or they can be saved as a PDF file and uploaded to the teacher's Web site. Students can return to the site at a later date and download the notes from class that day. This process is particularly helpful for a student who has missed school due to an illness or vacation. The student has immediate access to everything the teacher wrote on the board on the days that the student missed.

Since the IWB is touch sensitive, a variety of other possibilities are available. Here are a few examples:

- A Web site can be accessed that features mathematical content or applications and demonstrates a process for the class. For example, a site may feature an interactive visual tool that helps students to make sense of a mathematical concept such as viewing the process of solving an equation as similar to balancing a scale.
- A graphing calculator image can be projected onto the IWB, and the teacher can simply point to the appropriate keys to draw a graph or do a calculation. In this manner, students can actually see which buttons the teacher is pressing.
- Software, such as a spreadsheet, can be opened on the computer and displayed on the screen. The teacher (or students) can click on cells of the spreadsheet and interact with it directly on the IWB.
- The teacher can create a diagram for a problem-solving activity in advance, save it on the computer, and launch the image at the appropriate time in the lesson. The diagram, therefore, can be professionally generated, and the teacher does not to have use class time attempting to draw the image on the board. By using a "transparency slide" function, the teacher (or students) can mark up the diagram by using a virtual pen.

The possibilities for use of an IWB are almost endless. The technology actively engages students, provides visual models, allows for instant access to Web sites that can be used for instruction (including sites that feature streaming videos), and, most importantly, is fascinating and interesting to students. As the use of IWBs becomes more prominent, the chalkboard is rapidly becoming a thing of the past. Although little research at the present time links academic progress to use of the IWB, this technology unquestionably is the wave of the future in mathematics classrooms.

---

product. This situation is a teachable moment in which the teacher can point out that the distributive property can enable them to find this product mentally, since

$$17 \times 8 = 8(10 + 7) = (8 \times 10) + (8 \times 7) = 80 + 56 = 136$$

If the students can think of the multiplication problem as a distributive property situation by rewriting 17 as $10 + 7$, they can determine the product with ease, without using a calculator. Furthermore, suppose that a student is asked to multiply $4 \times 3\frac{1}{5}$. Many students respond by doing the following:

$$4 \times 3\frac{1}{5} = \frac{4}{1} \times \frac{16}{5} = \frac{64}{5} = 12\frac{4}{5}$$

However, the student who recognizes the computational implications of the distributive property might think:

$$4 \times 3\frac{1}{5} = 4\left(3 + \frac{1}{5}\right) = 12 + \frac{4}{5} = 12\frac{4}{5}$$

Essentially, the 3 and the $\frac{1}{5}$ each have been multiplied by 4, and this simple product can be computed in one's head, without having to utilize the procedure of changing the mixed number to an improper fraction.

The key, then, to promoting deep learning is to teach for understanding. Students should remain focused on conceptual ideas while also practicing fundamental skills. Most importantly, they need to be engaged in making connections among mathematical topics so that they make sense of how mathematical ideas are interrelated. This focus on learning and student thinking is the topic of Chapter 3 and is also woven throughout the book. Also, the "Classroom Dialogues" feature in each chapter explores a content issue and raises questions about how to respond to student misconceptions.

Assessment

To many, "assessment" is synonymous with "testing" and "giving grades." It is often viewed as something that is done *to* students in order to classify them by measuring their competence. But the NCTM takes a much more holistic view of this area. Assessment is a process by which information is gathered about students in order to improve the instructional process. Although this information may be collected through the formal administration of a test, it also may be the result of student journal writing, presentations given to a class, or even simple informal observations of students as they work together in a group, attempting to solve a problem. As a result of the assessments, both students and teachers are provided with information that can be used in a positive manner. For example, observations may reveal that students are confused, and in turn, the teacher may choose to intervene by posing a new problem or spending an extra class period on a particularly difficult concept. As such, assessment is an ongoing process that should not be viewed as an interruption and done exclusively "at the end of a unit."

Providing students with timely and helpful feedback is an essential component of effective classroom assessment. A student who completes a homework paper, writes a journal entry, or creates a project deserves to know how the work could have been improved, as well as the mathematical accuracy and potential misunderstandings that are evident in the work. With this feedback, students can improve their level of competence with more focus on what they need to improve. Again, the assessment should serve to improve the teaching and learning of mathematics in the classroom. The topic of assessment, including details on its purposes and how to use

Students investigate angle measures by collecting data with a protractor and reflecting on the results.

various measures of student progress, is the focus of Unit 4, which includes Chapters 10 and 11.

Technology

Think about the options available to a teacher who is beginning a unit on parallel lines and the angles formed when parallel lines are intersected by a third line. In a traditional classroom setting, the teacher may draw two parallel lines on a chalkboard, crossed by a third line (transversal). Then the teacher might identify the angles formed by the transversal cutting through the lines, pointing out which angles are congruent and which are supplementary, often writing definitions or rules on the board. In other classes, students may be asked to draw the lines on their own papers, be given protractors, and asked to measure the angles that are formed. The teacher then can ask the students to share their angle measures and to discuss the relationships that they have found.

Another alternative that the teacher has for this lesson is to take the students to a computer lab (or use one computer with an overhead display in the classroom) and use a dynamic geometry software package to help students determine the relationships. A student created the diagram shown in Figure 2.4 on a computer. It shows two parallel lines, cut by a transversal, and the angle measures have been determined by the computer for discussion.

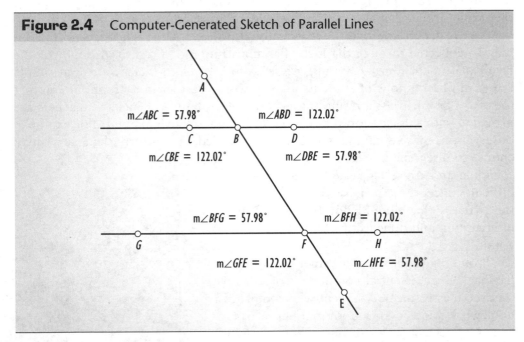

Figure 2.4   Computer-Generated Sketch of Parallel Lines

Using the image in Figure 2.4, students will notice that, although eight angles are formed when the transversal cuts the parallel lines, there are only two angle measures in the picture. They are also likely to notice that the adjacent angles are supplementary (i.e., add up to 180°) and that the vertical angles are congruent. From this point, the teacher can begin to give names to pairs of angles, such as referring to $\angle ABC$ and $\angle BFG$ as corresponding angles or $\angle CBE$ and $\angle BFH$ as alternate interior angles. By dragging transversal $\overline{BF}$, students can see that the same angle relationships exist, regardless of the steepness (slope) of the crossing line. Finally, the teacher can move one of the two parallel lines so that the lines are no longer parallel, and students can see that the angle relationships, such as alternate exterior angles being congruent, are no longer true.

The technology in this example provides a rich opportunity for students to interact with a geometric figure and formulate their own conjectures about relationships and what is causing them. Although the other two methods of instruction described—the teacher showing students the relationships on the board and the students drawing pictures on paper—are options for instruction in this lesson, the use of technology is much more likely to motivate students and to help them make sense of what happens when lines are intersected by a transversal.

The use of technology in the mathematics classroom is essential and goes far deeper than "checking answers" after paper-and-pencil work has been completed. Instead, students should be actively engaged in their learning through the use of graphing calculators, computers (including handheld computer devices), interactive whiteboards, and the Internet. Explorations such as the one described here can be particularly helpful for visual learners, as well as for students with learning disabilities who are unlikely to make sense of a teacher's lecture at a chalkboard. The appropriate use of technology should influence both *what* the teacher is teaching and *how* the concept is taught. In each chapter of the book, a feature entitled "Spotlight on Technology" will provide concrete examples of how technology can be used effectively in the teaching and learning process, and other technological examples are woven throughout the text.

Classroom Dialogues

On a quiz involving multiplying monomials and raising monomials to powers, a student wrote the answers shown in Figure 2.5.

The teacher called the student up to the desk and conducted a short interview to probe the answers more deeply.

Teacher: Can you explain to me how you found the answer to the first question?
Student: It's just a multiplication problem. So, you take 3 and 5 and multiply them to get 15. Then you multiply the exponents together, so 2 times 4 is 8.
Teacher: What about the second problem?
Student: In this one, you're raising the monomial to the third power. So, you take 2 times the power of 3 and you get 6. Wait a minute. It should be 2 to the third power, but that's not 6, is it?
Teacher: No, what should it be?
Student: Well, 2 times 2 is 4, and 4 times another 2 is 8. So, it should be 8. Then you just add 4 plus 3 and 5 plus 3 to get the exponents of 7 and 8. So, it should have been $8a^7b^8$.

Figure 2.5   Answers to Quiz Questions

$(3x^2)(-5x^4)$ $-15x^8$

$(2a^4b^5)^3$ $6a^7b^8$

(continued)

What do you believe is the student's understanding of these problems? What misconceptions does this student have and how might you help correct them? Often, the student views an error such as multiplying the exponents in the first problem as a "dumb mistake," but it may go deeper than that, indicating that a major conceptual misunderstanding is at the core of the incorrect answer. To help this student, it may be necessary to go back and rework the problems as if there were no rules to follow at all, as it appears that the student has incorrectly applied the power rules.

The teacher might help the student write the first problem out without using exponents at all:

$$(3x^2)(-5x^4) = 3 \cdot x \cdot x \cdot (-5) \cdot x \cdot x \cdot x \cdot x$$

Rearranging the factors and then rewriting the product of the six x terms by using an exponent, the student would find:

$$3 \cdot (-5) \cdot x \cdot x \cdot x \cdot x \cdot x \cdot x = -15x^6$$

The exponent rule says to *add* the exponents when multiplying, but the student originally multiplied the exponents. Expanding the problem into a form that does not use exponents at all can help the student not only to recognize how the rule was incorrectly memorized but also to see how the problem could be solved if the rule were forgotten entirely—a way to reconstruct or "invent" the process.

The second problem can be explored in a similar way:

$$(2a^4b^5)^3 = (2 \cdot a \cdot a \cdot a \cdot a \cdot b \cdot b \cdot b \cdot b \cdot b)^3$$

This expression *means* to repeat the factor in parentheses three times:

$$(2 \cdot a \cdot a \cdot a \cdot a \cdot b \cdot b \cdot b \cdot b \cdot b)^3 = (2 \cdot a \cdot a \cdot a \cdot a \cdot b \cdot b \cdot b \cdot b \cdot b)$$
$$(2 \cdot a \cdot a \cdot a \cdot a \cdot b \cdot b \cdot b \cdot b \cdot b)(2 \cdot a \cdot a \cdot a \cdot a \cdot b \cdot b \cdot b \cdot b \cdot b)$$

Multiplying these expressions results in an answer of $8a^{12}b^{15}$. Another way to look at the problem is to simply think of the original monomial as having been repeated as a factor three times:

$$(2a^4b^5)^3 = (2a^4b^5)(2a^4b^5)(2a^4b^5) = 8a^{12}b^{15}$$

This method uses the multiplication rule developed in the previous example. Again, the key to the student understanding the process is to see the problem written out in expanded form. Fortunately, the student discovered when talking through the problem that a mistake had been made with raising 2 to the third power. But the issue of dealing with the exponents of the product was still unclear to the student.

Too often, students in mathematics classes are shown an example or two and are expected to immediately generalize the rules, or worse yet, are simply "given" formulas on the chalkboard such as:

$$(x^a)(x^b) = x^{a+b} \text{ and } (x^a y^b)^c = x^{ac}y^{bc}$$

Students write down the formulas and rules into their notes but never really understand where they come from. As a result, we should not be surprised when they make the kinds of mistakes shown in Figure 2.5. When students explore several examples and are expected to extract their own rules and generalizations, they "own" the formulas and are more likely to understand and remember them. Then, if they forget the rules later on, the teacher can always go back and help the students reconstruct them based on examples as described here.

Connecting the Principles

Although the six principles described in this chapter are individual components of an effective mathematics program, they should be thought of as connected to one another. For example, a higher level of learning can be achieved through the use of technology, and using a variety of assessment tools can promote equity. One image to consider is the diagram shown in Figure 2.6.

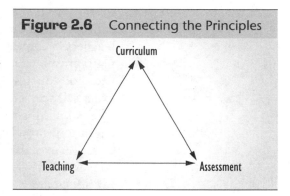

Figure 2.6   Connecting the Principles

The graphic in Figure 2.6 illustrates the connections among curriculum, teaching, and assessment. These three major components of the mathematics teaching profession are linked to one another and are almost impossible to separate. The arrowheads point in both directions to show that each principle affects the others. Suppose, for example, that the state or school district adopts a new set of standards (such as the *Common Core State Standards*) or a local curriculum. The adopted curriculum inevitably will have instructional implications, as the document is likely to point out the use of technology, hands-on materials, or other teaching strategies. So, to begin to use the new curriculum, the teacher will need to rethink classroom teaching practices. The same is true when a district adopts a new textbook series. Likewise, a new curriculum ordinarily implies a different focus in terms of what students are expected to know or be able to do. As a result, this curriculum will make a teacher (as well as the district and state) rethink the assessment practices utilized in the classroom and what factors are emphasized in evaluating student progress. In short, the curricular change brings about changes in teaching and in assessment.

Taken from another angle, suppose that the mathematics faculty from a school attend a workshop and decide to more aggressively implement the use of technology and hands-on materials in their teaching. As the teaching strategies are updated and modified, curricular emphasis is altered as well. For example, more emphasis may be placed on mathematical processing skills and practices, as described in Chapter 1. More attention also may be paid to the visual aspects of problems and to the collection of student-generated data, which also impact the curriculum because students are learning different things as a result of the change in teaching strategies. Furthermore, if greater emphasis is placed on visualization and mathematical processes and practices, teachers will need to restructure their classroom assessment practices to effectively measure them when tracking student progress. So, in the end, the agreement to change teaching practices, by default, affects the curriculum as well as classroom assessment strategies.

As a final illustration, consider what happens when a teacher redesigns the assessment strategies being used in a classroom. For example, suppose that the teacher decides to assign a project for each semester or begins to have students write in a mathematics journal two or three days per week. When the assessment practices change, the curricular emphases in the classroom, as well as the teaching strategies being used in the classroom, are likely to change as a result. In fact, research suggests that one of the best ways to bring about reform in the teaching of mathematics may be to have teachers in a school district study and adopt alternative assessment strategies (Brahier, 2002). All of the principles of the mathematics teaching profession described in this chapter are linked together. It is important for a teacher to recognize this connection and to view the profession as an integrated whole of several important components.

Conclusion

In the *Standards*, NCTM states, "Teaching mathematics well is a complex endeavor, and there are no easy recipes for helping all students learn or for helping teachers become effective" (2000, p. 17). Indeed, if there were a universal teaching plan, proven to be completely effective, that everyone could use, there would be no need for courses in teaching methods or field experiences. But teaching is not an exact science. The project that was a major success with last year's class may not work at all this year. A lesson plan that was a disaster in first period, with a slight alteration, may become one of the best that is taught all year in the fifth-period class. An explanation provided to one parent may be acceptable, whereas the same conversation with other parents may not be.

An analogy can be made with work conducted in the medical field. Perhaps the antibiotic prescribed for an illness that you had was successful in one instance but did not cure you the next time you had the exact same sickness. And the surgery that saves one person's life may not be effective in another case. When we deal with people—whether physically or psychologically—the results of our work are never certain. In the end, teaching is all about making the best use of current research on how students learn, putting it to practice in the classroom, believing firmly that every student can learn, and reflecting on practice so that improvements in teaching can be made with experience over time.

The principles described in this chapter—equity, curriculum, teaching, learning, assessment, and technology—are fundamental aspects of the profession that one must consider and address when becoming a mathematics teacher. And, of course, "becoming" a teacher is a career-long process. These principles are interrelated but can be considered individually. In the remainder of this book, for example, the three major components of curriculum, teaching, and assessment are the focal points of Units 2, 3, and 4, respectively. The current unit relates primarily to learning, and Unit 5 explores equity, as technology is woven throughout the entire text. As you read and think about each component of the mathematics teaching profession, remember that your success in teaching mathematics will rely on your ability to apply and refine these principles in the school setting. In the next chapter, we turn our attention to how students learn and what teachers can do to foster positive attitudes and dispositions toward mathematics in their students.

For bibliographic references and additional resources, see page 401

Glossary

Curriculum: A combination of all of the experiences that a student has throughout an educational career, which includes but is not limited to courses taken and textbooks used.

Equity: The assumption that all students have a right to equally access all areas of the mathematics curriculum as well as high-quality instructional materials and teaching.

Implicit Curriculum: The idea that students learn as much by virtue of the way that teachers structure their classroom as from the books that they use. Students learn about the nature of the content area by the way the classroom is arranged, the psychological environment established by the teacher, the way that lessons are arranged, the manner in which learning tools such as calculators are used, and so on.

Principles: The NCTM *Standards* list six principles, which are equity, curriculum, teaching, learning, assessment, and technology. These are the six features of a mathematics program.

Discussion Questions and Activities

1. Observe multiple mathematics classes with teachers and/or schools by visiting the schools or through video. Discuss the degree to which the teaching strategies employed are more traditional, like that of Mr. Dussan in the introduction of this chapter, versus more contemporary views of teaching, as reflected in the remainder of the chapter.

2. Consider the following statement: All students are capable of learning mathematics. What are your beliefs about this assumption, and how do your beliefs impact your teaching? What might be the impact when teachers in the same mathematics department disagree on the answer to this question?

3. Discuss the notion of an *implicit curriculum*. Provide examples of what you learned about the nature of mathematics and problem solving by virtue of the way your teachers ran the classes when you were in middle or high school. How closely does this match the vision that you now hold about the field of mathematics?

4. Obtain copies of several professional development books, such as NCTM products, that can be used by teachers to enhance their knowledge of mathematics and teaching strategies. How might you use these materials in your career as you refine your teaching practices?

5. Locate a Web site that can be used for professional development or for teaching, such as NCTM's *Illuminations* (NCTM, 2011) site or *Learner.org* (Annenberg Media, 2011). Explore the site and make a brief presentation on how it can be used to help a teacher improve classroom teaching practices.

6. Identify a mathematical concept, such as finding the area of a trapezoid or area under a curve, using the Pythagorean Theorem, or solving quadratic equations. Research and present methods to teach the mathematical idea in a meaningful way so that students develop not only the *skill* but also deep conceptual understanding.

7. Consider the following scenarios: One teacher of a mathematics class gives the students daily homework and weekly tests, and bases grades on these products. Another teacher of the same course has students write in journals, assigns them quarterly projects, and has them keep a portfolio of their work, in addition to giving them homework and administering tests. Discuss the differing messages that students get about what is valued and important in each of these classrooms.

8. An interesting equity issue surrounds the use of graphing calculators in that some districts do not have enough wealth to purchase them. Make a list of options that you might have if you were hired in such a district, particularly if you feel strongly that students should be using this technology.

9. Visit a classroom (or view a video) in which the teacher is using an interactive whiteboard. How does the teacher use the board, and how do the students respond? What are potential benefits and drawbacks of using this technology?

10. Obtain a copy of your state's standards for mathematics. After reviewing the document, describe the ways in which its contents are likely to influence the teaching and assessment practices of teachers within the state.

Learning Theories and Psychology in Mathematics Education

After reading Chapter 3, you should be able to answer the following questions:

- How is research conducted in mathematics education, and how does it impact trends in curriculum, teaching, and assessment?
- What are the key components of learning theories, such as those of Vygotsky, Bruner, and the van Hieles? What are the principles underlying the constructivist model of teaching and learning?
- How do the use of inquiry and an inductive approach to teaching differ from the traditional model that emphasizes deductive methods? Explain why there has been a shift toward this inquiry-based approach.
- What is motivation, and what can teachers do to help "motivate" students?
- What does it mean to develop a positive mathematical disposition? Describe some strategies that might be used to promote positive dispositions and to counter mathematics anxiety in students.

helsea is a sophomore student in Mr. Metzger's third-period Geometry class. On standardized tests, she has demonstrated the potential to be a high-achieving student. Mr. Metzger knows her and is aware that she is an intelligent girl with a promising future, but she is failing his class. At the beginning of the school year, when many of the problems used equation solving from algebra and simple formulas from middle school, Chelsea performed quite well. However, as the year progressed and the class started to work with increasingly more difficult definitions and theorems and to write two-column proofs, she began to struggle and eventually gave up. She rarely does her homework and finds her mind drifting off during class, unable to focus on the problems and proofs being demonstrated by the teacher at the board. After class one day, Chelsea apologized to Mr. Metzger and said, "I really want to do well in your class, but I don't understand it. I'm just not as interested in this class as I have been with other math classes in the past." She urged him not to take it personally, but as he watched her walk out the door, he knew that it couldn't be entirely her fault.

Perhaps you have known a Chelsea in your mathematics career (or maybe you *were* a Chelsea at some point). Every class includes students who have the potential to be successful but are struggling nonetheless. A common reaction is to dismiss Chelsea's problem as a personal issue that only she can fix. After all, if she is not consistently paying attention in class and doing her homework, how can the teacher expect her to achieve acceptably in the course? However, the classroom is a two-way street that involves both the teacher *and* the learner, and there are ways in which a classroom teacher can help a student such as Chelsea. First of all, if she has been having problems with two-column proofs all year long and is one of the smartest students in the class, her peers are probably struggling as well. It is entirely possible that the content is too difficult for many students in the class—developmentally beyond what they are ready to handle at this point. Second, Mr. Metzger should examine how he spends his class time and what he expects his students to be able to do. Chapter 1 discussed the importance of including problem solving, reasoning and proof, communication, connections, and representation in every lesson and emphasizing the eight mathematical practices. It may be that his chalkboard-based teaching style is simply not interesting to his students and that they need the sort of problems and activities that evoke curiosity and, therefore, motivate the class to want to do the work. When it comes to the personality and family concerns of the student, much is beyond the realm of what a teacher can do. After all, the National Research Council (2000) estimates that only 14 percent of students' time is spent in school. The other 86 percent of their time is spent in family and community settings or sleeping. But after close examination and reflection, every teacher should be able to identify areas for improvement in the way that a class is run that may, in turn, help students such as Chelsea get back on track.

This chapter turns to the psychological concerns in the teaching and learning of mathematics. Because theories of educational psychology result from years of research in the classroom, the role of mathematics educational research is explored before some current theories about how students learn are discussed. Then a definition of motivation is discussed, as well as what the teacher can do to help motivate students to learn. Finally, the chapter discusses what the National Council of Teachers of Mathematics calls mathematical disposition—the attitudinal side of teaching mathematics—and how it develops over time.

Research in Mathematics Education

The announcer of a nationally televised professional football game stated that quarterbacks of ages 25 and under have a 35 percent winning percentage whereas quarterbacks over age 33 win 74 percent of their games. He used the data to argue that older players are better at what they do and that teams often "recycle" quarterbacks because their performances tend to improve significantly as they gain experience. What he failed to realize—or at least he never mentioned it—was that only the best quarterbacks in professional football are still playing when they are more than 33 years old. As a result, the data should be no surprise to the viewer— we would expect that the *reason* a quarterback would still be playing beyond age 33 is that he has been very successful and has a high winning percentage. Less-successful quarterbacks have already left the game by the time they are 30 years old and are no longer included in the data. In short, the statistics were mathematically accurate, but conclusions drawn from the data were questionable.

Similarly, a newspaper recently reported that "90 percent of all divorced adults blame the breakup on the other person," and another headline stated that at a famous university, 94 percent of the faculty considered themselves "above average" instructors. Not only do headlines such as these sometimes make us chuckle—after all, shouldn't 50 percent of the teachers be at or above average and 50 percent be at or below average?—but also they inevitably make us ask questions such as, "How do they know that? Who did they ask? Are these statistics reasonable for the whole population? Does the conclusion make sense?" Research is the process of gathering and analyzing data so that the results can be used to inform decision-makers. For example, if a state raises its maximum driving speed from 65 to 75 miles per hour, and research data show a significant increase in highway fatalities during the following year, the legislature may use the research to argue that the speed limit should be lowered again. Decisions are made based on mathematical information every day in our world.

However, we must use caution because some data and, therefore, the results of some research reports are flawed. Let's suppose you ask five of your best friends whether they generally vote Democrat or Republican, and four out of the five say that they are Democrats. Is it logical to assume that 80 percent of all adults are Democrats? Of course not! The sample size you chose was too small to generalize from, and you selected a unique and, therefore, biased part of the population—college-educated and, perhaps, all of the same gender and living in similar situations. If you really wanted to know what percentage of the population belonged to each party, you would need to take a large national survey that included a reasonable mix of geographic regions, socioeconomic groups, gender, and so forth. In addition, you might want to compare your results to data from similar studies to look for patterns, similarities, and inconsistencies. You hope that you would never have to make a significant life decision based on one, potentially flawed, study.

Just as the legislature makes speed limit decisions based, in part, on fatality-rate research, educators ideally should write curricula and select teaching and assessment methods with current research in mind. Chapter 1 looked at the results of the TIMSS, PISA, and NAEP assessments. Once you are aware that fewer than one in twenty twelfth graders could respond acceptably to the movie theater problem, you may begin to ask more questions that require reading, analysis, and a clearly communicated response in your classes in order to give students more experience with this type of problem. In fact, a school district may use research such as the TIMSS, PISA, or NAEP reports to influence the topics taught in school and the type of expectations established for student progress.

Quantitative and Qualitative Methods

In general, two major types of research in education guide our decision-making—quantitative research and qualitative research. **Quantitative research** deals with gathering numerical data and analyzing them. For example, Slavin et al. (1990) described a quantitative study in which some high school students were placed in heterogeneous (mixed-ability) classes, and others were placed in homogeneous (ability-grouped) classes. At the end of a school year, the students in mixed classes significantly outperformed their peers. In short, they scored higher on achievement tests when they were members of heterogeneous classes. Similarly, a study conducted with junior high school students in Israel showed that although high achievers performed about the same in heterogeneous and homogeneous groupings, students at average or low-average levels achieved significantly higher while participating in heterogeneous groupings (Linchevski & Kutscher, 1998). In this article, the authors argued against ability grouping and tracking practices. On the other hand, quantitative research can also argue in favor of ability grouping. For example, a study by Rogers (1998) suggests that all students, particularly those who are gifted, benefit from homogeneous grouping. Therefore, decision-makers need to thoroughly explore a large base of research before reaching any conclusions and acting on the data.

Historically, educators first used quantitative methods. If we wanted to know, for example, whether calculators improve the learning of a particular concept, we could pretest two classes to establish that they are similar in background and proceed to teach them—one with calculators (the experimental group) and one without (the control group). Then, we could compare scores on a posttest to determine whether the calculator-based class actually outperformed the other and report those results to the education community. Recently, however, there has been a trend toward more qualitative research in education as researchers have become skeptical about the degree to which we can describe student performance based solely on numerical data. There has been a similar trend in the assessment of students in mathematics classes as is discussed in Chapters 10 and 11.

Qualitative research involves the collection and analysis of non-numerical data such as videotapes of classroom episodes, scripts of student–teacher conversations, audio recordings of interviews, or written summaries of student journal entries. For example, a qualitative study involving first- and second-year algebra classes in high school showed that teachers who prompted their students to write a five-minute response to a problem or question at the beginning of class several days per week tended to adjust their lesson plans accordingly, gaining more insight into student understanding than they would have without the prompts (Miller, 1992). The data for this study consisted of written student responses, written teacher reactions, and notes from meetings and interviews with participating teachers. In another study, a researcher concluded that students generally do not gain sufficient experience with justification and proof in mathematics at the middle school level. She presented two possible explanations for this conclusion: (1) Teachers often eliminate the discussion of students' reasoning due to lack of class time, and (2) teachers do not tend to provide students with adequate feedback when an answer is shared in the classroom (Bieda, 2010). In this middle school research, multiple case studies were conducted in seven schools that involved observation of classes, as well as written and interview reflections provided by classroom teachers. Although it is possible to attach numbers to qualitative raw data (e.g., one can count how many times students responded in a particular way), the research is primarily involved with "words" taken from observations and interviews, rather than "numbers" from tests.

On the other hand, a study does not have to be purely quantitative or qualitative, as some research employs both in a "mixed" method. By employing qualitative and quantitative methods in the same study, data from a variety of sources can be compared (a process researchers refer to as *triangulation* of the data). For example, a study conducted by Watson and Moritz (2003) studied beliefs about probability with students in grades 3 through 12. The students were interviewed about the fairness of dice and asked to verify their conjectures. Although interviewing is considered a qualitative research method, the researchers collected data from student responses and categorized the information to generate tables of quantitative data. Then, three or four years later, many of the same students were interviewed again. The researchers showed that only 45 percent of the students responded to the questions at a higher level than they had in the first interview. More than half of the students had not progressed in their understanding of fairness over the three- or four-year period of time. The authors concluded by suggesting that secondary and middle school students need more hands-on experiences with **manipulatives**, such as dice, to help them make sense of the need for significant sample sizes and fairness in the study of probability.

How Would You React

SCENARIO

You have planned a blocked, 2-hour lesson in which students will explore geometric figures with dynamic geometry software in the computer lab. Your students gather in your classroom, and you escort them to the lab, only to discover that the room has accidentally been "double booked" with an English class, and the students in that class are using the computers. Your response is to

a. Return to the classroom and teach the lesson anyway, but use a projector with a single computer to demonstrate the geometry, rather than having students manipulate the figures themselves.

b. Return to the classroom and teach the lesson anyway, but omit the use of any technology. Instead, illustrate the geometric properties by drawing diagrams on the board rather than by using software.

c. Scrap the lesson for today. Instead, teach an alternate lesson on a related topic that does not require the use of technology and reschedule the lab to do the original lesson at another time.

d. Compromise with the English teacher to split the lab use time and attempt to teach your 2-hour lesson in 1 hour in the lab.

e. Other.

DISCUSSION

One of the keys to effective teaching is learning to be *flexible*. Unexpected events, from fire drills to emergency assemblies to P.A. announcements, occur on a regular basis in schools. Particularly when it comes to teaching with technology, teachers should always be prepared with a backup plan. Many schools do not even have a computer lab, and any use of such technology may be restricted to small groups of students working on a limited number of classroom computers.

Current research points favorably toward the use of technology for exploration of numerical, algebraic, and geometric problems. For example, Laborde (1999) found that using dynamic geometry software allows students to solve problems that are impossible when only pencil and paper are used. The results of the study showed that students engaged in computer tasks that generated "intriguing visual phenomena that [were] not expected by students" (p. 300). Of course, when students are surprised by the results of an experiment, they are *motivated* due to interest and curiosity and will work harder on the task.

As a teacher who is the victim of a double-booked computer lab, you might find yourself asking, "Is the use of computers necessary to teach this lesson?" Although you will often hear some people emphasize the importance of cooperative learning and the use of technology, others do not agree. Some believe that manipulatives are always helpful, and others believe that lecture methods work best. The National Research Council (2000) provided an analogy in response to these arguments: It does not make sense to ask a carpenter whether a hammer or a screwdriver is the best tool because the choice of a tool depends on its purpose and context. A carpenter knows that it is appropriate to hit a nail with a hammer and to insert a screw with a screwdriver. In the same way, teaching strategies should be selected based on the needs of the students. Some geometry lessons are more effectively taught using a compass and straightedge, whereas others require a calculator or computer. No teaching method or tool used in a lesson is inherently "good" or "bad"; the choice depends on the intent of the lesson. So, whether the teacher in this scenario chooses to split the time in the lab, to teach another lesson, or to teach the lesson using a chalkboard will ultimately be decided by the context of the situation and what the teacher intended the students to gain from the experience.

Experimental and Descriptive Research

Some research in mathematics education is an attempt to prove that one teaching or assessment method is better than another, as was described earlier in the calculator example, and is referred to as **experimental research**. This type of research has its roots in agriculture: A farmer would apply a particular brand of fertilizer to one field and not to another to see whether the field with the treatment produced a heartier crop. In a study conducted by Whitman (1976), it was reported that students who learned to use the "cover-up" method of solving equations—as described in the TIMSS example for solving the equation $3(x + 5) = 30$ in Chapter 1—along with traditional symbol manipulation outperformed their peers who were only taught to manipulate the symbols with pencil and paper. A teacher can translate such a study into practice when deciding how to approach equation solving in a middle school classroom or in an algebra course.

In making educational decisions, it is often helpful to simply have a base of information. A study that is undertaken for the purpose of generating statistics and information for discussion, but not necessarily for comparison purposes, is **descriptive research**. The following are some examples of the results of descriptive studies: Stiggins (1988) found that teachers spend 20 to 30 percent of their work time designing and implementing assessments of student progress. In 1999, 91 percent of U.S. eighth graders' schools surveyed in the TIMSS–R study reported having access to the Internet, whereas only 41 percent of their international peers had network access (Gonzales et al., 2000). Another TIMSS report showed that 83 percent of the eighth graders in the United States were in classes of between 1 and 30 students, whereas 93 percent of the students in Korea were enrolled in classes with 41 or more students (Beaton et al., 1997). It is interesting to note, however, that Korean eighth graders significantly outscored U.S. eighth graders on the TIMSS achievement tests. The information presented in this paragraph is not intended as a foundation for arguing one position over another; it is purely a description of what is going on in the schools. Descriptive research frequently results from surveys or interviews and serves to inform the education community about the status of some program or situation.

Table 3.1 provides a generalized summary of the types of research that can be conducted in education and illustrates the way in which research can take on several different formats, depending on the intent of the researchers.

Table 3.1   Comparison of Research Methods

	Experimental	Descriptive
Quantitative	Experimental study conducted by comparing quantitative data	Descriptive study containing quantitative data
Qualitative	Experimental study conducted by comparing qualitative data	Descriptive study containing qualitative data

Most experimental studies are quantitative, and much of the descriptive research in mathematics education is qualitative. However, as previously noted, any study can contain both quantitative and qualitative elements. In fact, some of the most powerful research conclusions can be drawn when, for example, test results of student performance can be extended through a series of open-ended interviews with students. Interviews often allow researchers to probe students' thinking more deeply than they could using a written test and to quote student comments in the research results.

Research in mathematics education serves as either a catalyst for change or an affirmation of current practices. After several studies have been conducted and patterns about teaching and learning begin to emerge, an educational theory is often formulated. We will now explore some of the theories on teaching and learning that have evolved over many years of educational research and address the question of how a student actually learns mathematics.

Learning Theories in Mathematics

Think back to some of the teachers you have had in your educational career. Were any of them extremely knowledgeable in the area of mathematics but ineffective in the classroom, leaving you or others in the class confused? Perhaps you spent the semester or the year feeling as though the teacher was teaching mathematics but not teaching the students. Clearly, there is a difference! It has been said that the best mathematics teachers are those who have not only an understanding of the content but also a firm grasp of how mathematics is learned—teachers who are knowledgeable about theories of child development and can appreciate how students learn and become able to do mathematics. Richard Skemp, who wrote a popular book entitled *The Psychology of Learning Mathematics* (1971), stated that "problems of learning and teaching are psychological problems, and before we can make much improvement in the teaching of mathematics we need to know more about how it is learned" (p. 14). His comments are backed by research that suggests that teaching teachers to reflect on how their students think can have a significant effect on student achievement (an example is the discussion on cognitively guided instruction by Fennema and Franke, 1992).

Skemp also stated that "the learning of mathematics (is) . . . very dependent on good teaching. Now, to know mathematics is one thing, and to be able to teach it—to communicate it to those at a lower conceptual level is quite another" (Skemp, 1971, p. 36). A study conducted by Ball (1990), for example, described the difficulty that elementary and secondary preservice teachers had in representing the problem $1\frac{3}{4} \div \frac{1}{2}$ in a form that promoted understanding of the process. Although the undergraduates could "do" the problem, only about half of the secondary mathematics majors (and none of the elementary preservice teachers) could put the problem into a form that helped students understand what they were doing. Using this same division problem, another study showed that 10 out of 23 elementary school mathematics teachers (most of whom were considered above average teachers) were able to find the correct answer. Furthermore, only 1 of these 23 teachers was able to generate a reasonable word problem that used the calculation (Ma, 1999). (An example of a word problem might be, "How many half-pound burgers can you make out of $1\frac{3}{4}$ pounds of hamburger?") So, as we think about teaching secondary and middle school students, it is important to focus on how they think and develop as learners of mathematics. Let's look at some current learning theories that are influencing reform in mathematics education. We begin by tracing the development of general learning psychology and then elaborate on the theories of Jerome Bruner and the van Hieles as well as the constructivist model, which have their most direct application in the teaching and learning of mathematics.

Development of Learning Theory

Traditional classroom teaching, which features the teacher providing examples and the students taking notes, is primarily driven by the **behaviorist theory** of psychology—the predominant learning theory in the United States from 1920 until 1970 (Hofstetter, 1997). In classical behavioral psychology, the belief is that learning can be controlled by the application of external rewards and punishments. B.F. Skinner (1938), probably the best known of the behaviorists, described, for example, how a dog could be taught to sit by giving it food treats. In a similar manner, people can learn to perform various tasks by the consequences of their actions. So, if we wanted students to learn to convert fractions to decimals, we would show them the procedure, have them practice it over and over, and then give them a test. A high score on the test (and perhaps a sticker next to the student's name) would constitute a reward, and a low score would be a form of punishment. As a result, students would work harder to perfect the skill in order to earn a reward. In this sense, the student will have been "conditioned" to act in a particular manner. One major shortcoming of this model is that Skinner paid much less attention to internal stimulation than does modern psychology. His model was more about modifying behavior in humans and animals than accounting for the complex mental (cognitive) processes that occur in the brain when people learn (Hofstetter, 1997).

In a more contemporary view, psychologists such as Piaget (1969) held that people learn best when they can experiment and invent their own generalizations rather than simply being "told" what to do or how to think by a teacher. Similarly, Lev Vygotsky (1896–1934), a Russian-born psychologist, held that students actively construct their own knowledge (Santrock, 2004). Vygotsky is famous for defining the **zone of proximal development**, which is "the range of tasks that are too difficult for children to master alone but can be mastered with guidance and assistance from adults" (Santrock, 2004, p. 51). Vygotsky stated that the zone is between what the student already understands and what he or she is capable of comprehending through conversations with a more knowledgeable person (Steele, 2001; Vygotsky, 1978). As a result, learning depends on social interaction with others, whether that be the teacher or another peer. Riddle and Dabbagh (1999) noted that teaching strategies such as *scaffolding* (the teacher asking a series of structured questions that lead the students to higher levels of understanding) and *peer teaching* are natural applications of Vygotsky's theory.

Subsequently, Howard Gardner (1983, 1991) suggested a theory of multiple intelligences. Intelligence, he argued, can be defined among seven different areas: logical–mathematical, linguistic, spatial, musical, bodily–kinesthetic, and inter/intra-personal intelligences (Brualdi, 1996). In the traditional classroom, mathematics teachers have addressed primarily—if not exclusively—the logical–mathematical intelligence. But using Gardner's learning theory, we recognize that students have other strengths that can be incorporated in planning and teaching lessons. For example, the use of visual models in teaching can appeal to students' spatial intelligence, whereas the use of cooperative learning groups can tap into their interpersonal intelligence. Getting students to physically move around the room to collect data or to conduct a problem-solving activity may be a way to engage their bodily–kinesthetic intelligence. Gardner's theory spotlights what we have intuitively known for a long time—that to appeal to the needs of all students, teaching mathematics needs to move beyond lecturing and note taking.

Bruner's Stages of Representation

Another cognitive theory of learning, **Bruner's stages of representation**, was formulated by Jerome Bruner. Bruner, who was born in 1915 and received his doctorate in 1941 from Harvard, theorized that learning passes through three stages of representation—enactive, iconic, and symbolic. His theory has led to the extensive use of hands-on materials—manipulatives—in mathematics classrooms. We can illustrate these three stages of cognitive development with an example of combining similar terms in algebra.

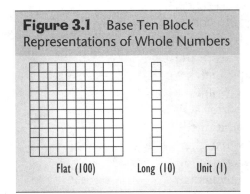

Figure 3.1 Base Ten Block Representations of Whole Numbers

Flat (100)   Long (10)   Unit (1)

In the primary grades, children often use a manipulative known as **base ten blocks** for exploring basic operations and place value. A set of base ten blocks (see Figure 3.1) is made up of cubes that measure 1 cm on a side; rods, often called *longs,* that are 10 cm × 1 cm × 1 cm; and *flats,* which are 10 cm × 10 cm squares with a depth of 1 cm. Each unit cube can represent a "1," whereas the long is a "10," and the flat is a "100."

When children are asked to add 124 + 235, they can represent the numbers with base ten blocks, as shown in Figure 3.2:

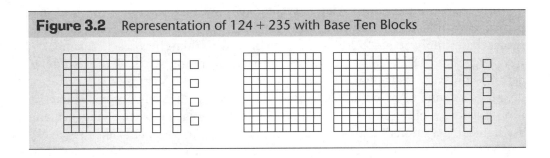

Figure 3.2   Representation of 124 + 235 with Base Ten Blocks

The child can readily see that there are 3 flats, 5 longs, and 9 unit cubes, so the sum of 124 and 235 must be 359. No pencil-and-paper computation is needed to do the problem (remember that for early elementary children this is still a problem, not an exercise!), and the design of the blocks makes it intuitively obvious to children which digits to add, as they simply combine the blocks that have the same shape and size.

Older students can allow the 10 × 10 flat to represent "1," which makes the long a representation for "0.1," and the smallest block, which is one-tenth of a long, becomes "0.01." Using this model, students can think about what it means to add 1.4 + 3.58 without being taught rules, such as to "line up the decimal places"— a rule that many students (and adults) follow but do not understand. Figure 3.3 shows how easy it is for students to group together blocks of the same size to find that the sum of 1.4 + 3.58 is 4.98.

Figure 3.3 Representation of 1.4 + 3.58 Using Base Ten Blocks

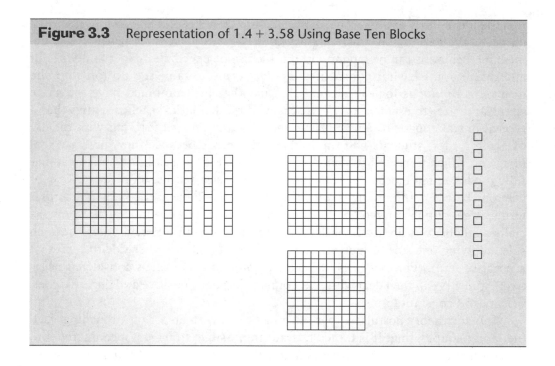

Similarly, this notion can be extended to the teaching of algebra in the secondary or middle grades. The manipulatives often used are referred to as **algebra tiles**. A standard set of algebra tiles as shown in Figure 3.4 includes three shapes—a unit that is 1 cm on a side, a long that is 1 cm wide and several cm long, and a square flat whose sides are the length of a long.

Algebra tiles are based on an area model, so we assume that the small square is 1 cm $\times$ 1 cm representing 1 square unit of area. The rectangular long is 1 cm $\times$ x, so it stands for x. The flat is $x \times x$, so it represents x^2. So, let's say that a student is trying to simplify the expression $(2x^2 + 3x + 5) + (x^2 + 6x + 7)$. A representation of the problem with algebra tiles would resemble Figure 3.5:

Figure 3.4 Algebra Tiles

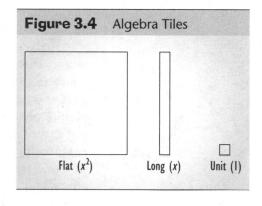

Flat (x^2)   Long (x)   Unit (I)

Figure 3.5 Representation of $(2x^2 + 3x + 5) + (x^2 + 6x + 7)$ with Algebra Tiles

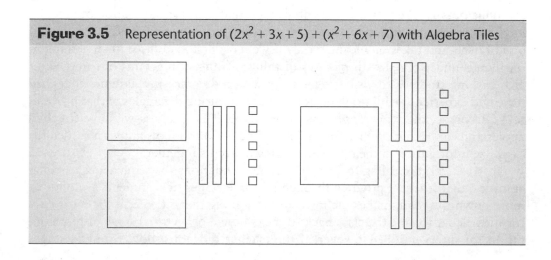

A student can fairly easily recognize that the sum consists of 3 flats, 9 longs, and 12 units, so the expression must simplify to $3x^2 + 9x + 12$. This process and the meaning behind it can be taught without the use of pencil and paper and without any discussion of what constitutes similar terms. Again, the notion that the terms are *similar* is logical because the tiles that are combined have the same shape and size (the same area). The seasoned mathematics teacher knows that a typical mistake made by students is to take $3x + 6x$ and get $9x^2$, but with the use of algebra tiles, students will rarely make this error because they have a visual image on which to rely. If students' previous teachers have skillfully and meaningfully used base ten blocks, the transition is even easier because students make connections between adding digits with the same place value and combining similar terms. Algebra tiles can model other concepts as well. For example, most commercially available sets are made of flat pieces of plastic with different colors on each side, allowing one side to represent a positive term and the other side to represent a negative term. (For most sets, the red side of an algebra tile is considered negative.) Students can then deal with polynomials that have positive and negative coefficients and constant terms.

Bruner's theory postulates that learning begins with an action—touching, feeling, and manipulating. It is difficult, if not impossible, to have a meaningful conversation about apples if one has never actually held an apple. This first stage is the *enactive* or concrete stage. Students are operating in the enactive stage when they learn to count, add, and subtract using base ten blocks in the first grade. They are also in the enactive stage of learning about similar terms when they manipulate algebra tiles on their desks to "feel" what it means to combine the terms.

The second stage of learning, according to Bruner, is the *iconic* or pictorial phase. This stage depends on visuals, such as pictures, to summarize and represent concrete situations. For the middle school student, this may mean that the child puts away the base ten blocks, is given a piece of paper, and is asked to draw a picture of what it means to add $2.57 + 4.3$. By analyzing the picture, the teacher can determine the degree to which a child is able to visualize number operations. Essentially, the students draw on paper what they already know how to do with the concrete manipulatives; but again, it is virtually impossible to draw a picture of an apple if we don't hold a real one in our hands first. So, the enactive phase is followed by an iconic phase in which the picture represents a physical object and serves as a further abstraction.

Bruner's third stage of learning is the *symbolic* or abstract phase. It is called symbolic because the words and symbols representing information do not actually have any inherent connection to the information. The numeral 3 has no meaning in and of itself and takes on meaning only if we have first held three of something in our hands and worked with pictures of things arranged in groups of three. Similarly, asking students to visualize an angle with a 45° measure assumes that they have had experience with drawing angles and measuring the angles with a protractor. Of course, the word *apple* has no meaning either, unless we have touched apples and can recognize them in a picture. The use of symbols allows a student to organize information in the mind by relating concepts together.

It is critical, according to Bruner's recommendations for sequencing teaching episodes, that learners progress through all three stages. If a student, a month or more down the road, makes the mistake of thinking that $3x + 6x$ is $9x^2$, it is easy for the teacher to take the class back to the concrete or pictorial stage of representation for intervention. However, if the teacher did not follow Bruner's stages initially and instead started by teaching the topic with the symbolic manipulation, the student has no model on which to fall back. It is also important that the teacher allow students to progress gradually from one stage to the next, which is not as simple as it may seem. If students are ready to move on to the next level but are continually asked to function at the concrete stage on assignments, they will most certainly become bored with the work. Similarly, if the teacher tries to get the students to a symbolic level before they are ready to proceed, the students might be able to demonstrate the skill on paper but will still have significant gaps in their understanding of the concept. The amount of time that a teacher spends at each of the three levels will vary, depending on the backgrounds, ages, and ability levels of the students, the difficulty of the topic, and a variety of other factors. Maybe you have heard someone say, "I could do it and got through the class, but I'm not sure I really learned very much, and I don't even remember what we did anymore!" It is likely that this student was rushed through the stages without enough time to allow the concepts to fully develop.

Historically, the lack of conceptual understanding has been a major problem in mathematics education, as we saw in the discussion of the learning principle in Chapter 2. Perhaps you were taught this way and, before reading this section, would have been hard pressed to visualize what it means to combine similar terms. For many students, mathematics is nothing more than a set of rules and procedures because they have been taught almost entirely on the symbolic level or in a classroom in which *getting the answer* was valued over *making sense* of the mathematics. A unit on similar terms that progresses through the phases allows the child to reason out *why* terms are added together, to communicate the process through the use of models and pictures as representations, and to connect the idea of place value to algebra. This unit goes beyond procedural knowledge to an understanding of the process. And although some students can be taught at the symbolic level and be successful in school, many cannot and are in need of other representations of problems.

A middle school student wrote in her mathematics journal:

> I really like using algebra tiles. I'm at the point now where I almost always do polynomial problems with pencil and paper or in my head. But sometimes I get confused on a problem, and I like to know that I can pull out the tiles so that I can see what I am doing. I guess I'm just a visual person, but I know that algebra tiles give me a way to reconstruct how to do the problems.

Her journal entry is consistent with the theory of Jerome Bruner. He pointed out that students with well-developed symbolic systems might be able to bypass the first two stages when studying some concepts, but he warned that their teachers take a risk because these students will not possess the visual images on which to fall back if the symbolic approach does not work (Bruner, 1966).

The van Hiele Model

A considerable amount of research has been conducted to specifically study the way that geometry is learned. The most well-known theory of geometric development is the **van Hiele model**. This cognitive theory was developed in the 1950s by a husband-and-wife team of mathematics teachers in the Netherlands, Pierre van Hiele and Dina van Hiele-Geldof. They attempted to explain why students have so much difficulty with high school geometry even if they have been successful in other mathematics experiences. After a considerable amount of quantitative and qualitative research (for details, see the NCTM monograph on the van Hiele model by Fuys, Geddes, & Tischler, 1988), they theorized that children pass through five stages, or levels, of geometric reasoning. Determining the level on which students function can help teachers understand how to meet the needs of their students.

The first level, Level 0, is the *visualization* phase. At this stage, a child will look at a square and identify it as a square. When asked how the child knows this, a typical response would be "because it looks like one," but the student will not know the properties of a square. The child simply recognizes the shape. At the second level, Level 1 or the *analysis* stage, students begin to recognize the attributes or properties of a shape. A child at Level 1 might say, for example, that a square has four sides, opposite sides that are parallel, and four right angles. However, the child will not be able to relate two geometric figures to one another. Looking at the diagram in Figure 3.6, the child generally will say that the figure on the left is a square, that it has four equal sides, and so forth. The student will also say that the figure on the right is a parallelogram, that it has two pairs of opposite parallel lines, and so on, but the child at Level 1 will not be able to recognize that the square is a special case of a parallelogram. The figures are seen as seemingly unrelated geometric shapes, although each has its own important properties.

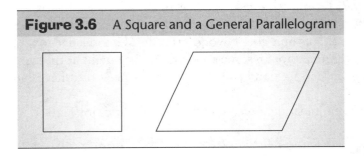

Figure 3.6 A Square and a General Parallelogram

When a child advances to Level 2, *informal deduction,* the student will begin to compare geometric shapes and construct simple proofs. At this level, the child will be able to recognize that the square is a special case of a parallelogram or that a parallelogram does not necessarily have to be a rhombus and why this is the case. However, at Level 2, the child is still unable to construct significant proofs. The ability to accept postulates and theorems and write proofs emerges at Level 3—*deduction*. This level, the one at which high school geometry historically has been taught, focuses on the assumption of various postulates and emphasizes two-column, paragraph, or indirect proofs of theorems. The highest level, Level 4, is *rigor*. This level is associated with the student's ability to work in other geometric systems, such as non-Euclidean geometry, in which virtually all of the work is done on an abstract, proof-oriented level.

If you browse through traditional high school geometry textbooks, you often will find an emphasis on postulates, theorems, and two-column proofs. Perhaps you used these texts in high school geometry. These textbooks assume that the student is ready to function at Level 3; however, research has shown that more than 70 percent of students enter into high school geometry functioning at Level 0 or 1 and, furthermore, that only those students who are at Level 2 or above are prepared well enough to be successful at writing proofs in the course (Shaughnessy & Burger, 1985). One research study found that after students in the United States had completed a geometry course that emphasized proofs, only 30 percent of those students were able to score at least 75 percent on a test of their ability to write reasonable proofs (Senk, 1985). In short, there is a serious mismatch between the students' ability levels coming into a geometry course and what the teacher is expecting them to do. It's no wonder so many people have negative memories of high school geometry classes. Brumfield (1973) conducted a study with 52 high school students who had just completed an accelerated geometry course. When asked to pick one interesting theorem and prove it, 42 of them did not even attempt to prove the theorem they stated, and of the remaining 10 students, only 1 was able to write a correct proof. So, even for the best students in the school, the traditional geometry course did little for their mathematical development.

The van Hieles also found that the geometric development of students was sequential: One had to pass through Levels 0 and 1 to get to Level 2. They recognized that students can slip back to a lower level and need to work their way back up. Finally, and most importantly for our purposes, they determined that the quality of mathematics *instruction* and not simply the chronological age of the student determined advancement. The van Hieles pointed out that some levels of thought may not even be accessible to students because of the lack of effective teaching at these levels. In other words, it is the skill of the teacher that makes the difference and helps the student to progress from one level to the next.

The research of the van Hieles has brought about several recommended changes in the teaching and learning of school geometry. Elementary school textbooks and curricula have begun to include a greater emphasis on geometry so that students have more time to develop their understanding, and the NCTM has emphasized the role of geometry in *Principles and Standards for School Mathematics* for grades Pre-K–2, 3–5, 6–8, and 9–12, as has the *Common Core State Standards*. But although the van Hiele model has existed since the 1960s, we still see many traditional, proof-oriented high school texts and courses. Clearly, there is much to be done in this area if we are to truly embrace the notion of mathematics for *all* students. Fortunately, many current secondary and middle school textbooks emphasize hands-on geometry lessons, in which students discover theorems for themselves rather than being "given" a theorem and asking for a two-column proof (an example is Serra's [2008] popular *Discovering Geometry* textbook).

The advent of software packages, such as Geometer's Sketchpad, GeoGebra, Geometry Inventor (which is similar to Sketchpad but more commonly used in the middle school setting), and Cabri Geometry, for the computer and graphing calculator, have now made it possible for students to manipulate geometric shapes on a computer screen. Such software is known as **dynamic software** because students interact with it, playing out various scenarios and making observations before drawing conclusions. With access to a computer or a graphing calculator, students can explore mathematics problems that historically were either tedious or even impossible to solve with pencil and paper.

Let's suppose, for example, that a teacher wanted students to examine the relationship of a radius of a circle drawn perpendicular to a chord in the circle. Using the dynamic geometry software, students can construct Circle A, with A as its centerpoint. Then, radius $\overline{AB}$ and chord $\overline{CE}$ can be constructed such that $\overline{AB} \perp \overline{CE}$. Students can label the intersection point of the radius and chord D and use the software to measure the lengths of CD and DE. They will discover that these segments are congruent, and can conjecture that a radius drawn perpendicular to a chord also bisects the chord.

The image in Figure 3.7 was constructed using Geometer's Sketchpad software. The measuring tools indicate that $\overline{CD} \cong \overline{DE}$ because their lengths are both 2.17 cm and that $m\angle ADC = 90°$.

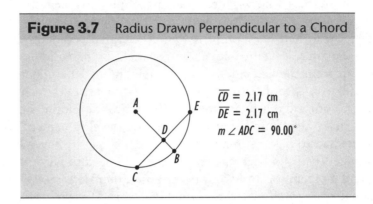

Figure 3.7 Radius Drawn Perpendicular to a Chord

$$\overline{CD} = 2.17 \text{ cm}$$
$$\overline{DE} = 2.17 \text{ cm}$$
$$m\angle ADC = 90.00°$$

By placing a pointer on point C and then on point B, students can slide the points around the circle and discover that wherever the chord lies, as long as the radius is perpendicular (a 90° angle is formed), the chord is always bisected. As a result, students make their own conjecture—a theorem—and can then prove it as a generalization ($\Delta ACD \cong \Delta AED$ because they are right triangles that share side $\overline{AD}$ and have congruent hypotenuses because $\overline{AC}$ and $\overline{AE}$ are radii of the same circle. The triangles are congruent by the Hypotenuse-Leg Theorem, and $\overline{CD} \cong \overline{DE}$, because they are corresponding parts of congruent triangles).

Many resource books that accompany texts highlight the uses of software such as dynamic geometry programs. Again, the power of these software packages lies in the fact that students can make conjectures, look for patterns, and manipulate pictures and data to test their ideas. In this way, students are actively involved in generating the mathematics—in a sense, they are reinventing theorems and properties rather than being told that the properties exist. Even something as simple as finding that the three angles of a triangle always sum to 180° can be exciting when the students construct their own triangle on the computer screen, have the computer find the sum of the three angles, and then manipulate a vertex to stretch and move the triangle around the page before conjecturing that the sum is a constant. These investigations are made possible by contemporary software.

The Inquiry Approach and Constructivist Model

Authors of recent texts and resources, even beyond the study of geometry, have developed effective implementations of learning theory in the design of their lessons. Let's look at an example of a hands-on problem and see how it can be used to help students arrive at their own conclusions.

Take a sheet of paper and fold it in half. Then take the half sheet and fold it in half again, and again, and again. How many times can you continue to fold the paper in half before it becomes impossible to fold it again? Is this true for all pieces of paper or just the one you were folding? What if your "piece" of paper was a 25-foot stretch of cash register tape? What if it was a sheet of newspaper? What patterns do you see?

If you have actually tried this, you might have found it simple to make the first and second folds, but by the fourth or fifth fold, it becomes difficult. Regardless of what kind of paper you used, you were probably unable to fold it more than about 8 times. Why does this happen? Let's organize the data in Table 3.2:

Table 3.2   Paper-Folding Data

Number of Folds	Number of Layers of Paper
0	1
1	2
2	4
3	8
4	16
5	32
6	64
7	128
8	256
9	512
10	1,024

As is evident in this table, by the time you try to fold the paper for the fifth time, you are folding 32 pieces of paper, and by the eighth time, you are folding more than 250 sheets. A standard phone book is about 900 pages, so folding the piece of paper in half 12 times would be like attempting to fold a stack of four phone books in half. But let's look at the problem with some more depth. How would we determine the number of thicknesses of paper if we knew only the number of folds? Students may recognize the numbers in the right-hand column of Table 3.2 as powers of 2 and determine that the fold number, n, used as the exponent, determines the thickness in terms of the number of sheets of paper (e.g., sheets = 2^n). So, if we wanted to fold the paper in half 17 times, we would find that it requires 2^{17} = 131,072 layers of paper, which is the thickness of about 145 phone books—a stack of paper that is more than 25 feet (7.6 meters) high.

Looking at the table again, what do we get when we take 2^0? Because the exponent tells us how many times to fold the paper, and the simplified result equals the number of thicknesses of paper, it is logical to assume that $2^0 = 1$, and now we have a *reason* for *why* this is true. If we trust the structure of mathematics and the consistency of patterns in problem solving, then raising to the zero power makes sense. Perhaps when you were in high school or middle school, you were *told* that any number raised to the zero power is equal to 1 but could not explain why this is the case. A simple paper-folding activity such as this can help students reach that conclusion for themselves.

Now, let's probe even deeper into the mathematical implications of the problem. Suppose that you were to extend the table further, in both directions (Table 3.3):

Table 3.3	Extended Table for the Paper-Folding Problem
n	**2^n**
−3	$0.125 = \frac{1}{8}$
−2	$0.25 = \frac{1}{4}$
−1	$0.5 = \frac{1}{2}$
0	1
1	2
2	4
3	8
4	16
5	32
6	64
7	128
8	256
9	512
10	1,024
11	2,048
12	4,096

Students use hands-on materials as an aid to construct their understanding of mathematical principles.

What patterns do you see as the n values decrease in Table 3.3? Think about it before reading on. Students may recognize that the values double as you move up the table, but they are divided in half as you move down the table. We can compare, for example, the fact that $2^2 = 4$ but $2^{-2} = \frac{1}{4}$, and that $2^3 = 8$ but $2^{-3} = \frac{1}{8}$. Can we predict the relationship between taking 2^4 and 2^{-4}? Using the logical order of mathematics, students will *discover*—without being told—that negative exponents produce reciprocals and will be able to generalize this to simplify, for example, 5^{-3}. Again, the effect of negative exponents does not need to be taught as a rule to be memorized; instead, the relationship can be discovered by students as they explore patterns in a table.

The paper-folding problem is used to teach an **inquiry lesson** in which students work through the activity and essentially invent their own mathematical rules. The teacher's role is not to provide direct instruction but to select a rich task and to guide the students in their exploration of that problem. An inquiry lesson can produce a deeper and longer-lasting conceptual understanding than can traditional lecture-type methods. It is consistent with a theory of teaching and learning known as the **constructivist model**. The constructivist model is an outgrowth of the work of Jean Piaget, although he himself did not use the term. There are three central components to the constructivist viewpoint. First, a constructivist believes that knowledge cannot be passively transmitted from one individual to another. Rather, knowledge is built up or constructed from within as we have experiences in our lives. Second, a constructivist believes that children create knowledge not only by *doing* but also by *reflecting* on and discussing what they have done. A hands-on lesson is not inherently constructivist—it only becomes so when accompanied by significant discourse or processing along the way. Finally, a constructivist generally views learning as a social process in which students compare and contrast their ideas about the patterns they see and what they believe about particular problems or concepts.

In a way, constructivism appeals to common sense. Most people would agree that it is more desirable, for example, for a middle school student to discover the need for common denominators when adding fractions than to be told that "you must find a common denominator any time you add two fractions." There are many mathematical rules, such as "invert and multiply," "count up the total number of decimal places and move it over that many in the answer," "FOIL to multiply the binomials," and "multiply the exponent and the coefficient and reduce the exponent by 1 to find the derivative," that many people have memorized, but few can explain why they work because most have been educated in traditional, lecture-oriented environments. Most people's mathematical knowledge, thus, relies on rote, pencil-and-paper procedures rather than on conceptual understanding.

However, putting constructivist research into practice requires a great deal of skill, both in selecting appropriate activities and in guiding students as they explore new concepts. Paul Cobb, in his research on the constructivist model of teaching and learning, stated that "although constructivist theory is attractive when the issue of learning is considered, deep-rooted problems arise when attempts are made to apply it to instruction" (Cobb, 1988, p. 87). Because using an inquiry approach is generally more difficult than "teaching as telling," more classroom teachers are still using traditional approaches even though they often acknowledge that the teaching techniques are not working. A publication from the Association for Supervision and Curriculum Development (ASCD) (Brooks & Brooks, 1993) outlines the difference between what might be observed in a more traditional classroom versus what is seen in the constructivist classroom (Table 3.4).

It should be noted that the constructivist classroom can and should include some individual work, pencil-and-paper tests, and even lectures. In fact, the model is often misconstrued as one in which it is "never appropriate to lecture or provide direct instruction," but that is simply not the case. The issue is the *frequency* with which various teaching techniques are used and whether the student's background (knowledge and beliefs) and thinking processes are the focal point of the classroom. Essentially, whereas the curriculum has been historically content centered, the constructivist approach is student centered. The examples used throughout this textbook are rooted in constructivist theory because it underlies much of the reform effort in curriculum, teaching, and assessment.

Table 3.4 Comparison of Traditional and Constructivist Classrooms

Traditional Classrooms	Constructivist Classrooms
Curriculum is presented part to whole, with emphasis on basic skills.	Curriculum is presented whole to part, with emphasis on big concepts.
Strict adherence to fixed curriculum is highly valued.	Pursuit of student questions is highly valued.
Curricular activities rely heavily on textbooks and workbooks.	Curricular activities rely heavily on primary sources of data and manipulative materials.
Students are viewed as "blank slates" onto which information is etched by the teacher.	Students are viewed as thinkers with emerging theories about the world.
Teachers generally behave in a didactic manner, disseminating information to students.	Teachers generally behave in an interactive manner, mediating the environment for students.
Teachers seek the correct answer to validate student learning.	Teachers seek the students' point of view in order to understand students' present conceptions for use in subsequent lessons.
Assessment of student learning is viewed as separate from teaching and occurs almost entirely through testing.	Assessment of student learning is interwoven with teaching and occurs through teacher observations of students at work and through student exhibitions and portfolios.
Students primarily work alone.	Students work primarily in groups.

(From J. G. Brooks & M. G. Brooks (1993), *In Search of Understanding the Case for Constructivist Classrooms* (Alexandria, VA: Association of Supervision and Curriculum Development). Copyright © 1993 ASCD. Reprinted by permission.)

Inductive versus Deductive Teaching

When it comes to investigating mathematical procedures, there are distinctly two different approaches a teacher can use. One is to simply "give" the students the rule and ask them to apply it to various situations (a traditional approach), while the other is for the students to use inquiry to "invent" the rule for themselves. While both methods have their merit, the latter one that involves students drawing their own conclusions is much more in keeping with the constructivist theory of teaching and learning.

Each time a teacher prepares a lesson, consideration of what the students already know, how the students learn, and how to best meet their needs should be the foundation of that lesson. Research supports the work of Bruner, the van Hieles, and the constructivist model, and if you concur, these theories should drive your teaching decisions. Suppose, for example, that you were teaching a review lesson on subtracting fractions and posed the following problem:

> *You have a cookie recipe that calls for $2\frac{1}{3}$ cups of flour. If you have a bag with 6 cups of flour in it, how much flour will be left after making the cookies?*

First, students must recognize this as a problem requiring subtraction. Then they need a basic knowledge of fraction subtraction. Most of us have been shown how to take 6 and change it to $5\frac{3}{3}$, then subtract to get the solution of $3\frac{2}{3}$. But any

SPOTlight on Technology

In recent years, the Internet has become an invaluable tool for both the planning and implementation of mathematics lessons. A search for the descriptor "algebra tiles" revealed more than 1.3 million "hits"—pages on the World Wide Web that had some type of information about the use of algebra tiles. Teachers often use these searches (involving search engines such as Yahoo.com or Google.com) to assist them in thinking through their lesson planning processes.

In addition to providing lessons and teaching ideas, many Web sites host on-line software that students can use to conduct mathematical investigations. Consider the following problem that was posed in a second-year Algebra course:

Using the green triangles from a set of pattern blocks, build progressively larger equilateral triangles. After building a few, identify visual and numerical patterns that you see. Express numerical patterns in general terms using a variable.

Instead of handing out sets of pattern blocks in class, the teacher grouped her 20 students in pairs and placed each team of students at a computer with Internet access. Searching on the Web ("interactive + pattern blocks"), the students identified several Web sites that featured a work mat and virtual pattern blocks for problem solving, such as the one shown in Figure 3.8.

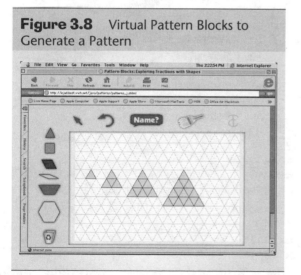

Figure 3.8 Virtual Pattern Blocks to Generate a Pattern

(Reprinted by permission of Jacobo Bulaevsky from http://arcytech.org/patterns/patterns_j.html)

One such Web site is the National Science Foundation–funded National Library of Virtual Manipulatives, located at http://nlvm.usu.edu.

What patterns do *you* see? As two of the algebra students created the images shown in the figure, they recognized a visual pattern: Each successive equilateral triangle is the previous triangle onto which a new row has been added. After discovering this recursive process, they also realized that the number of new triangles required to build the extra rows is a progression of odd numbers—3 triangles, then 5, then 7, and so forth. Finally, the students constructed a table, such as the one shown in Table 3.5.

Table 3.5 Relationship of Triangle Number to Number of Blocks

Triangle Number	Number of Blocks
1	1
2	4
3	9
4	16
5	25
x	x^2

Using the generalized pattern, students recognize that the relationship between the triangle number and the number of blocks is quadratic and can use the formula to predict the number of equilateral triangles needed to build, say, the tenth triangle in the sequence ($10^2 = 100$ green triangles).

Using the virtual manipulatives, students did not have to worry about running out of blocks or using up too much desk space. Building even the first 5 triangles of the sequence would require 55 wooden blocks, which is more triangles than most individual sets of pattern blocks even contain. Triangles on a computer screen can readily be rotated, inserted, or deleted. Also, the teacher can follow up by asking students to conduct the same investigation to find progressively larger blue rhombi and red trapezoids and to generalize those patterns as well. This type of inquiry lesson is enhanced by using the Internet to access Web sites hosting virtual manipulative software.

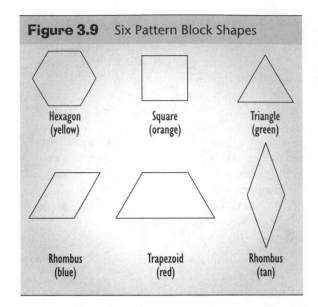

Figure 3.9 Six Pattern Block Shapes

Hexagon (yellow)

Square (orange)

Triangle (green)

Rhombus (blue)

Trapezoid (red)

Rhombus (tan)

teacher with some classroom experience has observed many students doing the problem $6 - 2\frac{1}{3}$ by taking away 2 from the 6 to get $4\frac{1}{3}$ as an answer. The student has forgotten the rule and made essentially the same mistake a primary child makes when taking 30 − 19 to get an answer of 29 (i.e., taking the 10 from the 30 to get 20, and because the 9 is being subtracted from nothing, just bringing it down). If the teacher wants to intervene, as we discussed earlier in the chapter, the student may have no concrete or pictorial images on which to fall back.

Suppose, instead of teaching a rule, we had given the student the problem and a set of **pattern blocks**. Pattern blocks are wooden or plastic sets of geometric shapes that are used for a variety of purposes in the mathematics classroom, including, but not limited to, teaching fractions, similarity, congruence, symmetry, numerical and visual patterns, angles, and graphing. A set of pattern blocks consists of six shapes as shown in Figure 3.9—a small rhombus (tan), a larger rhombus (blue), a square (orange), an equilateral triangle (green), a trapezoid (red), and a hexagon (yellow).

Each of the six pieces has sides of the same length, except for the base of the red trapezoid, which is twice the standard length. We will let the area of a hexagon represent one unit, so that the trapezoid is $\frac{1}{2}$ of the unit, and so on. The student can model the cookie problem by laying out six hexagons to represent the 6 cups of flour. Then $2\frac{1}{3}$ hexagons need to be taken away. Removing 2 of the hexagons leaves 4, but an additional $\frac{1}{3}$ must also be removed. Trading 3 blue rhombi for 1 of the hexagons, the student can then remove 1 blue rhombus, leaving 3 hexagons and 2 blue rhombi, or $3\frac{2}{3}$ as shown in Figure 3.10.

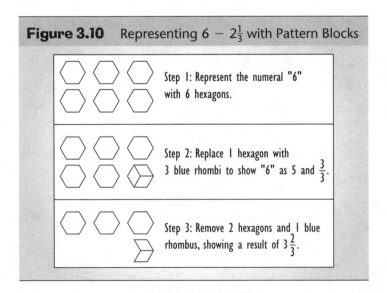

Figure 3.10 Representing $6 - 2\frac{1}{3}$ with Pattern Blocks

Step 1: Represent the numeral "6" with 6 hexagons.

Step 2: Replace 1 hexagon with 3 blue rhombi to show "6" as 5 and $\frac{3}{3}$.

Step 3: Remove 2 hexagons and 1 blue rhombus, showing a result of $3\frac{2}{3}$.

In the constructivist model, the students will do several problems like this one, using the pattern blocks as needed until they eventually invent a rule for doing problems that require some form of regrouping. A student will recognize that three of the thirds can be traded for one of the wholes and will be able to do similar examples such as $12 - 5\frac{4}{5}$ by applying the same procedure. In this way, not only has the student created a rule that is more likely to be remembered than if the teacher told the class what to do, but the student also has formed a visual image that ultimately enhances understanding. According to Bruner, pattern blocks and picture drawing on problems of this type should be used long before any pencil-and-paper abstractions are initiated.

This method is often referred to as **inductive teaching** because the student thinks through several examples and then generalizes a rule at the end. The more traditional form of teaching, in which the teacher states a rule or definition and then expects the student to apply it to a worksheet or set of problems, is called **deductive teaching,** meaning that a generalization serves as the starting point, and specific examples are applied later. Many teachers of traditional geometry courses in high school have relied on deductive thinking—give the students a definition and see if they can apply it—rather than inductive methods, which place the students at the center of the process and expect them to invent some of their own rules and procedures.

One classroom technique that promotes inductive thinking is the **concept attainment** method. This strategy was actually devised by Bruner as a way to help students make their own generalizations. Consider the 18 geometric figures in Figure 3.11:

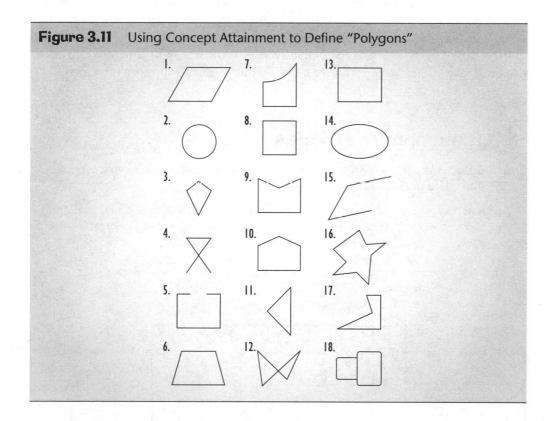

Figure 3.11   Using Concept Attainment to Define "Polygons"

The teacher would begin the lesson by telling the class to remain silent and not share ideas with anyone until instructed to do so. Then the teacher would tell the class, for example, that 3 is a "yes," but 15 is a "no"; 11 is a "yes," but 2 is a "no." The class should be challenged to start thinking about the rule that the teacher is using to classify the "yes" and "no" figures. At this point, the class can be given one more example, such as 9 is a "yes," but 18 is a "no." If a member of the class appears to have the rule figured out, that student should give an example of a "yes" and a "no" to the rest of the class with no explanation of why this is the case. Eventually, the class would be asked to list some common characteristics of "yes" figures versus "no" figures. Students realize that the "yes" figures have line segments as sides, that the segments must be joined at their endpoints, and that the figures must be closed or connected. Of course, the class has just defined a *polygon*, and the teacher can write this word on the board after the definition has been invented.

The concept attainment method tends to be challenging and fun for the students while giving them the responsibility for creating the definition. They have looked at a series of examples and nonexamples to generalize a rule, so the teaching method is said to be inductive. Contrast this teaching episode with the traditional geometry lesson in which the teacher walks up to the whiteboard and writes "A POLYGON is a geometric figure in which ..." and asks the students to copy it down. Later, the class in this traditional situation is generally presented with some drawings and asked whether they represent polygons. Because the teacher started with a definition or generalization and then attempted to have students apply it to specific examples, the lesson is deductive. Most teachers would agree that the inductive lesson is preferable and embodies the current learning theories just discussed. But again, the inductive approach often requires more time and creativity on the part of the teacher than does simply giving a definition on the chalkboard. In making instructional decisions, we try to think about what is best for the student, which is not necessarily what is easiest for the teacher. Someone once said that recent reform efforts in mathematics education were not intended "to make teaching easier; they were meant to make learning easier and more meaningful."

 lassroom Dialogues

In the process of solving a problem that required a calculator, the following conversation took place in the classroom:

Student 1: I just noticed something. I put in 12 divided by 0, and it says that there is an error. (The student goes to the overhead graphing calculator and shows the class the screen displayed in Figure 3.12.)

Figure 3.12   Error Message Displayed on a Graphing Calculator

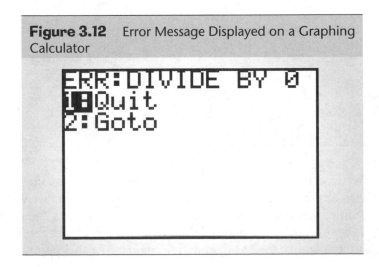

Student 2: That's because you're never allowed to divide by zero. It's a rule.

Student 1: I know it's a rule, but I don't understand why it's not allowed. Why can't the answer just be zero?

Teacher: Does anyone have an answer to that question?

Student 3: I remember being told that the denominator of a fraction can never equal zero.

Teacher: Exactly. Any number that can be written as a fraction, in which the numerator and denominator are both integers, is called a rational number. But the definition also states that the denominator may not equal zero, even though zero is an integer.

Student 2: Now I'm confused. Which numbers are integers?

Student 1: I know that one. It's just all of the regular numbers and their opposites, like −3, −2, −1, 0, 1, 2, 3, and so forth.

Teacher: What do you mean by "regular" numbers?

Student 1: Numbers that start from zero and go on to one, two, three, and so on.

Teacher: Does anyone know what we call those "regular" numbers?

Student 2: I think those are the whole numbers.

Teacher: Exactly! So, the whole numbers include zero, one, two, three, and on, and if we include their opposites, we have the integers. If you create a fraction in which the numerator and denominator are both integers, you have a rational number.

Student 1: I know that you're not allowed to have zero in the denominator, but I still don't understand why.

The students in this scenario are caught up in a tangle of misunderstood definitions and vocabulary. The names of number systems, including whole numbers, integers, and rational numbers, cause the confusion. Students acknowledge that there is a rule about dividing by zero but do not know why it exists, and in an attempt to answer the question, their lack of other content knowledge surfaces. How important is it for students to know basic mathematical terms and definitions? How much emphasis should be placed on using proper mathematics vocabulary in the classroom? How would you respond to the last student's comment?

One way to address the concern about division by zero is to present a simple list of examples, as follows:

$$12 \div 3 = 4 \text{ can be checked by computing } 4 \cdot 3 = 12$$

$$30 \div 6 = 5 \text{ can be checked by computing } 5 \cdot 6 = 30$$

Now suppose that we take $12 \div 0$. If we claim that $12 \div 0 = 0$, then it must be true that $0 \cdot 0 = 12$, which of course is false. Or we could say that $12 \div 0 = 12$, but then $12 \cdot 0 = 12$, but this is false as well. In fact, any number that is claimed to be the quotient, when multiplied by the divisor (0), will result in a product of 0, so division by zero results in a solution that creates other inconsistencies. The following situation can be used to help students to further appreciate what happens when division by zero is permitted:

$$\text{Suppose that } a = b.$$

$$\text{Multiplying both sides by } a, a^2 = ab.$$

$$\text{Subtracting } b^2 \text{ from both sides, } a^2 - b^2 = ab - b^2.$$

$$\text{Factoring both sides, } (a + b)(a - b) = b(a - b).$$

$$\text{Dividing both sides by } (a - b), a + b = b.$$

$$\text{Substituting } a \text{ for } b \text{ (since } a = b), a + a = a.$$

So, $2a = a$

Dividing by a, $2 = 1$.

Students now have to determine what mathematical mistake resulted in an incorrect conclusion. After some discussion, students will realize that dividing both sides by $(a - b)$, since a and b are equal, is division by zero. This division breaks a mathematical rule and results in a conclusion that is false.

Another inaccurate use of terminology when describing numbers occurs at the upper grades, where we frequently hear students use the terms *imaginary* and *complex* interchangeably. Yet, by definition, a *complex* number is the sum of a real and an imaginary number, such as $-3 + 5i$. The set of complex numbers constitutes a field, and real numbers are a subfield, as they are a subset of the complex numbers. In the case of $-3 + 5i$, -3 is the real part, and $5i$ is the imaginary part. Allowing students to use the terms *imaginary* and *complex* as if they were synonyms can lead students to the misconception that all complex numbers are also real, which is false.

Helping students pay attention to the accuracy of their vocabulary is part of the mathematics teacher's responsibility. But the teacher must also decide the degree of emphasis on the proper use of terminology, from the day-to-day classroom discussions to what is measured on tests. If students get overly caught up in memorization and correct use of key terms in the classroom, the resulting distraction may keep them from focusing on big ideas and problem solving. Yet to ignore key terms and reasons why various rules exist may equally deprive students of making sense of mathematics. How can a balance be maintained in your classroom? How can you ensure that students understand basic definitions and terms yet not allow pure memorization to clutter the problem-solving emphasis in the class?

Motivation

An activity such as the concept attainment polygon lesson is often enjoyable and memorable for students. Clearly, if the teacher can capture the imagination of the students, the potential for a successful lesson is much greater than if the class appears disinterested with the same old routine. Although psychologists do not have a universal definition of **motivation**, we know that it is an affective attribute that influences the degree to which students want to engage in some activity or choose to become involved. A student who is *motivated* to do a mathematics activity has a desire to do the work for a variety of reasons. Three interacting components constitute the psychological construct called motivation according to Ford's model—goal orientations, emotions, and self-confidence (Ford, 1992).

Individuals are motivated by either ego goals or mastery goals. Students who have primarily **ego goal** orientations do their work to gain favorable judgments from other people. They work for extrinsic rewards, such as grades or teacher approval, and they measure their success according to whether they have outperformed their peers. Suppose that a senior in high school scores 92 percent on a calculus test and is initially excited by the grade. If a student who has an ego goal orientation discovers that many other students in the class scored above 95 percent, that student's excitement will typically turn to disappointment as a result of a perceived inability to outdo everyone else. However, students with a **mastery goal** orientation emphasize the intrinsic value of learning and self-improvement. These students value learning for its own sake, and success depends on how much effort they put into a project. If a student with mastery orientation works as hard as possible and learns a great deal from a unit, then a test grade of a C may be as acceptable as a B or an A because it was not the grade that the person sought in the first place. Although the mastery goal orientation is certainly more desirable, students with ego goals are more commonly found in mathematics classrooms.

Although many students enter our classrooms with ego goal orientations, one of our greatest challenges as educators is to help these students develop a mastery goal orientation—to show them that mathematics can be inherently interesting and that they should want to learn. A teacher can do specific things in the classroom to make this happen. For example, if teachers select problems and activities for the classroom that elicit participation and spark debate, students will solve the problems not only because they are required to but also because they view the work as worth doing. In fact, research suggests that students in classrooms where inquiry approaches to teaching are being employed are more likely to develop mastery goals than are their peers who are learning in more traditional settings. In short, for students in inquiry classrooms, success is not about getting good grades but is defined as "working hard to understand mathematics" (NRC, 2000, p. 13).

Another strategy that teachers can use to promote mastery goal orientations is to keep student grades confidential at all times. Posting grades by code number, reading test scores aloud, or in any way comparing grades of students in the classroom feeds ego goals and only reinforces the drives of students to learn so that they can avoid looking stupid in front of their peers. Seemingly innocent teaching techniques, such as running board races, playing "around the world," or writing the class average for a test on the chalkboard, can seriously undermine efforts to get students to be self-motivated because they promote competition among students and the comparison of performances to determine success levels. Teachers need to examine what they do in their classrooms and whether their actions promote an intrinsic desire to do mathematics.

A second component of motivation in the classroom is **emotion.** Ford (1992) pointed out that interest and curiosity are two of the important emotions that constitute this component of motivation. We say that a student has **interest** in an academic topic when the individual believes that the study of that topic will be beneficial in some way. Hidi (1990) defined two types of interest—personal and situational. Personal interests are those that we have all the time, such as stamp collecting or watching football. Situational interests, on the other hand, can be evoked by posing a problem or reading a book. You may not have any inherent interest in coins, but you might become interested if you were asked whether the Empire State Building or a stack of 1 million pennies is higher. Students can become interested in the study of mathematics when teachers identify problems and projects that either appeal to the personal interests of the students or pose eye-catching puzzles to solve or present problems that students find meaningful. In fact, the constructivist approach emphasizes that students work at their optimal level when presented with tasks that are *meaningful and relevant* because they will choose to expend effort on that which interests them.

Two types of **curiosity** are addressed in the research literature—cognitive and sensory. Cognitive curiosity results when a student realizes that there is a difference between what was expected and what actually happened. For example, cognitive curiosity may be evoked by posing the birthday problem in Chapter 1, in which the students try to figure out how the teacher was able to determine their birthdate and ask, "How did the teacher know that?" Sensory curiosity can be thought of as inherent curiosity triggered by something in the environment. This is the curiosity we see when a student is handed a set of pattern blocks or a graphing calculator for the first time and wants to play with them and figure out how they work. In a sense, the tools themselves serve as the motivators just as the visual and auditory appeal of a hand-held baseball game might entice a person to want to play it. Posing paradoxical problems and using manipulatives and technology can evoke curiosity in the classroom, thus motivating the student to want to work on some problem or activity.

The third component of motivation is **self-confidence** or self-efficacy. This refers to the degree to which students believe that they will be able to succeed at a task or in a class. If a student has been historically unsuccessful in a mathematics class and is posed a problem that is even moderately difficult, that student is likely to think, "I can't do this" and may almost immediately give up. This student believes that the work will be impossible to complete successfully and that the ability to do it is lacking. Research has shown that individuals tend to choose tasks that are neither impossibly difficult nor overly simple—within their comfort zone (Malone & Lepper, 1987; Nicholls, 1984). As a reference point, one study found that a student must be successful about 70 percent of the time to consider tasks to be challenging enough to be interesting but not so difficult that they appear impossible to complete (Dickinson & Butt, 1989). This point is important for planning instruction in the classroom because students will appear unmotivated if a task appears easy and a waste of their time, and they may refuse to attempt a task or simply give up if it appears to be too difficult. The teacher's role, then, is to select tasks that challenge and build self-confidence for more difficult concepts later in the semester or school year.

The effective teaching of mathematics, then, depends on appealing to the needs of students in a way that motivates them. Motivating students means helping them to develop a mastery goal orientation, appealing to their interests and curiosity, and building their confidence so that they will be successful in the class. The effective teacher must pay attention to how a child develops and how that student can be motivated to complete tasks. If a teacher displays enthusiasm and attempts to appeal to the interests and curiosity of the students, then we would also hope that students would develop not only their mathematical content knowledge but also their positive attitudes and beliefs about mathematics. The National Council of Teachers of Mathematics has referred to the affective (feeling) side of mathematics as mathematical **disposition**.

The authors of the *Curriculum and Evaluation Standards* (NCTM, 1989) stated, "Learning mathematics extends beyond learning concepts, procedures, and their applications. It also includes developing a disposition toward mathematics and seeing mathematics as a powerful way for looking at situations. *Disposition* refers not simply to attitudes but to a tendency to act in positive ways" (p. 233). The authors of the document also stated the following:

The assessment of students' mathematical disposition should seek information about their

- confidence in using mathematics to solve problems, to communicate ideas, and to reason;
- flexibility in exploring mathematical ideas and trying alternative methods in solving problems;
- willingness to persevere in mathematical tasks;
- interest, curiosity, and inventiveness in doing mathematics;
- inclination to monitor and reflect on their own thinking and performance;

- valuing of the application of mathematics to situations arising in other disciplines and everyday experiences;
- appreciation of the role of mathematics in our culture and its value as a tool and as a language. (p. 233)

These dispositions develop in students most effectively when teachers model the dispositions. For example, research both in the K–12 arena (Zimmerman & Blotner, 1979; Zimmerman & Ringle, 1981) and at the college level (Brown & Inouye, 1978) has shown that when teachers model persistence in problem solving, their students become more persistent in solving problems as a result. Again, this may be a common-sense issue because we would expect that when teachers frequently use real-life, applied problems, their students will begin to appreciate the usefulness of mathematics. Similarly, teachers who are enthusiastic about the topics they are presenting are likely to instill the same interest in their students. Ask students who "like math" where this feeling came from, and you'll often find that one teacher at a particular grade level got them excited about math, and that excitement impacted their attitudes for the rest of their lives. Unfortunately, the same situation can be, and often is, true for those who dislike mathematics or even fear it—the math-anxious students.

One semester, one year, or a lifetime of undesirable experiences in mathematics courses can produce what is referred to as **mathematics anxiety**. Although this term is defined differently by various researchers, mathematics anxiety is generally thought of as both a fear of mathematics and a negative attitude toward its study. This fear often exhibits itself as the test-taking anxiety of a student in a mathematics class, but it may also surface as an unwillingness to volunteer answers or to participate in a learning team in the classroom. Research shows that this anxiety is ordinarily the result of low academic performance in mathematics and can be treated, in part, by attempting to change the students' beliefs about the nature of mathematics (Hembree, 1990). When we consider the high incidence of mathematics anxiety in our world, it becomes critical that we, as teachers, not only deliver content but also become actively involved in the shaping of attitudes and beliefs—dispositions— toward mathematics in the classroom every day. The Seventy-Third Yearbook of the NCTM—entitled *Motivation and Disposition: Pathways to Learning Mathematics* (Brahier, 2011)—features an entire book devoted to the theory and practice of developing positive dispositions in the mathematics classroom.

Conclusion

The National Council of Teachers of Mathematics publishes the quarterly *Journal for Research in Mathematics Education,* which disseminates the latest research findings for educators to consider when making curricular, teaching, and assessment decisions. Other organizations have similar publications or feature articles that address the need to put research into practice, such as the journals *School Science and Mathematics* (published by the School Science and Mathematics Association) and *Investigations in Mathematics Learning* (published by the Research Council on Mathematics Learning). As mathematics teachers, it is our responsibility to stay current with the latest research and its implications. Just as salespersons are expected to attend conferences and update themselves on current research on marketing techniques, a teacher needs to know what classroom strategies are supported by data and attempt to put them into practice. We address the issue of ongoing professional development in Chapter 13.

In this chapter, several current learning theories and their implications in the classroom have been described. Steffe and Cobb (1988) wrote that "the teacher will be far more successful in accommodating children's growth in conceptual understanding if he or she has some notion of what the child's present structures and ways of operating are" (p. viii). Indeed, what we do as teachers daily will be rooted in what we believe about the way that our students learn. If we accept the notion that learning is an active process that involves discussion and allowing students to reach their own conclusions, we accordingly will organize our classroom in an inquiry mode that emphasizes cooperative learning and active, hands-on lessons. An administrator who spends even 20 minutes in your classroom should not have to ask you what you believe about mathematics education; it will be evident by virtue of the lesson you teach and the role you assume in the classroom.

It has been said that the teacher who accepts the constructivist theory of teaching and learning is a "guide on the side" rather than a "sage on the stage." But being a guide is not as easy as it sounds. The examples described in this chapter, such as the polygon-definition activity or the inquiry lesson on using paper-folding to explore exponents, show that the questions the teacher asked and the way in which the lessons were organized were key to implementing the lessons. Although the students were actively engaged in the activities, the teacher played an important role in selecting and organizing the tasks, guiding the process through careful questioning techniques, and assessing student progress along the way. The hope is that, as students take part in active lessons that involve the invention or discovery of mathematical concepts, they will develop a view of mathematics that includes more than its content. They also should come to recognize the role of the mathematical processes and practices and the notion that mathematics can be thought of as a verb—as something one *does*. As students' dispositions toward mathematics change, we should also see a decline in mathematics anxiety and an increased appreciation for the study of mathematics.

In Chapters 4 and 5, we turn our attention to the mathematics curriculum. We examine what topics are studied in secondary and middle school mathematics, how the material is sequenced, and how those decisions are made while keeping in mind that all curricular decisions should be based on research.

For bibliographic references and additional resources, see page 402

Glossary

Algebra Tiles: Algebra tiles are manipulatives that are used to model variable expressions and equations. A standard set of tiles contains three shapes as shown:

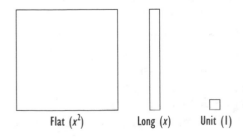

Flat (x^2)   Long (x)   Unit (1)

Most commercially available algebra tiles are a different color on each side: One color represents a positive term, and the other color represents a negative term. Mathematical processes from solving equations to simplifying expressions can be modeled with algebra tiles to enhance visualization skills and to promote conceptual understanding.

Base Ten Blocks: Base ten blocks are manipulatives that are frequently used to model numbers and number relationships. A standard set of blocks contains three shapes as shown:

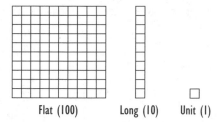

Flat (100)   Long (10)   Unit (1)

Most commercially available base ten blocks have standard measurements: A unit cube measures 1 cm on a side; a long or rod is 10 cm long; and a flat measures 10 cm × 10 cm. Mathematical concepts from place value to decimal operations can be modeled with base ten blocks to enhance visualization skills and to promote conceptual understanding.

Behaviorist Theory: The belief that learning can be controlled by the application of external rewards and punishments—consequences for actions.

Bruner's Stages of Representation: Jerome Bruner, an educational theorist, described cognitive development as passing through three stages: enactive, iconic, and symbolic. His theory emphasizes the importance of hands-on, concrete experiences in the early stages of learning a new concept. These experiences provide a foundation on which more abstract concepts can be built later. He is also recognized for having developed the concept attainment teaching strategy.

Concept Attainment: Concept attainment is a teaching strategy developed by Jerome Bruner. Students inductively create their own definitions as they are presented with a series of "yes" and "no" examples and counterexamples. The teacher's role in the process is to carefully select the examples that will allow students to invent their own definitions and rules. The students must reflect on the common characteristics of elements in a set and make generalizations.

Constructivist Model: The constructivist model is a teaching and learning theory in which educators view students as active participants who construct their own understanding of concepts rather than empty vessels into which knowledge is poured. The teacher in a constructivist classroom places student interests at the center of the curriculum and often employs cooperative learning strategies and a variety of assessment techniques. The roots of constructivism are found in the research and publications of Jean Piaget.

Curiosity: Curiosity is an emotion and an important mathematical disposition that students usually develop over time. Two types of curiosity are addressed in the literature—cognitive and sensory. Cognitive curiosity results when students realize that there is a difference between what they expected and what actually happened, and sensory curiosity can be thought of as an inherent curiosity that is triggered by something in the environment.

Deductive Teaching: A teacher who uses a deductive teaching strategy provides students with rules or generalizations and expects the students to apply those rules to particular cases. Deduction is a process that moves from the general to the specific. Emphasis is placed on students being able to use a rule in specific cases.

Descriptive Research: Descriptive research is undertaken for the purpose of generating statistics and information for discussion but not necessarily for comparison. Descriptive research efforts do not ordinarily make claims that one method is more effective than another as is the case with experimental research.

Disposition: Disposition refers to the affective (feeling) side of the teaching of mathematics. It is important not only to teach students mathematical concepts but also to promote positive attitudes toward the content area. The National Council of Teachers of Mathematics noted that disposition refers to "a tendency to act in positive ways" (NCTM, 1989, p. 233).

Dynamic Software: Computer software is referred to as dynamic if it involves human interaction with what is viewed on the screen. For example, a geometry program would be considered dynamic if the user can draw a quadrilateral, grab one of the vertices, and view the effects on the shape of the polygon as the vertex is dragged around the page. This type of software is different from traditional drill-and-practice software that simply displays a question and requires the user to input an answer.

Ego Goal: A student is said to have an ego goal orientation when the individual considers a performance to be successful if it is better than that of the others in the class. The student is generally more interested in earning extrinsic rewards, such as grades or teacher approval, than actually learning the mathematical concepts.

Emotion: An emotion is an affective attribute—a feeling—that is considered one of the elements of motivation. Ford (1992) pointed out that interest and curiosity are two of the important emotions that constitute this component of motivation. A student who is *interested in* or exhibits *curiosity about* a problem or lesson in the mathematics classroom will appear to be motivated to learn.

Experimental Research: Experimental research is undertaken to attempt to prove that one teaching or assessment strategy is more effective than another. Generally, this research effort uses a control group that receives no treatment and an experimental group that experiences a unique teaching approach, and a statistical comparison of effectiveness is used to argue in favor of one strategy over another.

Inductive Teaching: A teacher who uses an inductive teaching strategy tends to provide students with many specific examples and expects the students to generalize the examples into broad rules or definitions. Induction is the process of going from the specific to the general. Emphasis is placed on students inventing their own rules and definitions that are consistent with presented examples or counterexamples.

Inquiry Lesson: A teacher employing an inquiry lesson will typically pose a problem to a class and allow students to investigate and explore rather than provide direct instruction through lecture methods. Students involved in an inquiry lesson ordinarily use induction to generalize patterns and rules that arise while conducting the investigation. Teachers who adhere to the constructivist theory of teaching and learning usually employ inquiry lessons.

Interest: Interest is an emotion associated with motivation and a disposition that develops in students over time. We say that a student has *interest* in an academic topic when the individual believes that the study of that topic will be beneficial in some way. Hidi (1990) defines two types of interest—personal and situational. Personal interests are those that we have all the time, whereas situational interests can be evoked by, for example, posing a problem or reading a book.

Manipulatives: Manipulatives are hands-on materials used as tools in the mathematics classroom to promote understanding of a concept or to explore a problem. Algebra tiles, base ten blocks, and pattern blocks are examples of mathematics manipulatives. According to the cognitive theory of Jerome Bruner, students should have concrete experiences with manipulatives when they begin to learn new concepts.

Mastery Goal: A student is said to have a mastery goal orientation when the individual places an intrinsic value on learning and self-improvement. For students possessing mastery goals, learning is valued for its own sake, and success depends on how much effort they expend on a project.

Mathematics Anxiety: Mathematics anxiety is both a fear of mathematics and a negative attitude toward its study. This fear often manifests itself as the test-taking anxiety of a student in a mathematics class, but it may also surface as an unwillingness to volunteer answers or participate in a learning team in the classroom.

Motivation: Motivation can be thought of as an affective attribute that influences the degree to which students want to engage in some activity or choose to become involved. Motivation can be viewed as having three components—goals (ego and mastery), emotions (such as interest and curiosity), and self-confidence (or self-efficacy).

Pattern Blocks: Pattern blocks are manipulatives that are used to model geometric designs and patterns. A

standard set of pattern blocks contains six shapes as shown:

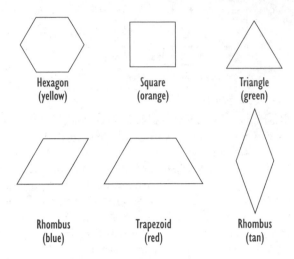

Hexagon (yellow) Square (orange) Triangle (green)

Rhombus (blue) Trapezoid (red) Rhombus (tan)

Most commercially available pattern blocks have standard colors, and the lengths of the sides are all the same, except for the base of the trapezoid, which is twice the standard length. Mathematical concepts from fraction skills to angle measurement can be studied using pattern blocks, which enhance visualization skills and promote conceptual understanding.

Qualitative Research: Qualitative research involves the collection and analysis of non-numerical data, such as videos of classroom episodes, scripts of student–teacher conversations, audio recordings of interviews, or written summaries of student journal entries. Descriptive studies often use qualitative data to paint a picture of a classroom situation or to enhance numerical data with quotes from a student interview.

Quantitative Research: Quantitative research involves the collection and analysis of numerical data, such as test scores or the number of times a person behaves in a particular way. Experimental studies often rely heavily on quantitative data to demonstrate the effectiveness of one teaching strategy over another.

Self-Confidence: Self-confidence or self-efficacy refers to the degree to which students believe that they will be able to succeed at a task or in a class. It is an important component of motivation, because students who perceive an inability to complete a mathematical task may simply give up and appear unmotivated.

van Hiele Model: The van Hiele model describes the stages a student passes through in learning geometric concepts. The van Hieles—a Dutch couple—theorized that students pass through five levels of development—visualization, analysis, informal deduction, deduction, and rigor. Advancement from one level to the next appears to be heavily dependent on effective instruction rather than on maturity or chronological age.

Zone of Proximal Development: An idea advanced by Lev Vygotsky, it is the range of tasks that lie between what the student currently knows and what can be learned through interaction with a more knowledgeable individual (either a teacher or a peer tutor).

Discussion Questions and Activities

1. Obtain several recent articles from an education research publication, such as the *Journal for Research in Mathematics Education* published by the NCTM. Scan the article abstracts and describe some of the issues that are currently being studied. Does most of the recent research appear to be qualitative or quantitative? Descriptive or experimental?

2. Not all research is necessarily conducted in a formal manner, and a current trend is to view the teacher as a researcher (generally referred to as *action research*). On a practical level, discuss what kinds of research can be carried out by a teacher in the classroom, including questions the teacher might try to answer and what kind of data could be collected to answer those questions.

3. Obtain a secondary or middle school mathematics textbook. Choose a unit or chapter and review it in light of current learning theory. Does the book, for example, appear to follow Bruner's stages of learning by suggesting an initial concrete experience? Does the book provide student activities that appear to be inquiry based or constructivist in nature?

4. Describe your own experiences with high school geometry. In light of the van Hiele model, discuss the degree to which your geometry course addressed your needs as a learner.

5. We have all heard the expression "practice makes perfect." Discuss the role of rote practice of skills in the mathematics classroom. Is there a place for the traditional worksheet in a classroom that emphasizes inquiry and an inductive approach to teaching and learning?

6. When a student chooses not to complete required assignments or refuses to pay attention in class, we often hear it said that the student lacks motivation. In light of the three components of motivation described in this chapter, identify several possible reasons why the student might be failing to do the necessary work. Discuss some practical strategies that a teacher might use in an attempt to motivate the student.

7. Because you have chosen mathematics as your teaching field, you probably have a very positive disposition toward the content area. Identify and discuss experiences that have influenced your attitudes and dispositions toward mathematics over the years. What specific strategies can you use in the classroom to improve the dispositions of your mathematics students?

8. Obtain copies of the *Curriculum and Evaluation Standards for School Mathematics* (1989) and read the complete Evaluation Standard 10 on disposition (pp. 233–237). Discuss the various components of a student's disposition and how a teacher can assess the degree to which a student is developing a positive disposition.

9. Conduct some additional research on the topic of mathematics anxiety. Describe some of the factors that cause individuals to become math anxious, and find some research-based suggestions on how to help students counter mathematics anxiety.

10. Preview a dynamic geometry software program on a computer or graphing calculator, such as Geometer's Sketchpad or GeoGebra. Devise a list of several geometric concepts that could be explored in more depth by using this software than with pencil and paper. Explain the degree to which these explorations are consistent with current learning theory.

Chapter 4

Curricular Models

After reading Chapter 4, you should be able to answer the following questions:

- What are the NCTM and the Common Core curriculum Standards? Why and how were they developed?
- What are the similarities and differences between a state curricular model and a set of national Standards?
- Why is it becoming increasingly important for *all* students to have a significant mathematical background?
- What is the core curriculum concept, and what are some models that schools may follow to achieve this?
- What are the advantages and disadvantages of the traditional versus an integrated sequencing of mathematical content?

Take a piece of paper and write down 10 things that you believe every student should know after completion of a Pre-K–12 mathematics program. Keep in mind that, because your list can include only 10 items, you need to focus on the skills and concepts that you believe are critical for success in life beyond high school (which may or may not include college—sometimes referred to as *college and career readiness*). Then ask a friend to do the same and compare your lists. Although you may agree on simple issues, such as the need to be able to add and subtract, you probably will put several items on your list that are not on your friend's, and vice versa. For example, does your list include the Pythagorean Theorem or the use of right-triangle trigonometry? Is it important that every person be able to use a ruler to accurately measure the length of an object? Should every student become proficient with using a calculator for problem solving, or should all critical outcomes require only the use of a pencil and a piece of paper?

Some people argue that it is important to learn to factor trinomials in algebra, but others believe this skill is a waste of time and is more efficiently done by a handheld computer. Some believe that every student should be well grounded in topics from the area of discrete mathematics, but others contend that a comprehensive exploration of calculus (a study of continuous functions) is more important. As you travel from district to district and state to state, you may find that what people consider to be significant content varies. Some countries, such as Russia and Japan, have a national curriculum with a set list of topics that *every* child must master in mathematics; this is not the case in the United States. The authority to write curricula, by virtue of the U.S. Constitution, is delegated to the states. Therefore, each state is free to determine its own curriculum, which means that each state has the power to develop its own list of objectives that every student should master in a Pre-K–12 mathematics program. ■

NCTM Curriculum Standards

Recognizing the differences in curricula from state to state and the need for the reform of mathematics education programs, the NCTM initiated a process of developing national standards for mathematics curriculum. A standard is a benchmark against which a state or local school district's curriculum can be compared to determine the degree to which the curriculum addresses nationally recognized critical outcomes. The first standards-writing process began in the mid-1980s with a writing team drafting a document that was scrutinized and eventually endorsed by thousands of educators, business leaders, and other professionals and organizations throughout the United States. In 1989, the NCTM *Curriculum and Evaluation Standards* were published, and they served as the driving force behind curricular reform at the national, state, and local level for more than 10 years. In 2000, the NCTM updated and refined the document into *Principles and Standards for School Mathematics,* which addressed societal needs for mathematics education.

Let's think for a minute about our world—a world much different from the one in which our parents and grandparents grew up. Today's society has shifted from an industrial age to an information age—driven by computers, the Internet, and a host of other technology. The assembly line, for example, on which the role of each worker is to place a bolt in a hole, has all but disappeared and been replaced by a workplace that requires an understanding of computers and an ability to problem solve when a system breaks down. Studies such as that conducted by the Bell Laboratory (Pollack, 1987) have consistently shown that, above all else, businesses need employees who can solve problems. Other studies of employers have indicated the importance of workers having not only the skill to do a job but also the ability to participate as a member of a team and to communicate effectively with others (Lawrenz & Strumpf, 2001). Indeed, the need for effective committees and working teams in industry has never been higher. Also, employees frequently undergo additional schooling and training. Businesses consolidate or refocus their directions, and workers must adapt to the resulting changes and learn new skills. The days in which a person would take a job, work on the job for 30 years, and then retire are all but gone, so one needs to prepare for a lifetime of education.

Historically, white males have been most successful in school mathematics. With the significant rise in minority populations comes the social responsibility to prepare all children—minorities and females equally included—to be successful in this changing world. Finally, it has long been the goal of education to prepare citizens to make reasoned choices and to contribute effectively to the democracy. Decision-making in a complex world requires the consideration of a vast amount of data and the ability to construct logical arguments with supporting data.

In light of what we know about our rapidly changing society, NCTM (2000) recognized in *Principles and Standards for School Mathematics* how important it is that students have significant mathematical backgrounds. Specifically, the authors of the document stated four primary reasons why students need to possess mathematical competence:

> *Mathematics for life.* Knowing mathematics can be personally satisfying and empowering. The underpinnings of everyday life are increasingly mathematical and technological. For instance, making purchasing decisions, choosing insurance or health plans, and voting knowledgeably all call for quantitative sophistication.
>
> *Mathematics as a part of cultural heritage.* Mathematics is one of the greatest cultural and intellectual achievements of humankind, and citizens should develop an appreciation and understanding of that achievement, including its aesthetic and even recreational aspects.
>
> *Mathematics for the workplace.* Just as the level of mathematics needed for intelligent citizenship has increased dramatically, so too has the level of mathematical thinking and problem solving needed in the workplace, in professional areas ranging from health care to graphic design.
>
> *Mathematics for the scientific and technical community.* Although all careers require a foundation of mathematical knowledge, some are mathematics intensive. More students must pursue an educational path that will prepare them for lifelong work as mathematicians, statisticians, engineers, and scientists. (NCTM, 2000, p. 4)

Clearly, 13 years of mathematics worksheets presenting isolated skill-based practice, such as fraction addition, denominator rationalizing, two-column proofs, parabola graphing, and distance = rate $\times$ time problems, simply are not sufficient to meet the goals identified by the NCTM. Instead, the vision was to develop a curriculum that would be rich in mathematical content—cutting across all content areas, from numbers to algebra, geometry, and statistics—as well as one in which mathematical thinking and processes were valued (as discussed in Chapter 1). Additionally, the NCTM believed it was important for students to develop positive beliefs about the nature and usefulness of mathematics.

The NCTM was the first professional organization in the United States to develop a list of recommended curricular topics with its groundbreaking document *Curriculum and Evaluation Standards for School Mathematics* in 1989. Eleven years later, *Principles and Standards for School Mathematics* was released. It is important to remember that the *Standards* were not written as *mandatory* curricular benchmarks but as a list of recommendations for states and school districts to voluntarily use as a basis for determining student outcomes at each grade level. As such, it was assumed that not every state or district would necessarily adopt every detail of the *Standards* but that at least a framework with a solid research base would be available for deliberation and decision-making processes. (To explore the research base behind the *Standards,* see Kilpatrick, Martin, and Schifter, 2003.) However, over the years following the release of the documents, virtually every state adopted a model curriculum or some form of state standards that aligned with NCTM's model (we discuss state models later in the chapter). In addition, other professional organizations, such as the National Science Teachers' Association, have also written their own sets of standards with the NCTM's process as their model. *Principles and Standards for School Mathematics* was written with the input of tens of thousands of readers of its draft document released in both paper and Web-based formats in 1998. Table 4.1 lists the curriculum standards for all grade levels, Pre-K through 12, as recommended by NCTM in the final document of 2000.

Table 4.1 NCTM Curriculum Standards for Grades Pre-K–12	
Standard Number	**Standard Topic**
Standard 1	Number and Operations
Standard 2	Algebra
Standard 3	Geometry
Standard 4	Measurement
Standard 5	Data Analysis and Probability
Standard 6	Problem Solving
Standard 7	Reasoning and Proof
Standard 8	Communication
Standard 9	Connections
Standard 10	Representation

(NCTM, 2000. Reprinted with permission.)

The first five of these topics refer to mathematical content that is recommended as developmentally appropriate for each grade-level band, where the bands include grades Pre-K–2, 3–5, 6–8, and 9–12. These mathematical topics are referred to as the **content standards.** Also, as was discussed in Chapter 1, the last five of the 10 standards are the mathematical **process standards**—problem solving, reasoning and proof, communication, connections, and representation. None of the standards were intended as course titles, per se, but are to serve as a collection of content and processes that should be addressed every year that a child is in school.

The content and process standards for each grade cluster in the document not only outline mathematical topics for student exploration but also illustrate the major concepts through classroom vignettes and examples that have a constructivist, student-centered approach at their core. Therefore, the document not only provides direction on mathematical topics but also includes insights on how to present these topics in a manner that would be meaningful and relevant to students. The *Standards* also present a major challenge to curriculum planners who have historically offered algebra or geometry courses primarily to the more advanced students, leaving only general mathematics courses for the non-college-bound population. The *Standards* essentially assert that *every* student needs to explore topics from algebra, geometry, discrete mathematics, probability, and so forth, regardless of academic ability, gender, or culture as described in Chapter 2. The notion of "mathematics for all students" is very difficult for many educators to accept or put into practice. Yet this has always been the challenge of the teacher, even back in the days of the one-room schoolhouse—to select activities that address the needs of all of the learners in the classroom while maintaining the basic belief that all students are capable of achieving.

NCTM Focal Points and Related Documents

As discussed in Chapter 1, TIMSS reports described the U.S. curriculum as "an inch deep and a mile wide," suggesting that in an attempt to address a multitude of learning outcomes, we may be shortchanging students by lacking depth of exploration. As a response to this issue, the NCTM released a book in 2006 entitled *Curriculum Focal Points for Prekindergarten through Grade 8 Mathematics: A Quest for Coherence*. A writing team of mathematicians and classroom teachers wrote the document "as a starting point in a dialogue on what is important at particular levels of instruction and as an initial step toward a more coherent, focused curriculum in this country" (NCTM, 2006, p. vii). In order to clarify the curricular emphasis at each grade level (through grade 8), three critical outcomes per grade were identified and discussed. These outcomes were selected because they were considered important mathematically, in terms of their applicability and their connections to mathematics topics studied before and after the grade level. *Curriculum Focal Points* (2006) provides states and school districts an additional level of detail on what is expected at each grade—a level of specificity that is not included in the original *Standards* (2000) publication.

In order to provide more specific information for secondary and middle schools that are preparing students for higher education, the College Board produced a document in 2006 entitled *College Board Standards for College Success: Mathematics and Statistics*. NCTM's *Principles and Standards for School Mathematics* (2000) was one of several publictions that were reviewed in the process of designing this document. In the book, the authors outlined key mathematical topics that should be studied from middle school mathematics courses through pre-calculus that are critical to a student's success in a first-year college mathematics course. For example, four standards are set forth for a high school geometry course, including the following: (1) geometric reasoning, proof, and representations; (2) similarity and transformations; (3) direct and indirect measurements; and (4) two-stage experiments, conditional probability, and independence. Note that the fourth standard is a data analysis and probability **strand**—a content area that is woven throughout the program, included in both algebra and geometry courses.

For the geometry course, each of the four standards has from two to four objectives, and each objective includes two to six performance expectations. For example, under the standard on similarity and transformations, an objective and its performance expectations are as follows:

Objective G.2.2
Student identifies congruent figures and justifies these congruences by establishing sufficient conditions and by finding a congruence-preserving rigid transformation between the figures. Student solves problems involving congruence in a variety of contexts.

Performance Expectations
G.2.2.1   Analyzes figures in terms of their symmetries using the concepts of reflection, rotation, and translation and combinations of these.

G.2.2.2   Compares and contrasts equality, congruence, and similarity.

G.2.2.3   Identifies and differentiates among sufficient conditions for congruence of triangles (SSS, SAS, ASA, AAS, and HL), and applies them.

G.2.2.4   Uses coordinate geometry and rigid transformations (reflections, translations, and rotations) to establish congruence of figures.

(From *College Board Standards for College Success—Mathematics and Statistics*, copyright © 2006–2007. The College Board, www.collegeboard.com. Reproduced with permission.)

Furthermore, the College Board also publishes a syllabus (Course Description) for Advanced Placement Calculus that is taught at the high school level. Most high schools that offer a calculus course follow this syllabus. In the document (College Board, 2007), the first calculus course includes the topics of (1) functions, graphs, and limits (including analysis of graphs, limits of functions, asymptotes, and continuity), (2) derivatives (concept, at a point, as a function, second derivatives, applications, and computation), and (3) integrals (interpretations and properties, applications, fundamental theorem of calculus, techniques and applications of antidifferentiation, and numerical approximations). Again, the purpose of this document is to provide a framework that ensures consistency among institutions offering calculus courses for high school students.

How Would You React

SCENARIO

You are teaching a lesson on a topic such as the rules of exponents and logarithms or how to multiply and divide fractions. A student in your class raises a hand and asks, "When would we ever have to use this stuff in our lives?" In your response you

a. Point out to the class that there are many topics in mathematics that are not necessarily "real life" but that serve as good mental exercises that teach us to think.

b. Remind the class that, although the topic is rather abstract, teachers in future classes will expect them to have mastered the skill.

c. Explain to the class that standardized tests—from state-level graduation tests to the SAT—often feature problems of this type, so they need to know how to do them.

d. Challenge the student (and the class) to research the topic and see if they can bring back examples of problems that might involve these skills.

e. Other.

DISCUSSION

The question of "why do we have to know this" is familiar to veteran teachers in all content areas. In the scenario, responses A, B, and C are typical responses that mathematics teachers have given through the years. However, in the mind of a secondary or middle school student, none of them is an acceptable response because students in these age ranges live in the here and now and generally have difficulty with learning something today that will not benefit them for another year or more. Similarly, Choice D appears to be appealing,

but most students will not take the initiative to research and answer their own questions, unless some form of extra credit is offered or a class project requires this additional work.

A simple benchmark for a teacher to keep in mind is that if a student has to ask why a topic is being explored, the lesson planning is probably flawed because mathematical content is being taught out of context. In *Principles and Standards for School Mathematics,* the NCTM (2000) states that "the contexts of problems can vary from familiar experiences involving students' lives or the school day to applications involving the sciences or the world of work" (p. 52). But the point is that the skills being taught—whether they are rules of logarithms or operations on fractions—should be couched in a problem-solving context that helps students to see, from the very beginning, that the skills are worthwhile.

Logarithms, for example, are used routinely by scientists who deal with sound (decibels), acidity of liquids (pH), and the study of earthquakes (the Richter scale). Similarly, architects and carpenters use operations on fractions when doing measurement as regular parts of their jobs. Instead of teaching students the basic skills and then demonstrating an application at the end of a lesson or unit (or not at all), teachers are encouraged to design lessons and experiences for students that *use* the skills in a meaningful way. The frequent occurrence of students wondering who would ever need to know the topics being studied should serve as a red flag for a teacher that the students are not experiencing the level of problem solving and application that is recommended in the NCTM and *Common Core State Standards.*

Finally, a nonprofit organization known as Achieve was established in 1996 to help "states raise academic standards, improve assessments and strengthen accountability to prepare all young people for postsecondary education, work and citizenship" (Achieve, 2011). As part of the organization's work, the American Diploma Project Network was established, out of which a set of high school–level mathematics benchmarks were written. These benchmarks are archived and can be downloaded from their Web site at www.achieve.org. Furthermore, Achieve was involved in the writing of another set of national Standards released a decade after NCTM's *Principles and Standards*—the *Common Core State Standards*.

The Common Core State Standards

The National Governors Association and the Council of Chief State School Officers initiated the Common Core State Standards (CCSS) Initiative in 2009. The goal of this project was to write and implement national standards that would be identical and mandatory for all states that approved them. Agreeing to use these Standards, in turn, qualified states to apply for federal funds, which served as an incentive to adopt the Standards. The *Common Core State Standards for Mathematics* (as well as for English Language Arts) were released in the summer of 2010, and most states began to use the document as their new Standards soon thereafter.

The design of the CCSS includes a significant emphasis on big ideas of mathematics. While some states had previously featured 50 or more objectives for students to master at each grade level, the CCSS generally includes fewer than 30 Standards for each grade level. The document was designed to help teachers and administrators appreciate the main ideas of mathematics and how they are connected. For the first time in history, a publication including specific statements of what a student should know and be able to do at each grade level began to be used in nearly every state across the country, using the same language in each instance. The idea was that a student could, for example, move from Boston, Massachusetts, to Las Vegas, Nevada, and know that the mathematics content being studied at a particular grade level would be exactly the same.

In Chapter 1, we discussed the eight mathematical practices described in the CCSS. These practices are intended to be modeled and emphasized across all grade levels. However, the CCSS also includes very detailed statements of mathematical content that students should be learning. At the elementary and middle school levels, there are several Domains—content areas—at each grade level, and within each Domain is a list of Clusters, where each Cluster includes one or more Standards. Let's consider a specific example.

At Grade 6, the CCSS begins with an overview that includes a description of four *critical areas* to be addressed by each student, including the following:

1. connecting ratio and rate to whole number multiplication and division and using concepts of ratio and rate to solve problems;
2. completing understanding of division of fractions and extending the notion of number to the system of rational numbers, which includes negative numbers;
3. writing, interpreting, and using expressions and equations; and
4. developing understanding of statistical thinking. (CCSS, 2010, p. 39)

Critical areas outlined for each grade level draw heavily upon NCTM's *Curriculum Focal Points,* described earlier in the chapter. After these critical areas are listed and described, the document lays out five main content Domains for Grade 6: Ratios and Proportional Relationships, The Number System, Expressions and Equations, Geometry, and Statistics and Probability (CCSS, 2010). Note that these Domains somewhat parallel the NCTM Standards in that they focus on number, algebra, geometry, and statistics/probability. In turn, each of these Domains includes one to three Clusters of Standards, where each Cluster groups together one to four more specific Standards. So, for example, in Grade 6, one of the five Domains is Statistics and Probability. Detail in this area is provided as follows:

Domain: Statistics and Probability

Cluster: Develop understanding of statistical variability.

Standards:

1. Recognize a statistical question as one that anticipates variability in the data related to the question and accounts for it in the answers. *For example, "How old am I?" is not a statistical question, but "How old are the students in my school?" is a statistical question because one anticipates variability in students' ages.*

2. Understand that a set of data collected to answer a statistical question has a distribution which can be described by its center, spread, and overall shape.

3. Recognize that a measure of center for a numerical data set summarizes all of its values with a single number, while a measure of variation describes how its values vary with a single number.

Cluster: Summarize and describe distributions.

Standards:

1. Display numerical data in plots on a number line, including dot plots, histograms, and box plots.

2. Summarize numerical data sets in relation to their context, such as by:
   a. Reporting the number of observations.
   b. Describing the nature of the attribute under investigation, including how it was measured and its units of measurement.
   c. Giving quantitative measures of center (median and/or mean) and variability (interquartile range and/or mean absolute deviation), as well as describing any overall pattern and any striking deviations from the overall pattern with reference to the context in which the data were gathered.
   d. Relating the choice of measures of center and variability to the shape of the data. (CCSS, 2010, p. 45)

Thus, there are five Standards for Grade 6 that fall under the Domain of Statistics and Probability, grouped together into two Clusters. In all, there are 29 mathematics Standards at the sixth grade level. Other grade levels are laid out in the same manner, with 26 Standards for fifth grade, 24 for the seventh grade, and 28 for eighth grade.

Recognizing that some high schools (and states) follow a traditional track of algebra and geometry courses, while others integrate the curriculum (which will be discussed later in this chapter), the development of CCSS for grades 9 through 12 was more difficult. Instead of using specific grade levels, the writers divide the content into six Conceptual Categories, including Number and Quantity, Algebra, Functions, Modeling, Geometry, and Statistics and Probability. Then, each

Conceptual Category includes Domains, Clusters, and Standards. Here is a specific example, taken from the Conceptual Category of Algebra:

Conceptual Category: Algebra

Domain: Creating Equations

Cluster: Create equations that describe numbers or relationships.

Standards:

1. Create equations and inequalities in one variable and use them to solve problems. *Include equations arising from linear and quadratic functions, and simple rational and exponential functions.*

2. Create equations in two or more variables to represent relationships between quantities; graph equations on coordinate axes with labels and scales.

3. Represent constraints by equations or inequalities, and by systems of equations and/or inequalities, and interpret solutions as viable or nonviable options in a modeling context. *For example, represent inequalities describing nutritional and cost constraints on combinations of different foods.*

4. Rearrange formulas to highlight a quantity of interest, using the same reasoning as in solving equations. *For example, rearrange Ohm's law $V = IR$ to highlight resistance R.* (CCSS, 2010, p. 65)

In this case, the Domain includes only one Cluster, which is subdivided into four specific Standards. The general organization of the CCSS is summarized in Figure 4.1.

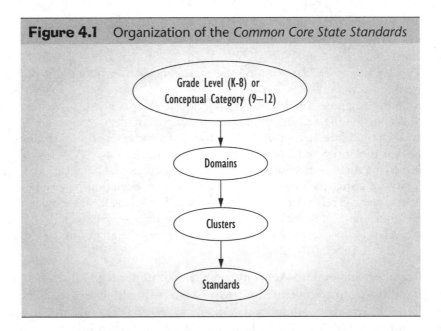

Figure 4.1   Organization of the *Common Core State Standards*

In addition, the high school portion of the *Common Core State Standards* includes several items that are designated as advanced topics intended primarily for students who plan to take courses in calculus or discrete mathematics but are not required content areas for all students. In turn, each state or school district is to use the entire pool of Standards for high school to design a three-course sequence of mathematics referred to as the **core curriculum**, organizing the content in whatever manner makes most sense for the situation. The *Common Core State Standards* document also provides an appendix sometimes referred to as the *pathways*. The appendix outlines suggestions for courses that can be built using the three-year core Standards.

State Models

The NCTM *Principles and Standards for School Mathematics* present an achievable national philosophy of mathematics education, given the school's resources and willingness to support the programs. As such, they are characterized by broad, theoretical statements of what students should be able to achieve in each grade-level band. However, what the *Standards* do not do is to prescribe *exactly* what a student should know or be able to do *at each grade level*. This task is left up to each state or district that chooses to use the *Standards* as its overarching model. Essentially, if a state chooses to embrace the vision of the NCTM *Standards,* then its task is to write a grade-by-grade, sequenced curricular model that provides districts within the state with a more specific design for each grade level. In those states that have adopted the *Common Core State Standards for Mathematics*, the year-by-year objectives (Standards) are prescribed, yet states still have the option to add to the core Standards and to provide teachers with additional detail to assist with implementation. Supporting documents such as *Curriculum Focal Points* (2006), recommendations made by the College Board, Achieve, and other professional organizations, or even curricular publications from other countries are sometimes used as guides for designing state-level Standards.

When reading a state model rooted in the *Standards,* one should be able to recognize the spirit and intent of the national view, despite the need to be more specific about objectives for each grade level. For example, Standard 3 on geometry for grades 9–12 in the NCTM *Standards* states that "all students should use trigonometric relationships to determine lengths and angle measures" and should "use geometric ideas to solve problems in, and gain insights into, other disciplines and other areas of interest such as art and architecture" (NCTM, 2000, p. 308). The Texas Mathematics Standards, based on the NCTM standards, makes a more specific statement for high school geometry students, stating that they should "determine the lengths and measures of angles in a right triangle by applying the trigonometric ratios sine, cosine and tangent in mathematical and real-world problems" (Texas Education Agency, 2011, p. 77). In this respect, the topics that are to be developed are clearly delineated for educators in the state and are attached to particular courses or grade levels. State standards are created to provide curricular direction to the local districts, so they tend to be much more specific about content, grade levels, or even instructional suggestions than do the NCTM or the *Common Core State Standards*. In turn, states that have some type of competency or proficiency testing program, then, draw the objectives for these assessments from their state models. The issues of assessment and its implications are discussed in more detail in Chapters 10 and 11.

Ultimately, as a state develops curriculum standards or frameworks, the important mathematical concepts to be mastered by all students must be identified. At the high school level, prescribing a curriculum can be particularly difficult because historically a number of "tracks" of mathematics study have been made available, depending on student interests, future needs, and ability. In the next section, we explore the issues surrounding the establishment of a core curriculum for all students.

The Core Curriculum

Suppose that two students each decided to take four units of high school mathematics courses and followed the sequence shown in Table 4.2:

Table 4.2	Possible Curricular Sequences for Secondary Students	
	College Bound	**Non-College Bound**
Grade 9	Algebra I	General Mathematics
Grade 10	Geometry	Applied General Math
Grade 11	Algebra II	Technical/Vocational Math
Grade 12	Pre-Calculus	Pre-Algebra

Upon graduation, each student's transcript would indicate that he or she had taken 4 years of mathematics. But how do you believe the students would compare if given a standard achievement test or an SAT or ACT exam? Are their mathematics backgrounds equivalent? Clearly not. The college-bound students have a distinct advantage in having studied a more diverse and higher-level set of concepts than other students. Yet this sequence and all of its inequities were very common in schools around the country even into the late 1980s; in fact, in some places, they still exist. Interestingly, in the 1970 NCTM *Yearbook,* the authors, speaking of changes in mathematics between 1920 and 1945, stated that it became an "increasingly common requirement that everyone take at least one year of mathematics in grades 9–12" and that "this new general mathematics [course] developed as the most popular alternative to algebra in the ninth grade. Down to the present day this course has been ill-defined and often poorly, or at least unwillingly, taught" (Jones & Coxford, 1970, p. 53). The General Mathematics course, indeed, still exists today—some 75 years later! The NCTM and *Common Core State Standards,* however, challenged us to reconsider what mathematical topics were being developed with whom and to think of ways to make mathematics accessible to all students as we have discussed. But why is this so important? Why not keep the curriculum the way it has always been?

As the world has moved into the information age, physical skills have been replaced by technical and problem-solving skills, and the workforce continues to require updating as industry changes. The U.S. Department of Labor (2007) estimates that two-thirds of all jobs being created today require a postsecondary education, resulting in a higher demand for individuals with critical thinking skills and creativity. The average worker will change jobs at least 4 or 5 times over a 25-year period (NCTM, 1989), and most experts agree that a job stays the same for only about 5 years, so a need for retraining is inevitable (Meiring, Rubenstein, Schultz, Lange, & Chambers, 1992). The National Research Council (1989) reported that 75 percent of all available jobs require at least a basic understanding of algebra and geometry. A basic understanding of statistics is also necessary in many career areas, just as knowledge of how samples are taken and statistics are analyzed is essential for following debates in politics (Konold & Higgins, 2003). And the need for students to be exposed to discrete mathematics topics, such as recursion and graph theory, is rapidly increasing because of the growth of computer technology and the relevance of discrete mathematics in industry (Dossey, 1991). It is unrealistic to believe that one segment of the population needs algebra "and beyond," and another segment will never need more than basic arithmetic; this simply does not appear to be the case anymore.

Consequently, the Common Core State Standards mandate that schools establish a core curriculum—a 3-year high school sequence with common objectives or outcomes—for *all* students. It is important not to confuse the "Common Core" with the notion of a "core curriculum." As we have discussed, the *Common Core State Standards* is a K–12 publication that describes desired outcomes for each grade level of schooling. The core curriculum, on the other hand, is simply a term for a 3-year program of study intended for all high school students. The core curriculum is discussed at length in an NCTM resource book published far ahead of its time, entitled *A Core Curriculum: Making Mathematics Count for Everyone* (Meiring et al., 1992). The authors make the case for developing a curricular model that would ensure that every secondary student has exposure to important mathematical topics that extend well beyond arithmetic. They suggest that college-bound and higher-achieving students will visit many concepts in greater depth than some of their peers but that at least the curriculum would ensure equal access to various areas of mathematics for all students. Meiring et al. suggest three possible models for schools to consider in restructuring their curriculum: the crossover, enrichment, and differentiated curriculum models.

The **crossover model** is probably the easiest to adopt if the school is currently on a very traditional tracking system. Two parallel tracks are established, one for college-bound students and one for students not planning to go to college. There is a 3-year sequence of courses with basically identical content objectives in both tracks. However, although the college-bound students may visit the topics at an advanced level with plenty of abstraction, including the exploration of some optional topics (many of which are included in the CCSS document), the student not planning to attend college will explore these concepts at a more concrete level with, perhaps, an increased emphasis on the use of technology. This is the "crossover" model because if a student decides, after a year or two of high school, to go to college after all but has not been in the college-bound track, that student can still switch to the other sequence and know that classmates have explored essentially the same objectives. Compare this situation to more traditional models in which the student in a low-average mathematics class visits less material in a watered-down fashion, making it virtually impossible for that student to ever get out of a low track. The minute a teacher, parent, counselor, or administrator labels the student as below average, the door is shut on the student's chances for exposure to significant mathematics. In traditional basic mathematics courses, often reserved for low-achieving students, the classes do no more than review elementary and middle school arithmetic. Also, in the crossover model, the student who is not successful on the college track can switch to the other without a loss of continuity. Finally, the model suggests a fourth-year advanced course for college-bound students. Figure 4.2 illustrates this with a simple flow chart.

Here is a specific example of how a high school might use the crossover model when teaching all first-year students

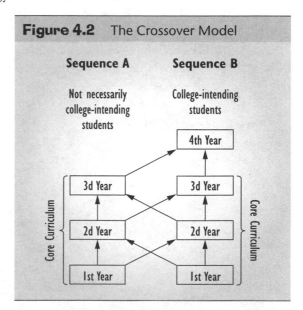

Figure 4.2 The Crossover Model

how to multiply polynomials. The students not planning to attend college might begin with a concrete experience involving algebra tiles. An analogy could be expressed as follows: *Think of what it means to multiply 12 × 13.* Geometrically, this multiplication problem can be expressed as the process of finding the area of a rectangle measuring 12 by 13. The tens and units pieces of a set of base ten blocks have been separated for emphasis in Figure 4.3.

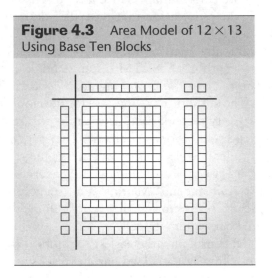

Figure 4.3   Area Model of 12 × 13 Using Base Ten Blocks

Think of the traditional algorithm. Four multiplications take place: 10 × 10, 10 × 2, 3 × 10, and 3 × 2. The diagram shows one flat that represents 100, 5 longs that represent 50, and 6 units, modeling the product of 156. Using base ten blocks, a child can visualize what it means to multiply. Similarly, the secondary class might consider $(x + 2)(x + 3)$. This problem is nothing more than a generalization of 12 × 13, where $x = 10$. So, with algebra tiles, as described in Chapter 3, the polynomial multiplication would look like the diagram in Figure 4.4.

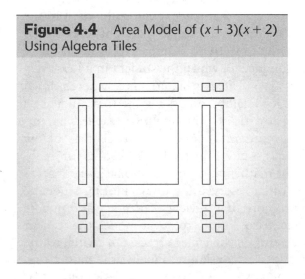

Figure 4.4   Area Model of $(x + 3)(x + 2)$ Using Algebra Tiles

The area of the rectangle is made up of one x^2 tile, five x tiles, and six unit tiles, so the product would be $x^2 + 5x + 6$. Students can work through several examples of polynomial multiplication problems like this, involving positive and negative numbers, without having to memorize a rule of any kind. Actually, every student should be exposed to this visual model, because many leave high school knowing "how to FOIL" without realizing that FOIL (First, Outside, Inside, Last) has no mathematical meaning beyond serving as a mnemonic for remembering an algorithm that applies only to binomials and without being able to explain *why* the problem is done that way. Eventually, the non-college-bound students will be able to move on to an iconic level, according to Bruner, and sketch freehand pictures of tiles that represent polynomial multiplication problems. Finally, the student will invent a procedure for multiplying polynomials without using concrete materials or drawing pictures. But the series of lessons that develop the abstract symbol manipulations are appropriate to the students and allow them to generalize their own rules, based on observations, which is at the core of the constructivist model for learning and teaching, as described in Chapter 3. The students might also try their hand at writing a function that describes the orange grove problem from Chapter 1 to see an application of binomial multiplication.

In the college-bound track, the students will explore the same concept but may be ready to move from concrete to abstract levels within a couple of days, thus leaving them additional time to explore extensions of the concept, such as how to develop a rule for multiplying and factoring the difference of squares or perfect cubes. They may also begin solving higher-level applied problems, such as those that involve maximizing volume. Perhaps you have solved the problem in which you are given an $8\frac{1}{2} \times 11"$ sheet of paper and asked how big the four squares you cut off from the corners should be in order to maximize the volume of the resulting open-top box formed when the sides are folded up. Figure 4.5 helps you visualize this.

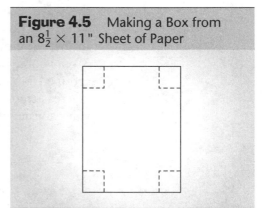

Figure 4.5 Making a Box from an $8\frac{1}{2} \times 11"$ Sheet of Paper

If the original dimensions of the paper were $8\frac{1}{2} \times 11"$, and the squares cut out measure $x \times x$, then the volume of the resulting box could be found by examining the function $y = x(11 - 2x)(8.5 - 2x)$, where x represents the height of the box, and the expressions $(11 - 2x)$ and $(8.5 - 2x)$ represent the length and the width of the base, respectively. Students can readily view the function's graph (Figure 4.6) on a graphing calculator.

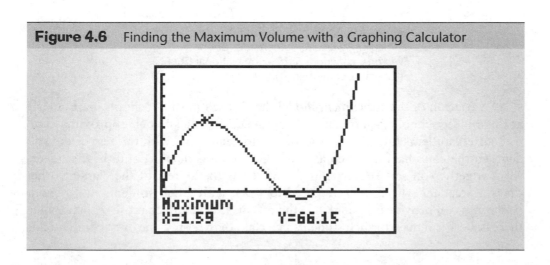

Figure 4.6 Finding the Maximum Volume with a Graphing Calculator

By tracing the curve using the TRACE function or using the CALC (calculate) button, they can locate the local maximum of the function at about $x = 1.59$ and calculate the volume by taking $1.59(11 - 3.18)(8.5 - 3.18) \approx 66.15$ cubic inches (or by simply using the y-value). This entire problem represents a rich, realistic application of polynomial multiplication that would engage the college-bound classes and extend their understanding of the use of variables for generalizing and solving problems. But again, in the crossover model all students still visit the same major core objectives.

A second curricular alternative suggested in *A Core Curriculum* is called the **enrichment model.** Under this model, students are arranged into small groups at the beginning of each unit throughout the 3-year common core. If a group of students completes the core content of a particular unit before the rest of the class, they can be assigned an enrichment topic to explore. These enrichment topics may include historical considerations of the content, such as the history of π; further exploration of a concept, such as studying fractals in a unit on area and perimeter; or looking at new situations, such as an application of a mathematical concept to a career area. In this way, all students are assured of a common core of mathematical concepts, but students who are more able have the opportunity to expand their knowledge even further. The enrichment model, similar to the crossover model, provides a common 3-year core. But these models differ in that classes are heterogeneously (mixed) grouped in the enrichment model, with small groups formed within the class, whereas students choose one of two tracks in the crossover model. Figure 4.7 provides a visual description of the enrichment model.

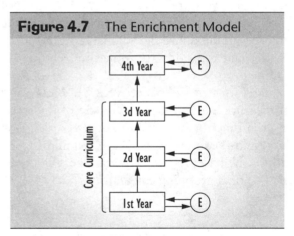

Figure 4.7 The Enrichment Model

A variation of the enrichment model that is used in some schools, particularly at the middle school level, is called **clustering**. Using this model, approximately 6 to 8 gifted students are selected and placed in each class, with the rest of the students in the class having mixed abilities. Grouping is flexible, and these students work together on some topics but are mixed with the rest of the class at other times. A teacher who is well prepared to work with gifted students in a regular classroom can provide challenges for them. This is often much more realistic when there is a critical mass of such students in a class than if only one or two individuals are in need of additional challenges. A book by Susan Winebrenner and Dina Brulles entitled *The Cluster Grouping Handbook* (2008) provides details on how to manage cluster groups in a regular classroom. Clustering is viewed by many as a preferred alternative to the more traditional grouping of students into full classes of honors or gifted students, while other classes serve average or struggling students. Unlike tracking practices, neither gifted nor struggling students are isolated from one another so that the diversity of thinking can enhance learning for all students (Winebrenner & Devlin, 2011).

Cooperative learning strategies are used to promote interaction among students.

The third curricular sequence suggested by the NCTM is the **differentiated model.** As is the case with the enrichment model, students are heterogeneously mixed into a shared 3-year core of mathematics courses, with a possible common fourth-year experience as well. Within each class, students are organized into small groups at the beginning of each unit. However, instead of all students completing a core of objectives and some moving on to additional topics, all students explore the same topics but at a variety of levels, as was described in the crossover model. So, there might be one group of students working on multiplying polynomials with algebra tiles, while another group is devising a shortcut for finding the square of a binomial in a more abstract manner. Both groups would be learning to multiply polynomials, but the content would be at a level appropriate to each particular group. Figure 4.8 illustrates how all students explore the same core of objectives but at a different level of depth in the differentiated model. The differentiated model organizes classes in a heterogeneous manner similar to the enrichment model but structures the work of each group by depth of coverage as the crossover model does.

Common to all of these models is the notion that every student deserves to explore the same core of objectives regardless of perceived ability level or future plans. Lessons should be rich in the use of hands-on materials (manipulatives) and technology and are taught with the students' needs in mind. The idea of a core curriculum for all, however, can be difficult to implement, particularly at the high school level, because it requires a radical change from the curriculum of the past—the idea that the "best" students get algebra, geometry, and pre-calculus, and the less-able students take basic math and, perhaps, a pre-algebra or algebra course. In a core curriculum, algebra, geometry, statistics and probability, and some discrete mathematics topics are given equal weight, so the secondary and middle school curriculum should provide experiences in all of the content areas. In order for a wide array of mathematical

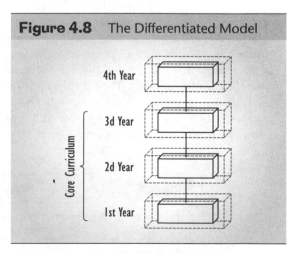

Figure 4.8 The Differentiated Model

4th Year

3d Year

2d Year

1st Year

Core Curriculum

(Reprinted with permission from *A Core Curriculum: Making Mathematics Count for Everyone*, copyright © 1992 by National Council of Teachers of Mathematics. All rights reserved.)

topics to make sense to students and to appear to be connected, many schools have dropped the traditional Algebra I–Geometry–Algebra II sequence and replaced it with an integrated high school mathematics program. The next section explores the traditional and integrated curricular sequences.

SPOTlight on Technology

A popular tool used for teaching mathematics is the computer spreadsheet (or the table function on a graphing calculator). Suppose that a teacher posed the following problem to a class:

A local video store offers the following plans for renting videos: For Plan 1, customers join the Rental Club for $20 per year and can rent each video for $1.50. For Plan 2, the customer does not have to pay a membership fee but pays $2.95 for each movie rental. Under what conditions is Plan 1 better than Plan 2? Which would you choose and why?

Using a spreadsheet application (such as Excel) on a computer, a student can input the number of video rentals in Column A and write formulas for calculating the total cost of video rentals using Plan 1 in Column B and Plan 2 in Column C, as illustrated in Figure 4.9.

Using the FILL DOWN option on the spreadsheet, the students can create a table (see Figure 4.10) that shows the relative cost of renting from 0 to 15 videos a year. Students can scan the table to look for patterns and to draw conclusions. They should notice, for example, that the total costs for 10 video rentals under Plan 1 and Plan 2 are $35.00 and $29.50, respectively. More importantly, the values in the spreadsheet allow them to compare the relative costs of the options and find the break-even point. They should notice that Plan 2 is cheaper until about 14 video rentals, at which point the costs are almost the same. At 14 videos or more, Plan 1 becomes the less expensive choice. In fact,

if the table is continued even further, a family renting an average of one video per week will save more than $50 per year if they choose Plan 1.

The spreadsheet, then, serves as a tool for comparing the costs of the options, given a particular number of video rentals. Students gain experience in setting up and reading a table, looking for patterns, and using algebraic symbols to define the spreadsheet formulas. The last of these activities is extremely important because a significant amount of time is generally spent on the representation of patterns and functions with variables at the secondary and middle school levels. In addition, the spreadsheet saves the students from having to guess and check their way through 14 different video rental scenarios to find the break-even point. Once the cost of an option has been calculated, the spreadsheet allows the calculation to be mechanically repeated to display a wide variety of possibilities. Finally, the spreadsheet option allows the teacher to ask such a question as, "What if the video store raised the membership fee to $30 but dropped the cost of renting tapes to $1.25 for members? What is the new break-even point?" With a quick change in the spreadsheet formula, students discover that members need to rent 18 or more videos to make the new Plan 1 the better choice. The spreadsheets allow a class to examine a number of scenarios to gather data and draw conclusions, with the computer doing each of the individual calculations. The focus of the problem, then, becomes the analysis of data and the formulation of an answer rather than computation. Furthermore, research supports the use of spreadsheets in teaching mathematics, indicating that spreadsheets help students generalize patterns and make connections between arithmetic and algebra (Hershkowitz et al., 2002).

Figure 4.9 The Video Problem Solved on a Spreadsheet

	A	B	C
1	VIDEOS	Plan 1	Plan 2
2	0	=20+(A2*1.5)	=A2*2.95
3	=A2+1		

Figure 4.10   Comparison of Plan 1 and Plan 2 for 15 Video Rentals

	A	B	C
	A	**B**	**C**
1	VIDEOS	Plan 1	Plan 2
2	0	$20.00	$0.00
3	1	$21.50	$2.95
4	2	$23.00	$5.90
5	3	$24.50	$8.85
6	4	$26.00	$11.80
7	5	$27.50	$14.75
8	6	$29.00	$17.70
9	7	$30.50	$20.65
10	8	$32.00	$23.60
11	9	$33.50	$26.55
12	10	$35.00	$29.50
13	11	$36.50	$32.45
14	12	$38.00	$35.40
15	13	$39.50	$38.35
16	14	$41.00	$41.30
17	15	$42.50	$44.25

Traditional versus Integrated Sequences

If you peruse the table of contents of a fairly traditional Algebra I textbook, you will usually find a couple of sections near the end of the book that address the Pythagorean Theorem and then introduce the distance formula based on that theorem. Generally, the section on the Pythagorean Theorem exists only to set up a proof to justify why the distance formula works. However, as we know, there are many interesting spin-offs to a discussion of triangles and the lengths of their sides. For example, students can draw pictures of obtuse triangles, measure the sides, and try to apply the Pythagorean Theorem, only to discover that $c^2 > a^2 + b^2$ (where c represents the length of the longest side of the triangle) and possibly conjecture that the reverse is true for acute triangles. Using computer software, such as Geometer's Sketchpad or Cabri Geometry on a handheld computer, the student can further explore these relationships and generate corollaries to the Pythagorean Theorem. It is important to note that some calculators have large viewing screens and are able to sketch graphs of functions and be programmed; these are generally referred to as *graphing calculators*. However, other handheld technology allows students not only to sketch curves and write programs but also to perform symbolic manipulations (such as solving equations or simplifying expressions), and it contains built-in software (such as interactive geometry software); these machines are ordinarily called *handheld computers*.

Figure 4.11 shows a screen of a TI Nspire handheld comparing the square of the length of the longest side of an obtuse triangle to the sum of the squares of the lengths of the shorter sides.

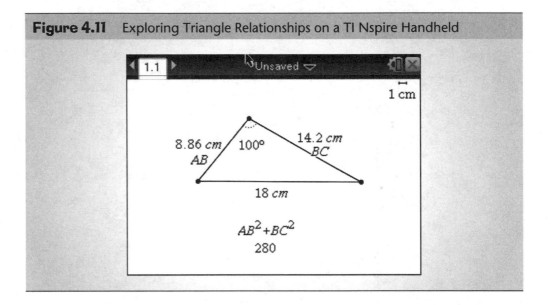

Figure 4.11   Exploring Triangle Relationships on a TI Nspire Handheld

When students realize that the sum of the squares—rounded to 280—is less than the square of the length of the longest side ($324 = 18^2$), a conjecture or hypothesis can be made about the lengths of sides in obtuse triangles and the way to determine whether a triangle is obtuse when given the lengths of its sides.

Furthermore, because algebra is, in part, a study of patterns, students often enjoy exploring Pythagorean Triples and searching for number patterns in the context of an algebra course. Take a look at this ordered list of triples:

3, 4, 5

5, 12, 13

7, 24, 25

Each list of numbers is referred to as a Pythagorean Triple because the sum of the squares of the legs equals the square of the hypotenuse or longest side (e.g., $3^2 + 4^2 = 5^2$), and all of the lengths are positive integers. Can you predict the fourth triple in the sequence? Take a few minutes to do this before reading ahead. How did you find the next triple, and what patterns did you notice? You might have noticed that the shortest leg is always an odd number, that the longest leg and the hypotenuse always differ by 1, and that you can find rules for generating triples, such as noticing that the 12 of 5–12–13 comes from adding the 3 and 4 of the first triple to the 5 of the second triple. Similarly, the 24 of the third triple comes from adding 5 and 12 of the previous triple to the 7 of the third triple. Some other discoveries actually made by students in a ninth grade mathematics course are the following:

Sarah: I looked at the triple 3–4–5 and took the first number, 3. If you add 1, then divide by 2, and then subtract 1, you get 1, which, when you multiply it by the (3 + 1), gives you the second number of the triple. In other words,

$3 + 1 = 4$

$4 \div 2 = 2$

$2 - 1 = 1$, and

$1 \times 4 = 4$

The last number of the triple is one more, so it would be 5. For the next triple, I know that it starts with the next odd number after 3, which is 5. Using the same process:

$5 + 1 = 6$

$6 \div 2 = 3$

$3 - 1 = 2$, and

$2 \times (5 + 1) = 2 \times 6 = 12$

The last number is one more than the middle number, so the triple would be 5–12–13.

Klaus: I noticed that the first numbers of the triples are consecutive odd numbers. If you take the length of the shortest leg, add 1, and multiply that sum by the number of the triple, it gives you the length of the longest leg. Then, the hypotenuse is always one more unit longer than the leg. So,

Triple 1: 3–4–5 because $(3 + 1) \times 1 = 4$

Triple 2: 5–12–13 because $(5 + 1) \times 2 = 12$

Triple 3: 7–24–25 because $(7 + 1) \times 3 = 24$

Jessica: Earlier in the year, we learned about **triangular numbers** and how they follow the sequence of 1, 3, 6, 10, 15, and so on. I noticed that if you multiply 4 times each consecutive triangular number, you always get the length of the longest leg in the next triple. Then, the hypotenuse is 1 more than that. The first number is always the next largest odd number, based on the previous triple. So,

Triple 1: 3–4–5. Then, $4 \times 3 = 12$ tells us that the next triple is 5–12–13.

Triple 2: 5–12–13. Then, $4 \times 6 = 24$ tells us that the next triple is 7–24–25.

Triple 3: 7–24–25. Then, $4 \times 10 = 40$ tells us that the next triple is 9–40–41.

Notice how these students made use of prior knowledge, such as triangular numbers, and their ability to identify and extend patterns to solve a rich problem. Many of the issues surrounding acute and obtuse triangles, as well as Pythagorean Triples, are typically found in a high school Geometry course. However, the context for discussing these topics may be more appropriate when the Pythagorean Theorem is first introduced and, in a sense, it may not be educationally sound to make the student wait until that chapter in the following course before making some of those connections. In fact, some schools place the Algebra II course immediately after Algebra I, and these students may explore the Pythagorean Theorem while learning the distance formula in Algebra I and not even encounter Pythagorean Triples or acute or obtuse triangles again for at least two more years!

Similarly, students in a high school Geometry course ordinarily study reflections, rotations, and translations. And although the topic of matrices is often deferred until Algebra II or a Discrete Mathematics course (if brought up at all), the geometry student is in a position to discover that you can represent the coordinates of the vertices of a triangle, such as $\triangle ABC$, with the coordinates $(3, 7)$, $(5, -1)$, and $(-2, 4)$ in a matrix:

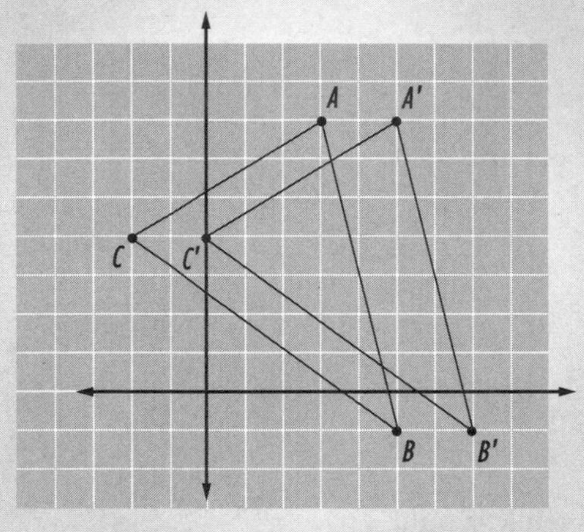

$$\mathbf{A} = \begin{bmatrix} 3 & 5 & -2 \\ 7 & -1 & 4 \end{bmatrix}$$

If matrix **A** is added to the matrix **B**, the result is a matrix whose entries represent a triangle that is translated 2 units to the right on the x-axis, as shown in Figure 4.12.

$$\mathbf{B} = \begin{bmatrix} 2 & 2 & 2 \\ 0 & 0 & 0 \end{bmatrix}$$

Similarly, multiplying matrix **C** by matrix **A** results in a matrix representing another new triangle, $\triangle A''B''C''$.

$$\mathbf{C} = \begin{bmatrix} 0 & 1 \\ -1 & 0 \end{bmatrix}, \text{ so } \mathbf{C} \times \mathbf{A} = \begin{bmatrix} 7 & -1 & 4 \\ -3 & -5 & 2 \end{bmatrix}$$

If you draw a ray from the origin through point A in Figure 4.13 and another ray from the origin through point A″, you will find that the rays form a 90° angle. The same relationship is true for the other two points of the triangles as well. Therefore, multiplication by matrix **C** results in a clockwise rotation of 90°.

With the aid of a graphing calculator, matrix operations can be done quickly and accurately and allow students to discover how adding or multiplying matrices can affect a geometric shape. Yet students rarely, if ever, make this interesting and natural connection in traditional mathematics course sequences.

The topical areas of algebra, geometry, statistics and probability, discrete mathematics, and so forth are merely content organizers that were never intended to build walls between those areas of study. In fact, one could argue that mathematics itself should be studied in conjunction with the other content areas. Virtually any algebra problem can be represented geometrically, and geometry problems can be represented by algebraic expressions or equations. For example, we used algebra tiles to create a geometric representation of similar terms in Chapter 3 and to relate area to polynomial multiplication in this chapter. Furthermore, although the study of combinatorics is a typical discrete mathematics topic, the patterns generated when studying combinations and permutations can lead to the generation of some interesting algebraic formulas and graphs. Yet topics such as probability and combinatorics have been historically absent from most secondary and middle school curricula. The NCTM and

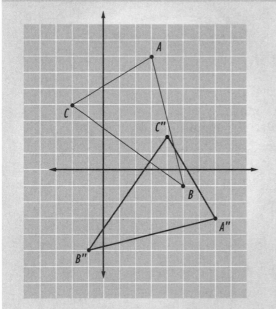

Figure 4.12 Matrix Addition Translating $\triangle ABC$ 2 Units to the Right

Figure 4.13 Matrix Multiplication Rotating $\triangle ABC$ Clockwise 90°

Common Core State Standards not only call for a robust set of concepts to be taught in the Pre-K–12 mathematics program but they also encourage the exploration of connections along the way. In an attempt to make connections and help students recognize that boundaries between content topics are generally artificial, many schools have begun to move from a traditional sequence of Algebra I to Geometry to Algebra II to an **integrated curriculum.** In an integrated curriculum, all of the major mathematics strands—generally, algebra, geometry, statistics and probability, and discrete mathematics—are visited every year from the middle through the high school levels. In addition, students in an integrated program use mathematics to analyze problems in a real-world context.

Classroom Dialogues

In a unit on coordinate geometry, the teacher asks the class to prove that the diagonals of an isosceles trapezoid are congruent, as shown in Figure 4.14.

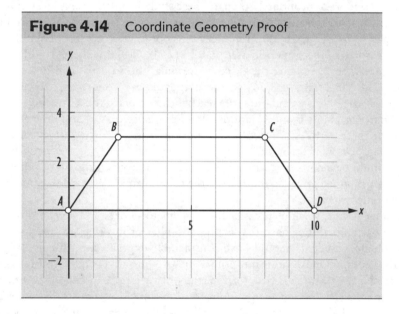

Figure 4.14 Coordinate Geometry Proof

Typically, in the study of coordinate geometry, proofs are generalized by using variables for coordinates. So, in Figure 4.14, the coordinates of the trapezoid could be represented as A(0, 0), B(c, b), C($a - c$, b), and D (a, 0).

Teacher: How could we find the length of $\overline{BD}$?

Student 1: You would have to use the coordinates of B and D and use the distance formula.

Teacher: Right. So, can you do that for me?

Student 1: I don't even understand where those coordinates came from. How do you know that B is represented by (c, b)? What is the c?

Teacher: Well, c is the horizontal distance of point B from the origin.

Student 2: I thought b was the horizontal distance. Isn't that why we're using the point (a, 0) for D?

Teacher: It is, but that's the distance all the way to D, not just to B.

Student 3: Then what does b stand for? Is that the coordinate of B?

Teacher: No, it's the vertical distance from the origin to point B.

Student 1: Vertical? I thought you said "horizontal."

Teacher: I did. For the point, (c, b) c is the horizontal distance, and b is the vertical distance.

At this point, the students are totally confused, and it seems that no matter what the teacher says, the level of understanding continues to diminish. Ultimately, the teacher would like the students to find the length of $\overline{BD}$ by taking

$$BD = \sqrt{(c - a)^2 + (b - 0)^2} = \sqrt{(c - a)^2 + b^2}$$

and the length of $\overline{AC}$ by taking

$$AC = \sqrt{((a - c) - 0)^2 + (b - 0)^2} = \sqrt{(a - c)^2 + b^2}$$

Of course, since $(c - a)^2 = (a - c)^2$, these two distances are equal; therefore, the diagonals are congruent.

However, the students are caught up in a common point of confusion that occurs when they attempt to abstract a situation using variables. How would you handle the situation? What should be the teacher's next step? The students in this class do not appear to be ready to write a generalized proof for the congruence of the diagonals in the trapezoid. But they are already familiar with the formulas for distance, slope, and midpoint. To more appropriately prepare these students for the next level, it is necessary for the teacher to return to a more familiar situation by using specific numbers.

Instead of using variables to represent the coordinates, the teacher could simply label the vertices of the trapezoid as A(0, 0), B(2, 3), C(8, 3), and D(10, 0) as shown in the figure. Then, applying the distance formula, the students can determine that $BD = AC = \sqrt{8^2 + 3^2} \approx 8.54$, so the diagonals are congruent. Once students have made sense of this calculation, the teacher can go back and show how "3" is the y-coordinate for points B and C (and becomes generalized as b) and how the x-coordinates for these vertices are two units from the origin and two units short of the x-coordinate for point D. Since point D is represented by $(a, 0)$, the x-coordinate of point C would be c units less, or $(a - c, 0)$, making the x-coordinate of point B be c. The teacher can then go back and rewrite the proof, using these variable quantities as vertices of the trapezoid.

In other words, it is much easier for students to understand a generalized proof involving variables if they have first analyzed similar proofs that use specific numerical coordinates. Students should have considerable experience with calculating specific distances, slopes, and midpoints before moving on to more abstract generalizations. The same is true for the study of variable expressions in general, as initial emphasis should be placed on numerical examples so that students can gradually comprehend abstractions. Can you think of other examples in the study of algebra or geometry in which specific examples might help students make further abstractions?

The idea of integrating the curriculum is no stranger to the middle school classroom. In fact, many middle schools attribute student progress to teachers' ability to help students make connections within the content area, as well as across disciplines. In some cases, the school day is even organized so that teachers team with others to create thematic units incorporating multiple disciplines, such as the use of mathematics to analyze problems from science or social studies. The National Middle School Association's famous document *This We Believe: Keys to Educating Young Adolescents* (2010) describes 16 characteristics of successful middle schools, and one of these qualities is that curriculum should be challenging and integrated. Since the mid-1980s, educational reformer James Beane has researched and spoken on the importance of students *using* their content knowledge to solve real-world problems, rather than focusing solely on individual content areas and units of study within those courses. He argues the need for integrated curriculum in his well-known book, *Curriculum Integration: Designing the Core of Democratic Education* (1997).

Although the major advantage of an integrated sequence of content is that students can make connections among topics, it has other benefits as well. As students learn the mathematics in context, they continue to sharpen skills, such as order of operations, graphing lines, and so forth, along the way. Consequently, the traditional notion of doing a chapter on square roots and then moving on to something else might be replaced by the idea of looking at square roots in the context of a quadratic equation and revisiting them a few weeks later when determining a geometric mean. Integrated textbook series and resource books tend to contain regular, ongoing applications of mathematical skills rather than entire chapters, units, or worksheets focusing on an individual topic. Finally, because the integrated topic includes ongoing review and application, less time tends to be spent reviewing material at the beginning of a school year or semester. A quick look at a traditional Algebra II book will reveal that approximately the first one-third of the text is often devoted to content that students already visited in Algebra I and are being asked to brush up on before moving forward. And this should not be a surprise, given that many students study geometry for a year between algebra courses and have forgotten many of the concepts. With less time lost on extensive reviews and a broader range of topics to be explored, the student in an integrated sequence tends to visit more mathematical topics than has historically been the case. Topics such as probability and recursion can become the norm for *all* students rather than being relegated to an upper-level course for a few select students.

So, why wouldn't a school or district choose to use an integrated approach? Kennedy (2003) cites several reasons, including "textbooks, SAT scores, college preparation, mathematics competitions, compatibility with other schools, consistency among generations, basic skills, cognitive development, [and] job preparedness" (p. 33). In addition, the topic is somewhat controversial because there is not a universal agreement on what it means to "integrate" a mathematics curriculum or how it should be done (Lott, 2001). Although there are many reasons why an integrated approach to teaching mathematics is often criticized, we discuss three in some detail here—tradition, lack of research, and availability of resource materials.

Probably nothing gets in the way of reform more powerfully than does tradition—the way it has always been done. Imagine a school district with a mathematics department made up of five teachers who have been teaching a traditional sequence of courses out of the same textbook series for 20 years. Unless some incredible professional development program comes along to convince them otherwise, they will assume that their way is best and continue to do it despite trends or research to the contrary. Simply put, it is safer and easier to continue to do something the old way than to change. That is why innovations from automatic transmissions in automobiles to mp3 players didn't catch on right away; people needed time to adjust and rethink.

Tradition is an interesting player in the change process, however. The state of New York, for example, began to use a unified or integrated approach to teaching mathematics in the early 1970s. So, to a teacher in that state, the tradition has been to teach an integrated sequence, and it may be difficult to convince some educators that it could be done differently. A mathematics education student from New York recently asked her classmates in another state, "Did you really just study algebra for a whole year?" and added, "I can't imagine doing that!" However, the State of New York has now abandoned their integrated sequence and reverted back to a traditional program of algebra and geometry courses. At the same time, the State of Georgia moved in the opposite direction, requiring that all students follow an integrated sequence, only to modify the rule, allowing schools to choose their own course sequences beginning in 2011 (Newnan Times-Herald, 2011). Clearly, there is not just "one way" to deliver the high school curriculum, though most of the rest of the world from Japan to Europe uses an integrated approach.

The traditional sequence of algebra and geometry has not always been the norm in the United States either. In the 1940s, for example, many schools in the United States were using an integrated approach. A report published by the Joint Commission to Study the Place of Mathematics in Secondary Education in the 1930s "emphasized the spiraling of instruction by including a grade-placement chart that displayed the attention given in *each grade* [emphasis added] to each of what were called major subject fields, namely: number and computation, geometric form and space perception, graphic representation, logical thinking, relational thinking, and symbolic representation and thinking" (Jones & Coxford, 1970, p. 55). However, a discriminatory system eventually developed in which vocational students were relegated to integrated courses, whereas college-bound students took the algebra–geometry sequence. By the early 1960s, the New Math reform movement had emerged, and the integrated approach fell to the wayside. So, when someone talks about this "new idea" of integrating the mathematics content, we need to realize that it's not really new at all—it's a return to the past. A look at historical perspectives in any curricular area will reveal a pendulum effect—the tendency to try something for a few years and then abandon it for another trend, only to return to the original plan several years later, as we now see in New York. Some educators choose to maintain the status quo and hope that, eventually, the pendulum will swing back to what they believe.

The second reason why a school district may follow an algebra–geometry program is that there is not a significant amount of research to support the fact that integrated mathematics sequences impact students more effectively than do the traditional course sequences. A 1979 study conducted in New York showed no measurable difference between students who were enrolled in an integrated sequence and those in a traditional sequence (Paul & Richbart, 1985). This study confirmed others that have shown that the integrated approach was not harming students, but it didn't appear to be helping them significantly either. More recent studies in New York show that, using an integrated curriculum, students continue to be successful on Advanced Placement and SAT exams and that more students than ever are successfully completing upper-level mathematics courses (Richbart, 2001). Also, work done with curriculum projects funded by the National Science Foundation (discussed further in Chapter 5) has shown several positive effects of integrating content. One longitudinal study tracked 145 students whose schools used an NSF-funded, integrated high school program into college, taking courses through Calculus II. In general, these students completed a similar course of study with success rates statistically equivalent to those of their peers who took traditional mathematics courses while in high school (Western Michigan University, 2007). However, the absence of a consistent, long-term body of research to support the change makes many educators hesitant to move toward an integrated approach.

Chapter 3 discussed the importance of making educational decisions based on research, and there simply is not enough evidence to convince many mathematics teachers or administrators that a change will benefit them and their students.

The last drawback to an integrated approach to the mathematics curriculum is a lack of resource materials. Because the traditional sequence has been with us for so long, most schools have texts, software, resource books, videos, and other media that support this approach. Moving toward an integrated program requires not only a great deal of time for faculty reorientation but also the selection and purchase of thousands of dollars worth of books and materials. Because the materials are not as abundant in the integrated sequence, teachers feel they have fewer choices in decision-making and this, together with the cost, can hold a school district back from making a change. When the *Curriculum and Evaluation Standards* were first published in 1989, some states adopted models that called for an integrated approach, but textbooks did not yet exist to support the Standards. Now that several National Science Foundation (NSF) projects have produced some outstanding materials, schools are able to at least view the resources in their decision-making deliberations.

Conclusion

In order to move toward a core of mathematics outcomes for all students, there must first be some agreement on the objectives that are essential. Identifying these objectives, however, is not an easy task—as we said at the beginning of the chapter, any two people making a list of important content issues are likely to come up with different objectives. Another quick look at some history as we close this chapter again reveals the pendulum effect—that the more things change, the more they stay the same.

In the *Curriculum and Evaluation Standards* (1989), the NCTM stated that "decreased emphasis" should be placed on trinomial factoring, simplifying radicals and complex fractions, and solving quadratic equations by hand. Compare this to a statement made by William Reeve in the *Fourth Yearbook of the NCTM* in 1929. Reeve, speaking of "recent" changes in the U.S. curriculum, stated that "among the first topics to be eliminated from elementary algebra were the highest common factor [of polynomials] by division . . . complex fractions of a difficult type . . . and complicated radicals. . . . One might here raise the question why the study of quadratic equations beyond the pure type such as $x^2 = 4$ should any longer be required of everybody in the ninth grade . . . those who do not [continue the study of mathematics] will never have any use for the kind of work that is traditionally given. It is artificial and ought to be omitted" (Reeve, 1929, p. 159). He went on to note that the 1930 syllabus for the state of New York made trinomial factoring optional and that, although using factoring and completing the square to solve quadratic equations were in the 1910 syllabus, the study of quadratics was made optional in 1930 as well. As you can see, curricular changes never come easy, and determining a common list of core objectives for a state or school district can be much more difficult than it may appear on the surface. However, if a discussion does not begin on this issue at some point, the mistakes of the past that have created generations of individuals with poor mathematics skills and attitudes will continue to perpetuate themselves.

In this chapter, we have examined the nature of the mathematics curriculum at the secondary and middle school levels. *Principles and Standards for School Mathematics* and the *Common Core State Standards* were described as visionary guides for states to follow as specific objectives are written for each grade level in a school district. Both Standards documents are somewhat radical in that they promote mathematics for all students, which includes a significant background in algebra, geometry, statistics and probability, and some discrete mathematics. At the secondary and middle school levels, the NCTM *Standards* recommend an integrated approach to the content rather than the traditional sequence of Algebra I, then Geometry, and so forth. To achieve this end, three curricular models of implementation were suggested, including the crossover, enrichment, and differentiated models. The authors of the *Common Core State Standards* left the course sequencing for high school up to the individual states and districts, providing both traditional and integrated options. The chapter included a discussion of the fact that many of the general principles embraced in recent Standards documents are not entirely new and that suggestions from curricular content to sequencing of courses have been with us for nearly 100 years.

In the second chapter of this unit—Chapter 5—we discuss the process by which a school district drafts a course of study, including the selection and writing of general goals and more specific objectives. Because the curriculum is heavily influenced by textbooks and resource materials, we also describe how teachers can use these sources to plan and implement curriculum. As you read the remainder of this textbook and ponder your position on the purposes of mathematics education, try to focus on these questions: Why do we teach mathematics, and what are the most important outcomes from a Pre-K–12 mathematics education? Do you view mathematics as a process, as content, or both? If you were on a curriculum committee, appointed to determine the core objectives for a secondary and middle school program, which objectives would you select and why? Thinking about these issues will lead you to a philosophy of mathematics education and define your place in the classroom.

For bibliographic references and additional resources, see page 404

Glossary

Content Standards: Content Standards are national (or state) benchmarks associated with mathematics content that should be addressed in a school mathematics program, including number and operations, algebra, geometry, measurement, and data analysis and probability. The NCTM released national content Standards in 2000, and the *Common Core State Standards* were released in 2010.

Clustering: Clustering is an educational practice whereby gifted and talented students are deliberately selected and placed in a classroom with students of mixed abilities so that the classroom teacher can challenge the gifted students as a group when possible.

Core Curriculum: The core curriculum is a 3-year secondary mathematics program designed to ensure that all students have equal access to a variety of mathematics topics, regardless of future plans, ethnicity, gender,

or perceived ability. In an addendum to the NCTM *Standards,* three possible curricular models were outlined: the crossover, enrichment, and differentiated models.

Crossover Model: In the crossover model, all high school students address the same set of objectives in a 3-year sequence. The school has one sequence for college-bound students and another for students not planning to attend college, but both tracks feature the same core mathematics outcomes.

Differentiated Model: In the differentiated model, all high school students address the same set of objectives in a 3-year sequence. However, within a classroom, each learning team of students might address the same outcomes in different ways. Teachers may use manipulatives, technology, or deeper applied problems, depending on the readiness and needs of students in the class.

Enrichment Model: In the enrichment model, all high school students address the same set of objectives in a 3-year sequence. However, a team of students who have mastered a set of outcomes might be given an enrichment extension that goes beyond the common core. Enrichment topics would be optional in a class and explored only by those students who initially demonstrate an understanding of the common objectives.

Integrated Curriculum: An integrated curriculum is a sequence of mathematics courses that includes the development of algebra, geometry, statistics and probability, and some discrete mathematics each year that a student is in school. The integrated approach is an alternative to following a sequence of Algebra I, Geometry, Algebra II, and so forth. Likewise, integration in the middle school involves making connections not only within mathematics but also across content disciplines so that students can focus on the use of mathematics to solve real-world problems that exist in science, social studies, and so forth.

Process Standards: Process Standards are national (or state) benchmarks of process skills that should be addressed in a school mathematics program, including problem solving, reasoning and proof, communication, connections, and representation. The NCTM released national process Standards in 2000. The *Common Core State Standards* describes eight mathematical practices that mirror the process Standards.

Strand: A strand is a content area that is developed over a period of time. For example, if geometry is viewed as a content strand (rather than a course title), it is thought of as an area of the curriculum that is developed each year that a student is in school, and a district or state determines what content is developmentally appropriate within that strand for each grade level.

Triangular Numbers: The triangular numbers are a sequence of numbers that, geometrically, refers to the number of dots required to build successively larger triangles, as shown in Figure 4.15:

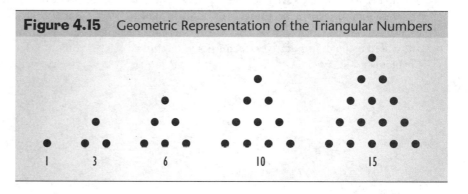

Figure 4.15 Geometric Representation of the Triangular Numbers

Therefore, the sequence of triangular numbers is 1, 3, 6, 10, 15, 21, 28, 36, 45, 55, and so on, where the nth term is $\frac{n(n+1)}{2}$. Triangular numbers frequently occur in problems that involve patterns or sequences and, when recognized, can be extremely useful in solving problems.

● Discussion Questions and Activities

1. Obtain a copy of the 1989 NCTM *Curriculum and Evaluation Standards* and compare this book to *Principles and Standards for School Mathematics* and the *Common Core State Standards*. Discuss the similarities and differences among these three documents in terms of content, style, and purpose.

2. Using a copy of the NCTM or the *Common Core State Standards* and a state curriculum model (of your own state or a sample accessed from the Internet), choose a specific content strand and compare the national Standard for a grade-level band to the specific outcomes listed in the state model. How would you characterize the differences and similarities between the national and state models?

3. Obtain a copy of your state's model curriculum or standards. Review and discuss the document and determine the mathematical content and processes that your state believes to be important by virtue of the outcomes emphasized in the model.

4. Divide into small groups and have each group generate a list of 10 mathematical outcomes that are critical for *every* high school graduate. Then compare the lists with those of other groups and with a list of critical outcomes in your state (which may include a list of graduation or proficiency exam objectives). Discuss the processes that might be used by a state or local school district in reaching consensus on what is important for students to know and be able to do in mathematics.

5. Using your state's Standards or other resource documents, identify three "focal points" (key ideas) of the curriculum for each of the middle and high school years. For each focal point, be prepared to explain why you believe the concept is so important in terms

of its applicability and its connection to the rest of the curriculum.

6. Divide the class into three teams and assign each team to one of the core curriculum models—crossover, enrichment, and differentiated. Each group should identify at least two major benefits of their model over the others and at least two potential drawbacks to adopting that particular model. The three groups then should be prepared to compare the advantages and possible disadvantages of the three models in depth.

7. The topic of multiplying polynomials was used as an example of how to deliver the same content at different levels for students at a variety of levels. Select another example of a secondary or middle school topic and show how that content area can be addressed using manipulatives, technology, or applied problems.

8. Compare the textbooks of a somewhat traditional Algebra I course and a first-year integrated mathematics course. Identify the algebra content included in the integrated text and discuss the degree to which all areas of the mathematics curriculum—including geometry, statistics and probability, and discrete mathematics—are addressed in the book. What are the advantages and disadvantages of the design of each course?

9. Invite the mathematics department chairs or principals of two schools—one having a traditional mathematics curricular sequence and one having an integrated sequence—to a panel discussion on the practical benefits and drawbacks of each model.

10. "The more things change, the more they stay the same." Discuss how trends in education have come and gone over the course of history and how this pendulum effect impacts the implementation of innovative curricular changes.

Implementing a Course of Study

Congratulations! You have just been hired to teach seventh grade mathematics at Oak Knoll Middle School in Monroe, Iowa. It is your first teaching position, and you walk into the department chair's classroom, excited about your new job, 2 weeks prior to the start of the school year.

You: So, what am I supposed to teach the seventh graders?

Chair: Well, it's really up to you. Teach them whatever you think they need to know. Oh, and feel free to teach and emphasize the things you're interested in. That's how I make my decisions.

You: You mean if I don't enjoy a topic like probability or three-dimensional geometry, I can just choose not to deal with it in my classes?

Chair: Yeah, that's correct. I mean, why not? If you've made it this far in your life without knowing much about a certain area of the math curriculum, they probably don't need to know much about it either. Teach what's in the book but leave out the stuff you don't want to do. Like I said, it's up to you.

A bit confused, you walk out of the room shaking your head and thinking, "This is my first job. I was really hoping that someone would give me at least a little bit of direction here."

As strange as this scenario appears, states and school districts have not always had models and prescribed curricula for teachers to follow. Remember that the United States did not have a widely accepted set of national curriculum standards in

After reading Chapter 5, you should be able to answer the following questions:

- What is a state or local course of study, and what does it generally include?
- What is the process by which a state or local course of study is written?
- What is the difference between a goal and an objective? Describe Bloom's Taxonomy (and its revision) and provide examples illustrating the levels at which objectives are written.
- What are the criteria by which textbooks are often chosen in a school district or state? Discuss the NSF-funded reform mathematics curricula.
- What are some examples of alternative sources of problems and activities outside of a textbook? Provide examples on how to organize a resource file of teaching ideas.

mathematics before 1989. In fact, as recently as the early 1980s, it was not unusual for mathematics teachers to be told that they would be teaching pre-calculus but be given few, if any, details on what it is that pre-calculus students are supposed to know or be able to do. In many cases, teachers were handed a textbook for a course, and the book *became* the curriculum because it was the only guide that was provided. Imagine the power that a textbook publisher has when a book *defines* the curriculum, from mathematical content to the sequence in which it is taught. But if you have no other assistance or guidelines, either a textbook or an educated guess may be all you have on which to base curricular decisions.

However, with more recent sweeping changes toward accountability—making local school districts responsible for student achievement—came the development of the **course of study**. A course of study is a document that prescribes the curriculum, by grade level, for a state, county, or individual school district. Instead of having a conversation like the one with the chair of the department, teachers now generally are handed a copy of a graded (by grade level) course of study to serve as the basis for instruction. The course of study should clearly define what a student should feel, know, and be able to do at each grade level. Chapter 4 addressed the general issues surrounding the NCTM and Common Core State Standards and the process of selecting appropriate curriculum. Chapter 5 focuses specifically on the writing and implementation of a course of study in a state or a local school district. We begin by looking at how the course of study is developed and then focus our attention on how one effectively uses resources such as a textbook or the Internet to support the course of study. ■

The Course of Study

As we have seen, the NCTM *Principles and Standards for School Mathematics* contains broad statements of what a student should be able to do across grade-range bands of Pre-K–2, 3–5, 6–8, and 9–12. But what if you are teaching a seventh grade class and want the students to explore some geometry? How do you know, specifically, what a seventh grader should know about two- or three-dimensional geometry? In most cases, you consult the course of study that has been written for a state, county, or local school district. The level at which a course of study is written varies by location. In some cases, a state or a county within a state may have a curriculum that is shared by many school districts. In other locations, each school district may have its own document, based on some standards, framework, or model written at the state level. On the other hand, states that have adopted the *Common Core State Standards* (CCSS) have already been given more specific outcomes for each grade level, though each state has the right to add to the core if they choose. Some argue that there *was* a national curriculum even before the CCSS—defined by *textbooks* used in the schools—but there is no federally mandated set of outcomes to which all states *must* adhere.

Suppose that your state has a model or framework that provides guidance to local school districts for writing their courses of study. Generally, at the local level, a curriculum committee is assembled to study national and state standards and to determine how to use them for writing a grade-by-grade document for teachers to follow. The curriculum committee might consist of central office administrators, principals, department chairs, guidance counselors, classroom teachers, curriculum supervisors, community members, or any combination of individuals representing various viewpoints. The curriculum committee usually begins the writing process by defining a **district philosophy** or statement of the beliefs held by educators in that system. This philosophy serves as the underlying foundation on which the rest of the document is built. It usually describes the role of mathematics in our society and establishes the need for students in the district to be well versed in the content area. Based on this philosophy, the committee then produces a series of overarching **goals** of mathematics education. Goals are broad statements about what a student should be able to accomplish as a result of participating in the district's program. A course of study may have 5 or 6 major goals or may contain a page or two of general statements of student outcomes. From these goals, curriculum writers define **objectives,** which are very specific statements that describe what a student should feel, know, or be able to do at each grade level. Finally, any of these objectives that are intended to be mastered by students at a particular grade level often have an associated **pupil performance objective (PPO),** which is an even more specific description of what a student should be able to do under a given set of conditions. These PPOs are often used to write classroom or districtwide assessment items, which may take the form of problems, questions, or projects.

Let's consider a specific example. Suppose the curriculum committee decides that it is important for every seventh grader to study the topic of probability because the NCTM recommended it in the *Standards* for grades 6–8 (NCTM, 2000), as does the CCSS (2010). The course of study, then, may identify a goal that says "The student will explore probability and its applications." Once this goal is stated, the classroom teacher knows that probability is important but is likely to ask, "What, specifically, do you want seventh graders to know about probability?" Consequently, the course of study is written to include objectives that fall under the general goal of probability. For example, the course of study might say that "The student will be able to determine the number of combinations and permutations for a set of concrete items." Furthermore, if this objective is to be mastered by a seventh grader, the document may state a PPO such as, "Given a set of 5 or fewer concrete objects, such as colored cubes, the student will be able to demonstrate and list the possible permutations of the cubes and the number of ways that 1, 2, 3, 4, or 5 of the cubes can be chosen from the set." The sequence of outcomes is set forth in Figure 5.1.

What did you notice about the wording of the objective versus that of the PPO? How are they similar? How do they differ? You might have noticed, for example, that neither the objective nor the PPO says anything about students being able to use formulas. Although the number of permutations of three items can be found by calculating 3! ($3 \times 2 \times 1 = 6$), the course of study recognizes that it is inappropriate for 12-year-olds to be memorizing factorial formulas at the possible expense of misunderstanding the concept of permutations. Instead, the document emphasizes visualization skills, which is consistent with the learning theories discussed in Chapter 3. Similarly, the number of ways that 2 objects can be pulled from a set of 5 can be determined by using a familiar formula and calculating $\frac{5!}{3!2!}$. However, developmentally, it makes more sense for the student to think of having 5 choices, then 4 more choices, so 5×4 will need to be calculated. And the student should recognize that the order in which you select the 2 blocks

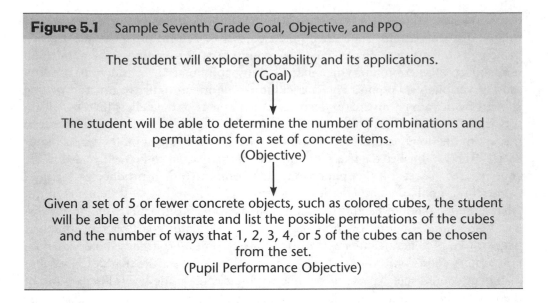

Figure 5.1 Sample Seventh Grade Goal, Objective, and PPO

The student will explore probability and its applications.
(Goal)

The student will be able to determine the number of combinations and permutations for a set of concrete items.
(Objective)

Given a set of 5 or fewer concrete objects, such as colored cubes, the student will be able to demonstrate and list the possible permutations of the cubes and the number of ways that 1, 2, 3, 4, or 5 of the cubes can be chosen from the set.
(Pupil Performance Objective)

does not matter, so 20 can be divided by 2 to find a solution of 10 combinations (i.e., it doesn't matter whether you pull the red block and then the green block, or the green and then the red; consequently, the number of combinations can be divided in half). At this point, it is more important for a student to know what it means to find all of the permutations of a set or to pull 2 blocks from a set of 5 than to possess the skill of using formulas to calculate a number of permutations or combinations.

To assess this PPO, a teacher might give the student 3 blocks—blue, red, and green—along with 3 colored pens and a piece of paper, and ask the student to move the blocks around on the desk to find all of the permutations and sketch them on paper. The child, then, is responsible for identifying the set of six permutations as illustrated in Figure 5.2.

Figure 5.2 Colored Blocks Representing Permutations

Permutation 1   R   B   G

Permutation 2   R   G   B

Permutation 3   B   R   G

Permutation 4   B   G   R

Permutation 5   G   R   B

Permutation 6   G   B   R

The child can also be asked to describe the strategy used in listing the permutations and how to be certain that all of the permutations have been listed. This type of teaching and assessment emphasizes conceptual understanding over procedural knowledge—an important and critical distinction. You also might have recognized that the goal is only useful inasmuch as it informs you that students should be studying the topic of probability at this grade level. But the objective and the PPO clarify in a very specific way what a student should know (the objective) and be able to do (the PPO) to demonstrate understanding of probability-related concepts in the seventh grade—specifically, permutations and combinations.

The objectives here are often referred to as *behavioral* because they describe specifically what a student should be able to do (i.e., how the student should "behave"). There has been a gradual shift in education away from the use of behavioral objectives in recent years. A course of study including nothing but a list of behavioral objectives often can resemble nothing more than a checklist of skills and may, at times, appear to be fragmented and rigid. Instead, many districts (and states) are now using NCTM or Common Core State Standards and "unpacking" them by describing what a student should know or be able to do after mastering a particular Standard. In general, **unpacking** a Standard can be thought of as a four-step process: (1) identify a Standard (such as from the CCSS); (2) generate a list of all of the skills that students will need to master and central concepts that will need to be taught; (3) determine the key questions that students should be able to answer; and (4) create a sequence and pace for instruction to ensure that the Standard will be met (Hamilton, 2011). As we discussed in Chapter 4, some state model curricula are designed to do the unpacking by listing each Cluster of Standards and providing details on how teachers should focus their attention to ensure their students meet the Standard.

The State of Pennsylvania provides a tool at their Web site to help teachers unpack objectives that will be assessed. For example, there is a general Grade 8 "big idea" stating that students will, "Understand and/or apply basic concepts of probability or outcomes" (Pennsylvania Department of Education, 2011). However, this objective is then made more specific to say that students must be able to "Determine the number of combinations and/or permutations for an event." To clarify this even further, the more specific objective is broken down into four subskills, including:

- Determine permutations for an event using up to four choices (e.g., organized list)
- Determine the number of combinations for an event using up to four choices (e.g., organized list)
- Show the number of combinations for an event using up to four choices (e.g., organized list)
- Show the number of permutations for an event using up to four choices (e.g., organized list) (Pennsylvania Department of Education, 2011)

Again, we see that each "big idea" has been broken down into more specific subskills to clarify what it will take for a student to master a Standard.

In their book, Grant Wiggins and Jay McTighe (2006) describe the idea of "understanding by design" or simply "backward design" of learning. Instead of viewing assessment as an afterthought, planning is viewed as a three-step process of (a) identifying the big ideas or outcomes, (b) thinking about what type of performance assessment would serve as evidence of mastery of the goal or standard, and then (c) planning the instructional sequence accordingly. So often in education, teachers have fallen into the trap of thinking about curriculum as a list of objectives and not focusing on the main ideas and thinking through in advance how they will know whether their students have reached an acceptable level of performance. In general, this is a reminder that the art of teaching is broader than simply getting students to master a "laundry list" of skills and competencies.

Returning to the goal dealing with probability, we might expect the school district to include an outcome in, say, a First-Year Integrated course, stating that "The student will be able to determine simple permutations and combinations" as a way of extending the related seventh grade outcome. The PPO for the course could state that "Given a problem requiring permutations or combinations, the student will be able to use multiplication or Pascal's Triangle to find the solution." The sequence of outcomes for the First-Year Integrated course is summarized in Figure 5.3.

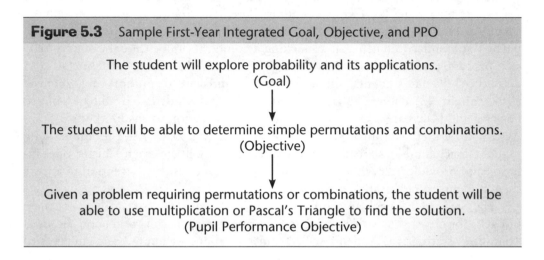

Figure 5.3   Sample First-Year Integrated Goal, Objective, and PPO

The student will explore probability and its applications.
(Goal)

The student will be able to determine simple permutations and combinations.
(Objective)

Given a problem requiring permutations or combinations, the student will be able to use multiplication or Pascal's Triangle to find the solution.
(Pupil Performance Objective)

In this First-Year Integrated course, if the student is asked to determine how many ways a subcommittee of 3 individuals can be selected from a board having 8 members, the student should be able to generate 8 rows of **Pascal's Triangle**, as shown in Figure 5.4.

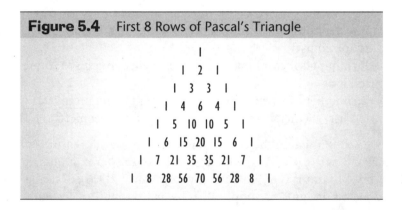

Figure 5.4   First 8 Rows of Pascal's Triangle

```
              1
            1   2   1
          1   3   3   1
        1   4   6   4   1
      1   5  10  10   5   1
    1   6  15  20  15   6   1
  1   7  21  35  35  21   7   1
1   8  28  56  70  56  28   8   1
```

The numbers in the eighth row indicate, in order, how many ways 0, 1, 2, 3, 4, 5, 6, 7, or 8 items can be chosen from a collection of 8 items. So, there are 56 ways to select 3 individuals from a board consisting of 8 people. (Note that there are also 56 ways to select 5 individuals from the board. Can you explain why the answers are the same?) Students would be expected to use Pascal's Triangle to find this combination, which is more complex than concretely counting blocks, as illustrated in the seventh grade example, but not to use any particular formula for completing a calculation for combinations.

Finally, as shown in Figure 5.5, by the time the student is in a Third-Year Integrated course or, perhaps, Algebra II or Pre-Calculus, the objective might read, "The student will be able to use formulas to compute permutations and combinations." The PPO might state, "Given a problem requiring permutations or combinations, the student will accurately use factorials and formulas to find a solution."

Figure 5.5 Sample Third-Year Integrated Goal, Objective, and PPO

The student will explore probability and its applications.
(Goal)

↓

The student will be able to use formulas to compute permutations and combinations.
(Objective)

↓

Given a problem requiring permutations or combinations, the student will accurately use factorials and formulas to find a solution.
(Pupil Performance Objective)

Consequently, a high school junior or senior should be able to solve a problem such as this:

A state lottery is run in the following manner: Thirty-six balls are placed in a container, numbered from 1 to 36. Six of the balls are pulled out at random. If an individual correctly guesses the 6 numbers on the balls, in any order, that person wins a grand prize of $1 million. What is the probability that the person who pays $1.00 and guesses 1 set of 6 numbers will win the grand prize?

For a student who has moved through the curricular sequence described in this section, it should be apparent that this problem can be solved by determining in how many ways 6 balls can be selected from a group of 36 without replacement. However, the problem is far too complex to be drawn by hand as was the seventh grade problem with colored blocks, and it is also unrealistic for a student to write out 36 rows of Pascal's Triangle. However, by using the formula for combinations, the number can be calculated as follows:

$$C_r^n = \frac{n!}{(n-r)!r!}$$

So, using the numbers from this problem,

$$C_6^{36} = \frac{36!}{(36-6)!6!} = \frac{36!}{30!6!} = 1{,}947{,}792$$

Therefore, the probability of winning the lottery in this state is nearly 1 in 2 million. We can expect that this state will take in almost $2,000,000 in revenues to play the game for every $1,000,000 that it gives back in prize money. Also, a careful examination of the formula reveals that there are 36 numbers to select on the first draw, 35 on the second, then 34, 33, 32, and 31. Because the order does not matter, the product of $36 \times 35 \times 34 \times 33 \times 32 \times 31$ needs to be divided by the number of ways to arrange 6 items, which is 6! The student might even be required to explain *why* the formula works as well as actually being able to use it to complete the calculation and solve the problem.

Perhaps, after reading how the topics of permutations and combinations can evolve over a 5-year period, you, too, have become more comfortable with these

How Would You React

S C E N A R I O

You have a rule in your classroom stating that students must bring a graphing calculator every day as a required supply. On the day of a test, one student forgets to bring a calculator and asks to borrow yours. Your response is

a. Remind the student that a class rule has been broken, so he or she will have to take the test without a calculator.
b. Lend your calculator to the student.
c. Allow the student to share a calculator with another person.
d. Have the student omit any items on the test that require the use of a calculator.
e. Other.

D I S C U S S I O N

Teachers are often confronted with on-the-spot decision-making when situations similar to this occur in the classroom. In this case, the teacher has made a rule for the class, and a student has neglected to bring an important supply. When grades are a factor in the decision, Choice A may not be the best. On one hand, "a rule is a rule," but on the other hand, the student's test score may very well depend on using the technology. In considering what you would do in this situation, you might also be tempted to allow the student to use your calculator. This choice is reasonable, but what if *five* students forget to bring their calculators, and you only have one calculator of your own to lend? Also, if students are using graphing calculators, it is easy for them to type in a hint—or even an answer—and pass the shared calculator to another student. It is much easier for students to cheat when they use graphing, rather than standard, calculators. Consequently, sharing calculators during a test is almost an open invitation to management problems in the classroom.

The key issue in this scenario is to think about the objectives from the course of study that are being measured by the test. In some cases, objectives emphasize paper-and-pencil symbol manipulation (such as solving equations or simplifying expressions), memorization of

terms and definitions, or writing explanations or proofs. In these situations, the calculator is probably not very useful, so the student can still perform acceptably without one. At other times, the objectives being tested may include language that suggests that students should be able to use technology in solving problems. For example, an outcome from the course of study in an Algebra II class might say that students should be able to draw a scatterplot of data on a graphing calculator and determine a line of best fit. In this case, it would be virtually impossible for the student to answer questions on the test without a calculator. So, to have the student either omit items or to attempt to answer questions without a calculator would most certainly result in failure on the test.

Another related issue to consider is the use of graphing calculators on standardized tests. In some states, passing scores on achievement tests are required for high school graduation, but the tests do not permit the use of graphing calculators. As a result, some teachers avoid using calculators for instruction, believing they are helping their students to prepare for the testing situation. However, this practice deprives the students of the opportunity to explore problems in which answers do not work out evenly, as well as to investigate problem-solving situations that involve visualization. It is best to have students use graphing calculators for instructional situations, even if the tools are not permitted on standardized tests. The teacher, of course, always has the option to allow or even require the use of this technology on classroom quizzes, tests, and projects.

Many schools have classroom sets of calculators that are shared by teachers in a building. When lessons are calculator intensive, the teacher simply distributes the technology to the students and then collects the calculators at the end of the lesson. If a school has shared sets of calculators, the best choice the teacher can make is to have the set available on test day so that if items require the use of technology, the calculators are available to all students. Ultimately, the teacher's decision on this question depends on the degree to which outcomes in the course of study that are being measured on the test require the use of technology.

concepts as you have looked at them through a number of developmental lenses. The point is that the local course of study serves as an important guide in that it describes what is *valued* at each grade level and helps the teacher to think about the ongoing development of important mathematical ideas as students progress from one course to the next.

In the process of writing curriculum, committees often deliberate for several months, thinking about what the appropriate mathematics content is for each grade level. The committees attend presentations, view videos, read curricular models and other documents, explore the Internet, and review possible textbooks and resources while making their decisions. Disagreements among committee members are common and are part of the decision-making process as they wrestle with deciding what is important, as we discussed in Chapter 4. When the document is completed, the course of study is submitted for approval to a governing body, such as the state, and it essentially becomes a legal document—a contract that school districts have with their communities in terms of what will be taught at each grade level. And to some degree, because the document includes objectives that may refer to the use of cooperative learning groups, calculator or computer explorations, or the use of manipulatives, the course of study often has implications for teaching strategies in the classroom as well. One of the most important tasks of a teacher who is new to a school district is to obtain a copy of the mathematics course of study to become familiar with *what* is to be learned and, often, *how* it is suggested that students in that district are to learn the mathematical content and processes. Because a local course of study consists of goals and objectives that rely on Standards, we explore these elements in some depth.

Writing Goals and Objectives

A goal is a general outcome that is addressed through a lesson, a series of lessons, a course, or even an entire Pre-K–12 mathematics program. Goals are stated broadly in terms of what a student is to achieve. The following statements are examples of goals in mathematics education:

- The student will appreciate the use of algebra in solving real-life problems.
- The student will develop a positive disposition toward the study of mathematics.
- The student will understand the connection between geometry and probability.

Suppose that you were in charge of assessing students in your school to ensure that they met each of these outcomes. Determining whether a student "appreciates," "develops," or "understands" is virtually impossible. Hence, goals are not necessarily statements that one can measure in some way to see if they have been accomplished. Instead, they provide a general direction for a lesson or even a program.

However, an objective is a very specific statement of what a student should feel, know, or be able to do. Again, such statements are sometimes referred to as behavioral objectives because they reflect the behaviors that a student should display to demonstrate an understanding of the skill or concept. The following statements are examples of objectives:

- Given the original cost and a percentage discount, the student will calculate the sale price.

- Given a compass and straightedge, the student will draw an angle and construct its angle bisector.
- Given the equation of a function, the student will determine the derivative of the function at a particular point and explain the meaning of the derivative at that point.

In contrast to the goals listed earlier, these objectives are very specific in terms of what a student should know and be able to do; furthermore, the degree to which the student has met these objectives can be measured through a variety of assessment techniques. A behavioral objective should be measurable, meaning that the statement should be clear enough so that a teacher can readily assess whether the student has mastered or met the objective. Objectives also generally contain a condition under which the student should perform. The conditions in the preceding list are the phrases that begin with "given . . ." so that the reader knows the conditions under which a student should be able to do something. These conditions often include specific directions in terms of materials the student should use (e.g., a compass and straightedge, pattern blocks, etc.) or whether technology is required to meet the outcome. Notice how the objectives also contain action words, such as "calculate," "draw," "explain," "show," "contrast," and so forth. Finally, objectives sometimes contain criteria by which one knows whether a student has mastered them. For example, the first objective in the presented list could read, "Given the original cost and a percentage discount, the student will correctly calculate the sale price 80 percent of the time." This means that if the student can accurately determine a sale price at least 4 out of 5 times, the teacher can check off the objective and conclude that the student has mastered that skill. However, keep in mind that this criteria-setting process is dangerous because a student can get 80 percent of the questions right and still not understand the skill, just as another student can fully comprehend the concept but make careless errors and miss 50 percent of the assessment items. This issue is pursued in depth in Chapters 10 and 11 dealing with assessment.

Classifying Objectives

Educators usually group objectives into three categories—affective, cognitive, and psychomotor. **Affective objectives** refer to attitudes or feelings; **cognitive objectives** reflect skills and concepts the student should understand; **psychomotor objectives** refer to things that a student should be physically able to do. When a curriculum is written, committees try to include a variety of objective types. We elaborate on affective and cognitive objectives in this section, because both are common in the mathematics curriculum, whereas psychomotor objectives are more common in physical education and the arts.

Affective Objectives

Although we often think of most mathematics objectives as being cognitive—something the student should know or be able to do—it is common for a mathematics curriculum to include affective objectives. In Chapter 3, we discussed mathematical disposition as described in the NCTM *Standards*. If we want our students to develop positive attitudes and beliefs about mathematics, such as interest, curiosity, perseverance, and an appreciation for the usefulness of mathematics, then those attitudes should be spelled out in a curriculum document. Therefore, it is not unusual to see a course of study or curriculum model display statements such as these:

- The student will appreciate the historical development of Pascal's Triangle.
- The student will display interest and curiosity in problem solving.
- The student will exhibit confidence in using technology to solve mathematics problems.
- The student will recognize the value of a mathematical background in virtually all career areas.

These objectives can be difficult to measure (e.g., it is not easy to know whether a student has developed an appreciation for something), but they prompt the teacher to consider the affective side of the mathematics classroom. The role of the teacher is not only to help the student to learn skills and concepts but also to develop important attitudes and beliefs about mathematics along the way. As was pointed out in Chapter 3, the best way that a teacher can foster positive dispositions toward mathematics is to model those dispositions in the classroom. When students observe a teacher who is persistent, curious, and flexible in problem solving, the student is likely to develop similar dispositions. So, if the course of study and individual lesson plans include affective outcome statements, the objectives serve as reminders that attitudes are important in the mathematics classroom.

Cognitive Objectives

In 1956, a committee led by Benjamin Bloom published a book that described a hierarchy of six levels of cognitive objectives (Bloom & Krathwohl, 1956). This classification scheme for the cognitive domain became known as **Bloom's Taxonomy**. The six levels of Bloom's Taxonomy are knowledge, comprehension, application, analysis, synthesis, and evaluation, shown in the form of a pyramid where knowledge is the foundation in Figure 5.6.

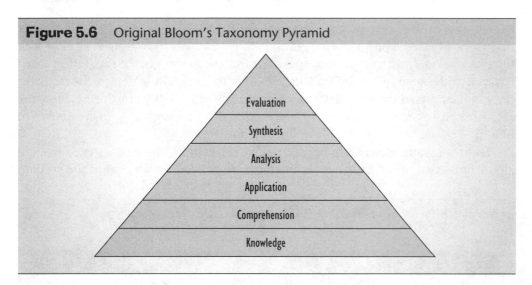

Figure 5.6 Original Bloom's Taxonomy Pyramid

Table 5.1 presents the six levels and their progression.

Subsequently, the taxonomy has been refined and rewritten (e.g., the Quellmalz Taxonomy in Stiggins, Rubel, and Quellmalz, 1988). One of the more commonly used revisions of the taxonomy was published in 2001 (Anderson, Krathwohl, et al.). The revised taxonomy includes four levels of knowledge: (1) facts that stu-

lessons

Table 5.1 The Six Cognitive Levels of Bloom's Original Taxonomy		
Taxonomy Level	**What the Student Can Do**	**Example**
Evaluation	The student can judge the value of materials or ideas using some form of criteria.	Determine whether the system of linear equations is best solved by graphing, substitution, addition–subtraction, or matrices and explain your reasoning.
Synthesis	The student is able to integrate several ideas together to form a new, original whole or product.	Design a process for classifying the graphs of functions based on their equations.
Analysis	The student takes a concept apart and is able to recognize how the components are organized.	Distinguish between a quadrilateral that is a rhombus and one that is a trapezoid.
Application	The student uses a concept in a new situation to solve a problem.	Use a compass and a straight-edge to construct a 30° angle.
Comprehension	The student demonstrates an understanding (the meaning) of information.	Give an example of an *irrational number* and explain how you know it is irrational.
Knowledge	The student can recall basic information that has been memorized.	Define *probability*.

dents must know, (2) concepts that relate the facts to one another, (3) procedures that must be used, and (4) metacognitive knowledge—self-awareness of how one thinks. Also, in an attempt to specify both a noun (knowledge that the student must possess) and a verb (what the student will do with the knowledge), the revised taxonomy uses a two-dimensional approach (Krathwohl, 2002). In this version, the cognitive processes are organized in a hierarchy, from remembering to creating. The two-dimensional taxonomy table is illustrated in Figure 5.7.

So, if we want a student to be able to divide fractions, there is a procedure—an algorithm—that we want them to remember. However, we also want the student

Figure 5.7 Revised Taxonomy with Two Dimensions						
The Cognitive Process Dimension						
The Knowledge Dimension	**1. Remember**	**2. Understand**	**3. Apply**	**4. Analyze**	**5. Evaluate**	**6. Create**
A. Factual Knowledge						
B. Conceptual Knowledge						
C. Procedural Knowledge						
D. Metacognitive Knowledge						

to *understand* why we take the reciprocal of the divisor and then multiply. Also, we want students to be able to *apply* the skill to solving real-world problems, and so forth. Objectives for lessons can essentially be placed in the cells of the table, depending on the type of knowledge and the processes that are desired.

In still another model, Marzano (2001) proposed a four-level hierarchy of cognition, where each level has its own set of verbs that describe what the students should be doing. The lowest level is retrieval, characterized by recognizing, recalling, and executing. The second level is comprehension, which includes integrating (e.g., summarizing, paraphrasing) and symbolizing (e.g., using a model, drawing). The third level is analysis, which involves matching, classifying, analyzing errors, generalizing, and specifying. The highest of Marzano's levels is knowledge utilization, which includes decision-making, problem solving, experimenting, and investigating.

When writing a course of study, committees are encouraged to develop objectives that fall into a variety of levels of whichever taxonomy is being utilized. Similarly, as teachers plan lessons and assess student progress, attention should be paid to ensuring that students are developing mathematical understanding that goes beyond basic recall of information or use of procedures. Indeed, one common criticism of school mathematics is that students tend to be taught and tested primarily at the knowledge and recall level. Consequently, students can find square roots, solve simple equations, and write definitions, but when faced with issues that require higher-level thinking skills, they often are unable to solve the problems. In short, being able to perform effectively at the lower levels of these taxonomies does not ensure that a student can apply and extend basic skills. Teaching and assessment, then, should be designed to address multiple levels of cognition.

In local courses of study, as well as in outcomes for standardized tests, it is common to see cognitive objectives subdivided into at least three levels—knowledge and skills, concepts (comprehension), and applications. We will explore these three levels in more detail. As you look at the examples that follow, think about what differentiates these objective categories from one another. Take a piece of paper and pencil and note the characteristics of objectives that might typically fall into each of the three categories.

▼ KNOWLEDGE AND SKILL

- Given a protractor and a diagram of a triangle, the student will measure each of the angles to within 5°.
- Given a piece of graph paper and a ruler, the student will accurately draw the graph of a linear function 9 out of 10 times.
- Given the length of one side of a 30–60–90° triangle, the student will determine the lengths of the other two sides without the use of a calculator.

▼ CONCEPT

- Given the general equation $y = A\sin(x + B) + C$, the student will describe the effects on the shape and position of the sine curve when values for A, B, and C are changed.
- Given a trinomial such as $x^2 - 5x + 4$ and a set of algebra tiles, the student will demonstrate geometrically what it means to factor the trinomial.
- Given a set of data, the student will determine whether the mode, median, or mean is the most appropriate measure of central tendency for the set and justify the response.

APPLICATION

- Given an object such as a cereal box or a cylindrical oatmeal container, a ruler, and a calculator, the student will determine the surface area and volume of the object.
- Given a problem involving probability, the student will devise a way to model the problem, collect data, and compare or contrast the experimental results with a calculated theoretical probability for the problem.
- Given a free-response question requiring computation with fractions, the student will respond to the question with explanations and diagrams and score at least a 3 on the district's rubric of 0 to 4.

After reading these examples, how did you characterize each of the three categories? You might have noticed, for example, that the knowledge and skill level is the simplest, the most straightforward, and the easiest to measure. If you want a class to be able to add a list of numbers containing decimals, you can give the students some exercises and see if they can add 4 out of 5 of them correctly. Keep in mind that the results of this assessment do not necessarily imply that the student understands *why* decimals are added this way, but understanding may not be the focus of that particular objective either. If, however, the objective is that "given a list of numbers with decimals and a set of base ten blocks, the student will show why the algorithm of lining up decimal places works," the objective has moved up a notch to the concept level. In general, concept-level objectives involve higher thinking levels and are used to emphasize understanding a process, rather than simply being able to do it. Most calculus students can differentiate a function, but far fewer can explain what the answer means or why the procedure works. In our discussion of learning theories in Chapter 3, we have already made the case that we live in a world in which people can perform mathematical skills but not necessarily understand *why* they are done that way or *when* one would have to use that particular skill. As a result, curriculum writers can and should write objectives so that particular levels of achievement are expected.

Consider, for example, the general outcome that students should be able to find the area of a circle. Table 5.2 illustrates how the same outcome might be translated at the three different objective levels.

Table 5.2	Comparison of Circle Area Objective at Three Different Levels
Knowledge and Skill Level	Given the diameter or radius of a circle, the student will be able to compute its area.
Concept Level	Given the formula for area of a circle, the student will be able to justify the formula by using a diagram and written explanation.
Application Level	Given a diagram of a figure containing rectangles, triangles, and fractional parts of circles, the student will determine the area of a shaded region.

At the skill level, nothing more is required than students' ability to substitute numbers into the formula $A = \pi r^2$ and to find a numerical answer. However, at the concept level, students are expected to know where the formula comes from so that it makes sense. Students might, for example, use a previously proven formula such as

$$\text{Area of a Regular Polygon} = \frac{1}{2} \text{Apothem} \times \text{Perimeter}$$

to explain how the apothem (the distance from the center of a circle circumscribed about a regular polygon to a side of the polygon) approaches the length of the radius, and the perimeter of the polygon approaches the circumference of the circle when the number of sides of the polygon tends to infinity. That is,

$$A = \frac{1}{2}a \times p \rightarrow \frac{1}{2}r \times C$$

And, because $C = 2\pi r$,

$$\frac{1}{2}r \times C = \frac{1}{2}r \times (2\pi r) \doteq \pi r^2$$

Finally, it requires yet another level of understanding and application to use the formula for area of a circle, together with the area of a rectangle, to find the area of the shaded region in Figure 5.8.

Figure 5.8 Find the Area of the Shaded Region

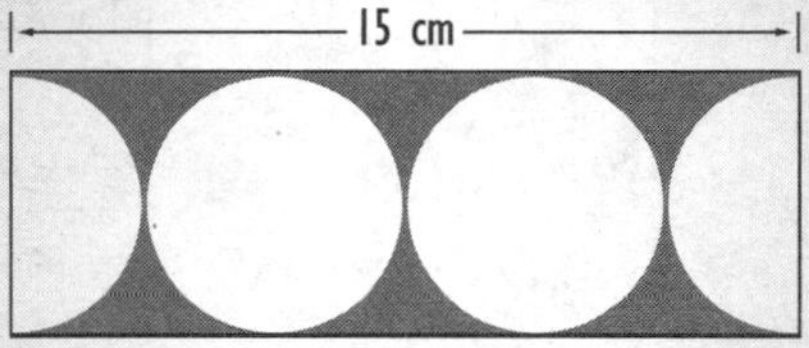

A teacher often asks, "In how much depth do my students need to understand this concept?" But a careful look at the course of study will generally answer this question and simplify the planning process. Objectives written at the skill level require students to perform some mechanical task or memorize a set of definitions, but objectives written at the concept and application levels emphasize the underlying reasons for mathematical processes and the consideration of when they are used.

As in the case of the circles-within-a-rectangle problem in Figure 5.8, an objective written at the application level requires the student to apply some concept to a problem-solving situation. In the following problem, a student not only needs to know how to weigh an object to the nearest gram on a balance but also must be able to use this skill in context to answer the questions:

There is an ancient story that says a man was put in prison for committing a crime, and the king said he would honor one wish for the man. The prisoner showed the king a checkerboard and asked that he put 1 grain of rice on the first of the 64 squares, 2 grains on the second, 4 grains on the third, 8 grains on the fourth, and so on. Then, he asked the king to give all of this rice to his family so that they would be well fed. Is his request reasonable? Will his family have enough to eat for the rest of their lives? Why or why not?

To solve this problem, one might begin by looking at the pattern of numbers representing the number of grains of rice on each square. The numbers are 1, 2, 4, 8, 16, 32, . . . , 2^{63}. So, the total number of grains of rice could be found by taking $1 + 2 + 4 + 8 + \cdots + 2^{63}$. Alternatively, students might use a spreadsheet containing the commands shown in Figure 5.9:

Figure 5.9 Spreadsheet Formula Representation of the Grains-of-Rice Problem

	A	B	C
1	Square Number	Grains on the Square	Total Number of Grains
2	=1	=2^(A2−1)	=B2
3	=A2+1	=2^(A3−1)	=C2+B3
4	=A3+1	=2^(A4−1)	=C3+B4

By using the FILL DOWN command on a standard spreadsheet program, the student can immediately have the computer calculate the number of grains of rice on each of the 64 squares and the total for all of the squares combined. The spreadsheet display would look like Figure 5.10:

Figure 5.10   Spreadsheet Calculations for the Grains-of-Rice Problem

	A	B	C
1	Square Number	Grains on the Square	Total Number of Grains
2	1	1	1
3	2	2	3
4	3	4	7
5	4	8	15
6	5	16	31
7	6	32	63
8	7	64	127
9	8	128	255
10	9	256	511
11	10	512	1023

But how much rice is this after 64 squares? How much does it weigh, and how much space would it occupy? First, one might want to weigh, say, 100 grains of rice and then use a proportion to determine an estimate of the total weight of all of the rice. Incidentally, the amount of rice produced in this problem is a quantity considerably greater than the total worldwide production of rice for an entire year! The important point is that this problem cannot be solved unless the student has the skill of using a balance and can apply this skill to solve the problem. An application-level objective often requires a student to explain how or why a problem was solved in a particular way so that the teacher can gain a sense of the student's ability to use a skill in context. Also, open-ended questions—questions that may have several possible solutions or problem-solving approaches—are often scored on a rubric, a grading scale that is discussed fully in Chapter 10.

You might have noticed that several references to assessment have been made throughout this chapter. This is not a coincidence; in fact, it is difficult to discuss the ideas of goals and objectives without referring to assessment. These terms are related because an objective should serve as a focus for a lesson or series of lessons, and teachers use assessment techniques, such as written tests, interviews, projects, and journal writing, to determine the degree to which students have mastered those objectives. When you think about the objectives you are addressing in a lesson or a longer-term plan known as a unit (discussed in Chapter 6), you should also think about what students should be able to do to demonstrate their understanding of a skill, concept, or application. Consideration of student assessment in the planning process is one of the main ideas of "backward design" that was discussed earlier in this chapter. Objectives that are vague are often difficult to measure and are of little use in planning. Here are some examples of poorly written objectives:

- Given a teacher-constructed board game, the students will win the game to show that they understand fractions.
- Given a set of algebra tiles, the student will show how to use them.
- Given a series of questions about triangles, the students will answer them with 75 percent accuracy.

In the first of these objectives, the emphasis is placed on the board game and not on the important mathematics. We know that the students are learning about fractions, but the objective does not specify what the students should be able to do with fractions (e.g., add, subtract, find common denominators, represent fractional parts with pattern blocks, etc.). In the second example, the focus is on the manipulatives and not on the mathematics. One might ask, "show how to use them *for what*?" Without being specific about the mathematical content, we have to assume that the purpose of the lesson will be to instruct the students on how to use algebra tiles and not necessarily to learn a polynomial or equation-solving skill. In the last example, we are not given any clues as to what kinds of questions students should be able to answer about triangles. The objective could apply to angle measures, lengths of sides, classification, area of the triangle, whether a triangle has symmetry, and so forth. Each of these three objectives is vague and would not give the teacher enough information about what students should know and be able to do to be helpful when planning a lesson. Keep in mind that objectives should reflect the mathematical content that the student is supposed to be mastering or the disposition that the student should be developing.

In many cases, teachers do not write objectives on a day-to-day basis. In reality, curriculum committees write objectives for a district, county, or state, and all of the teachers in that locale select objectives for lessons from the same list to achieve continuity across grade levels and courses. Otherwise, when a student enters a sophomore-level Geometry course, the content and processes explored when that student was a first-year student in Algebra I would be completely dependent on the instructor and the book used for the class. With a course of study or the use of a document such as the *Common Core State Standards,* the instructors and their strategies can vary, but at least teachers throughout the district know what is intended to be taught in other courses. The skilled teacher, however, should not only know how to write an objective but also should be adept at interpreting the meaning of objectives written by another person in a course of study. For this reason, some course-of-study writing committees even provide examples of problems throughout the document to key in on the types of questions that students should be able to answer at a particular grade level or in a certain course. These clues are also intended to keep teachers from "teaching the book" and, instead, turn them to teaching the students, using the textbook as a resource. We now explore the use of a textbook in the mathematics classroom and its role, from writing the course of study to making day-to-day instructional decisions.

An application-level objective on problem solving might incorporate an activity such as using a spinner.

SPOTlight on Technology

A topic that has gained in popularity since the advent of the graphing calculator is the process of *iteration*—that is, "[going] through the same routine over and over, using the output of one step as the input of the next step" (Schwartzman, 1996, p. 121). For example, if we take the square root of a number on a calculator and then continue to press the square root key again and again, the process involves successively taking the square root of the previous answer (the output or answer each time is called the *iterate*). Regardless of the starting number, a series of square root iterations will approach a value of 1.

On a graphing calculator, the ANS button allows the student to take the answer to a previous calculation and operate on it. For example, consider this problem:

Suppose that you had $5,000 to invest in the bank at 6 percent interest. In addition, you plan to invest an extra $500 on the first day of January each year. Determine how much money you would have in your account each year for 20 years.

On a graphing calculator, you would begin by setting the MODE at 2 decimal places because all of the answers will represent dollars and cents. Then, by entering 5,000 into the calculator and pressing ENTER, you give the calculator a starting point—an initial value. By calculating ANS * 1.06, you know how much money is in the account after the first year. This is where the power of the calculator takes over. By entering the general formula (ANS + 500) * 1.06, you are telling the calculator to continue to take last year's investment amount, add $500, and then have it earn 6 percent interest for a year to find the total investment for the end of that year, as shown in Figure 5.11.

Figure 5.11 Investment Problem as Explored on a Graphing Calculator

```
5000
                5000.00
Ans*1.06
                5300.00
(Ans+500)*1.06
                6148.00
                7046.88
■
```

The calculator shows that, after the first 3 years, the person would have $7,046.88 in the investment account. Continuing to press the ENTER button, the student finds that the account would have almost $34,000 after 20 years. Once the starting value and a general formula have been established, successively pressing the ENTER button allows the student to track the results over time.

In the reform mathematics curriculum materials developed with NSF funding, these types of explorations are common. For example, in *Contemporary Mathematics in Context: A Unified Approach* (the Core-Plus Mathematics Project), in Course 1 (generally for first-year high school students), students explore the iteration process in a unit on patterns of change. One problem posed in this unit is the following:

Recall that the Census Bureau estimates U.S. population growth based on birth, death, and immigration data. The 1990 U.S. population was 248 million, with a birth rate of 1.6 percent, a death rate of 0.9 percent, and about 0.9 million people immigrating to the U.S. each year. (Coxford et al., 1998, p. 115)

Students are then asked to use a graphing calculator to estimate the population in the years 2000 and 2010. Again, using the ANS button on the calculator, students can explore this problem as shown in Figure 5.12.

Figure 5.12 Population Growth Problem as Explored on a Graphing Calculator

```
248000000
             248000000
Ans+Ans(.007)+90
0000
             250636000
             253290452
             255963485
■
```

Notice that the formula takes the previous year's population, adds it to 0.7 percent of the population (the difference between the birth and death rates), and then adds the 0.9 million immigrants. After 3 years, we can project the population to be just under 256 million people and then continue to press the ENTER button to predict future populations. In another problem in this section, the authors ask the students to assume that the immigration rate was 2 million people per year, rather than 0.9 million, and they are asked to recalculate the results. Using the technology, this exploration is simple but interesting to students as they make population projections.

Selection and Organization of Resources

Textbooks

Let's listen to three mathematics teachers discussing the progress of their students:

> *Loretta:* How far is your math class?
>
> *James:* We're about halfway into Chapter 5. How about you?
>
> *Loretta:* That's what I had heard from my kids who have been talking to yours . . . we're barely into Chapter 4. My class is moving so slowly this year.
>
> *Juanita:* You two had better speed up if we're all going to make it to Chapter 7 by the end of the semester. We've already got that departmental exam made up for all of us to give our students in January, but you have to finish Chapter 7 to be able to use it.
>
> *Loretta:* I know. But my students always get hung up on the section that starts at page 115. By the time I give them a few worksheets on it and move on, we end up behind everybody else. That section gets them every year. And it kinda gets me, too, because I'm not sure why the book throws in those puzzle problems; my students always have a hard time with them.
>
> *James:* That's why I've decided not to even bother with the worksheets. If they don't get it, they should see me for help. Otherwise, I'll slow down too much, and we'll never make it to Chapter 7 by January.
>
> *Juanita:* It gets worse from there, too . . . it's impossible to finish the book by June unless you get to Chapter 7 by the end of the semester. But I'm determined to do it, and I've already warned my students to "hold on to their hats"!

Can you figure out what grade level or which course these three individuals teach? Do you know what the content is that they have been exploring with their students? Of course not. This conversation is so focused on *the book* that the relevant mathematics and the needs of the learners have been put aside. This is a very real problem in education that occurs anytime the users of a textbook decide that the book itself is the cornerstone of a class. In an attempt to gain consistency and to be thorough, educators sometimes forget that their purpose is to teach mathematics to real students. And if learning is not entirely linear (i.e., it is not important for every student to master Concepts A and B before exploring Concept C)—as suggested by the constructivist model in Chapter 3—we almost have to believe that it is sometimes appropriate to work problems in the back of a textbook before exploring some of the issues in earlier chapters. Finally, because no two classrooms of learners are exactly the same, why should we believe that three classes in a school would move at exactly the same pace, ending at the same chapter by the end of a semester? Decisions to follow a set program of timing for a course are often made for the convenience of the instructors, not for the benefit of the students they teach. We need to think of learning particular mathematical concepts as the constant and the amount of time it takes to do the learning as the variable, rather than making the historical error of viewing time as the constant and learning as the variable.

Despite what we know about student learning, however, some school districts engage in what is known as **curriculum mapping**—the process of scheduling the sequence and timing for teaching major topics throughout a school year. In fact, some districts have become so rigid that they publish pacing guides that tell teachers exactly which topic and page number is to be addressed on any given day. The benefit of mapping is the consistency achieved by knowing that every teacher is covering the same content at the same time and that objectives are not being skipped. The major drawback to the system is that students learn at different rates. So, if you are told that next Thursday's class must focus on area of a trapezoid, but your students have already discovered the formula, you are not permitted to move on to the next topic because of the requirement of following the map. This rigid approach to curriculum can limit creativity and meeting the needs of the students in an individual class. Likewise, strict adherence to sequence and content of textbooks can reduce flexibility in teaching. So, what is the purpose of a textbook in mathematics?

A textbook is a resource and a guide. It is a resource in that it serves the purpose of an encyclopedia—we may not need it every day, but when a visual or written explanation is needed or when a set of practice exercises is sought, the book can provide these items. But the book can also serve as a worthwhile guide for instruction. Particularly, the novice teacher can look to a textbook for direction in terms of how to sequence content and how much time one might need to spend on a particular concept. Teachers' manuals frequently contain charts that include teaching hints and field-tested timelines of teaching that can be very valuable to the less-experienced instructor. The book and its manual can be helpful for providing insights on how students might link previous knowledge to new concepts and for thinking about what types of activities and problems the students should pursue. We often hear of veteran teachers who are teaching mathematics without a book. In the constructivist model of teaching and learning, many experienced teachers find using textbooks constraining, making it difficult to pursue student questions. But a caution is warranted here. Most teachers who do not routinely use textbooks are experienced and had used books for several years before learning how students progress and how to address students' needs. Also, research shows that teachers who ignore textbooks altogether may be missing out on the positive effects of using field-tested materials, particularly those that have been produced with Standards and a constructivist model at their core (Ball & Cohen, 1996).

After the NCTM released *Curriculum and Evaluation Standards for School Mathematics* in 1989, the National Science Foundation (NSF) awarded millions of dollars to institutions to develop textbooks and curricular materials that would assist teachers and school districts in effectively implementing the standards across the grade levels. Textbooks were drafted, field tested, and refined, and by the mid-1990s, they began to become available in printed form. At the high school level, five standards-based programs were produced—Contemporary Mathematics in Context: A Unified Approach (CPMP), Interactive Mathematics Program (IMP), MATH Connections: A Secondary Mathematics Core Curriculum, Integrated Mathematics: A Modeling Approach Using Technology (SIMMS), and Mathematics: Modeling Our World (ARISE). All of these programs represent an integrated curriculum, as discussed in Chapter 4. A Web site has been developed for reviewing each of these programs and gathering additional information. This site, funded by NSF and entitled COMPASS (Curricular Options in Mathematics Programs for All Secondary Students), is located at www.ithaca.edu/compass. Contact information for each of the programs is also provided at the end of this chapter.

In addition, the NSF funded several middle school mathematics programs. Textbooks and materials were produced to support mathematics teaching from grades 5 through 8 with four projects—Connected Math Project (CMP), Mathematics in Context (MiC), MathScape: Seeing and Thinking Mathematically, and MATH Thematics. In 1999, the American Association for the Advancement of Science (AAAS) released the results of a study in which it evaluated 13 popular textbook series, based on the degree to which the series included significant mathematical topics and provided teaching strategies that would promote student learning. The study showed that only 4 of the 13 textbook series earned a satisfactory rating. And the 4 series that were rated favorably were the NSF-funded reform curricula. Not one of the commercially available textbooks met the rigorous criteria set by the researchers (AAAS, 2000). A Web site, funded by the NSF and entitled the Show-Me Center, features the details about all of these programs. The site is located at www.showmecenter.missouri.edu. Contact information about each program is also featured at the end of this chapter. (A similar Web site has been developed for NSF-funded reform mathematics curricula for the elementary grades, kindergarten through grade 6, at the Alternatives for Rebuilding Curricula [ARC] Center located at www.comap.com/elementary/projects/arc.)

We can see that there are some very worthwhile mathematics textbooks available on the market, several of which were written to support the NCTM *Standards*, with revisions and new books being produced to support the *Common Core State Standards*. However, even the authors of the best textbooks caution their users not to allow the book to *define* the curriculum. If you compare a typical course of study to the textbook used in that course, you will find that most books contain more content than is required in a course of study and that many courses of study require that students visit topics that are not present in the text for that particular class. Therefore, it is appropriate and even desirable for teachers to skip sections of a book that contain material not included in the course of study and to supplement the book with activities from other resources that address topics not included in the text.

One way to make effective use of the textbook is to sit down with the course of study and textbook and compare each objective or Standard in the curriculum with what is in the textbook. By placing a checkmark next to each section of the book that addresses an objective or Standard in the course of study and a star next to any intended outcome in the curriculum for which there does not appear to be a related section in the book, the teacher can quickly recognize which sections or units in the book can be omitted and which objectives or Standards will require resources beyond the textbook. Another suggestion on textbook use is to set up a meeting with a veteran teacher in the department, if possible, who has used the textbook in the past. Even one year of using a book can generate a great deal of insight into its strengths and shortcomings, and there is often no substitute for the personal advice of another individual who has actually worked with the text. However, it may not be helpful to pick the brain of an instructor who tends to rely entirely on the book for teaching a course.

A teacher at a workshop, during some active hands-on lessons, once said, "These lessons are nice, but I've got a 400-page book to cover." In reality, the teacher didn't have a book to cover at all; instead, this person had a classroom full of students to teach and had lost the focus of the course because the book had become more important than the students themselves and the course of study. Teachers are not expected to cover every page of every book. Instead, they are encouraged to use the book as a guide and a resource to help them teach to the objectives listed in the course of study. It has been said that the best way to cover a book is to have students sit on it!

A curriculum committee sometimes writes a course of study and defines the objectives with several possible textbooks as guides. That way, the committee can be confident that most of the objectives in the course of study are supported by text materials. So, one difficult decision of the committee—and, sometimes, of mathematics teachers within a particular building—is how to choose a textbook for a course. How do you distinguish a potentially effective text from a weaker one? The

**MAKING A MATHEMATICS TEXTBOOK SELECTION—
SOME QUESTIONS TO CONSIDER**

1. Does the book place the mathematical process skills (problem solving, reasoning and proof, communication, connections, and representation) and CCSS mathematical practices as major focal points? How do the authors of the textbook do this?
2. Do the authors approach mathematics holistically with investigations and problem solving as the context in which skills are developed, or is the book more skill oriented with occasional investigations suggested?
3. Do the problems and exercises, as well as assessments, throughout the book adequately address a mix of objectives from Bloom's Taxonomy and its revisions, such as knowledge and skill-, conceptual-, and application-level objectives?
4. Does the book take into account the developmental level of the students, using language and providing examples accordingly?
5. Is there evidence of a progression from concrete to pictorial to more abstract means of learning concepts as is consistent with current learning theories? Do the problems presented make effective use of manipulatives as tools for exploring and discovering mathematical principles?
6. How is technology used in the book? Do problems involve the regular, integrated use of calculators, computers, and other technologies for exploring concepts?
7. How close is the match between the objectives stated in the course of study and the contents of the textbook? Are the course of study and textbook compatible enough to limit the need to "skip" sections or to supplement the text?
8. Does the book appear to be free from gender bias and provide examples that demonstrate cultural diversity and acceptance of disabilities? How effectively have the authors addressed the issues of equity and equal access to mathematics for all students?

list of questions above can be asked when selecting a textbook. The list is only a sample and is not intended to be exhaustive, but it will provide some ideas to think about when reviewing textbooks for their relative strengths and weaknesses.

After questions such as these have been addressed, curriculum committees or the faculty within a school make a textbook selection and adopt a book for a course or grade level. Depending on the budget of a school district, a textbook may be used for many years, so a careful choice is important. But the effective teacher will not only use the textbook as a reference and a guide; the teacher will also look to resources beyond the textbook, including general resource activity books, journals, and the Internet. We discuss the use of these ancillary materials in the instructional process in the sections that follow.

Print Resources

Suppose that you were preparing to teach a series of lessons (a unit) on graph theory, a discrete mathematics topic. The textbook you are using is from a high school program that has a unit on discrete mathematics embedded in it. You look through the textbook and decide that students need more than the book provides—more hands-on experiences and richer problems to solve. You decide to go searching for additional teaching ideas. Fortunately, the National Council of Teachers of Mathematics has published an annual yearbook on *Discrete Mathematics across the Curriculum, K–12* (Kenney, 1991) that provides a number of practical classroom ideas, as well as a resource book entitled *Navigating Through Discrete Mathematics in Grades 6–12* (Hart, Kenney, DeBellis, & Rosenstein, 2008). Another book entitled *Discrete Mathematics in the Schools* (Rosenstein, Franzblau, & Roberts, 1998) also includes ideas that can be used to supplement textbook problems. Furthermore, a nonprofit organization known as the Consortium for Mathematics and Its Applications (COMAP) publishes a number of videos and teaching units, several of which key in on graph theory and contain reproducible masters and hands-on activities for classroom use. If you consult some of these sources as well as another textbook or two on discrete mathematics that you do not use for your course, you can suddenly find yourself equipped with dozens of problems and lessons from which to choose. Remember that teaching ideas are like recipes—the more you have to choose from, the more likely it is that you'll find one that is practical and effective. After all, a powerful activity or lesson is worth sharing, and an important role of the teacher is to seek out the most popular recipes, while recognizing that an activity that works for one teacher in a class may not work for another. When a teacher fails to seek out additional resource books, the result is a short menu of textbook-driven ideas that may be acceptable but are not nearly as powerful as is possible when additional sources are considered.

Of course, these books and videos are useful only if you know that they exist and know how to obtain copies of them. So, how do you find out about these resource books? Here are six suggestions to consider:

- Make sure that you are on the mailing list of several commercial publishers of teaching ideas. As new resources become available, the publishers highlight them in the catalogs. Many of these catalogs are available on the Internet, and having your name on a company's database is generally free. Often, resource books can be purchased on a 30-day trial basis, during which time you can determine whether the resource is worth the money. In many school districts, the school or department has a budget for these resources. If not, tell your family and friends that the books make great birthday gifts.

- Make regular visits to the NCTM Web site at www.nctm.org. Among other resources, NCTM has an on-line catalog service and publishes hundreds of books, videos, CD-ROMs, and other materials that support reform in mathematics education. For example, after the release of *Principles and Standards for School Mathematics,* NCTM released an entire series of books known as *Navigations* to support the document. Each *Navigations* book is geared toward a particular grade-level band (Pre-K–2, 3–5, 6–8, or 9–12) and a specific content area (e.g., algebra, geometry, statistics and probability). These books not only attempt to clarify the meaning of various content standards but they also provide specific lesson plans, ideas, and software on enclosed CD-ROMs to assist teachers in implementing the standards.

- Look for teaching ideas in feature articles of professional journals, such as *The Mathematics Teacher* and *Mathematics Teaching in the Middle School,* by the NCTM. These articles often include classroom-tested ideas from other teachers, complete with reproducible masters and step-by-step instructions on how to carry out a lesson. Also, these journals regularly review the latest resource books. These reviews describe available resources in some detail and point out strengths and weaknesses.

- Talk to your colleagues and friends in mathematics education. It is likely that a teacher down the hall or in a neighboring district has used a particular resource for years, and you have never heard of it. The more you talk with people about what they do and what they use, the more often exemplary resources will surface. And, in many cases, the teacher who owns an effective resource will be willing and excited about sharing it with you—borrowing one another's books is common among classroom teachers.

- Attend local, state, and national conferences of mathematics teachers. At these sessions, presenters often cite sources of effective teaching ideas that you can pursue when you return home. There is generally an exhibition area at conferences at which publishers display their teaching aids and resource books. These exhibitions give the teacher an opportunity to browse the available resources. The issue of professional development is discussed in Chapter 13.

- Visit curriculum libraries at universities or for local school districts. Often, libraries have places set aside for featuring the latest in teaching resource books that can be browsed or even checked out for use as supplementary sources of ideas. Curriculum supervisors at the district level frequently receive complimentary copies of new resource books and keep them on file in a curriculum library or holding area. These supervisors are generally very accommodating about allowing teachers to browse the sample copies for possible purchase.

Remember that teachers are the best when it comes to "stealing" ideas from one another. And why shouldn't they be? Many teaching ideas have been around for decades and continue to resurface in slightly reworked formats. The better you are at locating the resources and selecting the best teaching ideas, the more proficient you will become at supplementing the activities and problems in your textbook.

lassroom Dialogues

While studying a unit on algebra, including graphing and analyzing linear functions, the teacher displays the graph shown in Figure 5.13 for students to discuss.

Teacher: The graph shows the relationship between the amount of time that a car has been on the road and the distance it has traveled. What does the graph tell us about the car's trip?

Student 1: The graph is a line and has a *y*-intercept at the point (0, 0).

Teacher: So, what is the real-life meaning of the *y*-intercept?

Student 1: When the time is zero, the car hasn't moved anywhere yet.

Teacher: Good. Is there anything else that we know about this trip?

Student 2: Yes. The car's speed is increasing the further it travels.

Teacher: How do you know that?

Student 2: Well, look at the line. The greater the amount of time, the further the car has traveled. Since the line is going up to the right, it means that the car's speed is increasing as the person drives.

The teacher knows that the function is linear and has a constant rate of change, so the speed is not really increasing at all. But what is the best approach to use to help the student realize that the speed is constant? How would you respond to this student's question? Certainly, one way that the teacher could react is to simply tell the student that the function is linear and, therefore, the car is moving at a constant rate of speed. However, the student appears to have a conceptual misunderstanding about the nature of the function and is in need of a more careful explanation.

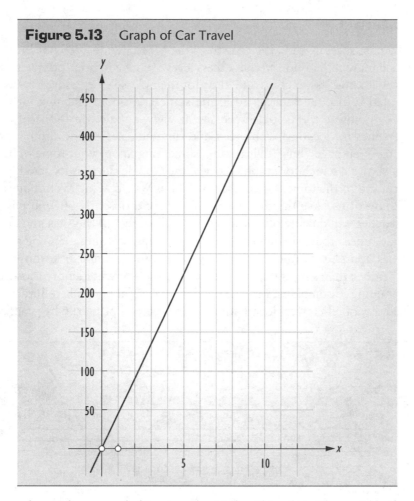

Figure 5.13   Graph of Car Travel

The teacher might approach this misconception by asking the student to identify two points on the line, such as the origin and the point (1, 45). The slope of the line between these two points is 45. Students should be able to describe this slope as a rate of change, explaining that the car is traveling at 45 miles per hour traveled (the vertical axis represents miles, while the horizontal axis represents hours). Likewise, the student could select another pair of points on the line, such as (3, 135) and (10, 450). Using the slope formula, $m = \frac{450 - 135}{10 - 3} = \frac{315}{7} = 45$. Therefore, for the second pair of points, the slope is still 45, indicating that the car continues to travel at 45 miles per hour. Regardless of which pair of points is chosen, the slope of the line will always be 45. After exploring two or more examples of this kind, students should recognize that the car is traveling at a constant rate of speed and is, therefore, not speeding up, as originally conjectured by Student 2.

A teacher may even choose to generate a table or to write an equation that describes the function ($y = 45x$) as further illustration that the slope remains the same. Most importantly, the teacher needs to recognize that the error in thinking is probably not a random mistake and has deeper, conceptual implications. Also, we have to assume that if one student has this misunderstanding, several others in the room are having difficulty as well. A careful exploration into the student's misconception can serve as a considerable help to the entire class as they try to make sense of linear functions. Often, students can calculate a slope but have little understanding of what the value of the slope actually means or represents. What are some other strategies that you might use to help this student and the class to gain a deeper understanding into the meaning of slope? Are there other quantities that students commonly "compute" by using a formula that they may not understand beyond memorization of the formula? What is the teacher's role in ensuring that students understand such quantities and are not simply *computing* their values?

The Internet

Over the past several years, the growth of the World Wide Web has been phenomenal. Teachers who had no Internet access a few years ago are, today, using the Web extensively to find lesson plans and ideas for their classes. Let's say, for example, that you wanted to use the Internet to locate some additional teaching ideas on graph theory. By going to the Google Web site at www.google.com—one of the popular search engines for locating Web sites—and running a search for "graph theory," the site locates Web page "hits" that contain something about your topic of interest. Figure 5.14 shows a search for graph theory at the Google site that located 883,000 Web pages relating to the topic. Of course, use of the World Wide Web requires patience because few of us have the time to actually view thousands of Web pages. So, the skilled teacher will quickly browse the titles and sources of the sites and click only on those that appear to have a high probability of being useful in planning and teaching. Sometimes, searches can be narrowed by typing, for example, "lesson plan + graph theory," rather than simply "graph theory," so the site will identify those Web pages also containing lesson plans. But like seeking out useful books in a library, the ability to efficiently and effectively locate sources is developed primarily by practice.

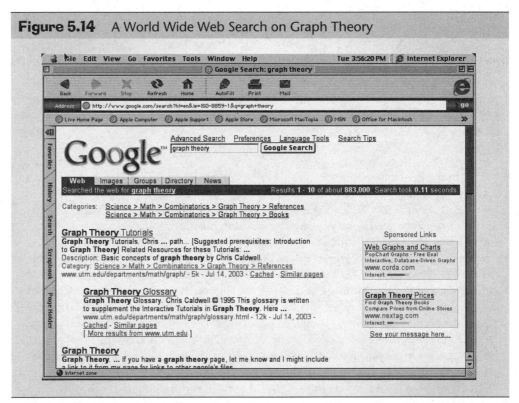

Figure 5.14 A World Wide Web Search on Graph Theory

(Reproduced with the permission of Google. Google and the Google logo are trademarks of Google Company.)

Several journals and most professional organizations now have Web sites that allow you to access supplemental teaching ideas from any computer with Internet access. If you are relatively new to the Internet, you may first want to visit the National Council of Teachers of Mathematics at www.nctm.org. At this Web site, you will obtain information about the NCTM and its affiliates and gain access to articles and ideas for teachers. The popular Math Forum site at http://mathforum.org has teaching ideas, problems of the week, links to other mathematics Web sites, and even a link to Ask Dr. Math, that allows students to leave questions to be answered by a mathematician. In fact, the future of teacher resources may very well reside with the Internet, as more materials are being made available every day and are easy to access with the click of a mouse. Some professional organizations have already begun to make their journals available on-line. A list of useful Web sites, including brief descriptions and addresses, appears in the Appendix.

Organizing a Resource File

Ultimately, most teachers accumulate a great deal of resource materials. It is not unusual for teachers to collect exemplary lesson plans, activities, classic problems, assignment ideas, useful handouts, and a wealth of other teaching resources from books, journals, the Internet, professional conferences, and colleagues. But although collecting these ideas is relatively simple, organizing them in a useful manner is not always so easy. We often hear teachers saying, "I know I have it somewhere because I took notes on that topic during a conference one time, but I have no idea where I put it." Therefore, it is important—particularly for teachers who are new to the profession—to establish a useful method for collecting and organizing resource materials. After all, what good is an exemplary hands-on activity if you can't find it on the day that you want to use it in class? Here are four practical suggestions for organizing a resource file:

- Obtain a box of file folders. Each time that you find a good problem, activity, or lesson, place a master copy in one folder and title the folder with a descriptor, such as "Grains of Rice" or "Orange Grove," on the label. Then organize the file folders in alphabetical order by content area. For example, you could place the grains-of-rice problem under Measurement because it involves weighing a sample of rice to estimate the total weight of the rice. You could file the orange grove problem under Algebra because the problem involves patterning and writing an equation that represents the problem. It is important, however, that you use a filing scheme that works for you. The grains-of-rice problem, for example, could just as easily be filed under Algebra because the solution can include an analysis of exponential functions. Consequently, some teachers file all of the problems and activities alphabetically. However you choose to organize the resources, it is important to place only *one* idea in each file folder. Otherwise, you may spend a great deal of time rummaging through a file to find one teaching idea that has been mixed in with a dozen others. And the process becomes simple: Each time that you encounter an idea that you think will be useful, give it a title on a file folder, place the idea in the folder, and file it in an appropriate location.
- Obtain several three-ring binders and a plastic storage tub or a small file cabinet. Label each binder for a particular content area, such as the conceptual categories in the *Common Core State Standards*—number and quantity, algebra, functions, modeling, geometry, and statistics and probability. Then, each time that you locate a useful teaching idea, three-hole-punch the pages, and place the idea in the appropriate binder. If you store all of the binders in a plastic tub or file cabinet, you will always know where to look for the teaching ideas. As new ideas are added, you may choose to change the organization scheme, and this is very easy when using binders and three-hole-punched pages. For example, if you decide to create a new binder on problem solving that includes some ideas you have already collected, you

only need to label a new binder and either move some activities from their former location to the new one or make a second copy of the activity and place one copy in each binder.

- Obtain a set of index cards and an index card file box. Each time that you discover a new teaching idea, write the idea title at the top of the card, a short description of the idea on the card, and file it in a file box by content topic (or by chapter of the textbook if your class uses a particular one over a period of time). Then keep one master file of all of the teaching ideas on paper in alphabetical order, titled at the top to match the titles on the index cards. Whenever you are going to teach a lesson on a particular topic, you can quickly thumb through the short descriptions on the index cards to locate a useful idea. Then go to the master file of ideas and pull it out for duplication or use in your class. It is often quicker and easier to locate a problem or lesson by looking through a small box of index cards than by flipping through binders filled with papers.

- Scan your favorite lesson ideas (or save them in PDF format) and put them on a flash drive or burn them onto a CD-ROM. The flash drive or CD-ROM can serve as an electronic file from which lessons and activity pages can be readily retrieved or printed. With a flash drive, each time a new idea is located, it can simply be saved and added to the drive. It is also easy to run a search for a particular lesson or key word when the resource file is saved in an electronic format. As an alternative, some teachers store their teaching ideas and Web links to lessons at free or subscription Internet sites, such as LiveText.com. Information stored at a Web site can be readily searched and downloaded when needed for a lesson. Updating the ideas at such a site is easy, and the lessons can be retrieved from any computer with Internet access, without having to physically take a CD or flash drive along to school.

Whatever method you choose—including, perhaps, some other scheme that is not listed here but makes sense to you—it is important to seek out exemplary problems, activities, and lessons from resource books, journals, the Internet, and other sources and to organize them for easy reference. These resources will facilitate your ability to meet the mathematical goals and objectives set forth by the school district for your grade level.

Conclusion

The teaching and learning process begins with a very specific set of statements about what a student should feel, know, and be able to do at each grade level in a Pre-K–12 program. Although national standards and state models provide a framework for teaching, a local course of study is generally written to prescribe the details of what students should be exploring each year they are in school. The course of study is essentially the contract between the school and the community in that it provides direction for the instructional process. Objectives within the course of study document vary from simple knowledge-level items to conceptual and higher-order application situations. The wording of these objectives can also suggest the type of teaching methods that are expected in a district, including the use of hands-on materials and technology.

After the NCTM published *Curriculum and Evaluation Standards for School Mathematics* in 1989, funding from the National Science Foundation brought about the writing of several reform mathematics curricula at both the secondary and middle school levels. These materials place the student at the center of the lessons, using inquiry and a constructivist approach to teaching as described in Chapter 3. Teaching units in these programs are rooted in real-life problems so that students can explore mathematical concepts in the context of problem solving. The materials emphasize the connections between content subjects and the use of technology in problem solving. Details on these programs can be found by accessing the COMPASS and Show-Me Center Web sites or by contacting the publishers directly using information at the end of this chapter.

But, although the active, hands-on engagement of students in the learning process makes sense on paper, this type of teaching becomes possible only when the teacher has access to lessons and activities that support a more constructivist approach. And although a textbook can be a valuable tool for providing direction and serving as a source for problems, often many additional ideas are found in resource books and on the Internet. Ideally, the teacher will use the textbook as a general guide for instruction but will supplement the book with a multitude of ideas from other sources.

With the release of *Principles and Standards for School Mathematics* in 2000, NCTM followed up by producing a series of resource books entitled *Navigations*, which provide educators with lessons and ideas that shed additional light on the meaning of the standards. Together with NCTM's secondary and middle school journals and Web site, these resources are available to assist teachers in implementing the standards in their classrooms. The thoughtful collection and organization of ideas from all of these resources are important skills for an effective mathematics teacher. The art of teaching is all about sharing ideas with one another so that we can use the experiences and successes of others in our own planning.

This chapter concludes our discussion of the mathematics curriculum. Chapter 4 explored the NCTM *Principles and Standards for School Mathematics* and the *Common Core State Standards,* the use of state-level curriculum models, and the notion of a core curriculum. In this chapter, we discussed the issues of writing courses of study; the use of goals and objectives in curriculum planning; and the selection, use, and organization of supplementary resource materials. In the four chapters that make up Unit 3, we turn our attention to the art of *teaching* mathematics. In Chapter 6, we discuss how daily lesson plans and long-term unit plans are prepared to meet the goals and objectives set forth in a course of study, and Chapter 7 deals with organization of the classroom and the role of the mathematics teacher. In Chapters 8 and 9, we look at some of the issues involved in teaching specific content areas, including number sense, algebra, geometry, statistics and probability, and discrete mathematics, in the secondary and middle school settings.

For bibliographic references and additional resources, see page 406

Glossary

Affective Objective: An affective objective is a statement of an outcome referring to attitudes or feelings that should be displayed by a student after experiencing a lesson, series of lessons, course, or mathematics program.

Bloom's Taxonomy: Developed in 1956, this hierarchy describes six levels of increasing complexity of cognition (thinking), which include knowledge, comprehension, application, analysis, synthesis, and evaluation. Other revisions of this taxonomy have been published since then. These levels should be considered when writing a course of study as well as when designing classroom lessons and assessments.

Cognitive Objective: A cognitive objective is a statement of an outcome referring to skills and concepts the student should understand after experiencing a lesson, series of lessons, course, or mathematics program. Cognitive objectives are often subcategorized as knowledge and skill, concept, and application-level outcomes.

Course of Study: A course of study is a document that prescribes the curriculum, by grade level, for a state, county, or individual school district. It includes a district philosophy, overarching goals, a list of objectives for each grade level, and pupil performance objectives for mastery-level outcomes.

Curriculum Mapping: Curriculum mapping is the process of scheduling the sequence and timing for teaching major topics throughout a school year. The idea is to keep all teachers of a course or grade level to follow the same syllabus and pacing schedule.

District Philosophy: A district philosophy is a broad statement of beliefs held by educators in that system. The philosophy should provide the underlying foundation on which specific objectives are written.

Goals: Goals are broad statements about what a student should be able to accomplish as a result of participating in a district's mathematics program. The goal statement should follow logically from the district's philosophy and provide a framework for more specific grade-level objectives.

Objective: An objective is a very specific statement that describes what a student should feel, know, or be able to do at a particular grade level. Objectives are the intended outcomes of a lesson or series of lessons. Objectives can be subcategorized as affective, cognitive, and psychomotor.

Pascal's Triangle: Pascal's Triangle is a triangle made up of progressively longer rows of numbers as shown in the following illustration:

$$
\begin{array}{c}
1 \\
1 \quad 2 \quad 1 \\
1 \quad 3 \quad 3 \quad 1 \\
1 \quad 4 \quad 6 \quad 4 \quad 1 \\
1 \quad 5 \quad 10 \quad 10 \quad 5 \quad 1 \\
1 \quad 6 \quad 15 \quad 20 \quad 15 \quad 6 \quad 1 \\
1 \quad 7 \quad 21 \quad 35 \quad 35 \quad 21 \quad 7 \quad 1 \\
1 \quad 8 \quad 28 \quad 56 \quad 70 \quad 56 \quad 28 \quad 8 \quad 1
\end{array}
$$

The numbers in each row are generated by adding the two numbers directly above and to the right and left of the location. Pascal's Triangle was named in honor of Blaise Pascal, a seventeenth-century French mathematician, although there is evidence that the triangle existed long before Pascal's lifetime. Patterns in Pascal's Triangle are numerous as one views numbers vertically, horizontally, and diagonally. Determining binomial distributions, finding combinations, and locating famous number patterns, such as the triangular numbers, are only a few of the uses of this valuable tool.

Psychomotor Objective: A psychomotor objective is a statement of an outcome referring to things that a student should be physically able to do after experiencing a lesson, series of lessons, course, or mathematics program. An example of a psychomotor objective is, "the student will be able to successfully do at least 10 consecutive jumping jacks," where the emphasis is on a physical activity required of the student. Psychomotor objectives are common in the areas of physical education and the arts and generally not associated directly with mathematics education.

Pupil Performance Objective (PPO): A pupil performance objective is a specific description of what a student should be able to do at a particular grade level. PPOs flow naturally from the objectives for a grade level, generally reflect those objectives, and are often used to write classroom or districtwide assessment items, which may take the form of problems, questions, or projects. A PPO often contains a condition under which the student should perform as well as criteria that are used to determine the degree to which a student has mastered the outcome.

Unpacking: A process by which one specifies what a student should know or be able to do to demonstrate mastery of a Standard. Unpacking is often part of the *backward design* process.

⬤ Discussion Questions and Activities

1. Obtain a copy of the mathematics course of study for a school district near you. Examine the document, looking for the philosophy, goals, objectives, and pupil performance objectives. How effectively does the document communicate to the teacher exactly what is to be taught at each grade level?

2. Discuss the potential advantages and disadvantages of including broad representation on a course of study writing committee. Why might a school district choose to have a curriculum supervisor and a small committee of mathematics teachers write the document rather than select a larger representative committee including administrators, guidance counselors, and community members?

3. One of the problems with including affective objectives in a course of study is that it can be difficult to assess the development of dispositions. Discuss some possible alternatives that teachers have for measuring affective outcomes in a lesson or throughout a course.

4. Suppose that you want students to become proficient at working with square roots. Write three objectives involving the use of square roots—one at the knowledge

and skill level, one at the concept level, and one at the application level.

5. Divide the class into small groups and have each group write a pupil performance objective that might accompany each of the following content objectives if mastery of the outcome is expected: (a) The student will determine the arithmetic mean of a set of numbers. (b) The student will graph a linear function. (c) The student will classify quadrilaterals. (d) The student will find the zeros of a polynomial function. Compare objectives and discuss the variety of ways in which an individual can interpret a given cognitive objective.

6. Obtain two available textbooks for a particular course or grade level. Using the questions and criteria described in this chapter, prepare a criticism of each book and a comparison that would allow an educator to select one text over the other.

7. Obtain copies of several resource books, such as the NCTM *Navigations* Series or other commercially available books of teaching ideas. How are the books organized, and what features might make one resource book more desirable to the classroom teacher than another?

8. Using a computer with Internet access and a search engine such as Google, run a search for teaching ideas on the mathematical topic of your choice. Then discuss the difficulties that may have confronted you while running the search and the practicality of using the Internet to find teaching ideas.

9. In a small group, discuss the options for organizing a resource file listed in this chapter. Which one appeals the most to you and why? What other ideas do you have for organizing resources?

10. Obtain a copy of one of the NSF-funded curriculum materials described in this chapter. Browse through the text materials and discuss the similarities and differences between this curriculum and a more traditional curriculum that you may have experienced. What are the benefits and possible drawbacks to using the NSF-funded curricula?

Planning for Instruction

After reading Chapter 6, you should be able to answer the following questions:

- What is a unit plan and what factors need to be considered when writing one?
- What are the essential components of a lesson plan? Describe each component.
- What features make one lesson plan better than another? Discuss some lesson-planning tips that increase the likelihood of success.
- What is the difference between a *lesson plan* and a *lesson image,* and how does teaching experience change the way that lessons are prepared?
- What are examples of key questions that can be addressed during reflection on a lesson, and why is it important for teachers to reflect on their teaching practice?

Suppose that you were an architect overseeing the construction of a new home. Before drawing up any plans, you would want to see the site and measure it, so you would know what kind of space is available and what it is realistic to build on the plot of land. Then you might carefully map out the project, scheduling each step of the process in an organized manner. It wouldn't make any sense, for example, to have the roofers show up with shingles on the same day the masons are laying the foundation, and you had better make sure that the carpenters have constructed the walls before the electrician comes in to wire the home. So, you design a general sketch of the process, including each of the major components of construction. And, although a general plan guides the building of the home, daily needs must be addressed. For example, if the carpenter is going to put on a roof on a Monday, then the plan must include not only a goal for what can be accomplished that day but the personnel and a list of supplies needed to construct the roof. The carpenter will have to secure plywood, nails, hammers, saws, tape measures, and so forth, and know, in advance, which step of the process will require which tools. Finally, as the house is being completed, an inspector will need to visit periodically to approve the construction and wiring before a family moves in.

The process of building a home is similar to the process that teachers go through each time they develop a series of learning experiences for students in a mathematics class. In a very general way, the teacher needs to identify a list of intended goals and objectives (discussed in detail in Chapter 5) and construct an all-encompassing plan. After all, the point of teaching a lesson or series of lessons is to attempt to address issues and concepts stated in a course of study. But, specifically, the teacher must also write detailed plans for how each day within the unit will be conducted, including daily objectives, materials, procedures, and a way to assess the degree to which students understand the major mathematical concepts. A well-engineered home-building project can save time and money and result in an excellent structure. Similarly, a carefully planned series of learning experiences for students can make all the difference as to whether students understand the outcomes in the course of study. In this chapter, we explore the major issues to be considered when planning long-term units and daily lesson plans.

 Unit Planning

A **unit** is a carefully planned set of learning experiences that are designed to address one or several goals and objectives over time. Generally, units are long term in that they may take several class periods or even several weeks to complete. However, there is no rule for the length of a unit—a unit may be taught in a couple of days, but it is not unusual for one to be planned so that it takes 3 or 4 weeks to complete. For example, a teacher may choose to insert a 3-day miniunit on fractals in a geometry course but design a 4-week unit on similar and congruent triangles later in the same course. A unit contains a few or several daily lesson plans, carefully sequenced to develop the goals and objectives of the unit. Following are some examples of secondary and middle school mathematics units and the topics of daily lessons within them. The individual topics may take 1 or more days to develop within the unit:

 SAMPLE UNIT 1

UNIT TOPIC: Probability
DAILY LESSON TOPICS INCLUDE:

Introduction: Explorations involving experimental probability

Probabilities in a real-world setting (e.g., weather forecasts and games)

Permutations and combinations to determine sample spaces

Calculating theoretical probabilities

Independent and dependent events—conditional probabilities

A geometric look at probability

Wrap-up: Review and discussion of the misuse of data in society

SAMPLE UNIT 2

UNIT TOPIC: Geometry/Right Triangles
DAILY LESSON TOPICS INCLUDE:

Introduction: Review of classification of right, obtuse, and acute triangles

Exploring right triangles (acute angles are complementary, etc.)

The Pythagorean Theorem

Converse and corollaries of the Pythagorean Theorem

Pythagorean Triples and patterns

The Distance Formula (and its proof, using the Pythagorean Theorem)

Simple right-triangle trigonometry (sine, cosine, tangent relationships)

Wrap-up: Review and stage setting for next unit on congruent triangles

▼ SAMPLE UNIT 3

UNIT TOPIC: Discrete Mathematics/Graph Theory
DAILY LESSON TOPICS INCLUDE:

Introduction: Konigsberg Bridge problem and networks

Explorations to determine whether a path is traversible

Euler Paths

Hamiltonian Circuits

Traveling Salesperson problem (i.e., counting the number of possible paths)

Representing circuits as adjacency matrices

Wrap-up: Review and stage setting for the next unit on matrix algebra

As you read these samples, you may have noticed that the first lesson in the unit sometimes opens by posing a problem or set of problems to get the students to begin to explore the topic at hand. Other times, a unit will begin with a brief review to help the students make connections between what is already known and what will be studied over the next several lessons. The last lesson of a unit often provides an opportunity for the teacher to review and to help the students make the connection between the current unit and the next topic to be explored. In a sense, a unit represents a block of teaching time, and it is important to remember that learning took place before the block and will continue after that block of lessons. Consequently, any time that a teacher designs a unit for a class, it is important to consider (1) the knowledge that students will bring to the new topics and (2) how the current unit will connect to the next one. These tasks are not as easy as they may appear on the surface, and, unless they are considered, a unit may be destined to fail.

Let's suppose that you were going to teach a unit on graphing lines. The first question you need to ask is, "What kinds of things do I expect students to know and be able to do by the end of the unit?" Although this inquiry may eventually result in the formulation of specific outcomes or objectives as described in Chapter 5, it is generally desirable to first think about the types of problems that students should be able to solve by the time they complete the unit. (You may recall the idea of "backward design" from Chapter 5, in which consideration of final assessments of student performance can serve as a starting point for designing a unit.) For example, you might look through the teacher's manual of your textbook or some other resource materials and decide that students should recognize the following situations as examples of linear functions:

- The cost of going to see a movie is $5.50. How much does it cost to see x movies?
- You agree to pay back a $250 loan at the rate of $15 per month. How much do you owe on the loan after m months?

- Create a table that relates the temperature in degrees Fahrenheit to the temperature in degrees Celsius.
- Draw a graph that shows how the circumference of a circle, *C*, depends on the diameter, *d*.
- Graph the function $y = 2x - 5$.

Once you have identified the skills and attitudes that the students should possess by the end of the unit, you can begin to think about what they should already know—a starting place—and how you might get them to the desired outcomes. You can begin by asking, "What types of experiences have they already had with linear functions, even if they have not specifically labeled them as such?" You may realize, for example, that every student has at least had exposure to graphing in the coordinate plane and to using a table of values to explore the relationship between two variables. Perhaps a study of the Cartesian plane was even the focus of a previous unit or chapter. The key issue here is to decide what **prerequisite knowledge** the students will need before studying the new unit. For the unit we are discussing, it may be necessary for the student to know how to graph in the plane, how to construct a value table, and how to use a variable to generalize a relationship. As long as you are confident that the students in your class possess those skills, you are ready to proceed. If not, they will need some additional preparation before moving into the new content.

Assuming that your class has the prerequisite knowledge to learn about graphing linear functions, you can ask, "As we explore this unit, what are the key concepts and skills that the students will encounter and need to understand?" Often, this analysis is done in the form of a **conceptual map** or a graphic organizer of how the content in a lesson, unit, semester, course, or even an entire program fits together as a whole. Figure 6.1 presents an example of a conceptual map for the linear function unit.

Figure 6.1 Conceptual Map for a Unit on Linear Functions

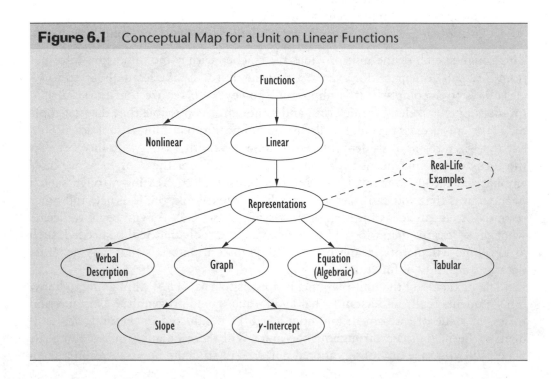

This conceptual map provides a visual "feel" for how all of the pieces of the unit fit together. The map is not only useful for planning, but students also find that this type of graphic helps them to appreciate the whole unit because students tend to get caught up in the details of a unit and lose the forest for the trees. A map may be presented at the beginning of the unit, as a review, or as an assignment to encourage students to think about the connections among content areas they have been studying. In the map in Figure 6.1, the unit focuses on linear functions and their multiple representations. In the unit, the student will develop the notion that some functions are linear but others are not and that a linear function can be represented through a verbal description, in tabular form, as an equation, or as a graph. Furthermore, students will explore the concepts of slope and y-intercept of a linear function and will make connections to the real-life uses of linear functions throughout the unit.

Once the unit is mapped out on paper, several questions become relevant and may be dealt with in no particular order:

- In what order should the key concepts be sequenced?
- What kinds of experiences should the students have to help them learn these concepts?
- How many lessons do I estimate it will take to accomplish the goals and objectives for the unit?
- What materials and tools will I need to support the lessons in this unit?

After reflecting on the map, you may decide that the sequence and timing for the unit would be as follows:

- Introduction: An exploration of real-life linear functions (2 days)
- Expressing linear functions as tables and graphs by hand (2 days)
- Exploring linear functions on the graphing calculator (1 day)
- Writing equations to describe linear functions (2 days)
- Examining the slope of a line (1 day)
- Discovering slope-intercept form (1 day)
- Linear versus nonlinear functions (1 day)
- Putting the pieces together: Four representations of a function (2 days)

This rough sketch of the unit provides the teacher with some important information. You can anticipate, for example, that the unit will take from about 10 to 15 class days to accomplish. It is important, however, to realize that the unit plan provides only a skeletal framework, and although it is possible that the first topic may take only 1 class period, the discussion of linear and nonlinear functions could expand—as a result of student interest—into 3 days rather than 1. Remember that the focus of the unit needs to be on the *student* and not the *content* as we have emphasized throughout this book. Another advantage to creating a rough sketch of the unit is that you can start to research your textbook, the Internet, and other resources to locate ideas for each of the lessons in the unit. As you begin to decide what those lessons might look like, you can list the tools that will be needed, such as graphing calculators, graph paper, and hands-on materials that may generate data for the study of functions.

The next step of the unit-planning process is to ask, "How am I going to know if my students really understand what I will teach them in this unit?" This question raises the issue of assessment and how it will be conducted in the unit. Will students write in journals throughout the unit? Will there be any quizzes along the way? Will you take any observational notes? Will students be assessed on a team project on linear functions, or will all of the work be done individually? Will there be a final test at the end of the unit? If there is a final test, are you certain that it will show you who has really mastered the objectives? A plan for assessing student progress should be roughed out as part of the planning process, keeping in mind that the best way to get a total picture of student understanding is to use multiple methods of assessment rather than restricting student assessment to a quiz or final test. Assessment is discussed in detail in Chapters 10 and 11.

The final decision to be made when crafting the total unit plan is to consider where students will move after its completion. You should ask yourself, "Once we have completed this unit, what is the next logical step in the students' learning sequence?" You have several options, and one is not necessarily better than another. For example, students in this unit on graphing linear equations might move on to study nonlinear functions, such as quadratics and exponential functions. Or you may choose to take them into a study of simultaneous equations, beginning with a graphing method and working toward more symbolic approaches, such as substitution or addition and subtraction methods. Or you may want to use this unit as a springboard to the study of function notation (e.g., $f(x)$) and to make generalizations about graphs of a variety of function types. To help you make this decision, you have a number of resources available to you, not the least of which is the textbook. However, considerable caution should be used here; a textbook is useful for providing direction and ideas, but it should not be considered the final word, as was emphasized in Chapter 5. Just because your textbook moves from graphing linear functions to studying simultaneous equations does not necessarily mean that your class has to go there. When all is said and done, you are the curricular leader in the classroom, and much is left to you in terms of deciding what sequence is appropriate for your class. Unless you teach in a district that follows a strict curriculum map that all are required to follow, administrators generally are not as concerned with how you sequence the content and use the book as they are with ensuring that you are teaching to the concepts and skills outlined in your course of study. Throughout the unit, keep your eyes and ears open—often, students ask leading questions that can assist the teacher in making decisions. For example, they might ask, "Do you ever need to graph two functions on the same set of axes?" You may be able to use this question to lead the class into a unit on simultaneous equations.

The following chart summarizes the major questions a teacher needs to ask when planning a unit of study:

UNIT-PLANNING QUESTIONS

- What kinds of things do I expect students to know and be able to do by the end of the unit? (goals and objectives)
- What types of experiences have they already had with this topic, even if they have not specifically labeled them as such? (prerequisite knowledge)
- As we explore this unit, what are the key concepts and skills the students will encounter and need to understand? (goals and objectives)
- In what order should the key concepts be sequenced? (sequencing)
- What kinds of experiences should the students have to help them learn these concepts? (lessons)
- How many lessons do I think it will take to accomplish my goals for the unit? (sequencing and timing)
- What materials and tools will I need to support the lessons in this unit? (tools)

> - How am I going to know if my students really understand what I want them to know after completing this unit? (assessment)
> - Once we have completed this unit, what is the next logical step in the students' learning sequence? (sequencing)

As a final note, it is important to realize that teachers do not necessarily go through this type of detailed unit planning for every unit in every class—time simply doesn't always allow it. Many textbook authors have already carefully considered the design of units included in the books, and teacher's manuals frequently discuss prerequisite knowledge, a suggested sequence, a list of outcomes, and so forth, so that a teacher is not really starting from scratch when planning a unit. In fact, the NSF-funded curricular materials described in Chapter 5 are generally packaged in predesigned units that have already been field tested to ensure that students make the connections, provide accurate estimates for the amount of time

How Would You React

S C E N A R I O

A note is being passed in your mathematics class, and you see it being handed from one student to another. Your response is to

a. Let it go.

b. Ask the student to put the note away.

c. Confiscate the note and destroy it.

d. Confiscate the note, read it, and then throw it away.

e. Notify the student's counselor, an administrator, and/or a parent so that others are aware that the student was passing a note in your class.

f. Other.

D I S C U S S I O N

Almost every teacher, at one point or another, has to deal with the classroom management issue of note passing in class. As students enter the middle school years, they become more social and prone to want to communicate with one another, even if it means breaking class rules such as writing notes or texting. (Another popular way for students to communicate is to type a message onto the screen of a graphing calculator and hand it to another student, disguising the note as an attempt to help another student with a problem!) To let a note go or to simply allow the student to put it away may communicate to the student that the teacher doesn't view the note as a distraction worthy of action. However, to make a "big deal" of the note may give the issue more attention than it deserves and actually cause more of a distraction than the note itself.

A true story shared among teachers involves a student passing a note in a high school geometry class. Rather than asking the student to put the note away, the teacher confiscated it and, after class, opened the folded paper. Folded inside the paper were two illegal pills—drugs were being passed in the classroom by way of "sending notes." In another case, a teacher took a note away from a student, glanced over it after class, and realized that the student was considering suicide. That teacher was able to contact a guidance counselor to take immediate action to help the student. Both of these teachers learned important lessons: Even something as innocent as a note may be more serious than it appears. Certainly, part of the decision of how you respond to this situation will depend on how well you know the student who is passing the note. As with any classroom management situation, a firm, consistent response should be the rule of thumb.

As you think about this scenario, you may also want to consider how the lesson itself may have propagated the writing of notes in the first place. A lesson without clear objectives, as well as a lesson that is primarily lecture oriented, can lead to off-task behaviors by students. Not only does research advocate the use of hands-on lessons but also students actively engaged in activities are far less likely to behave unacceptably. When planning a lesson, the teacher needs to consider the importance of keeping students involved in the lesson. This active involvement, in a sense, gives the students little "down time" in which to write or pass notes, to send text messages, or to cause any sort of disruptions.

the units will take, and describe the possible concerns that students will raise when they encounter the content of the unit. However, keeping in mind that a textbook's objectives are unlikely to be a perfect match for the course of study in your district, it is important not to assume that a preplanned unit is usable as is—modifications are inevitable as you consider the background of *your* students and the content of *your* course of study. A key to effective teaching is to work in harmony with the textbook, supplementing it with activities from outside resources when necessary and omitting sections or problems that do not advance objectives in the course of study. Similarly, teacher's manuals and resource books feature tips and suggestions for individual lessons, but they need to be regarded as just that—tips and suggestions; ultimately, teachers should tailor the ideas to fit the needs of their classes. In the next section, we explore the process of writing individual lesson plans.

Lesson Planning

Imagine inviting 25 children to your house to celebrate a younger sibling's birthday without having thought through what you wanted them to do. They arrive at your house to find that there are no organized games, few decorations, a cake but no forks or napkins, and no set ending time. What would happen? Most likely, you would end up with 25 screaming children looking for things to do and getting into a lot of trouble. Although the party may have been well intentioned, and the focus of the day was clear—to celebrate a birthday—the fact that it was not organized and prepared for in detail could very well have led to disaster. Similarly, when we walk into the classroom each day as teachers, we need not only a focus in terms of what we want the students to accomplish and be able to do, but also a blueprint for the class period—a road map of sorts—with details on how to most effectively spend class time. The document that details our objectives and the day's activities is referred to as the **lesson plan**. As we discussed in the previous section, the lesson plan should fit into a longer-range unit plan, flowing logically from the previous day's activities and preparing the students for future lessons. The effectiveness of a lesson depends significantly on the care with which the lesson plan is prepared. Although an excellent plan does not ensure a powerful lesson, you can be almost certain that the lack of a focused, detailed lesson generally spells disaster for the classroom teacher.

Let's think further about the road map analogy. When you set off in a car to travel from City A to City B, you have a route in mind. However, the actual route traveled may be very different from what was intended as shown in Figure 6.2.

We often encounter detours that force us off the intended path or onto side roads that are too tempting to be ignored. Consequently, we may begin at City A and end up at City B, but the roads driven are sometimes unplanned. Likewise, a good lesson plan sketches out a beginning point and an objective or list of objectives for the class period as well as a set of instructions for how to get a class to where the teacher wants it to go. However, the teacher needs to be flexible enough to recognize that there may be changes along the way—detours caused by unplanned student misconceptions or side trips suggested by questions or comments from the students. Midstream in a lesson, a student may ask a question that

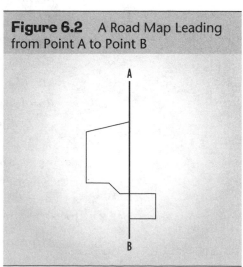

Figure 6.2 A Road Map Leading from Point A to Point B

leads to a **teachable moment**—a point at which the timing is perfect for addressing an issue other than what was intended in the lesson. Consider the following classroom situation mentioned briefly in Chapter 4.

A class of high school sophomores has been studying right triangles and leading up to a discussion of the Pythagorean Theorem. The teacher, Mr. Marks, has asked students to draw five right triangles and to measure the lengths of their sides to the nearest millimeter, square the lengths of the sides, and see if they can find a pattern developing. After about 15 minutes, Josette raises her hand:

Josette: I think I found it! When you add two of the numbers together, after you square them, you almost get the square of the third side.

Mr. Marks: Almost? What do you mean?

Josette: Well, it's like I get the feeling that it should be equal to the square of the third side, but the numbers aren't perfect.

Mr. Marks: Why not?

Sam: We noticed that too . . . it's because our rulers aren't exact enough, so you'll always miss it by a little.

Mr. Marks: How many people saw that pattern? (several students raise their hands)

Terri: We noticed that it didn't work for just "any" two sides . . . it's always the hypotenuse that when you square it equals the squares of the other two added together.

At this point, Mr. Marks feels as though his lesson has gone as intended. Time is running short, and he has planned to assign several practice problems for homework in which students will be given two sides in a right triangle and asked to calculate the length of the third side. Then Jason raises his hand:

Jason: Okay, so when we know it's a right triangle, we can square each of the sides, and the two legs added together will equal the hypotenuse squared, right?

Mr. Marks: Is that the pattern you were all seeing?

Jason: Yeah, but we were wondering . . . what if it's not a right triangle?

Sarah: Then, they wouldn't be equal anymore. So, it would be an acute triangle!

Jason: How do you know it wouldn't be obtuse?

Sarah: Well, I guess it could be, but I don't know.

Josette: That's a good point. We know that if it's a right triangle, $a^2 + b^2 = c^2$, but what if we discover that $a^2 + b^2 > c^2$?

Mr. Marks: Good question. Does anyone have any ideas?

Randy: I don't know, but it's possible that the sum could be less than the c-squared too, you know. But I'm not sure if that has any significance. I guess I'm a little confused now.

At this point, there are only 5 minutes remaining in the period. Mr. Marks can either work through an example with the class in which they are given two sides of a right triangle and have to calculate the third, or he can let go of his lesson plan to focus on student interests. He decides to choose the latter:

Mr. Marks: Well, you have certainly hit on an interesting idea here, group. Tonight, I would like for you to draw three different acute triangles and three different obtuse triangles on a piece of paper. Measure and square the side on all six of your triangles, and see if you notice any patterns for these. Maybe in tomorrow's class we can draw some conclusions about what happens when we have something other than a right triangle to work with.

Student participation is critical to the success of a lesson and can bring about teachable moments.

As the bell rings, and the class leaves the room, Mr. Marks knows that his objective for the day was not met. He had intended to make the point about how the Pythagorean Theorem could be used and allow students to practice the skill as an assignment. Instead, he took advantage of a teachable moment and allowed the students to lead the lesson in a direction in which they were interested. In the homework assignment, which he created on the spot, students will explore and most likely discover two important corollaries to the Pythagorean Theorem—that when the sum of the squares of the shorter sides is greater than the square of the longest side, the triangle is acute, and when the opposite is true, the triangle is obtuse. This can also be demonstrated with a simple model of two straws connected with a twist tie. As Figure 6.3 illustrates, when the straws are at a 90° angle, the Pythagorean Theorem holds true. If the angle is made greater than 90°, but the lengths of the short sides are fixed, the long side gets longer; therefore, the obtuse angle makes $c^2 > a^2 + b^2$. But when the angle is collapsed to less than 90°, the acute angle makes the third side shorter, so $c^2 < a^2 + b^2$. Thus, the students visually prove these corollaries for themselves.

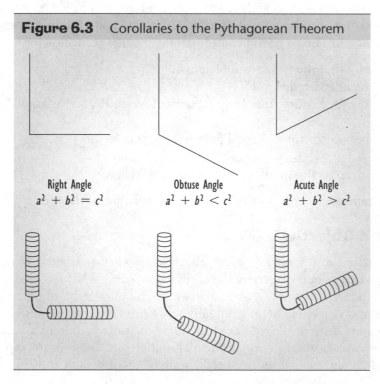

Figure 6.3 Corollaries to the Pythagorean Theorem

Right Angle
$a^2 + b^2 = c^2$

Obtuse Angle
$a^2 + b^2 < c^2$

Acute Angle
$a^2 + b^2 > c^2$

The important question is: How do you feel about Mr. Marks switching his direction midstream and following the student questions rather than his lesson plan? The answer probably depends on whether you are teaching a lesson plan or teaching real students in a mathematics class. When interest and curiosity have been generated, it is desirable to follow the path that the students view as important and worth exploring. So, we need to keep in perspective that a lesson plan is just that—a plan. It must be focused, with objectives and specific activities, but also be flexible enough to allow for modifications as students react to the activities. And, as we discuss in the next chapter, the real issue in this example is the task that the teacher provided for the class. It was during the process of working on the task of drawing and measuring five right triangles and generating subsequent classroom discussion (discourse) that students began to raise questions of their own. Instead of the teacher telling students what they were supposed to know, student opinions and questions were valued and used to redirect the instruction. Mr. Marks's lesson plan for the next day will need to be carefully crafted to give students an opportunity to discuss their conjectures about acute and obtuse triangles, while also taking the time to put some closure to a statement of the Pythagorean Theorem and explore some of its applications. So, in the end, Mr. Marks's objectives will be met, but like the road map analogy, the class will not follow the roads that he had intended.

There is no universal structure or framework for lesson planning; however, most teachers use the following **components of a lesson plan**: general considerations, goals and objectives, materials and resources, motivation, lesson procedure (including transition statements and ideas for meeting the needs of all students), closure, extension (optional), and assessment. After teaching a lesson, a teacher should also reflect on its implementation, which is discussed at the end of this chapter. We now explore each of these major components.

General Considerations

Because the reader of a teacher's lesson plan is often an administrator, an evaluator, or a substitute teacher, we begin by identifying some general information that frames the lesson. These general considerations include the following:

- The date that the lesson will be taught
- The intended grade level
- The intended course title (e.g., Integrated Math III, Sixth Grade Mathematics, etc.)
- The amount of time allotted for teaching this lesson (e.g., the length of the period)
- The approximate number of students in the class

These five items serve as a starting point for the writing of the lesson plan.

Goals and Objectives

As we discussed in Chapter 5, every effective instructional episode begins with clearly stated goals and objectives that delineate exactly what it is that the student is expected to feel, know, or be able to do at the end of a lesson or unit. Ordinarily, these goals and objectives are not actually written by the teacher; instead, they are pulled from the district-adopted graded course of study or from a document such as the *Common Core State Standards*. The goals are big-picture statements of learning outcomes; objectives are specific statements of what a student should feel, know, or be able to do. A reasonable rule of thumb is to include at least 1, but not more than 3, goals for a given lesson, as well as from 1 to 5 objectives. The number of goals or objectives for a lesson will depend on the content of the lesson, the needs of the students, and the amount of time the teacher has for the lesson. A teacher, for example, who is planning for a class period that is blocked for 90 to 120 minutes every other day is likely to address more objectives in a single class period than a teacher planning for a traditional schedule with a 40- to 50-minute slot of teaching time. Also, a lesson intended to help students make connections among several mathematical ideas might have more objectives than a plan that addresses a single main idea.

The goals and objectives should be the basis of all unit and lesson planning, and everything, from the activities or tasks selected to the way that the class is run, should flow from a statement of what is expected of students. Remember, also, that teaching mathematics transcends content and should include processing skills, as described in Chapter 1. So, when thinking about the intended outcomes for the lesson, a teacher should always be thinking about how the lesson will advance the problem-solving skills of the students, as well as the other processes and mathematical practices. In a lesson plan, the goals are often directly linked with specific NCTM STANDARDS or Common Core State Standards and should provide direction for the lesson, keeping both the teacher and the students focused on the key issues. It is not unusual for a teacher to actually explain the main goals and objectives to a class when initiating a new unit or lesson to make clear to everyone what is expected of them and what they are intended to learn. Some teachers even present a conceptual map, such as the one shown in Figure 6.1, to help students visualize the direction that the unit will take.

Materials and Resources

When an activity is selected for a lesson, it is likely to involve the use of tools, such as calculators, rulers, graph paper, a videotape, and so forth (see Chapter 7 for further discussion of tools). The lesson plan, therefore, should completely describe the materials necessary for the presentation. When appropriate, it should also refer to the location of materials and how many are required per class, per learning team, or per student. For example, a plan may state that the lesson requires "6 sets of algebra tiles (1 for each group of 4 students), graph paper (1 sheet per student), and 6 graphing calculators (1 for each group of 4 students)." This listing helps ensure that the activity will be organized and smooth. There is nothing worse than getting to the middle of a lesson and realizing that each student needs a pair of scissors, but you didn't bring a box of scissors today because it wasn't in the plan. As a result, the lesson falls apart, and so does the behavior of your students. So, be prepared by including a detailed listing of materials in the lesson plan.

Also, because many lesson ideas come from outside sources, such as the Internet, journal articles, or resource books, this section of the lesson plan should cite the sources of the activities in the lesson. The URL (Web site location and title), journal article citation, or resource book citation should be included here, along with a copy of any reproducible page (e.g., an activity page or worksheet) that the class will be required to use in the lesson from a source other than the textbook. This component communicates to the reader the source of "borrowed" teaching ideas that are included in the next three sections of the lesson.

Motivation

Every good lesson should open with an attention grabber that gets students thinking about the topic for the day's lesson while also sparking their curiosity and interest, which will make them want to engage in the learning process. Let's face it: How excited do you get when the teacher walks in and says, "Good morning. Open your books to page 147 and take out your homework"? If students are invited to engage in an interesting lesson right away, you have them in the palm of your hand. Otherwise, your students may shut down within the first 5 minutes, and you will have lost them for the entire period. So, arguably the most important task of the planning process is to think of a short activity that will motivate the lesson.

Sometimes, the **motivation**—also referred to as initiatory activity, engagement, or springboard—can be a book that is displayed or partially read to a class; at other times, it's a problem that is posed, a newspaper clipping that is displayed, or some other visual aid or activity that evokes interest and curiosity. For example, one teacher who was about to conduct a lesson on three-dimensional geometry brought in a sack of mineral crystals, leading the students to a discussion about how geologists classify minerals based on the shape of their crystals as they occur in nature. The students were fascinated by the shape of calcite and quartz crystals and were immediately drawn into the geometry lesson introduced by the solids. Another teacher, wishing to motivate a discussion of the trigonometric functions, presented the class with a graph of the average monthly high temperatures in their area over the course of 3 years. As the students viewed the graph of the temperatures, they recognized the cyclic behavior of the weather, and the teacher had set the stage for the discussion of the sine and cosine curves as examples of periodic functions. An example is shown for the city of Chicago between June of 2008 and June of 2011 in Figure 6.4.

A third teacher brought in an advertisement from a local department store and, displaying it to the class, asked what it means for the store to "take off an additional 20 percent on all sale items."

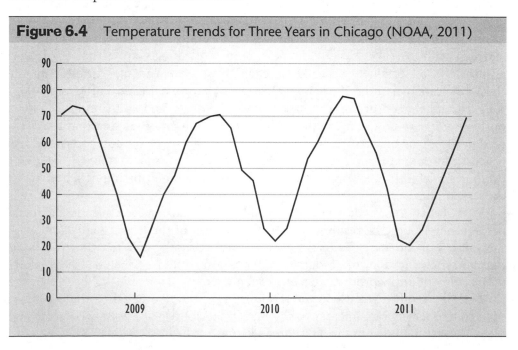

Figure 6.4   Temperature Trends for Three Years in Chicago (NOAA, 2011)

The motivation for a lesson can be brief, usually lasting only a few minutes, but it should be linked to the lesson content and give the students a reason for studying what they are about to encounter. The rest of the lesson becomes considerably easier to teach if the students are engaged from the beginning. However, most experienced teachers find the motivation to be the most difficult part of the lesson to plan because you have to know your students well enough to understand what will get their attention and make them want to engage in the lesson for the day. This is one of many reasons why it is important for teachers to have a firm grasp of adolescent development and learning psychology. Keep in mind that opening a lesson by stating that "Today, we're going to study rational functions," or "We're going to study polygons today, and I think you'll find them interesting," or, simply, "Take out your homework" is not motivational, and you will probably turn off your students from the start.

Lesson Procedure

The **lesson procedure,** a set of instructions for the teacher, is the heart of the lesson plan. Generally, the lesson procedure is an outline, a step-by-step description of what the teacher and the students will do in the lesson. The procedure should be detailed enough to give the teacher very specific directions on what to do and flexible enough to allow for student interactions and redirections along the way. The teacher writes a lesson plan for personal use in the classroom. However, particularly when you are first learning to write lessons, it is often useful to think of the audience as the principal or a supervisor, who may walk into class that day and want to read about what you are doing. Or think of the audience as a substitute teacher, who will be called on to teach your lesson if you are ill. You certainly can't make any major assumptions about a principal or substitute's ability to read into a lesson and ad lib. The plan needs to contain carefully written procedures so that one could pick it up and teach it without wondering what the writer meant by a particular step. Consequently, vague phrases such as "show the students how the distance formula works" should be avoided because this statement does not help the teacher to prepare for *how* to develop the distance formula with a class. Likewise, instead of a step that says "ask the students some questions about the diagram," the plan should include a list of specific questions to ask the class during that step of the lesson.

It is important that students recognize the connection between parts of the lesson and the sequencing of examples and experiences. Therefore, the lesson plan should include throughout the lesson procedure **transition statements** that the teacher can use to assist students in moving from one activity to the next. Something as simple as saying, "Let's see how the game we just played relates to number theory" can help students recognize that the discussion will shift from a game to a discussion about the Real Numbers. If you just say, "Take out your notebooks" after playing a game, students will have no idea what the focus of the next discussion will be. The beginning teacher often includes transition statements throughout the lesson plan, before and after each major activity, so that the plan progresses smoothly and coherently. Without these transition statements, the lesson can feel very choppy to the students, who might see it as nothing more than a series of disconnected activities and pieces. Following are additional tips to keep in mind when writing the lesson procedure component:

- Include statements about what the *student* will do as well as what the *teacher* will do throughout the lesson. A common flaw of lesson plans is that they often focus almost entirely on the teacher's actions, virtually ignoring the anticipated role of the learners in the lesson. A grid can even be used for planning, where each statement about what the teacher does is complemented by a statement of what the student does.

- Include descriptions of how students will be assessed on their understanding throughout the lesson. For example, if the teacher will be observing students as they work, or students will be asked to conduct a free writing in their journals during the lesson, these steps should be included in the procedure section. Chapters 10 and 11 address the area of assessment in detail.
- The lesson should demonstrate flexibility. This flexibility is often expressed with statements indicating that "if the students do X, then . . . but if they do Y, then. . . ." Remember that the plan is a road map, and teachers need to be prepared to take side trips that students suggest.
- Recognizing that the needs of students will differ within a class, include modifications that will be necessary to address various cultural or learning differences in the lesson. The issue of differentiating instruction and suggestions on how to try to meet the needs of all students is discussed in detail in Chapter 12.

Veteran teachers become very adept at writing plans as outlines in less detail, but beginning teachers need to spell out specific examples, questions, and comments to make the lesson flow. We discuss how veteran teachers "lesson image" instead of lesson plan later in this chapter.

Closure

When the bell rings as the teacher is in the middle of an example, the class is left hanging, and the teacher does not always know whether the students understood the major concepts. Just as an effective lesson begins with a motivational activity, the lesson should be carefully planned to conclude with a logical wrap-up activity, known as the **closure**. The closure gives the teacher an opportunity to assess the progress of the students through a series of specific questions, a journal prompt, or one final problem to solve. In many cases, the closure is a problem or set of questions that is linked to the original issue or problem posed in the motivation at the beginning of the lesson. Students view the lesson as a unified whole if the opening and closure are related in some way. For example, the teacher who began the lesson with an advertisement from the local department store might close the lesson by displaying three actual prices from the ad, asking the students to determine the new price after an additional 20 percent discount.

In other cases, teachers use the closure as a time to raise a final thought or question that may set the tone for the next class period. For example, a teacher who is concluding a lesson on measures of central tendency—mean, median, and mode—might put up a transparency bearing this statement:

A person can drown in a lake with an average depth of one inch.

Then, students could either be invited to comment on the statement in the last 5 minutes of class, or be asked to reflect on it in a journal entry as a homework assignment. Class-ending statements such as "Close your books," "Your homework is . . . ," or "See you tomorrow" should not be confused with the closure of the lesson; they are statements that a teacher might make after the lesson has been concluded.

Extension

The extension component of a lesson plan is an activity that provides the teacher with an option if students catch on more quickly than anticipated or are in need of an additional challenge. Veteran teachers know that there is probably nothing worse than having a classroom full of students with nothing to do when there are 15 minutes to fill after a lesson has concluded. Sometimes, teachers in this position will ask students to begin their homework, but most students resist this request and proceed to get into trouble. If an extension is planned, and it's clear that the lesson will run short, then the teacher has an option on how to proceed. The extension might be another deeper problem to explore or might involve an examination of a different representation of a problem solved in class. As such, the extension goes beyond the lesson and is only used if needed. If the teacher does not get to this activity, it can always be moved into the following day's lesson or simply deleted altogether. As a general rule of thumb, it's better to overplan with an extra activity "in your back pocket" than to have extra time and wish that you had brought something more for the students to do.

Assessment

A teacher should think through the process of how to most accurately measure student understanding whenever planning a lesson. As the lesson proceeds, students are often informally assessed by simple observation and monitoring of their answers to questions. In turn, these *formative* assessments help the teacher to decide how much time to spend on an idea, whether to skip or resequence steps or the lesson plan, whether to use the extension, and so forth. More formal assessments, such as carefully designed checklists or journal entries, may also be used in the lesson. Assessment of student understanding is pivotal in the teaching process and, therefore, planning for assessment in the written lesson plan is essential. These assessments are often summarized as a separate statement near the end of the lesson plan. The main idea here is that the lesson plan began with a listing of objectives to be achieved by the students, so it is important to identify, in advance, how the teacher will know if the learners have met those outcomes. Additional detail on assessment strategies is provided in Unit 4.

The lesson plan components described here are generalizations of how most teachers plan their class time. However, it is not unusual to find that three teachers in a mathematics department have three different formats for writing their plans, but the elements described here are typically included. A lesson-planning format that is popular among science teachers, for example, is called a **5-E lesson plan**. In this formatting model, the plan includes five stages: engage, explore, explain, extend (or elaborate), and evaluate. Although, at first glance, these steps may seem different from the ones we just discussed, "engage" is another word for "motivate"; "explore" and "explain" are part of the lesson procedure and closure steps; "extend" is, of course, somewhat analogous to the extension (although it is not viewed as an optional step in the 5-E lesson plan); and "evaluate" is the assessment component. Activities in the NCTM *Navigations* books (discussed in Chapter 5) include three steps—engage, explore, and extend. So, the language varies from one content area or source to another, but the basic components of a lesson plan are always essentially the same.

While planning a hands-on lesson, teachers frequently include some sort of activity that involves the collection and analysis of data. The use of technology can enhance lessons so that students can collect considerably more data in a shorter period of time than would be possible solely through the use of manipulatives. Consider this example:

> *A cereal company produces a set of 6 commemorative cards containing pictures of wild animals. The cereal boxes have a message on the outside saying:* **Special free card inside. Collect all 6!**

This classic probability problem centers around students trying to determine how many boxes of cereal they should buy at the store to make it almost inevitable that they will actually collect all 6 cards. Of course, one could buy 6 boxes and get a different card in each, but this is possible, not probable. One could purchase 100 boxes of cereal and still get only 5 of the 6 cards, but if equal numbers of the cards are randomly distrib-

uted, this isn't very likely either. So, how many boxes will maximize the chances? Probably the best way to approach the problem is to have students model the purchasing of boxes of cereal and record their results. Using a bag with 6 different-colored cubes in it, students can draw a cube, record the color, replace it in the bag, and continue this process until they have chosen all 6 colors at least once. Another way to model the problem is to roll a fair number cube until all 6 faces have shown at least once. In either case, students collect classroom data to refine their predictions about the optimal number of boxes of cereal to purchase.

Another way to have students model the problem is to visit the problem on the Internet. At http://mste.illinois.edu/reese/cereal/cereal.php, there is a simulation of the problem. Students select the total number of cards that a child would want to collect, and, by clicking on RUN SIMULATION, activate software that generates and logs the data so that students can use the Internet as their software source. The software runs a random selection process and tells the students how many boxes of cereal were needed to collect all of the cards. Figure 6.5 shows an example in which 19 boxes of cereal were needed for the buyer to eventually collect all 6 cards.

Figure 6.5   A Simulation of the Cereal Box Problem on the Internet

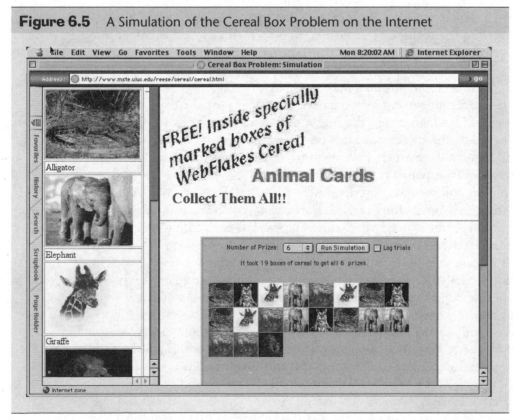

(Reprinted by permission from George Reese from www.mste.uiuc.edu/reese/cereal/cereal.html)

Many such Web sites contain software that sketch graphs, draw fractal designs, compute statistics, run simulations, and perform a host of other applications. The software is often referred to as an *applet* (mini application). Therefore, the school does not have to purchase the software; it is already available and able to be run from a site on the Web. Some sites also contain free software packages (sometimes called "shareware") that can be downloaded onto a computer and run locally by students in a school.

Another way to simulate the problem without using computers or the Internet is by running software on a graphing calculator. An application program called Probability Simulator is available for the TI-84 Plus SE graphing calculator. The home screen, shown in Figure 6.6, shows that the software can be used to simulate tossing coins, rolling number cubes, choosing marbles, spinning spinners, drawing cards, or simply generating random numbers.

By selecting the second menu item, a student can count how many times the number cube has to be rolled before all 6 numbers appear at least one time. Again, the simulation could be done by hand, but the calculator or

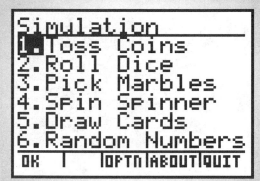

Figure 6.6 Simulating Probability on a Graphing Calculator

computer simulation allows the students to gather more data in a shorter period of time than is possible using manipulatives alone. Often, teachers allow individual students to use a physical model to collect a few samples and then to turn to the technology to generate a larger pool of data for analysis by the class.

Sample Lesson Plans

In order to make you think about the issue of lesson planning, two plans are presented here. Sample Lesson Plan 1 is an example of a flawed plan. As you read it, think about the components of effective lesson planning as discussed and make a list of potential weaknesses in this plan. Sample Lesson Plan 2 is an example of a well-constructed lesson plan. Again, think about what makes the plan useful and complete. In both cases, a standard lesson planning format has been used.

SAMPLE LESSON PLAN

1

Name: Brian Pack
Date: 11/11/12
Grade Level: 7
Course: Seventh Grade Mathematics
Time Allotted: 45 minutes
Number of Students: 23

I. **Goal(s):**
- To develop the concepts of perimeter/circumference and area

II. **Objective(s):**
- The student will learn about π.
- The student will work with another student.
- The student will use string to measure circles.
- The student will use a calculator to find the ratio of circumference to diameter.
- The student will complete a worksheet involving the measurements taken from several circles.

III. **Materials and Resources:**
  - Several circular objects
  - Pieces of string
  - Calculators

IV. **Motivation**
  1. Hold up a piece of string and say, "What do you think we'll use this string for today?"
  2. Explain to the class that they will be using it to measure the circumferences of several circles today.

V. **Lesson Procedure**
  3. Have students work in pairs. Give each pair of students a piece of string, a ruler, and a calculator.
  4. Distribute copies of the worksheet that contains lines on which to record the diameters and circumferences of the circles. Show the students where the circles are and tell them to measure the diameter and circumference of each. Then they should write those numbers down on the worksheets and use their calculators to figure out the ratio of the 2 numbers.
  5. Ask if there are any questions.
  6. After the students have finished collecting all of their data, ask the class several questions to see what they noticed.
  7. Tell the class that the actual value of π is about 3.14. Do several examples of circumference problems using π.

VI. **Closure**
  8. Give the class their homework assignment. They will do page 89, numbers 1–22. If they don't understand how to do the problems, do a couple of them on the board.
  9. Ask if there are any final questions before the period is over.

VII. **Extension**

VIII. **Assessment**

Circulate throughout the classroom as students work. Ask questions to check understanding.

SAMPLE LESSON PLAN
2

Name: Katherine Bronson
Date: 10/2/12
Grade Level: 9
Course: Algebra I
Time Allotted: 50 minutes
Number of Students: 27

I. **Goal(s):**
  - To develop an understanding of functions as applied to authentic data (NCTM algebra standard: "Understand patterns, relations, and functions") (NCTM, 2000, p. 296)

II. **Objective(s):**
  - The student will collect and organize real-life data from an experiment.

- The student will represent a function as a table, an equation, a graph, and with a verbal description.
- The student will describe the meaning of the slope and *y*-intercept for a linear function involving real-life data.

III. **Materials and Resources:**
- Each team of 3 students will need (1) a meter stick; (2) a superball, a golf ball, a Ping-Pong ball, and a tennis ball; (3) a sheet of centimeter graph paper; and (4) a ruler.
- Each student will need a graphing calculator.
- The teacher will need a superball and 27 playing cards—one each of a 6, 7, 8, 9, 10, jack, queen, king, and ace in the suits of hearts, diamonds, and clubs.

IV. **Motivation**
1. Bounce a superball on the floor and tell the class about how "we used to skip these off the elementary school building when I was a kid" and how the older children would try to throw them on the roof.
2. Raise the question, "But I'm wondering . . . just how 'super' is a superball, really? Does it have more bounce than, say, a golf ball?" (Let the class discuss how they think a superball bounce compares to the bounce of a golf ball.)
3. Ask the class how we might design an experiment to find out. (Lead them to think about how a number of different balls could be dropped from a given height to determine how high they bounce.)

Transition: Explain to the students that they will be working in teams, so I will randomly hand out playing cards to establish the working groups.

V. **Lesson Procedure**
4. Deal out one card to each student, randomly. Ask the students who received the same kinds of cards to sit together (e.g., a 10-team, a king-team, etc.).
5. Describe the experiment that the class is to conduct, as follows: Each team will be given a superball, a golf ball, a Ping-Pong ball, and a tennis ball as well as a meter stick. Placing a meter stick along the wall, each team should drop each ball from at least 5 different heights, and each height should be attempted twice for accuracy. Each time, the height from which the ball was dropped and the height to which it bounced should be recorded in a table until 4 data tables—one for each ball—have been produced. Before beginning, each team should have one person in charge of dropping the ball (the one holding a heart), one person to measure the heights (holding a diamond), and one person to record the data in a table (holding a club).
6. Ask the class if they have any questions about the procedure before moving ahead.
7. Ask the person in charge of dropping the ball to come to the front table and pick up a meter stick and one of each of the four balls. After collecting all necessary data, each team should return to the front of the room for further instructions. Teams should now collect their data. (Circulate through each of the teams, listening to comments and keeping students on-task. It may be helpful to prompt teams to retry some of the drops and/or to attempt more than 5 drops of the ball to more accurately depict the characteristics

of the ball. Record anecdotal notes of significant comments made by individuals or discussions within teams.)

8. As each team returns to the front of the room, give the data recorder a piece of centimeter graph paper and a ruler. The person who recorded the data is to draw a graph of each set of data points, where x is the height from which the ball was dropped and y is the height to which it bounced. The data for all 4 balls should be recorded on the same sheet. The other 2 team members should enter the data into their graphing calculators so that the technology can display the picture as well. The team should then come up with a linear equation that describes the bounce of each of the 4 balls. When all of the groups have finished, each will be asked to identify which ball had the "best bounce" and how they knew that.

9. Allow each of the 9 groups to briefly present its picture and findings to the class. Encourage debate among the class by asking appropriate questions, such as, "Why do you suppose that their golf ball bounced better than yours?" or "Why didn't we all find the same ball to have the best bounce?" (Flexibility will be important here because the data from all five groups may be very similar or very different and require much discussion.)

Transition: "Let's compare the class's data a little more formally now."

10. On the chalkboard, make a table:

	Super	Golf	Ping-Pong	Tennis
Team 1				
Team 2				
Team 3				
Team 4				
etc.				

Ask each group to write down the slope of their equation for each of the 4 balls. As a class, compute the mean slope for each ball and discuss how the class results may have deviated from what individual teams found.

11. Ask the class to state the equations describing the bounce of each ball. What is the meaning of the slope? (They should note that the slope is a ratio, in this case, comparing the amount of bounce per unit of height dropped. Thus, the greater the slope, the steeper the line, and the more bounce the ball has.) What is the y-intercept? (The y-intercepts should all be 0 or very close to 0. This means that if the ball isn't dropped, it doesn't bounce.) Can you use the equation to predict the height each ball would bounce if it were dropped from higher than you actually measured? How? Is this prediction realistic? (Students should recognize that dropping the ball from a mile-high cliff may not have the same result because the data may change dramatically with extremely high or low numbers.)

VI. **Closure**

12. We started the class today by asking whether a superball is really all that super. Do you think so now? Why or why not?

13. Take out your journal and spend the last 5 minutes of class writing a paragraph that starts with the phrase, "The most interesting mathematical idea that I learned today was. . . ."

14. Assign five homework problems from the textbook (p. 86, #2, 3, 5, 8, 10)

VII. **Extension**

If time allows, before Step 11, have students look at the data on their graphing calculators. Using an overhead, enter the class averages for the slopes and have the calculator draw the 4 graphs. Switch back and forth between the equations, tables, and graphs, and use the graphs to trace each function to make predictions about dropping the ball from heights other than those used in the experiment.

VIII. **Assessment**

Assessment in this lesson takes four different forms:

- Anecdotal comments are written on sticky notes as students work in groups (Step 7).
- Specific questions (about slope, y-intercept, etc.) during the class discussion of the data are asked (Step 11), so observation is being used.
- Students conclude the lesson by writing journal entries, which will be read tomorrow to measure their levels of understanding (Step 13).
- Students will complete a five-problem homework assignment that will be discussed and collected tomorrow.

These lessons both use a standard format, as we have discussed in this chapter, but the lessons are very different in terms of what they tell the reader and how they are written. What did you notice as you read them? Suppose that you were a substitute and were called on to teach either of these lessons. Would you consider one to be more clearly written and easier to follow? You might have noticed that both lessons are hands-on and actively involve students in the learning process. The intent here was not to differentiate between teaching philosophies but to illustrate the different ways in which lessons are actually written.

Analysis of Sample Lesson Plan 1

Let's look at Sample Lesson Plan 1. Mr. Pack is teaching a middle school class about circumference and the value of π. Although his overall goal appears reasonable, the objectives are far less useful. For example, the first objective, "The student will learn about π," is vague. What does it mean to "learn about" something? If the purpose of the objective is to say that "the student will define π as the ratio of circumference to diameter in a circle," then it should have been stated as such. As we discussed in Chapter 5, objectives need to be clear and are usually measurable. The other objectives listed in Mr. Pack's lesson are not really worthwhile either. They are simply statements about what the student will *do* in the activities for today's class—work in pairs, use string, use a calculator, and complete a worksheet—rather than statements of what the student should *know* by the end of the lesson. In reality, this lesson only has two major objectives. The first is the student's ability to define π and use it to determine the circumference of a circle, and the second, which should have been included, is that "the student will collect and analyze real-life data from an experiment."

A substitute (or even the teacher who wrote the plan) might find the materials and resources section confusing. First, we do not know what the writer means by "several circular objects." If this item is to include plastic container lids, a pie tin, a bicycle tire, and a quarter, then they should be listed. Otherwise, the teacher would have no idea about which items to gather, how many items to use, and so forth. Also, the materials and resources section does not say how many pieces of string and calculators will be needed. We know that students work in pairs, and because there are 23 students in the class, we can determine that 12 pieces of string and 12 calculators will be needed, but this should have been included in the materials and resources section. Also, the lesson later tells us that students will use a ruler and a worksheet, but neither of these items was included in the materials listing.

What did you think of the motivation for Sample Lesson Plan 1? Did it capture your imagination and make you eager to proceed with the lesson? Probably not. The teacher could have given the class the diameter of the earth and asked them whether they could figure out the distance around the earth, given this information. When the class realizes that they have no method of doing this, the teacher could proceed by explaining that today's experiment will give them the power to do this by the end of the period and return to that question in the closure. In the lesson procedure, students are to work in pairs, but the reader is not told how those pairs are formed. Are students already seated in pairs, or are they to select their own partner? Or will the teacher assign them to a partner? This needs to be spelled out in the lesson plan. In general, the lesson procedure is vague. For example, in Step 6, the reader is told to "ask the class several questions," but the plan does not list any possible questions. If the teacher plans to ask, for example, "What was the smallest ratio that anyone found?" then this question should be specifically stated; otherwise, the teacher is likely to forget to ask the question. The direction to "do several examples" is another common error of lesson planning by novice teachers. It is not a useful step because the specifics of which examples, how many, and in what sequence are critical to the success of the lesson. If the teacher plans to work two sample problems with the class, then those problems should be written and sequenced in advance, included in the plan, and not left to chance.

Finally, the closure for Sample Lesson Plan 1 does not really close the lesson at all; it is simply a statement of the homework assignment. How does the teacher know whether the students understood the main message for the day? And what does "do a couple of them on the board" mean? The closure is unclear and does not allow the teacher to assess the progress of the students over this lesson. Also, the lesson does not include transition statements at all. The class abruptly moves from a discussion about a piece of string, to measuring circles, to a homework assignment and is in need of teacher statements to ease students from one step of the lesson into the next. Flawed because of a lack of detail, the lesson would be very difficult to implement, and it leaves more questions unanswered than it provides direction for a principal conducting an observation or a substitute replacing an ill teacher.

Analysis of Sample Lesson Plan 2

Sample Lesson Plan 2 is a high school lesson prepared by Ms. Bronson for 27 Algebra I students, focusing on functions and, specifically, the slope and y-intercept of a linear function. The goal is linked to the NCTM Standards, and the objectives are clear in that they contain action statements, with words such as "collect," "organize," "represent," and "describe the meaning." There is enough detail in the materials and resources section to make it useful, including a description of the tools that each student and team will need to conduct the activity. The motivation for Sample Lesson Plan 2 is almost certain to gain the attention of adolescents, as the teacher bounces a superball on the floor and asks students to design an experiment to determine just how "super" it is. In Step 3, the teacher has made a note to herself in terms of where she wants to lead the students in the discussion, so that the stage is set for the lesson procedures that follow. Placing a hint or reminder into a lesson plan can be very helpful, particularly for the novice teacher.

The lesson procedure is very specific in terms of what the teacher and the student will do. For example, playing cards are used to determine randomly selected teams and to assign responsibilities in the project. Contrast this to Sample Lesson Plan 1 in which we were told neither how the pairs were selected nor what the role of each person was to be in the experiment. Notice, also, how Step 7 in Sample Lesson Plan 2 gives the teacher a specific direction about what she is to do as the class is conducting the experiments. By noting that she will "record anecdotal notes," the teacher is reminding herself of the assessment strategy to be used during the class period to ensure that students are on-task and are comprehending the major concepts.

The steps that follow serve as a logical extension to the collection of data. After the students have collected their team data, the lesson is completed by compiling class data and looking for patterns. Again, in Step 11, the teacher has provided herself with a note of what she hopes that students will realize about slopes and y-intercepts, which will be helpful in leading the class discussion. The last step of the lesson is a logical closure, which links the end of the lesson to the first question raised in Step 2 and allows students to reflect in their journals as a means to assessing their understanding. Finally, the teacher of Sample Lesson Plan 2 has included an extension to increase her flexibility. The final section on assessment summarizes the four strategies she will use to measure her students' understanding—anecdotal notes, questioning techniques (observation), a journal entry, and a homework assignment.

Looking at these two lesson plans, you can see how, on the surface, they both appear to be mathematically solid. They both use an appropriate planning format, key in on a couple of major mathematical ideas, and use hands-on, minds-on instructional strategies and technology. However, a careful study of the details reveals that one lesson is vague and leaves much to the imagination of the reader, whereas the other is clear, coherent, and very user friendly. As is true for a blueprint for a house, the more detail we put into the planning process, the more likely it is that we will teach a successful lesson. The following checklist can be used by a teacher in the process of preparing a lesson or by a supervisor who is assessing the components of a teacher's lesson plan. The checklist summarizes the major elements of each component, as described in this chapter.

General Considerations
- Include the date that the lesson will be taught
- Include the intended grade level
- Include the intended course title (e.g., Integrated Mathematics III, Sixth Grade Mathematics, etc.)
- Include the amount of time allotted for teaching the lesson (e.g., the length of the period)
- Include the approximate number of students in the class

Goals and Objectives

- At least 1 (no more than 3) broad goal(s) is/are clearly stated, often linked to NCTM or Common Core State Standards
- Approximately 1 to 5 clear objective(s) is/are stated
- Objectives are measurable and relate to mathematics *content* (as opposed to statements about students working together, playing a game, using a manipulative, etc.)
- Objectives are drawn directly from the local course of study or Standards and coded accordingly (e.g., Geometry, 8.12—indicates the objective is from the Geometry Strand, Grade 8, Objective 12)

Materials and Resources

- A complete list of materials needed for the lesson is included
- The materials list is detailed and specific to the class (e.g., "one calculator for each pair of students," rather than simply listing "calculators")
- Ordinary supplies, such as a pencil, textbook, and chalkboard, are assumed and need not be listed
- If any outside resources—such as a Web site, resource book, or journal—have been used as sources for ideas in the lesson, a citation is to be provided in this section (include a complete bibliographic citation with author, publisher, date, etc.)
- If an activity page, worksheet, or other type of handout is to be used in the lesson, it is listed here as a required material, *and* a copy of the page(s) is/are included with the lesson plan

Motivation

- A brief motivational activity is included (usually only a few minutes)
- The activity is designed to capture the interest and curiosity of the students
- The motivation connects in a meaningful way with the mathematical content of the rest of the lesson
- The motivation is not a mundane routine, such as reviewing homework, giving a quiz, passing out manipulatives, or making a statement, such as "Let's talk about triangles"

Lesson Procedure

- A detailed, step-by-step description of what is anticipated to happen in the lesson is outlined
- The procedure is written clearly enough for a principal or substitute teacher to follow
- Progression from one step to the next is logical and mathematically accurate
- Include statements of what the *teacher* will do throughout the lesson (sometimes including "quotes" of what the teacher plans to say, though the plan need not be merely a script)
- Include statements of what the *students* will do throughout the lesson
- Include examples of *assessments* the teacher will use to ensure that students are making sense of the lesson (e.g., observing their work, having students share answers at the chalkboard, students writing in a journal, etc.)
- Demonstrate a constructivist environment by having students actively engaged in the lesson ("hands-on" and "minds-on")
- Key *questions* asked by the teacher are included throughout the procedure section

- Sample problems or any examples to be explored with the class or individually are clearly spelled out (i.e., do *not* simply say "go over a few examples with the class" because it would not be clear to the reader what it means to "go over" or what examples the teacher had in mind)
- Transition statements that contribute to the flow of the lesson are included to connect major sections of the lesson or activities
- Illustrate flexibility by including occasional statements such that "if the students do *X*, then the teacher will do this, but if the students do *Y*, then the teacher will . . ." (do something different)
- Include ideas for differentiating instruction—modifications that will address the diverse needs and learning styles of the students

Closure
- Include a brief conclusion to the lesson (usually less than 10 minutes)
- Assess whether students have achieved the intended outcomes for the lesson
- Lay the groundwork for the next day's lesson
- Possibly relate back to the problem or issue raised in the motivation section
- The closure is not a mundane routine, such as giving a homework assignment, collecting papers, or telling students to "have a good day"

Extension (optional)
- An additional activity is included that can be used in the event that the lesson runs short (either because of a planning error or the inability of students to "catch on" quickly)
- The activity builds or goes into greater depth on an issue raised during the lesson
- Students are challenged to explore a topic more deeply than was originally intended in the lesson

Assessment
- Include a summary of how student understanding will be measured
- The summary illustrates more than one way of assessing student knowledge
- Assessments are woven throughout the lesson (as opposed to being included only near the end or in the lesson closure)
- If a checklist or some other type of assessment form is to be used in the lesson, it is described here, *and* a copy of the page(s) is/are included with the lesson plan

Someone once said, "Show me a classroom in which the students are misbehaving and off-task, and I will show you a teacher who does not know how to write a lesson plan." Although we cannot attribute all classroom management problems to planning, we can certainly curtail much potential classroom disruption through effective planning. So, why is it that veteran teachers can plan effective lessons without writing out all of the details? What happens when you practice detailing procedures, including specific questions and transitions? The answer is simple: You gain experience. Schoenfeld (1998) and others have written about how experienced teachers generate "lesson images" rather than "lesson plans," something we discuss in the next section.

Classroom Dialogues

A mathematics teacher was leading the class through a problem in which they were designing a recipe for cookies. One part of the directions called for one-third of a cup of flour and one-fourth of a cup of sugar. The teacher led the following class discussion.

Teacher: Will the total amount of dry ingredients here be more or less than a full cup?

Student 1: It'll be less than a cup. The way I think about it is that one-third is less than a half, and one-fourth is also less than a half. So, if you add two things together that are each less than half, then the total will be less than a whole—a whole cup.

Teacher: That's a good way to reason it out. Did anyone else think of it differently? Or does anyone disagree with this answer?

Student 2: I pretty much did the same thing except I actually added the fractions and found it to be less than 1.

Teacher: How did you do that?

Student 2: Well, I took one-third and added it to one-fourth, and that gives you two-sevenths, which is definitely less than 1.

Teacher: I'm not sure that I follow how you did the addition. Can you show us?

Student 2: (goes up to the whiteboard and writes)

$$\frac{1}{3} + \frac{1}{4} = \frac{2}{7}$$

Like that. You just add the fractions together.

Student 3: That doesn't seem right to me. Two out of seven is actually less than two out of six, and we know that one-third equals two-sixths. So, you added something to two-sixths and then actually got an answer that was less than what you started with!

Teacher: How did that happen? What went wrong here?

Student 1: I think you have to find a common denominator first, don't you?

Student 2: No, I don't think so. It's just like multiplication. When you multiply one-third times one-fourth, you just multiply the ones in the numerator and the three and four in the denominator, and you get one-twelfth. I just did the same thing here by adding the top and bottom numbers together.

Teacher: I can follow your thinking, but I think we already have a good argument on the table for why your answer doesn't make sense.

Mathematics teachers who are relatively new to the profession are often surprised by the difficulty that students have with understanding basic fraction operations, even at the secondary level. High school teachers do not generally see it as "their job" to teach fraction skills, yet most students struggle with adding, subtracting, multiplying, and dividing fractions. If you teach secondary or middle school mathematics, it is inevitable that you will need to teach or remediate students who do not understand the basics of working with fractions. In the case of this dialogue, it is clear that students do not have a firm grasp of how to add the fractions in the recipe problem. How would you handle the situation? What questions or examples might the teacher provide the students to assist them?

The students in this scenario are probably in need of a visual approach to help them see what is happening. The student's logic about why the answer does not make sense is a good start, and the teacher uses that comment to focus the class. But now the class needs to look at how to find the correct answer. In Figure 6.7, a 3-by-4 portion of a geoboard (a square board with pegs) is marked off with a rubber band, with those dimensions chosen because the problem deals with thirds and fourths.

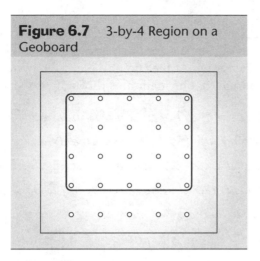

Figure 6.7 3-by-4 Region on a Geoboard

Students should recognize that each of the squares (made by the pegs) in the 3-by-4 region represents one-twelfth of the whole. So, in Figure 6.8, the top four squares that are shaded represent $\frac{4}{12}$ or $\frac{1}{3}$ of the whole. The next three squares represent $\frac{3}{12}$ or $\frac{1}{4}$ of the whole. So, if $\frac{1}{3}$ is added to $\frac{1}{4}$, the total shaded region represents 7 of the 12 squares or $\frac{7}{12}$. Therefore, $\frac{1}{3} + \frac{1}{4} = \frac{7}{12}$ and is certainly not the answer of $\frac{2}{7}$ that was originally suggested. The geoboard's area model also helps students see how it was necessary to look at 12 regions to work through the problem, as 12 is the common denominator used to work the addition problem.

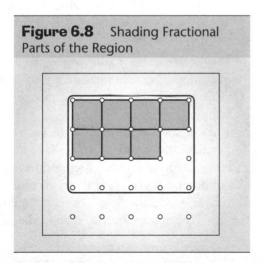

Figure 6.8 Shading Fractional Parts of the Region

In general, when students have difficulty with operations on fractions, it is essential to go back to hands-on models that help them to visualize the problem. Too often, fraction operations are memorized as rules, and students do not have the conceptual knowledge to make sense of the problems. The use of geoboards, Cuisenaire rods, fraction pieces, and other such models is encouraged to assist students in understanding the underlying concepts and to eliminate misconceptions. Can you think of other areas of the mathematics curriculum that involve fractions and may also require this type of intervention? How important is it for students to be comfortable with fraction concepts and operations?

Lesson Imaging versus Lesson Planning

Suppose that Mr. Pack attempts to implement his lesson on circumference of circles, using Sample Lesson Plan 1 as his guide. As the class period progresses, he realizes that his plan is not detailed enough and that his students are off-task and missing the point of the lesson. At the end of the day, he writes a brief reflection on his experience in a journal that he maintains throughout the year:

> *I just wasn't pleased with my lesson this morning. First of all, I realized that the motivating question did not motivate the class much at all, and I wish I had posed a real-life question that involved circumference instead. Then, I had several vague steps in my lesson, and I wasn't prepared enough to know what examples to explore with my class. I think they missed the point and still don't understand the formula for circumference or how to use it. I will need to approach the topic again tomorrow but from a different angle. Finally, we have a computer lab across the hall, and I have access to several handheld computers. I never thought about it at the time, but I could have used Geometer's Sketchpad or Geogebra in the lab or the handheld computer in my classroom to have students measure circumferences and diameters on the screen—they really enjoy using technology—I could have played to their interests. There is so much I would change next time around.*

You can bet that before Mr. Pack teaches the lesson again, he will rethink the examples he uses and, perhaps, attempt to use technology to help him make his point. If the students use Geometer's Sketchpad on a computer to explore circle relationships, the screen might resemble Figure 6.9.

In Figure 6.9, the student has created a circle, and the software has measured the circumference to be 13.02 cm and the diameter to be 4.14 cm. Using the CALCULATE command, the student can find the ratio of circumference to diameter to be about 3.14 and test circles of other sizes to see if the relationship is always true. If Mr. Pack has success with the revised lesson, it may become incorporated as part of his routine. Consequently, it will be much easier to plan in the third year because

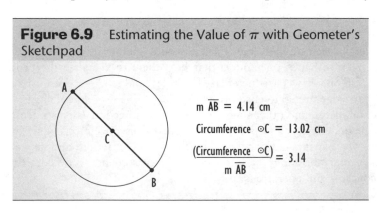

Figure 6.9   Estimating the Value of π with Geometer's Sketchpad

$m\ \overline{AB} = 4.14$ cm

Circumference $\odot C = 13.02$ cm

$\dfrac{(\text{Circumference}\ \odot C)}{m\ \overline{AB}} = 3.14$

he has seen that the lesson worked much better on the second try when technology was used in addition to hands-on measuring of circular objects. But experience is the key, and after you have taught and retaught a lesson a number of times, you begin to picture the lesson in your mind.

This mental picture of the lesson includes the kinds of comments that the teacher needs to make to clarify the task and help students identify the major mathematical ideas; it includes the errors that students are likely to make and concrete ways to respond to those misconceptions, and it includes a sense of how long the lesson will take and what parts can be shortened or lengthened. The mental picture is often referred to in the literature as a **lesson image**, the sense that a teacher carries into the classroom of what to expect from students, how they are likely to react, and what the teacher can do to make the lesson work. The lesson image differs from a lesson plan, which is a written document that guides instruction. But although a plan can be prepared by the novice teacher, it takes an experienced educator to image a lesson; and the more experience you gain with teaching a particular lesson or teaching toward a certain concept, the closer you will come to being able to create a lesson image. Individuals who have had considerable experience can write a fairly sketchy lesson plan on paper and still teach the lesson with artistry because they carry a mental image into the classroom. As you teach, over the course of several years, you will watch your skills progress from planning lessons to creating lesson images, but only *experience* can teach you how to do that.

It is important to realize the distinction between plans and images, however, because novice teachers are often surprised by the brevity of lesson plans of veteran teachers and wonder why they are being asked to write out every step. Like a musician who has learned which song to save for last after seeing how audiences respond to that song throughout an entire tour, anticipating audience reactions in the classroom also becomes much easier when you have an experience base. It's necessary not only to have the experience of teaching a lesson but also to take the time to reflect on its effectiveness, as we saw when Mr. Pack wrote his journal entry. In the next section, we discuss the final step in the planning and teaching of a lesson—reflection.

Reflecting on a Lesson

As we discuss further in Chapter 7, one of the things that good teachers of mathematics do is reflect on the effectiveness of their lessons. In describing the teaching principle (discussed in Chapter 2), the NCTM (2000) stated, "Opportunities to reflect on and refine instructional practice—during class and outside class, alone, and with others—are crucial in the vision of school mathematics outlined in *Principles and Standards*" and "to improve their mathematics instruction, teachers must be able to analyze what they and their students are doing and consider how those actions are affecting students' learning" (p. 19). Perhaps you have heard the statement that "nothing ever goes as planned," and this is often the case with planning a lesson in mathematics. One day, a teacher organizes what appears to be a simple review lesson and then discovers that the class has very little or none of the anticipated background. Another day, the lesson includes a seemingly complex task that the students complete in half the time allotted, leaving the teacher without a plan for 15 minutes or more. Earlier in the chapter, we discussed the issue of how to deal with student questions or misunderstandings, which, in some cases, may cause a teacher to put the plan aside and pursue a totally different direction. Of course, if we place students at the center of the teaching, we can expect and anticipate that their questions and concerns will often change the direction of our lessons. At the conclusion of the lesson, however, the teacher needs to return to the plan, think about how the class actually reacted to it, and address three key question areas:

1. What did I set out to do in this lesson, and why did I plan to do it that way?
2. Did I accomplish my goals and objectives for the lesson? How do I know (i.e., how did I measure the success of my lesson)?
3. What have I learned about my students and myself that will help me to be a better teacher tomorrow, next month, or next year? How would I change the lesson next time?

The answers to these questions will lead the teacher to write an even more effective lesson the next day and, certainly, the next year when another class studies the same content.

After implementing a lesson plan, the teacher should always reflect on or assess the plan and its effectiveness. If the students appeared to understand the content, was it because of the lesson itself or something that wasn't even in the plan? If the class was restless, confused, or off-task, can this be attributed to the students, or was it a flaw in the planning? Although it is sometimes difficult to be self-critical, examination of the plan may reveal gaps that could have been avoided or opportunities that should have been pursued. Over time, with experience, teachers create a collection of "best lessons" that work with their classes. Although some of these best lessons can be found in resource books or on the Internet, teachers begin to "own" a lesson only after planning, teaching, reflecting on, and reteaching it. As a result, the teacher becomes increasingly proficient in lesson imaging, anticipating student responses, and attaining the desired flow and success of the lesson. A well-planned set of lessons, then, becomes the cornerstone of coherent, meaningful units.

One form of professional development that has gained considerably in popularity in recent years is a lesson study group. In this model, a small group of mathematics teachers gather to write a lesson as a team. Then, one person teaches the lesson while the others observe. After discussing the strengths and weaknesses of the lesson, the study group refines the plan. Then, another member of the team reteaches the lesson, and the group convenes to discuss it further. This study group process (as described by North Central Regional Educational Laboratory [NCREL], 2002, and by Stigler and Hiebert, 1999) allows teachers to work together in the process of planning, teaching, and reflecting, which can be considerably more powerful than one person working alone.

Conclusion

The ability to plan a good lesson is one of the most fundamental of all teaching skills. In this chapter, we explored the role of planning both long-term units and daily lessons. Frameworks for the construction of units and lessons were presented, with examples and analyses of poorly written and well-written lesson plans. (Additional examples of detailed lesson plans can be found in Chapters 8 and 9, where we explore the issues involved in teaching specific content areas.) We acknowledged that the textbook and local course of study often drive the planning process but noted that teachers can supplement these with additional resources to make lessons more meaningful for students. We also emphasized the importance of assessing the strengths and weaknesses of the plan and its implementation. We improve only when we look back at previous lessons—individually or with a group of other teachers— and ask ourselves how the lessons could have been taught more effectively. Using our experience in the classroom, we develop our skills from planning lessons extensively on paper to imaging lessons in our minds, and our organizational abilities progress from the need to write out details to the ability to sketch outlines.

Throughout your career as a student of mathematics, you have inevitably experienced some very interesting and worthwhile lessons. Perhaps those lessons involved you actively in a cooperative learning team or required that you use manipulatives or technology in the learning process. Maybe you were challenged with thought-provoking questions and were expected to struggle somewhat to try to make sense of a problem. However, behind every one of those worthwhile lessons was a caring teacher who was responsible for planning, implementing, and reflecting on your classroom activities. So, what are "good" teachers, and what kinds of experiences do they provide for their students? These questions are pursued in Chapter 7 as we continue Unit 3 with a detailed discussion of the role of the mathematics teacher in the classroom.

For bibliographic references and additional resources, see page 409

Glossary

Closure: Closure is the final step of a lesson plan during which the teacher wraps up a lesson. Often, the closure includes an opportunity to assess student understanding of the lesson and may tie back to an issue raised in the lesson's motivation or pose a question for students to consider for the next class period.

Components of a Lesson Plan: Although there is no universal agreement on a structure for all lesson plans, the following simple outline and components may be helpful in constructing plans:
(General Considerations)

    I. Goal(s)
    II. Objective(s)
    III. Materials and Resources
    IV. Motivation
    V. Lesson Procedure (including transition statements and ideas for meeting the needs of all students)
    VI. Closure
    VII. Extension (optional activity or teaching idea)
    VIII. Assessment

Conceptual Map: A conceptual map is a graphic organizer of how the content of a lesson, unit, semester, course, or even an entire program fits together as a whole. Figure 6.1 indicates how various concepts are connected and suggests a possible instructional sequence.

5-E Lesson Plan: Used extensively in the teaching of science, this model of planning is designed for teachers to think through the development of a lesson in five stages—engage, explore, explain, extend (or elaborate), and evaluate.

Lesson Image: A lesson image is a mental picture that is held by an experienced teacher of what is expected of students in a lesson, how the lesson is likely to progress, and what the teacher's role will be in the teaching and learning process. Novice teachers spend most of their time writing lesson plans in detail on paper, but veteran teachers are more likely to be able to "image" a lesson and work from a more general outline for a plan.

Lesson Plan: A lesson plan is a written document that details the goals and objectives, the necessary tools, and the activities to be used in a particular classroom teaching episode. It is a road map that can be used by the teacher to provide structure to the lesson. Formal or informal reflections should follow the implementation of the plan. Prospective and less-experienced teachers must write extensive lesson plans that detail their classroom activities and attempt to anticipate student questions and misconceptions.

Lesson Procedure: The lesson procedure is a set of instructions for the teacher, generally written as an outline, with step-by-step descriptions of what the teacher and the students will do in a lesson. The procedure should feature specific instructions but be flexible enough to allow the teacher to move in a different direction if the students raise questions or concerns during the lesson.

Motivation: As it pertains to lesson planning, the motivation is an activity used at the beginning of a lesson to gain the attention of the students. Taking the form of a problem, a visual aid, or an activity, the motivation is intended to set the stage for the lesson and to evoke interest and curiosity in the intended topic. The motivation is often the most difficult part of a lesson to plan because it depends on the teacher knowing the students well enough to understand what will get their attention. Sometimes, the motivation is also referred to as an initiatory or engagement activity or as a springboard.

Prerequisite Knowledge: Prerequisite knowledge refers to the competencies and skills that students should already possess before the beginning of an instructional unit. It is important for a teacher to identify the prerequisite knowledge of students before designing a unit so that the students can connect the new content to concepts they have developed in the past.

Teachable Moment: A teachable moment is a class situation in which a student has answered a question in a particular way or raised a certain concern that leads the teacher naturally into the discussion of an unplanned example or topic. Students indicate their interest in the topic by making comments in class, and the teacher decides that it is better for the class to pursue the issue than to leave it alone.

Transition Statements: Transition statements are statements included in a lesson plan that are intended to help students recognize how the activities in the lesson are connected. These statements, generally included in the lesson procedure, are often written as direct quotes for the teacher to say so that the plan progresses smoothly.

Unit: A unit is a set of learning experiences designed to address one or several goals and objectives over time. Generally, units are long term in that they may take several class periods or even several weeks to complete. A unit may contain several individual lesson plans with a common theme or general topic.

Discussion Questions and Activities

1. Choose a general unit topic, such as exponential growth, area of a polygon, or total surface area and volume of three-dimensional solids, and create a conceptual map indicating the possible components of the unit and how they are connected.

2. Examine a textbook unit in a small group and discuss the length of time it might take to explore the unit and the degree to which your group agrees with the suggested sequence of topics.

3. Sample Lesson Plan 1 was presented as an example of a poorly written lesson. Rewrite the lesson to address the weaknesses described in this chapter.

4. Obtain a copy of a teacher's manual for a mathematics textbook. Identify and discuss the suggestions for lessons that are described in the manual. How helpful is the manual in the lesson-planning process for a novice teacher?

5. Run a search for mathematics lesson plans on the Internet in a topic area of your choice (or locate a resource book containing sample lessons). Evaluate the strengths and weaknesses of the lesson plans based on the criteria described in this chapter. To what degree do the lessons illustrate the lesson-plan components discussed in the chapter?

6. The motivation of a lesson—the activity conducted with a class in the first few minutes of a lesson—was identified as probably the most important yet most difficult part of the lesson plan to write. Generate several examples of questions, problems, activities, or situations that you could use at the beginning of a class to immediately engage your students in the exploration of a topic or topics of your choice.

7. View a videotape of a mathematics lesson. Then, in a small group, try to sketch out the teacher's lesson plan. Identify the goals, objectives, materials and resources, motivation, lesson procedure, closure, extension (if any), and assessment. What transitional statements did the teacher use? How did the teacher attempt to address diverse learning styles in the classroom? Describe anything in the lesson that appeared to be unplanned, including perhaps a student concern that was pursued by the teacher.

8. Most teacher candidates and inservice teachers are familiar with spiral-bound lesson planning books that have a grid of small squares (roughly 2 inches on a side) into which the plan for a given day is to be written. Do you believe that lesson plan books of this kind are ever appropriate? Why or why not?

9. View a videotape case or read a case study of a classroom teaching episode. Play the role of the teacher in the case study and write a reflection on the lesson. Be sure to include the three components of lesson reflection described in this chapter.

10. It has been said that there are teachers with 20 years of experience and teachers who have 1 year of experience, repeated 20 times. What does this statement suggest about the reasons for reflecting on lessons in the teaching and learning process?

Teaching Tools and Strategies

n a mathematics class, Anne Kelley is helping her students estimate the value of the square root of a number and compare the estimate with an answer on the calculator.

Ms. Kelley: Can anyone give me an estimate of $\sqrt{52}$?

Luke: It's about 7.5.

Ms. Kelley: Explain your thinking on that, Luke.

Luke: Well, I know that $\sqrt{49}$ is 7 and that $\sqrt{64}$ is 8. So, I knew it had to be between those, since 52 is between 49 and 64.

Elise: That's true, but 52 is a lot closer to 49 than it is to 64, so I would guess it would be more like 7.2 or 7.3.

Ms. Kelley: Does anyone else have any thoughts on this one?

Terry: Well, look at it this way . . . the average of 49 and 64 is 56.5. So, we can figure that $\sqrt{56.5}$ is halfway between 7 and 8 . . . um . . . 7.5, right?

Ms. Kelley: How can we check to see how close 7.5 is to the answer?

Luke: Find 7.5^2 and see if it's 56.5.

Ms. Kelley: Good. Why don't you go ahead and find 7.5^2 on your calculators.

(The class keys 7.5 into their calculators and squares the number.)

After reading Chapter 7, you should be able to answer the following questions:

- What are the NCTM Standards for Teaching and Learning Mathematics and the related principles from *Principles and Standards for School Mathematics*? Why and when were they developed?
- What are the criteria according to which a teacher selects activities and problems (tasks) for the classroom?
- What are some of the tools of mathematics instruction, and how are they helpful in the teaching and learning process?
- What are some specific strategies that teachers can use to develop a positive learning environment in the classroom and create community? Discuss these strategies.
- How can the teacher use questioning skills and cooperative learning to enhance the level of discourse in the classroom?
- What is the role of reflection on student learning and teaching practice?

Joshua: No, 7.5^2 is equal to 56.25, not 56.5.

Terry: Close enough, wouldn't you say, Ms. Kelley?

Ms. Kelley: I don't know. Why don't you go ahead and take $\sqrt{52}$.

(The class finds the square root with their calculators.)

Elise: I knew it! It's only 7.21-something. It's like I said; it's closer to 7 than to 8.

Ms. Kelley: Do we know "exactly" what it's equal to?

Luke: Yeah, it's exactly 7.211102551. That's what my calculator shows anyway.

Terry: So does mine. But I still think it's close enough if we call it 7.21.

Lakisha: Does it go any further than 7.211102551? I'm just wondering because we've seen other times where the calculator cuts a number off because it doesn't have enough space . . . like that one time we tried to change a fraction to a repeating decimal that had, like, 12 decimal places before it started to repeat.

(The students in the class start to look confused and wonder if Lakisha is on to something. They look up at Ms. Kelley and wait for her response.)

Now, put yourself in Anne Kelley's position. How would you handle this situation? Think about what you would do before reading ahead. In this short episode, a couple of significant issues have surfaced—let's discuss each of them.

First, Terry has the misconception that the square of a number should fall exactly between the square of the two whole numbers that bound it. Ms. Kelley could run with this point and, for example, show that whereas 11^2 is 121 and 12^2 is 144, 11.5^2 is 132.25 and not 132.5, as Terry might predict. But this might result in a question as to whether the average of the squares of two consecutive integers is always 0.25 more than the square of the average of the two integers (in this case, 132.5 − 0.25 and in the classroom situation, 56.5 − 0.25). This conjecture is correct and could be proven as follows:

Let x be an integer and $x + 1$ be the next consecutive integer. Then the squares of the two numbers would be x^2 and $(x + 1)^2 = x^2 + 2x + 1$. The average of the two original numbers would be $\frac{x + (x + 1)}{2} = \frac{2x + 1}{2} = x + \frac{1}{2}$. Therefore, the square of the average of the original numbers would be $(x + \frac{1}{2})^2 = x^2 + x + \frac{1}{4}$. But the average of the squares of the original numbers would be $\frac{x^2 + (x + 1)^2}{2} = \frac{2x^2 + 2x + 1}{2} = x^2 + x + \frac{1}{2}$, which is exactly $\frac{1}{4}$ or 0.25 larger than the square of the averages. So, although this conjecture is true and the class might be able to prove it, Ms. Kelley has to decide whether she wants to pursue the issue.

Second, the class may be on the brink of discovering that the square root of a number that is not a perfect square is irrational, and Lakisha's question about whether the calculator is actually displaying the entire number is interesting. Ms. Kelley could, for example, ask the class to key π into their calculators. If they have some background with π, they might already know that it neither terminates nor repeats, yet the graphing calculator displays only "3.141592654." This may prompt students to ask about how many digits the calculator actually has for π in its memory. But how can we find out? One simple approach is to key in $10*\pi$ on the calculator and then subtract 30. The display will be as follows:

π	3.141592654
10π	31.41592654
-30	1.415926536

Subtracting 30 gives the student's calculator the room to display another digit of the decimal because it can display only 10 digits at a time. Now, the students know that it originally rounded 3.1415926536 to 3.141592654. So, the question might be, "If you multiply by 100 more and subtract 140, can we find out if the calculator knows even more digits?" Repeating this process again and again, students will find that their particular calculators "know" the value of π up to 3.1415926535898. Finally, the same process could be used for determining an approximation for $\sqrt{52}$, and students can discover whether the decimal repeats or terminates within the first 13 decimal places. When they discover that it neither terminates nor repeats, the stage is set for a discussion of square roots as irrational numbers. Again, this is an interesting problem-solving excursion, but Anne Kelley has to make an on-the-spot decision about whether it is worth the class time to pursue Lakisha's question, particularly if it was unexpected and not part of her lesson plan or the curriculum as described in her course of study.

Although it would be relatively easy to dismiss Terry's answer as "close enough" and Lakisha's question as "interesting, but something you'll look at in another class in high school," this may also be a perfect opportunity for exploring something about which a student has expressed interest—what educators often call a teachable moment as discussed in Chapter 6. But the decision about how to proceed is up to Anne Kelley, and the master teacher knows whether the students can handle a further investigation and whether the time would be productively used before proceeding. Just as two musicians can perform the same song very differently, each having a different interpretation of the music, the implementation of a teacher's lesson plan depends on the teacher's ability to pick up on student interactions and adjust the plan in a meaningful way. In this chapter, we discuss the art of teaching and the role of the teacher in posing problems and orchestrating discussions that challenge and interest the students. We begin with a discussion of the NCTM Standards for Teaching and Learning Mathematics (NCTM, 2007) and the related principles from *Principles and Standards for School Mathematics* (2000).

Teaching Standards and Principles

The NCTM Standards for Teaching and Learning Mathematics

In the summer of 2007, the NCTM released a document entitled *Mathematics Teaching Today: Improving Practice, Improving Student Learning* (NCTM, 2007). This book was an updated revision (second edition) of *Professional Standards for*

Teaching Mathematics, which was originally published in 1991. The purpose for these publications was to assist those individuals involved in preparing or providing professional development for classroom teachers. *Mathematics Teaching Today* paints a picture of effective teaching and encourages readers to think about the degree to which their teaching skills are aligned with suggested benchmarks.

Mathematics Teaching Today features the graphic that is displayed in Figure 7.1.

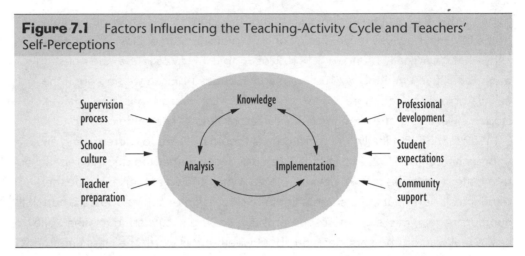

Figure 7.1 Factors Influencing the Teaching-Activity Cycle and Teachers' Self-Perceptions

The diagram shows how mathematics teachers are constantly involved in a learning cycle, which involves gaining new information (knowledge), utilizing their knowledge of mathematics and pedagogy in the classroom (implementation), and reflecting on the effectiveness of their practice (analysis). These factors interact with one another and are informed by the six influences on the outside of the diagram, including supervision, school culture, teacher preparation, professional development, student expectations, and community support. The authors noted that there are two assumptions that underlie the document: (1) "Teachers are essential figures in improving the ways in which mathematics is taught and learned in schools" and (2) "Such improvements require that teachers have long-term support and adequate resources" (NCTM, 2007, p. 6). In short, although it is important to have a well-written course of study, state-level standards, and texts and materials, it is the skill of the teacher that ultimately drives the academic performance of students in a school.

Mathematics Teaching Today is divided into three major sets of standards. The first set is the Standards for Teaching and Learning Mathematics, which we will use as an organizer for much of this chapter because those Standards are concerned with the way that a teacher conducts a class and analyzes student progress and his or her own teaching effectiveness. The second set of standards, Standards for the Observation, Supervision, and Improvement of Mathematics Teaching, presents a vision of how administrators and other individuals can be involved in the process of improving one's teaching practice. We will return to these standards in the last chapter of this book, Chapter 13. Finally, the last group of standards is entitled Standards for the Education and Continued Professional Growth of Teachers of Mathematics and is directed at those involved with providing professional development for practicing teachers.

So, what does it mean to be a "good teacher" of mathematics? Think back to your school experiences and jot down five things that your best teachers were able to do. Perhaps you remember the types of activities or projects in which you were engaged in the class, the classroom climate that felt inviting and made you want to learn, or the conversations that took place during class. In its effort to define what good teaching is all about, the NCTM put forth seven Standards for Teaching and Learning Mathematics: knowledge of mathematics and general pedagogy, knowledge of student mathematical learning, worthwhile mathematical tasks, learning environment, discourse, reflection on student learning, and reflection on teaching practice (NCTM, 2007). As you read the text of these standards throughout this chapter, think about whether your mathematics teachers measured up to each of the benchmarks and what you can do to meet the criteria.

Knowledge Standards

The first two Standards for Teaching and Learning Mathematics are rooted in the teacher's knowledge about mathematics and how students learn. The text of these two Standards is as follows:

STANDARD 1: KNOWLEDGE OF MATHEMATICS AND GENERAL PEDAGOGY

Teachers of mathematics should have a deep knowledge of—

- sound and significant mathematics,
- theories of student intellectual development across the spectrum of diverse learners,
- modes of instruction and assessment, and
- effective communication and motivational strategies.

(NCTM, 2007, p. 19)

Teachers themselves need to have a sound content knowledge, as well as a deep understanding of the psychological, social, and cultural factors that influence the teaching and learning process. Chapter 3 explored teaching and learning from a psychological perspective, and Chapter 12 will further explore equity and addressing cultural differences.

STANDARD 2: KNOWLEDGE OF STUDENT MATHEMATICAL LEARNING

Teachers of mathematics must know and recognize the importance of—

- what is known about the ways students learn mathematics;
- methods of supporting students as they struggle to make sense of mathematical concepts and procedures;
- ways to help students build on informal mathematical understandings;
- a variety of tools for use in mathematical investigation and the benefits and limitations of those tools; and
- ways to stimulate engagement and guide the exploration of the mathematical processes of problem solving, reasoning and proof, communication, connections, and representation.

(NCTM, 2007, p. 25)

Methods courses are designed to address the concerns raised by this standard. Teachers need to possess an arsenal of different teaching ideas so that the needs of students who all think differently can be addressed. At the heart of these ideas are specific problems and tasks that can be utilized to spark interest and build conceptual understanding, as well as the use of tools, such as hands-on materials and technology. The issues of tasks and tools will be discussed further in this chapter.

The Teaching and Learning Principles

In Chapter 2, we explored the six principles put forth by NCTM in *Principles and Standards for School Mathematics* (2000). Two of these were the teaching principle and the learning principle, and you might have noticed how they are clearly reflected in the Standards for Teaching and Learning described here. The authors of *Principles and Standards* asserted that "effective mathematics teaching requires understanding what students know and need to learn and then challenging and supporting them to learn it well" and that "students must learn mathematics with understanding, actively building new knowledge from experience and prior knowledge" (NCTM, 2000, p. 11). The teaching and learning principles express the common theme of meeting students "where they are" and making lessons meaningful, relevant, and challenging.

As we think about the design and implementation of lesson plans and units, we need to determine how closely our efforts as mathematics teachers measure up to the principles. While exploring the role of the classroom teacher in this chapter, we use *Teaching Mathematics Today* and its Standards for Teaching and Learning dealing with tasks (including the appropriate use of tools), learning environment, discourse, and reflection on practice as organizers and intersperse comments on how the Principles can be addressed as well.

electing Activities and Problems

As we discussed in Chapter 6, lesson planning should always begin with the process of identifying and clearly stating the goals and objectives that a teacher intends to address. At the same time, it is important to consider the various problems and activities—tasks—that can be used in teaching the lesson to carefully select the type of experiences that the teacher believes will be the most effective in developing the relevant mathematics. Standard 3 of the Standards for Teaching and Learning Mathematics outlines a description of criteria that can be used when selecting classroom tasks.

▼ STANDARD 3: WORTHWHILE MATHEMATICAL TASKS

The teacher of mathematics should design learning experiences and pose tasks that are based on sound and significant mathematics and that—

- engage students' intellect;
- develop mathematical understandings and skills;
- stimulate students to make connections and develop a coherent framework for mathematical ideas;
- call for problem formulation, problem solving and mathematical reasoning;

- promote communication about mathematics;
- represent mathematics as an ongoing human activity; and
- display sensitivity to, and draw on, students' diverse background experiences and dispositions.

(NCTM, 2007, pp. 32–33)

Let's look at a specific example. Suppose that the teacher wants the class to think about the graph of an absolute value function such as $y = |x|$. The instructor can ask the students to construct a table of values and sketch a rough, simple graph as shown in Figure 7.2.

Then the students can be given additional functions, such as $y = 2|x - 3| + 5$, and challenged to sketch their graphs by hand as well. In the end, students gain experience with making tables and sketching graphs, but the teacher has to wonder whether the students actually understand *why* the graphs have a V-shaped appearance. Additionally, the students may or may not have developed enough of an understanding to allow them to graph more complicated absolute value functions.

If the students have access to graphing calculators or computers with a graphing utility, they can be asked to use technology to draw graphs of such functions as

$$y = |x|$$
$$y = |x| + 3$$
$$y = |x| - 5$$
$$y = -|x|$$
$$y = -|x| - 3$$

By observing graphs such as the one in Figure 7.3, students can look for patterns and make generalizations about how the parameter changes affect the shape of each graph.

Figure 7.2 Table and Hand-Drawn Sketch of the Absolute Value Function

x	y
0	0
2	2
−2	2
5	5
−5	5

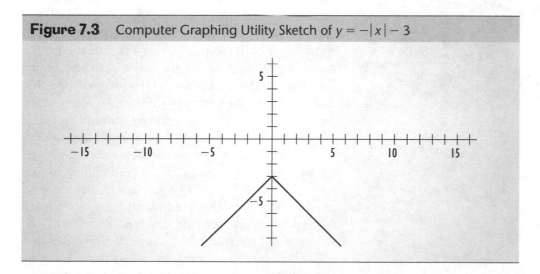

Figure 7.3 Computer Graphing Utility Sketch of $y = -|x| - 3$

Figure 7.3 was generated using a desktop graphing utility in a student computer lab. Again, students are likely to recognize characteristics of graphs that, for example, have negative coefficients multiplying the absolute value term, but they may or may not appreciate why the graph is shaped in this manner.

The teacher might also ask students to construct the graph of $y = |x|$ with graph paper and a straightedge and compare it with the graph of the line $y = x$. Students will recognize that the portion of the graph lying in Quadrant III has been reflected over the x-axis and can discuss the fact that the absolute value function takes all of the coordinates of the points and makes the y-coordinates (ordinates) positive. Then, students can use a manipulative known as a **mira,** an I-shaped plastic tool that, when laid on a piece of paper containing a picture, allows one to see the reflection of the picture in its window. Students can lay the mira on the x-axis

Figure 7.4 A Mira Used to Show a Reflection in the Absolute Value Graph

and see how the Quadrant III piece of the line $y = x$ is reflected up to Quadrant II in the graph of $y = |x|$. In Figure 7.4, the mira, placed on the x-axis, allows the reflection of the line $y = x$ to be viewed.

The advantages of using the mira are threefold. First, the students have a visual image of how the absolute value function is generated from the related linear function. Second, a geometric connection can be made, allowing students to appreciate the role of reflection in an algebraic context. And third, the stage is set for students to graph other absolute value functions by starting with their linear "parent." For example, the student can be asked to graph the function $y = |2x - 3|$ by sketching $y = 2x - 3$ on graph paper, using the mira to locate the reflected part, and completing the sketch of the absolute value graph. After concretely laying the groundwork with a manipulative such as a mira, additional explorations on a graphing calculator might follow so that, in a short period of time, students can appreciate how the parameters A, B, C, and D affect the graph of the function $y = A|Bx + C| + D$.

Therefore, by choosing to conduct a hands-on investigation of how absolute value functions are related to linear functions, the teacher can encourage visualization and the use of geometry in an algebra problem. The decision to take this route, rather than to simply sketch a few absolute value functions by using a value table, gives the students a considerably richer experience and allows them to make significant connections to previous learning. The lesson addresses the needs of the visual learner and, therefore, advances the learning principle. In this principle, NCTM has written that "when challenged with appropriately chosen tasks, students become confident in their ability to tackle difficult problems, eager to figure things out on their own, flexible in exploring mathematical ideas and trying alternative solution paths, and willing to persevere" (2000, p. 21). The teacher is the one who ultimately selects those tasks and problems such that students are actively engaged in lessons that appeal to their interests. Even an objective that appears to be rather mechanical, such as sketching an absolute value graph, can become an enticing activity for students if it is planned carefully. As we discussed in Chapter 5, there are a number of

A carefully selected task will generate interest and actively engage students.

resources that a teacher can use to find these types of problems and activities, including, but not limited to, the textbook, resource books, journal articles, and the Internet. Whenever an activity or problem is posed, you should look for a stimulus to evoke curiosity and interest on the part of the students. Also, keep in mind that a carefully selected classroom task may take students 5 minutes to complete or may be designed to take one or several days.

How Would You React

SCENARIO

You pose a problem in your mathematics class and randomly call on a student to start the problem-solving process. The student's face becomes red with anger and, snapping back at you, he or she says, "I have no idea. Why do you always call on me?" and looks down at the desk. Your response is to

a. Give the student a demerit (or some type of disciplinary response) for disrespect and call on another student.
b. Calmly remind the student that you don't always call on him or her, but call on another student for an answer.
c. Tell the student that he or she was chosen randomly, like everyone else, and insist that he or she give some kind of response to at least get the class moving toward a solution to the problem.
d. Ignore the response and call on another student, but take this student aside after class and discuss the situation.
e. Other.

DISCUSSION

The expectation of a teacher who is promoting mathematical discourse in the classroom is that every student will be actively involved in solving problems. However, we all know that there are some students in classes who are much more likely than their peers to raise their hands and interact in class discussions. If a teacher relies only on volunteers—students with their hands raised—the chances are fairly high that the same students will be called on time after time. However, if a teacher relies heavily on "calling on" students, despite their sometimes shy personalities and lack of interest in participating, confrontational situations such as these can arise in the classroom.

The *Standards* have made it very clear that *every* student should be actively engaged in learning mathematics.

Therefore, it makes sense for teachers to bring students into discussions who might be timid about participating. One technique that many teachers use is to put the name of one student on each of a stack of index cards (or to write the name of each student on a separate popsicle stick). Then, whenever the class is being asked a question for which there is no volunteer or the same students have done all of the volunteering, the teacher reaches down and pulls one card out of the deck. That student is called on, and the card is placed in a discard pile. That way, the student will not be randomly selected again until every other student in the class has been chosen at least once. This strategy curtails students' feelings that "you always call on me" because the students recognize that the system is designed to spread out the volunteers evenly.

Another point to keep in mind is that students who do not raise their hands either (1) have an answer but do not want to volunteer or (2) simply do not have an answer. In either case, the teacher needs to be sensitive to the fact that the student may lack the self-confidence either to participate at all or to believe that a thought is worth sharing. (You may recall that, in Chapter 3, we described self-confidence as one of the components of motivation.) Therefore, another suggestion is to "call on" (i.e., when they do not volunteer) students who tend to be less vocal at times when you know that the question is either fairly simple or so open-ended that students realize there are no "wrong" answers. In this way, students' self-confidence can be enhanced, thus increasing the likelihood that they will participate voluntarily in future discussions. To ignore the student, respond with a disciplinary penalty, or force the student to answer may cause a rift between the teacher and student that will be difficult, if not impossible, to mend for the remainder of the school year. Teachers who are patient and responsive to student needs create the type of environment that can make students excited to learn mathematics and to volunteer to share their thoughts.

Classroom Tools

Hands-On Manipulative Materials

Describing the importance of presenting worthwhile tasks in the classroom, the authors of *Mathematics Teaching Today* stated, "Tasks can be designed to incorporate a wide range of tools available for teaching mathematics, such as Web-based resources, computer software, manipulative materials, calculators, puzzles, or interactive electronic devices" (NCTM, 2007, p. 33). We now turn our attention to how mathematics teachers select and utilize a variety of tools to help students develop rich content knowledge, as well as the mathematical processes and practices. Specifically, we will explore the use of hands-on manipulative materials, technology, diagrams, graphs, and other discussion starters.

Any good carpenter knows that if a nail is to be driven into wood, not only is a tool required, but also it makes more sense to drive the nail with a hammer than with a screwdriver. To hit a screw with a hammer doesn't make much sense either, but most people would never choose to drive a screw into wood with their bare hands. The problem-solving process in the classroom often lends itself to the use of tools that can foster the development of mathematical thinking and stimulate discussion among students. But just as the carpenter chooses between a hammer and a screwdriver, the classroom teacher must decide which tools are most appropriate for exploring particular mathematical concepts. There are times when the use of hands-on materials, such as algebra tiles or miras, is important and other times when manipulatives may actually inhibit the classroom conversations. Sometimes students can get so caught up in determining what the physical model looks like that they lose the mathematical intent in the process. Likewise, there are times when a graphing calculator is appropriate in solving a problem and other times when the problem is more readily solved with pencil and paper. So, teachers need to think about the concept to be presented and determine which tools might be most useful to the students.

Let's revisit the concept of adding decimals in a middle school setting, as discussed briefly in Chapter 3. The issue of teaching decimals for understanding is particularly important in light of research on the topic. A study published by Hiebert and Wearne (1986), for example, showed that only 1 out of every 3 seventh graders was able to explain why he or she "lined up" the decimal places for adding and subtracting decimals. Simply put, students often can *do* the computation (simplify the expression, solve the equation, etc.) but have no idea of *what* they are doing or *why* they are doing it.

In getting students to think about what it means to add 3.25 to 5.7, you could choose to use a calculator in your instruction. When the students key the numbers into the machine, it will deliver an answer of 8.95, and the problem is solved. But is this the best way for students to explore the concept of adding decimals? Probably not, unless considerable discussion takes place afterward about how the calculator arrived at that answer. Instead, the teacher may choose to use base ten blocks as a manipulative to drive the exploration. The unit cube can represent $\frac{1}{100}$, so the long represents 10 of these or $\frac{1}{10}$, and the flat would represent 10 of the longs, or 1. Therefore, the problem could be represented as in Figure 7.5.

By putting together the flats, the longs, and the units, the student can visualize the sum as 8.95. Furthermore, the class can discuss why the 0.7 needed to be added to the 0.2, which will generally cause students to devise their own rule about lining up decimal places to ensure that proper place values are being added.

Figure 7.5 Base Ten Block Representation of 3.25 + 5.7

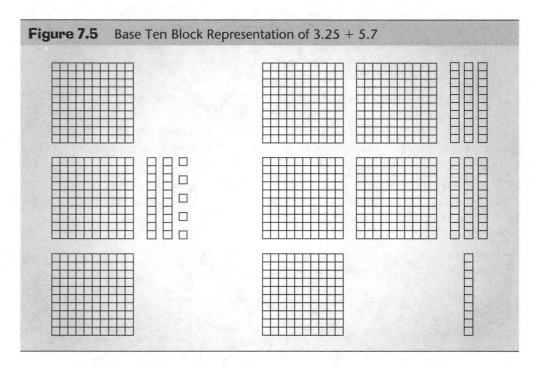

As an alternative to base ten blocks, the teacher might choose to give the students a piece of graph paper and have them shade a 10 × 10 grid to represent the number 1. Similarly, a student can shade a 1 × 10 grid to represent 0.1 and a single square to represent 0.01. The problem could be modeled just as with the base ten blocks but by drawing the pictures on the graph paper grid instead. This approach might benefit a student who is better served by creating a model than by being handed a commercial set of materials. It is also a low-cost alternative for a school that does not have an adequate supply of base ten blocks.

Another teacher may choose to use money as a model for the problem. By viewing the problem as $3.25 + $5.70, the students can use a visual such as the one in Figure 7.6.

Figure 7.6 Representation of 3.25 + 5.70 with Currency

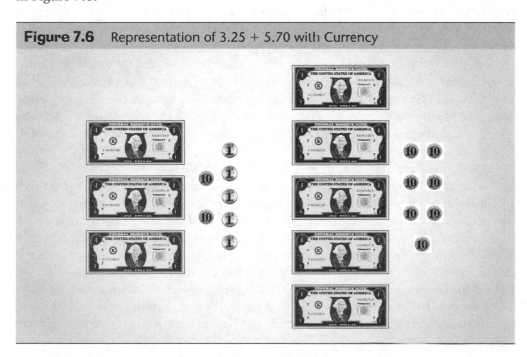

Recognizing that the dollars, the dimes, and the pennies can be combined, the student will see that the sum of the money is $8.95. Once again, students can discuss why the dimes cannot be combined with the pennies and justify the need for aligning decimal points when adding decimal fractions.

Making connections to an earlier measurement unit, still another teacher might give each student a ruler marked with decimeters (dm), centimeters (cm), and millimeters (mm) (see Figure 7.7). Because there are 10 millimeters in each centimeter and 10 centimeters in each decimeter, students could represent the number 3.25 with a line segment whose length is 3 dm, 2 cm, and 5 mm—the unit is 1 decimeter. Similarly, another line segment would have the length of 5 dm and 7 cm. When these two segments are placed side by side, the total length can be read off the ruler as 8 dm, 9 cm, and 5 mm, or 8.95.

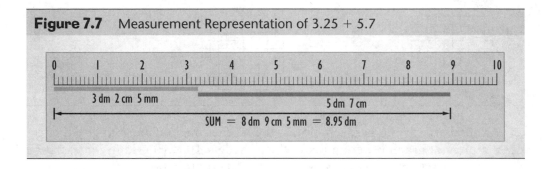

Figure 7.7 Measurement Representation of 3.25 + 5.7

The measurement model works for many students because it relates to reading a ruler, a skill that is very familiar to most students by the secondary and middle grade levels.

So, which tool is the best for getting a student to visualize and think about a decimal addition problem—calculators, base ten blocks, graph paper sketches, money (dollar bills, dimes, and pennies), or a ruler? You may have guessed by now that there is rarely a best way to teach a concept, one that will work for all students. Because a mathematics classroom is made up of many individuals, who each think in a different way, one model may be effective for some people, and another may work better for others. If students have had enough exposure to money problems before this class period to visualize coins in their heads, they may feel most comfortable with modeling the problem in terms of dimes and pennies. Another student who has been successfully thinking about whole number addition using base ten blocks may prefer to stay with that model. As teachers, we need to be prepared to use any of a number of different tools to promote learning and equity in our classrooms.

Each time we plan a lesson, we ask ourselves, "What is my class like this year, and what do I know about how they've responded to the use of various tools that might help me choose the best place to start?" For example, if you have just completed a series of lessons on metric measurement, and the students had a very difficult time with the material, probably the last thing you would want to do is to begin the unit on decimal operations with a ruler. However, introducing the metric model later in the unit might be just the reinforcement that your students need to help them view measurement in a different context—one that allows them to make a connection between number sense and measurement. Finally, it is important to acknowledge that what worked last year in your class or what works for another teacher in another classroom may not be effective in your current situation. The NCTM made this point in the learning principle, stating, "Teaching mathematics well is a complex endeavor, and there are no easy recipes for helping all students learn or for helping all teachers become effective" (NCTM, 2000, p. 17). Furthermore, the authors of *Mathematics Teaching Today* (NCTM, 2007) asserted, "No single 'right way' exists to teach all mathematical topics in all situations; teachers must balance their knowledge of mathematics, knowledge of pedagogical strategies, and knowledge of students to help students become independent mathematical thinkers" (p. 19). Educators often refer to teachers possessing **pedagogical content knowledge (PCK)**. Schulman (1986) is credited with introducing the term, and while PCK has many definitions, the National Council for the Accreditation of Teacher Education defines it as, "The interaction of the subject matter and effective teaching strategies to help students learn the subject matter. It requires a thorough understanding of the content to teach it in multiple ways, drawing on the cultural backgrounds and prior knowledge and experiences of students" (SFA State University, 2011). In other words, effective teachers are those who have knowledge of the mathematical content *and* the type of teaching strategies that are most effective in the classroom.

Think of teaching tools used in the classroom as a collection in a carpenter's toolbox. Sometimes, carpenters reach in and pull out a pair of needle-nose pliers, but if that doesn't work, they may reach back into the box and try a bolt cutter instead. You might begin a lesson with base ten blocks and very quickly realize that the manipulative you have selected is not working and that you need to pull back and display a set of coins on projector document reader instead. This decision is generally made during class—a real-time choice—and is based on an assessment of the degree to which students are mastering your planned objective. Consequently, flexibility is crucial; we must be prepared to shift gears in the middle of a lesson or to work individually with a student who appears to need a different tool than the rest of the class. As was pointed out in Chapter 6, our lesson-planning process should allow for the possibility that a particular model may not work for all of the students in a class.

Throughout the book, we have referred to a number of different classroom materials available to the secondary and middle school mathematics teacher, such as base ten blocks, pattern blocks, algebra tiles, miras, rulers, and play money. Keep in mind that these tools do not automatically ensure a successful lesson. As we mentioned earlier, hands-on materials can, in some cases, actually get in the way of learning. Students may, for example, get so involved in trying to properly model a fraction-addition problem with pattern blocks that they become proficient at using blocks but miss the major mathematical concepts of the lesson. In a sense, the proper use of the manipulatives can almost become more important in the student's eyes than mastering the mathematical content. We need to be very careful in selecting and using hands-on manipulative materials and recognize that their proper use in the classroom is a teaching skill that is developed over time. A surgeon can spend years studying books about how to repair a damaged liver, but the first time the physician is handed a scalpel, everything goes back to zero—the skill of actually using the scalpel is much different from having memorized the properties of the scalpel and its proper use. And as a surgeon spends several years learning to use the scalpel properly to make incisions, the mathematics teacher needs time to learn how to properly use manipulatives in the classroom.

The list that follows contains a series of recommendations and practical suggestions for the use of manipulatives in the secondary and middle school mathematics classroom. It includes both a summary of the discussion in this chapter and a few additional ideas to consider when planning to use hands-on materials in the classroom:

GENERAL TIPS ON MANIPULATIVE USE

1. Always *allow students "free play" time* with manipulatives the first couple of times that they are distributed. Students often need up to 15 to 20 minutes the first time that they encounter manipulatives, such as pattern blocks, or technology, such as a graphing calculator, simply to explore and experiment with them. Giving students time for free play reduces the likelihood that they will be exploring the materials while you are trying to teach the lesson.

2. It is important to realize that manipulatives can tempt students to exhibit off-task behavior. Therefore, *establish specific rules* for the use of hands-on materials. For example, you might specify that students cannot touch the materials during a whole-class discussion unless the teacher says that they may. Furthermore, if a student throws a manipulative, such as a base ten block, there must be a consequence. The consequence may be that the student loses the privilege of using hands-on materials for a week for a first offense, and the second offense results in a phone call to parents.

3. *Establish a routine for distributing and collecting materials.* For example, if students are working in learning teams, one person should be designated to get the materials, and another student should be responsible for cleaning up and returning the tools to their storage space.

4. *Don't ask students to memorize procedures with the manipulatives.* The hands-on materials should be used as a teaching aid but not as another process to be memorized. Students have enough problems with learning the mathematics without worrying about whether they are modeling the problem with the manipulatives in a way that satisfies the teacher.

5. *Remember that manipulatives are tools but are not the focus of instruction.* Lessons that teach students "about" algebra tiles or calculators are not useful in and of themselves. Instead, the materials should be used as a means to promote mathematical ideas.

6. Remember that students learn the mathematics as they discuss what they are doing with the materials; *they do not inherently learn simply because they use manipulatives.* In Chapter 3, the processes of reflection and communication were described as critical in the learning process. We cannot assume that the students mastered an outcome simply because they used hands-on materials; instead, the tools should promote the discussion and interaction that bring about the learning.

7. *Not every child will find manipulatives the easiest or the best way to solve certain problems.* Hands-on materials are merely an aid for those students who tend to learn best visually or tactilely, and provide a concrete experience.

8. *Work with other teachers in the building to determine a central location for storage of manipulatives.* When teachers need a set of graphing calculators or metric rulers for a lesson, they often don't know where the tools are located in the building. Consequently, some people avoid hands-on problems because it hardly seems worth the effort to try to find the materials. A tools closet with a sign-out system makes the use of manipulatives much more practical.

Use of Technology

The NCTM Standards for Teaching and Learning Mathematics listed calculators, computers, and other technology as important tools for generating discussions in the mathematics classroom. Furthermore, one of the principles from *Principles and Standards for School Mathematics* is the technology principle, which states that "technology is essential in teaching and learning mathematics; it influences the mathematics that is taught and enhances students' learning" (NCTM, 2000, p. 24). Throughout this book, a number of references have been made to the use of technology to support everything from curve sketching to exploring rational and irrational numbers. As is the case with manipulatives, there are times when a calculator or computer is appropriate, and other times when they are not useful. The diagram shown in Figure 7.8 is taken from one of the NCTM documents.

Figure 7.8   NCTM Problem-Solving Model

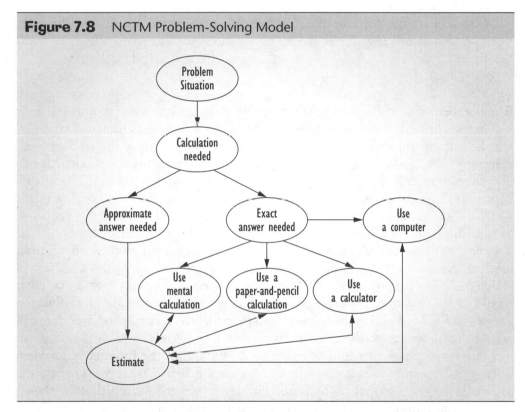

(Reprinted with permission from *Curriculum and Evaluation Standards for School Mathematics,* copyright © 1989 by National Council of Teachers of Mathematics. All rights reserved.)

This graphic reminds us that there are times when a calculator or a computer is appropriate in solving a problem and other times when mental or paper-and-pencil methods are best. For example, if you were multiplying the cost of a gallon of gas by the number of gallons to determine the total cost of a tank of gas, here are possible multiplication problems you might encounter:

A. $3.49 × 10
B. $3.50 × 2.2
C. $3.59 × 14.36

Most people would calculate (A) mentally by moving the decimal to get $34.90. Although some people might also prefer to do (B) mentally, a quick paper-and-pencil calculation shows a solution of $7.70. It would be rare to find someone who preferred to perform the calculation in (C) by hand and even more unusual to find someone who could do it mentally. So it makes sense to use a calculator for (C), keeping in mind that the answer should come out to somewhere between $45 and $55, because a number greater than 14 is being multiplied by a number between 3 and 4. This last example also reminds us that it is extremely important to teach students to mentally estimate an answer before pressing calculator keys, so that they will know if their answer is at least in the ballpark. There has probably never been a period in history in which it was more important for students to develop number sense and be able to make mental approximations because we need to ensure that answers calculated using machines make sense. But to ask students to do calculations such as that shown in (C) by hand tends to consume more time in the classroom than it is worth in the long run. So, allow technology to take over only when it is appropriate.

Let's look at another example. Suppose that a student in a high school mathematics course is solving a linear system of equations such as

$$\begin{cases} 2x + 5y = -3 \\ y = -3x + 15 \end{cases}$$

If the student chooses to solve the system by addition and subtraction, the individual may begin by adding $3x$ to both sides of the second equation and multiplying the bottom equation by 5. When doing this multiplication, the student must determine 5×15. At this point, we often see students reaching for a calculator to find the product. It then becomes the teacher's responsibility to step in and say, "Let's see if we can do that one in our heads. Can anyone think of how we might do that without having to reach for a calculator?" Using the Distributive Property, as was discussed in Chapter 2, students can then be led to think of 5×15 as $5(10 + 5)$ and can mentally add $50 + 25$ to get 75. Not only does this conversation teach students how to do simple mental arithmetic but it also provides a context in which to review the power of the Distributive Property. The point here is that most would agree that it is inappropriate for students to use a calculator to find the answer to 5×15, and it is the teacher's job to model the mental processes that will enable the student to do the calculation without technology.

The same argument could be made about the use of the Internet in problem solving. Although a student might be able to use the World Wide Web to find the price of a car for a project on budgeting, it may be easier just to pick up a phone, call the local auto dealership, and ask. In the classroom, it is critical that we take the leadership role and help students recognize when it is appropriate to use technology. If algebra students are asked to find $(-9) + (-3)$ and reach for their calculators, it is our responsibility to remind them that they should be able to do this calculation mentally. Students learn how to use technology properly when their instructors demonstrate and model proper use of the tools. And as the NCTM stated, technology is merely a tool. A calculator may be able to draw a graph and solve an equation, but only its user knows when a graph is needed or how to set up the equation that needs to be solved in the first place.

The technology principle states that "the effective use of technology in the mathematics classroom depends on the teacher. Technology is not a panacea. As with any teaching tool, it can be used well or poorly. Teachers should use technology to enhance their students' learning opportunities by selecting or creating mathematical tasks that take advantage of what technology can do efficiently and well—graphing, visualizing, and computing" (NCTM, 2000, pp. 25–26). If our classrooms are dominated by real-life, application-oriented problems, our students will be able to spend more time reasoning and problem solving, thus allowing the technology to be the means that it was designed to be—not the end that many believe it has become.

Diagrams, Graphs, and Other Discussion Starters

The final classroom tool that we will discuss here is the use of a picture to generate a classroom discussion. Often, students can be motivated by a graph, a diagram, a picture, or some such visual image that involves mathematical principles. Consider this problem as illustrated in Figures 7.11 through 7.13, adapted from the University of Hawaii Geometry Learning Project (Curriculum Research and Development Group, 1997):

SPOTlight on Technology

Calculators have been used in mathematics classrooms since the mid-1970s. However, many graphing calculators, computers, and handheld computers on the market now also feature **computer algebra systems (CAS)**. A calculator or computer with CAS not only is able to do numerical calculations and draw graphs but also can manipulate algebraic (symbolic) expressions that involve variable expressions. Computer algebra systems, for example, can simplify expressions, solve equations and inequalities, and manipulate vectors and matrices. With a single stroke of a key, the irrational roots of the quadratic equation $2x^2 - x = x^2 + 7$ are identified.

Some educators and community members fear that if students use a calculator to solve most of the problems contained in a traditional algebra book with a press of the button, the students will no longer understand what they are doing. Furthermore, if the calculator can solve equations and simplify expressions, one might wonder if there are any paper-and-pencil algebra skills that are still worth teaching. Research, however, counters many of the apprehensive feelings about CAS that are typical of mathematics teachers. For example, Heid, Blume, Hollebrands, and Piez (2002) showed that, in 8 out of 9 research studies, students who used CAS in school—whose teachers deemphasized paper-and-pencil manipulations—performed as well or better on achievement tests requiring symbolic procedures than did their peers who did not learn through use of the technology. Furthermore, the research also indicates that students who use CAS in their mathematics classes tend to possess higher levels of conceptual understanding of the algebra and to become better problem solvers than their peers who do not use technology.

Examples of the use of CAS are plentiful in resource publications. See, for example, the November 2002 focus issue of *Mathematics Teacher* journal and *Computer Algebra Systems in Secondary School Mathematics Education* (Fey, Cuoco, Kieran, McMullin, & Zbiek, 2003). Let's consider two simple exercises. Suppose that you were teaching students how to solve linear equations, such as $3(x + 5) - 2x = 4x - 8$. The equation can be entered into a calculator or handheld computer with CAS, as shown in Figure 7.9, which was produced on a TI Nspire CX-CAS.

Figure 7.9 Solving an Equation on a Handheld Computer with CAS

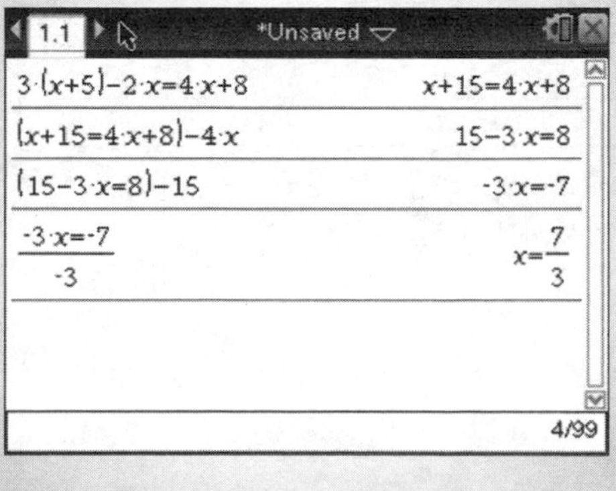

Instead of using the SOLVE command, the student transforms the equation, step by step, by telling the computer what to do (e.g., to subtract $4x$, subtract 15, and then divide by -3). Edwards (2003) noted that students can solve equations in this fashion without fear of making a mechanical error, such as subtracting incorrectly. Consequently, the student can focus on the steps necessary to solve the equation for the variable.

In another example, think of how you might approach teaching the binomial theorem in a second-year algebra or pre-calculus course. By using a calculator with CAS, students can generate several binomial expansions, as shown in Figure 7.10, which were created with the TI-89 graphing calculator with CAS.

As students expand the binomial $(x + 1)$ to progressively higher powers, the teacher can ask the class to report on patterns that they see. Students will notice a decreasing pattern in the exponents and, if they have studied Pascal's Triangle, will also note that the coefficients are rows of numbers from the Triangle. Although it is true that this same lesson could be conducted without a calculator, think of how long it would take for a student to expand an expression such as $(x + 1)^8$. The CAS allows the students to focus on the pattern and "invention" of the binomial theorem, rather than spend the time manipulating symbols on a page and hoping not to make a minor mistake that would throw off the entire patterning process.

The use of calculators and computers with CAS is revolutionizing the teaching of mathematics. In the process, teachers need to rethink what is important in terms of necessary paper-and-pencil skills. Goldenberg (2003) pointed out that "a new emphasis must be implemented because some algebra skills that are no longer needed for

Figure 7.10 Using a Calculator with CAS to Discover the Binomial Theorem

(a)
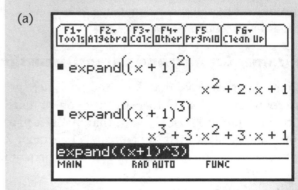

(b)
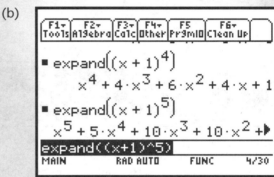

finding answers still remain essential for *understanding* answers or the methods by which the answers are found" (p. 17). Educators ultimately will need further professional development on the appropriate uses of technology in the teaching and learning of algebra because they are being challenged to teach in ways that are different from how they learned mathematics as students.

Figure 7.11 Picture Representation of a Table

Figure 7.12 Picture of the Scratch Made by Moving a Table

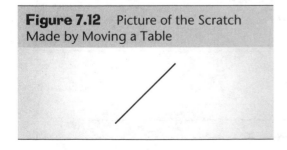

Jill's mother asked her to move a heavy metal table. Its top view is shown, with the positions of its legs at the vertices.

After moving the table, Jill sees to her horror that the lower right leg of the table has made a deep scratch mark on the wooden floor, as shown.

Draw the position of the table before and after Jill moved it.

How would you draw the picture? Make a sketch before reading ahead. Figure 7.13 illustrates three different possible interpretations that students may have of the image.

Students may also argue about whether the table started at the upper right and was pushed down and to the left or whether it started from the lower left and was pushed up and to the right. They may eventually conclude that there is an infinite number of solutions to the problem because the table can also

Figure 7.13 Interpretations of How the Scratch Was Made

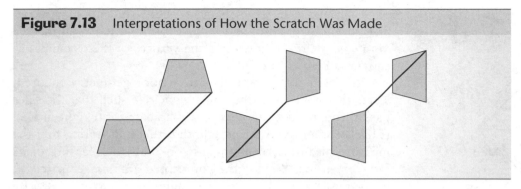

(Figures 7.11, 7.12, and 7.13 from the Geometry Learning Project, Curriculum Research and Development Group, University of Hawaii. Reprinted with permission.)

be rotated 360°, pivoting on the lower right leg. The point here is that, although the lesson focuses on the geometric notions of a translation (slide) and a rotation (turn), the picture lends itself to considerable discussion in the classroom, as students try to determine how the scratch might have been created. As such, the picture and its related problem become tools that have the potential to generate a classroom debate and discussion.

A similar problem for a mathematics class is to present the students with a line segment as shown in Figure 7.14 and present the following problem:

Figure 7.14 Find the Rectangle for Which This Line Segment Is a Diagonal

———————

Draw a rectangle such that this segment is one of its diagonals.

Some students will often immediately jump to the conclusion that there is only one answer to the problem and draw a rectangle such as the one shown in Figure 7.15:

Figure 7.15 Rectangle with the Segment as Its Diagonal

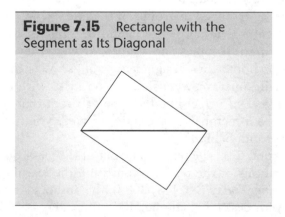

But, on further inspection, they will realize that there are some other solutions, such as the general rectangle and the square illustrated in Figure 7.16.

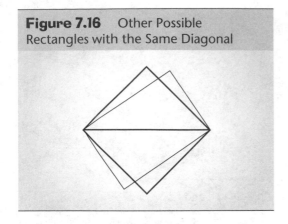

Figure 7.16 Other Possible Rectangles with the Same Diagonal

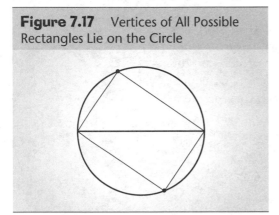

Figure 7.17 Vertices of All Possible Rectangles Lie on the Circle

Continuing the generalizing process, students may recognize that a diagram of several possible solutions will include points on a circle representing the vertices of the rectangles as shown in Figure 7.17.

Interestingly, a typical high school geometry theorem states that angles inscribed in a semicircle such that the sides pass through the endpoints of a diameter form right angles. (This theorem follows from another theorem stating that the measure of an inscribed angle is one-half the measure of its intercepted arc. Because the intercepted arc is a semicircle, it measures 180° so the inscribed angle must measure 90°.) By exploring this problem, students are likely to discover the theorem for themselves. In this case, we see that a single drawing of a line segment serves as a tool for a rich classroom discussion about rectangles, right angles, and, eventually, circles and inscribed angles.

The tools that teachers choose to employ—manipulatives, technology, diagrams, or others—are intended to serve as the basis for discussion of important mathematical topics. The tools, therefore, are not inherently valuable. Tools *become* valuable when they are carefully selected and effectively used in a positive learning environment to generate classroom discussion or discourse. In the following sections, we look at learning environments and what it means to promote meaningful discourse in the classroom.

Learning Environment

Try to visualize some mathematics classrooms that you have visited. When you looked around the rooms, what did you see? Were they cluttered and messy with stacks of books and papers? Did you see posters on the walls, suggesting mathematical themes, or were the walls antiseptic, with nothing on them? Were the desks arranged in neat parallel rows of individual workstations, or were tables or sets of desks arranged in groups of four or six? Were there tables with chairs, or were there individual desks? Were the bulletin boards colorful and suggestive of mathematical topics and themes, or were they bare or simply displaying calendars or homework assignment listings? Was the teacher shouting at the class to remain quiet, or were students on-task, with the teacher helping those who needed it? Did it feel like the type of room that invited you in and made you want to be a member of the class, or were you happy to get out the door and leave the room behind?

All of these factors, from the physical layout of the classroom to the attitudes, beliefs, and expectations of the teacher, constitute the **learning environment**. In *Mathematics Teaching Today* (NCTM, 2007), the authors state, "More than just a physical setting with desks, bulletin boards, and posters, the classroom environment is suggestive of a hidden curriculum with messages about what counts in learning and doing mathematics" (p. 40). Furthermore, the authors declare that the environment should encourage students to justify solutions, to persevere in problem solving, and to support one another in the teaching and learning process. We generally don't need more than a 10-minute visit to a mathematics classroom to know exactly what the teacher values in that room. What we absorb as we look around and listen is the environment. The NCTM standard on the learning environment is as follows:

STANDARD 4: LEARNING ENVIRONMENT

The teacher of mathematics should create a learning environment that provides—

- the time necessary to explore sound mathematics and deal with significant ideas and problems;
- a physical space and appropriate materials that facilitate students' learning of mathematics;
- access and encouragement to use appropriate technology;
- a context that encourages the development of mathematical skill and proficiency;
- an atmosphere of respect and value for students' ideas and ways of thinking,
- an opportunity to work independently or collaboratively to make sense of mathematics;
- a climate for students to take intellectual risks in raising questions and formulating conjectures; and
- encouragement for the student to display a sense of mathematical competence by validating and supporting ideas with a mathematical argument.

(NCTM, 2007, pp. 39–40)

The physical environment in the classroom can be a very important motivator. When students walk into a classroom and see a poster showing the first 2,000 digits of pi or an unsolved problem such as the triangle-trisection problem, students often can't help but get caught up in the wonder of mathematics. One of the features of an attractive classroom is the bulletin board. Bulletin boards often are used for utilitarian purposes, such as posting announcements, bulletins, schedules, homework assignments, and calendars, but they also can be used to promote mathematical understanding. For example, the bulletin board could display the ancient Egyptian numeration system, with the symbols that represent a few numbers. Underneath might be a series of questions, such as "How does this differ from our system?" and "How would you write 1,247 in hieroglyphics?" This type of bulletin board is interactive in that students learn something from reading it and might be challenged by a problem posed on it.

Similarly, some teachers put a "Problem of the Week" on the bulletin board. Changing the problem each week, they challenge students to turn in a solution by the end of the week, often offering extra credit points or some other incentive. Several excellent Internet sites (see, for example, http://mathforum.org/pows) can be used as resources from which to draw problems of this type for a bulletin board. In fact, a simple search of the Internet for "Problem of the Week + mathematics" can reveal more than twenty-six million Web pages of problems! Also, students often solve problems as part of classroom projects and can display their solutions on a bulletin board. The displays not only showcase student work but also are attractive reminders of the work that has been taking place in the classroom. A simple piece of corkboard can generate excitement in the mathematics classroom.

The physical arrangement of desks in the classroom is also an environmental issue to consider. Historically, desks are placed in straight, parallel rows. However, the straight rows suggest a lecture-style lesson and send a message that students should not be talking to one another. If the teacher values teamwork, student interaction, and hands-on lessons, desks are rarely placed in rows. You might consider putting four desks together to form a "table," so that all four students face one another.

Figure 7.18 Classroom Design of Desks Arranged in Tables of Four

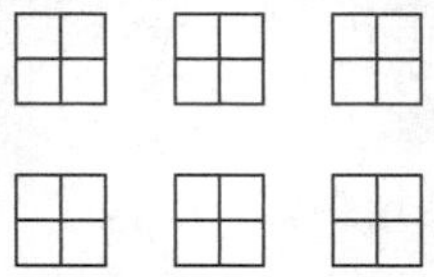

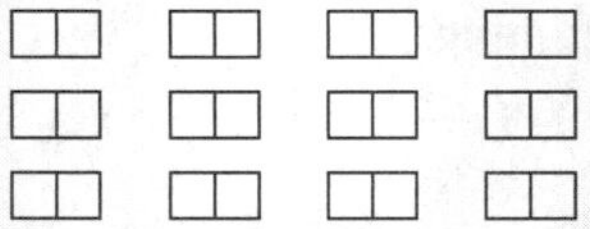

The arrangement shown in Figure 7.18 promotes student interaction while, at the same time, it creates more floor space around tables and makes the room feel more open and inviting.

Some teachers find it useful to arrange the room with rows of desks placed in pairs as shown in Figure 7.19. In this configuration, each student has a buddy with whom to work during routine classroom activities, and, whenever needed, two pairs of students can be joined to form a team of four.

Figure 7.19 Classroom Design of Desks Arranged in Pairs

Teachers who frequently employ cooperative strategies (discussed later in this chapter) sometimes find it best to leave individual desks in straight rows and ask students to move the furniture before a cooperative activity. This method has students sitting by themselves for some teacher-led lessons, which is conducive to classroom management and positive discipline. In addition, students are less prone to copy others' papers in quiz and testing situations if their desks are separated. However, this factor must be weighed against the amount of time spent moving desks around and the noise and distractions of desks being dragged across the floor into pairs or groups of four. Most importantly, the teacher needs to think about the message sent about the nature of the mathematics class and the invitation to learning by the placement of the furniture within the room. Maybe that's why kindergarten teachers often have rugs on the floor and few, if any, desks.

As we discussed in Chapter 3, in the sections on motivation and disposition, students develop their attitudes toward mathematics by virtue of how the classrooms are structured. A sixth grader who was asked to "write a letter to a friend, explaining to that friend how we add $\frac{1}{3} + \frac{1}{4}$" responded to the teacher, "You've got to be kidding! That's what you do in English class; it's not what you're supposed to do in math!" Why did the student respond that way? Probably because it was the first time a teacher had ever expected that student to write in a mathematics classroom. As soon as the teacher begins to require that students justify their thinking in words and with pictures, the students understand that this is what will be expected of them within the particular classroom environment. Indeed, the types of questions the teacher asks, the way they are asked, and the way the teacher responds to correct and incorrect answers all affect the classroom environment. Let's look at a simple example.

Ms. Barry is leading a discussion on Pascal's Triangle in her third period Integrated Mathematics 3 course for juniors. She has just looked at the first row containing 1, 1, the second row containing 1, 2, 1, and the third row containing 1, 3, 3, 1.

Ms. Barry: Does anyone know what numbers will be in the fourth row? Pat?

Pat: 1, 4, 4, 4, 1?

Ms. Barry: No, that's not it. Anyone else?

Juan: 1, 4, 6, 4, 1.

Ms. Barry: Very good, Juan. That's it!

In this situation, Pat was incorrect but was neither rewarded for attempting the solution nor revisited to see if Juan's answer made sense. And, in the end, the class now knows the correct answer but may still wonder how Juan solved the problem. Now, look at the possibility for a discussion in another way:

Ms. Barry: Does anyone know what numbers will be in the fourth row? Pat?

Pat: 1, 4, 4, 4, 1?

Ms. Barry: How did you get that, Pat?

Pat: In the second row, we put a 2 in the middle, and in the third row, we put a 3, 3, so I figured that the next row should have three 4s. It fits the pattern, doesn't it?

Ms. Barry: Can others see how Pat found that pattern? What other kinds of patterns did you find? Juan?

Juan: I got 1, 4, 6, 4, 1.

Ms. Barry: What pattern did you notice, Juan? How did you get that?

Juan: Well, the 3 came from the sum of 2 + 1 above it, so in the fourth row, the 4 comes from 1 + 3 above it; the 6 comes from 3 + 3, and the other 4 comes from 3 + 1 above it. That's the pattern I saw.

Ms. Barry: Hmmm . . . that pattern seems to work too. How many others got the same answer and pattern that Juan found? (Several students raise their hands.) Did anyone else get the solution that Pat got? (Two other students raise their hands.)

Brian: I actually got them both and couldn't decide when to raise my hand. I think it works either way.

Melissa: Me, too. I wasn't sure which was right.

Ms. Barry: Did anyone else get a third solution or see another pattern? (No hands are raised.) Well, let's go back to the coin-tossing problem we looked at the other day and see if we can figure out which answer would fit the real-life problem we were working on.

At this point, Ms. Barry would return to a previous day's problem and have students look at the possible outcomes for tossing four coins. Once students realize that they can get four heads (1 way), three heads and one tail (4 ways), two heads and two tails (6 ways), one head and three tails (4 ways), or four tails (1 way), they will recognize that Juan's solution fits the real-life problem and can argue that Pat's version fits a reasonable pattern but would not actually be the next row of the triangle. The idea here is that in the first version of this classroom scenario, the teacher was exhibiting a value on correct answers over student thinking. In the alternative version, however, the students' thinking took the center stage, and Ms. Barry allowed her students to explain their reasoning and encouraged them to defend their solutions. In the second case, the classroom environment is much more open and supportive of student interaction and thinking. If teachers want students to actively participate and share ideas, they must model a willingness to listen to student responses and value interactions.

The following list was distributed to students and posted by a mathematics teacher as a way to help students to think about the importance of building a supportive, nonthreatening mathematical community in the classroom.

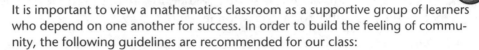

BUILDING A MATHEMATICAL COMMUNITY

It is important to view a mathematics classroom as a supportive group of learners who depend on one another for success. In order to build the feeling of community, the following guidelines are recommended for our class:

- View our class as a community in which each person wants all of the others to be successful in their learning experiences. Try not to see the classroom as a competitive environment in which your role is to outdo others.
- Criticize ideas, not people (e.g., say, "I disagree with the way you solved that problem because . . .," rather than, "You're so stupid; I can't believe you got that answer!").
- Make frequent contributions to classroom discussions by asking questions, answering questions, and reaffirming or disagreeing with comments made by others.
- Take responsibility for the learning of other students. If you understand a concept, take it upon yourself to help others (at your table or in the whole class) understand it as well.
- Ask questions and let the teacher and teammates know when you don't understand something. Remember that no one can read your mind—you will need to communicate your lack of understanding to get someone to help you.
- Encourage classmates to participate. Don't let individuals sit, day after day, without contributing their thoughts (e.g., encourage the person sitting next to you to raise the question with the class that the individual has expressed to you).
- Recognize that there is no such thing as a wrong answer in a mathematics classroom. It has been said that students never give a wrong answer; they simply answer a question different from the one the teacher intended. Seemingly wrong answers are actually opportunities for the class to explore new ideas.
- Realize that it is natural to fear failure in the classroom, but recognize that your classmates have this same fear and that risk-taking is important for success. For this reason, never laugh at the response of a classmate: laughter erodes confidence and feeds that fear. Also, you may be in the same position on the next day.
- Use first names. It creates a much more supportive environment when you say, "I think Frances is correct, but I disagree with Joseph's answer, and here's why . . ." than to refer to classmates simply as "he" and "she."
- Support one another. When you respond in a class discussion, make use of previous points made by saying, "I agree with Mark. And I also think that. . . ." If someone comes up with a unique approach or solution to a problem, it is appropriate to applaud and affirm that person.

Keep in mind that any time students are encouraged to contribute and debate their ideas, the teacher is likely to have some discipline concerns and classroom management issues, particularly when the classroom's desks are arranged in pairs or groups of four. However, we find that in many cases, if the students are provided with a combination of a nurturing environment and worthwhile, hands-on problems to solve, the disciplinary concerns are kept to a minimum. Simply put, students are much more likely to act out and be uncooperative when they are asked to do repetitive worksheets in a lecture-style classroom than when they are allowed to solve interesting problems in learning teams. However, some simple strategies can promote positive classroom management.

1. As was mentioned previously, students need specific directions for the use of classroom materials. If they are to measure circles with string, tell them up front that the string and rulers are the tools of the mathematician and are not toys. If students know, in advance, that the teacher expects appropriate use of the tools, this awareness will go a long way in curtailing management problems. As teachers, we need to anticipate potential misbehavior so that we can address our concerns with students before beginning an activity. Then, if students do not follow the prescribed rules of the classroom, the materials can be taken away or the student told to work alone on the project as a consequence. When students are working in learning teams, they need to be reminded that they are expected to speak no louder than they would if they were simply sitting at the kitchen table talking to their parents. Although it seems simplistic to tell 17-year-olds to keep their voices down in small-group interactions, just explaining what you want before an activity can significantly reduce problems.

2. When distributing materials for use in a hands-on activity, always try to explain to the students what they will be doing and review the directions *before* handing out the materials. If you hand some algebra tiles to a student and then start to explain what the class will be doing with them, the student often will start building a castle with the materials before you even finish explaining that you don't want the class to do that.

3. If your room is arranged in pairs or fours, have the students pull their desks apart and face them forward before handing out test papers. You can more easily monitor the classroom, and students are much less likely to attempt to cheat. Remember that each class is different, so the management strategy that works for one group using hands-on materials or cooperative learning may or may not work for another class or another teacher. However, the "good teacher" reflects on what works and what doesn't and uses the experience to improve classroom situations in the future.

4. When having a full class discussion, emphasize to the students that only *one* person can contribute to the conversation at a time. Students should not be speaking over one another, just as the teacher should not attempt to talk over student voices. Allow plenty of wait time and make sure that *every* student is quiet before answering or posing a question. In an environment of mutual respect, both students and the teacher value one another's thoughts enough to listen to all exchanges of ideas.

lassroom Discourse

The Role of Discourse

At the beginning of the chapter, we presented Anne Kelley's discussion about square roots with her students. After she had posed a problem to the class, several points were raised by students, forcing her to decide what to pursue and what to leave alone. In a contemporary mathematics classroom atmosphere that invites student interaction and emphasizes conjecture and validation of thinking, the teacher has an important role in directing the communication process. In *Mathematics Teaching Today* (NCTM, 2007), the authors stated that **discourse** as "the ways of representing, thinking, talking, agreeing, and disagreeing . . . is central to what and how students learn about mathematics" and that "discourse represents both what the ideas entail and the way ideas are exchanged: Who talks? About what? In what ways? What do people write? What do they record, and why? What questions are important? How do ideas change? Whose ideas and ways of thinking are valued? Who determines when to end a discussion?" (p. 46). Discourse in the classroom is largely driven by the tasks and tools selected by the teacher as well as the environment that has been established. The text of the standard on discourse follows:

▼ STANDARD 5: DISCOURSE

The teacher of mathematics should orchestrate discourse by—

- posing questions and tasks that elicit, engage, and challenge each student's thinking;
- listening carefully to students' ideas and deciding what to pursue in depth from among the ideas that students generate during a discussion;
- asking students to clarify and justify their ideas orally and in writing and by accepting a variety of presentation modes;
- deciding when and how to attach mathematical notation and language to students' ideas;
- encouraging and accepting the use of multiple representations;
- making available tools for exploration and analysis;
- deciding when to provide information, when to clarify an issue, when to model, when to lead, and when to let students wrestle with a difficulty;
- monitoring students' participation in discussions and deciding when and how to encourage each student to participate.

(NCTM, 2007, p. 45)

A book by Smith and Stein (2011) entitled *5 Practices for Orchestrating Productive Mathematics Discussions* outlines five ways that teachers can use student responses to promote discourse, including the following:

1. **anticipating** likely student responses to challenging mathematical tasks;
2. **monitoring** students' actual responses to the tasks (while students work on the tasks in pairs or small groups);
3. **selecting** particular students to present their mathematical work during the whole-class discussion;
4. **sequencing** the student responses that will be displayed in a specific order; and
5. **connecting** different students' responses and connecting the responses to key mathematical ideas. (p. 8)

Using this model, the teacher is instrumental in posing rich tasks for the class and then carefully using students' thinking to advance the lesson.

However, although the teacher generally directs the discourse in a mathematics classroom, students must realize that they have an important role in the process as well. They need to learn to listen to one another, to share their thinking, and to challenge or affirm the thinking of others. In Chapter 3, we discussed how learning often happens in a social environment as students affirm or refute the mathematical reasoning of others. As students listen to one another and say, "yes, that's what I think, too" or "no, I disagree because . . . ," they are engaged in the type of discourse that brings about learning. Students have a responsibility to actively engage in classroom discussions and problem solving, and teachers are charged with the task of assessing student interactions to determine whether the students are fulfilling that obligation. Assessing students in team interactions using checklists and self-evaluations is discussed in Chapter 10.

Questioning Skills

Much of the discourse in the classroom is the result of effective questions raised by the teacher. In fact, the difference between a strong lesson and a weaker one often lies in the teacher's ability to raise clear but critical questions with artistry. This is why Chapter 6 emphasized how specific, key questions to be asked of students should be written in advance and included in the lesson plan. Entire books have been written on questioning skills in the classroom because the way that teachers ask questions determines whether students actively engage in a discussion or shy away from it. For example, a teacher exploring permutations with a class could ask, "How many ways can you arrange 6 pictures on a fireplace mantel?" Students should respond that there are 6! or 720 possible arrangements. This is a **closed question** in that it has only one expected and correct response. Now, suppose that the teacher had said, "I have 6 pictures to arrange on the fireplace mantel. I'll bet there are at least 500 ways to do that. I need you to prove that I'm right or to prove that I'm wrong." If a student raised a hand and responded, "There would be 6! ways to arrange them, so there are more than 500," the teacher might reply, "Why should I believe that there are 6! arrangements? How do you know that?" With these questions, the student is pressed to explain *why* the formula works. The teacher then can direct the class in a discussion that leads to the conclusion that there are 6 choices for the first location, then 5 for the second, and so forth. And, even when the students have drawn this conclusion, the teacher can ask, "But why do you multiply $6 \times 5 \times 4 \times 3 \times 2 \times 1$ rather than add those numbers together?" This pushes students even further as they defend why multiplication makes sense, perhaps by drawing a tree diagram to convince the teacher and one another. In this second line of questioning, we refer to these as **open or open-ended questions** because responses are not limited to one correct answer. Students may react in a variety of ways, and the teacher can use those responses to make related points about permutations. In fact, open-ended questions in the classroom may have one correct response but several ways of explaining how to get to it, or the questions may have several acceptable answers.

Wiggins and McTighe (1998) posited that there are six "facets" of understanding a concept and proposed that teachers ask questions to elicit student thinking in each dimension. Table 7.1 illustrates each of the six facets with an example of a question for each.

In their book, the authors argue that development of all six facets is required for an individual to truly understand a concept. While each facet is distinct, they are also interrelated. Teachers can use these dimensions as guidelines for writing questions into lesson plans.

Table 7.1 Six Facets of Understanding

Facet	Sample Questions
Understanding	It appears that the three angles of a triangle always sum to 180°, but why does that happen? Can we prove it?
Interpretation	How does the formula for the area of a trapezoid relate to finding the area of a parallelogram?
Application	How can we use the skill of solving simultaneous equations to solve a problem involving making a choice of a cell phone plan to purchase?
Perspective	How can two politicians from different parties look at the exact same set of data but make entirely different predictions when forecasting the economy?
Empathy	Why do you think that a lot of people confuse the formulas for the circumference and the area of a circle?
Self-Knowledge	What are you most confused about in this unit on decimals, and why is it so difficult for you to make sense of it?

Another way to plan for effective questioning is presented in the original version of the *Professional Standards for Teaching Mathematics* published in 1991. In this document, the NCTM pointed out five different purposes for asking questions in the classroom, together with examples. These purposes and two examples of each are represented as follows.

PURPOSES FOR QUESTIONS IN THE CLASSROOM

1. **Helping students work together to make sense of mathematics**
   "What do others think about what Janine said?"
   "Can you convince the rest of us that makes sense?"
2. **Helping students to rely more on themselves to determine whether something is mathematically correct**
   "Why do you think that?"
   "How did you reach that conclusion?"
3. **Helping students to learn to reason mathematically**
   "Does that always work?"
   "How could you prove that?"
4. **Helping students learn to conjecture, invent, and solve problems**
   "What would happen if . . .? What if not?"
   "Can you predict the next one? What about the last one?"
5. **Helping students to connect mathematics, its ideas, and its applications**
   "How does this relate to . . .?"
   "What ideas that we learned before were useful in solving this problem?"

(NCTM, *Professional Standards for Teaching Mathematics*, 1991, pp. 3–4.)

When orchestrating classroom discourse, it is important to pay attention to the levels of questioning. You might ask yourself, "If someone were keeping track of my questions, placing each question I ask into one of the categories suggested in this chapter, how much variety would he or she observe? Am I asking frequent knowledge-level questions at the expense of higher-level questions? Or is it the other way around?" Students will respond to a question only in the depth that is expected; that is, if you ask a simple knowledge-level question, you'll get a simple answer back. If you expect to generate a meaningful discussion about a mathematical concept, you need to ask a significant question.

On a very practical level, the seemingly slightest change in the way that a question or statement is phrased can make a dramatic difference in the way that students respond. For example, strange as this may sound, teachers should always ask questions that can be answered. As an illustration, consider these two questions that a teacher might ask of an entire class when distributing paper and scissors for a hands-on activity:

Question 1: Did everyone get a sheet of paper and a pair of scissors?

Question 2: Raise your hand if you did not receive both a piece of paper and a pair of scissors.

Which question is preferable and why? You should recognize that Question 1 is a well-intended question, but it has no answer. If you were a student in the class and were asked that question, how would you respond? How do you know whether the other 25 students in the class got paper and a pair of scissors? The question is vague and will lead to confusion about how to respond, and the confusion often leads to behavioral problems. However, Question 2 is a very specific direction to which each person in the class can respond. If you did not receive, for example, a pair of scissors, you will raise your hand. Teachers often make this type of mistake when they work through a mathematics problem with the class and conclude the example by asking, "Does everyone understand this now?" Similarly, the teacher tells students to take out a homework assignment and asks, "Were there questions on the assignment?" The students don't know whether to raise their hands, to shout, "Yes" or "No," or simply to look around and see how other people are responding. Again, the response is entirely different when the teacher concludes an example and asks, "May I have a volunteer come up to the board and reexplain this problem in your own words?" On telling students to take out their homework assignments, the teacher can ask, "How many of you found that at least one problem confused you on the assignment last night?" These direct questions provide the teacher with valuable information and are clearly stated so that students know how they are to respond.

Reading and Literacy

While some may be reluctant to admit it, *every* mathematics teacher is also a reading and literacy teacher. A trend that became popular in the 1970s was to teach "reading in the content area"—in other words, to infuse reading and literacy skills within every subject area, including mathematics. In fact, Barton and Heidema (2002) found that mathematics textbooks tend to include more concepts per sentence and paragraph than do books from any other content area. For many students, learning mathematics is much like learning a foreign language in that it has its own set of terms, definitions, symbols, and syntax. Compounding the problem, some words have multiple meanings in mathematics (e.g., cube can be "third power" or a three-dimensional shape); some words sound similar (e.g., intersect and intercept); while other words are easily confused (e.g., permutation/combination and complementary/

Figure 7.20   Graphic Organizer Relating Number Systems

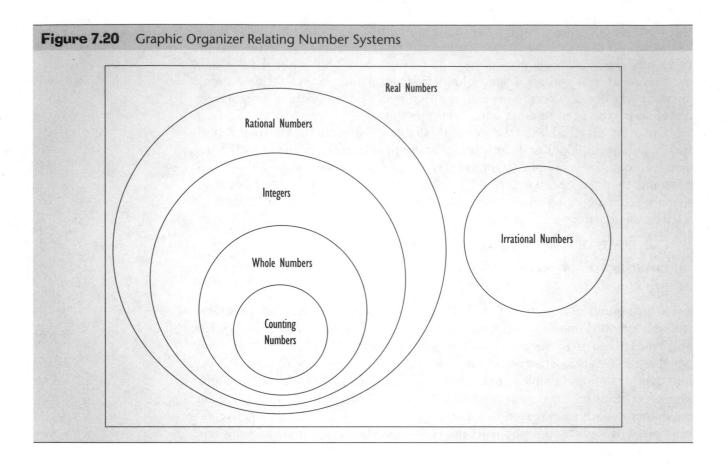

supplementary) (Rubenstein, 2007). Because of these language difficulties, many mathematics teachers do not require their students to read a book at all and, instead, simply spoon-feed all of the terms and definitions to their students.

In the spirit of developing reading and literacy skills, mathematics teachers at all levels are encouraged to incorporate reading and writing in the classroom. One example of a way to promote literacy is to help students use graphic organizers to make sense of terms and definitions. In Chapter 6, for example, we discussed how a conceptual map can be used by the teacher and the students to visually understand connections between the big ideas of a lesson or unit. Other graphic organizers can be equally helpful to the student. Figure 7.20 presents a visual in which students can relate the various number systems.

Figure 7.20 makes it fairly easy for students to see how the Real Numbers are made up of the Rationals and Irrationals and that, for example, the Whole Numbers are contained within the Integers. This visual can be much more effective than simply defining each of the number systems and having students copy the definitions into their notebooks. Similar graphics, such as charts and grids, can be generated to show relationships among quadrilaterals, as well as properties they share, as illustrated in Table 7.2.

The table helps students organize the properties of each quadrilateral for easily comparing shapes to one another, rather than listing the characteristics vertically in a notebook. Other books, such as *Improving Adolescent Literacy* (Fisher & Frey, 2012) and *Teaching Tools for Content Literacy* (Allen, 2004) provide numerous specific ideas for how to incorporate reading and literacy skills in the mathematics classroom. Most importantly, teachers should make every effort to have students read and write about mathematics, rather than avoid textbooks and communication skills.

Table 7.2 Chart to Graphically Represent Quadrilateral Properties

	Parallelogram	Rectangle	Rhombus	Square	Kite
Both pairs of opposite sides parallel	X	X	X	X	
Both pairs of opposite sides congruent	X	X	X	X	
All sides congruent			X	X	
Opposite angles congruent	X	X	X	X	
Diagonals perpendicular			X	X	X

Through a teacher's modeling, the students can learn to read a textbook, design a graphic organizer, or ask questions of one another that have considerable depth and clarity. With time, the students should rely less on the teacher and begin working more frequently with one another when justifying their thinking. Learning teams or cooperative learning strategies can facilitate this process. Cooperative (or collaborative) learning can also greatly enhance the level of discourse that takes place in the classroom.

Classroom Dialogues

A mathematics class was in the middle of a unit on probability. The teacher had led several demonstrations in which students tossed coins, rolled number cubes, spun spinners, and simulated events on a computer. On a quiz problem, the students were asked the following question:

Suppose that two fair coins are tossed at the same time. What is the probability that both coins will display Tails?

In response to this question, one student's work is displayed in Figure 7.21.

Figure 7.21 Student Response to Coin-Tossing Question

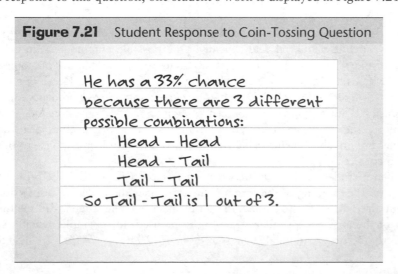

He has a 33% chance because there are 3 different possible combinations:
Head – Head
Head – Tail
Tail – Tail
So Tail - Tail is 1 out of 3.

Of course, the teacher was looking for an answer of $\frac{1}{4}$ (25%), so the student's response is incorrect. What does the student appear to know about probability, and what misconceptions are apparent when reading this response? How might you help this student make sense of the problem?

Interestingly, on this same question, another student in the same class responded, "The probability is one-half because everything is one-half—both the chances of getting a Head and of getting a Tail." Clearly, despite physical manipulations and computer models, students in the class are still making fundamental mistakes. One important message here is that just because a class was actively involved with doing hands-on problems does not automatically imply that all of the students understand how to use their observations to draw accurate conclusions on related problems. The class could benefit from looking at the problem from different perspectives. For example, the teacher may want to go back and have the class view the coin-tossing problem in a tree diagram or a matrix format, as illustrated in Figure 7.22.

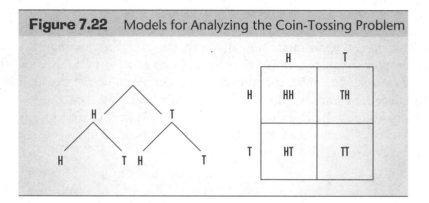

Figure 7.22 Models for Analyzing the Coin-Tossing Problem

Using either the tree or the matrix model, students can see that there are four possible outcomes, not three. The misconception illustrated in the response shown in Figure 7.21 is that the student did not recognize a combination of Head-Tail as being distinct from a result of Tail-Head. The student was simply thinking that the outcomes could be the same (Head-Head or Tail-Tail) or different (Head with a Tail). The tree and matrix, however, indicate otherwise. This mistake is common when students are rolling number cubes as well, as students will often say, "There is only one way to get a sum of 3," thinking of a 1 with a 2. However, a 1-2 and a 2-1 are distinct and represent two different ways to get a sum of 3 when rolling the number cubes.

Another teaching strategy that can be helpful here is to show the class two different coins, such as a quarter and a penny. One possible outcome results when the quarter displays a Head, and the penny comes up a Tail. But another outcome occurs when the quarter displays the Tail, while the penny comes up a Head. Similarly, by using two different colors of dice, such as one green and one red, students can readily see a green "1" and a red "2," or a green "2" with a red "1," and conclude that these outcomes in the sample space are different. In this manner, it becomes clear that four outcomes are possible when tossing two coins, and the student response to the question is incorrect.

When a student writes an incorrect answer on a paper, it is helpful to probe deeply into the meaning of the error. It then becomes the teacher's responsibility to seek out alternative ways to model the problem so that the student can see the inaccuracy of the answer. A similar strategy can be used, for example, when a student incorrectly factors a trinomial such as $x^2 - 4x - 12$ into $(x - 4)(x + 3)$. The teacher could, for example, have the student draw the graphs of $y_1 = x^2 - 4x - 12$ and $y_2 = (x - 4)(x + 3)$ simultaneously on a graphing calculator to show that neither the tables nor the graphs of these two functions match, indicating that there must be a mistake in the factoring. Teachers should refrain from simply marking an error as "wrong" without using the incorrect answer as an opportunity to inform instruction and provide the student with multiple ways to rethink the problem.

Cooperative Learning

John Goodlad's (1984) research showed that, on average, 80 percent of a typical class period is devoted to "teacher talk"; the other 20 percent of the class time, students are actually talking. Consider a typical 50-minute mathematics class: Out of this 50 minutes, 20 percent amounts to 10 minutes of student talk. If you consider that a classroom typically has 20 or more students, this means that the average student is allotted about 30 seconds per day to speak in your class. If we assume that knowledge is, in some way, constructed by the learner, often through interactions with others, then 30 seconds per day is simply not acceptable for student talk time. By using cooperative learning, teachers achieve what is referred to as **simultaneous interaction**, when several students in the classroom share their thinking at the same time. If a classroom of 28 students is divided up into teams of 4 students, and each team is given time to discuss a problem, 7 students can communicate simultaneously. This situation generates 7 times as much student talk time as can be achieved in a traditional classroom setting. The mathematics of talk time is simple, but the results can be striking.

A summary of research studies on cooperative learning published in *Social Education* (Guyton, 1991) showed that the appropriate use of cooperative learning in the classroom results in the following:

- increased achievement and long-term retention
- development of higher-order processing skills
- improved attitude toward school and subject area
- development of collaborative competencies and an increased ability to work with others
- improved psychological health
- liking for fellow classmates, including respect for students with different racial or ethnic backgrounds or disabilities
- increased self-esteem

More recent research found that cooperative learning strategies had a more profound effect on low-income students than high-income students and had significantly more positive effects on urban than suburban students (Ginsburg-Block et al., 2006). So, not only is the student's academic achievement generally enhanced through cooperative learning but also a variety of social and psychological goals can be addressed as well. The key issue here is the appropriate use of cooperative learning in the classroom.

Suppose that Mr. Read poses this problem:

If I were to roll a number cube and toss a fair coin at the same time, what is the probability that I will roll a 6 and toss a head on the same trial?

He gives each table of students a number cube and a coin and tells the students to "figure it out in your groups." Typically, the highest achiever at the table will take the materials, roll the number cube and toss the coin, and tell the rest of the group what is happening. Or, even worse, this student might reason out the sample space—a head with a 1, 2, 3, 4, 5, or 6 or a tail with a 1, 2, 3, 4, 5, or 6—and announce to the group that the probability has to be 1 in 12, eliminating any need for the group of students to actually conduct an experiment and make a conjecture. This traditional way of handling group assignments is often referred to as "groupwork," and it is not equivalent to cooperative learning as defined in the contemporary classroom. We often hear seasoned educators say, "I have used groupwork for years," which translates as "I give a problem to 4 students and tell them to work on it together." But we know exactly what happens—the best student does all the work, and everyone else gets credit for it.

In a cooperative learning environment, the activity should be *structured* so that every student has no choice but to be actively involved in the problem-solving process. Also, each student has **individual accountability**, which means that even though the work is done as a team, in the end, each student is required to individually demonstrate an understanding of the concepts through an interview, a written test, or some other means. So, in the number cube and coin problem (adapted from an NCTM publication, *How to Use Cooperative Learning in the Mathematics Class* [Artzt & Newman, 1997]), the teacher might divide the class into learning teams of three. In each team, one person is assigned the task of rolling the number cube, one person tosses the coin, and one person records the results on paper. Then, after the team has collected the data and come to a conclusion, the teacher randomly selects one person on the team to be responsible for sharing the results of the experiment and explaining the conclusions for the team. By using a random selection at the end, the teacher emphasizes that *every* student on the team must understand the problem because no one knows who will be selected to discuss the results. You will notice how this approach to cooperative learning is entirely different from simply telling a few students to work together. The structure for *how* the students are required to work as a team is provided, so there are no free riders in the process—every student gets involved in the process and is accountable for learning the mathematics. A study conducted with middle school students in Australia showed that when groups of students were given *structured* cooperative learning activities, as opposed to control groups of peers who were simply asked to work as a group, the structured groups were more willing to work together and provided considerably stronger help and support to one another (Gillies, 2004).

Mathematics teachers often use several other cooperative learning structures as well. For example, a *corners* strategy can be used. Suppose that a teacher realizes that students came up with three or four different answers to a homework problem. The individuals who found one solution would be asked to get up and move to one corner of the classroom, while those who found a different solution would move to a different corner. While in those corners of the room, students should share with one another how they found the common answer and why they think it is correct. Then each "corner" is asked to share their solution and an explanation. After all of the explanations, students are permitted to move to a different corner if they have decided to reject their own answer and accept another. Eventually, the students should arrive at the correct answer through these discussions.

Another commonly used cooperative learning structure is called *think-pair-share.* Let's suppose that the teacher has posed a problem to the class. Instead of asking students to immediately discuss the problem, they are individually given, say, three minutes of "think time." After this initial time period, students pair up with other students and discuss their initial thoughts about the problem with another person. Finally, each pair of students is asked to join up with another pair to share their thinking. In this manner, students can progress from individual thinking, to discussion with a partner, to sharing in a small group within a few minutes. Following the four-person table discussions, the full classroom discourse is generally much richer because students are better prepared to talk about the problem after having first shared in smaller group settings. Many other cooperative learning techniques are available to teachers through print resources, Web sites, and professional development workshops. For example, Spencer Kagan's book, *Cooperative Learning* (1994), features numerous structures and practical collaborative strategies that can be used across the curriculum.

You may have heard it said that you never completely understand a concept unless you can explain it to someone else, and that is where cooperative learning can be particularly powerful. When students explain their thinking to others, the result is "win–win" in that the student who is confused gets to hear an explanation from someone other than the teacher, and the students who are helping their peers clarify their own thinking by having to explain it to someone else. Students working in pairs can be a powerful strategy for checking homework assignments as well. Too often, several students go to the chalkboard to demonstrate problems that most other people already know how to do, and valuable class time is wasted. Instead, students can compare and discuss homework solutions at a table and correct one another's errors so that class time is spent only on those items with which students need help. The topic of assigning and checking homework is discussed in more depth in Chapter 11. Following is a list of practical tips and suggestions for implementing cooperative learning strategies.

PRACTICAL TIPS ON IMPLEMENTING COOPERATIVE LEARNING STRATEGIES

1. Rarely, if ever, should a teacher use student-selected or random grouping for learning teams. Instead, a teacher should carefully assign the members to each team. Sometimes, teams of four students are made up of a high achiever, a low achiever, and two average students. Other times, it may be more appropriate to group students of similar ability or performance levels when, for example, a teacher is implementing an enrichment or differentiated curricular model as described in Chapter 4. Whenever possible, a learning team should include a mix of males and females.

2. Once learning teams are established in a class, they should stay together for at least 4 to 6 weeks. A team generally needs a couple of weeks simply to learn how to work together and deal with each others' personalities. Teams should also be changed periodically because students need opportunities to work with others and can grow tired of always working with the same individuals.

3. The process of changing to a cooperative environment can be difficult for some students and should be gradual. If a ninth grader has rarely worked in cooperative teams in middle school, then that student is likely to resist, may prefer to work alone, and will need time to adjust to a collaborative environment.

4. Reading a manual or going to a short workshop on cooperative learning can be helpful in preparing a teacher to use the techniques effectively. However, nothing is more helpful than regular practice and acceptance of the idea that cooperative structures often require several "trials" before the teacher and the class begin to feel comfortable with this way of organizing the classroom.

5. Be prepared for some chaos and disorder when you initially introduce cooperative assignments. Cooperative learning is frightening to many teachers because they feel that they are losing control. Keep in mind that the teacher's role in a cooperative classroom is to guide and not to dispense knowledge.

Classroom discourse, therefore, needs careful analysis by the teacher in terms of the roles of the students and teacher, the effectiveness of questions that are being asked, and the ways in which students communicate and interact in a cooperative classroom. And, as we have mentioned, the way that the teacher runs the classroom—the environment—is critical to enhancing the discourse that occurs within it.

eflective Practices

The final component of effective teaching that we discuss in this chapter is reflection on practice. We discussed this issue in Chapter 6, because reflection should always follow implementation of a lesson plan. **Reflection** is revisited here because there are two standards devoted to this practice—reflection on student learning and reflection on teaching practice.

▼ STANDARD 6: REFLECTION ON STUDENT LEARNING

The teacher of mathematics should engage in ongoing analysis of students' learning by—

- observing, listening to, and gathering information about students to assess what they are learning

So as to—

- ensure that every student is learning sound and significant mathematics and is developing a positive disposition toward mathematics;
- challenge and extend students' ideas;
- adapt or change activities while teaching;
- describe and comment on each student's learning to parents and administrators; and
- provide regular feedback to the students themselves.

(NCTM, 2007, p. 55)

STANDARD 7: REFLECTION ON TEACHING PRACTICE

The teacher of mathematics should engage in ongoing analysis of teaching by—

- reflecting regularly on what and how they teach;
- examining effects of the task, discourse, and learning environment on the students' mathematical knowledge, skills, and dispositions;
- seeking to improve their teaching and practice by participating in learning communities beyond their classroom;
- analyzing and using assessment data to make reasoned decisions about necessary changes in curriculum; and
- collaborating with colleagues to develop plans to improve instructional programs.

(NCTM, 2007, p. 60)

Following these two standards, teachers should be constantly analyzing both the progress of their students and their own teaching practices. Reflection on student learning requires accurate formative and summative assessment strategies, which we will explore in some depth in Unit 4. In terms of reflection on teaching, a piece of conventional wisdom is that many teachers have 20 years of experience, while others have 1 year of experience, repeated 20 times. One of these teachers learns from successes and challenges, and the other ignores the past and tends to make the same mistakes over and over. But learning from experience does not happen automatically; it is part of the teaching and learning process known as reflection, as we first discussed when describing the teaching principle in Chapter 2.

The effective classroom teacher develops the ability to look back on a lesson or teaching episode and analyze it from every angle, thinking about what worked and what didn't. Specifically, you might first look at the task you chose and determine whether students viewed it as worthwhile and whether it fit within the overall scope of the curriculum. Second, you might consider the tools that students used in the lesson—were they appropriate? Should you have selected an additional tool or simply used another? For example, if students used graphing calculators to sketch quadratic functions, might the lesson have been more effective if they had drawn a few hand sketches first? Third, you might think about the learning environment that has been established. Do students feel free to participate? What are they learning about the nature of mathematics by being a member of your class? How might you have managed the classroom more effectively to maintain better discipline? Finally, you can reflect on the classroom interactions. How did the discourse flow? What type of questions did you ask? What kind of questions did the students ask?

As you reflect on these questions, you want to think about the major lesson-planning questions that were raised in Chapter 6: (1) What did I set out to do in this lesson, and why did I plan to do it that way? (2) Did I accomplish my goals and objectives for the lesson? How do I know (i.e., how did I measure the success of my lesson)? (3) What have I learned about my students and myself that will help me to be a better teacher tomorrow, next month, or next year? How would I change the lesson next time? These rather loaded questions constitute what we refer to as *reflection,* the process of thinking through what we have done in the classroom to improve our practice in the future. Ideally, reflection is carried out with colleagues who share their hits and misses with us as we attempt to grow together as a staff. Some details on the issue of interacting with colleagues are included in Chapter 13 in a discussion of professional development.

Conclusion

Near the beginning of this chapter, the question was raised as to what it means to be a "good teacher." Unfortunately, despite centuries of educational practice and countless books, we still don't have a working definition of good teaching. But we do have research on best practices of classroom teachers as well as guidelines set forth by professional organizations to assist us in the teaching and learning process. As you continue to develop your picture of the good teacher, think about what the Standards for Teaching and Learning Mathematics of the NCTM promote—selection of worthwhile tasks, the use of classroom tools, establishment of an effective learning environment, promotion of teacher and student discourse, and ongoing analysis of the teaching and learning process. Furthermore, *Principles and Standards for School Mathematics* emphasizes the importance of the caring teacher in promoting the learning of mathematics for all students.

It has been said that "good teaching is 75 percent planning and 25 percent theater" (Godwin, 1974). When we think about that, it makes sense. Many "B" movies have become major box office hits, not because the scripts were very interesting but because the acting and theatrics were appealing to the audience. Conversely, many potential blockbusters have lost considerable amounts of money because, although they had great scripts, the actors and actresses didn't excite the audiences. Similarly, a well-written, interesting activity can still be a bomb if the classroom teacher doesn't carefully orchestrate the discourse in the classroom. On the other hand, a simple question, such as, "Can anyone give me an estimate of $\sqrt{52}$?" can generate a classroom discussion that continues in depth for an hour or more. In the end, it is neither the content nor the lesson alone that makes the difference; it is the way that the teacher guides the process that matters.

Principles and Standards for School Mathematics and the *Common Core State Standards* recommend a broad range of mathematical content to be taught to all students at the secondary and middle school levels (as described in Chapter 4). In order to effectively teach this diverse content, a teacher needs to plan active, student-centered lessons that make use of the tools and strategies described in the current chapter. In Chapters 8 and 9, we conclude Unit 3 by turning our attention to the teaching of five specific content strands—number, algebra, geometry, statistics and probability, and discrete mathematics.

For bibliographic references and additional resources, see page 411

Glossary

Closed Question: A question is said to be closed if it has only one expected and correct response. Closed questions have their place in the classroom, but they rarely lead to an in-depth discussion because such questions generally do not invite speculation or differences in reasoning.

Computer Algebra Systems (CAS): Calculators or computers with computer algebra systems are able to manipulate algebraic (symbolic) expressions that involve variables, in addition to drawing graphs and performing numerical calculations. CAS can, for example, simplify, factor, or expand algebraic expressions;

solve equations and inequalities; and manipulate vectors and matrices.

Discourse: Discourse is the exchange of ideas in the classroom. Discourse can take place between the teacher and the students or within a group of students. It involves conversation, conjecturing, and sense-making of mathematical ideas and is closely related to the tools used by the teacher and the environment established in the classroom.

Individual Accountability: In using cooperative learning, individual accountability means that, although the work may be done as a team, each student is ultimately required to individually demonstrate an understanding of the concepts through an interview, a written test, or some other means.

Learning Environment: The learning environment is the classroom atmosphere in which a student is immersed. The environment includes both the physical features (e.g., the arrangement of the classroom) and the mood or tone that is set by the teacher.

Mira: A mira is an I-shaped plastic manipulative tool that, when laid on a piece of paper containing a picture, allows one to see the reflection of the picture in its window. A mira is helpful in exploring geometric properties, such as symmetry and reflection, and studying the graphs of functions, such as absolute value.

Open (or Open-Ended) Question: A question is said to be open (or open-ended) when it has several possible answers or one correct answer with several ways to reach the solution. The use of open-ended questions in the classroom can lead to rich discourse as students attempt to make and defend conjectures.

Pedagogical Content Knowledge (PCK): Introduced by Schulman in 1986, this term refers to the importance of teachers possessing both knowledge of the mathematical content they teach *and* an understanding of how to most effectively deliver that content in the classroom.

Reflection: Reflection is the process by which a teacher carefully analyzes a lesson, a unit, a teaching episode, or student progress to determine whether the stated goals and objectives are being met. The "lenses" of worthwhile tasks, tools, classroom discourse, and learning environment can be helpful in reflecting on the teaching practice. Over time, reflection should enable a teacher to fine-tune skills and determine what strategies tend to work best.

Simultaneous Interaction: In cooperative learning situations, simultaneous interaction refers to the idea that many students can interact or share ideas within the classroom at the same time. Simultaneous interaction is a major benefit of cooperative learning. In a traditional model, only one person in a classroom can speak at a given time.

● Discussion Questions and Activities

1. Observe a mathematics class or view a videotape of a teacher in the classroom. Assess the strengths and weaknesses of the lesson by discussing the tasks with which students are engaged, the use of tools, the perceived learning environment, and the flow of discourse in the classroom.

2. Select a topic such as measuring angles or determining a limit. Consult at least three different sources, for example, journals, the Internet, resource books, or a textbook, and choose what you consider to be the best activity for developing the concept. Support your choice by explaining what makes your choice more worthwhile than other possible activities.

3. Select a classroom manipulative from the following list: algebra tiles, base ten blocks, color tiles, Cuisenaire rods, fraction pieces, geoboards, miras, pattern blocks, and tangrams. Research the proper use of the selected manipulative and find examples of lessons and activities that make effective use of the tool. Demonstrate your selected materials to a small group.

4. The Standards for Teaching and Learning Mathematics state that tools that enhance classroom discourse include more than manipulatives and calculators. Locate several examples of other tools—pictures, tables, diagrams, and graphs—that can be used to enhance classroom discourse. Discuss the context in which each of these tools might be used in the classroom.

5. List several specific ideas that teachers can use to help establish a positive learning environment—including both physical and psychological environments. When making the list, reflect on your own experiences as a student and the characteristics of mathematics classrooms that were particularly inviting for you.

6. Observe a mathematics lesson or view one on tape. While watching the lesson, record the level of questions asked by both the teacher and the students, using the questioning levels described in this chapter. What patterns do you notice in the type of questions typically asked by teachers and students? How could those questions be changed to enhance the level of discourse in the classroom?

7. Locate a mathematics textbook for a particular grade level or course. Examine the content and layout of the book. Discuss the textbook in terms of its readability and the degree to which the authors use graphic organizers to help students understand key ideas. How much of the book would you expect your students to read and understand? How can you promote reading and literacy skills through use of the book?

8. Locate an example of a lesson plan or activity in a textbook or other resource that is written for students working alone. Rewrite the lesson plan or activity in a format that incorporates cooperative learning. Be sure to structure the lesson so that every student is actively involved.

9. Observe a mathematics class and interview the teacher and a sample of students from the class. Ask both the teacher and the students what they thought was the greatest strength of the lesson and what should have been changed. Compare the responses of the teacher to the opinions of the students in the class. How well does the teacher appear to be aware of the needs of the students in the room?

10. In this chapter's conclusion, the following quote was cited: "good teaching is 75 percent planning and 25 percent theater." What does this quote mean to you about the art of teaching?

Teaching Number Sense and Algebra

I f you ask most adults to describe key events in their school mathematics experiences, you are likely to hear stories about the fear of standing up in front of others while playing Around-the-World in first grade or the tense emotions felt while taking a timed test in the third or fourth grade. If you press them further to tell you about secondary or middle school mathematics memories, they are likely to describe, in some detail, their experiences with manipulating fractions or trying to make sense of negative numbers. In many cases, people will also tell you about their algebra or geometry classes. People typically remember "algebra" as being the gatekeeper course that kept many students in their schools from moving forward to more advanced classes. They view algebra as "the study of x and y" and recall solving linear equations, factoring trinomials, and simplifying rational expressions—doing page after page of exercises and assuming that no one actually uses those skills in the real world. Similarly, they are likely to remember "geometry" as "that class where we memorized a ton of theorems and postulates and wrote two-column proofs that I never did understand." Despite geometry involving the study of shapes, they will not recall doing anything "hands on" and, instead, only remember simply answering questions from a book. The release of the NCTM *Standards* in 1989 and in 2000, as well as the *Common Core State Standards* in 2010, however, painted a much different picture of the study of school mathematics.

Instead of viewing "number sense" and "algebra" as *courses* to be taken in secondary or middle schools, the

After reading Chapter 8, you should be able to answer the following questions:

- What does it mean to promote "reasoning and sense making" in the mathematics classroom?
- What is the current philosophy of how the mathematics topical areas of number sense and algebra are to be included in the school curriculum?
- What does it mean to develop number sense and what are the key mathematical ideas in the high school and middle grades?
- What are the major components of the study of algebra and how has the vision of the teaching of algebra changed as a result of reform documents?

standards described them as content *strands*—ideas to be revisited and further developed each year that a student attends school, from kindergarten through the senior year of high school. The authors of *Principles and Standards for School Mathematics* noted that "because mathematics as a discipline is highly interconnected, the areas described by the Standards overlap and are integrated. . . . Rich connections and intersections abound" (NCTM, 2000, pp. 30–31). The graphic in Figure 8.1 is taken from the standards and illustrates the relative emphasis of each content area for the grade-level bands.

In Figure 8.1, the NCTM is communicating that the topic of "number," although important throughout the curriculum, decreases in emphasis as students progress across the grades. Conversely, a topic such as algebra becomes increasingly important as students move from elementary into the middle and secondary grades. Of course, topics should connect to one another through the years, but the spirit of the document is that these five content areas are revisited throughout a student's mathematics education although the relative emphasis of the topics varies across the years.

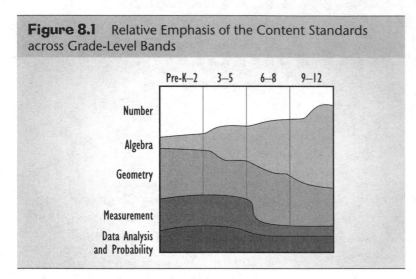

Figure 8.1 Relative Emphasis of the Content Standards across Grade-Level Bands

Additionally, in 2009, NCTM released another important document entitled *Focus in High School Mathematics: Reasoning and Sense Making* that described how the various content areas should be used as tools to promote mathematical thinking. Instead of recommending specific content for each grade level, as did the *Curriculum Focal Points* (2006) book (described in Chapter 4), the authors discussed how developing students' ability to think and problem solve should be the main emphasis of the high school curriculum, regardless of the sequence of courses that are taught. Of course, the following year, the *Common Core State Standards* (2010) delineated eight mathematical practices that describe what it means for a student to think mathematically.

In this chapter, we begin with a discussion of what it means to promote reasoning and sense making. From there, we examine the teaching of number sense and algebra. In each area, we feature a brief discussion of the content topic, followed by a sample lesson plan and several classroom-tested teaching ideas that support the strand. The lesson planning format from Chapter 6 and teaching strategies from Chapter 7 are incorporated in the lessons and activities presented in each section. In Chapter 9, we continue this discussion to include the topics of geometry, statistics and probability, and discrete mathematics. ▪

Reasoning and Sense Making

Consider the following problem posed to a high school mathematics class:

The flip sides of the three coins shown in Figure 8.2 contain a digit between (and including) 1 and 9. No digit may be repeated. When tossed, the sum of the three coins will always be a number between and including 15 and 22. Each sum must be possible. Determine which digit is on the reverse of each of the coins.

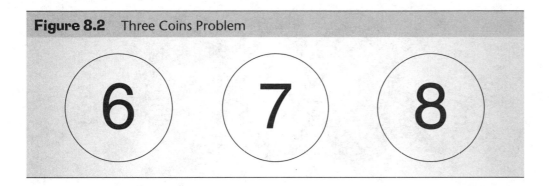

Figure 8.2 Three Coins Problem

Before continuing to read, think about how you might solve this problem. Most people approach the problem by thinking about the extreme values—what it would take to get a 15 and a 22. So, for example, since $6 + 7 + 8$ results in a sum of 21, the only way to get 22 is if the flip side of the "8" is a "9." Now, we might continue this thinking to look at ways to get 20. If an 8 is on one coin, then the other two have to sum to 12. The other two sides cannot be 4 and 8 because 8 is already taken, nor can they be 6 and 6 because a digit cannot repeat. But $5 + 7 = 12$, so perhaps the back of the 6 is a 5. Or, we might want to think of ways to get 15, given that one of the three addends must be an 8 or a 9. Clearly, there are multiple ways to analyze the problem, and most people end up making an organized list of possible addends that result in 15 through 22. The solution to this problem is left for you to think about, but one hint is that there is not necessarily one unique solution. How many solutions are possible? How do you know when you have them all?

The Three Coins activity is most certainly a *problem* as defined in Chapter 1 because the solution and process to determine the solution is not readily apparent. Guess-and-check, making an organized list, or looking for patterns might be appropriate strategies to find the solution. More importantly, this type of problem promotes mathematical thinking. In the NCTM document *Focus on High School Mathematics: Reasoning and Sense Making* (2009), the authors define *reasoning* as "the process of drawing conclusions on the basis of evidence or stated assumptions" (p. 4). By examining different number combinations and working within the constraints of the problem, we draw conclusions about the flip sides of these coins. We employ similar reasoning skills when we try to solve a statistical problem by conducting a survey to collect data and attempt to make reasonable inferences. On the other hand, *sense making* is defined in the book as "developing understanding of a situation, context, or concept by connecting it with existing knowledge" (p. 4). The authors also acknowledge, however, that these two processes—reasoning and sense making—work together when solving problems, as illustrated in Figure 8.3, which is taken from the NCTM publication. The diagram shows that not only are reasoning and sense making often used together, but these processes can extend from an informal investigation with manipulatives all the way to a more formal situation such as writing an algebraic or geometric proof.

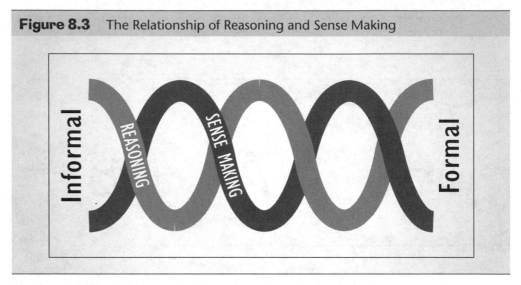

Figure 8.3   The Relationship of Reasoning and Sense Making

(NCTM, 2009. Reprinted with permission.)

Upon reflection, these definitions may be helpful in thinking about what we are really trying to accomplish with the teaching of mathematics. When teaching students to approach a problem, we want them to examine the data to draw conclusions and to connect the situation with ideas they have already developed. Perhaps you have already studied, for example, ways to obtain various sums when rolling a pair of dice and see the Three Coins Problem as simply an extension of what you know. And while teaching for reasoning and sense making may appear to be "common sense," this doesn't always happen in mathematics classrooms. The authors of the document note, "historically, 'reasoning' has been limited to very select areas of the high school curriculum, and sense making is in many instances not present at all" (p. 5). An emphasis on mathematical thinking can help students better understand and retain mathematical ideas.

So, practically speaking, what can teachers do in their classrooms to promote healthy reasoning habits in their students? NCTM provides ten tips for teachers that can be considered in the lesson planning and teaching processes:

- Provide tasks that require students to figure things out for themselves.
- Ask students to restate the problem in their own words, including any assumptions they have made.
- Give students time to analyze a problem intuitively, explore the problem further by using models, and then proceed to a more formal approach.
- Resist the urge to tell students how to solve a problem when they become frustrated; find other ways to support students as they think and work.
- Ask students questions that will prompt their thinking—for example, "Why does this work?" or "How do you know?"

- Provide adequate wait time after a question for students to formulate their own reasoning.
- Encourage students to ask probing questions of themselves and one another.
- Expect students to communicate their reasoning to their classmates and the teacher, orally and in writing, through using proper mathematical vocabulary.
- Highlight exemplary explanations, and have students reflect on what makes them effective.
- Establish a classroom climate in which students feel comfortable sharing their mathematical arguments and critiquing the arguments of others in a productive manner. (NCTM, 2009, p. 11)

Just as we discussed mathematics as a process in Chapter 1, the main idea here is that when considering what should be taught in the mathematics classroom, it is essential to think about how each lesson will promote reasoning and sense making. While the major topic may be finding the percent of a number or graphing a step function, it is the mathematical thinking developed along the way that will have the long-term effect of students understanding and retaining the concepts. Using the tips discussed here, we can create a classroom environment in which the emphasis is on discovery and thinking, not simply mastery of procedures. One of the topics that extends across the curriculum is the development of number sense, which we will explore in the next section.

How Would You React

SCENARIO

As a forward-thinking mathematics teacher, you take pride in using textbooks as guides, but not necessarily following the order of their chapters, and frequently supplement the book with ideas you have in your files from workshops and colleagues. As the school year unfolds, you discover that students in your class, as well as their parents, are upset because "not following the book" makes it difficult to catch up after an absence, and concepts not included in the text have no examples or practice problems on which students can rely. Your response is to

a. Ignore the reactions of your students and their parents and move forward, continuing what you are doing because you know it is the right thing to do.

b. Through the use of a newsletter or e-mail, contact the parents of your students and communicate why you are not following the book page for page, but do not change the format of your class.

c. Change your strategy by relying more on the textbook, at least for the sequence of topics and problems assigned for homework.

d. Abandon your plan and teach the class "by the book" because the concerns of students and parents are not worth the difficulties you are facing.

e. Other.

DISCUSSION

A common problem in the teaching of mathematics occurs when, on the one hand, the teacher wants to be innovative and help students make connections among topics, whereas on the other hand, the textbook for a class is overly traditional or outdated. In an attempt to better meet the needs of the students, the teacher either alters the sequence or content of the textbook or chooses not to use the book at all. Unfortunately, the plan often backfires, and the teacher finds the students upset because the class has lost its predictability—something that has been a mainstay of many of their previous mathematics courses. Unless a teacher is fortunate enough to be working in a school district that has *both* an innovative curriculum *and* an exemplary textbook series, important decisions will have to be made to bridge the apparent dilemma of choosing to use or to ignore the textbook.

Several of the curriculum materials available on the market today are supported by research and were developed through grant-funded programs, such as the National Science Foundation projects described in Chapter 5. A teacher using these types of materials often has little need to look elsewhere for good lessons because the best of the field-tested activities are incorporated in the book. There is a pervading mentality among many creative teachers that "using a textbook is always bad," and that is simply not true. A well-designed book can serve as a core and a direction for instruction. And although no textbook is perfect, a worthwhile book can serve both the teachers' and the students' needs.

However, there are poorly designed textbooks and books that do not meet the needs of students on the market as well. Also, budget-cutting efforts in some districts have forced schools to use books that are 10 or 20 years old, rendering features such as word problems and the use of technology irrelevant. In these cases, the teacher needs to take responsibility by drawing on outside resources for ideas to supplement the book's content. Most importantly, however, the students and their parents have a right to know what direction the teacher is taking and why those decisions are being made. Communication to students and parents, together with sensitivity to their need for structure, are extremely important factors in adapting a textbook to the needs of the class. Research suggests that the perceptions of parents and students regarding what they believe the students should be learning and how the teacher should be structuring students' learning experiences tend to impede teachers from attempting to implement creative classroom ideas (Clarke, 1994). Giving in to the pressure of "how we did it last year" or "how the teacher across the hall does it" has thwarted the plans of many innovative mathematics teachers.

The Teaching of Number Sense

A popular game that is often played in the mathematics classroom to develop number sense is called The Factor Game. The game can be played online at the NCTM Illuminations Web site or on paper with a simple number grid. A screen shot of the beginning of an online game is shown in Figure 8.4.

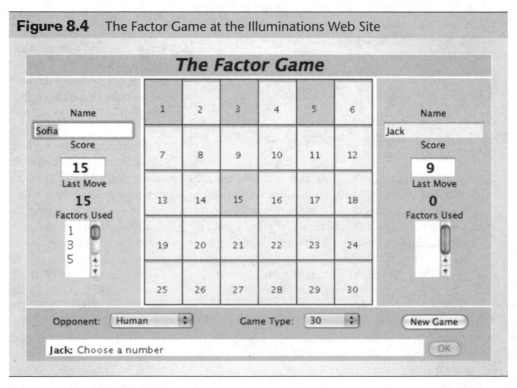

Figure 8.4 The Factor Game at the Illuminations Web Site

(NCTM, 2011. Reprinted with permission.)

The game is played between two individuals or two teams of students. In the case illustrated in Figure 8.4, Sofia and Jack are competing. Sofia's first move was to select (click on) 15 as her starting number. She receives 15 points for this move, which is recorded by the computer. In turn, Jack selects all known factors of 15 (other than 15 itself)—in this case, 1, 3, and 5. He earns 9 points for his move (because $1 + 3 + 5 = 9$). With a score of 15-9, it is now Jack's turn to select a number. If he were to select a prime number such as 7, he would lose a turn because the only other factor of 7 is "1", but that number has already been used in the previous play. Instead, he would want to choose a number that would give him the most possible points, while limiting the number of points Sofia would earn. For example, if he chooses 24, Sofia could click on 2, 4, 6, 8, and 12 (remember that 3 was already used), and she would earn 32 points—8 more than Jack! But if he chooses, say, 21, then she would earn only 7 points, giving him a 14-point advantage for the move. Play continues until there are no more possible moves, and the person with the highest number of points is the winner.

What are some potential benefits of playing this game? Where does it fit in the curriculum? First and foremost, games are engaging. Most people enjoy a game, and the activity plays into the interests of the students. Mathematically, the game has the potential to develop numerous conceptual ideas. As students recognize that some number choices have a host of factors, they recognize that some numbers are wiser choices than others. In some cases, the sum of the factors even equals the number itself, such as 6 ($1 + 2 + 3 = 6$). When the sum of the factors (other than the number itself) equals the original number, we call it a **perfect number**. On the other hand, a number like 10 is called a **deficient number** because the sum of the factors (8) is less than the number itself. When the sum is greater than the number—such as 24—this is referred to as an **abundant number**. In this game, students are really searching for deficient numbers and can be asked questions such as, "What patterns do you see?" "If 6 is a perfect number, what is the next perfect number?" "Sofia earned a 'net' 6 points for her first move because she earned 15 points while Jack earned 9. What would have been Sofia's best choice for a first move to maximize the net gain of points?" "What is the worst choice for a first move?"

As students analyze this game, they grow in their understanding of number, learn new terminology within the context of the game, and develop reasoning and sense making skills along the way. A middle school teacher can use this game when helping students think about products, factors, perfect squares, and other number theory, while a high school algebra teacher can use it as an introduction to a unit on factoring trinomials because it gives students a refresher on thinking about possible factors of a given number (e.g., when one factors a trinomial such as $x^2 - 7x - 30$, the first issue to consider is all of the factors of 30). The idea is to develop an understanding of number along with reasoning skills at the same time.

The *Common Core State Standards* (2010) require that students work heavily with fractions and decimals—including understanding what they represent in the base ten system and performing operations with them—in grades 5 and 6, building an understanding of rational numbers, including negative numbers. By grade 7, they are relating decimals, fractions, and percents and performing operations on negative and positive numbers. By grade 8, students extend their understanding of number to include irrationals. In high school, students explore imaginary numbers and develop an understanding of the set of complex numbers. The authors of the Common Core State Standards state:

> With each extension of number, the meanings of addition, subtraction, multiplication, and division are extended. In each new number system—integers, rational

numbers, real numbers, and complex numbers—the four operations stay the same in two important ways: They have the commutative, associative, and distributive properties and their new meanings are consistent with their previous meanings" (CCSS, 2010, p. 58).

Principles and Standards for School Mathematics (2000) outlines the following Standards for the study of Number and Operations:

Instructional programs from prekindergarten through grade 12 should enable all students to—

- understand numbers, ways of representing numbers, relationships among numbers, and number systems;
- understand meanings of operations and how they relate to one another;
- compute fluently and make reasonable estimates. (p. 32)

While it is important for students to add and subtract fractions and decimals, it is equally important that students look for structure or patterns in numbers. In this regard, reasoning and sense making can be promoted in the context of the study of number concepts. The next section provides a sample lesson plan and 12 classroom activities that promote number sense.

SAMPLE LESSON PLAN

Number Sense

I. Goal(s):
- To develop an understanding of the difference between rational and irrational numbers. (NCTM number and operations standard: "Compare and contrast the properties of numbers and number systems, including the rational and real numbers") (NCTM, 2000, p. 290)

II. Objective(s)
- The student will approximate the golden ratio through data collection.
- The student will recognize the difference between a rational and an irrational number.
- The student will draw a scatterplot of tabular data.
- The student will use technology to generate a line of best fit and interpret the slope.
- The student will use technology to generate a box plot and interpret the shape of the graph.

III. Materials and Resources (for each student)
- Meter sticks with centimeter markings (two per pair of students)
- A pack of small sticky notes
- Graphing calculator or handheld computer (one per student)
- Data collection handout (one per student—attached)

IV. Motivation
1. Display an image of a Vitruvian Man from the Internet. (This is a famous picture of a man with his arms outstretched in which his height and armspan appear to be equal.) Have you ever seen this picture? What does the picture suggest? (Students should recognize that the artist is implying that the ratio of one's armspan to height is 1.) It is said that Vitruvius influenced the work of Leonardo da Vinci, as

artists often use proportions—fractions—to determine the sizes of images they draw (Phi: The Golden Number, 2011).

2. Explain to the class that, throughout the course of human history, scientists, artists, and mathematicians have used a number referred to as the golden ratio (also referred to as the golden section, the divine proportion, or the golden mean) to design buildings (e.g., the Parthenon), to describe planetary motion (such as in the work of Johannes Kepler), to paint pictures (e.g., da Vinci's *Last Supper*), and a host of other applications. (Display images of the Parthenon, the planets, and the *Last Supper* from the Internet.) The golden ratio has a value of $\dfrac{1 + \sqrt{5}}{2}$, which is approximately equal to 1.618. Even today, something as simple as a notecard is designed so that the sides that measure 3-by-5 and 5-by-8 have ratios of about 1.6. Rectangles with sides having this ratio appear to be aesthetically pleasing to the eye and, therefore, are natural in the design of architecture and artwork.

3. Explain that in Greek art, statues often were designed so that the ratio of the height of the statue to the height from the ground to the figure's belly button was roughly equal to the golden ratio (Museum of Harmony and Golden Section, 2011). Say to the students, "This makes me wonder how close our class is to what the Greeks would have considered the ideal ratio when making their statues."

Transition: Explain to the students that they will be gathering some data to analyze and then using that data to approximate the golden ratio. They will be plotting points and analyzing the graph on a calculator.

V. Lesson Procedure

4. Explain the general directions to the class for today: Working in pairs, each person will use a meter stick to measure his/her total height and height from the floor to the belly button. Each person will write his/her two measurements on a sticky note and come up and stick the note on the front board. Once all the data have been collected, we will enter it into graphing calculators and begin to analyze the information.

5. Distribute a copy of the data collection sheet and one sticky note to each student. Point out to students that the first step is to measure their heights, recording the numbers on the handout and the sticky note.

6. Give time for students to measure one another and place the sticky notes on the board. (As students work, walk around the room to ensure that measurements are accurate.)

Transition: "Let's enter the data into our graphing calculators and see what we came up with."

7. Remove the sticky notes from the board, one at a time, and read the values. Ask students to enter the data into two lists on their graphing calculators while doing the same using the overhead graphing calculator with the class.

8. After all data have been entered, ask students to use the graphing calculator to generate a scatterplot where the x-value is the belly button height, while the y-value is the individual's total height. (There

may need to be a discussion about the appropriate window size to ensure that all data points are visible.)

Transition: "Now, we will take a look at our graphs and see what's going on here."

9. What do you notice about the points in the scatterplot? (They should be roughly linear.) Why do you think these points tend to lie on a line? (Students should be able to explain that the ratio of total height to belly button height is somewhat the same for everyone.) How can we figure out what that ratio is? (Students may choose to use the slope of the line or to go back to the original data. Assuming they will want to go back to the original data in the table, return to these values. If they want to explore the slope first, then follow their lead.)

10. Returning to the original lists, create a formula for another column that is the ratio of list #2 (the y-value) to list #1 (the x-value). By using the "mean" command, a graphing calculator can instantly determine the mean of the ratios. Ask, "What value did you find?" (This value should be close to the golden ratio.) Does this surprise you? How close are we to being the "ideal" class, as the Greeks saw it? (They should discuss how close to approximately 1.61 the ratio came out for the class.)

11. Returning to the scatterplot, ask the students to have their calculators determine a line of best fit. What is the equation of this line? What do you notice about this equation? (Students should recognize that the slope of the line is an approximation of the golden ratio.) Why might we have expected this slope to be so close to the value of the golden ratio? (The slope is a rate of change that compares total height to belly button height, so its value would be close to that of the golden ratio.)

12. Explain to the class that throughout this lesson, we have talked about approximating the golden ratio. Is it possible to know the exact value of the golden ratio? (No. Since the expression representing the actual value includes a square root, the golden ratio is actually an irrational number. Therefore, any value attached to it is simply an approximation.)

Transition: "Let's take a few minutes to explore how the ratios from the data we collected varied from one person to the next."

VI. Closure

13. Have the class return to the values in list #3, which are the ratios of total height to belly button height for each person. Using the box plot command, have students generate a box-and-whisker plot for the list. What do you notice about the shape of the box? What is the median value for our class? How close is this to the actual golden ratio?

14. Ask, "Would you expect this box plot to look different if the group of people we measured were older? Younger?" (The idea here that there is much more variability in body shapes when children are younger and growing than when they get older. We might expect the box plot to be wider, possibly including outliers, for younger children but less variable for adults.)

15. Ask one person from each table to return the graphing calculators and meter sticks.

4. For homework, ask each student to respond to the following in his/her journal: What did you learn about the golden ratio today? How would you describe the difference between a rational and an irrational number in your own words?

VII. Extension

If time allows, organize students into groups of four and send them out to measure any three rectangular objects, either in the room or throughout the building. They might measure a whiteboard, picture frame, window, television or computer screen, bulletin board, etc. Students should gather the data and then calculate the ratio of the longer to the shorter side of the rectangle. Gather back together as a class to compare and discuss the results. Are rectangular objects in our classroom and building constructed in a golden ratio?

VIII. Assessment

Assessment in this lesson takes three different forms:

- Anecdotal notes will be collected as students work to measure themselves and enter the data into graphing calculators.
- Informal observation will be used as students respond to questions raised throughout the lesson.
- Journal entries require students to summarize their learning from the lesson and will be collected and read the following day.

Number Sense—Activities Sampler

1. **Fibonacci Numbers:** Around the year 1200, an Italian mathematician, Leonardo of Pisa, posed a puzzle in a book that involved the growth of a population of rabbits. Assuming that a female rabbit can begin to give birth to rabbits after 2 months, that the rabbit bears a male and a female each month, and that a rabbit could live forever, he explored the growth of the population. Students can explore this puzzle by considering 1 pair of rabbits in the first and second months, but by the third month, another pair is born so that there are 2 pairs. In the fourth month, the original pair gives birth to another, so there are 3 pairs of rabbits. Continuing this pattern results in one of the most famous of all number sequences—the Fibonacci numbers, which are 1, 1, 2, 3, 5, 8, 13, 21, 34, 55, and so forth. Students can examine the pattern to find that each number in the sequence is the sum of the two previous numbers. With a search of the Internet, numerous applications of this number sequence can be found. For example, most flowers tend to have 3, 5, or 8 petals, but few have a number of petals that is not a Fibonacci number. Another interesting exploration is to have students divide successive numbers from the sequence. For example, $\frac{1}{1} = 1, \frac{2}{1} = 2, \frac{3}{2} = 1.5$, and $\frac{5}{3} \approx 1.67$. Continuing this process, students should recognize that the ratios oscillate back and forth, with their limit being the golden ratio of about 1.61, which was discussed in the lesson plan in this chapter—a surprising result that most students find fascinating.

2. **"War" with Integers:** A standard deck of playing cards can be used for students to practice their skills with positive and negative numbers. Take a deck of cards and remove the face cards, assigning a value of 1 to the Aces. Black cards are considered "positive," while red cards are "negative." Two students

are randomly dealt 20 cards apiece. Turning up one card at a time, the person with the greater number wins the round and takes the two cards. So, if one person turns up the 7 of Hearts, and the other turns up the 5 of Diamonds, the 5 of Diamonds wins because -5 is greater than -7. After all 20 rounds are completed, the person with the greatest number of cards wins the game. A variation of this game involves addition. Again, each player is dealt 20 cards, but instead of laying down a single card for each round, each player lays down two cards and adds them together. The person with the greater sum gets to take all four cards. This version of the game allows students to practice addition of integers and comparison of the magnitude of numbers at the same time.

3. **Constructing Irrationals:** A compass and straightedge can easily be used to construct a number line that shows where 1, 2, 3, and the other whole numbers are located (by simply not changing the size of the compass setting). By using a perpendicular bisector construction, students can also readily locate numbers such as $3\frac{1}{2}$ or $5\frac{1}{4}$ on the number line. Challenge students to determine the location of an irrational number, such as $\sqrt{5}$, on the number line. One way to accomplish this is to construct perpendicular lines and then use the 90° angle to construct a right triangle whose legs measure 1 and 2 units. According to the Pythagorean Theorem, if the legs are 1 and 2, the hypotenuse would measure $\sqrt{5}$. Using the compass, the students can measure the length of the hypotenuse and copy it back onto the number line to show its location. Using this same process, students should be able to readily locate numbers such as $\sqrt{2}$, $\sqrt{10}$, and $\sqrt{13}$ on the number line. They can also construct the location of $\sqrt{20}$ by using a triangle whose legs are 2 and 4 and can verify with a compass that the distance is the same as $2\sqrt{5}$, which sets the stage for discussing how square roots can be simplified (i.e., recognizing that $\sqrt{20} = 2\sqrt{5}$).

4. **Large Numbers with String:** This activity can help students to appreciate large numbers and the significance of changing an exponent. Take a large ball of string and put a piece of electrical tape at the end to designate 0. Measure 1 cm and put another small strip of electrical tape around the string to designate the location of 1. Measure 10 cm from the end and place another strip of tape around the string, as well as at 100 cm, 1000 cm, and 10,000 cm. Be advised that the 10,000 cm strip will be about 328 feet from the end! Take the students to a playground or parking lot and have one student hold the end of the string with the rest coiled up. Unravel the string to reveal the location of the 10 cm mark. Ask the students how far the string will need to be unraveled to find the 100 cm mark and have someone hold the string at that location. Allow students to estimate where the 1,000 cm and 10,000 cm marks are located. After estimates have been made, unravel the string to show their locations. Discuss these locations as the differences between 10^1, 10^2, 10^3, and so on. Students often have the misconception that "I only missed the exponent by 1" without realizing the significance of a single change in an exponent. This activity provides a visual to help address the misconception.

5. **Adding Percents:** Several years ago, an article appeared in a local newspaper regarding the viewing of public television. The article claimed that the preschool audience viewing of Public Broadcasting System (PBS) programming was up 37% over the previous year and that similar data indicated growth of 40% the previous year. The writer concluded by stating that viewership had, therefore, increased by 77% in two years (40% last year, 37% this year, so 77% altogether in two years). Have students explore this claim. Can percents

be added in this manner? A related problem is to discuss what happens if a store lowers the price of a product by 10% one day and then raises the price by 10% a week later. Is the final price the same as the original price? What happens to an investment that sits in the bank earning 5% interest per year? Does it earn 25% in five years? This discussion can lead students to an understanding of compounding interest over time.

6. **Divisibility Rules:** Exploration of divisibility rules can be an excellent way to engage students in mathematical reasoning. For example, the rule for divisibility by 3 is that if the sum of the digits is divisible by 3, then the original number also is divisible by 3. So, 237 would be divisible by 3 because the sum of the digits is 12, which is divisible by 3. But why does this rule work? One way to think about it is to visualize the number 237 formed by base ten blocks—2 flats, 3 rods, and 7 units. Think of each flat as having $99 + 1$ units. Each 99 is evenly divisible by 3, with 1 unit left over. Likewise, each rod can be thought of as having $9 + 1$ units and, again, each 9 is divisible by 3 with 1 unit left over. So, when 237 is divided by 3, there are 2 units left over from the 2 flats, 3 units remaining from the 3 rods, and 7 more additional units—a total of 12 units that are also divisible by 3. The rule for divisibility by 9 can be explained in a similar manner. Students can research other divisibility rules on the Internet and present explanations to classmates for why they work.

7. **Square Roots as Irrationals:** As students explore irrational numbers, why square roots (of numbers that are not perfect squares) are irrational can be discussed. This fact was proven by the ancient Greeks and can most easily be understood as a proof by contradiction, as follows: In order to prove that $\sqrt{2}$ is irrational, we begin by assuming it is rational and that it can be written as a fraction $\frac{a}{b}$ where a and b are integers. If $\sqrt{2} = \frac{a}{b}$, then squaring both sides implies that $2 = \frac{a^2}{b^2}$ and, therefore, that $a^2 = 2b^2$. So, for this to be true (since any number multiplied by 2 is even), a must be an even number. If a is even, it can be written as the product of 2 and some other number, c. So, $a = 2c$. By substitution, $(2c)^2 = 2b^2$, so $4c^2 = 2b^2$ making $b^2 = 2c^2$. But this means b is also an even number. However, if a and b are both even numbers, they are both divisible by 2, which contradicts the assumption that $\frac{a}{b}$ is in simplest form. Therefore, $\sqrt{2}$ is an irrational number. A similar argument can be made about the square root of other numbers. This exercise can help students to appreciate the role of proof in justifying why a number belongs to a particular set.

8. **Approximating *e*:** While pi is arguably the most famous irrational number, e is another example that students encounter in a second-year algebra or pre-calculus course. An interesting way for students to discover this number is by investigating a compound interest problem. Suppose that one dollar is invested at 100% interest per year. At the end of the year, the amount in the bank would be calculated by taking $1(1 + 1) = 2$—the money is doubled. But suppose the money were compounded twice in the year. This means the person would receive 50% interest midway through the year and another 50% interest at the end of the year or $1(1 + \frac{1}{2})(1 + \frac{1}{2}) = (1 + .5)^2 = 2.25$. Compounding 4 times in a year (quarterly) would be calculated as: $(1 + \frac{1}{4})^4 = 2.441$. Monthly compounding would result in the following calculation: $(1 + \frac{1}{12})^{12} = 2.613$. Following this same process, daily compounding would result in a total of $2.715 in the bank, while compounding every second—31,536,000 times a year—produces a total of 2.718, which is not even a penny more than compounding daily. The limit of this calculation is the value of e, which is an irrational number approximately

equal to 2.718. This number was investigated and named by the mathematician Leonhard Euler (though it is likely he named it after the word "exponential" rather than the initial of his last name). In order to calculate the maximum (continuous) interest rate on an investment, we can simply calculate e to the power of the rate. For example, if the interest rate is 5%, $e^{0.05} \approx 1.05127$ tells us that the maximum possible earnings for the year (effective annual yield) when compounding would be 5.127%.

9. **Richter Scale:** The use of scientific notation and logarithms (which are exponents) can be taught in the context of applications. Students may be interested to know how the Richter Scale that is used to report the strength of an earthquake is a logarithm—a power of 10. When an earthquake measures a "4" on the scale, it is considered a light earthquake and the number represents the amplitude of seismic waves that are measured, which ultimately have to do with the degree of shaking of the ground. If another earthquake measures a "6", it would be considered a strong earthquake that would cause considerable damage. While there may not appear to be much difference between a "4" and a "6", these numbers represent powers of 10, which means that an earthquake with a magnitude of 6 produces seismic waves that have 100 times greater amplitude than those produced by an earthquake measuring 4 on the Richter Scale. Students may want to investigate what this means in terms of energy released by an earthquake and how exponents are also used for other purposes, such as determining pH of a substance in chemistry.

10. **Engineering Notation:** In addition to featuring scientific notation (SCI), most graphing calculators also include engineering notation (ENG). As students examine their calculators and use the tool to solve problems, it is common for them to ask how the ENG setting is used. This question presents an excellent opportunity—either in the context of a question raised in class or a planned lesson on the topic—for students to investigate engineering notation. Ask students to activate the ENG setting and to type in a variety of numbers, large and small, to record and discuss how the graphing calculator reports the results. As students look for patterns, they should recognize that the exponents are always divisible by 3. The reason for this is that we put commas between every 3 digits, so it is easy to identify large (and small) numbers using this notation. For example, while the value of 2.5×10^7 may not be obvious, seeing the same number written as 25×10^6 makes it clear that the number is 25 million because we can more readily "see" 6 zeros after a number (and recognize the number as being millions) than mentally move the decimal and change the exponent. With engineering notation, the multiplier is between 0 and 1,000, and the exponent is always divisible by 3.

11. **Sums of Evens and Odds:** In earlier grades, students often recognize that, for example, the sum of two odd numbers is always even. In the high school and middle grades, however, they can more formally prove why this is true. One way to approach the proof is to represent even numbers as 2 times some other number (such as $2a$), while an odd number can be written as 1 more than an even number (such as $2b + 1$). So, if we add any two odd numbers, the sum can be represented by the expression $(2a + 1) + (2b + 1)$. The sum is $2a + 2b + 2$, and factoring out a 2, the expression becomes $2(a + b + 1)$. Since the product of 2 and any other number is even, our sum must have been even, so we have proven that the sum of two odd numbers must be even. Similar proofs can be done to show why the product of an even and an odd number must be even

and so forth. These proofs can help students to justify rules by using more formal mathematical language and notation.

12. **Difference of Consecutive Squares:** Students are often fascinated by what appear to be "random" rules of arithmetic—results that "always happen," leaving students to wonder why. An example is the fact that the difference between the squares of any two consecutive whole numbers is equal to the sum of the numbers. Consider 7 and 8, whose squares are 49 and 64. Note that $64 - 49 = 15$ and that $7 + 8 = 15$ as well. As another example, consider 11 and 12. Their squares are 121 and 144, so the difference is 23, which is the same as the sum of the original numbers. After examining some examples, students may become curious about why this relationship is always true. Here is a simple proof that can be explored: Suppose x and y are consecutive whole numbers. The squares of these numbers would be x^2 and y^2. However, since y is 1 more than x, it can be written as $(x + 1)$. So, the sum of the original two numbers would be $x + (x + 1) = 2x + 1$. If we square the original numbers and find the difference, the calculation can be done as follows: $(x + 1)^2 - x^2 = x^2 + 2x + 1 - x^2 = 2x + 1$. Therefore, the same expression—$2x + 1$—results from adding the original numbers and from subtracting their squares and proves why the rule always works.

SPOTlight on Technology

One of the greatest challenges of teaching algebra is to assign problems that are applied to the real world. When students can see a use for the mathematics they are studying, they are more likely to engage in finding solutions. Both the *Common Core State Standards* and the NCTM *Standards* provide numerous examples of applications that can be employed. Fortunately, with advancements in technology, we are more able than ever to allow students to investigate real-world phenomena. Suppose, for example, that your students are exploring quadratic functions. Instead of simply graphing parabolas by hand, as a teacher, you are interested in having your students investigate more interesting applications.

One tool that can be used is computer software or handheld technology that allows students to upload a photograph and explore the mathematics in the picture. The image shown in Figure 8.5 was downloaded onto a TI-Nspire handheld (one of the sample photographs included with the software).

After downloading the picture, one question that can be raised to a class is, "What is the approximate equation of the parabola that describes the shape of this arch?" Students can explore this question in a variety of ways. First, by grabbing the axes on the screen, the origin can be moved to any convenient location. If the students want the origin to be at the location of the vertex, this can easily be done. In Figure 8.5, students

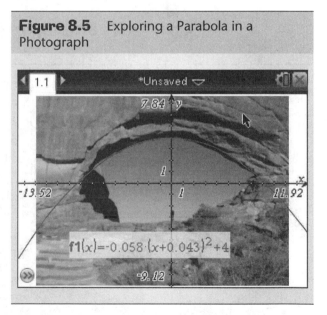

Figure 8.5 Exploring a Parabola in a Photograph

$$f1(x) = -0.058 \cdot (x + 0.043)^2 + 4$$

(Image used with permission from Texas Instruments.)

chose to locate the vertex as closely as possible to the point (0, 4). In turn, students can conjecture as to the equation of the parabola. They may notice, for example, that the parabola turns downward. Therefore, the coefficient of the quadratic term in the equation must be negative. Furthermore, if the vertex is at the point (0, 4), students can infer that the general equation for the parabola would be $y = -Ax^2 + 4$. Finally, since the parabola has a wide opening, they may determine that the coefficient must be a fraction between -1 and 0.

The power of the technology is that students can test multiple hypotheses for the value of A until the parabola most closely matches the curve. Initially, they may try a coefficient such as −0.5 and discover that the parabola is far too narrow. As they investigate this problem, students begin to recognize how the coefficient affects the shape of the curve but in the context of a real-world photograph. Also, after determining a best-fit equation for the parabola, the teacher can move the axes to a new location and ask students how the equation would be affected by the shift. In the case of the image shown in Figure 8.5, students began by placing the curve described by the equation $y = -x^2 + 4$ onto the picture and then used the pointer tool on the handheld to drag the curve until it fit the shape of the arch. In turn, the handheld dynamically displays the equation as the curve is moved, resulting in the final equation shown in the figure. Students can be asked, for example, why 0.043 is being added to the x-value and conclude that the actual vertex is located slightly to the left of the y-axis.

As technology becomes increasingly sophisticated, almost endless strategies for exploring problems arise that might have been impossible even when the teacher was in school. In the case of the example described here, students can use digital cameras or cell phones to snap pictures of shapes that appear to be parabolic, upload them to their handhelds, and determine equations of best fit. A student in one class took a picture of water coming from a drinking fountain, while another pulled out a picture of the fountains in the World War II Memorial from a class trip to Washington, DC, to upload and explore. The use of such images provides yet one more way to creatively use technology to help students connect mathematics to their world.

The Teaching of Algebra

In a junior high school mathematics class, Mr. Ritter gave a birthday candle, mounted on a plate with a small piece of modeling clay, to each small group of students. The groups were also provided with metric rulers, stopwatches, and recording sheets. He proceeded to walk around the room, lighting each team's candle. The students' first task was to measure the initial height of the candle, to the nearest millimeter (tenth of a centimeter), and then to measure and record the height of the candle after each minute of elapsed time. One group's data are displayed in Figure 8.6.

Figure 8.6 Time and Length Relationship for a Burning Candle

Time (min)	Length (cm)
0	6.0
1	5.7
2	5.4
3	5.0
4	4.7
5	4.5
6	4.2
7	3.9
8	3.6

Other teams of students in the class recorded similar results. After all of the information had been collected and candles were extinguished, Mr. Ritter asked each student to use the data in the table with a piece of graph paper to sketch a simple scatterplot for a visual picture of the time–length relationship. When the scatterplots had been drawn, he led the class in a discussion about the experiment.

> *Mr. Ritter:* What do you notice about the points that you graphed in your scatterplot?
>
> *Miyagi:* Ours lie almost exactly in a straight line. (Other students in the class express agreement.)
>
> *Mr. Ritter:* Good point, Miyagi. So, what does that tell us?
>
> *Miyagi:* It means that the two variables are related.
>
> *Mr. Ritter:* Can anyone tell me which is the dependent variable and why?
>
> *Marcus:* The length of the candle is the dependent variable because it depends on the amount of time it's been burning. That makes time the independent variable. In science class, we call that the control variable.
>
> *Mr. Ritter:* So, if we use x to represent the time in minutes and y as the length in centimeters, can we find an equation that relates the variables?
>
> *Vanessa:* We would have to know two points that are on the line to find the equation, wouldn't we?
>
> *Sarah:* No, not really. If you look at the tables, the candle basically burns about 3 millimeters every minute. So, the slope of the line would have to be 0.3, right?
>
> *Vanessa:* Wouldn't it be *negative* 0.3 since the length is getting shorter as it burns?
>
> *Mike:* Yeah, it would. And since the candle was 6 centimeters long when we started, the y-intercept would be at the point $(0, 6)$.
>
> *Mr. Ritter:* So, what is the equation of the line?
>
> *Miyagi:* It would be $y = -0.3x + 6$!

The students in this class have explored a fundamental component of the teaching and learning of algebra, which is the relationship of various representations of a function. From the middle grades through high school, students should be challenged to flexibly move between these representations, as shown in Figure 8.7.

Although there are subtle differences in the ways that *algebra* is defined in mathematics education, it is important to think of it as a language and a content area, rather than a *course* that one takes in secondary or middle school. Usiskin (1997) pointed out that the study of algebra began to be considered a kindergarten-through-high-school experience by 1990, just as the study of geometry became the responsibility of teachers at all grade levels beginning in the early 1960s. Furthermore, he identified five major components that comprise the language of algebra: unknowns (variables), formulas, generalized patterns, placeholders (such as cells on a spreadsheet), and relationships between variables. Similarly, Kaput (1997) defined five types of algebraic reasoning: (1) generalizing

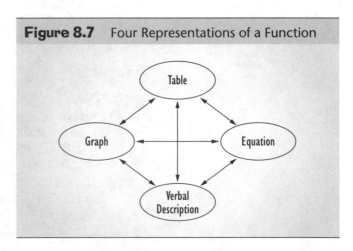

Figure 8.7 Four Representations of a Function

Students investigate physical models to make sense of numerical, algebraic, and geometric relationships.

patterns; (2) manipulating variables; (3) studying structures abstracted from computation; (4) studying functions, relations, and joint variations; and (5) using algebra for modeling and as a language.

The *Common Core State Standards* (2010) include a domain on Operations and Algebraic Thinking at Grade 5, while Grades 6 through 8 feature a domain on Expressions and Equations, and Grade 8 also includes a domain entitled Functions, which includes defining, evaluating, and comparing functions, as well as using them to model real-world phenomena. In high school, two conceptual categories include algebraic concepts—Algebra and Functions. Each year, algebraic ideas build upon previous knowledge so that the study of algebra extends throughout the curriculum.

Principles and Standards for School Mathematics (NCTM, 2000) draws on similar themes in the algebra standard, which states the following:

Instructional programs from prekindergarten through grade 12 should enable all students to—

- understand patterns, relations, and functions;
- represent and analyze mathematical situations and structures using algebraic symbols;
- use mathematical models to represent and understand quantitative relationships;
- analyze change in various contexts. (p. 37)

The NCTM *Standards* also emphasize that the study of algebra and geometry should be integrated, particularly in the middle grades, so that a more extensive study of algebra is possible in high school. And the authors of the document note that *all* students should have access to the study of algebra, as opposed to some slice of the population who has historically taken a "course" in algebra. The next section provides a sample lesson plan and 12 classroom activities that promote algebraic reasoning.

SAMPLE LESSON PLAN

Algebra

I. Goal(s):
- To develop the concept of writing and graphing linear and two-dimensional inequalities. (NCTM algebra standard: "Represent and analyze mathematical situations and structures using algebraic symbols") (NCTM, 2000, p. 296)

II. Objective(s)
- The student will represent a real-life situation by writing an inequality.

- The student will graph a two-dimensional inequality by hand and with a graphing calculator.
- The student will interpret numerical data in a table.
- The student will draw a scatterplot of tabular data.

III. Materials and Resources (for each student)
- A copy of the "How Well Do You Know Yourself?" data sheet
- Graph paper and a straightedge
- Graphing calculator (an overhead graphing calculator is also needed)

IV. Motivation
1. Say to the class, "On the way to school today, I saw a sign that said, 'Speed Limit 55'. What does that mean? How fast or slowly am I allowed to drive?" (Students should note that any speed is possible as long as it does not exceed 55 miles per hour [mph].)
2. Ask the class to write a mathematical statement that represents a speed, s, that may not exceed 55 mph ($s \le 55$). (We may get into a discussion about whether this is reasonable because a car has to be moving faster than 0 mph. Therefore, it may be more accurate to say $0 < s \le 55$.)
3. On another stretch of road, the sign also reads, "Minimum 45." What does that mean? How can we express the acceptable speed at which you can drive on that road? (Students may need to review the notion of a compound inequality and the meaning of $<$ versus $\le$. They should find the inequality: $45 \le s \le 55$.)

Transition: Explain to the students that the focus of today's lesson is on writing and graphing two-dimensional inequalities. They will learn to do this by hand and on a graphing calculator.

V. Lesson Procedure
4. Remind the class that when they took a 50-point quiz last week, they predicted their scores. After grading the quizzes, a data sheet entitled "How Well Do You Know Yourself?" was typed up. The sheet contains a random list of student scores with a prediction in one column and an actual score in another.
5. Distribute a copy of the sheet to each student. Ask the class to take a minute to look over the data. Have one person explain what the table reveals. (Someone should be able to describe, for example, that Student 3 predicted a 40 on the quiz but actually scored a 35 out of 50.) Then ask the students what they notice about the data in the table. (They should notice that most students predicted slightly higher than their actual scores, but the actual average for the class was almost identical to the predicted average.)

Transition: "Let's see if we can construct and analyze a graph of the data."

6. Ask the students to take out a piece of graph paper and a straightedge and to draw a scatterplot of the data, where the x-values are the predicted scores, and the y-values are the actual scores. (Walk around the room to informally assess their skill in constructing scatterplots.)

Transition: "Now, we will use your scatterplots of the data to answer some questions."

7. Raise the questions, "What if everyone in our class had predicted exactly the same score that they earned? What would the scatterplot

look like?" (Students should realize that the points would lie on a diagonal line containing [50, 50], [49, 49], etc.) "What would be the equation of the line if the predictions had been perfect?" (Students should realize that if the actual equals the predicted, then the equation must be the line $y = x$.)

8. Discuss the fact that, unfortunately, our predictions were not perfect. Some people earned an actual score that was lower than the predicted score. Can you show me where those people's data points are located? (Students should point out that these points lie "beneath" the line $y = x$.) What do the points that lie beneath the diagonal line have in common? (In each case, the y-value is less than the x-value.) How might we represent that set of points, all of which lie underneath the line $y = x$? (Students should recognize that these points satisfy the inequality $y < x$.) How about the points that lie above the line (where the actual score was higher than the predicted score)?

9. Have one student from each table come up and get enough graphing calculators for each person at the table. Using the overhead graphing calculator, demonstrate how to graph $y < x$ with the technology. As it shades one side of the line, explain to the class that when we do these by hand, we will use a colored pencil or marker to shade the appropriate area. Ask a student to explain why it is shading and what this means. (Try to reiterate that these are points that have y-coordinates that are less than the x-coordinates.)

10. Tell the students to turn off their graphing calculators and set them aside. Ask them to draw on graph paper a graph of each of the following:

$$y > 2x + 5$$
$$y \geq 2x + 5$$
$$y \leq -\tfrac{2}{3}x - 4$$

(As students work, encourage them to talk to one another about their solutions, and walk around the room to assist and observe how they are thinking about the problems.)

11. Once everyone has finished, ask the students to talk about the differences and similarities between the first two problems. (When they recognize that the only difference is whether the boundary line is included in the graph, introduce them to the notation of using a dotted versus a solid line in the graph.) Have a student come to the chalkboard and draw a quick sketch of the third inequality.

12. Have students turn their graphing calculators back on and graph the inequalities. They will notice that the first two look the same, and we will discuss how the "calculator doesn't tell you everything" and how we need to know how to handle the borderlines ourselves.

VI. Closure

13. Say to the students, "We have been working with inequalities today, both by hand and on the graphing calculator." Ask the students to write down a set of instructions in their journals for how to graph a two-dimensional inequality and share the instructions at the table. Before class ends, ask one or two students to share their instructions with the whole group.

14. Ask one person from each table to return the graphing calculators

back to the front table and assign the homework problems (textbook, p. 237, #1, 5, 9, 14, 20, 22–24).

VII. Extension

If time allows, before the closure, ask the students to draw a sketch of $y > 7$ and $x \leq -3$ on graph paper. Discuss the meaning of these two inequality graphs in two dimensions and how they compare to the graphs of inequalities that we constructed on number lines earlier this year. (This question comes up again on the homework assignment, but if there is time to address it in class, that would be helpful.)

VIII. Assessment

Assessment in this lesson takes four different forms:
- Students' abilities to construct scatterplots are assessed through an informal observation in Step 6.
- As they begin to draw graphs of inequalities, observational notes will be taken in Step 10.
- The journal writing from Step 13 will assess their ability to communicate the process of sketching an inequality.
- The homework problems that are due the following day will also assess students' ability to sketch an inequality.

Classroom Dialogues

A student drew the graph of a line, as shown in Figure 8.8.

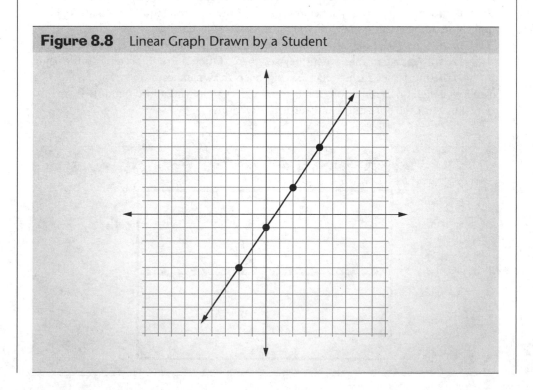

Figure 8.8 Linear Graph Drawn by a Student

As a follow-up to the graphing activity, the teacher sat with the student and conducted a short interview, as follows:

Teacher: Can you tell me about the graph that you drew?

Student: Yeah, it's a line. I graphed it using the slope and the *y*-intercept.

Teacher: What is the *y*-intercept here?

Student: It's at the point (0, −1), right here. (points at it)

Teacher: How am I supposed to know the coordinates of that point?

Student: It's just one square below the origin, so it has to be at the point (0, −1).

Teacher: What if the scale on the *y*-axis were set up so that each square represented five units instead of one?

Student: Then the *y*-intercept would be at (0, −5), but that's not what I meant.

Teacher: How am I supposed to know what you meant? Let's assume that the *x*-axis was constructed so that each square represented two units. Then what?

Student: Well, the rise would be 15 units because it's three squares where each one stands for 5 units, and the run would be 4 units because it's two squares in the *x*-direction. So, the slope would be $\frac{15}{4}$, but it's really supposed to be $\frac{3}{2}$.

Teacher: Why?

Student: It's 3 units up and 2 units to the right.

Teacher: So, how can you be sure that I know the slope is $\frac{3}{2}$ instead of something else, like $\frac{15}{4}$?

Student: You would have to mark the scale on it somewhere.

Teacher: Ah, now you're getting the idea! If the axes aren't labeled, how would I be able to interpret your graph? Using my scale ideas, the equation of your line could be $y = \frac{15}{4}x - 5$ but I don't think that's what you meant.

Student: No, I meant it to be $y = \frac{3}{2}x - 1$. But I need to make sure I label the scale the next time so that you'll know.

Notice in Figure 8.8 that the student has drawn an accurate representation of the linear function $y = \frac{3}{2}x - 1$. However, since the axes are not labeled, there are many different ways that the graph could be interpreted. How important do you believe it is for a student to accurately label graphs and other diagrams in mathematics? How might you address this issue with your students?

One of the typical objectives in a mathematics course of study is for students to recognize misleading graphs when they see them. Often a graph becomes misleading due to labeling issues rather than having been drawn inaccurately. Figure 8.9 is a graphing calculator's rendition of the graph of $y = x^2$ in a standard window from −10 to +10 in both the horizontal and vertical directions.

Figure 8.9   Graph of $y = x^2$ with a Standard Window

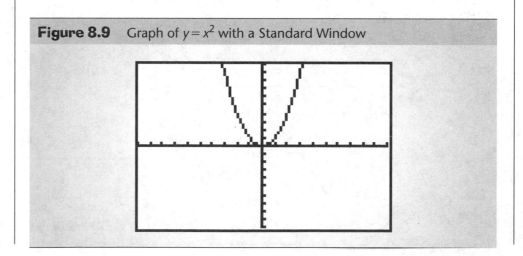

In Figure 8.10, the graph of $y = x^2$ is shown once again, but this time the scale on the x-axis is stretched out from -3 to $+3$. The function, however, is exactly the same.

If students were asked to describe what they see in these two graphs, they might be inclined to say that the graph in Figure 8.10 is flatter and does not increase as rapidly. However, the scale is the only difference between these graphs, as they represent the same function. Demonstrating this difference can help students understand the importance of communicating scale to a reader by labeling units and names of axes in a graph. Can you think of other mathematical situations in which labeling of any kind is essential when solving the problem? In general, how insistent should a teacher be to ensure that students are paying attention to labeling details?

Figure 8.10   Graph of $y = x^2$ with the x-Scale Changed

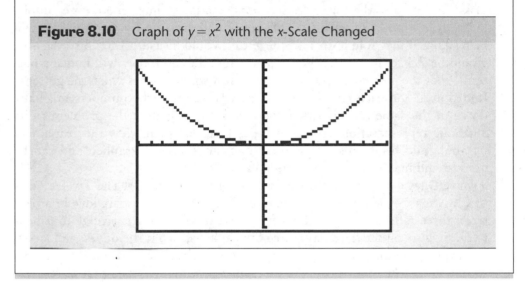

Algebra—Activities Sampler

1. **Fist Size and Height:** Provide students with tape measures or yardsticks (meter-sticks) and ask them to carefully measure (a) the distance across their knuckles when making a fist and (b) their height in inches (or centimeters). Each student should write the measurements on a sticky note and place it on the chalkboard. Read the measurements to the class and have each student make a scatterplot of the data for everyone in the class. The points should be roughly linear, and this will lead to a discussion of selecting two of the plotted points to use for finding a line of best fit. By counting off the slope between the two selected points, students can find the slope of the line, and by extending the line until it intersects the y-axis, they can find the y-intercept and determine an equation for the line of best fit. Similar explorations can be carried out to compare height with shoe size, length of the forearm with diameter of the head, and so forth. This activity gives students practice with collecting and representing data while they think about equations that describe lines in real settings.

2. **Numbers from Dates:** Give students the digits that form the current month and day, and have them use those digits, together with the four operations, square roots, exponents, and grouping symbols to generate a list of expressions that simplify to answers from 1 to 20. For example, suppose that it is March 15. The date would be 3/15, so students would be allowed to use 3, 1, and 5 in their calculations. Here are some examples of possible answers: $5 - (1 + 3) = 1$,

$(5 - 3)^1 = 2, 5 - \sqrt{(3 + 1)} = 3, 5 - 1^3 = 4$, and so forth. Students can determine (a) whether it is possible to write an expression for every number from 1 to 20 and (b) how many possible solutions they can find for each of the numbers. This experience can be repeated on a regular basis (e.g., once per month) to help students practice order of operations and to develop general problem-solving skills.

3. **Bending Aluminum:** Give students a piece of paper that measures $8 \times 10"$. Explain that the paper represents a piece of aluminum, out of which a rain gutter for a house will be formed. They need to fold up the 8" width on both sides so that the cross-section is a rectangle (with no top, similar to a gutter). The task is to fold it so that the cross-sectional area is maximized. So, for example, if they fold it up 1" on each side, the gutter will measure 1×6 so the area will be 6 sq. in. If they fold it up 1.5" the gutter would measure 1.5×5 so the area would be 7.5 sq. in. As they continue the investigation, they will notice a pattern—that the area goes up until it peaks at 8 square inches when the gutter is folded at 2" on each end—and are likely to see that the numbers fall back down at the same rate that they increased. By extending the problem to its algebraic representation, $Area = x(8 - 2x)$, students can view the graph as a parabola and begin to see how quadratic functions are graphed and can be used to find maximum and minimum values.

4. **Twelve Days of Christmas:** A traditional Christmas song—"The Twelve Days of Christmas"—describes receiving one gift the first day (a partridge in a pear tree), three gifts the second day (two turtle doves *and* a partridge in a pear tree), six gifts on the third day (three French hens, two turtle doves, and a partridge in a pear tree), and so forth. Have students review (and sing?) the words to this song. The task, then, is to determine how many gifts a person receives on each of the 12 days and how many gifts they receive altogether over this time span. Students will discover a number of patterns, shortcuts, and formulas for finding the answers and may be surprised to discover that a person would receive 78 gifts on the twelfth day and 364 gifts altogether! As an extension, have students research the cost of each gift (the costs are published annually during the holidays) and determine how much it would cost to actually give someone that many gifts over 12 days. A similar problem can be solved by placing it in the context of the 8 days of Hanukkah.

5. **Functions Stations:** As a group project, have students visit learning stations over the course of 2 days, at which they collect some type of data and estimate a line of best fit. Stations might include the following: (a) Provide a tape measure and several circular objects and have students graph and find a line of best fit comparing the diameter (x) to the circumference (y). (b) Set up a water jug containing a tap, a yardstick, and a bucket under the tap. Students should turn on the tap, empty the water into the bucket, and compare the amount of time (x) that the tap has been opened to the height of the water level (y) in the jug. (c) On the Internet, find another set of statistical data, such as a comparison of the number of people in a country who smoke (x) to the incidence of coronary heart disease (y). In each of these cases, students collect data, draw scatterplots by hand or on a graphing calculator, and determine a line of best fit.

6. **Real-Life Systems:** As an individual project, have students identify and solve a real-life problem that involves a system of linear equations. For example, they might compare the cost of two long-distance carriers, and by writing equations or drawing graphs of the payment plans, determine how many minutes a

person would have to call long distance in a month for one plan to be better than the other. Students can use the same process to compare Internet service providers (ISPs) or the value of free compact discs by mail, when the shipping charges and the cost of making a required purchase may be more than simply going to the store and buying the products off the shelf. Then, students can generate a written paper and make a presentation to the class on their results.

7. **Bicycle-Rotation Trick:** Here is a mathematical trick called the bicycle-rotation problem that students may find interesting: Start with two numbers, such as 3 and 5. Then, follow this sequence of steps: (a) Take the greater number (5), add 1, and divide by the lesser number ($\frac{5 + 1}{3} = 2$) (b) Take the result (2) and add 1 again, this time dividing by the previous number that was added to 1, which was 5 ($\frac{2 + 1}{5} = 0.6$) (c) Take the new result, 0.6, add it to 1, and divide by the previous number added to 1, which was 2 ($\frac{0.6 + 1}{2} = 0.8$). Continuing this process, the next two steps would be (d) $\frac{0.8 + 1}{0.6} = 3$ and (e) $\frac{3 + 1}{0.8} = 5$. Notice that the last two numbers that were generated were the original two numbers with which you started. Choose any two integers and follow this process; you will find that the fourth and fifth steps will regenerate the original numbers. Of course, the algebra appears when the students attempt—using specific numbers at first, then x and y later—to show why this process always works. Many students find the exercise interesting, and it provides plenty of practice in simplifying rational expressions.

8. **Infinite Series:** Students often have difficulty understanding why the infinite series $\frac{1}{2} + \frac{1}{4} + \frac{1}{8} + \frac{1}{16} + \cdots = 1$. Here is a way that they can see what is happening. Provide each student with a square piece of paper and a pair of scissors. Ask them to fold the square in half and cut it into two congruent rectangles. Because the original square was 1, they could model $\frac{1}{2} + \frac{1}{2} = 1$ by putting the two rectangles back together. Tell them to set one rectangle aside and cut the other one in half. Each of these halves represents one-fourth of the original square. Putting all of the pieces together, students can model $\frac{1}{2} + \frac{1}{4} + \frac{1}{4} = 1$. Now, ask them to take the one-fourth piece and cut it in half so that the two new pieces each represent one-eighth. Putting the pieces together again, students can see that $\frac{1}{2} + \frac{1}{4} + \frac{1}{8} + \frac{1}{8} = 1$. Finally, the class takes the leap of assuming that if they were to keep cutting the remaining pieces in half infinitely, the sequence would continue, but there would still always be the original square of paper with which they started. Therefore, the sum of all of the pieces would still equal 1.

9. **Pendulums:** Students can make a connection to physics and the use of formulas by exploring a pendulum. Materials required include a 50-cm string marked every 5 cm, a weight (such as a nut from a bolt) tied to the end, and a stopwatch. The *period* of the pendulum is the amount of time it takes for the pendulum to swing from a given position back to its starting place. Holding the pendulum at the 5-cm mark, a student lets the pendulum swing for 30 seconds while another student counts and records the number of swings. Dividing 30 by the number of swings allows them to calculate the period (length of time for one swing). Then, students should repeat the process with the pendulum held at 10 cm, 15 cm, 20 cm, and so forth, to 50 cm. Students can then put the collected data into a graphing calculator, where $x =$ the length of the pendulum (L) and $y =$ period (T). They will notice that the data points are not linear and can discuss how much more sensitive a pendulum is when it is shorter in length (i.e., a change from 5 cm to 15 cm makes a greater difference in the period

than a change from 40 cm to 50 cm). Also, students can attempt to fit a curve to the data by doing a Power Regression on the calculator, and they may recognize it as a square root function. If they are given the information that the function can be generalized as $T = k\sqrt{L}$ they can substitute their T and L values for each pendulum length and approximate the value of k. In physics, the actual equation for period (T) is: $T = 2\pi\sqrt{\frac{L}{980}} = 0.2\sqrt{L}$. By using collected data, students should be able to approximate this formula and will gain an appreciation for the usefulness of the square root function. Finally, they may also want to try using different weights on the pendulum and will discover that the period has nothing to do with the weight on the end—only with the length of the pendulum.

10. **Tagging Fish:** Biologists often face the problem of determining how many of a particular variety of fish live in a body of water or how many species of animals live in a particular woods or mountain range. They may be interested in knowing how many trout live in a lake. Of course, it is impossible to count them all, so they catch a sample of fish and tag them on the gills. Then they throw the fish back into the water and allow them to mix with the other fish. Taking another net, they catch a second group of fish and compare the number of tagged trout to the total number of trout caught. Using a simple proportion, they can estimate how many trout are in the lake (i.e., $\frac{TT}{N} = \frac{tt}{n}$, where TT is the number of tagged trout released into the water; N represents the total number of trout in the lake; tt is the number of tagged fish that were recaptured; and n represents the total number of trout that were caught on the second try). Give each pair of students a paper bag containing an unknown number of "fish" (you can use Goldfish Crackers, colored tiles, colored cubes, etc.). Students should reach into the bag, pull out a handful, count them, "tag" them (i.e., exchange a goldfish with a pretzelfish or a blue cube with a red one), and put them back in the bag. After shaking up the bag, students should reach in and pull out another handful. By counting the total number of fish in the handful and noting how many of them are tagged, they can set up and solve a proportion to estimate the number of fish in the bag. If every pair of students has the same (unknown) number of fish, it can generate an interesting class discussion about the different answers that students produced after their sampling process and then a conversation about how this method is moderately effective but only generates estimates, some of which may not be very accurate.

11. **An Unusual Polynomial Equation:** The following problem was posed in *The Ideas of Algebra, K–12* (Coxford, 1988). Ask students to solve this equation:

$$(x^2 - 5x + 5)^{x^2-9x+20} = 1$$

Students should begin with small-group, peer discussions and then analyze the problem as a class. They should recognize that three issues need to be considered: (1) Since an expression is being raised to a power, and the result is 1, the exponent could be 0. Therefore, two solutions can be found by solving the resulting equation, $x^2 - 9x + 20 = 0$. (2) However, another way to think of the problem is that anytime a quantity is raised to a power, if the result is 1, then the base could also be 1, regardless of the value of the exponent. Therefore, students will also need to explore the equation $x^2 - 5x + 5 = 1$, which results in two more solutions. (3) Finally, if the base is -1 and the exponent is an even number, then the expression will also equal 1. So, the last equation for students to consider is $x^2 - 5x + 5 = -1$. A graphing calculator can also be useful for exploring this problem, as the TABLE function reveals solutions when the equations $y_1 = (x^2 - 5x + 5)^{x^2 - 9x + 20}$ and $y_2 = 1$ are entered as the two functions to explore. The problem is almost certain to spark debate and discussion in the classroom.

12. **Laundry Line Limits:** Students need visual approaches to help them appreciate how the terms in a sequence can converge to a limit. Present the class with an expression such as $\frac{n - 5}{2n + 1}$. In the front of the classroom, hang a string that looks like a laundry line and has clothespins on it that hold small cards with integers on them, from -3 to $+3$, making a number line. Give each of several students a small card with an n value on it, from $n = 1$ to $n = 100$ (including, perhaps, 1, 2, 3, 4, 5, 6, 7, 8, 9, 10, 20, 50, 75, and 100). Each student should evaluate the expression for the given n value and write the answer on the card. Then, moving from the least n to the greatest, students come to the front of the room and use a clothespin to hang their calculated expression values on the laundry line. As students proceed to hang up their cards, they will see the values increase from $-1\frac{1}{3}$ (when $n = 1$) to $-\frac{3}{5}, -\frac{2}{7}, 0, \frac{1}{13}$, and then eventually to $\frac{95}{201}$. Students should recognize that no matter how great the n-value becomes, the value of the fraction will never exceed $\frac{1}{2}$. Therefore, the limit of the sequence is $\frac{1}{2}$. The number line can be reset for other sequences, and students can follow a similar procedure to observe the trends in the calculated values and predict the limits in each case.

Conclusion

Suppose that you were hired to teach a general mathematics course in a large school district. As you open the book, you begin to scan the table of contents and notice that Unit 1 focuses on whole number operations, Unit 2 explores fractions and decimals, Unit 3 is on algebra, Unit 4 is on measurement in customary and metric units, Unit 5 involves graphing lines and solving equations, and Unit 6 includes a study of statistics and probability. As you begin to plan your instruction, you might be tempted to work your way through the text, one unit at a time. When you "finish" with the study of number operations, you can move on to fractions and decimals. And when rational numbers are "completed," you can begin to study algebra, and so forth. The flaw in this plan, however, is that students are likely to view the content of the course as a series of disconnected facts and skills. The very design of the textbook and your course can suggest false walls between content areas, creating the illusion that each branch of mathematics stands alone. You may also notice that an important topic is not even included in the textbook at all, despite having objectives from this field in your course of study.

As we have described in this chapter, the content of a mathematics program should illustrate for students the inherent connections between content areas, between mathematics and other subject areas, and from one year of study to the next. Instead of viewing algebra as a course, we conceptualize it as a content strand that takes many years to explore. The same is true for geometry, statistics, and probability as well, and these will be discussed in some depth in the next chapter. Chapter 9 specifically focused on reasoning and sense making, as well as the content areas of number sense and algebra. These topics are particularly challenging when designing courses and individual lessons for secondary and middle school students because they are at the core of the curriculum, yet they are often misunderstood in terms of what it means to study each area and how to address the content.

We have described mathematical reasoning, as well as each of these content areas, as a prekindergarten through high school responsibility and have emphasized how teachers need to spend adequate time on each topic, each year that a student is in school. In Chapter 4, we described integrated curricular models that are designed to promote the notion of "every topic, every year." And even within a district that uses a more traditional approach with algebra and geometry courses, connections can be made between content areas by a teacher who is prepared to, for example, use algebra tiles when teaching polynomial operations, promote the meaning of fractions and percents while studying probability, and emphasize the representation of geometric figures and their translations through the use of matrices.

As students see the connections between the major content areas, they begin to appreciate "mathematics" as an integrated whole and can become flexible in choosing representations to solve real problems. In the next chapter, we continue to explore mathematical content taught in middle and high school by focusing on geometry, statistics and probability, and discrete mathematics.

For bibliographic references and additional resources, see page 413

Glossary

Abundant Number: A number is said to be abundant if the sum of all of its factors (other than the number itself) is greater than the number.

Deficient Number: A number is said to be deficient if the sum of all its factors (other than the number itself) is less than the number.

Perfect Number: A number is said to be perfect if the sum of all its factors (other than the number itself) is equal to the number.

Discussion Questions and Activities

1. In a small group, discuss your experiences with learning number sense and algebra in school. Discuss whether you had distinct courses (or major units) in these topics or whether they were part of an integrated curriculum and how the curriculum design influenced your learning.

2. Obtain one of the NCTM *Navigations* books or a similar resource and examine the types of activities and software suggested for the promotion of content topics. Discuss similarities or differences between the types of activities suggested in these books and the classroom experiences you had in school.

3. High school teachers often feel that it is not their responsibility to teach fractions and decimals—that these skills and concepts should have been mastered in middle school. But this is often not the case, as high school teachers often intervene when students lack sufficient background in number sense. Research how hands-on materials such as base ten blocks can be used to remediate high school students who are not yet proficient in working with rational numbers.

4. Obtain a secondary or middle school general mathematics textbook, such as a typical eighth grade mathematics book. Scan the table of contents and then the rest of the book. Determine which topics are emphasized and whether there is any significant effort on the part of the author(s) to connect ideas from the content areas together.

5. Obtain an integrated mathematics textbook and analyze its content. Determine roughly how much of the book is devoted to the studies of number sense and algebra. Are the topics woven together so that algebraic ideas arise from the study of number, or are they presented in separate chapters? Is one content area emphasized considerably more than another?

6. Using a copy of the *Common Core State Standards*, your state's curriculum standards, or a local course of study, examine the outcomes for the secondary and

middle grades and highlight the objectives that would be identified for the study of number sense and algebra. What are the "big ideas" that are emphasized in these two content areas?

7. Using a traditional algebra textbook, select a section of the book or an individual lesson that appears to be purely teaching an algebra skill. Rewrite the section or lesson in a way that might help students connect this idea to at least one other area of the mathematics curriculum.

8. In a team of students, have each person select one of the 12 recommended activities from each of the two content areas in this chapter and "peer teach" it to the rest of the group. After the presentations, reflect on the activities by discussing the manner in which they address the spirit of that content area as described in the *Common Core State Standards*.

9. Examine the contents of one or more high school mathematics textbooks. In what ways do the authors of the texts attempt to promote reasoning and sense making? What evidence can you find to support your answer?

10. Obtain a copy of the *Common Core State Standards* or the NCTM *Principles and Standards for School Mathematics*, or access the documents on-line. Examine how mathematical content in number and algebra develops across the grade levels, and compare and contrast this vision of school mathematics with your experiences through elementary, middle, and high school.

Teaching Geometry, Statistics/Probability, and Discrete Mathematics

After reading Chapter 9, you should be able to answer the following questions:

● How has the research of the van Hieles influenced the teaching of geometry? Identify the areas of study that are included in the geometry content area.

● Why has the study of statistics and probability become increasingly important in the secondary and middle grades? Describe the major components of this content strand.

● What are the characteristics of a discrete mathematics problem? Identify the types of problems that are included in this branch of mathematics. Explain how the vision of teaching discrete topics has evolved over time.

● What is the role of pre-calculus and calculus courses in the curriculum?

At professional development meetings for mathematics faculty, teachers tend to be surprised to hear about the role of statistics and probability in the *Common Core State Standards* (2010). While the NCTM *Standards* (2000) called for data analysis and probability to be content strands studied across all years, kindergarten through grade 12, the CCSS suggest that students should only have informal introduction to data analysis before grade 6, at which time a more formal study of statistics begins that includes an understanding of variability and ways to describe distributions. Furthermore, the study of probability is not introduced in the CCSS until grade 7, representing a major shift in thinking about what content is most important for students to explore in each year of school. The idea is to limit the number of topics examined each year so that fewer concepts can be studied in more depth. But no matter which topics are moved to different grades, someone is going to be upset about the sequencing. This change has sparked much debate about what it is important for students to learn, as was discussed in Chapter 4.

However, regardless of the specific grade levels at which various topics are studied, the mathematics curriculum at the secondary and middle school levels continues to feature the study of number, algebra, geometry, measurement, statistics, and probability. In addition, topics from discrete mathematics are often infused in the curriculum, though most parents of school-age students will tell you that they rarely, if ever, studied statistics and probability in school and have no idea what you mean by "discrete mathematics" (e.g., "Is it a secret?").

In this chapter, we continue our discussion from Chapter 8 about specific mathematics content, including the big ideas of each topic and examples of lessons that can be used to teach them. After an introduction to the idea of promoting reasoning and sense making, Chapter 8 focused on number sense and algebra, while in this chapter we will examine the teaching of geometry, statistics and probability, and discrete mathematics. The study of geometry is a major emphasis in both the secondary and middle school curricula. The other two areas had been historically lacking (or, at best, underplayed) but were given increased emphasis at all grade levels in both the NCTM and *Common Core State Standards* documents. We conclude the chapter with a brief discussion of the role of pre-calculus and calculus courses in high school. ▧

The Teaching of Geometry

In Chapter 3, we discussed the influence of research conducted by the van Hieles and how their work defined stages that learners pass through as they develop geometric ideas. As a result of their studies, we have become much more sensitive to student needs as we attempt to design lessons that match the developmental levels of the students. Most importantly, the teaching and learning of geometry naturally lend themselves to hands-on experiences, which include the use of pattern blocks, geoboards, algebra tiles (to establish a link between algebra and geometry), three-dimensional solid models, paper folding, and computer explorations. Historically, much of the teaching of geometry has been restricted to plugging numbers into formulas at the middle school level and writing two-column proofs in high school, leaving students confused and turning them off to a content area that should be attractive to visual learners.

The NCTM *Navigations* books, described in Chapter 5, began to be released in 2001 and were written to support classroom teachers in their implementation of the standards. Specifically, four of the resource books in the series are devoted to the teaching of geometry—one for each grade-level band (Pre-K–2, 3–5, 6–8, and 9–12). These books describe the developmental nature of geometric thinking, provide classroom activities for teachers, include electronic copies of articles on teaching geometry, and furnish computer software on a CD-ROM. One of the activities included in the high school book (Day, Kelley, Krussel, Lott, & Hirstein, 2001) engages the student in investigating **fractal** images on a computer. Fractals are relatively recent mathematical discoveries and involve a family of geometric shapes that are generated by beginning with a *seed* (initial image) and then applying some rule to that image in successive iterations. An important property of fractals is that they are **self-similar**: Regardless of how closely or how distantly a fractal is viewed, the same shape is always seen. Secondary and middle school students enjoy fractal explorations, in part, because they recognize that they are studying a topic in geometry that is current in the field of mathematics.

In one of the *Navigations* activities, students explore Koch's Snowflake Curve, which is a fractal image that begins with a triangle and successively has "bumps" added to its sides. The illustration in Figure 9.1 was generated with the software that is used in this investigation.

Figure 9.1 Koch Snowflake Curve Generated with *Navigations* Software

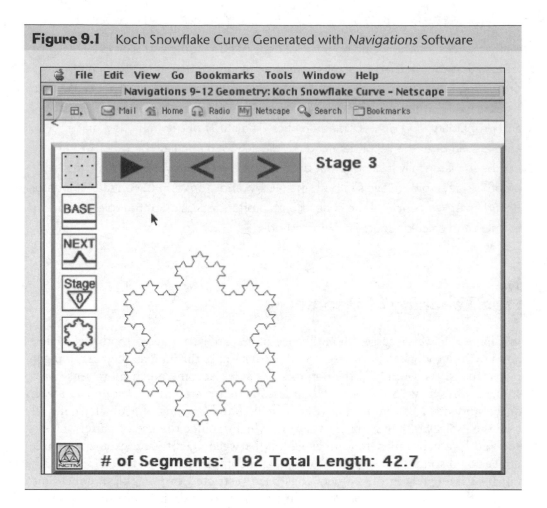

Each time that the computer's mouse is clicked, another iteration is performed on the fractal image. Additionally, at the bottom of the screen, the student is provided with a count of how many segments compose the picture together with a readout of the image's current perimeter. Students discover that, although the fractal remains within a bounded area, the perimeter increases infinitely, without bound—a paradox of the snowflake. The activity helps students to visualize changes and to connect the geometry of the problem to related issues in extending patterns (algebra) and quantifying lengths and areas (measurement).

As with the study of algebra, the NCTM and Common Core State Standards call for teachers to continually integrate geometry in the mathematics curriculum—to provide geometric models of problems from algebra, probability, and so forth. In the middle grades, teachers can use geometric representations to advance ideas of number, including fractions, decimals, percents, and ratios. As students develop their geometric-reasoning skills, they prepare themselves for a more axiomatic approach to the topic in high school. The *Common Core State Standards* (2010) document states, "During high school, students begin to formalize their geometry experiences ... using more precise definitions and developing careful proofs. Later in college some students develop Euclidean and other geometries carefully from a small set of axioms" (p. 42). The authors of the *Common Core State Standards* expect students to explore geometry both from a synthetic (without using coordinates) and an analytic (using coordinates) viewpoint.

The authors of the NCTM *Standards* (2000) also emphasize that students need experiences with geometric shapes in both two and three dimensions. The geometry standard states that

Instructional programs from prekindergarten through grade 12 should enable all students to—

- analyze characteristics and properties of two- and three-dimensional geometric shapes and develop mathematical arguments about geometric relationships;
- specify locations and describe spatial relationships using coordinate geometry and other representational systems;
- apply transformations and use symmetry to analyze mathematical situations;
- use visualization, spatial reasoning, and geometric modeling to solve problems. (p. 41)

Students' exposure to geometry should be rich and developmentally appropriate according to the levels of thinking outlined by the van Hieles. In time, students will realize the value of using geometric models in analyzing mathematical situations and solving problems. The next section provides an example of a lesson plan and 12 classroom activities that promote geometric reasoning.

SAMPLE LESSON PLAN

Geometry

I. Goal(s):
- To analyze the characteristics of two-dimensional geometric figures. (NCTM geometry standard: "Analyze characteristics and properties of two- and three-dimensional geometric shapes and develop mathematical arguments about geometric relationships.") (NCTM, 2000, p. 308)

II. Objective(s)
- The student will accurately measure an angle with a protractor.
- The student will use proper polygon terminology (e.g., sides, vertices, angles, quadrilateral, pentagon, hexagon, etc.).
- The student will collect, organize, and interpret data.
- The student will generalize and apply a formula for determining the sum of angle measures in a polygon.

III. Materials and Resources (for each student)
- Sheet of white paper
- Straightedge
- Protractor
- Handheld computer (1 for each pair of students)

IV. Motivation
1. When you write a number such as 23, what does the "2" represent? Why do we group things together by 10s? (More than likely, it was because we have 10 fingers, so it made 10s convenient.)
2. People have not always grouped things by 10s, however. In ancient times (more than 2,000 years ago), the Babylonians viewed 60 as the perfect number and grouped things by 60s. So, their number 23 would have stood for 2 groups of 60 and 3 left over—our 123! Can

you think of any modern-day examples of how we still think like the Babylonians? (Students should recognize 60 minutes in one hour and 60 minutes in a degree as a carryover from ancient times.)

3. How many degrees, altogether, are there in a triangle? (180°) It is easy to remember that there are 180° in a triangle when we think of an equilateral triangle as having three 60° angles—the ideal triangle in the days of the ancient Babylonians.

4. Draw an irregular quadrilateral on the board. How many degrees are there, altogether, in this figure? (Most students probably realize that a rectangle contains 360° but don't know that this applies to all quadrilaterals.) What if the figure had 10 sides? 20?

Transition: Explain to the students that today our class will focus on determining the total number of degrees in a polygon. We already know the answer for a triangle, but what about the rest?

V. Lesson Procedure

5. As the desks are arranged in pairs, have one person from each pair (the person with the latest birthdate in the year) come up and pick up 2 blank sheets of paper, 2 protractors, 2 straightedges, and 1 handheld computer. Remind the students that they may not use the computers until instructed to do so.

6. Using the straightedge and blank paper, each student should draw three polygons on the paper. Tables 1, 2, 3, and 4 should all draw pentagons. Tables 5, 6, 7, and 8 should all draw hexagons, and Tables 9, 10, 11, and 12 should all draw heptagons. After they have drawn their figures, each student should use the protractor, measure, and sum all of the angles in each of the three diagrams.

7. When the students have completed the drawing, measuring, and adding, make a chart on the board such as this:

	Polygon	No. of Angles	Angle Sum
Table 1			
Table 2			
Table 3			
and so forth			

Ask each pair of students to find the mean (average) of their measured sums and to report them to the class. As they read their answers, record them on the table on the board. What do you notice about the numbers on the board? How do the answers from different students compare? (The answers are likely to be different because of measurement errors, but it will at least get students thinking about how increasing the number of sides increases the angle measures.)

Transition: "On the board, we have measured estimates, but, of course, they are only as accurate as our protractors and students who use them. To get a more precise set of data, we will turn to our handheld computers."

8. Ask the students to open and turn on their computers. Pressing the APPS button will get them to a menu from which they can open the Geometer's Sketchpad software. Using the program, students

can draw polygons, measure their interior angles, sum the angles, and interact with the polygon so that vertices are dragged around. They should make observations and take notes about what they see. Beginning with a quadrilateral, students should test each polygon up to a decagon and record any patterns or trends that they notice.

9. After students have explored the different polygons, ask them to turn off their computers and set them aside. Have one person from each pair (the person with the earliest birthdate in the year) bring the protractors, straightedges, and computers back to the front table. Set up the following table on the chalkboard and have students volunteer answers to complete the Angle Sum column (they should have noticed that each polygon has a fixed angle sum, regardless of how it was oriented, dragged, or stretched on the screen):

Polygon	No. of Angles	Angle Sum
Triangle	3	180°
Quadrilateral	4	360°
Pentagon	5	540°
Hexagon	6	720°
Heptagon	7	900°
Octagon	8	1,080°
Nonagon	9	1,260°
Decagon	10	1,440°

10. Ask the students to describe patterns that they see. (They should notice that each time another side is added to the polygon, another angle and 180° are also added.) Without drawing or measuring a dodecagon (12 sides), can you tell me the interior angle sum? How do you know? (Students should see the interior angle sum as increasing by two more sets of 180°.)

Transition: "Let's see if we can generalize the formula for any polygon."

11. What if the polygon had n sides? How could we find the number of angles and the sum? (Students should recognize that if it has n sides, it must also have n angles. The sum is found by taking $(n - 2) \times 180°$ and this becomes the rule for finding an interior angle sum.)

VI. Closure

12. You have just developed a very useful and important formula for the study of geometry. With your partner, try each of the following:

    (a) Find the sum of the interior angles for an 18-gon.
    (b) How many sides does a polygon have if the sum of its interior angles is 4,500°?

13. Observe students working on the two problems to assess their understanding of the formula. Invite two students to come to the chalkboard and explain how they found their answers.

14. Assign the homework problems (textbook, p. 145, #2, 4, 6, 12, 15, 18, 26).

VII. Extension

If time allows, before the closure, ask the students to figure out why this formula makes sense (i.e., why 180° per side?) by drawing some polygons and analyzing them. Students should recognize that a diagonal drawn in a quadrilateral divides it into two triangles, each of which contains 180°. A pentagon, likewise, can be divided into three triangles, and so forth. If we do not get to it today, it might make a nice place to begin tomorrow's lesson.

VIII. Assessment

Assessment in this lesson takes three different forms:
- As students draw polygons by hand in Step 6 and on computers in Step 8, informal observations will be conducted.
- In Steps 12 and 13, observation notes will be taken as students attempt to solve two problems using their newly discovered formula.
- The homework assignment—checked the following day—will provide an assessment of students' abilities to apply the formula to other problems.

How Would You React

SCENARIO

In your mathematics class, you are committed to promoting reading and writing skills in the curriculum. Consequently, one of your assignments is to have students write a paper about a mathematical topic of their choice. One student writes about the history of π, while another writes about the development of fractal geometry, and still another writes about the use of probability to design casino games. While reading a student's paper, you see words used in the essay that appear to be beyond the level of the student. You copy and paste a sentence from the paper into the Google search engine and discover that the sentence has been lifted word-for-word from a Web site but has not been cited by your student. Clearly, the student has cheated by copying full sentences from another source. Your response is to

a. Ignore the problem, as the essay was generally well written and the number of direct quotes from another source appears to be minimal.

b. Grade the paper as if nothing had been copied but individually speak to the student about the problem at a later time.

c. Call the problem to the attention of the student and require that the paper be resubmitted with proper citations to be accepted.

d. Give the student a "0" on the paper and contact the principal to see that the student is punished for breaking the school's plagiarism policy.

e. Other.

DISCUSSION

Students cheating on homework assignments have been—and continue to be—one of the many issues that mathematics teachers confront on a regular basis. Whether two students have copied each other's papers at the lunch table, a student has copied another person's response during class time, or a student has texted an answer to another classroom during an exam, cheating is prevalent in our schools. Sadly, even teachers themselves have been involved in changing student responses on standardized tests to show artificial gains on scores in order to preserve their jobs. While most school districts have policies regarding how to handle cheating, individual teachers tend to have their own approaches.

One issue to consider is the severity of the offense. Did the student simply copy one sentence from another source and insert it into a 3-page paper, or did the student copy an entire paragraph of a 1-page essay? Also, the teacher must consider whether this is a first offense or the student has been warned of similar situations in the past. Perhaps the student is warned the first time that a solution to a problem is copied but given a "0" for a second offense. In some cases, the student may simply not be aware that there is anything wrong with copying a sentence or two from another source. And, in fact, there *is* nothing wrong with quoting directly from another document, *provided that a bibliographic citation is given*. Teachers can use this type of incident as a teachable moment to help students understand the importance of citing sources. Students may even be aware of this rule in an English class but not realize that the same rule applies to the mathematics classroom.

One way to prevent these types of problems on student writing projects is to use computer software such as Turnitin and Viper. These are Internet-based programs that allow students to scan their own papers for an originality check. The computer will search for direct quotes from other sources so the student can ensure that the quotations have been cited. Further-more, when the teacher grades the paper, the student can already be aware of its "originality index," and the teacher can scan it to ensure that proper credit has been given for quoted work. This software, of course, does not solve the problem of students copying homework papers but can be very useful for essays and long-term projects. With daily work, teachers must be vigilant to observe students working in class and to look for directly copied work. Students must also learn to distinguish between collaborating on a problem (i.e., discussing the problem and how to solve it, but writing down their own versions of the work and solution) and directly copying a classmate's work. In some ways, this may appear to be paradoxical because on one hand, students are often encouraged to work together and build cooperative teams, while on the other, they are expected to be accountable for their own learning, as we discussed in the section on cooperative learning in Chapter 7. The difference between collaborating and cheating is one of the many life skills that students can be taught in the context of a mathematics class.

Geometry—Activities Sampler

1. **Rectangle Folding:** Provide each student with a rectangular strip of paper ($2 \times 8''$ works well). Ask the students how many rectangles they see. Of course, there is 1 rectangle, so have them fold it in half and ask the same question. They now should be able to identify 3 rectangles—the original rectangle plus 2 smaller ones that were formed when the paper was folded. Now, take half of the strip (one of the smaller rectangles) and fold it in half again. At this point, they should see 6 rectangles. Continue this process several times, and have students generate a table of values (i.e., 0 folds = 1 rectangle, 1 fold = 3 rectangles, 2 folds = 6 rectangles, 3 folds = 10 rectangles, etc.). Engage the students in a discussion on how they do the counting and how they can be sure that they have counted *all* of the rectangles. Then, ask the students to generalize the number of rectangles for *n* folds. The resulting sequence is the set of triangular numbers, generalized by the formula $\dfrac{(n + 2)(n + 1)}{2}$, where *n* represents the number of folds. This activity allows students to develop spatial reasoning skills in identifying rectangles while analyzing a recursive pattern and generalizing a formula.

2. **Perimeter and Area:** Provide the students with a set of colored tiles (or some other square tiles or cubes). Ask them to arrange a set of tiles on the table so that the perimeter of the shape is 24 units and to record its dimensions (length and width) and its area, where each tile has an area of 1 square unit. Then, they should rearrange tiles to find another rectangle with a perimeter of 24. Students should continue this process until they have identified and recorded the dimensions and area of all of the possible rectangles. They will discover

that the area is changed each time, and the perimeter remains constant. Which dimensions generate the greatest area? (They will find that the dimensions can be $1 \times 11, 2 \times 10, 3 \times 9, 4 \times 8, 5 \times 7,$ or 6×6, and the greatest area is formed when the figure is a square.) To extend the problem, use x to stand for one of the dimensions. Because $2x$ added to twice the other dimension will sum to 24 units, the other dimension must be $(12 - x)$. Therefore, the equation $y = x(12 - x)$ describes the possible areas, and students can generate the parabola on a graphing calculator, noting that the maximum is at (6, 36). This problem allows students to connect the concepts of perimeter, area, and quadratic functions.

3. **Straw Triangles:** Provide each pair of students with a bag containing 5 straws cut to the following lengths: 1", 2", 3", 4", and 5". Begin by asking the students to reach in the bag, randomly pull out any 3 straws, and try to put them together to form a triangle. Then, place the straws back into the bag and repeat the process. One person should serve as the recorder, keeping track of how many times a triangle could be formed and how many times it could not, whereas the other person will be in charge of pulling out the 3 straws each time. After 20 trials, students should calculate and compare experimental probabilities. Then, ask students to make an organized list of all of the possible combinations of straw lengths that could be pulled out 3 at a time. They should try to make a triangle out of each combination and note when this is possible and when it is not. (Students should discover that there are 10 possible combinations and that only three of them—2-3-4, 2-4-5, and 3-4-5—actually form triangles.) Students can determine that the theoretical probability of drawing a triangle from the bag is 0.3 and compare this to the experimental probability from the beginning of the investigation. Finally, students should discuss any patterns that they noticed regarding the relative lengths of sides when it is possible, and not possible to form triangles. They most likely will discover the triangle inequality that states that the sum of the lengths of any two sides in a triangle must be greater than the length of the third side. Students then can use this generalization to determine whether, for example, a 5-7-9 triangle can be formed without actually trying to make one. This problem helps students develop an important triangle relationship while they are dealing with key concepts in the study of probability.

4. **Matrices, Trigonometry, and Transformations:** The coordinates of the vertices of a triangle can be written in a 2×3 matrix format, where each column contains a vertex's coordinates (x is the first row, and y is the second row). Multiplying a 2×2 matrix such as $\begin{bmatrix} 0 & -1 \\ 1 & 0 \end{bmatrix}$ by the 2×3 triangle matrix has the effect of generating three new triangle vertices that represent a 90° clockwise rotation or turn of the original triangle. Have students use a graphing calculator that can handle matrix multiplication, a piece of graph paper, and a protractor to try to find a transformation matrix that would rotate the original triangle 90° *counterclockwise* or one that would rotate it by 180°. If students have a background in trigonometry, they can determine that sin(90°) = 1, and cos(90°) = 0. Then, they can try to use this information, along with the original transformation matrix, to figure out how one might use sin(60°) and cos(60°) to find a matrix that rotates a triangle by 60° clockwise. This matrix is

$$\begin{bmatrix} \cos(60°) & -\sin(60°) \\ \sin(60°) & \sin(60°) \end{bmatrix} = \begin{bmatrix} 0.5 & -.87 \\ .87 & .87 \end{bmatrix}$$

Using sine and cosine values, students can generalize the process to find a transformation matrix that will rotate a triangle for any given number of degrees. This exploration involves several connected mathematical topics, such as geometric transformations, matrix algebra, and right-triangle trigonometry.

5. **The Scarecrow:** In the movie *The Wizard of Oz*, when the scarecrow receives his brain, he holds a diploma in his hands and announces that "the sum of the square roots of any two sides of an isosceles triangle is equal to the square root of the remaining side." Obtain a copy of the video and show this brief segment to the class. Then, have students analyze the statement to determine whether it is true. At first glance, it appears to be a pronouncement of the Pythagorean Theorem, but it deals with the *square roots* of the lengths of the sides, not the squares. Students will need to consider two cases: (a) The case in which the sides being added are the legs of the isosceles triangle and (b) the case in which the sides being added are a leg and the base. If the lengths of the sides are x, x, and y, then for the first case to be true, $\sqrt{x} + \sqrt{x} = \sqrt{y}$. However, for this statement to be true, $4x = y$, so $y = \frac{1}{4}x$. However, if $y = \frac{1}{4}x$, the triangle inequality would not be true because the sum of the lengths of the legs would be less than the length of the base, so the construction of this triangle is impossible. For the second case to be true, $\sqrt{x} + \sqrt{y} = \sqrt{x}$, but this is only true when $y = 0$, which is not possible either. Therefore, the Scarecrow's statement is false—maybe he hadn't received a brain after all. This activity leads to a rich discussion of isosceles triangles, the use of proper geometric terminology, and the generation of a deductive proof.

6. **How Many Diagonals?** A triangle has no diagonals. If a quadrilateral is drawn on a piece of paper, it will contain 2 possible diagonals. If a pentagon is drawn, 5 diagonals can be formed. Students should continue to draw polygons with an increasing number of sides to look for patterns in the number of diagonals that are possible. Students should discover that, in any polygon containing n sides, there are n choices for the endpoint of a given diagonal. Then the other endpoint can be any other point in the polygon, other than the point itself or the two points adjacent to the selected point. Therefore, there are $(n - 3)$ possible endpoints for the diagonal. Consequently, if we multiply $n(n - 3)$, this product will tell us how many diagonals can be formed *except* it assumes that, for example, the diagonals $\overline{AC}$ and $\overline{CA}$ are distinct, which they are not. Therefore, we must divide the product by 2, and the formula that students can derive for the number of diagonals in a polygon is $\dfrac{n(n - 3)}{2}$. The process of deriving this formula involves sketching and analyzing polygons and their diagonals, collecting data to identify patterns, and using a variable to generalize the pattern.

7. **Pattern Block Angles:** A fairly simple but rich activity can be conducted by giving each student (or pair of students) 1 of each of the 6 standard pattern blocks—a hexagon, trapezoid, rhombus, smaller rhombus, square, and triangle. The task is for the students to find the angle measures for every angle of every pattern block without using a measuring device such as a protractor. Students might decide, for example, that the square has four right angles and that the equilateral triangle has three 60° angles, and use those angles to measure the others. If they know that the angles of a quadrilateral sum to 360° and that the blue rhombus contains two 60° angles, they can determine the remaining two angles by performing the calculation: $\dfrac{360 - 2(60)}{2} = 120°$. Have

students demonstrate a variety of methods of determining each angle measure—there are *many* different ways to find the angles. This problem involves an exploration of angle measure but can quickly develop into a discussion of anything from the properties of polygons to angles formed by the intersection of parallel lines.

8. **Greatest Volume:** Provide each student with a 3×5 index card and pose the following problem: We would like to fold the card into a rectangular prism. One way to fold it is by making it tall and skinny, and the other way is make it short and wide. Which of these designs would result in a container with the greater volume? Or would the volumes be the same? Distribute tape, a paper plate, and a cup of rice to each group of students and have them fold and tape their cards and fill them with rice to compare the volumes. Then, ask whether a "short and wide" container would have the greatest volume if made into a triangular prism, a rectangular prism, or a cylinder. Again, allow the students to build the shapes and compare their volumes with rice. Many students will begin the investigation by assuming that any two containers made out of the exact same size card will have the same volume, and they will quickly be surprised to find that this is not the case. By studying the relative volume of the containers, students can generalize that the more sides the prism has, the greater the volume, and a circular base will maximize the volume. This investigation can lead to a discussion of why soup and soda cans are cylindrical; after all, their manufacturers make efficient use of a sheet of aluminum to maximize profits. The activity is primarily an exploration of volume but also involves the construction and discussion of three-dimensional objects and the application of estimation and problem-solving skills.

9. **Euler's Formula:** Begin by having the students construct a number of three-dimensional solids with materials such as straws. (Students can use a bendable straw, cut a slit in the short end, and insert it into another straw to build polygons that can be taped together to form solids.) After students have constructed solids such as cubes, tetrahedra, and square-base pyramids, collect classroom data on the number of base edges, the total number of edges, the total number of faces, and the number of vertices for each solid. Students then should analyze the data and look for patterns. They will rediscover Euler's formula, which states that the sum of the total number of faces added to the total number of vertices is always 2 more than the total number of edges in a right prism or pyramid (or, $f + v = e + 2$). Students can also cover the solids with newspaper and fill them up with materials such as rice or candy to explore the relative surface areas and volumes of the solids. This investigation allows students to explore the properties of three-dimensional solids and to use proper terminology, such as "face," "vertex," and so on. At the same time, students are collecting and analyzing data, generalizing patterns using algebraic expressions, and exploring concepts of measurement such as surface area and volume.

10. **Squares on a Geoboard:** Give each student a 25-peg geoboard, a recording sheet with pictures of geoboards on it, and several geobands (rubber bands). The task is to find all of the possible squares that can be formed on the geoboard. Each square must be a different size (i.e., a student cannot count a 1×1 square 16 times by simply sliding [translating] it around the geoboard). This task is not as simple as it sounds. Most students will find the first four squares (1×1, 2×2, 3

× 3, and 4 × 4) rather quickly because they are oriented the same way as the board itself; however, students generally have a more difficult time locating the rest of the squares, which are offset from the horizontal. In all they should find 8 different squares. Then, students can be challenged to determine the area of each square. The 4 less-obvious squares will require either a thought process involving moving pieces of the square to visualize the area or using the Pythagorean Theorem to determine the lengths of the sides. The possible areas of the 8 squares are: 1, 2, 4, 5, 8, 9, 10, and 16 square units. Finally, students can look at each square and record the number of pegs located inside and outside the square. Noting these peg numbers for each of the 8 squares, they should notice patterns such as the number of inside pegs progressing as a list of squares from 1, to 4, to 9. This activity emphasizes problem solving and visualization while pushing students to identify squares, determine areas, use the Pythagorean Theorem, and identify and generalize patterns.

11. **What's My Area?** Students generally are surprised to find out that all of the standard area formulas are based on the area of a rectangle. Students should review why the area of a rectangle can be found by multiplying base times height (by drawing rectangles on a piece of graph paper and recognizing that the grid determines the number of squares making up the shape). Because a square is a rectangle with base and height being equal, its area can be found by multiplying side times side or s^2. A parallelogram is a rectangle with a triangular piece translated, as shown in Figure 9.2.

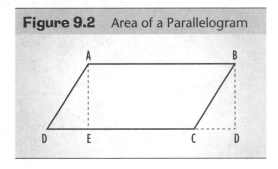

Figure 9.2   Area of a Parallelogram

The area of parallelogram *ABCD* would be the same as the area of rectangle *ABDE* because triangle *ADE* has been translated to the location of triangle *BCD*. Therefore, the area formula for a parallelogram must be the same as the formula for area of a rectangle, base times height. Similarly, a triangle can be thought of as a parallelogram with a diagonal drawn in it, so its area must be half of the area of the original parallelogram or $\frac{1}{2}bh$. When two parallelograms are joined together, a trapezoid is formed. Hence, the area formula for a trapezoid is also based on the parallelogram and rectangle models. A similar argument can be made for the area of a rhombus. Therefore, by using drawings, a geoboard, or tangrams, students can see that the area formulas for square, parallelogram, triangle, trapezoid, and rhombus are all rooted in the area of a rectangle. Investigating these relationships can help students to review the properties of various geometric shapes, while also setting them up to reinvent their own area formulas in the future if they forget one or more of them.

12. **Pick's Theorem:** Students can explore and reinvent a famous theorem discovered by Georg Pick in the late 1800s. Ask students to make several shapes on a geoboard and to record (a) the number of pegs on the inside of the shape, (b) the number of pegs that make up the boundary of the shape, and (c) the area of the shape. For example, the rectangle formed in Figure 9.3 has 3 pegs on its interior and 12 pegs on its boundary. The area of this shape is 8 square units.

Figure 9.3   Boundary and Interior Pegs for a Rectangle

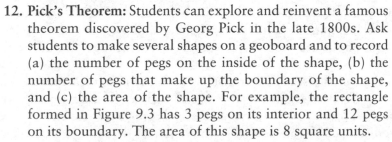

Students should generate numerous examples and try to find the relationship between the numbers of boundary pegs and interior pegs and the area. Eventually, they should be able to determine what is known as Pick's Theorem, which states that the area, A, can be found by using the formula $A = I + \dfrac{B}{2} - 1$, where I is the number of interior pegs, and B is the number of border pegs. There are a number of proofs for why this theorem is true (see, for example, Grunbaum & Shephard, 1993). Exploration of this relationship can be a rich problem as students collect and analyze the data to "invent" the theorem.

The Teaching of Statistics and Probability

"There is a 40 percent chance of rain tonight."

"At the current growth rate, the city's population will double within 6 years."

"The basketball team has a 0.675 winning average."

"Climatic trends suggest that this year's summer will be hot and dry."

"Astronomers calculate the chances of the asteroid striking the earth at 1 in 909,000."

"The median annual salary for the county is $46,236."

These news headlines are typical of the information with which our society is bombarded every day. What do they have in common? They are all statements based on the collection and analysis of some type of data, whether climatic, population, athletic, scientific, or financial. Enhanced technological capabilities have made it much easier for professionals to collect and analyze data than at any point in history. Consequently, society expects its employees (and its citizens, in general) to have a fundamental understanding of data analysis and probability that surpasses the needs of previous generations. A report from a conference on the teaching of statistics, funded by the National Science Foundation, defined *statistics* as "the science of learning from data" (Lindsay, Kettenring, & Siegmund, 2003, p. v). The authors of the report indicated that undergraduate course taking in statistics classes increased by 45 percent in the decade from 1990 through 2000. As a result of the societal need for statistics education, the *Common Core State Standards* recommend a formal study of statistics beginning at grade 6 and of probability at grade 7. The NCTM *Standards* advocate the inclusion of a significant content strand focused on statistics and probability throughout a student's prekindergarten through high school experience.

As students engage in the study of statistics, they encounter various ways that information can be collected (through the use of various sampling methods) and then communicated through graphs and statistical measures. Students at the secondary and middle school levels need the experience of debating which type of graph is appropriate for a given situation. For example, monthly attendance figures for an amusement park may be displayed best as a bar graph, whereas

SPOTlight on Technology

Perhaps the most famous problem from the field of discrete mathematics is called the traveling salesperson problem (TSP); it has perplexed mathematicians for more than 100 years. Here is an example of a TSP: Suppose that a salesperson lives in Chicago (C) and has to travel to New York City (N) for a sales call. There is a certain cost associated with that trip—dominated by airfare—that the traveler will incur. Now, suppose that the traveler also has to visit Orlando (O) and Las Vegas (L) on the same trip. The question that the salesperson must pursue is this: Is it cheaper to fly to New York first, and then to go on to Orlando and Las Vegas before returning home? Or would it be better to fly to, say, Orlando first, then one of the other two cities next? Checking airfares for each possible trip and comparing them can solve this problem fairly easily.

To analyze the problem, consider the diagram in Figure 9.4.

Figure 9.4 is a graph on which the vertices represent the cities, and the edges (segments) are labeled with the cost of travel (sometimes referred to as the *weights*) between the cities located at the endpoints. Although there are only three cities to be visited, a student attempting to solve this problem may begin by exploring six different routes (C–N–O–L, C–N–L–O, C–O–N–L, C–O–L–N, C–L–N–O, and C–L–O–N). By adding the total cost of travel for each of the six routes, a least-expensive alternative can be determined. Students also will discover that the number of routes to be checked can be found by taking $\frac{(n-1)!}{2}$, where n stands for the number of cities. In this case, we have three choices for the first city to visit, then two, and then one, so the total number of routes to check by "brute force" (as the method is referred to by mathematicians) is $\frac{3!}{2} \cdot (\frac{3 \times 2 \times 1}{2} = 3)$. Note that the route from Chicago to New York to Orlando to Las Vegas would be assumed to cost the same as a trip from Chicago to Las Vegas to Orlando to New York (the reverse of the same route). As a result, $(n-1)!$ includes duplicated routes, so we have to divide $(n-1)!$ by 2 to determine the actual number of routes to be checked.

Now, suppose that the salesperson found out that a fourth city was added to the business trip—San Diego. With four cities to visit, there will be $\frac{4!}{2}$ or 12 different routes to explore to find the least expensive trip. Computer programs are available that can run the numbers to find the cheapest route. However, students can explore the problem further to discover that if the trip, for example, takes the traveler to nine different cities, there are 181,440 routes to consider. Fortunately, computers can crunch those numbers and come up with a solution in less than 1 second (Cozzens & Porter, 1987). However, suppose that the salesperson wanted to visit 25 cities. In this case, even some of the fastest computers would require 10 billion years to check all of the possible routes (Leake, 1998)!

The traveling salesperson problem lends itself well to exploration with calculators and computers. For example, a student can be given a five-city route and, using a commercial airline's Web site, find the airfares between the cities to solve the "optimal route" problem. Likewise, many of these problems involve distances that one drives in an automobile. Again, a student could select some cities or towns in the school's locale and use a mapping program on the Internet to determine the distance between each pair of cities to find the route with the shortest driving distance. There is even a site on the Internet devoted entirely to exploration of the TSP, which is located at www.tsp.gatech.edu. Students often are amazed by the mathematical challenges presented by a problem that appears so simple on the surface.

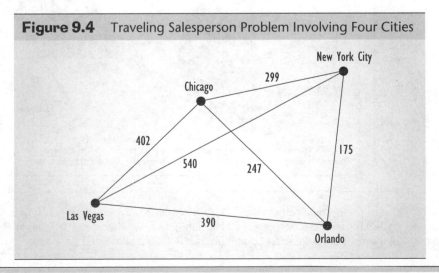

Figure 9.4 Traveling Salesperson Problem Involving Four Cities

the height of a plant over the course of a month can be illustrated with a line graph. Likewise, as we discussed through a sample test item in Chapter 3, students must not only learn *how* to calculate an arithmetic mean, a mode, and a median but also know *when* it is appropriate to use a particular statistic. Finally, students should have experiences with using data displayed in a variety of formats to draw conclusions and make predictions. Notice that the title of the NCTM standard is Data *Analysis,* which implies that the study of this strand involves not simply collecting and displaying information but also using the data to make decisions.

One of the richest experiences for students within this content area is the study of probability. Misconceptions abound in the classroom when "chance" and "likelihood" are the topics. In problems that involve probability, students are called on to think through a situation, to list the possible outcomes, and to determine—either mathematically (theoretically) or experimentally—how likely it is for a particular event to occur. In Chapter 5, we described several curriculum products that were created through funding by the National Science Foundation. One of these programs, the Connected Math Project, was developed at Michigan State University. In a unit entitled "What Do You Expect?" seventh graders explore probability through a series of problem situations. In one case, students are presented with the spinners and question featured in Figure 9.5.

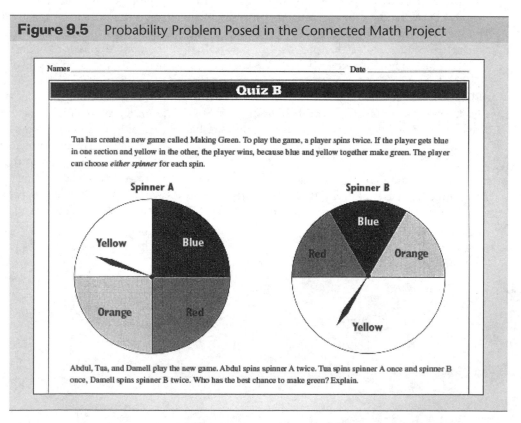

Figure 9.5   Probability Problem Posed in the Connected Math Project

Names _____   Date _____

Quiz B

Tua has created a new game called Making Green. To play the game, a player spins twice. If the player gets blue in one section and yellow in the other, the player wins, because blue and yellow together make green. The player can choose *either spinner* for each spin.

Spinner A

Yellow   Blue

Orange   Red

Spinner B

Blue

Red   Orange

Yellow

Abdul, Tua, and Damell play the new game. Abdul spins spinner A twice. Tua spins spinner A once and spinner B once. Damell spins spinner B twice. Who has the best chance to make green? Explain.

As students explore a problem such as the one shown in Figure 9.5, they might begin by actually spinning a spinner to run trials and collect data. One way to do that is to place the open end of a paper clip at the center of the circle, then put the point of a pencil on the center point and spin the paper clip. If each student in a class of 25 individuals conducts 20 trials, these 500 results can be pooled and discussed as a class to discover and describe trends. Also, by using a program on a graphing calculator, as described in Chapter 6, students can simulate the spinning of a spinner hundreds, or even thousands of times to look for trends. The American Statistical Association (1997), however, has written about the difficulty that students have in learning about probability. They stated that whereas small-scale simulations (such as using a spinner) can lead to inaccurate data and conclusions, computer and calculator simulations can mask the connection between the real problem and what the technology is doing. Students, then, need experiences on both levels. In fact, research suggests that a powerful way to work students up to the study of probability is through looking first at data sets and then using the data to suggest probability questions (Shaughnessy, 2003). Eventually, of course, we want students to look at the spinner on the left and conclude that the probability of spinning a blue and a yellow is $\frac{1}{8}$ ($2 \times \frac{1}{4} \times \frac{1}{4} = \frac{1}{8}$), whereas the probability of spinning this combination with the right spinner is $\frac{1}{6}$ ($2 \times \frac{1}{2} \times \frac{1}{6} = \frac{1}{6}$). Students make sense of the situation by comparing and discussing the results of their experiments to those of their mathematical calculations.

In addition to middle school introductions to the study of statistics and probability, the *Common Core State Standards* devote an entire high school conceptual category to these topics, emphasizing how every student needs to develop statistical thinking. There are four domains for high school that focus on statistics and probability: (1) interpreting categorical and quantitative data, (2) making inferences and justifying conclusions, (3) conditional probability and the rules of probability, and (4) using probability to make decisions. The document states, "Decisions or predictions are often based on data—numbers in context. These decisions or predictions would be easy if the data always sent a clear message, but the message is often obscured by variability. Statistics provides tools for describing variability in data and making informed decisions that take it into account" (2010, p. 79). Furthermore, the CCSS call for the use of technology to generate graphs and simulate probability situations.

The NCTM standard on data analysis and probability reads as follows:

Instructional programs from prekindergarten through grade 12 should enable all students to—

- formulate questions that can be addressed with data and collect, organize, and display relevant data to answer them;
- select and use appropriate statistical methods to analyze data;
- develop and evaluate inferences and predictions that are based on data;
- understand and apply basic concepts of probability. (p. 48)

As with the other content areas, the study of statistics and probability presents a rich environment in which to connect ideas of fractions, percents, and geometry (such as determining geometric probabilities) and should be viewed as a content strand that extends across all grade levels. A sample lesson plan and 12 classroom activities that advance this standard are presented in the next section.

Statistics and Probability

I. Goal(s):
- To develop skills of collecting and analyzing data. (NCTM data analysis and probability standard: "Formulate questions that can be addressed with data and collect, organize, and display relevant data to answer them.") (NCTM, 2000, p. 324)
- To determine and use probabilities in problem solving. (NCTM data analysis and probability standard: "Understand and apply basic concepts of probability.") (NCTM, 2000, p. 324)

II. Objective(s)
- The student will determine the probability of an event.
- The student will apply the fundamental counting principle.
- The student will use the problem-solving strategies of generating a table, listing all possibilities, and extending a pattern.

III. Materials and Resources (for each student)
- Sheet of paper and pencil
- TI-84 Plus graphing calculator (including an overhead model for the class)

IV. Motivation
1. Begin the class by asking students to clear their desks and take out a sheet of paper for a quiz. Ask them to number their papers from 1 to 5 for a five-question true–false quiz.
2. Once students are organized and ready to begin the quiz, look at the lesson plan book as if confused, and admit to the class that the quiz questions are at home. Tell the students that they will have to guess at the five answers because, luckily, there is an answer key in the plan book.
3. When students have finished the "quiz," ask them to exchange their papers with a partner and grade them. Read the answers as F, F, T, T, F. Have students write the number correct at the top of the page and hand the papers back to their owners.

Transition: "You might have guessed by now that I'm not planning to count this quiz today. Actually, I was just making up the part about forgetting to bring the questions, and I would like for us to take some time today to analyze this quiz and the results."

V. Lesson Procedure
4. Ask for a show of hands to determine how many people in the class got all 5 correct, then 4, 3, 2, 1, and 0. Record the results on the board. Is this the number of people that you would have *expected* to get those scores? Why or why not? (The answers to this question will depend on the results of the quiz and whether the class is surprised by them.)
5. Display the following three questions, and tell the students to discuss them at their tables for about 10 minutes. Be ready to share your answers and reasoning at the end of that time.

   (a) How many possible answer keys are there to this quiz?
   (b) What is the probability that you will score 100 percent when guessing?

(c) How does the theoretical probability compare with the experimental probability for our class?

(As students work, walk around with a Group Observation Checksheet and be sure to take careful notes about Groups 2 and 3 today, because the other teams received formal feedback earlier in the week.)

6. After about 10 minutes, ask for a volunteer to provide an answer for (a) and someone to write the possible answer keys on the chalkboard. (It is possible that someone will come up with $2 \times 2 \times 2 \times 2 \times 2 = 32$ because of experience with counting techniques.) Engage the class in a discussion, comparing the answers on the board to their group's solutions and discussing (b) and (c). (Students should have found 32 answer keys, so the probability of scoring 100 percent is $\frac{1}{32} < 0.03$. Thus, we would expect no more than 1 or 2 students in a class to score 100 percent.)

Transition: "Let's take a slightly different approach to determining the probability of getting a perfect score by randomly writing down answers."

7. On the chalkboard, make a table similar to this one:

No. of Questions	No. of Keys
1	2
2	4
3	8
4	16
5	32

Have students determine the number of answer keys, given the number of questions. After completing the five entries in the table, ask the students the following: What patterns do you see? How could we find out the number of answer keys for a 10-question quiz? Why does the number of keys double each time? (Students should be able to figure out that adding an extra question takes all of the previous keys and adds one new key ending in true and another that ends in false, so there would be twice as many keys.) What if there were x questions on the test?

8. When students determine that for x questions there are 2^x keys, ask them to take out their graphing calculators. How can we use the graphing calculator to help us explore this problem? (Students should recognize that they can key in $Y_1 = 2^x$, go to TABLE mode, and view the x-column as the number of questions and the y-column as the number of answer keys.)

Transition: "Let's take this example one step further. . . ."

VI. Closure

9. How can we use the technology to determine the probability of scoring 100 percent on a quiz with 10 multiple-choice items, where each question has 4 choices—a, b, c, and d? (Give students a couple of minutes to work at their tables and circulate around the room to check for understanding.) Ask a student to come up to the overhead TI-84 Plus and demonstrate the solution for the class.

2. For a homework assignment, answer the following questions:

   (a) Suppose that 60 percent or higher is passing. What is the probability of passing a five-question true–false quiz by randomly guessing answers?

   (b) If 60 percent or higher is passing, what is the probability of passing a 10-question multiple-choice quiz by randomly guessing answers?

VII. Extension

If time allows, an important discussion on sample size can be inserted into Step 6. In a class of only 20 students, we may or may not even have a 100 percent score on the quiz. To gain a more accurate experimental probability, we would need to pool our class's data with several other classes. We also could model additional trials by rolling a number cube (1–3 would be a true for the item, and 4–6 would be a false), which would make a possible extension for today or another exploration for tomorrow's class.

VIII. Assessment

Assessment in this lesson takes three different forms:

• A Group Observation Checklist has been developed for use with this lesson. In Step 5, this checklist is used, with particular emphasis on Groups 2 and 3.

• In the closure, students are observed as they try to extend the problem, and a student demonstrates the solution at the board.

• The homework assignment involves two additional problems that can be used to check for understanding the following day.

Statistics and Probability—Activities Sampler

1. **Which Letter?** Which letters are the most commonly used in the English language? Provide the students with a newspaper and have each person randomly select a paragraph anywhere in the paper. Have students count the number of times that each letter of the alphabet occurs in the paragraph and keep a tally of the totals. Then compile the whole class's data and construct a bar graph showing the relative frequencies of the occurrence of each letter. Students can consult a library resource book and check whether the most frequently occurring letters in the newspaper sample are the same letters that are reported to occur most frequently in the English language in general. How does this information influence the way that contestants play "Wheel of Fortune" or friends play Hangman by guessing letters? An extension to this data collection and analysis activity is to sample a paragraph from a book, magazine, or newspaper printed in another language and conduct a similar count. Are the same letters the most common in another language such as Spanish, or does the language affect the frequency of letter usage? Finally, students learning to use a computer can copy a passage from the Internet to the clipboard, paste it into a word processing document, and run a SEARCH or FIND on each letter to count the frequency. Then they can use a spreadsheet program to generate a bar graph of the frequencies for discussion. This is an activity that will engage students in collecting, representing, and analyzing data, as they learn about the nature of the English (or another) language at the same time.

2. **Carnival Guessing Game:** A common game played at carnivals and amusement parks is Guess My Birth Month. Generally, the game is played by asking the contestant to pay a certain amount of money and to write down the month in which the person was born. Then, someone has to guess the month of the person's birthday within one month. Model the game by having students pair up: When one person randomly chooses a month, the other person tries to guess it within one month. To keep the months truly random, students might put the names of the 12 months on cards and draw them from a bag each time. Collect enough class data to determine how often the contestant wins and how often the "guesser" wins. Ask students to determine the theoretical probability that the contestant will win. (When the guesser chooses a particular month, there are actually 9 months that will cause the contestant to win, so the contestant has a $\frac{9}{12} = 0.75$ probability of winning.) How does the theoretical compare to the experimental probability for the class? Suppose that the "guesser" charges $2.00 to play the game. What is the maximum value of each prize that can be given away so that the "guesser" at least breaks even on the game? (On average, the "guesser" will lose 3 out of every 4 games, so for the $8.00 collected, 3 prizes will be given out. Therefore, each prize should have a value less than or equal to $2.67. However, in the real world, the "guesser" also gets paid a few dollars per hour, so the prizes must also cover the cost of the person's salary and turn a profit for the carnival. The need to make a profit can lead to a rich classroom discussion about the nature of this game.) Finally, challenge students to think of what the "guesser" might do to increase the chances of winning the game. This activity is a real-life exploration of how probability is used by businesspeople for setting up a situation that turns a profit. Students will enjoy the familiar context of the problem and engage in determining experimental and theoretical probabilities while developing problem-solving skills along the way.

3. **A Probabilistic Approximation of π:** Assume that a circle has a radius of 1 and is inscribed in a square that measures 2×2. If the center of the circle is located at the origin $(0, 0)$, then Quadrant I contains a sector with an area of $\frac{\pi}{4}$ and a square with an area of 1. Suppose that the square that makes up Quadrant I was a dartboard. If you were to throw a dart at it, what is the probability of the dart hitting within the boundaries of the sector?

$$\frac{P(\text{hitting the sector})}{P(\text{hitting the square})} = \frac{\text{Area of the sector}}{\text{Area of the square}} = \frac{\frac{\pi}{4}}{1} = \frac{\pi}{4}$$

So, if we could find an experimental value for the probability, then multiplying this result by 4 would give us an approximation for pi. Using a random number generator on a spreadsheet or graphing calculator, students can generate coordinates of points that lie within a square having vertices at $(0, 0)$, $(1, 0)$, $(1, 1)$, and $(0, 1)$. Using the two random coordinates for x and y, students can determine $x^2 + y^2$. If $x^2 + y^2 \leq 1$ (i.e., it is located within the sector), then the point is a hit, and if not, it is a miss. After testing several random points, determine the ratio of hits to total points tried. This result, multiplied by 4, will result in an approximation for the value of π. This activity is a rich investigation that engages students in an exploration involving probability, while developing the geometric concepts of π, area, and the use of Cartesian coordinates.

4. **Misleading Graphs:** A common advertising trick is to take a set of data and attempt to mislead the public by graphing it using a scale that makes the

information appear more impressive than it really is. Students can see a simple example of the effects of changing scales by graphing the line $y = x$ on a graphing calculator with the window at a standard setting of -10 to $+10$ in the x- and y-directions. Changing the window to a Ymin at -100 and a Ymax at $+100$ will show a graph dramatically different from the first. Yet, both lines have the same equation. On a graphing calculator, students can enter a variety of function equations and explore how changes in the window size can affect the look of the graph. Then, students can be challenged to try to find newspaper or magazine advertisements that contain misleading graphs. For example, a company recently published an advertisement about how its product was 98 percent effective, and those of its competitors were 97 percent, 96.5 percent, and 95.5 percent effective. But when a bar graph of the four brands was drawn with the origin at (0, 95) and the vertical axis extended to (0, 99), the bars looked dramatically different. As an extension, students can also be given a set of data and asked to represent it as some type of graph that is deliberately misleading to emphasize some feature of the data. This exploration involves the representation and analysis of data in a real setting to which students can relate. The graphing calculator is an excellent aid in helping students view the effects of scale changes on a graph.

5. **The Birthday Problem:** One of the most famous probability problems is what is often referred to as the birthday problem: Suppose that N people are gathered together in a room. What is the probability that at least 2 of the N people were born on the same day of the year (i.e., share the same birthday)? Most students find this problem interesting because it defies intuition. If there are, for example, 20 people in a room, then the probability that at least 2 of them will have the same birthday is about 0.411, and by the time the group size is up to 41 people, there is more than a 90 percent chance that at least 2 of them will have the same birthday. Students should begin exploring this problem by collecting data from other classes in the school with N students with birthdays. Students can determine how the N-size relates to the number of birthday matches. Then students can explore the theoretical probability. Suppose that there are 10 people in the room. The probability that at least 2 people have the same birthday can be found by taking "$1 -$ (the probability that there are no matches)." The probability, then, would be calculated as follows:

$$P(\text{at least one match}) = 1 - \left(\frac{365 \times 364 \times \cdots 356}{365^{10}} \right) \approx 0.117$$

So, there is about a 12 percent chance of at least 1 match of birthdays in a room with 10 people. Extending the formula to a room with N individuals, the general probability would be

$$P(\text{at least one match}) = 1 - \left(\frac{365 \times 364 \times \cdots (356 - N + 1)}{365^N} \right)$$

If a class has 28 students, this formula shows that the probability of having at least 1 birthday match is 0.654. At a party with at least 68 people, the probability is 0.999. This problem is motivating because of the curiosity evoked when the expected answer does not match the actual solution, and it is rich in that it gives students experience with thinking about probabilities and generalizing a process into a general algebraic formula.

6. **What Is Average?** The word *average* is often misused because a central tendency can be expressed as a mode, a median, or a mean, and the term *average* can be

used with any of these measures. As a result, data can be misleading unless the public is clear about how the "average" was determined. For example, according to the U.S. Census Bureau (DeNavas-Walt & Cleveland, 2002), the mean household income in the United States in 2001 was $58,208. However, the median household income in the same year was $42,228, meaning that half of the households in the country earned less than this figure. The problem, of course, is that a few extremely wealthy people can boost a national "average" if the measure used is the mean, whereas individuals who earn a high income have little effect on the median. Students should generate sets of data in which (a) the mean provides an accurate picture of the data, but the median may be misleading; (b) the median provides the accurate picture, and the mean is misleading; and (c) the mean and the median are both fairly accurate measures of the data. The presentation of these sets of data, then, should result in a discussion of when it is most appropriate to use median versus mean. (Generally, when there are extremely high or extremely low outlier data points, the median is the most accurate measure.) Finally, students can search the Internet for data on populations, salaries, and so on, to locate an interesting set of data and properly use a measure of central tendency to generalize the data. Although the skills of finding a mean and a median are fairly simple and taught in the middle grades, the selection of the most appropriate measure is not as easy as it sounds. This activity will help students think about situations in which one would choose mean over median or vice versa when describing a data set.

7. **Winning the Lottery:** Most states have a lottery that is designed to make a profit for the state treasury. In many cases, up to 6 numbers are selected at random, and a match on all 6 numbers can entitle the winner to $1 million or more in prize money. However, mathematicians have dubbed the lottery as "a tax on the innumerate" because most people have no idea how unlikely it is to win a significant amount of money. Have students research the lottery process in your state or region and determine the probabilities of winning the grand prize. Then, they can put the probability into more understandable terms. For example, suppose that the chances of winning the lottery were "one in a million." If you were to place 1 million dollar bills end to end and walk along them, trying to pick up the "right one," the string of bills would extend nearly 95 miles—imagine walking 95 miles and hoping to stop at precisely the right time and pick up that *one* bill that is marked. Students can also explore other games of chance, such as the Powerball lottery that involves several states working together. This problem gets students actively involved in researching a situation in which the state uses probability to make money to fund such endeavors as education.

8. **Grades and Marbles:** Pose the following problem to the students: In order to determine grades this quarter, we will let your understanding of probability be our guide. Each person will be given 2 jars, 10 red marbles, and 10 white marbles. You can distribute the marbles into the 2 jars in any way that you wish, but you must use all 20 marbles. I will come to your desk and randomly select one of the jars and then randomly draw one marble from that jar. If I draw out a red marble, you get an A, and if I draw out a white marble, you fail. The question is, "How should you distribute the marbles in the jars to maximize your chances of earning an A?" Students typically begin to explore this problem by thinking about placing all 10 red marbles in 1 jar and all 10 white marbles in the other, thus making the probability of getting an A equal to 0.50. However, with some additional thought, they should also recognize that placing 5 red and

5 white marbles in each of the jars, or even 1 red and 9 white marbles in 1 jar and 9 red and 1 white marble in the other will always result in a probability of 0.50. After additional exploration and discussion, students probably will realize that they were in a mind set about having 10 marbles in each jar—by placing 1 red marble alone in 1 jar and 9 reds and 10 whites in the other jar, the probability increases to almost 0.74 (calculated by taking $\frac{1}{2} + \frac{1}{2}(\frac{9}{19}) \approx 0.74$). Interestingly, if there were 20 marbles of each color, and the same procedure were followed, the probability of drawing a red marble would still be about $0.74(\frac{1}{2} + \frac{1}{2}(\frac{19}{39}) \approx 0.74$). As a final step, students can generalize the marble problem by writing an equation that expresses the maximum probability of drawing a red marble (y) as a function of the number of marbles (x): $y = \frac{1}{2}\left(1 + \frac{x-1}{2x-1}\right)$. Graphing this function on a graphing calculator or computer can give students a visual image of how the probability approaches 0.75 as $x \rightarrow \infty$. An investigation that begins as a simple probability question becomes an exploration of patterns and the generalization of a pattern into a function that can be graphed and analyzed to determine its limit.

9. **Spaghetti and Probability:** Suppose that you randomly placed two points on a line segment so that it is divided into three smaller segments. Determine the probability that these three segments will form a triangle. Distribute several strands of thin spaghetti to each pair of students and ask them to randomly break the pasta into three pieces. Then, instruct the students to try to put the pieces together to form a triangle. As a class, tally the number of times that triangles could be formed and determine an experimental probability. In order to gather additional data, a graphing calculator can randomly assign two break distances for a segment that is 1 unit long. Then, using the triangle inequalities, a decision can be made as to whether the triangle can be formed with these random lengths. Finally, students can analyze the problem from a more theoretical perspective. Suppose that a line segment has endpoints labeled as 0 and 1 and contains two breaks at X and Y. The three segments would have lengths of X, $Y - X$, and $1 - Y$. Therefore, three triangle inequalities must be true if the new segments can form a triangle: $X + (Y - X) > 1 - Y, (Y - X) + (1 - Y) > X$, and $X + (1 - Y) > Y - X$. Solving these inequalities simultaneously, by graphing boundary lines and shading, can approximate the probability. Students should recognize, however, that it is possible for X to be greater than Y, and this results in three additional inequalities that must be graphed on the same set of axes. By finding the area of the shaded regions, the mathematical probability can be determined. Students should compare their answers from the physical breaking of spaghetti to the random number generated on the calculator and the theoretical value found from calculating the areas of the triangles. This problem connects the concepts of collecting and analyzing data to the calculation of probabilities, the application of triangle inequalities, and the graphing and interpretation of two-dimensional inequalities.

10. **World Series:** The World Series baseball championship requires that the "best" team win four out of a maximum of seven games. Suppose that two teams are evenly matched, in that the probability of either team winning a given game is 0.5. If they play each other in the World Series, what is the probability that the series will be completed in four games? Five? Six? Seven? Students can model this problem by tossing a fair coin. Working in pairs, one student tosses a coin while another student records the data. The two teams playing against one another are the Heads and the Tails. Each pair of students should play several

series so that the class can combine all of the data to determine the frequency with which the series ended in four, five, six, or seven games. Then move the students toward a more theoretical approach to the problem. Suppose that the Heads and the Tails want to finish the series in four games. The probability of the Heads winning four times in a row is $(\frac{1}{2})^4 = \frac{1}{16}$, and the Tails have the same probability of winning four games in a row, so the chances of the series ending in four games is $(\frac{1}{2})^4 + (\frac{1}{2})^4 = \frac{1}{8}$. If we want the Heads to win the series in five games, then the Tails must win one of the first four games. There are four possibilities for which of the first four games the Tails can win, so the probability of the Heads winning in five games is $4 \times (\frac{1}{2})^5 = \frac{1}{8}$ and because the Tails could also win four of five games, the probability of the series going exactly five games is $\frac{1}{8} + \frac{1}{8} = \frac{1}{4}$. Using similar logic, students can determine that the chances of having either a six- or seven-game series is $\frac{5}{16}$. Therefore, if the teams are evenly matched, we can expect the series to generally go six or seven games, but there is only a 1 in 8 chance that one team would win the first four games in a row. Students can compare their experimental and theoretical probabilities and discuss the similarities and differences. This activity is very real to young adolescents and can be very motivating because of their interest in professional athletics. The problem can be extended by having students determine what might happen if the teams were not evenly matched (e.g., Team A has a 0.6 chance of winning each game). The activity involves the collection and analysis of data, use of counting rules, and determination of experimental and theoretical probabilities.

11. **Chi Square Candy:** Chi square is a statistic used to determine whether categorical data are randomly distributed—in other words, whether theoretical and expected frequencies are roughly equal. For a real-life activity involving the chi square statistic, begin by giving each student a bag of M&Ms and have the students pour their bags of candy out onto their desks. Students should count the number of each color of candy and also calculate the expected number for each color if the colors are truly randomly distributed in the candy. A Pearson chi square statistic can be computed as follows:

$$X^2 = \sum_{i=1}^{k} \frac{(\text{Observed}_i - \text{Expected}_i)^2}{E_i}$$

Comparing this chi square value to numbers presented in a table of chi square statistics (readily available in appendices of books, as well as through Internet searches), students can determine whether there is a statistically significant difference between the actual number of M&Ms of each color in the bag and the number of each color that we would expect there to be if the colors were randomly distributed. A similar experiment can be conducted to compare the number of students in a class who own one brand of computer to another or any such situation in which data can be categorized.

12. **Your Chances:** A powerful way to get students to think about probability is to present them with information and ask the *students* to write associated probability questions. For example, consider the data presented in Table 9.1:

Table 9.1 Choice of Color Preferences

Student age	Red	Green	Blue	Yellow
Middle School	45	27	58	19
High School	83	41	103	56

Students actively participate in playing games they created as team projects, designed to illustrate basic principles of probability.

Students in a middle school and its connected high school were asked which of the four colors—red, green, blue, or yellow—they preferred to the others. Their responses were tallied and recorded in Table 9.1. The task is for mathematics students to develop a list of probability questions that could be asked based on the information presented in the table. Along with each question should be a solution and an explanation. For example, students might ask, "What is the probability that a middle or high school student prefers blue to the other colors?" or "Find the probability that a middle school student prefers red or green to the other colors." Students are given the freedom to generate any creative questions about the data that they wish. This process of developing probability questions based on data can be instrumental in helping students determine solutions to questions posed by someone else.

The Teaching of Discrete Mathematics

A field of mathematics that has significantly grown in popularity since the late 1980s is **discrete mathematics.** This content area involves problems from graph theory (networks), combinatorics (and probability resulting from combinatorics used to determine sample spaces), iteration and recursion, matrices, and several other related topics. Rosenstein, Franzblau, and Roberts (1997) noted that discrete mathematics "does not refer to a well-defined branch of mathematics—like algebra, geometry, trigonometry, or calculus—but rather encompasses a variety of loosely-connected concepts or techniques. Moreover, it is not a branch of mathematics which is generally familiar to the public" (p. xxv). In discussing which type of problems are considered "discrete," Dossey (1991) characterized three categories of problems—*existence* (determining whether a problem even has a solution), *counting* (deciding the number of possible solutions to problems that can be solved), and *optimization* (selecting the most desirable solution from a list of possible answers). Hart (1998) added that another important theme of discrete mathematics is determining whether an algorithm can be established to most efficiently solve a problem.

Let's illustrate these principles of discrete mathematics through a problem that appeared in an NCTM Yearbook (Hersberger, Frederick, & Lipman, 1991):

Four people wish to cross a river. They have a boat, but the boat holds at most two people. Each person takes a different amount of time to cross the river; person A takes 20 minutes, person B takes 15 minutes, person C takes 10 minutes, and person D takes 5 minutes. When two people are in the boat, it takes the maximum of their time to cross the river; that is, A and C together would take 20 minutes. What is the smallest crossing time required to get all four people across the river? (p. 52)

Before reading on, take a minute with a piece of paper and pencil to solve the problem yourself. Did you find a solution of 55 minutes? If so, then you have correctly solved the problem, probably by using a strategy of always sending the fastest person across the river. Now, let's solve the problem again but change the rules as follows: In your second problem, assume that the four people require 25, 20, 10, and 5 minutes to cross (as opposed to 20, 15, 10, and 5). Now, go ahead and resolve the problem. Did you find an answer of 65 minutes? If so, you have determined a solution to the problem but not the optimal solution. It is possible to get all four people across the river in this second scenario within 60 minutes, but to find that answer, you will have to "think outside the box" and not rely on simply sending the fastest person across each time, as you did on the first problem. The way to solve the problem so that you can get all four people across in 60 minutes is left to you!

The river-crossing example serves as an excellent illustration of a discrete mathematics problem because it involves the characteristics that define the content area. We know that it's possible for all of the people to get across the river, which establishes existence of a solution. Then, we focus our efforts on looking at a variety of ways to accomplish the task, while attempting to define a rule or process that will allow us to find the optimal (minimum) travel time. Other typical discrete mathematics problems that appear in the school curriculum include, for example, the following:

- Which path should a snowplow follow in a small town to clear all of the roads while minimizing the number of times that individual streets have to be traversed twice? (graph theory)
- If a traveling salesperson has to visit six cities, how many possible travel routes are there, and which requires driving the shortest distance? (graph theory)
- How many ways can you select five people to form a committee from a department of 30 employees? (combinatorics)
- If an adolescent is given a gift of a financial account of $4,000 and decides to add $1,000 to the account on the first day of each year and averages 5 percent annual interest on the account, how much money will be in the account at the end of 30 years? (iteration and recursion)
- What will the next iteration of a fractal, such as Koch's Snowflake Curve, look like, and what will be its perimeter? (iteration and recursion)

These types of problems are often motivating for students because they are applied, "real-life" examples of how mathematics is used every day. Also, the development of technology, such as computer simulations and graphing calculator explorations, has made these types of problems much more accessible to students. In the 1989 *Curriculum and Evaluation Standards for School Mathematics*, the NCTM included a standard for grades 9–12 entitled discrete mathematics. The standard stated the following:

In grades 9–12, the mathematics curriculum should include topics from discrete mathematics so that all students can—

- represent problem situations using discrete structures such as finite graphs, matrices, sequences, and recurrence relations;
- represent and analyze finite graphs using matrices;
- develop and analyze algorithms;
- solve enumeration and finite probability problems;

and so that, in addition, college intending students can—

- represent and solve problems using linear programming and difference equations;
- investigate problem situations that arise with computer validation and the application of algorithms. (NCTM, 1989, p. 176)

The inclusion of this standard provided curriculum writers with evidence that discrete mathematics had "come of age" and should be included in courses of study and textbooks. As the 1990s progressed, integrated mathematics materials began to include discrete topics, and some high schools began to teach a semester or full-year course on the subject. Likewise, many middle school programs began to feature the study of discrete topics. When the next set of national standards—*Principles and Standards for School Mathematics*—was released in 2000, it did not include a separate standard for discrete mathematics. Instead, the objectives were woven throughout the document. The authors of the standards noted the following:

> Three important areas of discrete mathematics are integrated within these Standards: combinatorics, iteration and recursion, and vertex-edge graphs. These ideas can be systematically developed from prekindergarten through grade 12. In addition, matrices should be addressed in grades 9–12. Combinatorics is the mathematics of systematic counting. Iteration and recursion are used to model sequential, step-by-step change. Vertex-edge graphs are used to model and solve problems involving paths, networks, and relationships among a finite number of objects. (NCTM, 2000, p. 31)

Consequently, discrete topics continued to be emphasized as an important part of the curriculum but were embedded within preexisting content strands, further indicating that discrete mathematics is not as distinct an area of mathematics as algebra or geometry. This trend continued in the *Common Core State Standards*, which also included topics that were discrete, but not set aside as individual conceptual categories or domains. State-level curriculum models and local courses of study often include objectives drawn from discrete mathematics, and many textbooks are available to support this topic, either as an individual course or as part of an integrated program (see, for example, *Discrete Mathematics through Applications* [Crisler, Fisher, & Froelich, 2000] or *For All Practical Purposes* [Brams et al., 2003]). A sample discrete mathematics lesson and 12 classroom activities are provided next.

SAMPLE LESSON PLAN

Discrete Mathematics

I. Goal(s):
- To develop recursive thinking skills and apply recursive thinking to mathematical problem solving. (NCTM algebra standard: "Represent and analyze mathematical situations and structures using algebraic symbols.") (NCTM, 2000, p. 296)

II. Objective(s)
- The student will provide an example and a description of the process of iteration.

- The student will use iteration to solve problems, including modeling iteration on a graphing calculator.
- The student will calculate compound interest, given the interest rate and the investment period.

III. Materials and Resources
- Glass pitcher filled with iced tea (or lemonade made from concentrate)
- Pitcher filled with water
- Drinking glass
- Two-problem activity sheet for each student
- Graphing calculator for each student

IV. Motivation
1. As class begins, show the students a pitcher filled with iced tea. Describe a situation in which I made a pitcher of tea and intended to use it for dinner when guests arrived last Friday, but I got thirsty at lunchtime and drank a glass of the tea. Then invite a student to the front of the room to model the problem. Pour a small glass of tea and have the student drink it. Explain how I was upset that the pitcher wasn't full anymore, so I just filled it with water (after all, tea starts out as water). Later in the afternoon, I got thirsty again, so I drank another glass, but I filled up the pitcher again. Have the student drink another small glass of the tea and fill the pitcher again. Continue this process about five times and ask the student to sit down.
2. At 7 P.M., the guests arrived, and I served the drink in the pitcher. Is it still iced tea? What if I continued to refill the pitcher throughout the evening, every time that someone drank another glassful? Would we ever reach a point at which the tea becomes pure water? Why or why not? (Students will struggle with this because the intuitive notion is that the tea will become so diluted that it will cease to be "tea," yet if there is some tea in the pitcher, there will always be some tea in the next mixture.)

Transition: "The process that we just illustrated is called *iteration* because it featured a repeated set of steps (i.e., pour out a glass, then fill up the pitcher). Today, we will explore several examples and applications of iteration as an introduction to the topic."

V. Lesson Procedure
3. Distribute a copy of a two-problem activity sheet. Explain to the students that they are to work with their partners and take about 10 minutes to solve both problems. The problems on the sheet are as follows:

(a) Suppose that the teacher started at the front desk and walked halfway to the door and stopped. Then the teacher walked halfway to the door once again and stopped, continuing this process over and over. How long would it take the teacher to walk out the door?

(b) A scientist put one bacterium into a jar at 11 A.M. She knew that bacteria divided into two cells (doubled) every minute. If the jar was completely filled with bacteria at 12:00 noon, at what time was the jar half filled with bacteria? Thinking fast, the scientist realized that the jar was going to be filled by noon, so she added three new jars for the bacteria to spill into. At what time were all four of her jars completely filled?

As students work on the problems, walk around the room and individually interview at least three pairs of students to get a sense of how they are viewing and attempting to solve the problems.

4. Once it appears that all of the students have explored both problems, ask each pair of students to join another pair and take 2 minutes to share their thoughts on the two problems. Then conduct a full-class discussion to process the results. (Students should realize that in (a) the teacher will never reach the doorway because "half of something" still leaves "something." In (b), the students should recognize that the jar was only half filled at 11:59 A.M. but full at noon. If the scientist added three new jars, they would be filled at 12:02 P.M.) Ask the students to explain how both of these problems involve the process of iteration. (In each case, there is some process—halving or doubling—that is applied to the situation and repeated over and over.)

Transition: "Let's take a look at how iteration can be modeled in a numerical way by using a graphing calculator."

5. Ask students to take out their graphing calculators and clear the screen. Suppose that the teacher's desk was 20 ft from the door. How far would the teacher walk on the first move? (10 ft) How far on the second move? (5 ft) The third? (2.5 ft) The calculator has a built-in function that allows us to quickly apply a recursive rule. Key in 20 and ENTER. Then key in ANS * 0.5 and press ENTER (actually, if students simply press * 0.5, the calculator will automatically display ANS * 0.5). The calculator automatically takes half of the previous answer (ANS). Press ENTER again, and the calculator will take half of the displayed answer once again. Each time that you press ENTER, it will continue to take half of the previous answer. Press ENTER 50 times. What do you see? (Students will discover that the answer is an extremely small distance but not equal to 0; therefore, the teacher still has not reached the doorway.)

6. In the second problem, we started with one bacterium, and the population doubled every minute. How can we model the doubling process on the graphing calculator? How many bacteria are there after 30 minutes? (Students should ENTER 1 and then use ANS * 2 to find subsequent populations. In 30 minutes, the population exceeds 1 billion bacteria cells.)

Transition: "Now, let's apply this process to something with which you are more familiar—earning interest on money invested in the bank."

7. Raise your hand if you have some type of savings account that earns interest on your investment. How does it work? (Students should be led to explain how the interest earns interest over time, and we will define this as compound interest.) Compound interest is an iterative process because, each year, the previous amount of money earns interest and is added to the principal.

8. Suppose that you had $10,000 and wanted to invest it at 6 percent interest per year. How can we model the compounding process on

the graphing calculator? Take a few minutes to discuss this with your partner. (There are a couple of ways the students can do this, but it will be acceptable if they come up with pressing 10,000, then ENTER, and then use ANS + ANS * 0.6 for the formula. They might even come up with 1.06 * ANS for the formula, which is probably better but not necessary at this point.) Have students share their thinking and then look at how much money would be accumulated after a 10-year, 6 percent investment of $10,000 (about $17,909).

Transition: "I would like you to use what you know about iteration, together with your graphing calculators, to explore a final problem today."

VI. Closure

   9. I am going to give you three possible ways to earn interest, and you need to choose the offer that would give you the most money:

   (a) I could give you $150 per year for the next 15 years with no interest being paid at all.
   (b) I could lend you $2,500 to invest at 6 percent interest for 10 years, and you could keep the interest at the end of that period and return the $2,500 to me.
   (c) I could lend you $2,500 to invest at 3.5 percent interest for 20 years, and you could keep the interest at the end of that period and return the $2,500 to me.

   Work the problem alone for a few minutes and then discuss your solutions at your tables. (Students should discover that, despite the low interest rate, the last choice yields the highest interest because of the time factor—$2,474.) Discuss the solutions and the effects of interest rates and time.

   10. For homework, assign page 114, #4, 7, 11, 15, 20 in the textbook.

VII. Extension

   If time allows, the class could explore the graphs and tables that result from applying an iterative process. Specifically, after Step 6, students could determine that the function can be represented by the equation $y = 2^x$, and they could use the graphing calculator to sketch its graph, describe the effects of compounding, and use the TABLE function to view the numerical data. Similarly, after Step 8, students could explore the function $Y_1 = 10,000(1.06)^x$ to generate a discussion about the benefits of long-term investments. By entering $Y_2 = 10,000(1.07)^x$, and viewing Y_1 and Y_2 simultaneously, students can use the TABLE function to readily compare the growth of an investment at 6 percent versus 7 percent interest over time.

VIII. Assessment

   Assessment in this lesson takes three different forms:

   - In Step 3, three pairs of students will be randomly interviewed to provide a snapshot of how the problems are being perceived by the class.
   - In the closure, students can be observed as they attempt to determine the best investment plan.
   - The written homework assignment will provide individual evidence of understanding on five additional problems, due the following day.

Classroom Dialogues

A teacher began class by holding up a paper cup and telling students that she was going to toss the cup and let it fall to the floor. Students were asked to discuss in their groups what the probability would be for the cup to land rightside up, upside down, and on its side. The groups were given about 5 minutes to conjecture, during which time some of the students borrowed a cup, tossed it, and collected some data.

Teacher: What did you come up with?

Student 1 In our group, we decided the probability is always one-third.

Teacher: How did you get that?

Student 1: When you toss the cup, there are three things that can happen: It either lands on the bottom, on the top, or on its side. Since there are three possible ways for it to fall, you have a one-in-three chance of any of them happening.

Teacher: Does everyone agree?

Student 2: No. We talked about that, but common sense says it's going to fall on its side more often.

Teacher: How much more often and why?

Student 2: We think it'll fall on the side about half of the time. If you think about the area of the cup, it has more surface around it than it has on the bottom or the top. It has to fall on the side more.

Student 3: That's pretty much what we thought too, so we took the paper cup and tossed it 15 times. It landed on its side every time, so we decided it was almost impossible for the cup to land on the top or the bottom. It lands on its side every time—100 percent.

Student misconceptions about probability abound in research literature. While students enjoy the study of probability because it tends to be applied and hands-on, the problems often are not as easy to understand as they might appear. What misconceptions did you notice as you read the short dialogue? Student 1 seems to understand the main idea that determining a probability relies on understanding a set of possible outcomes—the *sample space*. However, the student (and the group) fails to recognize that the three outcomes are not equally likely. While it's true that a tossed coin can land on heads, tails, or its edge, the probability of the coin landing on the edge is so negligible that, for all practical purposes, there are really only two outcomes to consider. So, the relative likelihood of each outcome needs to be considered. Student 2 uses a more intuitive explanation of how a cup has more lateral surface area than area on the top and bottom, yet merely guesses that the probability of the cup landing on its side will be one-half.

Comments from Student 3 illustrate what is one of the most common probabilistic misconceptions—a lack of understanding of how the number of trials affects the results of an experiment. To the group's credit, they refused to simply guess at a probability and decided to run an experiment instead. Unfortunately, the experiment did not involve enough trials, so it misled the group into thinking it was impossible for the cup to land anywhere but on its side. Perhaps if they had tossed the cup just 5 or 10 more times, they would have realized that while it's not *likely* the cup will land right-side up or upside down, it is *possible* for these outcomes to occur. Research conducted by Konold et al. (1993) describes how difficult it is for students to analyze a set of possible outcomes in an experiment. In most cases, students ignore the Law of Large Numbers (a rule that suggests that as we increase the number of trials, we will approach the actual probability). So, 15 trials are simply not enough to draw a conclusion on this problem. A famous "Hospital Problem" has circulated for many years in research literature that tends to illustrate similar misconceptions. The problem states:

Half of all newborn babies are boys and half are girls. If Hospital A records an average of 50 births per day while Hospital B records an average of 10, which hospital is more likely to record that 80% of their births are female?

In a study conducted with undergraduate education students, only 14% of the respondents correctly stated that Hospital B is more likely to experience such an event (due to the small sample size), and almost two-thirds of the education students believed that the 80% occurrence was equally likely for both hospitals (Godino, Cañizares, & Díaz, 2003). The point here is that probabilistic misconceptions are common not only in middle and high school students, but in adults as well. What kinds of experiences can teachers give students at the middle and high school levels to help address misconceptions, such as all outcomes being equally likely, or the importance of running a sufficient number of trials to draw accurate conclusions? What real-world contexts require an understanding of probability, and how might you use these applications in teaching the topic?

Discrete Mathematics—Activities Sampler

1. **Possible Burgers:** On a national television advertisement, a fast-food chain promoted its restaurant by saying that "there are 512 ways to have a burger" at its establishment. Have students investigate the underlying mathematics of this claim by attempting to explain how the fast-food restaurant did its calculation. More than likely, the restaurant chain had 9 different ingredients available for putting on its hamburgers (e.g., ketchup, mustard, mayonnaise, onion, relish, cheese, etc.). Because a customer can choose either to include or not to include the ingredient, the number of possibilities can be calculated by taking $2^9 = 512$. Interestingly, if there are 8 possible ingredients, then there are 256 different burgers that can be made, and if there are 10 ingredients, the number of possible burgers increases to 1,024. Students should recognize that the number of possible burgers doubles each time another ingredient is added and be able to explain why this happens. (Imagine the list of 512 possible burgers with "no olives" added to the end and another 512 with "include olives" added to the end, so the total number of burgers when olives are added as an option increases to 1,024.) Students should then be challenged to watch the media for similar advertisements, as they are typical for pizza restaurants and salad bars that make claims about how many different meals are possible. This problem engages students in a real-life situation that involves combinatorics, a major concept in the study of discrete mathematics.

2. **Matrix Representations:** The NCTM *Standards* call for the use of matrices in high school, and many local courses of study embed the topic throughout the middle grades as well. Students should be encouraged to take simple tables and represent them as matrices. For example, by accessing the win–loss record of the baseball teams in the American League during the past 5 years from the Internet, students can represent the standings in each season as a team-by-record matrix. Then, by adding or subtracting matrices by hand or using the matrix function on a graphing calculator, they can compile long-term data or track changes in records from one year to the next. Also, students can use what are referred to as Markov chains to represent probabilities as matrices and predict long-term results. For example, suppose that an athletic team has won

65 percent of their games and that whenever they win, they historically have won the next game 50 percent of the time. However, when they lose, they tend to come back to win the next game 70 percent of the time. We can represent their *initial state* with the matrix

$$I = [0.65, 0.35]$$

and their *transition matrix* for the future as

$$T = \begin{bmatrix} 0.5 & 0.5 \\ 0.7 & 0.3 \end{bmatrix}$$

By multiplying $I \times T$ on a graphing calculator, we get the result of

$$[0.57, 0.43]$$

This product matrix tells us that, although the team has a 65 percent chance of winning tonight's game, they have a 57 percent chance of winning tomorrow night. By continuing to multiply each product by matrix *T*, we can predict that, if the current trend continues, the team will win about 58 percent of its games. (See, for example, Crisler et al., 2000, for additional applications.)

3. **Handshakes:** A classic discrete mathematics problem is often referred to as the handshake problem. Suppose that all of the students in a classroom were to get up and shake the hand of every other person in the room. How many hand-shakes would take place altogether? The problem is sometimes framed in a different context, such as the following: If a tennis tournament involves each participant playing every other person for one match, how many matches will need to be played? This problem is also rooted in the same "handshake" principle. When students are initially posed the problem, they should be asked to make a conjecture about the answer and write it down. In a class of 25 students, a typical initial response is to multiply 25×25 but some will recognize that they can't shake their own hands and attempt to multiply 25×24 which is more accurate but still incorrect. Students can take their notebooks and walk around the room, having every other student sign their pages. Discussing this process, students generally realize that when "Dan signed Anne's notebook" and "Anne signed Dan's notebook," it actually took only one "meeting" or handshake. Therefore, the total number of handshakes can be determined by taking $\dfrac{25 \times 24}{2} = 300$. Some students may also discover that that they can find the same solution by adding $24 + 23 + 22 + \ldots 1 = 300$, and this can lead to a discussion of Gauss's method for quickly adding this string of numbers. By systematically exploring what happens when two, three, or four people are in the room, students can also generate a pattern in a table and generalize the handshake problem solution to $\dfrac{n(n-1)}{2}$, where *n* represents the number of people in the room (tournament, etc.). This problem is very rich because it involves the problem-solving skills of solving a simpler problem, organizing information into a table, and looking for patterns, while it emphasizes counting methods and can involve generalizing a pattern into an algebraic expression.

4. **The Game of Sprouts:** Students can explore the nature of graph theory by playing a popular discrete mathematics game called Sprouts. The rules are simple, but winning requires a great deal of careful planning and strategy. The game is intended to be played with two people. Sprouts begins with one person making

three dots on a piece of paper; all of the moves for the rest of the game will "sprout" from these three points. Opponents take turns, following these rules: Each will draw an arc (edge) that either connects two of the points (vertices) or loops around to connect a vertex to itself. After drawing the new edge, the player must draw another vertex somewhere on it. Players are never allowed to intersect an existing edge, and a vertex may not have any more than three edges "sprouting" from it. Whoever draws the last sprout, leaving the opponent without a play, wins the game. Sprouts is an enjoyable way for students to think about graph theory, to develop their reasoning and problem-solving skills, and to gain experience in using the proper graph theory terminology of vertices and edges.

5. **Write an Algorithm:** An important part of the study of discrete mathematics is the development of algorithmic thinking—the ability to spell out a process in a clear, step-by-step, procedural manner. Mathematics teachers can include this skill in the context of almost any topic studied through the secondary or middle grades. For example, suppose that a class has learned how to solve quadratic equations by factoring. Students may be asked to write an algorithm for solving quadratics, such as (a) add or subtract terms from the equation to arrange it in descending order and equal to 0; (b) factor the polynomial; (c) if the polynomial does not factor, discontinue this method; (d) if the polynomial *does* factor, then set each of the factors equal to 0; (e) solve the new equations to find the two solutions to the equation; (f) if the solutions are the same, then the equation has a double root. Students can write similar algorithms for many other mathematical processes, such as simplifying fractions, finding the missing side of a right triangle, or determining the limit of a function. It is not the intent of this activity to have students be given or simply memorize algorithms but, rather, to make them reflect on a mathematical process that they have learned and to try to put it into words in a systematic, step-by-step manner.

6. **Double the Money:** Ask the students to consider making this proposal to their parents: For my allowance this month, I would like 1¢ today, 2¢ tomorrow, 4¢ the next day, then 8¢, 16¢, and so forth. Or, I will settle for $100 in cash at the beginning of the month. Before doing some of the mathematics, it appears that $100 is rather expensive; after all, the parents will only have to pay a few cents a day during the first week. However, what effect does the doubling have throughout the rest of the month? This problem lends itself to exploration on a computer with a spreadsheet because a student can put 0.01 in the first cell, then *2 in the second cell, and have it fill down to show 30 days. Similarly, the ANS button on a graphing calculator can be used to do the iterations for 30 days of allowance collecting. On the tenth day of the month, the student would receive $5.12, which is still minimal compared to the $100 "up front" alternative. However, by the twentieth day of the month, the daily allowance climbs to more than $5,000, and the thirtieth day represents an allowance of more than $5 million. Students can use this problem to think about the effect of investing money over a long period of time and the rate at which the investment can grow. They can consider the cost of paying interest on a loan and the long-term effects of carrying a credit card balance or paying interest on a 30-year mortgage for a home. The activity serves as an interesting motivator for the discussion of iteration and interest rates, while making use of technology to generate the relevant numbers for discussion.

7. **Three Coins:** An interesting problem surfaced on the Internet that students will enjoy trying to solve (used as an example in Chapter 8). Suppose that you are

given three coins that have the numbers 6, 7, and 8 displayed on them. You are told that the flip side of each coin contains a digit between 1 and 9 and that no digit may be repeated. The sum of the three coins, when tossed, will always be a number between and including 15 and 22 (i.e., $15 \le \text{sum} \le 22$). Each sum from 15 to 22 must be possible. The task is to find which digit is on the reverse of each of the coins. Students generally begin the problem by realizing that if 6-7-8 is displayed, the sum is 21, so they can eliminate those three digits and one of the sums. In addition, the only way to get a sum as high as 22 without repeating a digit is to have the combination 6-7-9, so a 9 must be on the back of the 8. This means that the back of the 6 and the 7 must contain two of the digits 1, 2, 3, 4, or 5. There are two possible solutions to this problem, one of which is 6-2, 7-5, or 8-9. You and your students should be able to find the other solution. This problem is rich in that it tends to capture students' curiosity and is accessible because it involves reasoning skills but not a great deal of heavy mathematical background. It involves the discrete mathematics skill of counting all of the possible combinations and checking them to see which work. The problem can also be used as a motivator for a topic such as exploration of the traveling salesperson problem or factoring a polynomial, both of which rely heavily on guess-and-check methods to find workable solutions.

8. **You Have My Vote:** One of the content areas within the field of discrete mathematics is social choice, which includes the study of the mathematical fairness of various voting methods. At an organizational meeting of a professional group, nominations were taken from the floor for president. Three people were nominated and about to be voted on by the group of about 70 people in attendance. Just before the vote was taken, one of the candidates stood up and announced, "I want to withdraw my name. I think both of the other people are as well qualified as anyone, so there's no point in voting for me because I don't want the job anyway." Consequently, the election was held with only the two remaining candidates. The question for students to consider is this: What effect, if any, does a third-party candidate have in this type of election? Is it likely, or even possible, that this person's last-minute withdrawal changed the outcome of the election? Students can then explore presidential elections in the United States to determine the effect that independent-candidates have had on elections. For example, would Bill Clinton have defeated George Bush in 1992 if Ross Perot had not drawn away a significant share of the Republican votes? Should the United States have a policy whereby a run-off election takes place before the presidential election so that only two candidates remain? Students should be able to generate various voting scenarios that demonstrate cases in which the independent or third-party candidate does or does not have a significant effect on the outcome of the election. This activity is also a natural for collaborating with the social studies instructor to initiate an integrated social studies/mathematics unit.

9. **Reading Bar Codes:** Perhaps you have looked at an envelope and noticed the bar code at the bottom that represents your zip code. Students will enjoy breaking the code and determining which sets of bars represent which zip code digits. The codes are made up of a series of long and short bars; a string of 5 bars translates into 1 digit. Obtain some copies of postcards or envelopes containing zip codes and their related bar codes and provide students with the copies. Explain to the class that their task is to figure out which 5-bar sequence represents each digit. It will be helpful to know that a bar code for a 5-digit zip code always contains 32 bars (or 52 bars if it is a 5 + 4 zip code)—the first and the

last are long bars that tell the reader that the code is about to begin and that it has finished. In the middle are 30 bars that represent 6 digits—the first 25 bars (5 digits) are the zip code. The last 5 bars represent an error-correction number. The error-correction digit is the number that, when added to the sum of the 9 digits comprising a $5 + 4$ zip code, adds up to a multiple of 10. So, if the zip code is 48161-9978, then the error correction number would be 7 because $4 + 8 + 1 + 6 + 1 + 9 + 9 + 7 + 8 = 53$, and 7 has to be added to 53 to get a multiple of 10. With this information, students can figure out which set of bars stands for which number. They should also be encouraged to look for patterns when they study the sequence of bars and notice that every digit is made up of 2 long bars and 3 short ones. This makes sense because the 2 long bars can be placed in 10 different possible positions in a sequence of 5 bars $\left(C_2^5 = \dfrac{5 \times 4}{2} = 10 \right)$, and 10 different patterns are needed to represent the digits 0 through 9. Cracking a code makes for an interesting discrete mathematics activity that gives the students experience with counting rules, patterns, and making generalizations. Students might also be fascinated with the way that UPC labels on items in grocery stores or secret messages sent during wartime are coded and decoded.

10. **Meeting Schedules:** A student's ability to organize a schedule or sequence of events is a discrete mathematics skill associated with graph theory. Here is an actual meeting-schedule problem that was given to a manager of a business by the boss who was attempting to plan a day for employees in the business to connect with one another: The business has 12 full-time employees and 5 secretaries. The boss wants the 12 full-time workers to meet with one another for 20-minute meetings until everyone has met with everyone else. In addition, the 5 secretaries each need to meet with one another for 20 minutes, but they do not need to meet with the other 12 employees. A meeting day to accomplish this task needs to be planned. If the meeting day is to begin at 9:00 A.M., then (a) How many 20-minute meetings will have to take place altogether? (b) What is the earliest time that all of these meetings could be completed? (c) What is the latest time that the secretaries need to arrive so that they finish at the same time as the other 12? (d) Design an actual master schedule that shows who meets with whom during each of the 20-minute time slots. Students should work in small groups to complete this task, put their answers in writing, and be prepared to share their thinking and solutions with the rest of the class. (They should be able to determine, for example, that the 12 employees will need $C_2^{12} = 66$ meetings for all of the pairs to get together, and because 6 meetings can take place simultaneously, eleven 20-minute time slots—3 hours, 40 minutes—will be required.) A worthwhile extension to the activity is for students to contact a local business, such as a pizza place, and interview the manager of the store about how work schedules are determined and the factors that need to be considered when planning a master work schedule for a week or more. The meeting-schedule problem engages students in thinking about how many combinations (of meetings) are possible and necessary and how to organize the sequence of meetings so that all three of the conditions are met.

11. **Exploring Fractals:** One of the most famous fractal images is called the *Sierpinski triangle,* named after the person who first generated it in the early 1900s. Of the variety of ways to describe the creation of the image, one is the following: Begin with an equilateral triangle. Identify the midpoints of the three sides and

connect them together to form an interior triangle. Remove the inner triangle. Then take the three remaining triangles, identify the midpoints of the sides of each, connect those midpoints, and once again remove the interior triangles. This process would be continued infinitely many times. The diagram in Figure 9.6 shows the initial image (the *seed*) and the first two stages of this process.

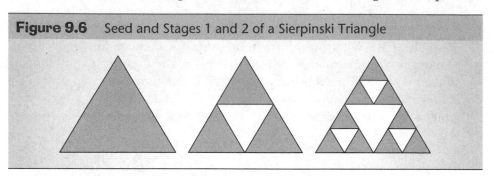

Figure 9.6   Seed and Stages 1 and 2 of a Sierpinski Triangle

After generating the first three or four stages of the Sierpinski triangle, challenge students to solve problems such as the following:

- How many triangles are there in the first, second, third, fourth, and nth stages?
- How many "holes" are there in the first, second, third, fourth, and nth stages?
- If the area of the seed is 1, what is the area at stage 1? 2? 3? 4? n?
- If the perimeter of the seed is 1 (one unit per side), what is the perimeter at stage 1 (including the interior perimeter)? 2? 3? 4? n? (Students should recognize that the area approaches zero, while the perimeter grows infinitely large.) The study of fractal geometry is a natural opportunity to visualize recursion problems. As students project what will happen to the image after infinitely many iterations, they also gain early experiences with determining limits. This topic lends itself to naturally connecting topics from algebra and geometry. (For an excellent source of fractal activities, see Peitgen et al., 1992.)

12. **Soft Drink Preference:** Provide the students in the class with paper ballots on which they can vote for their favorite soft drinks. Explain that the class will be having a holiday party and that there are five different soft drinks that are available, but only two will be chosen. Instead of voting for one drink, each student should identify his or her top choice as a "1," second choice as a "2," and so forth, so that the ballot represents a ranking. Collect all of the ballots and put the results together in a grid format, as shown in Table 9.2.

Table 9.2   Voting Results for Soft Drink Preference

Drink	Student 1	Student 2	Student 3	Student 4	Student 5
Coke	3	1	3	5	3
Pepsi	5	4	1	4	2
Mountain Dew	1	3	2	1	4
Sprite	2	5	4	3	1
Dr Pepper	4	2	5	2	5

Distribute a copy of the results in grid form, as represented in Table 9.2, and ask the students to decide, based on the data provided, which two drinks should be selected for the party. Some students will simply count the number of "1" votes to elect the winner and runner-up. Others will weight the votes by adding the numbers together, determining the winner by choosing the soft drink that accumulates the least number of points. Still others may eliminate any soft drink that had primarily "4" and "5" votes in the *preference schedules*. Students are likely to disagree on the final choices, even though they all have the same voting information in their hands! The theory of elections is a discrete mathematics topic that students enjoy because they discover that selecting a winner can go more deeply than simply "counting votes," as they realize that the soft drinks selected depend as much on the method of choosing the winner as the vote totals themselves. A natural extension of this exploration is to discuss the electoral college approach to choosing a president in the United States, which also serves as an excellent connection to social studies.

A Word on Pre-Calculus and Calculus

Most secondary schools offer a course that is titled either "Pre-Calculus" or "Analysis." The purpose of this class is to offer students a challenging mathematical experience that directly prepares them for the eventual study of calculus, either in college or while still in high school. A pre-calculus course is generally integrated in the sense that it involves multiple content areas and cuts across algebra, geometry, statistics, and so forth. However, there is no universally accepted syllabus or agreement on what such a course should include. The NCTM *Standards* (2000) describe a curriculum for all students in grades 9 through 12 but no details as to what constitutes a final course prior to calculus. The *Common Core State Standards* describes a set of optional topics for those intending to take advanced mathematics courses, but a syllabus for a pre-calculus course, per se, is not presented. Consequently, although the course title of "Pre-Calculus" may be on the transcripts of a dozen different students from various high schools as they move on to college, it is likely that the course was a different experience for each of them.

Although there is no generalized syllabus for all students, the College Board (2006) published standards for courses at the high school level that speak directly to the contents of a pre-calculus course. Specifically, the document suggests six general areas of study in the course: families of functions, trigonometric functions, conic sections and polar equations, recursion (series and sequences), vectors and parametric equations, and the study of lines of best fit (including median fit and linear regression, as well as correlation). Comparing this list of topics to the table of contents in a popular high school pre-calculus textbook (Foerster, 2007), we find a close match in content. The book includes functions, trigonometry, conic sections, series and sequences, vectors, and curve fitting, in addition to topics such as probability and matrices. The book finishes with an exploration of limits and the derivative, leading students directly to the study of calculus. In addition to these topics, it is not unusual for a pre-calculus course to also include the study of complex and real numbers, as well as combinatorics, inequalities, exponents, and logarithms. The point here is that there are many important building blocks that pave the pathway to the study of calculus, and it is essential that students have a firm grounding in these topics prior to taking a Calculus course.

In 1986, a joint statement made by the NCTM and the Mathematical Association of America (MAA) stated that, although many students feel pressured to take calculus in high school, they should never take the course in place of an opportunity to study algebra, geometry, and trigonometry in greater depth, as their preparation in these areas is more important than being exposed to concepts of calculus (Bressoud, 2007). The official position of the Michigan Section of the MAA, for example, states, "The fourth year of high school mathematics for college-intending students should extend the depth and breadth of their understandings in mathematics and prepare them for the mathematics needed for their respective college majors. Students should take calculus only if they have demonstrated a deep understanding of algebra, geometry, trigonometry, and coordinate geometry" (Michigan Section of MAA, 2001). Furthermore, there is agreement among college-level mathematics departments that if a student is going to study calculus in high school, the course should be taught at the level and depth of a college course in the subject. In other words, the AP syllabus for Calculus (College Board, 2010) should be followed.

In Chapter 4, we discussed the contents of the AP Calculus syllabus (first semester) in which students explore functions (and limits), derivatives, and integrals. Interestingly, between 1990 and 2004, the total number of students taking the AB Calculus course (first-semester AP course) nearly tripled, while the number of students taking the BC Calculus course (second semester) increased almost fourfold in the United States, with the total number of students taking the exam approaching 250,000 (National Science Board, 2006). In 2011, more than 340,000 high school students took either the AB or the BC Calculus AP exam (College Board, 2011a, 2011b). Clearly, the demand for advanced-level courses at the high school level has never been greater. However, regardless of the level of course that is being taught, teachers must always reflect on *how* to most effectively help the students to make sense of the content. The principles of effective teaching that were described in Chapter 7 are just as important when working with more advanced students as they are for those who have historically struggled with mathematics. The better we are able to utilize research-based teaching practices, the more likely it is that students will gain access to the full spectrum of mathematical topics discussed in this chapter.

Conclusion

A consultant from a state's Department of Education was giving a presentation to a county gathering of dozens of mathematics teachers. After presenting the state's new curriculum model and providing teachers with time for discussion and questions, she concluded the day by saying, "Let's face it . . . You can have the best course of study in the country and a winning lottery ticket to pay for all the textbooks and technology you want. But if you, as teachers, don't have the vision of a coherent math curriculum and an understanding of how students learn, we won't be able to change a thing." When you think about it, she is entirely correct. In the end, successful learning of mathematics depends more on the teachers' ability to interpret the curriculum and design masterful lessons than on the quality of the written curriculum itself. The *Common Core State Standards* and the NCTM

Standards present a vision but are still words on pages. It is then up to the teacher to interpret the documents and make them come alive in their classrooms. An effective teacher will focus on big ideas of mathematics and constantly look for creative ways to connect one topic to another.

Though Chapters 8 and 9 have presented specific areas of the mathematics curriculum, the emphasis has been on applying concepts to the real world and connecting ideas across units and courses. An idea as simple as multiplication of two-digit numbers—typically taught in third and fourth grade—can be used as a basis for exploration of how to multiply mixed numbers involving fractions at the middle grades and then extended into a process for multiplying binomials and other polynomials in high school. Along the way, visual representations of the multiplication can help students appreciate the use of geometry and measurement that underlie the multiplication process. Keep in mind that, as we discussed in Chapter 1 and have emphasized in these last two chapters, the focus of teaching mathematics should be on the development of problem solving and thinking skills, not simply the mastery of rules and procedures. Chapters 8 and 9 have provided explanations of each area of the curriculum as well as listing numerous lessons and activities that promote mathematical reasoning and sense making within each content strand. As the students develop their mathematical background, one of the important roles of the teacher is to assess their understanding of these topics—to measure the level of understanding and attitudinal changes of students over time. In Unit 4, we explore the topic of assessment. In Chapter 10, we examine several strategies that teachers can use to assess student progress. Then, in Chapter 11, we look into more of the details of the NCTM's views on assessment as well as practical considerations involved with assigning and checking homework and determining final grades in a course.

For bibliographic references and additional resources, see page 414

Glossary

Fractal: Fractals involve a family of geometric shapes that are generated by beginning with a *seed* (initial image) and then applying some rule to that image in successive iterations. An important property of fractals is that they are self-similar.

Self-Similar: A property of fractals that means that regardless of how closely or how distantly a fractal is viewed, the same shape is always seen.

Discussion Questions and Activities

1. In a small group, discuss your experiences with learning geometry, statistics, and probability in school. Discuss whether you had distinct courses (or major units) in these topics or whether they were part of an integrated curriculum and how the curriculum design influenced your learning.

2. Explore several dynamic geometry software programs, such as Geogebra, Geometer's Sketchpad, and Cabri Geometry. How can this type of software be used to help students "invent" geometric ideas?

3. Consider the role of proof in the teaching and learning of geometry. While many schools emphasize the use of two-column proofs, other formats may be more helpful to students, such as paragraph proofs, proof by contradiction, or visual proofs. Which types of proof is it important for a high school student to encounter? How much emphasis should be placed on writing proofs?

4. Obtain an integrated mathematics textbook and analyze its content. Determine roughly how much of the book is devoted to the studies of geometry, statistics, and probability. Are the topics woven together so that algebraic ideas arise from the study of number, or are they presented in separate chapters? Is one

content area emphasized considerably more than another?

5. Misconceptions in the study of probability are very common, and the topic is not as easy to teach as it would seem, though students often enjoy exploring probability. Use the Internet or library to identify recent research on how students learn probability, examples of common misconceptions, and classroom teaching strategies that can be used to counter these misconceptions.

6. Using a copy of the *Common Core State Standards,* your state's curriculum standards, or a local course of study, examine the outcomes for the secondary and middle grades and highlight the objectives that would be identified for the study of discrete mathematics. Can you find examples of outcomes involving graph theory? Combinatorics? Iteration and recursion? Matrices?

7. Using a copy of the *Common Core State Standards,* your state's curriculum standards, or a local course of study, examine the outcomes for the secondary and middle grades and highlight the objectives that would be identified for the study of geometry, statistics, and probability. What are the "big ideas" that are emphasized in these two content areas?

8. Obtain copies of two or more books that carry the title of "Pre-Calculus." Examine the contents of the books, in light of the Standards published by the College Board. How does the content of these books compare to the topics recommended in the board's Standards? How do the contents of the books compare to one another? Describe the differences and similarities in content that students may encounter in a pre-calculus course when using one book versus another.

9. In a team of students, have each person select one of the 12 recommended activities from each of the three content areas in this chapter and "peer teach" it to the rest of the group. After the presentations, reflect on the activities by discussing the manner in which they address the spirit of that content area as described in the Standards.

10. The conclusion of this chapter quoted a consultant who said, "You can have the best course of study in the country and a winning lottery ticket to pay for all the textbooks and technology you want. But if you, as teachers, don't have the vision of a coherent math curriculum and an understanding of how students learn, we won't be able to change a thing." How important is it to have a detailed course of study (or set of standards) to follow? What are the limitations of the use of a shared curriculum document? How is it that two teachers can use the same set of standards but emphasize very different ideas in their classrooms?

The Role of Assessment

How often have you been in the middle of a class and heard someone ask, "Is this going to be on the test?" Think about the ramifications of the teacher's response. If the teacher says "no," then the class has an excuse for shutting down and not participating because students know that they will not be held accountable for the information. However, a response of "yes" tells the students that they will need to know the material to succeed in the class, and the message is to stay alert and keep working. In other words, the teacher's response sends out a message about what is important—what is *valued*—in the classroom. And, after all, isn't that what the student is really asking? "Is this going to be on the test?" loosely translates to, "Is this important enough for me to have to worry about?" Ideally, virtually everything we do in the classroom should be "tested" because if students didn't need to know it, the material was probably not worth spending time on in the first place. As many experts on assessment have maintained, we should not be upset about students asking whether something is on the test; they are simply doing what is natural for human beings—determining whether mastering a particular skill should be a priority.

In mathematics education, not everything that is valued in the classroom can be measured or assessed by a written test. For example, suppose that, in keeping with the standards, problem solving and oral communication are priorities in the classroom. One cannot measure oral communication skills and ability to work with others on an individual paper-and-pencil test. So, the teacher either must abandon communication as a goal or devise another method by which to assess student

After reading Chapter 10, you should be able to answer the following questions:

- How is assessment defined, and what are some of its major purposes?
- What are some of the issues associated with the construction of tests in mathematics?
- Why might a teacher need to develop strategies for assessing student progress in mathematics other than paper-and-pencil tests and quizzes?
- What are several alternative assessment strategies available to teachers beyond the traditional tests, quizzes, and homework assignments? Describe them.
- What are some advantages and disadvantages of various assessment alternatives, such as journals, rubrics, interviews, and checklists?

progress in this area. Alternatives to traditional tests include such strategies as interviews, observations, and portfolios. These nontraditional assessment techniques allow the teacher to gather more powerful data about student progress than can be measured by most paper-and-pencil tests. In this chapter, we explore the issue of assessment, from the definition and purposes for assessment to the construction of mathematics tests and the use of alternative strategies for measuring progress. We begin by defining "assessment." ▪

What Is Assessment?

If your instructor told you that you were going to be assessed on your understanding of this chapter at the end of the week, how would you interpret that statement? What does it mean to assess someone? In a workshop for inservice mathematics teachers, the word *assessment* generated the following list:

evaluation	test	high stakes	portfolio
measurement	grades	proficiency tests	homework
classroom behavior	pass/fail	observations	standardized tests
achievement	accountability	report card	quizzes

Notice that the majority of these responses focus on the process of testing, quizzing, giving grades, and determining whether a student has passed or failed. These conceptions surface because most people associate assessment with testing and giving grades. But assessment goes beyond tests and grades; it includes gathering and analyzing information along the way as teaching occurs rather than *doing* something to students *at the end* of a lesson or a unit.

As we discussed in Chapter 5, teachers using backward design will consider assessment and what they expect as the "final product" of the instruction *before* creating any lessons for a particular unit. As such, consideration of assessment strategies can serve as more of a starting point in the planning process, rather than an ending point. In some cases, teachers conduct a **pre-assessment**—some sort of assessment activity conducted before designing a unit—in order to determine the needs of their students. If the pre-assessment indicates that students are deficient (or already well versed) in some area of the unit's content, the teacher may opt to emphasize or de-emphasize a topic accordingly. In this regard, assessment data can be used to drive the planning of a unit.

Educators generally differentiate between two types of assessment—formative and summative. **Formative assessment** is used throughout the teaching and learning cycle to determine whether an individual is progressing at an acceptable rate. Often, formative assessment provides students with some useful feedback on how they are doing and how they can improve their performance. Also, most formative assessments are informal. They may consist of students writing a brief journal entry, the teacher orally raising a series of questions in the classroom, or even the simple observation of facial expressions during a lesson. In addition to monitoring student progress, these formative assessments also give the teacher some insight as to whether the lesson is progressing at the right pace and how to make minor adjustments in the plan as the lesson unfolds.

Summative assessment, on the other hand, is a final evaluation of a person's performance. After all of the data have been gathered over time, the student is given a grade in the course, or the employee is rated to determine whether a promotion is warranted. The summative assessment places a value on student performance over time, often in the form of a letter grade or numerical scores on a grade sheet. This assessment also provides the student with feedback on performance, as well as helping the teacher reflect on the progress of each student or the class as a whole. We can think of formative assessment as having been conducted *along the way,* whereas summative assessment is done *at the end* as a *summary* of previously collected data. The issue of how to assemble assessment data to determine a final, summative grade will be explored further in Chapter 11. So, in a broad sense, what does it mean to assess a student in mathematics?

In 1995, the National Council of Teachers of Mathematics released *Assessment Standards for School Mathematics* (1995). In this document, **assessment** was defined as "the process of gathering evidence about a student's knowledge of, ability to use, and disposition toward, mathematics and of making inferences from that evidence for a variety of purposes" (p. 3). The authors noted that evaluation, a final judgment of progress, is only one of many uses for assessment. So, when we think of assessment, we need to frame it in a very broad sense as a data collection process. The nature of students' questions can be used to informally assess their understanding of the content. Assessment can take on many forms, from written tests to observations, interviews, and projects—anything that can be used to generate data that will be helpful to the teacher who is guiding the teaching and learning process. Let's explore some of the uses for data collected through the assessment process.

Purposes for Assessment

Consider the following assessments that were conducted in an Algebra II class studying a unit on probability during the past 2 weeks:

1. Students were given a pretest on their knowledge of probability before beginning the unit.
2. Students worked problems in teams as the teacher circulated around the room, listening to their conversations.
3. The teacher asked students to go to the board to explain their solutions to assigned homework problems.
4. The teacher collected homework assignments and checked them into the gradebook as having been completed.
5. The teacher walked around the room while students were individually attempting to solve a problem and selected three students to briefly question about their understanding of the problem.
6. Students were given a 100-point test at the end of the unit on probability.
7. Students wrote journal entries, summarizing the major points of the unit and discussing which lessons were most effective for them and why.

As you can see, a number of different assessments were used throughout the unit. Some were more formal, such as giving pre- and posttests and checking homework assignments, whereas others were more informal, observing students working in groups, briefly interviewing a sample of students, and asking students to write journal entries. Assessments may be formal or informal in nature, but the objective is always the same—*to gather information* about how students are performing. You may notice that the unit test is summative: It provides a final score that theoretically represents the degree to which students mastered the concepts (we deal with perception versus reality in testing later in this chapter). However, other assessments, such as students explaining problems at the board, correcting homework assignments, and being interviewed, provide the teacher with some ongoing or formative information about how the unit is progressing. Ideally, every teacher should use a combination of formative and summative assessments to monitor and validate student learning.

Although all seven of the items on the list would be considered some form of assessment, only two of them—checking homework into the gradebook and giving a unit test—were used to evaluate student learning and ultimately affected the students' grades. The other five assessments were used to pre-assess the students' background, to monitor progress, and to help the teacher more effectively guide the instruction. In fact, a journal entry about the relative strength of lessons in the unit is useful in two ways: (1) It helps the students reflect on their own learning experiences, and (2) it helps the teacher plan by providing insight into how the students in the class regard the lessons.

Certainly, one of the major reasons why a teacher assesses student progress is to have enough data to eventually make a final evaluation of student achievement in the form of a grade. This grade shows both the students and their parents to what degree the goals and objectives of the course have been mastered. But assessment also monitors student progress over time. A special education student, for example, may be on an IEP (an individualized educational plan), which consists of a number of mathematical and personal goals for the school year with strategies to accomplish them. The teacher, then, conducts regular assessments in a variety of ways to determine whether the student is on track toward reaching those preset goals. Similarly, a student who is being assessed with a portfolio, which we discuss in more depth later in this chapter, also frequently sets goals for the next unit, grading period, or semester, and those assessments can be used to track the student's progress toward those goals.

Another reason for assessing student progress is to evaluate the effectiveness of an entire mathematics program—within a building, school district, state, or country. In many states, students are required to take some form of proficiency tests, which are statewide exams at particular grade levels and are keyed to objectives in a state's model curriculum or standards. In some cases, students can't graduate from high school until they pass some sort of exit exam between grades 8 and 12. Scores on these types of tests are often published in the newspaper, so that the community can have a snapshot of how effective the school is in teaching the state's recommended curriculum. Proficiency tests are an issue of heated debate because a student's graduation—indeed, that student's entire future—often depends on the score on a single examination. Perhaps you had to take a proficiency test or two in school and have a few opinions of your own. One of the purposes for proficiency tests is to ensure that teachers are actually addressing outcomes stated in the curriculum, so scores may reflect the effectiveness of instruction as much as the achievement of students. With the release of the *Common Core State Standards* in 2010, many states began to collaborate to design assessments that parallel shared standards (e.g., see the Partnership for the Assessment of Readiness for College and Careers or PARCC at http://parcconline.org or the SMARTER Balanced Assessment Consortium at http://k12.wa.us/smarter). The debate on standardized testing and its effects continues as schools attempt to be accountable to the public that pays their bills.

Because proficiency exams are aligned with a set of standards and scores are based on the degree to which students have mastered those objectives, the proficiency tests are **criterion-referenced tests**. The criterion is the set of standards for that state or consortium of states. Similarly, some school districts give their own

competency tests, which are criterion-referenced tests based on the outcomes stated in the local course of study. These tests measure whether the objectives in the local curriculum are being mastered by students, pushing educators to stick to the script and follow the adopted course of study as we discussed in Chapter 5. Another type of test used to measure the success of a program is a **norm-referenced test.** Students in a particular district are compared against the norm, a sample of other students at the same grade level and age from around the country. The PSAT, SAT, and ACT are norm-referenced tests that measure whether a student or group of students is scoring at, above, or below the average when compared to a sample of other students. Children in the elementary and middle grades often take the ITBS, or Iowa Test of Basic Skills, yet another norm-referenced test that is given to determine whether a district's program is keeping up with other districts around the country. Standardized tests—both criterion referenced and norm referenced—are generally used to determine the effectiveness of an entire program for a school, district, or state.

Although it is frequently overlooked, probably the most important use of assessment data is to assist the teacher in making instructional decisions, before (pre-assessment) and throughout the unit. If, for example, the teacher in the probability unit of an Algebra II or Second-Year Integrated class observes several students making significant errors when solving a problem at their seats, a decision might be made to adjust the lesson plan for the next day to meet the needs of those students. If a series of random interviews indicates that students understand the concepts and could be challenged at a higher level, the teacher might choose to accelerate the pace of the unit or to assign some different tasks than originally planned. In Chapter 6, we discussed the importance of building assessments into lesson plans. Assessment should provide clear information about what students are thinking in order for the teacher to fine-tune the lesson or unit accordingly. When assessment depends entirely on an end-of-the-chapter test, the data regarding student progress come in too late—by the time the teacher realizes that the students are confused and need intervention, the unit has been finished. Formative assessments along the way put the teacher in a much better position to help students and, thereby, to enhance the teaching and learning process.

The diagram in Figure 10.1 is taken from the NCTM *Assessment Standards* and summarizes four major purposes for assessment—evaluating student achievement, monitoring student progress, evaluating programs, and making instructional decisions.

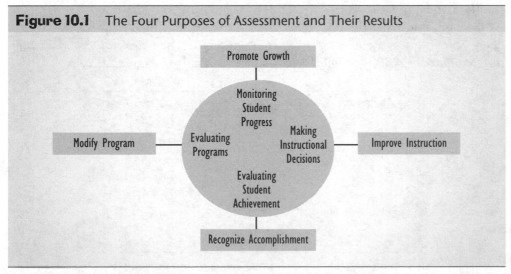

Figure 10.1 The Four Purposes of Assessment and Their Results

Because assessment is conducted for a variety of reasons, it makes sense that teachers would use several methods for gathering data about student learning. Some means of assessment are very formal, such as written exams, whereas others are more informal, such as observations or brief interviews. We examine some assessment strategies, beginning with the more traditional written tests and then exploring such alternatives as the use of journals and portfolios.

 Test Construction

After a 2-week unit on perimeter and area of polygons, the eighth grade mathematics teacher has decided to give the students a written test on their understanding of the major concepts. How does the teacher decide what to include on the test? What types of questions should be asked? How long should the test be? How can one ensure that a reasonable number of questions have been asked and yet not make the test so long that students are overwhelmed? The answers to these questions are not easy because there is no set formula for designing a test; therefore, teachers frequently struggle with this issue. Here are some suggestions to consider when constructing a written test.

Preparing Items

First, remember the purpose of the test—to determine the degree to which students have mastered the objectives set forth in the unit and lesson-planning process. Each item on the test should flow directly from the stated objectives or standards. If one of the objectives states that "given a polygon with the lengths of the sides labeled, the student will determine its perimeter," then the test needs to give the students an opportunity to demonstrate that they can do that. And unless the objectives talked about circumference and area of a circle, it would also be unfair to place items on the test that involved circles because the focus of the unit was on polygons. In Chapter 6, we noted that it is often useful, when sketching out a unit plan, to list some examples of the types of problems the student should be able to solve by the end of the unit. Doing this backward planning of the unit makes the test construction much easier because samples of problems students should be able to solve have already been written. The key element here is that every item on the test should match up with a stated objective or standard for the unit.

Second, construct the test items in such a way that the chances of a student being able to guess a correct answer are minimized. The *Curriculum and Evaluation Standards* (1989) document provides the example in Figure 10.2:

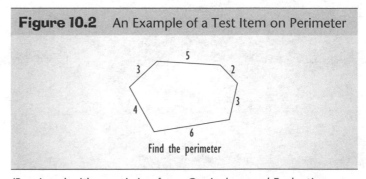

Figure 10.2 An Example of a Test Item on Perimeter

Find the perimeter

(Reprinted with permission from *Curriculum and Evaluation Standards for School Mathematics,* copyright © 1989 by National Council of Teachers of Mathematics. All rights reserved.)

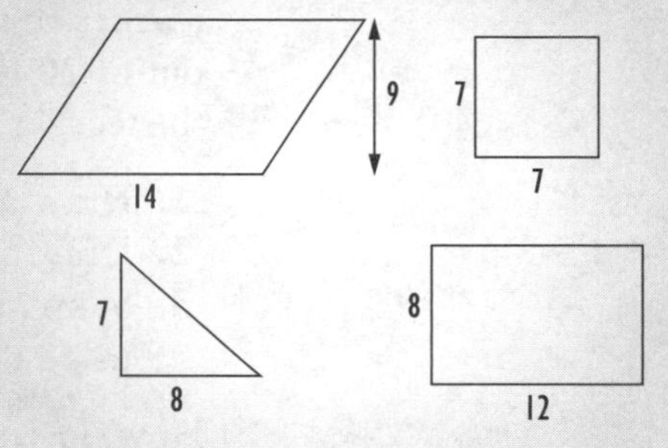

In a typical test on the topic of perimeter, students are asked to "Find the perimeter of this polygon." However, most students have learned enough about test taking to bluff their way through this type of an item. They realize that if the figure has 6 labeled sides, the only operation that makes sense is to add them all together, even if they have no idea what it means to find the perimeter! However, consider this problem: "Draw a 6-sided figure that has a perimeter of 23 units." This alternate item makes it very difficult for students to bluff their way through the drawing without knowing anything about perimeter. Similarly, think of what happens when you give students a set of four polygons (see Figure 10.3) and ask them to find the area of each.

Figure 10.3 Find the Area of Each Polygon

Because students may be well aware that area involves multiplication, if they simply multiply the two given dimensions together in each case and write the answers on a blank, they are likely to get 3 out of the 4 questions correct, missing only the triangle question. On a hypothetical 8-item test containing 4 perimeter problems and the 4 area problems presented previously, the student could get all of the perimeter problems and 3 out of 4 of the area problems—7 out of 8—correct without knowing anything about perimeter or area. A score of 7 out of 8 is the equivalent of 88 percent, which is a solid B on most grading scales. How do you feel about a student earning a B on a mathematics test without meeting any of the objectives of the unit? The point, of course, is that not only should the test items be carefully aligned with the stated goals and objectives of the unit but they also should be written in a way that makes it as difficult as possible for students to bluff their way through the test. This is not to say that an entire test should be made up of questions like the alternative suggested for Figure 10.2; in fact, it is often desirable to place straightforward problems, such as the four diagrams and direction in Figure 10.3, on the test. Likewise, it may make sense to include multiple choice and essay questions on the test as well. After all, we know that most standardized tests include multiple choice and free-response (essay) questions, so, in part, we can help students prepare for the high-stakes tests by incorporating similar items on regular unit tests. The point here is that a balance is needed in terms of variety of question types, and with enough nonroutine questions to help the teacher determine whether the student has mastered the concepts. This brings us to another important consideration when writing tests, the issue of length.

If you ask most secondary or middle school students about the ideal length for a test, they often will say that they prefer longer rather than shorter tests, because a longer test generally means that fewer points are deducted for each incorrect response. Yet, common sense tells us that if a test is unreasonably long, many students are likely to look at it and give up, too overwhelmed to even attempt the tasks. The teacher should ask, "What kinds of things will the students need to be able to demonstrate to convince me that they have met the stated objectives?" Sometimes, this question may result in a test of no more than 5 items, and other times, because of the nature of the skills and competencies being developed, a test may require 20 items or more. Of course, the length of the class period also needs to be considered. If a mathematics class is 45 minutes long, then the time factor will certainly drive the decisions about the nature and length of the test. Some teachers choose to spread a long test over 2 days, but this decision needs to be weighed against the loss of an additional 45 minutes of instructional time.

After completing a unit involving the area and perimeter of squares, rectangles, parallelograms, and triangles, one way to test the class is to provide a series of 10 diagrams involving these figures, labeled with dimensions, and ask students to find the perimeter and area of each. By providing the class with 20 answer blanks (10 for area and 10 for perimeter), the students write their responses on the blanks, and the teacher counts the correct answers to determine a final score. If the student had 17 out of 20 items correct, the final grade would be an 85. But suppose, instead, that the teacher asked the following questions on the test:

1. Draw a rectangle whose perimeter is 20 and whose area is 24.
2. Draw a square whose perimeter is equal to its area.
3. Show, with diagrams and words, why the area of a triangle can be found by using the formula $A = \frac{1}{2}bh$.

How do you feel about this three-item test? The problems attempt to assess student understanding in a way that transcends the demonstration of a simple skill, and they often give us greater insight into a student's understanding of area and perimeter than traditional items typically provide. Keep in mind that if teachers are addressing objectives that span the levels of Bloom's Taxonomy and its revision (Chapter 5) and ask questions in class that also require higher levels of thinking (Chapter 7), it follows that items on a test should measure more than simply knowledge and skills. What would you think of a test that contained the four diagrams shown in Figure 10.3, coupled with these three questions? Perhaps a combination of skill-based and concept- or application-level items might be the best way to assess student understanding on a written test. Regardless of how the questions are asked, the test does not have to be lengthy to measure student understanding; it merely has to match the objectives and reduce the likelihood of students guessing most of the answers correctly.

A third issue to consider is how closely the assessment aligns with the day-to-day instructional practices that have been used. **Alignment** refers to the consistency of the type of questions raised and the tools required on an assessment as compared to the question formats and tools used in day-to-day instruction. Suppose, for example, that a high school mathematics teacher allows students to use a calculator to find trigonometric values when studying a unit on right triangles. If, on the unit test, students were given a table of trigonometric values and told that they are not allowed to use a calculator, this would be like training an employee on a computer but evaluating that person's job performance by requiring proficiency with a manual typewriter. The skills and tools required in the classroom should be mirrored in the assessment situation for two reasons: (1) Students should see consistency between what is emphasized during class time and what the teacher expects them to be able to do on a test. (2) The test items are a reflection of what the teacher believes are important, and these values should be consistent in both the classroom and the test. Otherwise, students may become confused and ask, "We used a calculator in class yesterday, so why can't we use one on the test today?"

Widespread changes in the use of technology in the classroom, for example, spurred the creators of the SAT to change a rule that "calculators are prohibited" to "calculators are recommended." In fact, addressing the issue of alignment on the SAT, the College Board states that "all questions can be answered without a calculator," but "we suggest that you bring and use a calculator, especially one with which you are familiar. We recommend the use of a scientific or graphing calculator" and "Some questions on the Mathematics Level 1 and Level 2 Subject Tests cannot be solved without a scientific or graphing calculator. We recommend the use of a graphing calculator rather than a scientific calculator" (College Board,

2011). If a test is so computation driven that a student with a calculator can easily get most or all of the items correct, then the problem is not with the use of the calculator; it's probably with the design of the test. Alignment is all about consistency, and a teacher needs to be able to look at a test and ask, "Are the question formats and tools required for success on this test the same ones that I have emphasized in class during each day of the unit?"

Ensuring Validity and Reliability

Although this chapter will not discuss statistical measures in depth, it is important to note that any written assessment has a certain validity and reliability associated with it. **Validity** is a measure of the degree to which a test actually measures the content that the teacher intends it to measure. We often hear about students who do well in a class but then struggle on the written tests. This situation sometimes arises because the tests are not valid—they do not adequately measure the concepts emphasized in the class.

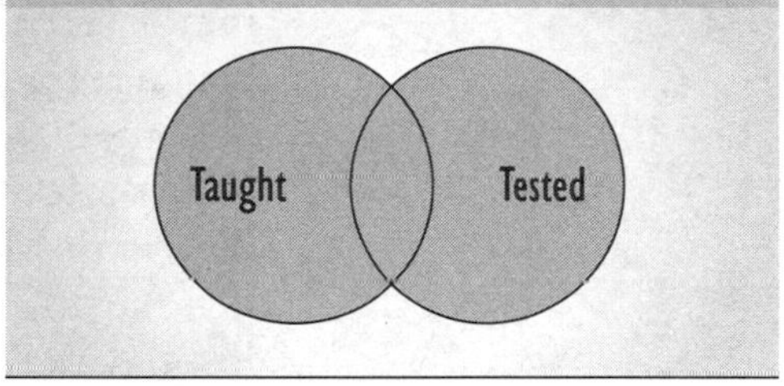

Figure 10.4 illustrates the relationship between concepts that are *taught* and those that are *tested* on written assessments. Ideally, that which is taught is equivalent to that which is tested, and the two circles merge into one. However, much more is often taught in the classroom than is ever actually measured on a written assessment. Also, a teacher preparing a test may inadvertently include items that do not align with instruction, so content is tested that was not directly taught. This error in measurement often happens when teachers in a department administer a "common exam" and some of the content includes

Figure 10.4 Relationship between Outcomes Taught and Tested

material that one class of students never had time to explore. The overlap of the circles represents those concepts that were both emphasized in the class and assessed on the test. The more these circles overlap, the greater the validity of the test. In designing tests, teachers are trying to ensure that the assessment actually measures the content that was taught and emphasized in the classroom.

The **reliability** of a test refers to the likelihood that a student will obtain roughly the same score if given different versions of the test multiple times. A good test is one that the student could take twice (or, more realistically, the student would take two similar versions of the same test because taking the exact same test twice will inevitably raise the score because of familiarity with the questions) and score about the same each time. A reliable test score will serve as a fair representation of a student's knowledge level of the content. When students boast that they bluffed their way through a test and pulled an A, then it's likely that the test was not reliable because the student could have just as easily bluffed and missed most of the items. Again, teachers should design tests so as to maximize the reliability of the instrument.

Scoring Student Work

Suppose that a student solved an equation on a written test in the following manner:

$$2x - 4(x - 3) = 10$$
$$2x - 4x - 12 = 10$$
$$-2x - 12 = 10$$
$$-2x = 22$$
$$x = -11$$

The correct solution to the equation, however, is +1. So, as a teacher, you have some choices to make in terms of scoring the item. Let's suppose the question is worth 10 points. You could insist on a perfect solution, put a line through the answer, and take off 10 points. In fact, some teachers tell their classes that the slightest error in calculation when designing a bridge can make the bridge tumble into the water; therefore, they do not accept even the most minor mistake. But let's analyze the error carefully. Notice that the only mistake the student made was on the first step, when −12, rather than +12, resulted from multiplying two negative numbers in applying the Distributive Property. From that point on, the rest of the steps and the solution are correct and consistent with one another. Consequently, you might say that the student was on the right track and understood the major concept and award the student half credit or 5 of the 10 points. Still another way to look at it is to consider each step of the equation as worth 2 points, and because one multiplication error was the only mistake made, you could award the student 8 of the 10 points. Of course, the choice that a teacher makes on scoring this type of item will significantly impact test scores and final grades. If a student made a minor error in each of 10 equations on a short test or quiz, one teacher might assign a grade of 0 to that student, but a second teacher might assign a score of 50, and another would give the student an 80. In the first two cases, the student who makes a few minor computational errors will receive an F on the test, but the student in the third class will earn a C or low B. Which grade is the most reasonable? Is it fair to give a student who makes these kinds of mistakes an F? To which philosophy do you subscribe?

How Would You React

SCENARIO

You have given a written assessment to a class of 25 students. With less than 10 minutes to go in the period, you realize that only about half of your students have completed and turned in the test and that the rest are not likely to have time to finish. After collecting all of the tests at the end of the period, your response is

a. Grade the tests but base each student's final grade on how many problems the student was able to complete.

b. Grade the tests, marking "wrong" any item that a student was unable to complete.

c. Do not grade the tests, but hand them back on the next day to the students who were not finished and give those students extra time to complete the test.

d. Do not grade the tests, but hand them back to all of the students the next day and give students an additional period of time to complete or correct their work from the first day.

e. Throw the tests away and create a new, shorter version to administer the next class period.

f. Other.

DISCUSSION

Estimating the amount of time it will take a group of students to complete a written assessment is a more difficult task than it would seem to be. Even novice teachers know that some students work faster (or slower) than others and that items the teacher perceives to be "simple" often are the very problems that take students the most time. If a written test is designed to be brief in duration, the students are likely to complete the work within a class period. However, the brevity of the test leads to the issue of each problem being weighted so heavily that even the slightest mistake can cost a student several points. Teachers are constantly struggling with creating written assessments that are challenging and can be used to provide accurate information about student progress, while not including so many items that students feel defeated and are unable to finish.

In this scenario, each of the possible multiple-choice reactions has a related consequence. For example, if the teacher establishes a policy of basing grades on the number of items the students complete, then the wise student will attempt only the easiest problems on the next test so that incorrect answers on more difficult problems will not affect the score. If the omitted items are simply marked as "incorrect," without students having had the time to attempt to answer them, the teacher will never know if the students had the skills to answer the questions. And if the teacher provides extra time for some students the next day, this practice would not be fair to students who hurried to complete their tests on the first day. But giving the whole class additional time may totally invalidate the results because students are likely to have discussed the problems in the intervening day.

As you think about this scenario—and about written assessments, in general—consider your philosophy on why written tests are administered in the first place. If the purpose of the test is to measure a student's ability to solve some type of problems, then is a time constraint part of what you are trying to assess? Time may well be part of your objective, but if it is not, then students need to have ample opportunity to complete their work. With some experimentation, tests can be designed to adequately fit in a given time period. Some teachers, for example, take the test themselves and then determine that students should have at least twice the amount of time it took the teachers to complete the problems. It is generally easier for a teacher to deal with a class that completed a written test earlier than expected than to have a few students who have not finished. As a rule, shorter tests create less anxiety among students and teachers. In the end, your personal style and philosophy will dictate how you handle this scenario of students who do not finish the work on time.

Deciding how to score student responses on a written test goes beyond gut feelings and opinion. Instead, think of the test as sending out a message to your students about what you value as a teacher. The first teacher values the student getting the right answers. We might wonder, for example, how that teacher would respond if the student simply wrote down +1 as an answer without showing any of the steps required to get to this answer. Would the first teacher award 10 points for the right answer or 0 points because no work was shown? Conversely, the second and third teachers emphasize and value the process involved in obtaining a correct solution. By scoring the item as 5 or 8 out of 10 points even though the final answer is incorrect, the teacher is essentially telling the student, "I value your thinking and because you know how to solve the equation, I will award some or most of the points to you." The emphasis, then, is not only on the correct answer but also on whether the student understands the process of solving an equation. The second and third teachers are likely to award few, if any, points if the student writes down a correct answer but does not show what steps were taken in order to get the answer.

So, your decision about how to score items on a written test should be based on your philosophy of what is important in the classroom. If you value mathematical processes, including thinking and reasoning, then this position will be apparent by the way that you assign points to partial or incorrect answers. A teacher who views mathematics as cut and dried and emphasizes only the "right answers," however, will grade accordingly. Of course, some questions such as definitions can have only one right answer. If a student who is asked for the name of a triangle in which each angle measures 60° answers, "right triangle," no teacher is likely to assign any partial credit to the answer. However, a written test should give students the opportunity not only to identify terms but also to demonstrate mathematical thinking. Making reasonable judgments about how to award points for mathematical thinking is up to each teacher and is not as easy as it sounds.

Including Review Items

Some mathematics teachers include review items on a written test to ensure that students continue to review and study skills and concepts from earlier units. If a middle school class has progressed from studying the metric system to exploring graphing, the teacher may choose to include a few items on the graphing test that review the metric system. Of course, these review items are not a surprise; the class should be told, in advance, what type of review items to expect. In this way, the review items motivate students to go back and review prior concepts, and class performance on these items can provide the teacher with evidence as to whether students are progressing or whether they have forgotten prior topics. Also, the incorporation of review items can help students make connections among mathematical topics as the students recognize that concepts being studied today often build on ideas that were explored earlier in the year.

The idea of including review items on tests has surfaced in some major textbooks and their test booklets. These authors see each test as a measure of everything that has been discussed since the first day of class. If teachers believe that the practice of placing review items on tests is worthwhile, then they have to decide how much of the test to devote to review. Again, there is no formula or typical way for teachers to make this decision. A rule of thumb might be to allow no more than one-third of the test to overlap with previously-studied content and let the other two-thirds assess students on new concepts that have been developed since the previous test.

Limitations to Written Tests

Unfortunately, no matter how valid or reliable the test is and no matter how the teacher scores the items, no individual test can accurately measure a student's achievement. A written test has a number of limitations. First, a test is a snapshot—a 45-minute glimpse of student performance on a particular day on a set of items written by the teacher or a textbook publisher. It cannot possibly capture all of the dimensions of learning and usually provides no opportunity for the student to react, ask a question, or follow up a response with a question or an explanation. Second, some students are simply not good test takers. As we noted in Chapter 3, many students have mathematics anxiety and freeze up when they are given a written test. They may understand the concepts but are unable to effectively demonstrate their comprehension in a written testing situation. Third, as we have seen, the score on a written test often has little meaning because two teachers will grade the same test differently. Teacher A may give the student 71 percent, and Teacher B may give the student 93 percent on the same paper because they employ different grading practices. In turn, the scores might cause a person to ask, "93 percent of what?" In a sense, the numerical scores are almost arbitrary because they depend not only on student performance but also on teacher opinion about how the tests should be graded.

Limitations on the value of written tests have sent educators in search of other methods to assess student understanding. In order to capture the diversity of thinking and the depth of comprehension, a number of other assessment strategies are available to teachers of mathematics. The next section describes a few of the more common assessment alternatives that a mathematics teacher can use in conjunction with or in place of more traditional test scores to paint a picture of student progress.

Alternate Strategies for Assessing Student Progress

Journals

Students in an introductory algebra course have been given the following task as illustrated in Figure 10.5:

> *Toothpicks are arranged on a table to create a string of squares as shown in Figure 10.5. Determine the total number of toothpicks required to build the structure 10 squares long. Also, find a formula for determining the number of toothpicks required if you know the number of squares, x. Explain your reasoning.*

Figure 10.5   Forming Squares with Toothpicks

Within a few minutes, one student raises a hand and says, "It would take 31 toothpicks to make 10 squares, and the formula is $3x + 1$." Other students nod their heads in agreement, and the bell signals the end of the period. As students leave the classroom, the teacher wonders whether every student in the class really understood how to solve the problem. Also, it is not clear how the student who answered the question found either the answer or the formula, and the teacher can't even be certain that other students used the same formula to solve the problem.

As an alternative, the teacher could have posed the problem near the end of the period and asked students to write their responses in a **mathematics journal,** a binder or spiral notebook containing student writing that reflects their thinking, problem-solving approaches, and opinions. The mathematics journal is considered an assessment tool because each student can write about a problem or classroom issue and know that these reflections are being "heard" by the teacher. The teacher can use the journal entries to determine the progress of the class and to make instructional decisions for the future. The following journal entries, for example, were generated in response to the toothpick-square problem.

Student 1

I made a list of values like this:

x	1	2	3	4	x
y	4	7	10	13	$4 + 3(x - 1)$

I saw that each one of the squares was the original square containing 4 toothpicks added to 3 toothpicks for each extra square. So, I took 3 times one less than the number of squares and added that to the first square with 4 toothpicks. From that formula, I could find the total toothpicks for 10 squares to be 31.

Student 2

For my formula, I found $4x - (x - 1)$. I pretended like each square took 4 toothpicks, and that's how I got my $4x$. Then, I figured that the left side of the square was missing a toothpick for every one of them except for the first, so I took away $x - 1$ toothpicks from the $4x$. If you put 10 into the formula, you get 31 toothpicks to form 10 squares.

Student 3

If you take off the last toothpick on the left, each square is really only made of 3 toothpicks, not 4. So, if you multiply 3 times x, that will leave you 1 toothpick short of the total. So, for my formula, I used $3x + 1$. If you put 10 in for x, you find that 10 squares will need 31 toothpicks.

Student 4

I looked at how many toothpicks it took across the top, along the bottom, and vertically. For x squares, you use x toothpicks across the top, x toothpicks across the bottom, and 1 more than x toothpicks vertically (you have to add 1 because of the toothpick on the left that starts the chain). So, for my formula, I used $x + x + x + 1$. Using 10 for x, you find that 10 squares will need 31 toothpicks.

Interestingly, all four of these students obtained the correct answer of 31 toothpicks and generated an acceptable formula. However, you may also notice that the mathematical thinking and what the students were visualizing were very different in each case. If we look beyond the answers, we discover individual differences that would not have been readily apparent if we had simply asked the class for a solution. Also, students can be creative in journal entries because they are not biased by the thinking of others. We often find that one student's explanation of a solution can hinder others from thinking divergently because others believe that if the person who contributed was "right," then their answer is either wrong or irrelevant. If students think that one particular student is always right, then they have little incentive to contribute a solution or process that differs from the answer of that individual. When students first address the problem in a journal, they are more inclined to share and express their approaches in class that day or in the future. Writing in the journal thus actually promotes rich classroom discourse.

Of course, the teacher gains valuable information from the students' journals as well. For example, the teacher of the class just described had not yet talked about similar terms in the course. But the four stated formulas, $4 + 3 (x - 1)$, $4x - (x - 1)$, $3x + 1$, and $x + x + x + 1$, provide an excellent opportunity to distribute algebra tiles to the class and explore why these four expressions are equivalent to one another—a teachable moment. In this way, the discussion of similar terms flows naturally from the toothpick-square problem rather than being viewed as a disconnected, new topic in a textbook chapter. If we read journal entries carefully, they can give us insights into student thinking that suggest patterns for intervening when misconceptions arise as well as determining teaching strategies for the future.

Mathematics journals can be written at virtually any grade level. Some teachers have students write in journals on a daily basis, whereas others require their students to do so once or twice a week. Often, students are given a **prompt**—a question or problem posed to a class, which is either to be addressed in class or for an assignment in the journal. Some generic journal prompts that can be useful to both the teacher and the student are as follows:

- *What was the most difficult topic we studied this week? What made it difficult for you?*
- *How do you think that you performed on today's test? What was the easiest part of the test and why?*
- *Complete this thought: Compared to the past 10 weeks, my recent performance in mathematics has been. . . .*
- *Which homework problem gave you the most trouble last night? What did you learn about this problem in class today?*
- *How much time did you spend on your homework last night? Describe how and where you did your work (e.g., at the table, in your room, working alone, working with a friend on the phone, with help from a parent, etc.).*
- *Comment on the teaching strategies used this week. Were the classes effective for you? Why or why not?*

Many secondary and middle school teachers have multiple classes and may teach 150 or more students. So, daily writing in and regular collection of the journals may be unrealistic. Each teacher needs to decide what is a possible and helpful schedule for collecting data about student progress and the effectiveness of lessons. Journal entries might be made once or twice a week and collected in rotating classes (e.g., Period 1 this week, Periods 2 and 3 next week, etc.) to make the task more manageable. Some teachers simply score a set of journal entries as "acceptable" or "not acceptable," whereas others assign points for the journals based on the depth and clarity of student writing. In either case, remember that the information gained by reading individual insights often allows the teacher to get to know each student far better than would be possible without this tool. Another example of a nontraditional or "authentic" assessment in mathematics is the use of open-ended (free-response) questions and rubrics on which to score student responses. We explore this strategy in the next section.

Open-Ended Questions and Rubrics

An **open-ended question** (or *free-response* question) is one in which there are either multiple acceptable answers or one right answer with multiple means of arriving at the solution. Teachers use open-ended questions to gather information about how students are thinking about a problem and to send out the message that student thinking processes are valued. So, instead of asking a student to find the probability of pulling the ace of hearts from a deck of ordinary playing cards, a teacher might challenge the student to describe a situation in which one would have a 1 in

4 chance of winning when pulling one card from a deck. The student is not being required to simply recall a fact or solve a simple problem. Instead, the student is expected to produce a game or situation. Sometimes this type of question is referred to as a **performance task** because the student has to make, display, create, or explain something—to perform.

In California, twelfth graders were asked to respond to the following question (California Assessment Program, 1989):

> *Imagine you are talking to a student in your class on the telephone and want the student to draw some figures. The other student cannot see the figures. Write a set of directions so that the other student can draw the figures exactly as shown in Figure 10.6.*

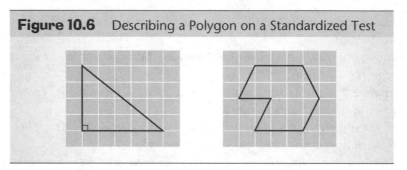

Figure 10.6   Describing a Polygon on a Standardized Test

(Reprinted by permission of the California Department of Education.)

This item tested students' abilities to use proper geometric language to describe a polygon. A number of misconceptions surfaced, and less than 15 percent of approximately 500 twelfth grade papers demonstrated an acceptable response. Most teachers would agree that even a middle school child should be able to effectively describe a right triangle, but relatively few of these high school seniors were able to do this. This information gives us a clearer picture of the type of communication that needs to occur on a regular basis in the classroom if students are to become adept at using proper mathematical terminology.

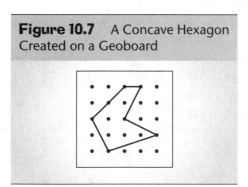

Figure 10.7   A Concave Hexagon Created on a Geoboard

Recognizing the difficulty that students may have in using proper terminology to describe polygons, the teacher could intervene by providing the class with a task using a **geoboard**, a square board, made of plastic or wood, that contains pegs that are generally arranged in a square. Many geoboards contain 25 pegs (5×5), but some are as large as 12×12 (144 pegs) or have pegs arranged in a circular pattern. By placing rubber bands (geobands) on the geoboard, students can produce images of such geometric figures as the polygon in Figure 10.7.

Suppose that the teacher arranges the class in pairs, gives each student a geoboard and a geoband, and asks each person to sit back to back with a partner. One person from each pair is asked to create any polygon on the geoboard. Then, that student has to describe it to the partner so completely that the partner eventually can create exactly the same polygon without ever having seen it. This exercise can be very powerful and requires students to use accurate terminology as they provide directions to their partners. We might expect that the activity would improve the performance of students on an item such as the one in Figure 10.6. The open-ended question then can provide data indicating that students need more practice in communicating mathematically and sends the teacher in search of an activity through which to provide the practice.

Considerably more is learned from the open-ended item in Figure 10.6 than would have been gained by asking a list of fill-in questions such as, "The triangle is an example of a(n) _____ triangle," which emphasizes recall rather than understanding. Generally speaking, open-ended or free-response questions, as they often are called, allow the teacher to ask richer questions that can tell us a great deal about how students think.

Because students often are able to respond in a variety of ways to an open-ended question, a simple right-or-wrong scoring strategy or even a partial-credit approach may not be appropriate. Instead, teachers often use a rubric, a generalized scoring standard that can be applied to an open-ended question as discussed in Chapter 1. A student's rubric score indicates the level at which a response can be placed. Some rubrics are simple, containing only three levels—high, middle, and low—whereas others may have as many as 10 levels. The National Assessment of Educational Progress (NAEP) exams include extended-response questions that are scored by using multileveled performance benchmarks. The descriptors of student's response categories from the 1992 NAEP, using a six-level rubric, are presented in Table 10.1. These general levels are still used on the exam today.

Table 10.1 Six-Level NAEP Scoring Rubric

Score	Level	Descriptor
0	No Response	There is no response.
1	Incorrect Response	The work is completely incorrect or irrelevant. Or the response states, "I don't know."
2	Minimal	The response demonstrates a minimal understanding of the problem posed but does not suggest a reasonable approach. Although there may or may not be some correct mathematical work, the response is incomplete, contains major mathematical errors, or reveals serious flaws in reasoning. Examples are absent.
3	Partial	The response contains evidence of a conceptual understanding of the problem in that a reasonable approach is indicated. However, on the whole, the response is not well developed. Although there may be serious mathematical errors or flaws in the reasoning, the response does contain some correct mathematics. Examples provided are inappropriate.
4	Satisfactory	The response demonstrates a clear understanding of the problem and provides an acceptable approach. The response also is generally well developed and coherent but contains minor weaknesses in the development. Examples provided are not fully developed.
5	Extended	The response demonstrates a complete understanding of the problem, is correct, and the methods of solution are appropriate and fully developed. Responses scored as a 5 are logically sound, clearly written, and do not contain any significant mathematical errors. Examples are well chosen and fully developed.

(Dossey, Mullis, & Jones, 1993, p. 89.)

Using the framework in Table 10.1, teachers can ask students an open-ended (free-response) question and score or place them at a particular level based on the categories listed. In this sense, the numbers actually mean something. In other words, a score of a 4 indicates a performance level that is clearly described in the rubric. Contrast this score with an 86 percent on a test, which does not tell us anything specific in terms of content mastery. It is important to remember that rubric scores generally have nothing to do with percentages. A score of 4 on an open-ended question does *not* imply 4 out of 5 or 80 percent of the points. Instead, the number merely places the response into a category, and by recording the response levels over time, the teacher can track a student's growth in answering these types of questions.

Notice also that this rubric can be used to score anything from an equation-solving task to a problem in which a student is to find the area of some irregular shape. Rubrics provide a *holistic* alternative to scoring a student's response because, instead of looking at each step of the process and assigning credit based on pieces of a solution (often referred to as an analytic grading scale), the teacher looks at and places the whole response into a category. Scoring papers on a rubric can be time consuming, particularly for the novice teacher. It also can be a shock to the student who has never been assessed in this manner. However, as the teacher becomes more adept at using a particular rubric, it can actually save time in the long run because it takes the guesswork out of assigning performance levels. After all, the rubric states what the student needed to do, and all the teacher is doing is determining whether the student met particular criteria. Then the score on the paper has meaning to the student because the rubric category of the paper provides feedback on what is needed for a better performance. Most importantly, the use of scoring rubrics allows student papers to be graded according to established and well-communicated criteria rather than by comparing one student's paper to another. The rubric communicates the expectations to students, and the subjectivity in scoring responses is minimized.

Let's look at a specific example of how a teacher might think through the development of a rubric to score a quiz or test item. Suppose that a class has been studying coordinate geometry and is given the diagram shown in Figure 10.8.

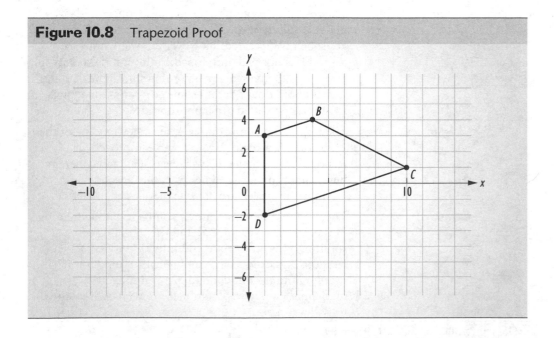

Figure 10.8 Trapezoid Proof

The problem given to the students is:

Prove that quadrilateral ABCD is a trapezoid.

The students are expected to write a paragraph, convincing the reader that the figure is a trapezoid. First, the teacher needs to make a list of all of the information that the student should include in the explanation, such as:

- A trapezoid, by definition, is a quadrilateral that has exactly one pair of opposite parallel sides. (Note that some use an inclusive definition of a trapezoid, in which the figure must have *at least* one pair of opposite parallel sides, but the major components of the proof are the same either way.)
- The slopes of sides $\overline{AB}$ and $\overline{CD}$ are both equal to $\frac{1}{3}$. Whenever two lines have the same slope, they are parallel, so these two sides must be parallel.
- The slope of $\overline{AD} = 0$, and the slope of $\overline{BC} = -\frac{1}{2}$. Since these slopes are not equal, the two sides cannot be parallel.
- We now know that $\overline{AB}\|\overline{CD}$ but that opposite sides $\overline{AD}$ and $\overline{BC}$ are not parallel. Because exactly one pair of opposite sides is parallel, the quadrilateral must be a trapezoid.

Now, the teacher must decide how many performance levels to assign to the rubric. Ordinarily, a relatively simple rubric to implement has five levels—from 0 to 4. In order for a student to score a "4" on the rubric, which is considered Excellent, the student needs to address all of the major points raised in the teacher's solution to the problem. On this rubric, the teacher might consider a "3" to be Acceptable, which allows for the student to have made a simple mistake or missed something in the problem. Specifically, consider the following response:

> *In order for a quadrilateral to be a trapezoid, it must have exactly one pair of opposite parallel sides. In this figure, sides AB and CD are parallel, because they both have a slope of $\frac{1}{3}$. The other sides are not parallel, so the figure must be a trapezoid.*

What is the problem with this response? You probably noticed that the student never convinced the reader *why* the "other sides are not parallel." We assume that the student knew that the slopes were not equal, but the slopes of the nonparallel sides were never calculated (as far as we know) or explained. Similarly, let's suppose that a student explains the definition and points out that $\overline{AB}$ and $\overline{CD}$ are parallel, whereas $\overline{AD}$ and $\overline{BC}$ are not parallel, making the figure a trapezoid. In this case, the student clearly knows the definition and recognizes that two sides are parallel but never convinced the reader that slopes were even calculated. In this instance, the student might earn a "2," which can be thought of as a Partial Answer. We are not giving the student "half credit"; we are simply recognizing that the answer is on the right track but includes some major gaps in the explanation. Finally, suppose that a student gives the following short response:

> *It has to be a trapezoid because of two sides being $\frac{1}{3}$.*

The student in this response must have explored the slopes of the sides or the number $\frac{1}{3}$ never would have been mentioned. However, in this answer, the student never explains what a trapezoid is, discusses that slopes are being calculated, or even mentions the nonparallel sides. This response is Minimal and, therefore, might score a "1" on the rubric. On a scale of 0 to 4, a "1" simply recognizes that the student knew *something* about the problem but was not able to adequately answer the question. Of course, the student would score a "0" for either leaving the answer blank, writing "I don't know," or writing something off-task, such as, "*ABCD* could be a trapezoid."

If a teacher wants this question to be more heavily weighted, then rubric scores could be doubled so that the problem is worth 8 points, and possible scores could be 8, 6, 4, 2, or 0. If you think about it, there are many mathematics problems that can be scored using this same principle. Think of a student solving a routine word problem, such as:

> *When the greatest of three consecutive even integers is tripled, the result is the same as twice the value of the least integer. Find the three integers.*

If the solutions to this problem are scored on a 4-point rubric, the teacher might expect the student to write an equation, solve it, and list the correct three answers ($-12, -10$, and -8) to earn a "4." It then would be up to the teacher to decide what kinds of responses would be allowable to score on the Acceptable, Partial, and Minimal levels. For example, a "3" might be an appropriate score for a student who writes and solves an equation but leaves "$n = -12$" as the solution rather than listing the other two consecutive integers. A "2" could be the score for a student who writes an incorrect equation but solves it correctly, resulting in three incorrect final integers. Or a student could also score a "2" by writing the correct equation but making a mistake when solving it, resulting in three incorrect integers for final answers.

Also, suppose that a student comes up with the correct answer but does not write an equation, simply using guess and check. If the teacher is going to require students to write equations, then that needs to be explained on the test with directions saying, "For each of the following, write an equation, solve it, and find the solution." If an equation is not required, then the teacher would need to score the item based on the clarity with which the student explains the guess-and-check procedure that was used to find the answer. With practice, scoring papers on a rubric can become a powerful way to use performance levels to objectively grade responses and to give the students feedback on their work.

Individual and Team Projects

As another alternative to more traditional written tests, the teacher has the option of assigning individual or team projects. Students in a high school geometry class, after completing an introductory unit on fractals, were asked to design their own fractal picture; draw the image to show 5 iterations; and generate and solve a mathematical problem using the algorithm, such as exploring what happens to the area or perimeter after n iterations. A scoring rubric was then developed that included mathematical rigor, creativity, and neatness of the work. The teacher employed this project in place of a test to obtain a more *authentic* look at student understanding of fractals than could be gained by asking students to answer a list of questions.

A middle school mathematics teacher who had just completed a unit on ratio and proportion, including unit pricing, assigned a project in which students were required to visit a local grocery store sometime within a 1-week time frame and collect price information on large and small containers of 20 foods. Then students

SPOTlight on Technology

One way to help students make the connection between a real-life activity and a graph is through the use of probes, such as tools that detect motion, temperature, light, and sound. These peripherals can be easily connected to graphing calculators or to computers, and they allow students to collect data for analysis. For example, suppose that students wanted to explore the cooling rate of water in a glass. Each pair of students could boil a beaker of water, place a temperature probe in the water, and use an application on the graphing calculator that records the temperature over some given period of time. A graph can be drawn that shows the relationship between time and temperature, and students can use the graph to determine the equation of a function that relates these two variables.

A popular probe that was released in the late 1990s was the Calculator-Based Ranger (CBR) from Texas Instruments. This peripheral measures, records, and graphs motion from a car driving down the street to a ball bouncing on the sidewalk. Software that drives the probe is either preloaded into the graphing calculator or can be downloaded from the Internet. Another popular use of the CBR is to get students to do the reverse—to look at the graph first and then try to perform the motion that simulates the curve. Consider the graph shown in Figure 10.9.

The graph in Figure 10.9 shows a relationship between time (in seconds) and distance (in feet). The CBR sensor is pointed toward a student for 10 seconds, and the student attempts to move at the correct speed and direction so that data points are plotted as close to the curve as possible. So, for example, the student needs to recognize that the initial distance should be

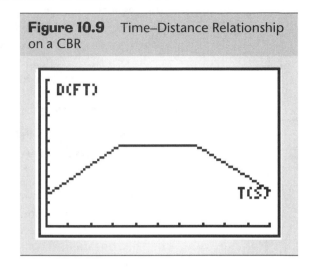

Figure 10.9 Time–Distance Relationship on a CBR

about 3 feet from the sensor. Think for a minute about how *you* would walk to simulate the graph and then read on. The student should walk away from the probe for 3 seconds (roughly 4 feet), stand still for 4 seconds, and then walk back toward the sensor at about the same speed as walking away from it. Students can either attempt to simulate the same curve multiple times or can progress to other scenarios.

Using this type of probe helps students appreciate the generation of real-life data and, in the case of Figure 10.9, to develop an understanding of piecewise functions, as described in Chapter 1 (a content issue in most algebra courses). Such tools help students make sense of dependent and independent variables and freely move between various representations of a function. Teachers can use these probes to assess student understanding of graphs before instruction or as tools for an activity in an instructional unit. The relatively low cost and portability of probes continue to make them popular in mathematics classrooms.

had to determine and compare unit prices, provide the data in a table, and write a short paper on their findings and observations. Finally, each student was required to make a 5-minute presentation to the class on the results of the study. The scoring rubric included accuracy of the calculations, depth of the data analysis, clarity of writing, and organization of the presentation. Not only did this project assess student understanding of unit pricing, but it also emphasized communication in written and oral forms and went beyond simply having students find the unit price for several items on a written exam.

The following problem-posing project was assigned by the teacher of a First-Year Integrated course during the last 2 months of the academic year to determine whether students could apply algebraic reasoning skills to some real-life problem-solving context. Students worked alone on the task and made presentations to the class. The characteristics of a good problem as well as the rubric used for scoring the project were developed by the students themselves as a class activity. Many teachers find that when students are actively involved in developing the task and its scoring rubric, they are more likely to assume ownership of the project. This ownership, in turn, results in a higher level of student performance because they helped determine the criteria for grading the project.

PROBLEM-POSING PROJECT: FIRST-YEAR INTEGRATED MATHEMATICS

Rationale
Throughout the school year, you have solved a wide variety of problems dealing with issues from predicting the death rate in a group of smokers to determining which of two local Internet services is the most economically feasible. But all of these problems had one thing in common: They were posed by an instructor for you to solve. The purpose of this assignment is to get you to identify and pose an interesting problem that someone else could solve by using the algebra skills we have developed this year.

Task
Your assignment is as follows:

- Identify/create and pose an interesting mathematics problem that can be solved by using the algebraic knowledge we have developed this year.
- Explain *why* you think this a worthwhile and interesting problem.
- Outline a process by which the problem can be solved (although you need not actually solve the problem in its entirety, partly because it may not be possible to do that—for example, some problems we posed this year could only be explored by collecting classroom data over time) and/or solve the problem.

A *typewritten* paper is to be turned in on the due date, and the paper must include all three parts previously noted.

A *classroom presentation* of your problem will be given to a small group of students on the due date. You will have 10 minutes to present your problem, reasons why you saw it as interesting, and its solution to the rest of the group.

Timeline
5/14	(Tuesday)	Explanation of rationale and task
		• Journal entry to consider scoring process
5/21	(Tuesday)	Development of scoring rubric
5/28	(Tuesday)	Problems are due

A Good Problem
The class has defined a good, worthwhile problem as one that

- makes you think
- is realistic (real life)
- requires algebraic thinking skills
- is interesting
- evokes curiosity
- is one that we can relate to
- does not necessarily have only one or any solutions
- lends itself to different ways of solving it
- has enough data presented and is worded appropriately to be solvable
- is unique and not merely a copy of another problem we have solved

Assessment Criteria

The project will be worth 50 points—half of a regular test score. You also have the option of doubling your project to be worth 100 points, but this choice must be made when you hand in the project. Your final grade on the assignment will be determined as follows: 40 points − written paper; 10 points − class presentation.

Written Paper

Your written paper will be scored on a five-level rubric as follows (it is possible for your project to fall between two categories as well):

40 Points (A)
- Must include all three sections (problem, explanation of why it is a worthwhile problem, and process for solving the problem)
- Not only are all three sections included but they are also all carefully written and clearly communicated
- Problem meets a majority of the good-problem criteria
- Contains a solution that makes sense to the reader
- If there are multiple solutions possible, this must be pointed out and discussed in the paper
- The problem and related writing are interesting to read
- Paper is neatly prepared and on time

35 Points (B)
- Must include all three sections
- Problem meets a majority of the good-problem criteria *or* the problem is not great, but the supporting writing is excellent
- The discussion about the value of the problem may be somewhat weak *or* the solution to the problem may be sketchy and unclear
- Multiple solutions may not have been discussed or recognized by the writer
- The problem and related writing are fairly interesting to read
- Paper is neatly prepared and on time

32 Points (C)
- Must include all three sections
- Problem may not meet most good-problem criteria and be only a fair problem
- The paper, overall, presents both a weak discussion about the value of the problem and a sketchy discussion of its solution
- The problem and writing are not particularly interesting
- Bare minimum requirements are covered, but the problem and its related discussion and solution could have been considerably strengthened
- Paper is fairly neat and on time

28 Points (D)
- May not include a significant discussion or solution at all
- Problem does not meet most of the good-problem criteria and is weak
- Discussion and solution are both sketchy and unclear
- Paper is not interesting to read overall
- It is evident that the point about what makes a good problem has been missed

0 Points (F)
- Assignment is not completed on time or at all

Class Presentation

This part of the grade will be provided by the peers in your small group who observe your presentation. Each member of your group will rate you on each of the following: (1) value of the problem, (2) discussion of its value, (3) presentation of the solution, (4) your overall attitude and presentation style.

One student in this class decided that, for her project, she would investigate whether it was better for her to count the project as being worth 50 or 100 points. She wrote equations based on her current grade in the class, graphed them, and found a break-even point in terms of the minimum score she needed to attain, above which making the project worth 100 points would be to her advantage. The intent of this project is clear: It challenges the students to think about real-life applications of the algebra that they have studied and to explore a problem of interest to them. As such, the project gives the teacher a unique window into the thinking of students.

More recent textbooks, particularly the NSF-funded curriculum project materials described in Chapter 5, tend to include assessment packages that provide teachers with performance tasks and projects that students can complete as alternatives to testing. In fact, many of the more recent resource books include the tasks, solutions, and suggestions for how to score the tasks on a rubric. Several resources that can be used as sources of these tasks and that provide further direction on how to design projects are included in the resource listing for this chapter. Sometimes, identifying worthwhile projects and organizing them can be time consuming for the classroom teacher. But, again, the key question that a mathematics teacher needs to ask is, "Can I learn more about my students by assigning a short-term or long-term project than by giving a written test?" This decision, in part, depends on what kind of message the teacher wants to send regarding the nature of mathematics. By assigning projects, the students not only engage in an alternative assessment task but they also gain firsthand experience with "doing" mathematics rather than simply solving a few routine exercises for the teacher.

Observations and Checklists

Perhaps the most powerful way to assess student understanding is to watch what the student is doing in class—to observe. In the 1993 NCTM *Yearbook* (Webb, 1993), which focused on the topic of assessment, the author quoted the following five recommendations about classroom assessment that have been offered by others over time:

1. In general, observation, discussion, and interview serve better than paper and pencil tests in evaluating a pupil's ability to understand the principles and procedures he [sic] uses.
2. Information is best collected through informal observation of students as they participate in class discussions, attempt to solve problems, and work on various assignments individually or in groups.
3. Evaluation of the thinking and procedures employed by students is usually better done by careful observation and interview than by objective testing.
4. From the standpoint of the classroom teacher in particular, frequent *informal* observations of student behavior have a vital role to play in the evaluation process. They neither replace nor are replaced by the more formal observations of student behavior that are made on the basis of tests and the like.
5. Observation of the pupil's oral and written work . . . [is] a very important testing procedure and should be encouraged. Closely associated with the observation technique is the interview with the pupil regarding his daily work or his solution or attempted solution of items of a test (Lambdin, 1993, p. 8).

Interestingly, these recommendations come from 1946 (Sueltz, Boyton, & Sauble), 1989 (*Curriculum and Evaluation Standards*), 1961(Sueltz), 1970 (Weaver), and 1951 (Spitzer), respectively. In other words, for nearly 70 years, educators have argued that observations and interviews with students are the best ways to determine whether the students are making progress in a mathematics class. Although written tests, journals, and projects certainly also provide a great deal of insight, there is no substitute for watching students work and asking them questions about a particular problem or task as they solve it. But observing students as they work is a skill and, as is true for any other assessment strategy, there are specific techniques for conducting effective observations in the classroom. There are several informal observation opportunities, such as watching students work at the chalkboard or asking for a show of hands, but other more detailed techniques are available as well. We discuss a few of them here.

Suppose that students are working on a problem in teams, and the teacher wants to make notes about how the individuals or teams are performing. If the teacher circulates about the room and takes notes on a sheet of paper, this will necessitate recopying the notes onto some other form or page later and is not time efficient. Instead, one popular observational strategy is for the teacher to carry a set of mailing labels on a clipboard. If, as students work, the teacher notices that Susan has observed that a pattern of numbers involves perfect squares, the teacher can write Susan's name, the date, and the following statement on the label:

noticed a pattern of perfect squares when others in the team did not

At the end of the period, the teacher simply pulls the label from the sheet and sticks it on a premade page with Susan's name on it for future reference. If this strategy is used regularly, over time, the teacher will amass a number of mailing label observations for each student. These labels provide the teacher with a picture of that particular student's participation and insights over the grading period. When it comes time for parent–teacher conferences, instead of having to describe Susan by reading off lists of numbers, the teacher has rich observational data and can report specifically what Susan did or did not do on particular days in class. Parents appreciate these details much more than numerical averages. As we have discussed, a number really doesn't convey how a student is performing on a day-to-day basis in the classroom. Similarly, some teachers make observations on sticky notes and stick them directly on the students' desks so that they are aware of what the teacher saw when passing by their workstations. Then, at the end of the period, the sticky notes are collected and placed on the student page in an assessment binder. Again, this process formalizes the observations so that teachers are not only watching how students are performing but also recording and compiling the data to look for changes throughout the semester or year.

It is sometimes helpful to have a checklist of anticipated behaviors or skills during the class period. Then, instead of writing anecdotal comments on labels or pages, the teacher assesses by determining whether a student meets the criteria spelled out on the checklist. For example, one teacher decided that she would try to observe process skills and told the students that she would be listening to their team conversations for evidence of problem solving, reasoning and proof, communication, connections, and representation skills. She sat down ahead of time and made a list of a few behaviors she might observe that would provide evidence of these processes being developed in the classroom. Table 10.2 presents some criteria from her list.

Table 10.2	Sample Checklist of Mathematical Process Skills
Problem Solving	☐ Uses a variety of strategies ☐ Demonstrates high level of thinking ☐ Shows persistence in problem solving ☐ Is able to analyze and understand a problem
Reasoning and Proof	☐ Is able to justify thinking ☐ Recognizes a reasonable solution ☐ Asks questions such as Why? What if? What would happen? Couldn't we?
Communication	☐ Is an effective listener ☐ Is willing to help others ☐ Presents thinking and results in an understandable manner ☐ Produces clearly written work
Connections	☐ Recognizes usefulness of concepts ☐ Recalls related tasks ☐ Uses prior knowledge effectively ☐ Asks "How is this different from . . . ?" ☐ Sees the connection between today's lesson and the past (or with other subject areas)
Representation	☐ Uses representations to model real-life data ☐ Is able to use multiple representations of the same problem ☐ Demonstrates effective mathematical communication with teammates by using proper representations

Another teacher was more interested in how well students were working together as a team on a problem-solving task and created the form in Table 10.3.

Table 10.3	Observation Checklist for Cooperative Learning Team Behaviors	
Student Name	**Behavior**	**Rating (−, ✓, +) and Comments**
	Assists others who are having difficulty	
	Remains on-task when problem solving	
	Open to hearing suggestions from team members	
	Discusses, rather than argues, with other team members	
	Works with others and does not move ahead of the team	

After placing the student's name in the box on the left, the teacher can record up to five characteristics of the individual's performance in teamwork. Making ratings or writing brief comments gives the teacher a framework with which to assess student performance in a cooperative learning environment. The observation checklist serves as a reflection of what the teacher values during classroom teamwork. Students should be given a copy of the form in advance so that they know what the teacher is planning to record, and they can reflect on what the teacher believes is important. As we know, the checklist can be particularly powerful when students become involved in designing the criteria. The teacher can ask, "I am about to observe you working in teams and want to make some notes about what I see. Can you help me to make a list of the types of behaviors that I would hope to see at your tables?" Students then make suggestions; the teacher writes them on the board or on poster paper, and the list is narrowed to a final form that is used as an observation sheet. Students who help develop their own checksheets will most certainly know what is expected of them because they wrote the criteria for participation themselves. The teacher, however, needs to keep in mind that any kind of observation is a glimpse of student performance; students often will point out that "you came by my desk at a bad time; I figured out the next problem by myself, and you weren't there to see it." Consequently, observation data need to be placed in context with other assessment data. Another way to gather data on performance is through formal and informal student interviews.

Interviews

As the teacher observes students at work on a problem alone or in a team, it is almost inevitable that the teacher will want to ask, "Why are you solving the problem that way?" or "Can you explain the table that you just constructed?" to gain additional insight into student thinking. As soon as these questions surface, the teacher moves into interview mode. Interviewing students is one of the best ways to find out what they are thinking because the technique involves a one-on-one discussion, and, unlike a written test, the interview allows the teacher to pursue particular points with follow-up questions.

Thomas has been exploring the graphs of quadratic equations on his graphing calculator, and Ms. Breckenridge approaches his desk:

> *Ms. Breckenridge:* Can you tell me about what you're doing, Thomas?
>
> *Thomas:* Yes, I'm trying to find a pattern, but I'm not seeing it.
>
> *Ms. Breckenridge:* What have you tried so far?
>
> *Thomas:* Well, we were supposed to graph $y = x^2$ and then compare that to the graph of $y = 2x^2 + 3$. I did that, but they pretty much look the same to me.
>
> *Ms. Breckenridge:* Pretty much? What does that mean?
>
> *Thomas:* I mean, they're basically the same shape, so I don't know where to go from there.
>
> *Ms. Breckenridge:* You said they're basically the same, so you must not think the two graphs are exactly the same, right?

Interviewing is a powerful assessment technique that allows the teacher to probe individual student responses.

Thomas: No, they aren't exactly the same . . . one is . . . I don't know. . . .

Ms. Breckenridge: One is . . . ?

Thomas: Well, one is, like, skinnier than the other one. When you graph the x^2 one and compare it to the $2x^2$ one, the second one is skinnier.

Ms. Breckenridge: Oh, so you *did* notice *something*. Do you have any predictions about what other graphs like this might look like?

Thomas: I guess I would predict that if you graph, say $y = 3x^2$, it would even be skinnier. (Thomas proceeds to draw the graph of the new function.) Yep, I was right. It's almost like that number that multiplies the squared term determines how skinny or steep it is.

At this point, Ms. Breckenridge can pursue the issue of how the *y*-intercepts change or make a note about how Thomas never brought it up and then move on to another student. The important point here is that Thomas started off the interview by saying that he couldn't find any pattern and that the two graphs were basically the same. If he had been given a written test about this exploration, he probably would have left the question blank, claiming that he never found a pattern. But, in reality, he *did* find the pattern and simply needed an external catalyst—the teacher— to prompt him and challenge him to communicate his thinking. The interview technique allows the teacher to pursue student thinking and to probe more deeply than a written instrument often can do. The interview is particularly useful when assessing students with learning disabilities, who may be unable to express their thoughts accurately in writing but can explain the thinking process and demonstrate understanding of the concept.

Interviews are also effective follow-ups of observations or written journal entries. For example, if a student's misconception appears in a journal entry, the teacher can conduct a brief interview the next day to see if the student has overcome the initial misunderstanding. Not all classroom interviews are formal; in fact, most are informal and consist of no more than a question or two asked by the teacher during a problem-solving situation. It would be unrealistic for a teacher to conduct weekly in-depth interviews with students; after all, an interview may take 5 to 10 minutes, and many secondary and middle school teachers have 100 or more students. But interview questions asked of even a small sample of students each week can provide a cross-sectional glimpse of how a class is thinking or in-depth information about how one student is developing.

Self-Assessment

Another helpful strategy to assess student knowledge and thought processes is through conducting self-assessments. Probably no one knows his or her strengths, weaknesses, concerns, and questions better than the student. There are several ways in which this process can take place:

1. The student can do self-assessment by virtue of responding to prompts given for writing tasks, including journal entries. For example, on the day that a class takes a written test, the students can be asked to write to the following prompt in their journals: *What was the easiest part of this unit for you? Which content was the most difficult? Why? How do you believe you performed on today's test? Explain.* The student's written journal entry can give students an opportunity to think about the concepts studied and to identify which areas

need more work while also providing a window for the teacher to reflect on the content through the students' eyes.

2. The teacher can administer a short survey to students in the class. The survey can have students respond to various statements using a rating scale of Strongly Disagree, Disagree, Agree, or Strongly Agree. These statements might include the following: (a) *I tried my hardest on homework this week.* (b) *I asked questions in class whenever I needed help.* (c) *I studied for the quiz for an appropriate amount of time.* (d) *I understand the content of this week's work.* (e) *I am generally confident in my ability to perform in this class.* This type of survey helps students to focus on their effort, learning, and confidence levels in the class while also giving the teacher insights into these same areas. Students can take a similar survey a few weeks later, and ratings can be compared to assess growth over time.

3. Through an interview, the teacher can directly ask the students questions about their own learning styles. For example, as a class is attempting to solve a problem in small groups, the teacher might ask an individual student, *"Do you feel that your team is helping you to make sense of this problem?"* and *"What might the others do that could be more helpful to your learning?"* This technique is particularly useful for a student with limited writing skills, such as one with a disability or with deficiencies in the English language.

4. At the end of a project or unit, students can assess the work of their peers by completing a rating or evaluation form. Ratings that they give to one another can be anonymously shared so that students can obtain direct feedback from their peers. Many teachers use this technique to assist them in assessing individual work in a team project setting, as students can write about the degree to which their peers contributed to the group effort.

Note that these strategies are directly connected to journal writing and interviewing, as well as taking on a new dimension of completing a survey about one's own performance or the work of peers. In Chapter 7, we discussed "self-knowledge" as being one of the six facets of understanding a concept, and this assessment strategy plays right into dimension. Research suggests that when students conduct self-assessment, the result is significantly higher academic achievement (Ross, Hogaboam-Gray, & Rolheiser, 2002). Essentially, the process of self-assessing puts students in touch with how they are learning and helps them to identify areas in which they need help, both in terms of content and in doing their daily work in mathematics. As students get to know their learning styles, strengths, and weaknesses, they can more adequately set goals that ultimately result in increases in learning. Self-assessments, then, can become part of a student's portfolio, which we will discuss in the final section of this chapter.

Classroom Dialogues

A class was exploring a problem that involved, in part, finding the area of a circle. The dialogue picks up as the teacher leads the class through questions about how to determine the area.

Teacher: To solve this problem, we're going to need to know the area of the circle that has a diameter of 16 centimeters. Who can tell me how to do that?

Student 1: I think the formula is pi times diameter, so you just take 16 times 3.14 to estimate the area.

Student 2: I thought the formula was pi times radius squared. So, wouldn't you take 3.14 and multiply it by 16 squared?

Student 1: I can't remember which formula it is, but if it's πr^2, then you wouldn't square the 16 because that's the diameter. You would only square 8—the radius.

Teacher: So, what *is* the formula for area of a circle?

Student 3: I know it's either $2\pi r$ or πr^2, but I can't remember which one!

Student 2: I'm almost certain it's πr^2. But one thing I've never understood is where that formula comes from in the first place. How do you get πr^2 for area of a circle? Or do we still have the formula wrong?

This dialogue is part of an actual conversation that took place in a mathematics classroom. There are two points of confusion in the classroom: First, although the students are familiar with both formulas, they do not know which one—$2\pi r$ or πr^2—represents the area of a circle. Second, they also do not understand the derivation of the formula (i.e., "where did it come from?"). Should the teacher attempt to address both of these issues at this point in the lesson? How might students remember which formula to use for circumference and which is used for area? Is the explanation of where the formulas come from too complex for secondary or middle school students to understand?

In many cases, a teacher might address this issue by simply asking students to page back in their books or their notes to find the required formula and move on. However, a quick search to retrieve the correct formula does not address the deeper issues of confusion in the classroom. For example, a simple thought that can be shared with the students is that circumference is the distance around a circle. Therefore, the unit of the answer must be inches, centimeters, miles, and so on. On the other hand, the area of any region is always expressed in *square* units; so two dimensions have to be multiplied together to obtain square centimeters, square inches, and so forth. So, the area formula has the "squared" in it, resulting in square units; the formula is πr^2. The circumference formula involves the use of only one dimension, so it would be $2\pi r$ (or rewritten as πd).

The derivation of the formula for area of a circle is fairly simple once the students have first determined that $C = 2\pi r$ (such as by measuring circular objects with string or tape measure, as suggested in the lesson plan in Chapter 6). If the students then view the circle as cut into pieces that are rearranged, as shown in Figure 10.10, they will notice that the new figure approximates the shape of a rectangle.

Figure 10.10   Deriving the Formula for Area of a Circle

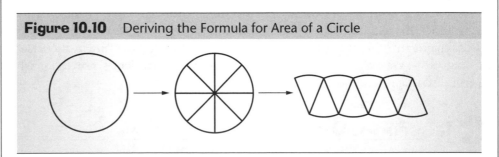

The rectangular shape at the far right in Figure 10.10 has a base length that is half of the circumference and a height that approximates the radius. Because the area of a rectangle is found by multiplying base times height, the following derivation can be demonstrated:

$$A = b \times h = \frac{1}{2}C \times r = \frac{1}{2}(2\pi r) \times r = \pi \times r \times r = \pi r^2$$

A recommended way to demonstrate this relationship is to give the students paper plates and scissors and have them cut the plate in half and in half again until eight pieces are formed. The students can place the pieces together as shown in Figure 10.10 as a tool for discussion of the formula.

Confusion over the appropriate use of formulas is common in mathematics classes. However, the source of the difficulty experienced by students is often a lack of careful, hands-on development of the formulas in the first place. Students should not be simply "given" formulas to use. Instead, when they are actively involved in generating the formulas, they are more likely to understand, remember, and know how to use them appropriately. Can you think of other examples of formulas that students are likely to memorize while in secondary or middle school that they may be able to recall but do not deeply understand how they were derived? What are some other benefits of engaging students in the derivation of these formulas?

Portfolios

As a student progresses through a school year, evidence of academic growth can be collected and assembled in a folder or a binder. A **portfolio** is a purposeful collection of work, produced by a student over time, that provides a glimpse of what the student is able to do and believes about mathematics. A portfolio might contain some or all of the following:

- Written tests, with errors corrected
- Sample homework papers demonstrating the mathematical process skills and practices
- A paper or project designed for the class
- A solution to an open-ended question or problem that illustrates a high level of mathematical thinking
- Sample journal entries that illustrate attitudes and skills
- Interview notes from a teacher
- Video- or audiotapes of teamwork or individual presentations
- Observation checklists completed by the teacher
- Self-assessment writing in which the student discusses growth over time

Generally, the student writes a short introduction to each section of a portfolio, explaining what can be found in that section and why it was selected. For example, one student wrote the following introduction to a sample test included in a portfolio:

I chose to include this test because I made a number of careless mistakes when I took it. But I went back and corrected my errors, and for each correction, I gave a short explanation of why I missed the item in the first place and what I need to remember for the next time. I believe that carefully correcting my mistakes on early tests helped me to achieve much better later on in the year. I still look at every wrong answer on tests and homework papers and ask myself, "Why did I miss that?" and "What can I do next time to make sure I don't do the same thing again?"

Finally, the student writes an introduction to the portfolio and creates a table of contents. The portfolio generally is put into a file box or a three-ring binder, or can even be scanned and burned to a disk that can be used by students to demonstrate their abilities to other teachers or at parent–teacher conferences. The portfolio represents students' growth over time and illustrates the way that the students solve problems and what they believe about the nature of mathematics. A portfolio is a much more concrete illustration of mathematical abilities than a percentage average in a course. Consequently, some teachers have begun to use portfolio assessment as a complement to current assessment procedures or as *the* determining factor in assigning grades. Some districts and states have mandated that a mathematics portfolio be created for every student beginning in kindergarten and that it be passed along from one grade level to the next so that teachers have an overview of student competencies before starting a new school year.

Stenmark (1991) suggested that portfolios themselves should be assessed on a rubric for their effectiveness. Such a rubric would have the following categories and descriptions:

RUBRIC FOR SCORING A MATHEMATICS PORTFOLIO

Level 4 (top level)

The Level 4 portfolio is exciting to look through. It includes a variety of written and graphic mathematical work, indicating both individual and group work. Projects, investigations, diagrams, graphs, charts, photographs, audiotapes or videotapes, and other work indicate a broad and creative curriculum that leads students to think for themselves. There is evidence of student use of many resources: calculators, computers, reference libraries, and conversations with adults and students. Papers display student organization and analysis of information. Although neatness may not be a primary requisite, clarity of communication is important. Student self-assessment is shown by revisions of drafts, letters that explain why the student chose certain papers, or student-generated assessment lists or reports. Improvement in communication over time is reflected in samples from the beginning, middle, and end of the term. Student work reflects enthusiasm for mathematics.

Level 3

The Level 3 portfolio indicates a solid mathematics program. There is a variety of types of work presented, as in the top level. Students are able to explain fairly well their strategies and problem solving processes. Some use of resources and group work may be evident, and students indicate good understanding, especially of basic mathematics concepts. Work over a period of time is included. The factors most likely to be missing are indications of student enthusiasm, self-assessment, extensive investigations, and student analysis of information.

Level 2

The Level 2 portfolio indicates an adequate mathematics program, somewhat bound by textbook requirements. There is little evidence of student original thinking as shown by projects, investigation, diagrams, and so on. Student explanations of the process by which they solved problems are minimal. There may be an over-concentration on arithmetic or similar algorithmic topics and a resulting lack of work from other content areas.

Level 1

The Level 1 portfolio includes almost no creative work and may consist mainly of ditto sheets or pages copied from a textbook. There is almost no evidence of student thinking. Papers are likely to be multiple choice and short answer and show no evidence that students are discussing mathematical ideas in class. Students do not explain their thinking about mathematical ideas.

(Reprinted with permission from *Mathematics Assessment: Myths, Models, Good Questions, and Practical Suggestions*, copyright © 1991 by National Council of Teachers of Mathematics. All rights reserved.)

As with the use of rubrics to score open-ended questions, it is important that the students help develop a portfolio-scoring rubric or at least that they are given the rubric well in advance so that they are aware of the teacher's expectations. Although some students resist the first time they are asked to assemble a portfolio, the benefit of being able to display growth ultimately makes the use of this assessment strategy very appealing to them. Many teachers also resist implementing portfolios in the classroom because of the perceived difficulty in organizing the assignment and in scoring the portfolios. However, the effort is certainly worthwhile when students are able to display their mathematics portfolio with pride and reflect on their accomplishments over a term or an entire year.

The use of multiple techniques of collecting assessment data provides the teacher with a broad, diverse methodology for determining the level of development for each student. As a filmmaker shows a scene from several angles in order to get the viewer involved in the action, a variety of assessment strategies can illuminate the many dimensions of mathematical development. If a primary aim of assessment is to determine student progress, there are certainly more ways to measure that progress than paper-and-pencil testing means.

 Conclusion

It has been said that the ultimate goal of the assessment process is to make students effective self-assessors who recognize quality work when they produce it. By asking students to create rubrics and to reflect on their performances in journals and portfolios, we are helping them to think about what it means to do mathematics and to monitor their own academic and attitudinal growth. When an external person, such as the teacher, does all of the assessment and tells you how you performed, you will naturally begin to expect someone else to monitor your growth, and that external assessment ultimately shifts the responsibility for reflection on work from you to the teacher. Self-assessment, however, places the students in an active role as they think about their own development and set goals for improvement. Similarly, we see a recent trend in business and industry toward employees setting their own goals for professional development based on their perceived weaknesses and planning a process for meeting those goals. In a sense, the use of alternative assessment strategies in the classroom not only provides the teacher with a richer view of the development of each student but it also helps students prepare for careers in which they may need to track their own professional growth.

In this chapter, we have discussed why, if inferences about student achievement are to be valid, a variety of data sources are necessary. Simply put, the Friday afternoon or weekly test or quiz does not provide enough information for a teacher to realistically gain a complete picture of each student's mathematical understanding. Consequently, we have seen the advent of a variety of nontraditional assessment strategies in mathematics, including techniques such as the use of journals, open-ended questions and scoring rubrics, individual and team projects, checklists and observations, interviews, self-assessments, and portfolios. Each of these strategies has been described at some length in this chapter. We must also realize that it may not be physically possible or desirable for a teacher to use all of these strategies to assess student achievement and attitudes. Instead, each classroom teacher must design a coherent assessment system that effectively monitors student progress.

The use of strategies such as writing and employing rubrics is not new in education. In fact, journals and rubrics have been standard assessment procedures in English and in the arts for decades. However, many of these strategies are in their infancy in mathematics, and this has led to some controversy. A local mathematics teachers' organization, for example, sponsors an annual mathematics contest for grades 6–12. Two open-ended items were added to the test after many years of administering a straightforward multiple-choice exam. Parents immediately complained that the decision as to who won the contest would be the result of a subjective score based on a rubric and that this process was not fair. Thinking quickly, the president of the organization asked the parents if their children had ever entered a writing contest, such as an essay competition for the Daughters of the American Revolution, or an art contest. After their affirmative replies, the president reminded them that scores for such contests are almost always based on rubrics, which are no more than predetermined performance standards—after all, you can't run a painting or an essay through a grading machine. In a similar way, a rubric for an open-ended mathematics question is predetermined and takes most of the guesswork out of assigning scores to papers. Once parents realized that the mathematics educators were doing what English and teachers in the arts have done for generations, the complaints almost immediately ceased. The problem, of course, is that these nontraditional assessment strategies are simply that—nontraditional, and, therefore, they are not within many people's comfort zones. Changing assessment practices, for many, involves realizing that assessment has other purposes than assigning grades and that traditional methods don't provide the total picture of student achievement and attitudes.

In the next chapter, we continue our discussion of assessment by exploring the *Assessment Standards for School Mathematics* (1995) and the assessment principle from *Principles and Standards for School Mathematics* (2000) from the NCTM. When we think about assessment strategies that teachers are now employing in an attempt to meet these standards, a number of other issues begin to surface as well. For example, on a practical level, how does a teacher select homework problems and assess the students' work? And what are the important issues to consider when determining final grades for a class? These questions are pursued in Chapter 11.

For bibliographic references and additional resources, see page 415

Glossary

Alignment: Alignment refers to the consistency between the type of questions raised and the tools required for an assessment, compared to the question types and tools used in day-to-day instruction. In other words, if the teacher regularly emphasizes problem solving and the use of technology in class, then a test with a high degree of alignment would also contain problem-solving items and expect students to use technology to answer some or all of the questions.

Assessment: The National Council of Teachers of Mathematics defines assessment as "the process of gathering evidence about a student's knowledge of, ability to use, and disposition toward, mathematics and of making inferences from that evidence for a variety of purposes" (1995, p. 3). Assessment is the process by which a teacher tracks student progress; it is a broad term that is often confused with *evaluation,* which refers to a final judgment of student performance.

Competency Tests: Competency tests, criterion-referenced tests that are generally given at the local level (such as an individual school district or county), measure the degree to which objectives in the local curriculum are being mastered by students as a means of encouraging educators to stick to the script and follow the adopted course of study.

Criterion-Referenced Tests: Criterion-referenced tests are aligned with a set of standards, such as a local curriculum, a state curricular model, or the *Common Core State Standards.* Scores on criterion-referenced tests are, then, based on the degree to which students have mastered the stated outcomes. Proficiency tests at the state level are examples of criterion-referenced tests.

Formative Assessment: Formative assessment is used during the teaching and learning process to determine whether an individual is progressing at an acceptable rate. Often, formative assessment provides the individual with feedback.

Geoboard: A geoboard is a square board made of plastic or wood on which pegs are arranged in square or circular patterns. The square on a geoboard varies from 25 to 144 pegs.

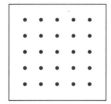 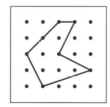

Geoboards can be used to study the properties of triangles, angle measurement, area, perimeter, the Pythagorean Theorem, and a host of other mathematical concepts.

Mathematics Journal: A mathematics journal is a notebook or binder in which a student reflects on learning experiences in the classroom. The journal generally contains some problem solving, reactions to problems and projects, reflections on the value of a team activity, and other self-assessments. By regularly collecting mathematics journals, the teacher can gain insights into how individual students are learning and viewing the class, which are difficult, if not impossible, to obtain by observation of student work in the classroom.

Norm-Referenced Tests: Norm-referenced tests compare the performance of students in a particular district or county to the norm, a sample of other students at the same grade level and age from around the country. The PSAT, SAT, and ACT are norm-referenced tests and measure whether a student or group of students is scoring at, above, or below the average when compared to a sample of other students.

Open-Ended Question: An open-ended (free-response) question is one in which there are either multiple acceptable answers or one right answer with multiple means of arriving at the solution. The most common reasons for using open-ended questions are (1) to gather information about how students are thinking about a problem and (2) to send a message that student thinking processes are valued. Open-ended questions are often referred to as free-response items.

Performance Task: A performance task requires the student to make, display, create, or explain a mathematical situation. An open-ended question constitutes a performance task as does the completion of a project in mathematics.

Portfolio: A portfolio is a purposeful collection of work, produced by a student over time, that provides a glimpse of what the student is able to do and believes about mathematics. Assembled into a folder or binder, a portfolio often contains samples of written tests (with errors corrected), homework papers, a paper or project, a solution to an open-ended question, sample journal entries, interview notes from the teacher, observation forms filled out by the teacher, and student self-assessments.

Pre-Assessment: A pre-assessment is an activity that is conducted prior to designing a unit. The assessment is used to determine the needs of their students.

Prompt: A journal prompt is a question or problem posed to a class, which is to be addressed in class or for an assignment. Sometimes, prompts are very specific problems or questions, and other times, they are open-ended and allow students to choose their own directions for responses.

Reliability: The reliability of a test refers to the likelihood that a student would obtain roughly the same score if given different versions of the test multiple times. Often, standardized test makers report a reliability measure, which indicates the likelihood that a student would score about the same if taking two equivalent tests on two different days.

Summative Assessment: Summative assessment is a final evaluation of performance. After all of the data have been gathered over time, the student is given a final course grade, or the employee is given a rating used to determine whether a promotion is warranted.

Validity: Validity is a measure of the degree to which a test actually measures the content that the teacher intends it to measure. A test is said to be valid when its content is consistent with the stated objectives or standards for the unit that the test is assessing.

Discussion Questions and Activities

1. Discuss the teachers' assessment strategies in several of your own recent courses. What did you learn about the values of your instructors from the way that your grades were determined?

2. Proficiency and other standardized testing is the topic of continual heated debates across the United States. In this chapter, several arguments in favor of and opposed to proficiency testing were presented. Take a stand for or against the notion that all students should pass a standardized proficiency test to graduate from high school and defend your position.

3. Obtain a copy of a test from the teacher's manual of a textbook series or from a mathematics teacher in the field. Critique the test by considering some of the issues described in this chapter, such as validity and reliability, length of the test, inclusion of review items, alignment with stated outcomes, and likelihood of students bluffing correct answers.

4. Previously in this chapter, a student response to an equation-solving question was discussed. The student did the following steps: $2x - 4(x - 3) = 10, 2x - 4x - 12 = 10, -2x - 12 = 10, -2x = 22, x = -11$. If the problem was worth 10 points on a 100-point test, how would you score it? What is a fair grade for this student, and what needs to be considered when making this decision?

5. Sketch out a conceptual map for a unit on the topic of your choice. Then, design two different assessments for the unit. One of the assessments should be a more traditional but well-written test, and the other assessment should be a performance task such as a project or interview. Discuss the benefits and potential drawbacks of each method of assessment. How can developing the assessment as the first step in planning (backward design) help the teacher create a conceptual map and individual lessons?

6. Interview a secondary or middle school student in depth about one particular mathematical concept or view a videotape of a student interview. You could begin by looking at some problem that the student's class may have done for homework and ask a series of questions to find out how much the student actually knows about that topic. In a small group, discuss the interview and what you learned about the student's understandings and misconceptions.

7. Create an open-ended question (or borrow one from another source) and administer it to a class of secondary or middle school students. Using the sample rubric from this chapter or some other similar rubric, grade the student papers by placing them into categories. Describe the difficulties you encountered while attempting to use the rubric for scoring the student papers. What are the benefits of this assessment strategy?

8. Select an alternative assessment strategy and generate a list of its advantages and disadvantages. In a team with three others who explored different strategies, compare notes and discuss which of the techniques described in this chapter are potentially the most useful and practical.

9. Interview English, social studies, or art teachers and ask them how essays and artwork are assessed in their classes. What type of rubrics do they use, and what can we learn, as teachers of mathematics, from assessment in the other content areas?

10. "Is this going to be on the test?" Recognizing that it is essentially impossible to assess every single mathematical point that is raised in the classroom, how do you react to the comment that "if it's not going to be on the test, there's really no point in my paying attention and taking notes on it in class"? How do you motivate students to engage in a mathematical discussion when they know that the conversation has strayed from the teacher's objective for the day and is not likely to be included on an assessment?

Principles of Assessment Practices

olleen was a student in Mr. McAlister's Calculus course in her senior year of high school. The students' "senior privilege" exempted them from their final exam if they were averaging an A or a B in the second semester. In the last week of class, Mr. McAlister read off a list of students' names who were exempted and called Colleen's name. Elated, she walked out of the room knowing that she would not have to take the Calculus exam. The following week, when grades were posted, she discovered that she had received a B in the class. She was upset because she thought that Mr. McAlister had read a list of the names of students who were exempted with an A, and if she had known that she had a B average, she would have elected to take the final exam to attempt to raise her score. She went home that night and told her parents about the situation. Her father called the teacher to ask what had happened. In his response, the teacher explained that Colleen had been averaging a B for the fourth quarter, and that with the level of material being studied, she should be proud of her performance. In response, her father said, "But if only she had known that you were going to give her a B. . . ." Mr. McAlister interrupted, "I didn't *give* her anything; she earned the grade that she received!" Upset and realizing that they had reached an impasse, they both hung up the phone, and Colleen graduated with the only B she had received in 4 years of high school mathematics.

Have you ever expected one grade in a class but were given another? Have you ever been in a class in which someone asked you, "What grade do you think you're getting in this course?" and your response was something like, "I have no

After reading Chapter 11, you should be able to answer the following questions:

- What are the six NCTM Assessment Standards and the Assessment Principle? Discuss the criteria that they establish as benchmarks for the effective implementation of an assessment system.
- What does it mean to achieve equity, and how can this issue be addressed through assessment?
- In what ways are the needs of individual students met through a variety of assessment strategies?
- What role do homework assignments play in the mathematics teaching and learning process, and how can they be used as assessment tools?
- What factors should be taken into account when managing grades and determining a student's final grade?

idea. I don't know how the number of points we get on tests and assignments relates to the final grade"? Colleen's situation is not unusual because there is often much confusion over how a student is assessed and where that student stands in terms of a final evaluation in the course. Mr. McAlister was absolutely correct when he stated that students are not *given* grades; instead, grades are *earned.* However, students have a right to know how their grades are determined and where they stand at any particular time in a class. Final grades should never be a surprise to the student; they should be a natural reflection of how the student has performed and be very predictable based on evidence collected throughout the grading period. In this chapter, we extend our discussion of assessment from Chapter 10 by turning our attention to some of the ramifications of developing a coherent system for assessing student progress. We begin with a discussion of the Assessment Standards (NCTM, 1995) and the Assessment Principle (NCTM, 2000) put forth by the National Council of Teachers of Mathematics. Then, we explore a few of the practical issues, including the use of assessment to meet the needs of individual students, assigning and checking homework as an assessment tool, and the process of keeping track of grades and determining final evaluative grades in a course.

NCTM Recommendations on Assessment

The Assessment Standards

Assessment Standards for School Mathematics was released by the NCTM in 1995. The book is divided into two major sections—the mathematics assessment Standards and the use of the assessment Standards for different purposes. In Chapter 10, we discussed the various uses for assessment data. Now, we visit the six assessment standards themselves and their implications. It is important to remember that these six standards are guidelines or benchmarks that can be used by a state, county, district, building, or even an individual teacher to determine the effectiveness of an assessment system.

▼ **THE MATHEMATICS STANDARD—Assessment should reflect the mathematics that all students need to know and be able to do**

Key questions that follow from this standard are:

- What mathematics is reflected in the assessment?
- What efforts are made to ensure that the mathematics is significant and correct?
- How does the assessment engage students in realistic and worthwhile mathematical activities?
- How does the assessment elicit the use of mathematics that it is important to know and be able to do?

- How does the assessment fit within a framework of mathematics to be assessed?
- What inferences about students' mathematical knowledge, understanding, thinking processes, and dispositions can be made from the assessment?

(NCTM, *Assessment Standards for School Mathematics*, 1995, pp. 11–12.)

The first standard relates to the idea that assessment should focus on what we value in the classroom. If process skills and mathematical practices, such as problem solving and reasoning and proof, are emphasized in the classroom, then the assessment program used by a teacher, district, or state should emphasize the same goals and objectives. The mathematical content in an assessment should provide a window into the content that a state, district, or teacher believes is important.

THE LEARNING STANDARD—Assessment should enhance mathematics learning

Key questions that follow from this standard are:

- How does the assessment contribute to each student's learning of mathematics?
- How does the assessment relate to instruction?
- How does the assessment allow students to demonstrate what they know and what they can do in novel situations?
- How does the assessment engage students in relevant, purposeful work on worthwhile mathematical activities?
- How does the assessment build on each student's understanding, interests, and experiences?
- How does the assessment involve students in selecting activities, applying performance criteria, and using results?
- How does the assessment provide opportunities for students to evaluate, reflect on, and improve their own work—that is, to become independent learners?

(NCTM, *Assessment Standards for School Mathematics*, 1995, pp. 13–14.)

Assessment is a data-collection process that goes well beyond simply assigning grades. Teachers should use assessment data to determine gaps in student understanding and then to target those areas for intervention when making instructional decisions. This standard is a reminder to teachers that assessment should help them assist their students by providing feedback that is important in the teaching and learning cycle.

THE EQUITY STANDARD—Assessment should promote equity

Key questions that follow from this standard are:

- What opportunities has each student had to learn the mathematics being assessed?

- How does the assessment provide alternative activities or modes of response that invite each student to engage in the mathematics being assessed?
- How does the design of the assessment enable all students to exhibit what they know and can do?
- How do the conditions under which the assessment is administered enable all students to exhibit what they know and can do?
- How does the assessment help students demonstrate their best work?
- How is the role of students' backgrounds and experiences recognized in judging their responses to the assessment?
- How do scoring guides accommodate unanticipated but reasonable responses?
- How have the effects of bias been minimized throughout the assessment?
- To what sources can differences in performance be attributed?

(NCTM, *Assessment Standards for School Mathematics,* 1995, pp. 15–16.)

Some students are good test takers, and others are not. Some enjoy getting up in front of a class and explaining their thinking; others would rather write their thoughts in a journal. The equity standard is a reminder that when students score low in a mathematics class, it doesn't necessarily mean that they don't understand the concepts, nor is the highest-performing student in the class necessarily the one with the highest level of understanding. One of the major reasons why we use a variety of assessment strategies is to give every student an opportunity to demonstrate an understanding of the content and processes. As we discussed in Chapter 10, a teacher who relies on written tests and quizzes as the sole tools for determining student progress is most certainly missing major dimensions of student learning, and, thus, an equal opportunity to demonstrate learning is denied to some students. We discuss the issue of how assessment can be used to promote equity in more detail later in this chapter.

 ## THE OPENNESS STANDARD—Assessment should be an open process

Key questions that follow from this standard are:

- How do students become familiar with the assessment process and with the purposes, performance criteria, and consequences of the assessment?
- How are teachers and students involved in choosing tasks, setting criteria, and interpreting results?
- How is the public involved in the assessment process?
- What access do those affected by the assessment have to tasks, scoring goals, performance criteria, and samples of students' work that have been scored and discussed?
- How is the assessment process itself open to evaluation and modification?

(NCTM, *Assessment Standards for School Mathematics,* 1995, pp. 17–18.)

In the short scenario at the beginning of this chapter, we saw a high school student—Colleen—who was earning a B in Calculus but thought that she was earning an A because the teacher's grading process was so confusing and unclear. The openness standard emphasizes that when students are being assessed, they (and their parents) deserve to know the criteria on which they are being assessed and the consequences of performing well or poorly. In the case of statewide proficiency testing as well as assessments required by the No Child Left Behind legislation (U.S. Department of Education, 2011), many states make it mandatory for students to pass some type of exit exam in mathematics in order to graduate from high school. With the stakes so high, students and their teachers have the right to be provided with a detailed set of outcomes, if not a list of sample test items, so that they know exactly what is expected of them. Similarly, if a teacher plans to use a rubric to score an open-ended question or a portfolio, students should at least be given a copy of the rubric in advance, if they do not assist in creating it themselves.

THE INFERENCES STANDARD—Assessment should promote valid inferences about mathematics learning

Key questions that follow from this standard are:

- What evidence about learning does the assessment provide?
- How is professional judgment used in making inferences about learning?
- How sensitive is the assessor to the demands the assessment makes and to unexpected responses?
- How is bias minimized in making inferences about learning?
- What efforts are made to ensure that scoring is consistent across students, scorers, and activities?
- What multiple sources of evidence are used for making inferences, and how is that evidence used?
- What is the value of the evidence for each use?

(NCTM, *Assessment Standards for School Mathematics*, 1995, pp. 19–20.)

The teacher eventually has to decide whether the student is doing A work, B work, and so forth. To make a reasonable judgment about a student's learning, a variety of data need to be collected. This standard emphasizes that generalizations or **inferences** can be made only if the assessment data provide a broad enough spectrum of information on which to make instructional and evaluative decisions. Again, we discussed in Chapter 9 how a variety of assessment strategies can be used together to generate a holistic sense of a student's progress over time.

THE COHERENCE STANDARD—Assessment should be a coherent process

Key questions that follow from this standard are:

- How is professional judgment used to ensure that the various parts of the assessment process form a coherent whole?
- How do students view the connection between instruction and assessment?
- How does the assessment match its purposes with its uses?
- How does the assessment match the curriculum and instructional practice?
- How can assessment practice inform teachers as they make curriculum decisions and determine their instructional practices?

(NCTM, *Assessment Standards for School Mathematics*, 1995, pp. 21–22.)

The last of the six assessment standards is designed to pull together the other five. It serves as a reminder that a state, district, or teacher's assessment system has to fit together and make sense. The assessment strategies employed should align with instruction and accomplish what they set out to do—evaluating students, charting progress, making instructional decisions, or serving as an accountability tool.

How Would You React

SCENARIO

A student in your class is struggling and averaging a near-failing grade of D–. The student missed several homework assignments, participates very little in class, and failed the first two tests of the quarter. Stopping in to see you after school, the student asks if there is any way that you could devise some extra credit assignments to help boost the grade. Your response is to

a. Answer "yes" and immediately generate some assignments that the student can do for extra practice to add to the point total for the quarter.
b. Answer "yes" but insist that the student complete the required assignments from the quarter first and then come back for extra credit work.
c. Answer "no" but tell the student to spend the time that would have been used for extra credit work to complete previously assigned homework.
d. Answer "no" but offer to work with the student after school to help the student catch up with the rest of the class.
e. Other.

DISCUSSION

There is considerable variation in the opinion of classroom teachers on the philosophy of assigning extra credit work. In some cases, teachers routinely provide opportunities for extra credit points to their students. For example, bonus points are often made available on tests, and extra assignments and projects are given to allow students to accumulate additional points that inflate their grades. In fact, some teachers even award extra points to students who keep their homework assignments and tests for a full academic term and can produce the documents at the end of the term. Other teachers provide opportunities for students to earn extra points if an individual student requests an assignment and the teacher believes that the student has earned the right to do extra credit work (for displaying a positive attitude, contributing to class discussions, and so forth). Still other teachers believe that students should spend their time doing the required classwork and assignments, and if the students do so, the grades will take care of themselves. Therefore, these teachers see no need for offering any extra credit at all.

Of course, any alternative chosen in this scenario will have a resulting consequence. One issue the teacher needs to consider is making a fair decision that gives all of the students in the class equal opportunities to earn extra credit points. For example, if the teacher in this scenario chooses A or B, then the rest of the students in the class probably deserve to be given the same opportunity. To allow one, near-failing student to earn extra points without making those points available to the entire class would be unjust to the other students. After all, shouldn't the student with a high B-average be given the chance to earn a few extra points to boost the grade to an A? However, if the teacher chooses to provide such an assignment, this decision creates a whole new set of issues, such as taking the time to design the assignment, deciding how many points can be earned, setting deadlines, collecting and grading the assignment, and dealing with the fact that many grades in the class could become artificially inflated because of the extra points.

Most teachers would be delighted with a student having the initiative to come forward and ask for help. So, if the teacher has philosophical and practical issues with assigning extra credit, the meeting with the student can be used to strategize how to help the student catch up with the class and to establish a plan for getting work done on time. In the long run, the student is much better served by learning the life skills of timeliness and responsibility than by being excused from doing past assignments and being "given" extra points. As is generally the case, the teacher's response to this scenario will be driven by that teacher's beliefs about the nature of assessment and the type of life skills that students should be learning.

Using the standards as benchmarks, teachers can evaluate their own systems of assessing student work and determine the degree to which their systems meet the criteria set forth in each of the standards. For example, if a teacher decides to use written journals as a major part of the assessment program, this may help in making more reasonable inferences but might also make the system less equitable because not all students are adept at expressing their thinking in writing. A teacher who uses only tests to assign grades may be very clear about expectations and be meeting the openness standard, but because the tests do not measure student ability to solve problems in teams or make oral presentations—which may be a major focus of the program—we might question whether the mathematics standard is being addressed. Ideally, an assessment system designed by a mathematics teacher at the secondary or middle school level should meet, to the highest degree possible, each of the six assessment Standards.

The Assessment Principle

Principles and Standards for School Mathematics (2000) includes assessment as one of the six principles in the teaching and learning of mathematics, as we discussed in Chapter 2. The Assessment Principle reiterates the NCTM's position on the use of assessment as a formative means of gathering information and as a summative manner of judging student performance. The principle states that "assessment should support the learning of important mathematics and furnish useful information to both teachers and students" (NCTM, 2000, p. 22). The authors cited a compelling article that summarized 250 research studies that consistently showed that students tend to achieve higher levels of learning in mathematics classes if their teachers routinely gather formative assessment data (Black & Wiliam, 1998).

In the principle, the process of assessment is described as cyclical, involving planning assessments and then using the data from the assessments to make decisions that result in modifying instructional practices. Formative assessment data that are collected on a regular basis to inform instruction is sometimes referred to as **short-cycle assessment**. Short-cycle assessments are often conducted daily, such as through the use of journals or checklists as discussed in Chapter 10. When assessment is viewed as a process over time, it becomes clearer that "counting points" to assign final grades in a class is only one of several components of a well-designed assessment system. The authors concluded the section on the assessment principle by stating that, "teachers must understand their mathematical goals deeply, they must understand how their students may be thinking about mathematics, they must have a good grasp of possible means of assessing students' knowledge, and they must be skilled in interpreting assessment information from multiple sources" (NCTM, 2000, p. 24). In the next section, we explore how equity and meeting the needs of individual students can be addressed through the assessment process.

Equity and Assessment

Throughout this book, from the discussion of learning theories to curricular and instructional models, we have operated under the assumption that *all* students have the capacity to learn mathematics. We have argued that no one is born with a mathematics gene; each of us has the potential to develop our mathematical reasoning skills. Whether we accomplish this is largely a function of our environment, including the home environment and the efforts of classroom teachers. The assumption that all students have a right to equal access to the study of mathematics is referred to as **equity**. According to Croom (1997), "equity in mathematics education implies fairness, justice, and equality for all students so that they may achieve their full potential, regardless of race, ethnicity, gender, or socioeconomic status" (p. 2). Although the general issue of equity and addressing the needs of all students is explored in some depth in Chapter 12, we will take a moment here to think about what it means to promote equity through assessment practices.

As we discussed in Chapter 10, some students prefer to make a presentation, whereas others would rather write a paper. Some students are better at taking tests, and others perform better on teams or by conducting individual projects. Achieving equity in assessment implies that students should have an opportunity to demonstrate an understanding of mathematical concepts in a way that is consistent with their learning styles. This point is evident in the equity standard, which states that "because different students show what they know and can do in different ways, assessments should allow for multiple approaches" (NCTM, 1995, p. 15). Furthermore, the Assessment Principle notes that "teachers must ensure that all students have an opportunity to demonstrate clearly and completely what they know and can do. For example, teachers should use English-enhancing and bilingual techniques to support students who are learning English" (NCTM, 2000, p. 24).

Addressing the issue of the promotion of equity through assessment practices, Belcher, Coates, Franco, and Mayfield-Ingram (1997) presented five suggestions for teachers to consider. They recommended that (1) assessment goals need to be made clear to students (which, of course, is an underlying principle of the openness standard); that (2) students should be assessed on the same principles that guide classroom instruction (e.g., if problem solving is emphasized on a day-to-day basis, then it should be a cornerstone of the assessment); that (3) equitable assessment tools should be used, in terms of their format and design; that (4) instruction should be connected to assessment; and that (5) self-assessment should be part of the information-gathering process. A classroom teacher who uses a variety of assessment strategies does so out of a desire to get to know each student in the classroom and see how well each student is progressing. If we look at the total person and give students the opportunity to demonstrate their mathematical knowledge in a variety of ways, we open new doors to students who might have opted not to take a course or might have been unsuccessful in a more traditional classroom and, thereby, promote equity.

Practically speaking, addressing equity might mean that a teacher includes several assessment strategies in the information-gathering process as was described in the previous chapter. So, a teacher might use journal writing, interviews, and a portfolio in determining grades along with tests and homework. In this way, students who have difficulty with written tests might have the opportunity to demonstrate their understanding through writing. Students who are poor writers still have an opportunity to show progress in oral interviews, and so forth. Moreover, a teacher might attempt to make a class more equitable by giving students a choice of assessment type. For example, suppose that a middle school mathematics class was completing a unit on angle measurement and triangles. The teacher might pose the following options to the students:

As an assessment of your understanding of angles and triangles, you may select one of the following:

1. *Take a traditional 25-item test issued on Friday.*
2. *Interview an architect or carpenter and ask that individual how angles are used in the profession. Write a 3- to 5-page paper about the interview,*

including diagrams that show examples of how triangles and angles are involved in that job.

3. *Come in during a study hall or before or after school for a 10- to 15-minute interview with the teacher. In the interview, you will be asked three questions involving angles and triangles. Each question will also have a follow-up question, based on your response.*

In each of these cases, the student is being asked to demonstrate an understanding of angles and triangles, and the assessment is worth 100 points. But the student can choose whether to be assessed in a traditional testing format, by way of a written paper, or orally, through an interview. Some students simply don't want to hassle with interviewing a professional and writing a paper and may feel content with taking a written test. However, if students believe that they can explain their thinking more readily in an interview than on a 25-item test, they may select the option of an interview. Then, on the day of the written test, the students who chose one of the alternative assessments might spend the test time preparing for their assessment, completing an assignment, or studying for another class.

Is giving a choice of assessment methods realistic for the teacher? The answer to this question depends on the teacher's class schedule and the experience that instructor may have had with various assessment strategies in the past. For example, after giving students this type of choice a number of times, a teacher might discover that only two or three students in each class consistently ask to use an alternative assessment; thus, the projects and interviews can be very manageable. The teacher may even wonder if it is worthwhile to offer alternative assessments, but for those few students, it could make the difference between failing and demonstrating competency. Also, the teacher may require some written tests or some projects for all students to complete, so it's not necessary to provide these options on every assessment.

Teachers must decide what is workable in their own particular cases and remember that any attempt to adjust for various learning styles promotes equity and can serve as a major improvement over what has historically been offered to students in the mathematics classroom. One of the more traditional ways to assess the formative progress of each student is to assign and collect homework. Individual assignments can be helpful to students as they explore or practice mathematical problem solving. At the same time, an examination of student performance on these assignments can provide the teacher with data on how students are progressing in their conceptual understanding. We now turn our attention to some of the practical issues associated with homework assignments in mathematics.

Homework Assignments

In the Trends in International Mathematics and Science Study (TIMSS) (Beaton et al., 1996), research on middle school achievement showed that 22 percent of Japanese students have mathematics homework three times or more per week, and 87 percent of eighth graders in the United States have homework at least three times per week. In addition, U.S. students' homework assignments affect their grades in 95 percent of the cases, whereas only 31 percent of the Japanese students' grades are impacted by homework. Simply put, teachers in the United States place a higher value on homework assignments and assign homework more frequently than do teachers from most other countries in the world. Yet, achievement test scores, as we discussed in Chapter 1, were well below the international average at the eighth grade level and even worse at the twelfth grade level in the United States, and the scores were near the top in Japan. Interestingly, eighth graders from both Japan and the United States reported an average of about 45 minutes spent on mathematics studying per night. Does that sound like a contradiction to the last statistic? Not really. Consider the following: Students in the United States are studying mathematics because the teacher gives a particular assignment; Japanese students *choose* to spend about the same amount of time working on mathematics, studying and reviewing class notes, but not because teachers require it. As much as anything, this might reflect a cultural difference in which Japanese parents encourage children to study mathematics every day, regardless of whether they have a formal homework assignment to complete for the next day. So, how much homework is reasonable, and how should it be checked?

Homework Amount and Frequency

Of course, there are no clear-cut answers to the questions of frequency and quantity of homework assignments. A survey of fourth and eighth graders on the 2000 National Assessment of Education Progress (NAEP) showed that about half of all fourth graders and 59 percent of eighth graders spent an average of 30 minutes or more on homework per night. More importantly, the study showed that, on the achievement test, eighth and twelfth graders who completed an average of at least 15 minutes of homework each night significantly outperformed students who never did any homework (Braswell et al., 2001). Similarly, the 2004 NAEP data indicated that 73 percent of 17-year-olds reported doing mathematics homework "often" (as opposed to sometimes or never) and that scores on the achievement test tended to be higher for students who did more homework (Perie, Moran, & Lutkas, 2005).

There are generally three reasons why a teacher may choose to give a homework assignment: (1) to lay the groundwork for a new lesson, (2) to allow students to complete a problem or project begun in class, or (3) to provide practice on some type of exercise that was explored during class time. Teachers should assign as much homework as they believe is necessary to assist in the teaching and learning process. If a teacher brings a topic to closure during class, has no particular skill for students to practice, and intends to introduce the class to a new concept the following day, there is probably no reason to assign any homework problems at all. But students need to be reminded that even though a teacher did not assign a written homework lesson to be collected the next day, it is always wise to go back and review the day's lesson, brush up on previous topics, or review one test to begin to prepare for another. The following are examples of homework assignments that complement the classroom routine:

LAYING THE GROUNDWORK FOR THE NEXT DAY

Suppose that Mr. Vail decides to have students conduct an investigation to approximate the value of π and to discover the formula for circumference, $C = \pi d$. To carry out the investigation, students will use a piece of string or tape measure and determine the circumference and diameter of each of three different circles. After placing the values in the form of Table 11.1, the students will calculate and average the ratio as shown:

Table 11.1 Data Collection Table for Approximating the Value of π

Item Used	Circumference	Diameter	C ÷ D
1			
2			
3			
Average			

After all of the classroom data have been collected, the students will discuss the values they found when dividing circumference by diameter and will average the averages to find a classwide value, which will serve as an approximation for the value of π.

The day before this discussion, as a homework assignment, Mr. Vail gives each student a piece of string. Each student is to take the string home and, along with a ruler or yardstick, select three circular objects in the house—a plate, a glass, a bowl, a wheel, a table, and so forth—and find each object's circumference and diameter, recording the measurements in the table (see Table 11.1) provided. Then, the next day in class, the students will be given calculators and asked to find the ratio of circumference to diameter, rounded to the nearest thousandth. After this, the class will discuss the numbers found, discover an approximation for the value of π and develop a formula for determining the circumference of a circle, given the diameter or radius.

In this case, Mr. Vail has used the homework assignment to get students involved in the investigation by using objects familiar to them in their own home environment. It is also a clever time-saving device because he could save as much as 20 minutes of class time, during which students would be roaming about the room, measuring predetermined circular objects. Of course, if the students do the measuring in class, he can also assess their ability to properly use a ruler and record the results, but he has decided that using objects at home is more advantageous.

COMPLETING A CLASSROOM PROBLEM

Ms. Aspen's geometry class is discussing the concept of a midpoint. She poses the following problem to the class:

If the endpoints of a line segment are located at (5, 9) and at (1, 3), find the coordinates of the midpoint joining the segment.

Having had no previous instruction on the midpoint formula, the students in the class begin to explore the problem. After about 10 minutes, several students are ready to share their solutions and explanations.

Ms. Aspen: Joseph, can you tell us what you found?

Joseph: Well, I got the point (3, 6) as the midpoint. I used a piece of graph paper and plotted the two points you gave us. I noticed that you eventually have to go 4 up and 6 over to get from (1, 3) to (5, 9). So, if you only go 2 up and 3 over, you'll be at the midpoint. I took the coordinates of (1, 3) and added 2 and 3, and I got (3, 6) as my answer.

Ms. Aspen: Did anyone else do anything different? Krissy?

Krissy: I think Joseph's right because it's just about like finding a slope. I did about the same thing except I figured that to get from 1 to 5, you have to go 4 units, and to get from 3 to 9 takes 6 units. So, I took half of each and subtracted those numbers from (5, 9), and that brought me down to (3, 6). That was my answer too.

Ms. Aspen: Thanks, Krissy. (seeing Angelia raise her hand) What did you get, Angelia?

Angelia: I got the same answer, but I used my graphing calculator. I had it draw a segment with those two endpoints and used the TRACE function to estimate the midpoint. Then, I figured it was common sense . . . it has to be sort of halfway between the points, so (3, 6) made sense to me.

Ms. Aspen: The answer was common sense to you. Good. Did anyone do anything else? Any different answers? (No one raises a hand.) Can you find the midpoint of the segment with its endpoints at (−13, 25) and (−7, 84)? (Students look puzzled.) What's the problem?

Joseph: There's no way I'm going to use graph paper on this one!

Angelia: (laughing) I don't think my graphing calculator will do much good either.

Ms. Aspen: Well, the old methods may not be the best here, right? Unfortunately, time is running out. . . . Here is your homework for tomorrow: First, I want you to find the midpoint for the segment joining (−13, 25) and (−7, 84) using any method that you choose. Second, analyze that question and the one we did today and see if you can write down a quick, easy shortcut that will allow us to do these problems without using graph paper or calculators, because I think we just found out that those methods aren't always going to be the best. (The bell rings.)

The intent of Ms. Aspen's lesson was for the students to discover and develop the midpoint formula. Acting in a constructivist mode, she does not want to simply tell her students the formula; instead, she values the process of students developing or inventing their own formula. But with time running out, she leaves one specific problem and an attempt to generalize a formula up to the students for homework. The homework assignment should put closure on a problem that was posed and partially investigated in class. Although she could have opted to tell students to close their books and come back tomorrow to finish the exploration, she decided that it would be valuable for students to explore on their own and allow the homework results to serve as tools for the development of the formula the following day. In the end, she wants students to recognize that for any two points, (x_1, y_1) and (x_2, y_2) the midpoint can be represented by the formula $\left(\dfrac{x_1 + x_2}{2}, \dfrac{y_1 + y_2}{2}\right)$. The homework assignment serves as the bridge between today's classroom discussion and the closure to the formula development planned for tomorrow. She fully expects that several, although not all, of the students will discover that the midpoint coordinates are merely the arithmetic mean of the coordinates of the two given points. From that point, the class can generalize the formula and move forward.

▼ PRACTICING A SKILL DEVELOPED IN CLASS

Ms. Estes-Park has completed a 2-day discussion of right-triangle trigonometry, and students have determined the three trigonometric ratios—sine, cosine, and tangent—and their inverses. One of the objectives in her course of study is for students to be able to solve a right triangle; that is, given the length of any two sides, the student should be able to find the length of the third side and determine the approximate measures of the three angles using the Pythagorean Theorem and the trigonometric ratios. As a homework assignment, Ms. Estes-Park gives the students the following information about five triangles:

Triangle 1: The lengths of the legs are 5 and 7.

Triangle 2: The lengths of the legs are 6 and 8.

Triangle 3: The length of one leg is 7; the length of the hypotenuse is 10.

Triangle 4: The length of one leg is $5\sqrt{3}$; the length of the hypotenuse is 12.

Triangle 5: The length of the hypotenuse is $15\sqrt{2}$; the triangle is isosceles.

For homework, students are asked to draw a rough sketch of each of the five triangles and to use the Pythagorean Theorem along with the trigonometric ratios to solve each triangle. The students are to bring the lengths of the three sides and the measures of the three angles for each of the five triangles to class the next day. Ms. Estes-Park wants students to practice a skill that was developed in class during the past 2 days. She recognizes that there is a place for skill-building and practice, as long as it does not dominate what goes on in the classroom and homework on a daily basis. In addition, through her selection of homework problems, she sets the stage for another discussion the next day.

In problem 2, notice how the lengths of the sides are 6 and 8; therefore, the hypotenuse must have a length of 10, and students will discover a Pythagorean Triple. The next day, she would like to engage her class in a discussion of Triples, so she purposely assigned that problem so that students would notice that, sometimes, the lengths of all three sides of a right triangle are integral values. Also, she assigned problems 4 and 5 to give students some practice working with radicals because they recently completed a chapter on irrational numbers, including simplifying radicals. Finally, problem 5 was assigned so that students would recognize that the relationship of the lengths of sides in a right isosceles triangle has a ratio of $1:1:\sqrt{2}$. Later, she will explore the lengths of sides in a 30-60-90 triangle so that students can discover a ratio of $1:\sqrt{3}:2$. In other words, even though the homework assignment appeared to be nothing more than a set of five practice problems to sharpen skills, the careful selection of homework items also set the stage for discussions in class for the next couple of days.

A mathematics teacher must purposefully and carefully select the homework problems. An easy way to create an assignment is to ask students to do the even-numbered problems at the end of a section of the book. But do the even-numbered problems ask students to practice what you think is important? Will those particular problems lead students to the discourse you intend to pursue on the following day? Is it necessary to do all of the even-numbered questions, or would a few of them be sufficient? Ms. Estes-Park could have given the students 10 or more triangles to solve for homework, but she realized that if a student already understood the concepts of the Pythagorean Theorem and the trigonometric ratios, five problems would provide sufficient practice, and that anything more than five problems might be busywork that wastes the students' time. However, if a student is confused and does not know how to find the angle measures, the student is likely to miss all of the problems and will need to redo the assignment anyway, whether it consists of five or 20 triangles. Students who need additional help do not have to struggle through 20 problems when five examples would be sufficient to make them realize that help is needed.

Teachers often pose rich problems during class that students can investigate as a homework assignment.

Therefore, teachers need to consider length of homework assignments in terms of what is really necessary for students to do on their own. A textbook publisher may provide 25-problem practice worksheets for sections on synthetic division, total surface area, or solving proportions, but it may only be necessary and reasonable for the teacher to assign 10 of the problems on the sheets if the pages need to be used at all. Remember that in Chapter 7, we discussed how effective mathematics teachers tend to assign worthwhile tasks: Each time we plan a homework assignment, we have to ask ourselves, "What is my purpose for giving this assignment?" and "Which problems are worthwhile for my students to solve?" If a teacher concludes that the assignment is essentially busywork that will not significantly advance the classroom discourse into the next day, there may be no need to assign homework at all for that day. If a teacher chooses to give the class a homework assignment, then the following day a decision is needed on how to check the work and use it to promote classroom discourse.

Checking Homework Assignments

There are many ways in which mathematics teachers typically handle homework assignments. The following is a list of possible options for checking homework and the advantages and disadvantages of each strategy:

1. Students put all of the problems on the chalkboard, discuss the solutions, and correct errors on their papers. Papers are handed in for the teacher to check and record.

   ADVANTAGE: Every problem assigned is discussed, and students have an opportunity to compare each problem on the chalkboard to the work on their papers.

   DISADVANTAGE: If every student in the class got a particular problem correct on the homework assignment, class time may be misused on discussions of common knowledge. If 3 students missed a problem, and 20 others got it correct, one has to question whether it's an effective use of class time for all 23 students to discuss that particular problem.

2. The teacher asks the students which problems were the most difficult for them, and those problems are put on the board by volunteers and discussed so that students can correct their own homework papers. Papers are handed in for the teacher to check and record.

   ADVANTAGE: Only those problems on which students had difficulty need to be discussed; relatively easy problems are not given class time. Students are actively involved in placing solutions on the chalkboard and defending their methods of solving the problems.

   DISADVANTAGE: Suppose that in a class of 25 students, one student does not understand problem 4. If that student asks for the problem to be worked through at the board, the other 24 students spend several minutes of class time sitting through the explanation of a problem that only one person missed.

SPOTlight on Technology

A recent trend in mathematics education is to assess students using short- or long-term projects. Some individual projects can be completed in a few days or a couple of weeks; however, other projects may involve teams of students working over extended periods of time, as was discussed in Chapter 10. An increasingly popular method of creating projects involves basing them on the collection of real-world data from the Internet. Students can search the Web to locate relevant information and then use the data to solve problems. Here are a few examples of projects for students using the Internet:

- Students can explore the difference between predicted weather and actual weather for a particular city over a given period of time. *In this project, teams of students might select a city, locate the forecasted high and low temperatures for that city each day on the Web, and record the actual temperatures from the Web each day. Then, drawing line graphs, over time, the students can determine the accuracy of the forecasts and compare their results to those of students who selected other cities. Forecasts and databases of meteorological information can be readily located on the Internet.*

- Students can research a mathematician or a historical topic, such as the history of π, but are restricted to the Internet as their source of information. *A considerable amount of factual information about individuals and events is available on the Internet. Students learn about mathematicians and the history of mathematics while developing their searching and problem-solving skills on the Internet.*

- Students can track the population growth rates in several cities, counties, or states and make predictions about future population sizes. *Databases of population information are plentiful on the Web, and students can look up information that can be used to draw graphs and determine the regression equations that allow them to make predictions.*

- Students can plan a summer vacation for a family of four on a $2,500 budget. *Using the Internet, students can determine the travel distance between major cities; the cost of admission to various points of interest; and the cost of motels, food, and gasoline. They can estimate travel time and costs, and design a reasonable family vacation within the budget.*

- Students can design personal health-conscious diets and justify their content based on mathematics. *There are Web sites that allow individuals to input their age, height, and weight, and the software tells the user what is an optimal number of calories that they should consume in a day. By accessing sites with nutritional information, students can plan meals based on their needs for caloric intake, maximum fat grams, and so forth. This investigation could be a joint project for a health class and a mathematics class.*

- Students can design their own Web pages focused on a problem of their choosing. *In collaboration with another teacher, such as an English, science, or social studies teacher, a team of students in a mathematics class can select a problem of interest, write it in an interactive manner, and create their own Web site that focuses on the topic. For example, students might design a Web site that allows the user to explore various applications of the trigonometric functions.*

In order to complete projects such as these, students are engaged in running and narrowing searches on the Web to gather the data, which is, in and of itself, an interesting exercise in problem solving and reasoning. Most students are fascinated with the Internet and its wealth of information, so these projects are natural extensions of their interests and curiosity. The most significant obstacle to conducting these types of projects is availability of networked computers in schools. Teachers often need to devise careful plans for small groups to use the computers while others work on different assignments because access to the Internet may be limited in a particular building. But for the teacher who is able to work through the issue of limited resources, these projects can be powerful means of assessing student understanding of mathematics.

Also, if a student lacking confidence (or, for example, a female student in a classroom dominated by male peers) misses a problem and is aware that most other students understand it, the problem may be avoided when it really deserved a full class discussion.

3. The teacher reads correct solutions from an answer book, and students check their papers, asking questions where necessary. Papers are handed in for the teacher to check and record.

ADVANTAGE: By providing the students with solutions, the teacher allows them to check their own work so that they know what questions to ask later. This is a relatively time-efficient method, and minor questions can be dealt with as the teacher reads the solutions.

DISADVANTAGE: Remember our discussion of the role of the teacher in Chapter 7? We once again see the teacher in the role of a dispenser of knowledge here. Giving students solutions to homework assignments tends to promote the notion that mathematics problems always have single solutions, that the authority in the classroom is the teacher, and that the students' job is to try to get the same answers the teacher was seeking. The method may appear to be efficient, but it may also send out the wrong message about the nature of mathematics and the role of the teacher in the classroom.

4. Students work homework problems in a notebook, ask the teacher to help them through the most difficult problems each day, and turn in the notebook with solutions corrected at the end of the week.

ADVANTAGE: With this technique, students can update and revise homework answers throughout the week. If they were confused about a skill on Monday, they can ask questions on Tuesday, knowing that they have until Friday to revise Monday's homework and submit their answers.

DISADVANTAGE: Teachers helping students through the homework again places teachers at the focal point of the classroom. Also, some teachers prefer to obtain daily written feedback on student progress, and a weekly notebook collection may not be sufficient to track student understanding of concepts. Finally, many students need daily feedback and reinforcement to keep them on schedule for completing required assignments.

5. Students compare solutions to homework problems in small groups, correct their own papers, and ask the teacher for help as needed. Papers are handed in for the teacher to check and record.

ADVANTAGE: Students are responsible for their own learning in this model. If all four members of a learning team agree on a homework solution, they can be reasonably certain that they understand the concept and can move on at their own pace, checking their own work. Conversely, whenever a question arises on which all of the team members need assistance, they can raise their hands and obtain the help they need as a group.

DISADVANTAGE: It is possible for a student to simply copy another team member's solution to a problem without understanding the concept. Of course, whether students are able to do this depends on how the cooperative learning tasks are structured as discussed in Chapter 7. Therefore, the teacher should actively monitor the homework checking process by moving from group to group using observation techniques (see Chapter 10 for details). Also, some groups will always finish checking homework assignments more quickly than others, so the teacher needs a plan to keep those students on-task while others finish checking their assignments. Sometimes, for example, the teacher may ask a student from an early-finishing table to put a problem on the board or to move to a different group to assist other students who are experiencing difficulty.

The decisions on how to handle homework assignments are largely a reflection of the values and philosophies held by the classroom teacher. For example, a teacher with a belief system rooted in the constructivist or student-centered model would not work through the problems for the students on the chalkboard because that teacher values the classroom discourse in which students argue and use mathematical reasoning to confirm their own solutions. A teacher who believes that it is important to view student work every day is not likely to allow students to hand in a notebook once a week because the teacher fears losing contact with the day-to-day development of the students. Finally, a teacher who places a high value on communication and teamwork might choose to have students compare solutions in small groups and spend that time monitoring, assessing teamwork, and tuning in to misconceptions. Because these decisions are based on values and beliefs, we see teachers using a variety of techniques to check homework. As with any decision regarding how to manage the classroom, you have to select the method that appears to be the most appropriate and is the closest fit for your belief system. And just as options exist for checking homework assignments, there are also several ways to count the homework toward a student's summative evaluation or final grade.

Using Homework Assignments in Assessment

Once a homework assignment has been collected, a teacher has several decisions to make: (1) How will I count this assignment toward the student's grade in the class, if at all? (2) Should I count it as complete or incomplete, or should I score the paper for correct answers? (3) Should I attempt to hand back homework papers daily or collect and hand them back every other day or weekly? Again, the manner in which a teacher handles homework assignment grading will vary, depending on the style and beliefs of the teacher. Here are examples of a few methods of scoring collected homework assignments and the advantages and disadvantages of each:

1. The teacher collects homework daily and scores the assignment as complete or incomplete/missing, based on whether the student has finished the entire assignment. At the end of the grading period, the student receives a homework percentage based on the number of complete assignments out of the total number collected. For example, if 20 assignments were given, and the student completed 18 of them on time, the student would receive a 90 percent (18/20) as a homework score.

   ADVANTAGE: This is a relatively straightforward method in terms of teacher work time. The teacher simply has to make sure that the student completed the assignment and to record it, not to score the paper in any detail.

   DISADVANTAGE: If a student has completed 13 out of 15 homework papers and simply skipped two assignments, the student would receive two incomplete/missing marks, as would a student who fails to complete all of the problems on two of the assignments during the grading period. Therefore, there is no way to numerically distinguish between a student who regularly almost completes assignments and one who rarely attempts the assignments at all.

2. Homework papers are collected daily and scored on a rubric. For example, the teacher might use a simple, four-level rubric such as

   3 = Complete, with all mistakes corrected

   2 = Complete, with minor errors on problems not having been corrected

   1 = Incomplete paper, but a majority of the problems have been attempted

   0 = Incomplete paper in that less than half of the problems have been attempted, or the student has turned in no paper at all

   Then, the teacher who has required 20 homework assignments for the grading period can use a scale for accumulated points—for example, a student earning a total of 50–60 rubric points earns an A for homework performance; 40–50 points earns a B, and so forth.

ADVANTAGE: This grading method differentiates between levels of student performance, and the rubric scores *tell* the students and their parents something about the type of work that has been submitted. Rubric scores have the advantage of providing valuable information about a student's performance beyond the fact that the student completed or did not complete an assignment, as was discussed in Chapter 10.

DISADVANTAGE: The rubric-scoring method can be more time consuming than simply determining whether a student has completed an assignment, and it also requires the teacher to develop a workable rubric and final grading scale.

3. Homework assignments are rarely checked in class, and the teacher uses answers on them to determine whether the students have mastered a concept. Assignments are graded in that students receive a percentage score based on how many problems were solved correctly. These percentages are averaged to determine the student's homework grade.

ADVANTAGE: By scoring homework problems, the teacher can save a great deal of classroom time that might otherwise be spent discussing problems that the students already know how to do. The teacher can gather information about what students know and can do outside of class time and keep homework checking time to a minimum.

DISADVANTAGE: The purpose of many homework assignments is to practice a skill that has been taught. If students misunderstand and miss several or most problems on a homework assignment, they are essentially punished in a final grade for making mistakes in the practice exercises. This would be akin to an athlete having deductions taken from an Olympic performance for mistakes in a practice session 2 weeks before the competition.

4. Homework assignments are rarely, if ever, collected, but every two or three days, students are given a "homework quiz." When taking this quiz, students are asked to take out their assignments from the past couple of days and then to write the problem and solution to two or three problems drawn directly from the assignments (e.g., "write down #5 from page 134 and its solution and then #17 on page 138"). Students are not allowed to open their books for the quiz, so if they do not have the problems written down and solved on homework papers, they get no credit.

ADVANTAGE: If students make mistakes on their homework, they can ask questions and correct errors for the next day. They can also leave confusing problems blank, knowing the paper won't be collected the following day. In turn, this process saves the teacher the daily work of collecting and looking through dozens of student papers.

DISADVANTAGE: Students can fairly easily get away with not doing their homework. Once an assignment is discussed, they can write down the correct answers and then bring the solutions to class on the quiz day. Also, when the teacher is not collecting papers each day, students are not receiving any feedback on their work, which may result in the teacher not knowing whether the students are really understanding the material.

There are other homework scoring strategies as well. For example, some teachers assign and collect homework but do not count it toward final grades. In one of the TIMSS reports (Beaton et al., 1996), for example, it was reported that although 46 percent of Japanese teachers sometimes or always collect, correct, and return assignments to their students, 32 percent of those teachers never use the homework as a factor in determining final grades. However, 80 percent of teachers of eighth graders in the United States sometimes or always assign homework, and 95 percent of those teachers use the homework in some way to determine final grades. Some teachers collect a weekly homework notebook from students and score it as complete or incomplete or on a rubric but only record a weekly mark, as opposed to scoring each day individually. Still other teachers occasionally assign homework but do not require or collect it—a practice not recommended here because students have little, if any, motivation to complete uncollected homework assignments. Also, if the teacher does not collect homework, valuable feedback about student progress is lost.

As we have seen, there are a variety of reasons why a teacher might assign homework, and, once it has been collected, there are also several ways to score and record the assignment before handing it back to students. When making a decision about what homework to assign and what to do with it when students hand in the assignment, keep the six Assessment Standards and the Assessment Principle in mind and ask yourself questions such as the following:

- Are the homework tasks worthwhile?
- Will the assignment enhance the mathematics teaching and learning process?
- Does the assignment promote equity?
- Have I been open with my students about the purpose for homework and how it will be assessed?
- Will this homework assist me in making reasonable inferences about each student's progress?
- Does this assignment "fit" in the grand scheme of how I teach and assess my students?

In the next section, we explore how a teacher combines all of the assessment data, from test scores to homework averages and portfolio rubric levels, and devises a system for organizing and determining final evaluative grades for students.

Classroom Dialogues

Students were shown the diagram in Figure 11.1.

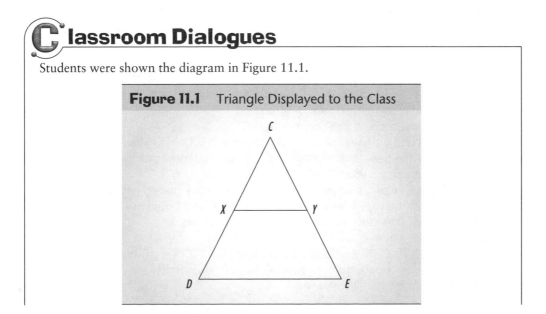

Figure 11.1   Triangle Displayed to the Class

Given the triangle displayed in Figure 11.1 and the information that $\overline{CD} \cong \overline{CE}$ and that X and Y are midpoints, students were asked to write a proof that $\overline{XY} \| \overline{DE}$. One student's attempt at this proof is shown in Figure 11.2.

Figure 11.2   Student Attempt at a Proof

Statements	Reasons
1) $\overline{CD} \cong \overline{CE}$ X and Y midpoints	1) Given
2) $\overline{CX} \cong \overline{XD}$ $\overline{CY} \cong \overline{YE}$	2) The midpoint of a segment divides the segment into 2 congruent segment
3) $\overline{CX} \cong \overline{CY}$	3) ??? (I just know that!)
4) ???	

As the teacher circulated through the room, the following conversation took place with the student who wrote the proof shown in Figure 11.2:

Teacher: It looks like you have a good start.
Student: Yeah, but I got stuck on the third step. I just don't get these two-column proofs.
Teacher: You wrote that segment *CX* is congruent to segment *CY*, which looks okay to me.
Student: Well, I know it's true, but I can't prove it.
Teacher: Can you tell me what you *do* know?
Student: It's just common sense. We know that segments *CD* and *CE* have the same length. If *X* and *Y* are midpoints, then they split two equal segments in half, so *CX* and *CY* have to be equal to each other.
Teacher: Why is that?
Student: Let's say that *CD* was 10 inches long. Then *CE* would also be 10 inches. If *X* and *Y* are midpoints, then *CX* and *CY* would both be 5 inches long. That's what I mean; it's common sense.
Teacher: So, where could you go from there?
Student: If *CX* and *CY* have the same length, then $\triangle CXY$ has to be isosceles, and that makes the base angles congruent too. So, we know that $\angle CXY \cong \angle CYX$.
Teacher: What else do you know?
Student: There are two triangles here—the big one we started with and the small one at the top. They have $\angle C$ in common and both have equal base angles. That means that all four of the angles are equal.
Teacher: Which angles?
Student: $\angle CXY$, $\angle CYX$, $\angle D$, and $\angle E$. Oh, wait! If $\angle CXY > \angle D$ (marks the angles on the paper), then they would have to be parallel.
Teacher: Which are parallel and why?

Student: XY and DE are parallel because these two angles (points to ∠CXY and ∠D) are corresponding angles. When the corresponding angles are congruent, the lines are parallel.

Teacher: Excellent. You got it!

There are several important messages related to this scenario. First of all, notice that the student was convinced that he or she was unable to complete the proof. It is very common for mathematics teachers to collect papers on which students have written little more than question marks for answers. What the student does *not* say is that the geometry is confusing, only that the format of the proof is making it difficult. Historically, this has been a major problem with the teaching and learning of geometry, particularly at the high school level: Students struggle with proof in general and two-column formats specifically. Ironically, in the college environment, as well as in mathematics research, proofs are rarely, if ever, written in two-column format. Instead, most proofs are written in paragraph form. After all, a proof is really nothing more than a structured argument that explains why something must be true. And most middle school and high school students write letters and verbally explain their thinking to friends all the time. So, by allowing students to write proofs through writing prose—in paragraph form—students are able to use communication skills they have already developed.

A common myth is that two-column proof writing will help students to think logically and properly sequence their arguments. However, for many students, this is simply not the case. Instead, they get confused about *how* to write the proof, and the format gets in the way of their thinking about the *mathematics* involved. This fear of proof is further intensified when the teacher insists, "The proof can be done in six steps," as if there is only one expected way that the argument can be written. You may have noticed how the student was perfectly capable of explaining why the line segments must be parallel. Although unable to complete the written, two-column proof, the student was able to verbalize the key geometric points in the situation and reason out to the correct conclusion.

Lastly, notice that the role of the teacher was to ask questions and guide the student through the proof rather than to "tell" the student what to do. In this case, the teacher is serving as a facilitator of learning by asking key questions and gently pushing the student to continue until the conclusion was reached. Without this guidance, and relying only on a paper-and-pencil, two-column approach, the student was convinced that he or she could not complete the work. NCTM and the Common Core State Standards have emphasized the need for students to develop their skills of reasoning mathematically and doing proof, but the notion that all students must be able to write two-column proofs in geometry is inaccurate and perhaps outdated. Instead, the spirit of reform in mathematics education calls teachers to encourage mathematical reasoning in a variety of formats, making paragraph proofs and verbal explanations important features in the classroom. How comfortable are you with writing proofs in two-column format? Do you believe that all students should become familiar with this approach? How important is it for students to be able to generate and communicate proofs, in general, in mathematics?

Evaluation: Maintaining and Determining Final Grades

Although some school districts, counties, and even states use portfolio and checklist assessments without letter grades, most mathematics teachers at the secondary and middle school levels will ultimately be responsible for reporting a letter (or numerical) grade for each student at the end of each grading period. Furthermore, most districts require teachers to file midterm reports as well, so that parents are informed about progress and possible deficiencies in their children's performance before the end of the formal grading period.

If a teacher uses several assessment strategies, then data will need to be entered into a grade book on a regular basis. Although some teachers still maintain paper record books, most use electronic means to keep track of student assessment data. In some cases, the school uses a grading software package that all faculty members use, and the grades are uploaded daily to a Web site that is accessible by parents who can routinely check the grades on-line. In other cases, the teacher keeps track of the grades throughout the term and simply reports a final numerical average at the end of the grading period. The record keeping can be conducted in a number of different ways. One method is to set up a spreadsheet with student names and simply type in scores on various assessments as the term progresses. However, one potential drawback to this process is that when it comes time for midterm grades to be determined, or when a parent or student wants to know an up-to-the-minute grade, the teacher often has to go into the spreadsheet and manually calculate the grades because the numbers have been preserved, but the weighting and calculation of scores change each time a new assignment is added.

As an alternative to spreadsheets, several companies offer computer software packages that help a teacher to maintain accurate, up-to-date records. One example of this software is called Easy Grade Pro, published by Orbis Software (2010). The screen shot in Figure 11.3 shows a teacher's grade book for part of the second quarter of the academic year.

Figure 11.3 Sample Grade Book on a Computer Screen

	Mi.	Overall	1	2	3	4	5	6	7	8	9	10	11	12	13	14	15	16	17	18	19	20	21	22	23	24	25
15 of 15 Students			1	1	1	10	1	1	1	10	1	100	6	1	1	100	1	1	1	1	20	1	1	1	100	1	100
1 Barry, Loretta	88	B	1	1	1	9	1	1	1	10	1	90	6	1	1	80	1	1	1	1	20	1	1	1	90	0	85
2 Bronson, Kathy	93	A-	1	1	1	10	1	1	1	10	1	100	5	1	1	92	1	1	1	1	18	1	1	1	98	1	93
3 Daniels, John	94	A-	1	1	1	10	1	1	1	7	1	90	5	1	1	92	1	1	1	1	20	1	1	1	99	1	94
4 Davis, Marcus	91	B+	1	1	1	10	1	1	1	10	1	100	6	1	1	77	1	1	1	1	13	1	1	1	94	1	83
5 Speer, Billy	98	A	1	1	1	9	1	1	1	10	1	100	5	1	1	97	1	1	1	1	16	1	1	1	96	1	99
6 Emerine, Janice	91	B+	1	1	1	10	1	1	1	5	1	90	5	1	1	87	1	1	1	1	18	1	1	1	95	1	78
7 Francis, Stephen	90	B	1	1	1	10	1	1	1	10	1	100	6	1	1	87	1	1	1	1	15	1	1	1	91	1	89
8 Gallagher, Debbie	93	A-	1	1	1	10	1	1	1	10	1	100	6	1	1	79	1	1	1	1	20	1	1	1	95	1	90
9 Joseph, Luke	93	A-	1	1	1	9	1	1	1	10	1	90	6	1	1	95	1	1	1	1	18	1	1	1	98	1	89
10 Kelley, Anne	93	A-	1	1	1	10	1	1	1	10	1	100	6	1	1	96	1	1	1	1	16	1	1	1	91	1	87
11 King, Angelica	92	B+	1	1	1	10	1	1	1	10	1	90	5	1	1	87	1	1	1	1	15	1	1	1	96	1	93
12 March, Kelley	93	A-	1	1	1	8	1	1	1	10	1	100	6	1	1	89	1	1	1	1	14	1	1	1	96	1	78
13 McArthur, Colleen	91	B+	1	1	1	9	1	1	1	10	1	80	5	1	1	66	1	1	1	1	15	1	1	1	96	1	96
14 Metzger, Joyce	96	A	1	1	1	8	1	1	1	10	1	100	4	1	1	94	1	1	1	1	18	1	1	1	91	1	95
15 Stephens, Mark	94	A-	1	1	1	9	1	1	1	8	1	100	6	1	1	89	1	1	1	1	18	1	1	1	98	1	85

2nd Quarter: Honors Grade B... 93%

(Reprinted with permission of Tom Pauly.)

Each time a new assessment is graded, the numerical score is entered into the computer. Immediately, the student's current average is computed, and the bar graph shows how many students are currently in each of the grade categories. In the example from Figure 11.3, the teacher knows that all of the students in the class have an average of an A or a B, and the page shows the results from graded homework assignments, quizzes, tests, journal entries, and a quarter project on functions. What is most important is that, regardless of how the scores are physically managed, teachers keep their record books updated so that student progress can be readily tracked and available when needed for conferences and for reporting final grades.

For the teacher's Honors Mathematics class displayed in Figure 11.3, tests, quizzes, and projects were weighted as 75 percent of the grade, whereas homework counted for 15 percent, and journal entries accounted for the final 10 percent of the grade. However, the decision on how to put all of the pieces of assessment data together to determine a student's final grade is almost always up to the teacher. Consequently, another teacher might have used the exact same scores but weighted them differently, resulting in a different set of final grades. In thinking about ways to calculate a student's final evaluative grade, let's consider the following vignette:

Julio is a student in Mr. Lieb's second period grade 7 mathematics class. He is an intelligent student who catches on to mathematical concepts quite easily. In the first quarter of the school year, Julio earned a solid B average (89 percent) on his tests and quizzes. However, because the mathematics comes easily to him, and he spends a great deal of time watching television, Julio turned in only half of his homework (50 percent) for the quarter. Mr. Lieb firmly believes that tests, quizzes, and homework alone should determine a student's grade, but he has been quoted as saying, "The most important parts are the tests and quizzes; if they can't show me how to do it on a test, they don't understand the material." Consequently, he weighs tests and quizzes as 90 percent of the grade and homework as 10 percent of the final grade. At the end of the quarter, he determines Julio's grade as follows:

$$90\%(89\%) + 10\%(50\%) = 85\%$$

In the school district, there is a prescribed grading scale, a common occurrence in many districts in the United States:

100%–93%	A
92%–85%	B
84%–77%	C
76%–70%	D
<69%	F

Because of the result of the calculation (85 percent) and the required grading scale, Mr. Lieb gives Julio a B for the first quarter.

Across the hall, Ms. Ward is teaching a seventh grader by the name of Ashleigh. Like Julio, Ashleigh does well on tests but generally forgets to do her homework assignments and rushes to finish them on the bus in the morning when she can. Coincidentally, she also averages 89 percent for tests and quizzes and has done 50 percent of her homework in the first quarter. However, Ms. Ward believes that homework is a sign of motivation, character, and disposition, and she weighs it as one-third of a student's final grade, whereas tests and quizzes account for the other two-thirds. At the end of the quarter, Ms. Ward does the following calculation:

$$\tfrac{2}{3}(89\%) + \tfrac{1}{3}(50\%) = 76\%$$

Using the scale required by the district, Ms. Ward gives Ashleigh a D for the first quarter because her average fell in the range of 70 percent to 76 percent.

Imagine how Julio and Ashleigh will feel at lunch when they discover that they both had an 89 percent test and quiz average and did half of their homework in mathematics, but Julio received a final grade of a B, and Ashleigh got a D in the same course. Because schools often use a generalized grading scale but seldom require a particular system of arriving at the numerical averages, these differences occur all the time. Which final grade do *you* believe is the most reasonable? The answer probably lies in what you value as a teacher. If you, like Mr. Lieb, believe that competencies measured by tests and quizzes tell most of the story, then you might be inclined to give the student a B. If, however, you want to reward students for doing homework and punish those who don't, you might find Ms. Ward's grade of a D more reasonable. But think about it—without knowing the students or their teachers, how do you feel about a student who maintains a high B average on tests and quizzes but does homework only half of the time? Is it reasonable to assume that this student should, at least, receive a C in the course? Or is Ms. Ward's grade of a D acceptable? This scenario paints a very realistic picture in terms of how students are assessed in school mathematics: Final grades are essentially arbitrary. *The final grades often depend more on the values and beliefs of the teacher than on the performance of the student.*

This story also holds another moral for us as we look at ways of determining student grades: Perhaps the example serves as a case for why more diverse assessment tools than tests, quizzes, and homework are necessary in determining a student's final grade. For example, if these students were required to write in journals twice a week and keep portfolios, we might discover that Ashleigh eloquently expresses herself in journal writing and portfolio reflections, but Julio does not, and we would obtain a further window into student thinking that allows us to more adequately evaluate their performance in a final grade.

Let's imagine, for example, that Ms. Ward agrees that her current system of determining grades is inadequate; all dimensions of student learning are not accounted for when only tests, quizzes, and homework are used. She has decided to have students write in mathematics journals twice a week and to collect, read, and react to the journal entries every 2 weeks. She has also decided to assign a team project each grading period. Finally, she will ask an open-ended question every Wednesday and score it on a holistic rubric to give students experiences with solving problems and defending their thinking. She has added these three assessment tools to gain a deeper understanding of how her students develop. The journal entries will allow students to express their thinking in writing and bring Ms. Ward more in touch with their opinions and learning styles. The projects will promote interpersonal communication and demonstrate for students that real mathematics problems are not always clearly defined or easily solved. The open-ended questions will give students practice in defending answers and communicating clearly and will serve as practice for state-level testing that includes free-response questions.

The journal entries can be scored as complete or incomplete or can be placed on a simple rubric. For example, a rubric from 2 to 0 could be used as follows:

2 – a journal entry has been completed, contains clear written communication, and illustrates depth and insight

1 – a journal entry has been completed but may be vague or entail surface-level thinking without the depth that was expected

0 – the journal entry was incomplete or not turned in at all

Because a grading period is 10 weeks, Ms. Ward will have collected the journals five times over that quarter. A student earning 8 to 10 total rubric points receives an A for journal writing, a total of 6 or 7 points earns a B, 4 or 5 points earns a C, 2 or 3 points is a D, and 0 through 2 points is an F. By using this type of conversion scale, the rubric points can be translated into more traditional percentage-type scores used in a final grade. Keep in mind, as was pointed out in Chapter 10, that rubric points should not be thought of as percentages. A score of a 1 on a journal does not indicate 1 out of 2 or 50 percent. A 1 simply places a journal entry in a category so that the teacher and student have an indicator of the quality of that particular journal entry.

Similarly, the open-ended questions could be scored on a 5-point rubric. Because a weekly question is to be given for 10 weeks, the students could earn up to 50 rubric points. Through experience, Ms. Ward can determine how many points out of 50 the student needs to accumulate to earn an A, a B, and so forth. The project grades can be based on a 100-point scale that includes data collection, a written report, and a classroom presentation. In this way, each of the areas in which she is assessing her students' progress can be quantified so that a letter or percentage grade—which is required by her district—can be determined.

The final grading scheme in terms of weight for each of the grade's components depends on what the teacher values. For example, the final grade could be determined as follows:

30%	Tests
15%	Quizzes
15%	Project
10%	Open-ended questions
10%	Journals
20%	Homework

Using this grading scale, Ms. Ward preserves a relatively heavy weighting for homework but builds in several other "pieces" that show the total progress of the student. With the new assessment system containing all of these additional assessments, Ashleigh's first quarter grade may be more likely to reflect her total performance in the class. Let's take a closer look at how her grade might be determined.

Suppose that Ashleigh's test average was 85 percent, and her quiz average was 95 percent for the first quarter. She also conducted a project on which she earned 80 points out of 100—an 80 percent. We already know that she completed 50 percent of her homework assignments for the grading period. The class was given 10 open-ended questions during the term, and each question was scored on a 5-point rubric. Based on previous experience with using rubrics to assess student work, Ms. Ward converted rubric scores into percentages by applying the following scale:

50–45 rubric points	→	A work	→	use 95% as the numerical score
44–35 rubric points	→	B work	→	use 88% as the numerical score
34–25 rubric points	→	C work	→	use 81% as the numerical score
24–15 rubric points	→	D work	→	use 73% as the numerical score
14–5 rubric points	→	F work	→	use 60% as the numerical score

She has never had a student earn fewer than 10 total rubric points for the quarter.

Suppose that Ashleigh accumulated a total of 32 rubric points. Using Ms. Ward's scale, she would receive a grade of a C or 81 percent for open-ended questions. Finally, student journals were collected five times, and Ms. Ward used the following conversion scale for journal grades:

10–8 total journal rubric points	→	A work	→	assign a score of 95%
7–6 total journal rubric points	→	B work	→	assign a score of 88%
5–4 total journal rubric points	→	C work	→	assign a score of 81%
3–2 total journal rubric points	→	D work	→	assign a score of 73%

Ms. Ward has never had a student earn less than 3 journal rubric points in a quarter.

For the first quarter, Ashleigh earned 6 total rubric points, so she is assigned a grade of 88 percent for journals. Therefore, all of the collected data can be used to determine her grade.

Tests:	30%(85%) = .255
Quizzes:	15%(95%) = .1425
Project:	15%(80%) = .12
Open-ended questions:	10%(81%) = .081
Journals:	10%(88%) = .088
Homework:	20%(50%) = .10

So, her grade can be calculated by finding $0.255 + 0.1425 + 0.12 + 0.081 + 0.088 + 0.10 = 0.7865$, which rounds to 79 percent and is a C on the school's grading scale. Contrast this grade to the original situation in which Julio received a B and Ashleigh earned a D when only test and quiz scores, along with homework assignments, were used in the assessment process. We might claim that Ms. Ward's revised grading system results in a fair and realistic assessment of Ashleigh's performance for the first quarter.

However, we need to be careful about assuming that this grading practice will water down grades. Some people automatically assume that if tests and quizzes count for a smaller fraction of the grade, the students will earn higher percentages in the class, and this will cause an inflation of grades. But some students are good test takers and would much rather have grades based on exam performance than have to complete projects and write in journals. In fact, many students who have been historically successful with tests and quizzes as performance indicators may earn considerably lower grades on this scale because they may not be as proficient at expressing their thoughts in writing and defending solutions. However, students who perform well in a team setting and appreciate the forum in which to discuss thoughts about the class may see their grades enhanced by the same system.

In the end, no grading system, per se, is perfect. In an attempt to meet the six criteria set forth in the Assessment Standards and the Assessment Principle, it is important to vary the assessment strategies. But how many strategies are ideal? Is it reasonable to assume that if observations are being used, formal interviews may not be necessary? If students are regularly answering open-ended questions, are quizzes necessary at all? These are decisions that each teacher has to make: No answers universally apply to all classrooms. The most important issue to consider is that once a grading system has been devised, the teacher needs to ask, "How well will I get to know the development of each of my students by using this approach?" If the system appears to maximize the teacher's window into each student's thinking, then it's probably on the right track. In the end, the values of the teacher will significantly affect the selection of assessment strategies, as well as the relative weighting of the components that comprise the final grade in a class. Julio and Ashleigh may earn final grades that are a letter grade or two higher or lower than they have earned under their current systems because of the use of other strategies for assessing their progress.

Conclusion

Equity and assessment have become focal points in mathematics education reform over the past couple of decades. The notions that every student should have equal access to important mathematics and that teachers need to provide a variety of assessment opportunities so that each student can demonstrate an understanding of the mathematics have become important to the reform process. However, research (Senk, Beckmann, & Thompson, 1997) shows that secondary teachers still rely heavily on tests, quizzes, and homework to assess student progress and that most test items tend to be low level and are not open ended. Another study by Garet and Mills (1995) suggested that assessment practices are still dominated by short-answer and multiple-choice tests and that there has been little change in the use of these techniques over time despite the recommendations of professional organizations and the availability of assessment ideas in mathematics education literature. So, although standards have been set to suggest changes in assessment strategies, many teachers are still comfortable with the old ways of collecting data on student progress and assigning grades. But why has it been so difficult to get mathematics teachers to alter their practices?

Research by Cooney, Badger, and Wilson (1993) suggests that teachers will use a variety of strategies to determine student progress only under three conditions: (1) The assessment tasks must be consistent with the teacher's own understanding of what it means to do mathematics, (2) the teachers must see the value of the tasks in determining student understandings of mathematics, and (3) teachers must believe that the outcomes these alternative assessment strategies measure are important. If mathematics is viewed as nothing more than a list of discrete, measurable skills to be learned over time, it is difficult to be convinced of the value of students writing in a journal or keeping a portfolio. And teachers who do not appreciate the value of communication in the mathematics classroom probably will not use team projects in a class. So, as we have previously stated, the assessment strategies that you choose will reflect what you believe about the nature of mathematics and what you think is important in your classroom. And students will pick up on your values and often make them their own. In the end, the assessment system we choose in our mathematics classroom and the way that we determine grades will teach students important lessons about the very nature of the subject area.

Keep in mind that any assessment is merely a snapshot of student performance on a particular topic on a certain day. Perhaps you have had the experience of looking at a picture of yourself and saying, "That's not *me*," demanding a retake wearing different clothes or looking in another direction. The same situation arises with assessment. It is only after taking several "pictures" from different angles that we can piece them together to get a holistic look at how students are performing. No single photograph—in fact, no single assessment strategy—can tell the entire story. As you conduct your classes, you will find that some strategies work better for you than others, and you are likely to change your thinking and refine your teaching practices. Just because you used a particular system in the past year doesn't mean that you have to feel committed to using it the following year. In fact, many teachers modify their assessment practices by trying one new technique each year and reflecting on whether they will adopt it and use it on a continuing basis. One of the many reasons for using multiple assessment strategies is to achieve

For bibliographic references and additional resources, see page 417

equity so that the needs of all students are addressed. In the next chapter, we explore the complex issue of meeting the needs of all students in the mathematics classroom. We discuss issues such as diversity (e.g., cultural and gender differences), students with special needs, and teaching practices that promote equity.

Glossary

Equity: Equity is the assumption that all students have a right to equal access to the study of mathematics. The term *all students* refers to students of various ethnocultural and socioeconomic backgrounds as well as students who are female and male. Equity is a key issue in the assessment process, as teachers look for ways to provide each student with an opportunity to demonstrate understanding of mathematical concepts.

Inference: An inference is a conclusion that is based on the collection and analysis of evidence or data. For example, in statistics, we might look at the value of a correlation coefficient and infer that two variables are

related, such as the performance of a student on the SAT and that student's eventual college grade point average. Similarly, when teachers collect assessment data, they make inferences about the progress that their students are making in terms of academic achievement and attitude development.

Short-Cycle Assessment: Collection of formative assessment data on a regular basis to inform instruction is often referred to as short-cycle assessment. Short-cycle assessments are often conducted daily, such as through the use of journals or checklists.

Discussion Questions and Activities

1. Obtain a syllabus from a secondary or middle school mathematics class that includes a description of how students are assessed. Using the six assessment standards as the criteria, critique the strengths and weaknesses of the assessment system for the course.

2. Identify a state that has a statewide assessment, such as a proficiency test or a graduation test that must be passed for a student to receive a diploma. Explore how the testing is conducted, and discuss the degree to which the statewide test addresses the six assessment standards. Consider questions such as the following: Does the test measure important mathematics? Is it equitable? Has the state been open regarding content and scoring of the test? Is it reasonable to assume that only students who can pass the test deserve to graduate?

3. Select a mathematical topic, such as constructing and interpreting circle graphs, and devise three assessment alternatives from which students could choose to demonstrate their understanding of the concept.

4. What is a reasonable amount of time for a secondary or middle school student to spend on a homework assignment each evening? How can you determine whether you are assigning too much or not enough

homework and whether the assignments are actually beneficial for the students in your class?

5. In the chapter, five methods of checking homework assignments were described and critiqued. Which methods appear to be the most desirable for you and why would you select them over the others? Small groups could each select a favorite and then compare their thinking with that of other groups.

6. Four methods of using homework assignments to contribute to final grades were discussed, and two other methods were mentioned in this chapter. In small groups, discuss which methods appear to be the most desirable, and why you would select them over the others.

7. Obtain an examination copy of a software package designed to serve as a grade book, or visit a teacher who currently uses such a program. What are some of the benefits of using this type of software to electronically record and manage student grades? What are some potential drawbacks to using this program rather than simply keeping a paper grade book?

8. The cases of Julio and Ashleigh were described in this chapter. Julio and Ashleigh are seventh grade students who are both carrying an 89 percent test

and quiz average but have completed only half of their homework assignments for the grading period. What final grade do you believe that they deserve in mathematics? Be prepared to defend your answer in terms of fairness to these students and the rest of the class.

9. Design a system for determining final grades in your class; include any categories of evidence that you wish and their weighing as percentages. Explain how the system is fair, equitable, and meets the cri-

teria in the Assessment Standards and the Assessment Principle.

10. Teachers devise their assessment systems based on their beliefs about the nature of mathematics and what they value in the classroom. What do you value in the teaching and learning of mathematics, and how are your values demonstrated in your plan for determining final grades for students in your classes?

Meeting the Needs of All Students

The secondary and middle school teachers from three fairly large school districts gathered for a joint professional development workshop after the first 2 weeks of their school year. The mathematics teachers began their meeting by gathering in a circle and describing their classroom situations to their peers. The following statements were compiled as the teachers shared experiences with one another, and the comments are typical of what teachers observe in their classes as they open a new school year:

- "I have a homeroom this year with 17 students. Of the 17, seven of them are on IEPs (individualized education programs), and ten of them are on some type of medication for behavior modification. Some of the students on medication are the ones on IEPs, but others are not."

- "One of my math classes this year has 21 females and only 3 male students. I'm trying to figure out how to meet the needs of a primarily female population while not ignoring the boys in my class. I'm sure that I can't do the same thing I always do when the class is about half male and half female."

- "I have one student in an Algebra II class who is legally blind. He has to be seated in the front row in my classroom, and anytime I give the class a handout, worksheet, or written test, I am required to modify his sheets by expanding them to 200 percent of their original size on the copy machine."

- "I have two first-year students in my high school class who just moved to the United States, one from Japan and one from India. Neither one of them can speak more than a few words of English. I know that they are working hard to learn English, but their parents are hopeful that their mathematics class will be one place where they can overcome the language barrier."

- "One of the boys in my class is extremely gifted in mathematics. The counselor has already contacted me and told me that the student will be meeting with a special education tutor once a week. I am to work with that tutor to help generate problems and projects that will adequately challenge this student who functions well beyond anyone else in his class."

- "Our building was redistricted during the summer, and we're now being fed by an area of town that is mainly African American. Last year, more than 90 percent of my students were Caucasians, and this year, almost 75 percent are African Americans. I have to believe that the difference in their cultural backgrounds will challenge me to teach in different ways than I have in the past."

- "There is one girl in my Calculus class this year who has a severe auditory disability. She wears a special headset, and I wear a portable clip-on microphone when she is in my class. I also try to face her whenever I am speaking so that she can see my lips to help her understand directions."

- "Because of budget cuts, our school dropped its honors program last year. So, this year, there is no ability grouping of students whatsoever. In each of my classes, there is a range of students that spans from students who are learning disabled all the way to those who are gifted, with everything in between. With class sizes of 25 to 30 students, I simply don't know if I'll ever be able to reach all of them, given the diversity of their needs."

The situations described in these comments are very familiar to seasoned veteran teachers; the statements highlight the challenges of teaching diverse populations of students. In an ideal world, class sizes are small, students are all eager to learn, and the ability and motivation levels of all of the students in each class are identical. But this "ideal world" does not exist, so teachers are constantly searching for ways to best meet the needs of students in what often can be difficult situations. Unfortunately, there is no prescription for success that works in all classrooms. Instead, educators use ingenuity, supported by ideas that have proven effective with others, in an attempt to find solutions to their classroom challenges.

In Chapter 3, in the discussions of learning theories, we emphasized that no two students think exactly alike and that their individual needs vary. However, the NCTM standards have emphasized that mathematics should be accessible to *all* students, so a fundamental responsibility of the teacher is to seek ways to engage all students in the learning process. In this chapter, we address the issues of meeting the needs of all students. We examine several specific diversity concerns, such as dealing with students with special needs, as well as situations involving gender and cultural differences. Finally, we take a general look at examples of strategies that teachers can use in the classroom to address these diverse needs.

Defining and Achieving Equity

As we discussed in Chapter 11, *equity* in mathematics is the assumption that all students have a right to equally access all areas of the curriculum as well as access high-quality instructional materials and teaching. In *Mathematics Teaching Today* (NCTM, 2007), the NCTM specifies that *all students* refers to:

- students who have been denied access in any way to educational opportunities as well as those who have not;
- students who are African Americans, Hispanics/Latinos, Native Americans, Alaskan Natives, Pacific Islanders, Asian Americans, First Nations people, and other minorities, as well as those who are considered to be a part of the majority;
- students who are female as well as those who are male;
- students who are from any socioeconomic background;
- students who are native English speakers and those who are not native English speakers;
- students with disabilities and those without disabilities; and
- students who have not been successful in school and in mathematics as well as those who have been successful. (pp. 7–8)

Therefore, any policy, curriculum, or classroom practice that limits access to an area of content to particular groups of students is seen as inequitable. An example of inequity was described in Chapter 4 when we looked at how some students can be "tracked" in such a way that they study nothing more than number-based arithmetic all the way through high school, whereas their peers take entire courses in algebra and geometry, and sometimes in statistics or discrete mathematics. In an attempt to address the issue of equity, many school districts have adopted core curricula or an integrated mathematics sequence to ensure that every student in that district has equal access to mathematics that spans the NCTM content standards or domains of the Common Core State Standards.

If all students were truly gaining equal access to the mathematics curriculum, to adequate instructional materials, and to quality classrooms and teaching, we might expect the research on student achievement and career trends to reflect consistency across gender, race, and ethnicity. But this has not historically been the case. Research has shown that males outperform females in mathematics achievement and that this might be explained, in part, because males are more likely to take upper-level secondary mathematics courses, such as probability and statistics, than are their female peers (see Leder, 1992, for details). Although more recent research indicates that females are taking more mathematics courses, career statistics show, for example, that only 9 percent of all engineers are female (NSF, 1994). Similarly, Caucasian students tend to outperform their Hispanic and African American peers. Malloy (1997) argued that African American students may learn differently than their white counterparts and that mathematics educators have not historically addressed these learning differences. She asserted that "mathematics educators have little knowledge of how African American students perceive themselves as mathematics students, how they approach mathematics, or the role of culture in their perception and mathematics performance" (p. 23). These learning differences, in turn, may account for some of the differences in performance. Certainly, the lack of financial resources in inner-city settings has contributed to a lack of equal access of all students to quality mathematics education as well.

In *Principles and Standards for School Mathematics* (NCTM, 2000), one of the six principles dealt with equity. In the equity principle, the authors of the document stated that "equity does not mean that every student should receive identical instruction; instead, it demands that reasonable and appropriate accommodations be made as needed to promote access and attainment for all students" (p. 12). The authors point out that students who live in low-income areas, as well as students who are female, nonwhite, and possessing disabilities, have historically been "victims of low expectations" (p. 13). The standards serve as a reminder that students are best served when the "bar is raised high" so that teachers adequately challenge all in their classes. The equity principle concludes with the following remarks:

> Achieving equity requires a significant allocation of human and material resources in schools and classrooms. Instructional tools, curriculum materials, special supplementary programs, and the skillful use of community resources undoubtedly play important roles. An even more important component is the professional development of teachers. Teachers need help to understand the strengths and needs of students who come from diverse linguistic and cultural backgrounds, who have specific disabilities, or who possess a special talent and interest in mathematics. To accommodate differences among students effectively and sensitively, teachers also need to understand and confront their own beliefs and biases. (NCTM, 2000, p. 14)

Let's examine some of the strategies that teachers can use to address the needs of all students. We begin with a discussion of teaching students with special needs—both those with learning disabilities and those who are gifted in mathematics.

Students with Special Needs

Mrs. Ruetz teaches a pre-algebra course in her school. In the class, students explore basic number concepts, ratio and proportion, coordinate graphing, and other concepts that prepare students for a course in algebra. One of the topics in her class is working with integers—operations with positive and negative numbers. In her class, she has two students who are on IEPs. **IEP** is an acronym for individualized education program. A student with learning disabilities typically has an IEP that describes the nature of the disability, provides a statement of how the disability affects classroom performance, provides short- and long-term goals for the student, and provides a plan for modifications or accommodations that will be needed for the student to be successful (Concord SPED PAC, 2003). Greenes, Garfunkel, and DeBussey (1994) noted that "it should be clear that the IEP is not just an 'educational plan' that well-meaning and skilled teachers develop and put into place in order to facilitate their teaching and the learning of their students. The IEP must specify objectives, goals, and time schedules for achieving them" (p. 119). At various times during the school year, IEP meetings involving teachers, parents, and other school personnel are held to review the plan and to make adjustments.

Through these meetings, Mrs. Ruetz has learned that her students with special needs tend to require hands-on experiences with physical materials to make sense of mathematical concepts. She was not surprised by this, however, because she recognizes that most students react positively to interactions with manipulatives as tools to generate classroom discourse. In the lesson, she provides each student with a collection of **two-color counters**—counters that are yellow on one side and red on the other. She explains to the class that the yellow side represents a positive number, whereas the red side represents a negative number. (Some teachers use lima beans, spray painting one side red and leaving the other side white.) One essential rule that she describes is the "rule of zero," which means that any time a yellow counter is combined with a red counter, they neutralize one another, and the result is 0. She models $(3) + (-3)$ on the overhead projector by using three yellow counting chips and three red chips. As they are combined in pairs, the result is 0.

For her next example, she models $(-6) + (2)$. The counters are placed on the overhead in the arrangement shown in Figure 12.1.

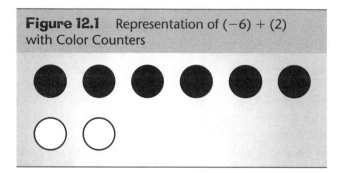

Figure 12.1 Representation of $(-6) + (2)$ with Color Counters

Using this model, students see six red counters in a row, with two yellow counters below them. Because the first two red counters cancel with the two yellow counters, the result is four red counters left in the display, so the solution is -4. Students are given similar examples of addition problems and asked to model them with counters at their desks.

After Mrs. Ruetz is fairly confident that the students can model addition problems with their counters, she asks the class to find the solution to $(-5) - (-2)$. First, students represent -5 with red counters, as shown in Figure 12.2.

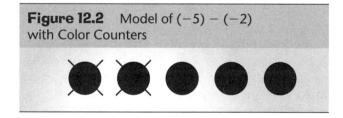

Figure 12.2 Model of $(-5) - (-2)$ with Color Counters

Because subtraction can be modeled as "taking away," students determine that they can simply remove two of the five red counters to model "take away -2," leaving them with three red counters (as shown in Figure 12.2 with Xs over two of the counters). Therefore, the answer to the question is -3. At this point, one of the students with special needs—Heather—raises her hand and asks, "But what if you have to take away more than you have? Like -3 minus -5?"

In response, Mrs. Ruetz asks her students to model -3 with three red counters. Of course, we are trying to "take away" five of them, but there are only three to remove. She asks the class, "What more do you *want* to have up here?" Heather replies, "Another -2." By placing an additional two red and two yellow counters on the overhead, as shown in Figure 12.3, "zero" has been added to the problem, so there are now enough red counters to remove five.

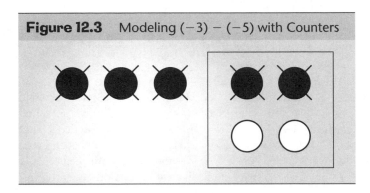

Figure 12.3 Modeling $(-3) - (-5)$ with Counters

When the two pairs of yellow and red counters were introduced, they did not change the value of the collection (because each pair was a "neutralized" zero). So, when the five red counters were removed, the two yellow counters remained. Consequently, students had the physical evidence that $(-3) - (-5) = +2$.

In this example, a pre-algebra teacher has used two-color counters to bring a physical and visual meaning to what is for many students the very abstract notion of operating with positive and negative numbers. Notice that students were able to explore a variety of addition and subtraction problems without the teacher ever introducing standard rules, such as "change the subtraction to addition and change the sign of the next number"—rules that are not only difficult for many students to remember but also fail to promote an understanding of *why* they work. In fact, research suggests that students with disabilities tend to achieve higher in mathematics when the problems are meaningful and suggests that students' difficulties often are the result of teachers not emphasizing the meaning of mathematical procedures (Cawley, 2002; Wright, 1996).

The teacher chose this physical model specifically to address the needs of special education students in her classroom because research supports the fact that students with disabilities should be encouraged to visualize problems that they solve by, for example, drawing pictures of the situation (Montague, Applegate, & Marquard, 1993). However, we know from Bruner's theory (explained in Chapter 3) that when students have an initial concrete experience, they can build on the example by eventually drawing pictures and then abstracting the process with numbers on a page. So, what could be considered a modification for a student with a learning disability may well be a strategy that is appropriate for other students, if not an entire class. Of course, at other times, a student who possesses a particular disability may require an entirely different approach from the rest of the class.

In November 1975, the U.S. Congress passed Public Law 94-142, now referred to as the Individuals with Disabilities Education Act (IDEA), and reauthorized it in 1997. IDEA was established to ensure that children with disabilities would have access to a free public education that provides the services necessary to meet their individual needs. As a result, many students with special needs are now placed in regular classrooms, with support services available—an educational practice known as **inclusion**. Sometimes, the student is "pulled out" from this regular classroom for individual tutoring—a practice that provides individual assistance to students but also has a tendency to undermine efforts to get them to share thinking strategies with peers in a classroom (Baxter, Woodward, Voorhies, & Wong, 2002). In other cases, a special education teacher or an aide is present in the classroom to assist with teaching the lesson. Slightly more than 13 percent of the student population in U.S. public schools has an identified learning disability (U.S. Department of Education, 2010). Since 1984, there has been a steady increase in the percentage of students with disabilities

How Would You React

S C E N A R I O

You believe firmly in the use of cooperative learning and seat your students in tables of four in your classroom. In an attempt to promote equity, you place two male and two female students at each table, as well as seat your special education students who are on IEPs at tables with regular education students. But you feel a great deal of pressure because the students repeatedly ask to sit with their friends, and parents of some of your stronger students are concerned that their children's energies are being spent "teaching" others in the group rather than learning new things. Your response is

a. Try to ignore the feedback from students and their parents and continue to diversify your learning groups.
b. Allow friends and students of similar ability levels to work together from time to time, but maintain diversity in the groups at other times.
c. Take the advice of the students and their parents and allow students to form their own groups so they are comfortable with the others with whom they work.
d. Given the diversity in your classroom, discontinue the use of learning groups and emphasize more individualized work.
e. Other.

D I S C U S S I O N

The use of cooperative learning is an excellent way to promote diversity in a mathematics classroom. Teachers can prearrange students into groups that give the students experiences working with the opposite gender as well as working with students who do not necessarily have the same abilities. Anyone who has taught others knows that it takes a high level of understanding of a concept to help someone else make sense of an idea. So, even the highest-achieving students in a class can be challenged by working with other students in a team.

The concern expressed by students and their parents in this scenario is very common. Students tend to get upset when they are not seated with their friends and people who think like they do. Consequently, it is easy for a teacher to give in to this pressure and abandon a grouping strategy that makes sense. Students need to be reminded that in many situations throughout their lives—from the ballpark to the boardroom—they will be expected to cooperate and function with other people, including people with whom they would rather not work. Diversity in designing cooperative learning groups not only helps students to learn mathematics but it also develops a life skill of compromising and dealing with other personalities.

It is generally not advisable to allow students to choose their own teammates in a classroom setting. Not only does this practice have ramifications in maintaining classroom discipline but it also promotes the idea that people should only work with those who are "like" themselves. The idea of inclusion for special education students is that individuals who are on IEPs have much to gain from solving problems with their regular education peers, and the other students benefit from the unique perspectives brought to a classroom by the special education students. Research supports the fact that high-achieving students often benefit from working with one another (see Chapter 3). As a result, a teacher may want to form groups with some of the best students from time to time for a particular unit, as described in the core curriculum model in Chapter 4. During that same school year, however, those students should also be mixed with their peers who function at different levels to ensure diversity. Moving students from one type of group to another is referred to as *flexible grouping* and can provide the students with a variety of experiences throughout the school year.

attending regular schools and being included in regular classrooms (U.S. Department of Education, 2001). As a result, almost all teachers have included special education students in their classrooms (LDEA, 2007). However, a report by the U.S. Department of Education showed that only about half of the teachers who have students with learning disabilities in their general education classes receive any consultation from special education teachers or staff members as to how to address the needs of those students in their classes (Wagner et al., 2003). Consequently, it is important for a teacher to be aware of the disabilities of special education students in an included classroom, as well as to have some specific strategies to help meet their needs.

A central philosophy with inclusion is that it is important for special education students to experience the same lessons and classroom environments as their peers. In fact, studies suggest that when students with learning disabilities are included in regular classrooms, they benefit from the experience, provided that the teacher has adapted lessons and assessments to their needs (Salend, 1994). However, in the process of teaching in an included classroom, the mathematics teacher generally has the responsibility of attending IEP meetings and making modifications or accommodations in the classroom to meet the needs of the students, such as the following:

- If a student is hard of hearing, the teacher may need to wear a special portable microphone so that the voice can be amplified. Also, the teacher will need to directly face the student when talking one on one so that the student can read the teacher's lips.

- If a student has a visual impairment, the teacher may have a camera in the room that the student can use to read notes from a chalkboard or overhead by zooming in on the pictures or writing. Also, the teacher may be expected to enlarge classroom handouts or test materials for the student.

- If a student has a reading or writing disability, the teacher may be required by the IEP to either read test questions aloud or to send the student to a tutor who can administer the items of the written test by way of an interview. In this case, interviews between the teacher and the student may also replace a written journal that is being used as an assessment tool for the rest of the class.

- If a student has an identified reading, writing, or mathematical disability, the student likely will have special accommodations when taking standardized tests, such as graduation or proficiency tests. In some cases, students are given extra time to complete the tests or frequent breaks in the testing process. In other situations, the tests may be read, may key in on a limited number of concepts, may require being completed in a setting outside the classroom, or the student may be exempted from taking the tests altogether.

- If a student has a severe behavioral disability, the student will benefit from active, hands-on lesson experiences and needs regular affirmation and praise from the teacher for accomplishments. Very specific directions for proper behavior when working in groups can help the student to interact in an acceptable manner with peers.

- If a student's disability makes it difficult to complete regular classwork or homework, assignments may be modified, including the teacher providing alternative work, fewer or shorter assignments, advanced notices of deadlines, and even audio recordings of printed text (Thurlow, 2002).

- If a student needs additional help (or challenges) with problem solving, the teacher may need to select or recommend computer or graphing calculator software that can be used for the student to individually explore, practice, or analyze mathematical situations.

- If a student is gifted, as opposed to possessing a disability, the teacher may group that student with others who are most likely to challenge the student. Also, the level of content addressed may be differentiated, as described in the core curriculum models in Chapter 4.

There is a vast array of disabilities that a student may possess, including, but not limited to, problems with reading, doing arithmetic, processing language, visual-spatial difficulties, or some combination of these (Wright, 1996). Also, some of these disabilities are short-term difficulties, whereas other disabilities last a lifetime, such

Interactive software can help students use computers to pursue conjectures and to validate their thinking.

as hearing impairments. *Windows of Opportunity: Mathematics for Students with Special Needs* (Thornton & Bley, 1994) was published by the NCTM and addresses this complex issue in detail. One of the book's editors noted that students with special needs are more "like" their peers than different and encouraged teachers to "help [special education students] to help themselves so they become as independent as possible" (Bley, 1994, p. 138). Books such as this, as well as professional development workshops on inclusion, are recommended for regular education teachers who inevitably will face the challenge of addressing the needs of these students in their classes. In the next section, we discuss the effects of gender differences on the teacher and learning of mathematics.

Gender

A guidance counselor helping a high school junior plan her class schedule for the following year recommended, "Don't worry about taking any math classes next year. You're a young woman, and you plan to go into nursing, so you won't need pre-calculus anyway." Similarly, a male mathematics teacher in a middle school announced that one of the females in the class had earned the highest grade on a project and proceeded to say that the "guys in this class should be ashamed of yourselves, allowing a *girl* to outperform you!" Sadly, both of these stories are true, and the messages sent to students are misleading and are likely to have long-term negative effects on students' beliefs about the nature of mathematics. Nursing students are generally required to take mathematics in college, as are students in almost all fields of study. And the middle school girl should have received praise for her performance, instead of having her grade used as a tool to "motivate" the boys.

Teachers frequently engage in conversations about the differences between the way that males and females learn and how they perform in the classroom. Some of these differences are perceived but not based on research, whereas other differences are very real. Since the 1970s, there has been an effort to reduce gender-related inequities and to mend the "gender gap." Here are a few examples of gender differences that have been documented with research:

- Both males and females at the twelfth grade level scored significantly higher on the NAEP mathematics test in 2009 than in 2005, but in both years, males outscored females (Nation's Report Card, 2011). And while average scores for males and females did not change significantly between 2007 and 2009 at fourth and eighth grades, males performed slightly higher than females at both levels (NCES, 2009).
- According to a report by the National Science Board (2006), there is not a significant difference in the high school course-taking mathematics patterns between males and females.
- Approximately two-thirds of eighth graders in 2000 were taking a regular eighth grade mathematics or a pre-algebra course, and this was true for both males and females (Braswell et al., 2001).
- Three out of five members of the National Honor Society are females, and more females than males take advanced placement courses (which is the opposite of the case in 1987) (Potrikus, 2003).

- Females spend more time on homework and less time watching television than their male peers (Potrikus, 2003).
- TIMSS results show that males and females in the fourth and eighth grades tended to perform at about the same level, but in 18 out of 21 countries studied, the males achieved significantly higher than their female peers in the senior year of high school (Mullis, Martin, Fierros, Goldberg, & Stemler, 2000).
- When males perform a task, they tend to attribute their successes or failures to their *ability* levels. However, females tend to attribute their performance levels to good or bad *luck* (Morris, 1995).
- In areas such as computer science, mathematics, and other science-related fields, women make up less than 15 percent of the scientists and engineers in the workforce (National Science Foundation, 1996).
- Traditional means of teaching mathematics generally are not compatible with the learning styles of most females (Becker & Jacobs, 2001).

Of course, this is only a sampling of what we know about gender differences. The major point here is that there *is* a difference between how males and females learn, attitudes that they hold, and careers that they tend to choose. Teachers of mathematics need to be sensitive to these differences and to conduct the teaching and learning process in such a way that equity between the genders is promoted. For example, the students who take the most and the highest-level mathematics courses tend to perform the best on standardized tests, such as the SAT. Consequently, male and female students alike should be encouraged to take higher-level mathematics courses. Also, as students take more-rigorous mathematics courses, the course work opens the doors to mathematics and science-related fields, such as medicine and engineering.

Similarly, students should have an opportunity to explore professions and the qualifications required for those jobs while still in middle or high school. One way to do this is to invite guest speakers to mathematics classes to describe their jobs and explain the role mathematics has in their day-to-day working situations. A female engineer speaking to a class can serve as an excellent role model to help girls recognize that even male-dominated careers are a possibility for them. Some teachers also assign career projects to mathematics students. In these projects, students are required to select a career area of interest and explore it in detail. As part of the project, the student is asked to carefully consider the mathematics requirements for the profession. As students make presentations to one another about the careers they explored, they learn about opportunities for their futures—opportunities that are open to *both* females *and* males. The following feature includes the details of such a career project that was assigned to students in a high school.

CAREER PROJECT

Rationale

Most individuals in the workforce would agree that there are very few professions that do not, in some way, require the use of mathematics. In fact, if we include "mathematical thinking" (i.e., "logical reasoning") and "problem solving" on the list of mathematical skills, then we could safely say that *every* job involves the use of mathematics. You are at a point in your life when you are carefully considering college and, ultimately, career options. As you think about the career you see yourself pursuing, it is important to think about the mathematics involved in the career. The purpose of this project is to get you to deeply explore your current career interest, including the college background required for the career and the skills you will be expected to possess in the workplace.

Requirements

You will research your career area and write a paper (approximately 3 to 5 pages) to be turned in on the due date. Also, you will be expected to make a 5-minute presentation to the class in which you briefly discuss your career area, how you gathered your information, and what you found out (the "highlights" of your paper). Your typewritten paper must include the following three sections:

The Profession

In this section, you describe the profession itself, including issues such as what a person does on the job, why you are interested in doing this job, what (or who) influenced you to have an interest in this area, the role that mathematics has in your career area, and the possibilities for advancement in this professional field.

College Requirements

In the second section, you will discuss the type of courses and/or experiences that will be required of you when studying this profession in college. Be sure to include specifics on the levels and content of mathematics courses that you will need to take, as well as other classes that seem to be required of most people in this career area. Is a bachelor's degree enough, or will your career area eventually require a master's and/or doctoral degree?

Reality of the Profession

After researching the profession on the Internet and conducting one or more interviews, you will begin to piece together a realistic view of this profession. In this section, you will address the details of the job, including items such as the number of hours per week a person typically devotes to this job, the working hours and conditions (e.g., nights and weekends, working days only, etc.), typical salary for a person in this profession, whether the job typically carries a high level of satisfaction (i.e., do most people in this career area seem to like what they're doing?), and so forth. Also consider the job market right now (i.e., is there a lot of competition for this job, or is it likely that you will get a job on college graduation?). Discuss what it would "really be like" to do this job.

Note: A bibliography must be included at the end of the paper, citing any Web sites, books, pamphlets, personal correspondence, or interviews used to gather your information. Use of formal rules for doing citations is not required.

Timeline

You have 5 weeks to complete this project. Do not wait until the last minute to begin your work—the project is intended to be completed a little at a time over several weeks. No excuses, such as "I was supposed to interview him on Friday, but he was sick," "I couldn't get on the Internet this weekend," or "my printer wouldn't work last night," will be accepted. Plan now to make sure all of the work is completed on time.

Assessment of the Project

This project will count the weight of 1.5 tests—150 points—toward your grade (this ends up being about 20 percent of your quarter grade). You will contract for the grade you intend to earn. Here are the contract requirements:

To earn a C (77–84 points, then multiplied by 1.5):

- Conduct enough Internet and/or book research to gather information about your profession to enable you to write the paper and make a presentation. At least two colleges must be contacted for information (by visiting their Web site and/or writing or calling their admissions offices).

- Interview one person in your career field, and include information from this interview in your paper. This could be a phone interview and may not be done with a parent or other close relative. In your paper, include the name of this person and a phone number where he or she can be contacted to verify the interview, if it would be necessary. (Parents can be asked for references of other people to interview, however.)
- Submit your paper with all three of the required sections and make an acceptable presentation to the class.

To earn a B (85–92 points, then multiplied by 1.5):

- Complete all of the required elements for a C.
- Interview a second person who works in your career area, comparing and contrasting his or her view of the profession with the other interview in your paper.
- Use *both* Internet *and* paper (books, journals, pamphlets, etc.) resources to gather your information and cite them in the bibliography.

To earn an A (93–100 points, then multiplied by 1.5):

- Complete all of the required elements for a B.
- Conduct an additional miniproject related to your profession and turn in the results of this work with your paper. This extra miniproject will require some creativity on your part. Some examples are as follows: If you were interested in a television broadcaster career, you could try your hand at being a newscaster by having "your" 10-minute news program videotaped and submitting the tape and its script with your paper. If you were interested in a career as an elementary school teacher, you could identify an elementary school student in need of help, tutor him or her, and write a 1-page reflection about your experience, submitting it with, perhaps, a photograph of you working with the child and/or a note from the child's parent, verifying that you did the tutoring. If you are thinking about a career as a pediatrician, you might identify a person in the field that you could "shadow" for a couple of hours on the job and submit a picture of yourself "on the job" with a short note/letter from the professional, verifying the time you were with him or her and a statement of what you did. Any type of tutoring, shadowing, and so on needs to be documented with a short note from the professional (or, you could write a note about what you did and have the person sign it and provide a phone number so that it can be verified).

Note: The final grade you earn will depend on the contract that you choose. The paper itself will be graded according to (1) meeting all of the requirements of the paper; (2) incorporation of the role of mathematics on the job in the paper; (3) punctuation, grammar, and neatness; and (4) effectiveness of your 5-minute class presentation on the highlights of your paper. A project that is late will have 10 points deducted for each day that it is late.

This is your opportunity to dig deeply into your intended profession and what it entails, including the mathematics of the job. Start early and enjoy the benefits of exploring. Good luck!

On a regular basis in the classroom, teachers can use other strategies that also promote gender equity. Because of females' tendency to attribute success in a class to "luck," the teacher can serve students well by affirming their performances and helping them build confidence that they are truly developing mathematical competence. Likewise, all students are verbal and social beings, and at the secondary and middle school levels, their needs are best served by providing cooperating learning settings that promote interaction among their peers. Research supports the fact that females prefer working with peers (rather than competing against them) and tend to achieve at higher levels in a collaborative environment (AAUW, 1992). Jacobs and Becker (1997) also emphasized that the promotion of gender equity depends on the use of writing in the mathematics curriculum (for students to clarify thinking and become independent thinkers) as well as building a classroom community in which students support one another.

Mathematics teachers need to be sensitive to gender differences and to plan lessons accordingly in order to promote equity. The idea that mathematics is for *all* students and that all career areas are accessible to both females and males is central to the way that the classroom environment is designed. For additional details and ideas on how to promote gender equity, the NCTM has published several resources, including *Changing the Faces of Mathematics: Perspectives on Gender* (Jacobs, Becker, & Gilmer, 2001), *Changing the Faces of Mathematics: Perspectives on Multiculturalism and Gender* (Secada, 2000), and the 1997 NCTM *Yearbook, Multicultural and Gender Equity in the Mathematics Classroom: The Gift of Diversity* (Belcher, Coates, Franco, & Mayfield-Ingram, 1997).

SPOTlight on Technology

Students in mathematics classes need experiences exploring problems and looking for patterns that result in generalizations. For example, as students solve integer problems with colored chips, they begin to realize that when two negative numbers are combined, the result must be negative "because you are simply adding up the total number of red counters." Through experience, they are able to generate their own sets of rules and properties. Likewise, the use of technology can help students explore various scenarios and note trends they see. If a teacher carefully structures an inquiry-based lesson, students can be led to significant conclusions. The following example is an exploration page designed by an algebra teacher for students exploring the shapes of parabolas and the characteristics of quadratic functions. The activity was designed to be conducted on a graphing calculator but could also be completed on a computer with graphing software. Notice how each question builds on the previous one and how mathematical understanding develops as a student completes the activity.

We have seen that the graph of the function $f(x) = x^2$ results in a U-shaped curve that we called a parabola. The purpose of this investigation is to use the graphing calculator to explore the effects of the values of a and c for the graph of the equation $f(x) = ax^2 + c$.

1. Turn on your calculator.
2. Press CLEAR.
3. Press WINDOW and set to:
   $Xmin = -20$
   $Xmax = 20$
   $Xscl = 5$
   $Ymin = -50$
   $Ymax = 50$
   $Yscl = 5$
   $Xres = 1$
4. Press Y = *key* and enter x^2
5. Press GRAPH to see your graph of $y = x^2$
   Draw a picture of what you see to the right:

6. Press Y = *CLEAR* and change the equation to $y = 3x^2$
   Draw a picture of what you see to the right:

7. Now, try $y = 5x^2$ and $y = 0.5x^2$
   Draw them on the same set of axes to the right:

8. Explain, below, what happens as the coefficient of x gets larger.
   What happens when it gets smaller?

9. What do you think will happen if the coefficient of x is a negative number?

10. Test your reasoning on question 9 by comparing the following graphs on your calculator:
    $Y_1 = x^2$ and $Y_2 = -1x^2$
    $Y_1 = 0.3x^2$ and $Y_2 = -0.2x^2$
    $Y_1 = 4x^2$ and $Y_2 = -4x^2$
    Was your prediction correct?

11. Look at the picture you drew for question 5. How would you predict that the graph from question 5 would change if you changed the equation to $y = x^2 + 20$?

    Try it on your calculator. Were you correct?

12. Draw a sketch of your prediction of what $y = x^2 - 15$ would look like.

    Try it on your calculator. Were you correct?

13. Now, let's put it together. Write a description of what you would expect this graph to look like: $y = 5x^2 + 12$.

Use your calculator to draw the graph. Were you correct?

14. Draw a picture of what you would expect this graph to look like: $y = \frac{1}{5}x^2 - 7$

Use your calculator to draw the graph. Were you correct?

15. Summarize what you have learned in this activity by completing the following statements:

When the coefficient of the x^2 term is positive, the graph. . .

When the coefficient of the x^2 term is negative, the graph. . .

When the coefficient of the x^2 term is a large number, it makes the graph. . . .

When the coefficient of the x^2 term is a small number, it makes the graph. . . .

When a constant is added, such as the $+3$ in $y = 2x^2 + 3$, this number tells us. . . .

Notice how these questions lead the students through an exploration of a variety of mathematical concepts, from quadratic functions to parabolas, parameter changes and their effects on graphs, reflections and translations, and making predictions, to name a few. With a graphing calculator (or a computer with graphing software), students can conduct much more in-depth explorations than can be accomplished by pencil-and-paper computations. Furthermore, exploratory activities such as these can motivate students by using visual cues to draw their own conclusions and "own" the mathematics by learning on a conceptual level.

Ethnic and Cultural Issues

Headlines in the newspaper and executive summaries of reports have echoed the same disturbing results for decades: Students of color and those from lower-socioeconomic settings tend to be taught by teachers who do not believe these students can succeed, and the students' achievement test scores are consistently lower than the scores of their Caucasian peers. For example, the 2000 NAEP results showed that at grades 4, 8, and 12, white students outperformed African American, Hispanic, and Native American students. Furthermore, although scores across all populations increased during the decade from 1990 to 2000, "the score gaps between white and black students, and between white and Hispanic students were large at every grade. There was no evidence in the 2000 assessment of any narrowing of the racial/ethnic group score gaps since 1990" (Braswell et al., 2001, p. xvi). Similarly, scores on the 2009 NAEP were higher at grades 4 and 8 for white students than for African American, Hispanic, or Native American students (NCES, 2009). Essentially, educators have known for decades that the curriculum and classroom settings cater primarily to the needs of middle- and upper-class white students, but we continue to see little progress in improving the situation for students of other colors and cultures.

In an article published by H. Richard Milner (2010) from Vanderbilt University, he discusses five factors or concepts that need to be addressed in teacher education programs in order to prepare teachers to understand diversity in the classroom, shown in Table 12.1.

TABLE 12.1 Milner's Five Concepts of Diversity
Color-Blindness
Cultural Conflict
Meritocracy
Deficit Conceptions
Expectations

Consideration of each of these concepts can help teachers to examine their beliefs about how to address diversity in a classroom. The first concept is *color-blindness*, in which he asserts that some teachers try so hard to avoid being considered biased or racist that they ignore the richness of diverse backgrounds when teaching. Instead, teachers need to recognize how different students experience the classroom and the world and capitalize on, rather than ignore the differences. The second concept is *culture conflicts*, which implies that some teachers believe it is important to get students to adapt to their way of organizing the classroom, rather than adapting lessons to meet the various needs of their students. The third factor is called the *myth of meritocracy* in which the teacher believes that everyone possesses the same opportunities and can be successful through hard work, rather than seeking to understand why some students do not pay attention in class or resist completing homework (often due to factors beyond effort, such as the student needing to work a full-time job to help support a family). The fourth concept is called *concept conceptions*, which means that some teachers tend to focus more on what students are lacking rather than what they can contribute to the classroom. In this case, teachers may, for example, give assignments that involve busy work to keep students quiet as a way to avoid allowing students to express their own ideas. Finally, the last concept is *low expectations* in which "teachers do not believe that culturally diverse students are capable of rigorous academic curriculum so they provide unchallenging learning opportunities in the classroom" (p. 127). At the heart of this last concept is the important question for all mathematics teachers to ask themselves: Do I truly believe that *every* student is capable of learning the content in my class?

In response to teachers' needs for more clearly understanding how to address ethnic and cultural differences and looking for ideas for their classrooms, the NCTM published an entire series of books directed toward educators. The series, called *Changing the Faces of Mathematics,* includes several volumes: *Perspectives on African Americans* (Secada, Strutchens, Johnson, & Tate, 2000), *Perspectives on Asian Americans and Pacific Islanders* (Edwards, 1999), *Perspectives on Gender* (Jacobs, Becker, & Gilmer, 2001), *Perspectives on Indigenous People of North America* (Hankes & Fast, 2002b), *Perspectives on Latinos* (Ortiz-Franco, Hernandez, & De La Cruz, 1999), and *Perspectives on Multiculturalism and Gender Equity* (Secada, 2000). Each book addresses the needs of an individual population of students and includes several articles written by experts in the field. The articles describe the students of each unique population and provide suggestions for teachers for changing classroom practices to promote equity.

In the book on indigenous populations, for example, one article describes the clear connections between the cultural beliefs of the Native American and the constructivist philosophy of teaching and learning (as described in Chapter 3). The authors point out that Native Americans prefer lessons that can be applied to their real lives and that the bonding of family members can be simulated through cooperative learning activities in the classroom—pedagogical strategies that are very familiar to the constructivist teacher (Hankes & Fast, 2002a). In another article, the authors present an example of a Rug Task that was designed for Navajo students, shown in Figure 12.4.

In this problem, students are challenged to connect mathematics to a skill with which they are very familiar—the skill of weaving a rug. Teachers extended the task by generating discussions on topics such as area and symmetry. The idea, of course, is to make the study of mathematics relevant and meaningful to the child by connecting activities to the life and culture of the community.

In the book on African American students, Strutchens (2000) described the issues confronting this population. Specifically, African American students are often placed in low-level mathematics classes and are taught by individuals who do not believe these students can achieve significant mathematical understanding— *low expectations* according to Milner (2010). Those teachers often are ill prepared to deal with the mathematical content and may lack an understanding of how African American students learn mathematics. This article provides a number of concrete suggestions for teachers, including the following:

- Focus on *conceptual* understanding.
- Let your students know that you *believe* they are capable of learning the mathematics.
- Use mathematics to explore issues related to race and ethnicity.
- Promote an atmosphere in the classroom in which students justify their thinking and challenge other students' responses.
- Develop partnerships with the parents of the students (e.g., newsletters or family math nights).

Figure 12.4 The Navajo Rug Task

Designing and Weaving a Rug

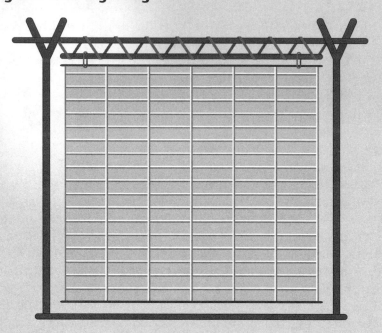

Instructions

You are spending the summer in the canyon with Grandmother. So that you can earn some money for new school clothes, Grandmother has offered to weave a rug for you to sell if you will create the design.

1. Design your rug in the grid on the following page [which shows a 5 × 7″ grid with $\frac{1}{4}$″ squares for the students to use in their work].
2. Grandmother says it will take her five minutes to weave each row. How many minutes will it take her to weave your rug? Count the number of rows and multiply by 5. [Some teachers eliminate this statement to make the task more appropriately demanding.] Show your work below.
3. A tourist to the canyon came through on a Jeep tour and stopped to watch Grandmother weave. She was so impressed with Grandmother's weaving that she asked Grandmother to weave her a rug using her favorite pattern. [A simple pattern involving four squares is shown.] Use the pattern to design a rug. Use only this pattern in as many ways as you want.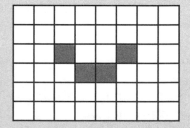
4. Color in the tourist's rug using two or three colors.

The Chinle rug task has three more parts that call on the student to make further calculations on the basis of the number of colors used and Grandmother's daily available time.

(Reprinted with permission from *Changing the Faces of Mathematics: Perspectives on Indigenous People of North America,* copyright © 2002 by National Council of Teachers of Mathematics. All rights reserved.)

As is the case with students with special needs and gender differences, the teacher who possesses a deep understanding of the students that are being taught will be more likely to enter their world and have a significant impact. Resources such as the *Changing Faces* books or a more recent series entitled *Mathematics for Every Student: Responding to Diversity, Grades 6–8 and 9–12* (Ellis & Malloy, 2008; Malloy, 2009) can help educators understand the populations they are teaching. Building bridges with those students and their families can ultimately raise achievement levels, which in turn may result in new career opportunities for populations that historically have been underrepresented in the professional workforce.

English Language Learners

According to the Pew Research Center (2011), about 50 million people in the United States in 2010 were Hispanic—more than 15% of the population—with Hispanics being the nation's youngest ethnic group, having a median age of 27, compared with a median age of 32 for non-Hispanic African Americans and 42 for non-Hispanic whites. Every day, immigrants from Latin America, India, Japan, and other non-English-speaking countries move to the United States, and the children enroll in schools. In turn, these students appear in classrooms around the country, seeking to learn mathematics but often inhibited by their lack of familiarity with the English language. The Education Alliance at Brown University (Brown University, 2011) defines an English Language Learner (ELL) as "a person who is in the process of acquiring English and has a first language other than English," adding that this population is often referred to as "language minority students, limited English proficient (LEP), English as a second language (ESL), and culturally and linguistically diverse (CLD)."

Historically, ELL students have been taught mathematics in a variety of ways, from receiving individual tutoring to being enrolled in remedial courses that would not be overly difficult for a student who has not yet mastered the language. For example, a freshman in high school might be prepared to study algebra but placed instead in a Basic Math course until language skills were well developed. However, the practice of placing students lower than their capabilities violates the equity principle and the notion that all students should have equal access to the mathematics curriculum. As a result, much has been written in recent years about **sheltered instruction**, which is the strategy of "making grade level academic content understandable and comprehensible to English language learners while at the same time promoting English language development (ELD) and literacy" (ELD Strategies, 2011). In other words, the idea is to place the ELL students in regular classrooms so that they explore the same mathematical topics as their peers, while also boosting their proficiency with learning English.

There are a variety of approaches to conducting sheltered instruction, but a commonly used model is known as SIOP—Sheltered Instruction Observation Protocol. This model consists of eight components, described in detail in a book entitled *Teaching Ideas for Implementing the SIOP Model* (Vogt & Echevarria, 2006). These components can be summarized as follows (Colorado Springs School District 11, 2011):

- **Lesson Planning**—Lessons should focus on both mathematics and language development and encourage ELL students to ask key questions such as, "Would you please explain to me how to solve that problem?"
- **Building Background**—Using strategies such as journals or KWL charts (What do I know? What do I want to know? What have I learned?), teachers

can help students connect knowledge to prior experiences while building vocabulary along the way.

- **Comprehensible Input**—Teachers need to make expectations of assignments clear to students by using familiar vocabulary.
- **Student Strategies for Success**—Using teaching techniques such as Venn diagrams and other visual approaches, ELL students can not only learn the content but also develop ways to understand new information.
- **Interactions**—By providing sufficient wait time, using cooperative learning, and incorporating other similar teaching strategies, teachers can maximize discourse in the classroom.
- **Lesson Delivery**—The target is to engage the ELL student in at least 90% of the lesson and make clear both the mathematical and language-based standards being addressed.
- **Practice/Application**—ELL students need hands-on experiences and practical applications to learn the mathematical content.
- **Review and Assessment**—A variety of strategies should be used to ensure that students adequately review both content and language ideas to ensure mastery.

Other books are available from the same authors providing detailed lesson ideas that implement the eight components of this model, such as *Making Content Comprehensible for English Learners: The SIOP Model, third edition* (Echevarria, Vogt, & Short, 2007), *The SIOP Model for Teaching Mathematics to English Learners* (Echevarria, Vogt, & Short, 2010), and 99 *Ideas and Activities for Teaching English Learners with the SIOP Model* (Vogt & Echevarria, 2007). Most importantly, we need to recognize that students with limited English proficiency are capable of learning the same mathematical content as their peers. In fact, if there is any such thing as a "universal language," mathematics may be a prime example because mathematical concepts and problem solving skills can transcend language. The key is to teach in such a way that we not only espouse the belief that ELL students can learn mathematics but we also help them to develop English literacy along the way.

As you read this chapter, you may be feeling overwhelmed with the responsibility of meeting the needs of such diverse classroom populations. But you also may have noticed that there are several principles for teaching all students that we can generalize from the discussions presented here. Following the Classroom Dialogues feature, we summarize a few concrete suggestions that contribute to addressing diversity in all classrooms so that *every* student has the opportunity to learn significant mathematics.

Classroom Dialogues

One of the most common mistakes that students make in pre-algebra or algebra classes involves the multiplication of binomials, as seen in this classroom discussion.

Teacher: What do we get when we multiply $(x + 2)(x + 4)$?

Student 1: That's easy! It's $x^2 + 8$.

Teacher: Can you explain how you got that?

Student 1: You're basically just multiplying two binomials together. If you take x times x, you get x squared. Then you take 2 times 4 and get 8. So, it's $x^2 + 8$.

Student 2: But don't you have to FOIL it?

Teacher: I don't know, do you?

Student 1: Oh, yeah, I forgot to FOIL. You get the *x* squared and the 8, but you have to multiply *x* times 4 and *x* times 2, so that would give you 6*x* in the middle. So, the answer would really be $x^2 + 6x + 8$.

Teacher: Are you sure about that?

Student 2: Yes, that's what I got. It's a FOIL problem.

Most mathematics students are familiar with what is sometimes called "the FOIL method" for multiplying binomials—First, Outside, Inside, and Last. The sum of the four products results in the solution to the multiplication problem. But do you know why the FOIL method works? Other than simply showing the students a rule to follow, how might the teacher in this scenario best help them to understand why the procedure works?

The process used to multiply two binomials has its roots in finding the area of a rectangle. Let's say that you wanted to find the area of a 3-by-5 rectangle. By multiplying the numbers 3 and 5, you can determine the total number of squares required to fill the rectangular region, as shown in Figure 12.5.

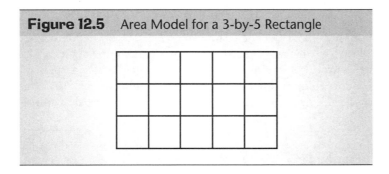

Figure 12.5 Area Model for a 3-by-5 Rectangle

Similarly, to find the area of a 12-by-14 rectangle, we might choose to divide the rectangle into four regions, as illustrated in Figure 12.6.

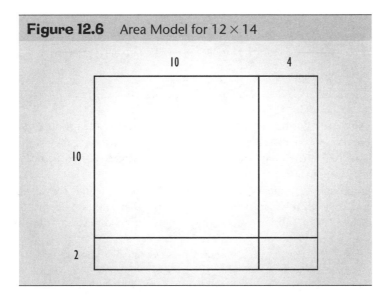

Figure 12.6 Area Model for 12×14

The total area is the sum of the areas of the regions: $100 + 20 + 40 + 8 = 168$, so the product of 12 and 14 is 168. Using the same strategy, let's suppose that we wanted to find the area of a rectangle that measures $(x + 2)$ on one side and $(x + 4)$ on the other. The area model shown in Figure 12.7 shows this process.

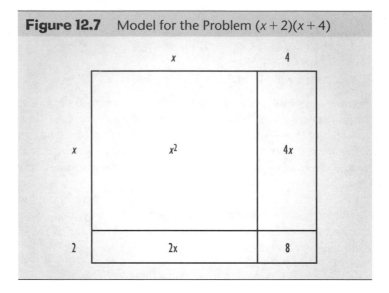

Figure 12.7   Model for the Problem $(x + 2)(x + 4)$

The use of this area model will help students to make a connection between the basic processes of multiplying two-digit numbers and determining the area of a rectangle, together with a process to multiply two binomials. Often teachers begin with students using algebra tiles to form rectangles with the given dimensions. With some practice, students can sketch charts to determine the products, such as shown in Figure 12.8, for multiplying $(2x + 3)(3x - 5)$.

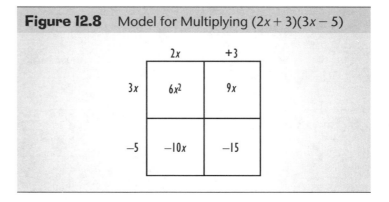

Figure 12.8   Model for Multiplying $(2x + 3)(3x - 5)$

Adding the similar terms in the chart, students determine that the product of the binomials is equal to $6x^2 - x - 15$. This process can also lead them to a mental procedure in which they visualize the chart or table shown in Figure 12.8 to rapidly determine products of binomials.

Most importantly, students come to an appreciation for the connection between mathematical ideas with which they are already familiar and the algebra that is being introduced. Instead of simply memorizing a FOIL procedure, they develop a visual process based on an area model and are able to understand why the multiplication process works. Furthermore, they invent a process that is expandable for more complex multiplications such as $(x^2 - 5x - 2)(2x^2 - 7x + 4)$, which can be rewritten by creating a 3-by-3 chart, multiplying, and combining the similar terms. How did you learn to multiply polynomials in school? Is there a place for using the term "FOIL" at all in a secondary or middle school mathematics classroom? Once students have memorized the FOIL method from a previous class, is there ever a place for going back and revisiting the multiplication process as described here, or might this confuse the class?

Ideas for Meeting Diverse Student Needs

Differentiated Instruction

If we stop to think for a minute about education in the United States, we quickly realize that grade level is one of the few things that students have in common in a typical classroom. At a given grade level, the students' ages often are different, due to having been held back or accelerated, or starting school early or late. Some students are males; some are females. Students in a class often represent a mix of racial, cultural, and socioeconomic backgrounds. Within the class may be students who are typically high achieving, whereas others may have a variety of identified learning disabilities. Combine this with a large class size, minimal teaching experience, potentially outdated textbooks, and high-stakes accountability that includes standardized achievement testing, and we have to ask ourselves, "How could a teacher honestly believe that standing in front of the class, using one standard teaching technique, will be successful for all—or even a majority—of the students in the room?"

Recognizing these differences within each classroom, there has been a renewed interest in ensuring that individual student needs are met. **Differentiated instruction** is a process by which teachers adapt their teaching strategies in an attempt to meet the diverse needs of students who possess a variety of academic, socioeconomic, cultural, and racial backgrounds. Differentiating instruction, then, implies the use of a variety of teaching techniques to meet student needs and emphasize critical thinking, as well as using a variety of assessment strategies that allow all students to demonstrate what they have learned (LDAA, 2004). Tomlinson (1995) noted that differentiation does *not* mean that some students should simply be asked to solve additional problems, do an extra report, or play computer games when they finish early. Instead, the teacher plays into student interests, using active teaching techniques that allow students to explore and draw some of their own conclusions. Differentiation can apply to the content being learned, as one idea may be pursued in greater depth by some students than others; it may involve the process of teaching, as some students explore information with others on a team, while others conduct individual Internet research; and it may involve differentiation in the way that students are assessed (Access Center, 2011).

Does all of this sound familiar? If you have read most or all of this book by now, it certainly should. The principles of differentiated instruction are "common sense" for educators who create a student-centered learning environment and adhere to the six Principles and the Standards for Teaching and Learning Mathematics described in Chapters 2 and 3, respectively. In *Mathematics Teaching Today*, the NCTM states:

> Various classroom structures can encourage and support . . . collaboration. Students may at times work independently, conferring with others as necessary; at other times students may work in pairs or in small groups. Students may use the Internet to research and collect data, use interactive geometry software to conduct investigations, or use graphing calculators to translate among different mathematical representations. Whole-class discussions are yet another profitable format. No single arrangement will work at all times; teachers should use various arrangements and tools flexibly to pursue their goals. (NCTM, 2007, p. 41)

This flexibility to change the classroom routine, including strategies such as using technology, developing learning contracts, designing tasks to appeal to multiple intelligences, providing graphic organizers for students (see, for example, Maccini & Gagnon, 2007), and engaging the students in relevant investigations, is at the heart of what differentiated instruction is all about (Tomlinson, 1995).

General Suggestions for the Classroom

Following is a generalized list of recommendations for strategies that teachers can use in an attempt to meet the diverse needs of students. Most of these strategies have been addressed elsewhere throughout the book but are listed together here as a summary of suggestions.

Recommendation 1: Make use of cooperative learning and group activities. Research has repeatedly shown that most students learn best when they discuss mathematics with one another. This practice can include everything from informal "sharing of thinking" with a partner on a particular problem to working with a team where each person has individual responsibilities. Collaboration can also be used as a way for a group of students to work together as a team on a project. In this way, students not only come to a deeper understanding of the content as they defend their thinking and challenge others but they also learn the basic life skill of communicating with others and being part of a team.

Recommendation 2: Select worthwhile, relevant tasks for students to explore. The heart of the constructivist model for teaching and learning is to make the content meaningful and relevant to the student. Consider the following two problems that both address the same general outcome:

1. Write the equation of a line with a slope of 3 and a y-intercept at $(0, 5)$.
2. Find an equation that describes the total amount of money earned mowing a lawn if a worker is given \$5 just to "show up" and another \$3 for each hour spent cutting the grass.

In both cases, the student is responsible for writing the equation of a line, and the result will be $y = 3x + 5$, but the context of the situation makes all the difference. Teenagers can relate to getting paid for doing jobs, and Problem 2, although not particularly rich, relates to student interests and provides real-life meaning for the skill. The books that have been written on meeting the needs of students with various ethnic and cultural backgrounds have been very clear about the need to write problems and lessons that align with the background and interests of students—*recognizing*, not ignoring their cultural backgrounds. Even subtle changes to the wording of problems can evoke the interest of students and motivate them to find the solutions.

Recommendation 3: Use multiple representations to illustrate problem-solving strategies. Students perceive problems in a variety of ways, and when we limit the approach to a problem to only one method, you can be sure that there will be at least a few students in the class who are not "seeing it" like the others. For example, earlier in the chapter, we looked at the use of two-color counters to simplify expressions with integers. Although this strategy can be quite effective for visual and tactile learners, there are likely to be students in a class who need other models to make sense of the operations. So, a teacher may also want to present a number line model, as shown in Figure 12.9.

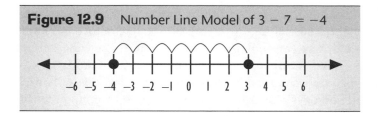

Figure 12.9 Number Line Model of $3 - 7 = -4$

As the student explores the problem $3 - 7$, instead of starting with three yellow counters and attempting to take away seven, the problem is modeled on a number line. In this case, we start at 3 on the line and interpret subtraction as moving to the left on the line, jumping back to a final location of -4. In some ways, the number line is a more abstract manner of representing the problem because it does not involve the use of a physical material. However, the model may simply make more sense to some students than the use of counters. Most importantly, both of these models provide a visual representation of the problem. A report by the U.S. Department of Education (2009) on research-based interventions in mathematics teaching states as one of their primary recommendations, "Intervention materials should include opportunities for students to work with visual representations of mathematical ideas and interventionists should be proficient in the use of visual representations of mathematical ideas" (p. 30).

In addition, other students may benefit from thinking about what happens if a person has \$3 and then promises to contribute \$7 toward the price of a gift. After spending the first \$3, the person would be another \$4 short, which justifies the answer to the problem as -4. The point here is that there are many ways to think about addition and subtraction of integers, and although none of them we have discussed here involves the memorization of any rules, the models illustrate a number of ways that students can represent—and, therefore, make sense of—these types of problems. Of course, this is why the NCTM devoted one of its ten Standards to the importance of representation.

Recommendation 4: Differentiate tasks and/or assignments. A core curriculum for all students implies that everyone addresses the same general outcomes. However, by targeting specific tasks and assignments to particular groups or individual students, common topics can be approached at different levels, and some students can even be given the opportunity to explore some optional topics that are above and beyond what others are doing. We have discussed, for example, how a student with a learning disability may investigate the same mathematical content but be given a shorter assignment or a different task. The same may be true for a full classroom of students who take a pretest on a topic so the teacher can group them for a short unit. In that unit, the problems that one group of students explores may be different from the problems of another group of students, yet all the students are studying the same concepts. Teachers are encouraged to treat each student as an individual, and the tasks that students are asked to perform may vary, even within the same classroom.

Recommendation 5: Provide extra assistance for students who need help and extra challenges for those who are high achievers. Caring teachers frequently arrive in their classrooms well ahead of the required school hours and often remain in school after hours to tutor individuals or small groups of students who need extra help. Often, student buses arrive before the start of the school day, and teachers can make use of this time to provide extra assistance to those who have questions. Some teachers establish study groups of students and even promote certain days of the week for extra help. For example, Tuesdays and Thursdays after school from 3:15 to 4:15 p.m. may be established as regular "help times" for students who have more questions than can be addressed in class.

Similarly, many schools have established mathematics clubs or take part in local, state, or national mathematics competitions to provide challenges for high achievers. These students can be forgotten easily because they often catch on to new content fairly quickly and do not qualify for any special services. So it becomes the responsibility of the teachers in a school or district to find ways to keep the students active. Mathematics clubs often feature special projects, competitions, guest speakers, and even tutoring for younger children, which can serve both the needs of the secondary or middle school students and the community.

Finally, many teachers have found other innovative ways to communicate with and help all of their students. Some teachers publish and e-mail a biweekly or monthly newsletter with simple study tips and information for students and their parents to promote an understanding of the mathematics and the sequencing of content. Other teachers create class Web sites where descriptions of what took place in class each day, together with a listing of assignments, are updated on a regular basis. In some cases, PowerPoint slides or class notes are made available for download. These Web sites can be particularly helpful to students who are ill and miss days of school because the Internet can serve as a tool to help them keep up with their peers. Most importantly, all of these strategies represent ways that teachers attempt to individualize to the needs of students.

Recommendation 6: Use a variety of assessment strategies. In Unit IV, we took an in-depth look at issues associated with student assessment. It is important to recognize that just as lessons should be relevant and include multiple strategies for solving problems, assessments should follow the same principles. As we discussed in Chapter 11, the use of authentic forms of assessment, such as asking free-response questions and assigning projects, promotes equity in the classroom. Students not only *learn* the mathematics through a variety of models, but they are also given the opportunity to *prove* that they learned the content through the use of a variety of assessment techniques. Not all students are good test takers, but they may be very polished in an interview. Some students struggle with participating in class but feel comfortable asking and answering questions in a journal. Meeting individual needs and promoting equity imply that teachers provide students with multiple means to demonstrate what they have learned.

These six recommendations are by no means an exhaustive list but can serve as a starting point as you think about how to promote equity in your own classroom. Fortunately, there are many excellent resources in print form and on the Internet to support those efforts as well. The resource listings at the end of this book provide citations to books and Web sites described in this chapter and others that will be helpful in developing strategies to meet the needs of all of your students.

Conclusion

Teaching a lesson on rational expressions, the instructor of a first-year algebra course designed a very creative sequence of problems that dealt with determining gas mileage for an automobile. For example, if x represents the number of miles, and y stands for the number of gallons of gas that are used, then $\frac{x}{y}$ would represent the gas mileage in miles per gallon. So, if the car used 5 more gallons of gas than anticipated, the new expression for mileage would be $\frac{x}{y + 5}$. The entire lesson was rooted in these real-life examples, but at the end of the 90-minute block of class time, the class walked out confused, and the teacher was frustrated. All of that work in planning had produced no better results than last year's dry presentation of the same content. As the teacher thought through the lesson, a hint of a smile appeared on her face. "Duh," she thought, "these students are mostly freshmen. They're only 14 years old, and they won't be driving for another 2 years. Even then, many of their parents will put the gas in the car. These problems are very real to *me*, but they have no relevance in my students' lives whatsoever." In short, the lesson *was* meaningful, but it was not meaningful *for the audience* in the classroom!

In Unit 3, we emphasized the role of reflection after teaching a lesson. It is not unusual for a teacher to present a lesson in which only a fraction of the class understands the concept. And the tendency of many educators is to blame the lack of success on the students (e.g., they weren't paying attention, they didn't work hard enough, etc.). However, if we are honest with ourselves, we can often find flaws in the structure of the lesson that made the content inaccessible to some portion of the class. Perhaps students were working alone but should have been discussing the examples with a partner. Or maybe the class drew diagrams on graph paper but would have been better served by using technology, such as a graphing calculator. In the case of the mileage examples, the connection did not resonate with the class because it did not relate to the students' lives.

The issue of mathematics courses not meeting the needs of students has been a cornerstone of debate in the discussion of equity for many years. The NCTM and Common Core State Standards acknowledge that *all* students should be addressing *all* areas of the mathematics curriculum. Speaking on the topic of algebra for all students as a central component of the equity issue, Strong and Cobb (2000) noted that "truly effective algebra instruction must be both historically accurate and culturally relevant" and that "mathematics programs [should] embrace equity, expectations, and effectiveness" (p. 3). In an attempt to address the Equity Principle, teachers are challenged to develop strategies to adequately meet the needs of a diverse population—a population of students that includes those with learning disabilities and gender differences, as well as ethnic and cultural diversity or limited English language proficiency. In this chapter, we have explored each of these populations and summarized with several concrete suggestions for how teachers can transform their classrooms into settings that address individual differences in their students.

In order to explore ideas and make changes, effective teachers of mathematics regularly return to school, attend conferences, and take part in a variety of other professional development opportunities so that their education is ongoing. In the final chapter, Chapter 13, we explore the role of the teacher in the school context. We discuss how teachers work with parents, administrators, and within a department, and the importance of participating in ongoing professional activities.

For bibliographic references and additional resources, see page 417

Glossary

Differentiated Instruction: Differentiated instruction is a process by which teachers adapt their teaching strategies in an attempt to respond to the diverse needs of students who possess a variety of academic, socioeconomic, cultural, and racial backgrounds.

IEP: IEP is an acronym for individualized education program. A student with a learning disability typically has an IEP that describes the nature of the disability, provides a statement of how the disability affects classroom performance, provides short- and long-term goals for the student, and provides a plan for modifications or accommodations that will be needed for the student to be successful (Concord SPED PAC, 2003).

Inclusion: Inclusion is a process by which a student with special needs is placed in a regular education class-room, with support services provided. In some cases, a special education teacher or an aide assists the regular teacher with the lesson. In other situations, the student is pulled out from the regular classroom for tutoring.

Sheltered Instruction: Sheltered Instruction is a strategy of "making grade level academic content understandable and comprehensible to English language learners while at the same time promoting English language development (ELD) and literacy" (ELD Strategies, 2011).

Two-Color Counters: A common classroom manipulative, two-color counters are yellow on one side and red on the other and can be used to explore everything from integer operations to fractions.

Discussion Questions and Activities

1. Obtain a prewritten mathematics lesson plan from a resource book or the Internet. Design a list of modifications that could be made to the lesson if students with special needs, such as reading, behavioral, or other disabilities, are included in the class.

2. Suppose that you teach a heterogeneously mixed class of students and have one individual who is gifted and solves problems well beyond the abilities of the rest of the class. This student is likely to become bored and even to create discipline problems if required to follow the exact same plan as the rest of the class. Discuss some strategies that you might use to challenge the student within the regular classroom.

3. In a small group of students, select one of the *Changing Faces* resource books to review. Then, develop a hands-on presentation for the rest of the class that summarizes the spirit of the book that was chosen.

4. The notion that everyone is capable of learning mathematics (barring severe learning disabilities) is not universally embraced by all teachers. What do *you* believe about the extent to which all students can learn mathematics? What experiences in your life have shaped those beliefs?

5. Interview two mathematics teachers who work in very different settings. For example, interview one person who teaches in a fairly wealthy suburb and another who teaches in a high-minority, inner-city setting. Compare and contrast their views on mathematics education and their strategies in writing lesson plans.

6. View the movie *Stand and Deliver* (Menendez & Musca, 1988), which is based on the true story of Jamie Escalante, an individual who overcame ethnic, cultural, and socioeconomic issues to become a highly successful mathematics teacher. Discuss the beliefs he held and the strategies he employed in his classroom that contributed to high achievement levels in his students.

7. Discuss reasons why female students have historically tended to take fewer mathematics courses and select careers that use less mathematics than their male peers do. What specific steps might teachers of mathematics at the secondary and middle school levels take to increase female participation in mathematically oriented career areas, in addition to the ones described in this chapter?

8. Obtain a copy of one of the resource books listed in this chapter that can be used to support sheltered instruction for ELL students in a mathematics classroom. Discuss some practical lesson planning and teaching ideas presented in the books. In what ways can mathematics be viewed as a "universal language"?

9. The last section of this chapter provided six specific suggestions of classroom practices that promote equity in the classroom. In a small group, brainstorm additional strategies that a teacher might employ to address diverse student needs. What types of activities and classroom environment characteristics promote equal access to mathematics for all students?

10. In an attempt to address a variety of levels of student abilities, some schools have adopted elaborate tracking systems. A secondary or middle school sometimes offers the same class at "basic," "average," "accelerated," and "honors" levels, placing students where they will be most appropriately served. Research the topic of tracking in education and be prepared to argue the benefits and the disadvantages of using this strategy to meet student needs.

The Teacher of Mathematics in the School Community

A teacher once said that he had 100 reasons to get out of bed and teach every day and that his greatest joy was greeting those 100 "reasons" and calling them by name 5 days a week in his classroom. In addition to being excited about mathematics, successful teachers who enjoy their jobs need to be equally excited about kids—after all, the development of thinking skills in students is the ultimate product of our efforts. It is very rewarding for a teacher to see a student volunteer a nonroutine approach to a problem, make an effective presentation to the class, or suddenly gain a profound insight on a task. Indeed, the teaching profession carries with it a great deal of interaction with children and young adults, which can be exciting and gratifying.

In the midst of that enjoyment in the classroom, however, many teachers still feel isolated and disconnected in their workplace. After the teacher greets the students and closes the classroom door, what occurs during the next 40 to 120 minutes is up to that teacher. There is generally not another colleague or adult in the classroom during the entire time period. Consequently, teaching is, for some, a lonely profession. But teaching also has the potential to be very connected because all the teachers in a school have a common purpose—educating young minds.

Although teachers may feel alone at times, they are part of a much larger education community that includes colleagues, parents, administrators, members of the community, and other mathematics teachers around the city, county, state, country, and world. None of us acts entirely alone, and everything we do in the classroom ultimately impacts a host of other people. In this

After reading Chapter 13, you should be able to answer the following questions:

- What can the teacher do to enhance communication between the parents of students and school personnel?
- What are the criteria by which the performance of teachers of mathematics can be supervised and evaluated?
- How do departments of mathematics function in a secondary or middle school? What is the role of the classroom teacher within the department?
- What psychological factors interact and affect the decisions that a teacher makes during class? Discuss these factors. Why is participation in professional development activities necessary?
- What are some opportunities that teachers of mathematics have for professional development? Why is it important for teachers to write professional development plans?

chapter, we discuss the context in which the teaching and learning of mathematics occur and the role of the teacher in that greater context. We begin by exploring the role of parents in the educational process. █

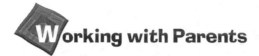

Working with Parents

Following is a list of actual contacts that parents of secondary and middle school students have made with their children's mathematics teachers:

- A parent called a teacher to express displeasure with perceived classroom instructional practices. The teacher frequently assigned homework problems and encouraged students to explain their approaches to others in the class. During the phone call, the parent was clearly upset and said, "It is apparent that you don't understand the mathematics yourself and are hoping that students will bail you out by having them explain the problems to one another."

- A parent sent a note to the mathematics teacher that called the teacher "the most significant positive influence on my daughter's life in her educational career."

- A parent called the principal to complain that the teacher had used a video-tape problem-solving program in class that day. He claimed that "the teacher is forcing students to watch television in class and calling it mathematics education." Later in the conversation, the parent stated that "kids watch too much TV at home these days, and they certainly don't need another hour of it in your classroom!"

- A parent shook a mathematics teacher's hand at parent–teacher conferences and said, "I don't know what you're doing in that classroom, but my son literally can't wait to get out of bed in the morning to get to your class. It's just surprising because he has never really liked mathematics that much in the past. Thank you!"

- A parent called the teacher because students had been using graphing calculators in class. He argued that "when students are using calculators, they're not learning math; the machine is doing all the thinking in that classroom" and asked the teacher, "Why are you allowing your students to cheat with those things?"

- A parent showed up at a mathematics teacher's house on the last day of school with a bouquet of flowers simply to say "thank you" to the teacher and his spouse for their support of the students in the class.

- A parent approached a teacher before school one morning and explained how her son had "always been good at mathematics until he got to your class" and that "his uncle is a math teacher, and whenever he works with my son, he says that he can't imagine why my son isn't getting an A." The parent truly believed it was the teacher's fault that her son's performance had declined during the past year.

- A parent approached her daughter's middle school mathematics teacher after her daughter had graduated from college with a degree in mathematics education and said, "It all started with you. . . . Your class inspired her to become a mathematics teacher."

Clearly, parents can be teachers' hardest critics, but they can also be our strongest allies. One thing that all of the preceding scenarios have in common is that the parents are interested in the development of their children and care enough to speak to the teacher about it, whether their comments are critical or complimentary. Teachers cannot begin to spend the same amount of time with a student that a parent or guardian does, and no one has invested as much time and energy into the students' lives as their parents. Whereas parents watch their children grow and change throughout their entire lives, the teacher only gets a glimpse of the students' total development. No one knows the students better than the people who live with them, and this puts parents in a position to help teachers understand the development of each child. But how can we solicit the help of parents and keep them supportive of our efforts? Here are some practical suggestions for working with them.

1. Communication with parents is extremely important. The more frequently and clearly that a teacher communicates with parents, the more likely they are to understand the focus in the classroom. In fact, in the NCTM *Curriculum and Evaluation Standards* (NCTM, 1989), the authors stated that "parents who expect students to do mathematics homework on paper at a desk rather than by gathering real data to solve a problem will be surprised. The best way to bring about reform is to challenge directly the perceptions held by many about the content of mathematics" (p. 255). There are a variety of ways to open these doors with parents and help them examine their perceptions. Some teachers e-mail informal newsletters to parents biweekly, monthly, or once per grading period. In the newsletter, the teacher describes the topics the class has been studying and provides examples of the type of activities and problems the students have been encountering. The newsletter often contains an article encouraging parents to call if they have questions. Other teachers have a family math night, in which parents can come to the classroom and engage in hands-on activities themselves to model what their children are doing in school. Sometimes, parents believe that "manipulatives are toys" or that "calculators are cheating devices" until they personally experience a lesson that involves the use of these tools. The family math night also gives the teacher an opportunity to explain and to model the philosophy of the classroom. Finally, some teachers make regular phone calls to parents simply to touch base and talk to them about student progress. A 5-minute phone call to each parent, once per grading period, can be time extremely well spent.

2. When parents do call or send a note, be sure to respond to their concerns immediately, and when you have a concern about a particular student, do not hesitate to call the parents. Many teachers believe that a phone call to parents is a last resort, used only when all else fails. In reality, however, most parents appreciate a phone call sooner rather than later. It is much easier to head off a problem at the start (e.g., if a student is not completing homework assignments) than to wait until it is too late and grades suffer. A conversation with a parent may result in changing the way the student's time is organized or securing a tutor to assist the student with the content of a particularly difficult unit.

3. In today's world, it is not unusual to have students in our classes whose parents either cannot read or cannot speak English or may simply not be able to read at all. When working with non-English-speaking families, remember that there is not only a language barrier, but cultural differences as well. For example, in the Hispanic culture, children often are taught not to make eye contact

with people in authority. Consequently, having a conversation with parents, sharing concerns about how their child refuses to look you in the eye in class would be confusing (if not upsetting) to the parent, as the child views you as an authority, and that is exactly the behavior they were taught at home. So, it is important to become familiar with the cultures from which your students come. Also, if there is a language barrier, contact school administrators about identifying a translator who may be able to mediate in a conference or assist you in writing a short note to send home. Finally, there are many stories told about teachers who send a letter home to parents and then find out later that the parents cannot read and discarded the paper. If parents do not respond to a written note within a reasonable time period, be sure to follow up with a phone call to ensure that they received, read, and understood the information.

4. Consider having each student keep a portfolio as an assessment strategy as was described in Chapters 10 and 11. Portfolios can be used to track students' progress over time, and they provide excellent tools with which to review students' work with parents during scheduled meetings, parent–teacher conferences, and so forth. When a parent comes in to discuss a child's performance, it is much more effective and desirable to show the parent a portfolio that highlights the student's work than to quote numbers representing test and quiz scores. Parents appreciate the fact that the teacher can show concrete evidence of what the student believes and is able to do rather than simply telling them that "your daughter has an 84 percent average in my class and is doing okay."

5. Whenever possible, involve parents in the process of problem solving and doing homework assignments. Suppose, for example, that you developed the concept of why the area of a circle can be found by taking πr^2 with your students. The homework assignment for the evening could be for the students to go home and reexplain this concept to their parents and bring a note back from the parents the next day indicating that the task was completed. Sometimes parents can be used to assist in the collection of data for a long-term project: Students might, for example, ask their parents how much electricity their family uses on a monthly basis according to old electric bills. Not only do these types of projects and assignments get the parents involved in the child's education but they also serve as a means of communicating to parents the mathematical content and processes the students are developing in school and bringing them on board.

6. Whenever possible, involve parents directly in the teaching and learning process. For example, some parents like to come into the classroom and observe a lesson now and then. With the principal's permission, parents should feel welcome to do this so that they can experience the classroom for themselves. Also, if you know the career areas of parents and guardians of your students, you might invite them to give presentations on particular topics. The class may be interested in hearing from Marge's father, who works for the Water Department and can explain how mathematics is used in the water-treatment process, or from Bill's mother, who is a surgeon and can describe the use of problem-solving and reasoning skills during an operation.

Parents and guardians play pivotal roles in the success of a mathematics class, so whatever you can do to involve them and communicate with them is likely to work to your advantage. Similarly, parents want to help their children in your class. So, a frequently asked question is, "How can I best help my child to learn mathematics in your class?" At the beginning of the school year, you may want to consider distributing a handout with tips for parents on how they can help their children at home. Here is an example of such a handout that was provided to parents of algebra students at a beginning-of-the-year parent night:

HINTS FOR HELPING YOUR CHILD IN ALGEBRA

- When assisting your child with a homework assignment, it is generally *not* helpful to show him or her how to do an individual problem. This is particularly true in a class in which hands-on materials and technology are emphasized. There is often a shortcut to an answer, but when the student is shown the trick, the underlying reasons why it is done a certain way are lost.

- When your child is struggling with a problem or concept, sympathize with him or her by saying, "That problem/concept is difficult for me to understand too" but *never* remark, "I don't know . . . I never was very good in math either." The latter statement sends a message that if algebra were not important and useful to you—and you got where you are today—then there's no real need for your child to know it either.

- You do *not* need to be an expert at algebra to help your child with homework or studying. The best way to do this is to ask leading questions. Ask such questions as "What is the problem asking you to figure out?" "How might you start the problem?" "Did you do an example similar to that in class today or this week? What did you do in that problem?" "Can you show me your notes from today and explain what you discussed in class?" Research shows that those parents in other countries who are excellent helpers tend to *motivate* and *monitor* the efforts of their children, but they also tend to harbor some fears of the math content of their children's classes.

- If you and your child are both stuck on a problem, make sure that he or she knows where the difficulty began and encourage him or her to ask about it in class the next day. Say to your child, "When you come home tomorrow, I want *you* to explain to *me* how to do that problem. I'll be curious to know how other people attacked it. . . ." In this way, you become part of the learning team at home, and your child knows you're concerned about his or her frustration and that you want to know how to solve the math problem, too.

- Encourage your child to work with other students in the class. Often, a short phone call to a classmate or friend can help a student realize that he or she is not the only one who has a certain question. A conversation with another person in the class may help to clear up the problem. It's not unusual for students to get together after school, in the evening, or on the weekend to work through a set of problems or study together. Mathematics can be a social activity—research shows that students learn math concepts best when they talk to other students about what they're doing. On the first day of class, students were asked to write down the name and phone number of one other person in their notebooks so that they could contact that person if needed.

- Completion of homework assignments and writing of journal entries are essential for success in the course. Students have been told that if they establish any kind of pattern of missing assignments or not completing them, you will be contacted.

- Ask and expect your child to bring tests, quizzes, projects, and so forth home and show you his or her progress with some regularity. As parents of an adolescent, you want your child to have some autonomy and personal responsibility. However, he or she is still at an age at which having parents watching over the shoulder now and then continues to be very helpful. You would be surprised how many students go through an entire quarter (or even semester) without showing a parent a single paper from class. When you look at a test, focus questions and comments on, "What have you been learning to do lately? Can you show me?" rather than focusing on the grade and questions that he or she missed on the test.

- Encourage your child to participate actively in class and not to be afraid to ask and answer questions. There is no such thing as a wrong answer in a mathematics class. Every incorrect response is simply a door that leads the class into another discussion, and students can learn more from a mistake than from a correct answer. Generally, the students who have positive attitudes and take active roles in class discussions are the ones who excel in their studies.

- No textbook is used for this course because the class is student centered. The approaches that we take depend on questions raised and the needs of the class. Before the year is over, we will have explored every algebra concept required by the course of study (and then some). If, however, your child wants or needs additional skill practice, algebra textbooks are available that can be checked out for a short time or the entire year. *Because of the student-centered nature of the class, assignments for upcoming days generally cannot be given in advance (for vacations, etc.).*

- It is important that students in this course feel successful, challenged, and confident in their study of mathematics. Often, students are very active in organizations, playing on athletic teams, helping with activities at church, and so on. Watch for signs that may indicate that your child is overloaded (e.g., a great deal of stress, work not being completed, late bedtimes, falling grades in other classes), so that we can work out a strategy to help.

- If, at any time, you have questions about your child's progress, please call me. I can be most easily reached by calling the office at (419) 555-8662. If I am not available, leave a voice-mail message, and I will return the call as soon as possible.

Parents and siblings participate in a family math night to promote active parental involvement in the educational process.

As you read this handout, you might have noticed that openness with parents is paramount. The teacher has explained how the classroom will be student centered and why homework assignments generally are not given in advance. Likewise, the teacher has explained why a textbook is not being used but offers to allow the students to check out a book if the parents or student would like one. Clear communication about rules, as well as suggestions for parents, are essential elements of a successful school year. As the teacher noted in the handout, parents help their children the most when they monitor what the students are doing and motivate them to do their best.

In *Family Math* by Stenmark, Thompson, and Cossey (1986), the authors make a number of recommendations as to how parents can help their children be successful in class. In addition to advice provided in the sample handout, the authors also suggest that parents communicate to their children that they have confidence in their children's abilities

How Would You React

S C E N A R I O

Your department requires each student to own a graphing calculator as one of the school supplies. The parent of one of your students e-mails you regarding the choice of calculators for the class you are teaching. In the e-mail, the parent questions whether students should be using calculators at all and expresses anger over having to spend money on the technology, claiming that it is "little more than an electronic game that is permissible to be brought to school." Your response is to

a. Ignore the e-mail to avoid an argument with the parent.

b. Reply to the e-mail, but do not directly answer the question. Instead, simply state that this is the school's policy and that you are sorry that his or her family does not agree.

c. Forward the e-mail to the principal or department chair and let that individual handle the question.

d. Call or reply to the e-mail, explaining in detail why each student is expected to own a graphing calculator as one of the school supplies.

e. Other.

D I S C U S S I O N

An excellent way to spur a debate among parents and members of the community is to bring up the use of calculators—or any technology, for that matter—in the classroom. Because the majority of the parents who currently have children in school did not use much, if any, technology in their school experiences, many caregivers have difficulty accepting the use of these tools in the teaching and learning process. We commonly hear parents remark, "When I was in school, we had to do everything by hand" and that "children will never learn the basics if they are allowed to cheat with a calculator." However, as we discussed in Chapter 1, research evidence suggests just the opposite—the use of calculators enhances academic achievement and enriches the learning experience. In 2003, high school students scored the highest in more than 35 years on the SAT in mathematics (The College Board, 2003), providing further evidence that current reform in mathematics education, which includes the use of technology, is having a significant impact.

Addressing the concerns expressed by parents is a routine but important function of the classroom teacher. Within the teaching community, workshops, classes, and publications advance the use of improved classroom strategies from cooperative learning to hands-on explorations. However, parents and other caregivers rarely have exposure to these trends and changes in education, and they often tend to believe that any teaching technique that is different from what they had in school must be inappropriate or unnecessary because "we made do without it." Consequently, one of the functions of the teacher is to communicate with community members by presenting research evidence and providing a rationale for why the classroom is being run in the manner chosen. In fact, it is educators' responsibility to provide this information to the community in a proactive manner, rather than simply defending decisions after the fact. So, for example, if a district does decide to require secondary or middle school students to purchase graphing calculators, there needs to be a public relations campaign that accompanies the stated requirement. The publicity would help parents to understand what children will be doing with the technology, why it is important to use graphing calculators, what current research suggests about the use of the tools, and how the district arrived at that decision. As is often said, "an ounce of prevention is worth a pound of cure," and in this case, some early information to the community may have averted the parental reaction.

The decision as to whether the teacher should handle the question or pass it along to an administrator or department chair depends on the policies or protocol within the school district. In some cases, this type of general parent concern that applies to many classrooms may be handled best through a single information source. However, a parent's question about how student journals are assessed would need to be handled by the individual teacher. Most importantly, *all* parent concerns need to be handled by *someone* and not simply ignored as insignificant. Questions from community members may put teachers on the defensive, but they also help educators to define what they believe and to produce evidence to support those beliefs. Furthermore, when the same concerns are frequently expressed, they may cause teachers and administrators to refine policies, making the school stronger in the long run.

to succeed. The authors encourage parents to provide a specific location for study, depending on the learning style of the student. A particular room or a special table in a well-lit room can help make the process of studying more of a regular routine. Finally, the authors ask parents to be models of persistence and to show enjoyment of doing mathematics. As we have seen in Chapters 3 and 7, students become persistent, confident, and interested in mathematics by working with people—such as parents and teachers—who espouse those same dispositions. Becoming a positive person generally results from associating ourselves with other positive people.

The success of a teacher in working with students and their parents may be measured and reported in a variety of ways. Generally, the principal is responsible for assessing the performance of teachers, although department chairs, assistant principals, or even central office supervisors also are often involved in the process. In the next section, we examine the process of assessing and evaluating teaching performance.

he Supervision and Evaluation of Teachers

It is Thursday morning, and you have just prepared the most exciting mathematics lesson of the year. Students will be rotating among learning centers, spinning spinners, dealing cards, and pulling marbles from bags to examine counting rules and probability. Even better, today is the day that the principal has decided to visit your classroom to observe and read through your lesson planning book. The students come to class and are oriented to the learning centers, but as they begin to circulate about the room, everything goes wrong. Prom weekend is rapidly approaching, and at the tables, students are more interested in talking about the band, tuxedos, and dresses than the chances of pulling a red marble from the bag. The spinner falls apart at one table, and a student drops a bag of marbles, spilling them all over the classroom floor. In your frustration, you try to stop the class and reorganize the activity, but it's too late—the students are laughing about the marbles on the floor and do not understand the point of what they are doing at the stations. As the bell signals the end of the period, you take a deep breath and watch the principal walk out the classroom door with a frown on her face. It's not that you haven't had a lesson bomb before, but the principal hasn't been there to witness it. You realize that your evaluation for the semester depended on her observation of this lesson, and you fear that your file will be adversely affected by this disaster. You think back to the day that Francine, one of your students, said to you, "It's too bad that one-third of our semester grade is based on this exam; I know so much more than the test measured, and I just had a bad day." Similarly, you are aware that you are a much better teacher than the one that the principal just observed, but you also had a bad day.

If you are fortunate enough to have an administrator who acknowledges that assessments are merely snapshots of the whole, then that person probably is going to use more data in an evaluation than observation notes from one classroom visit. Just as we emphasized throughout Unit 4 that it is important to use a diverse array of assessment strategies to determine student progress in mathematics, administrators should use several pieces of evidence to determine your effectiveness as a teacher. The ways in which teachers are assessed and evaluated often vary greatly from one school or district to another. The following is a list of some of the pieces of evidence that can be collected to determine your effectiveness as a teacher:

- Classroom observation notes from announced visits
- Classroom observation notes from unannounced visits
- An examination of your lesson plan and gradebooks
- Preobservation and postobservation interview notes
- Degree to which you have addressed your self-stated goals on your annual professional development plan (which we discuss later in the chapter)
- Formal or informal input from peers, including colleagues and a department chair, regarding your classroom performance, adherence to standards, use of technology or manipulatives, understanding of mathematics content, and so forth
- Letters from parents or students in support of your teaching performance
- Scores earned by students on standardized district- or statewide tests of achievement
- Professional activity within local, state, or national mathematics organizations
- Evidence of the establishment of positive classroom environments, including photographs of bulletin boards and student projects
- Other samples of student accomplishments, including project posters, video-clips of classroom presentations, and models (such as three-dimensional solids) constructed by students

Although few districts would use *all* of the pieces of evidence listed here, many use a combination of *some* of them to serve as a sample of your work in the process of evaluating teaching performance. Consequently (and luckily) a teaching evaluation for the file generally does not hinge on one classroom observation alone. As a result, if the principal saw your probability lesson going awry, she would also have a file that included a host of evidence to support that, despite the lack of success on that particular day, you are still an excellent teacher. In fact, many administrators would look at the probability lesson through a positive lens and compliment the teacher for at least attempting a hands-on activity that involved groups of students working in centers. They would also recognize the difficulty of teaching during the week of the prom and take that into consideration when reporting on your teaching performance. In the end, the analogy of assessing teaching performance to that of assessing student progress in mathematics is powerful. Any one of the assessment items on its own would be an insufficient base for an entire report on your teaching performance, just as test scores are not the only components of a grade when both teachers and students have other dimensions that are worth measuring and including in a final evaluation.

In many areas, beginning teachers are assessed to determine their abilities for licensing or certification. Many states have joined together into a consortium to develop and administer a Teacher Performance Assessment (TPA) for teachers entering the profession. The TPA involves the measurement of a combination of materials created through coursework and through a portfolio assessment of classroom teaching that includes videos and a variety of artifacts (AACTE, 2011). Another assessment, developed by the Educational Testing Service (ETS), is the Praxis III performance assessment. Using this tool, new teachers are evaluated in four "domains" of the profession, including (1) planning lessons that are appropriate to student needs; (2) creating a positive classroom environment;

(3) demonstrating effective classroom instructional practices; and (4) exhibiting professionalism as a teacher, in terms of reflecting on lessons, communicating with parents, and working with colleagues (Dwyer, 1998; ETS, 2003). Similarly, the Interstate New Teacher Assessment and Support Consortium (INTASC) established a set of 10 Standards that can be used to assess performance of teachers who are new to the classroom. These Standards include content pedagogy, student development, diverse learners, multiple instructional strategies, motivation and management, communication and technology, planning, assessment, reflective practice, professional growth, and school and community involvement (North Carolina Public Schools, 2003). Although each state reserves the right to feature its own process for licensing teachers, the TPA, Praxis III, and INTASC assessments are common and require that teachers be measured in a variety of professional dimensions. Also, the assessments use multiple pieces of evidence, including the review of written documents as well as observations of and interviews with the teacher.

In the second edition of the *Professional Standards for Teaching Mathematics,* entitled *Mathematics Teaching Today* (NCTM, 2007), the authors put forth Standards for the Observation, Supervision, and Improvement of Mathematics Teaching. The first three standards refer to the process of teacher observation, supervision, and improvement (*how* the process is conducted), and the latter three are the objects of focus in teacher observation, supervision, and improvement (*what* is to be measured). Let's take a look at each of these standards, as they delineate the expectations that a supervisor should have for a mathematics teacher. As you read these standards, note how they parallel the best practices of effective mathematics teachers that were described in Chapter 7.

 STANDARD 1: THE CONTINUOUS IMPROVEMENT CYCLE

The observation, supervision, and improvement of the teaching of mathematics should be a cyclical process involving—

- the periodic collection and analysis of information about an individual's teaching of mathematics,
- professional growth based on the analysis of teaching, and
- the improvement of teaching as a consequence of professional growth.

(NCTM, 2007, p. 69)

Like the assessment cycle for student progress described in Chapter 11, teacher evaluation should follow a sequential process of collecting data, analyzing it, and attempting to improve performance based on the analysis. Throughout the book, we have emphasized the importance of reflection in the teaching and learning process and made the point that teaching improves when we think about what we attempted to do in the classroom, how our plan actually played out, and what we might do to improve our lesson the next time. In *Principles and Standards for School Mathematics* (NCTM, 2000), the NCTM points out that effective teachers use student assessment data "to appraise how well the mathematical tasks, student discourse, and classroom environment are interacting to foster students' learning. They then use these appraisals to adapt their instruction." (p. 19)

STANDARD 2: TEACHERS AS PARTICIPANTS IN THE OBSERVATION, SUPERVISION, AND IMPROVEMENT PROCESS

The improvement of the teaching of mathematics should provide ongoing opportunities for teachers to—

- analyze their own teaching,
- deliberate with colleagues about their teaching, and
- confer with supervisors and administrators about their teaching.

(NCTM, 2007, p. 72)

The evaluation of teaching performances should not be *done to* the teacher; instead, it should be a cooperative venture involving the local administrator working *with* the teacher on long-term improvement of practice. Using the constructivist model, for example, the principal might ask the teacher to describe the observed lesson and how the students reacted and then to suggest three ways the lesson could have been improved—a very different approach from having the principal observe a lesson and then sit down and tell the teacher what should have happened and how the lesson could have been taught more effectively. As both the teacher and the student have roles in classroom discourse, the teacher and the supervisor have roles in the teaching evaluation process.

STANDARD 3: DATA SOURCES FOR THE OBSERVATION, SUPERVISION, AND IMPROVEMENT OF MATHEMATICS TEACHING

Improvement in the teaching of mathematics should be based on information from a variety of data sources including the teacher's—

- goals and expectations for students' learning and achievement;
- plans for addressing the students' achievement goals;
- lesson plans, student activities and materials, and means of assessing students' understanding of mathematics;
- analysis of multiple episodes of classroom teaching;
- analysis of classroom teaching;
- evidence of students' understanding of mathematics; and
- participation in collaborative activities with colleagues.

(NCTM, 2007, p. 76)

Does this sound familiar? In Unit 4, we argued in favor of using multiple assessment strategies to determine student progress and pointed out that test scores may not present a total picture of student achievement. Likewise, the assessment of teaching performances demands a variety of sources of information, more than a classroom observation or two. We now turn our attention to the objects of focus in the standards for the Observation, Supervision, and Improvement of Mathematics Teaching. Not surprisingly, these three standards mirror the standards for teaching and learning mathematics that were described in Chapter 7, including worthwhile tasks, learning environment, discourse, and assessment.

STANDARD 4: TEACHER KNOWLEDGE AND IMPLEMENTATION OF IMPORTANT MATHEMATICS

Assessment of the effective teaching of worthwhile mathematical tasks should provide evidence that the teacher—

- demonstrates a sound knowledge of mathematical concepts and procedures;
- represents mathematics as a network of interconnected concepts and procedures;
- emphasizes connections between mathematics and other disciplines and connections with daily living;
- models and emphasizes aspects of problem solving, including building new mathematical knowledge, applying and adapting a variety of appropriate strategies to solve problems, making and investigating mathematical conjectures, and selecting and using various types of reasoning and methods of proof;
- recognizes reasoning and proof as fundamental aspects of mathematics; and
- models and emphasizes mathematical communication to help students organize and consolidate their mathematical thinking.

(NCTM, 2007, pp. 84–85)

Teachers who possess a firm grasp of their content areas and their course of study tend to be the best at pursuing student questions, recognizing teachable moments, and helping students make connections. Although it is important for a teacher to have a strong background in education and psychology, a solid understanding of the mathematical concepts being taught is also an important component of effective teaching. Knowledge of the content area can help teachers select tasks and mathematical topics that are important for students to explore—an important consideration in the implementation of the curriculum principle in *Principles and Standards for School Mathematics* (NCTM, 2000). Examining several related pieces of research on teachers' understandings of mathematical concepts, Fennema and Franke (1992) concluded that "[mathematical] content knowledge does influence the decisions teachers make about classroom instruction" (p. 149). Therefore, it is important for supervisors of teachers of mathematics to consider the subject-area knowledge of the teacher. Also, in Chapter 1, we described mathematics as a combination of content and processes (practices)—something that one does as well as what someone knows. This standard emphasizes that, as teachers of mathematics, we must recognize and value the role of the process skills and mathematical practices in our day-to-day teaching routine. Ideally, a supervisor should be able to record evidence of promoting the mathematical processes and practices in almost every lesson that is observed. This makes an interesting criterion for reflection on one's own lesson: Watch a videotape of the lesson and ask yourself, "At which points in the lesson did I promote the process skills and mathematical practices?"

STANDARD 5: TEACHER KNOWLEDGE AND IMPLEMENTATION OF EFFECTIVE LEARNING ENVIRONMENT AND MATHEMATICAL DISCOURSE

Assessment of the student learning environment and the use of effective mathematical discourse should provide evidence that the teacher—

- engages students in tasks and representations that promote the understanding of mathematical concepts, procedures, and connections;
- engages students in mathematical discourse that extends their understanding of mathematical concepts, procedures, and connections;
- engages students in mathematical tasks that select, apply, and translate among mathematical representations to solve problems;
- engages students in mathematical discourse that communicates their mathematical thinking coherently and clearly to peers, teachers, and others, that analyzes and evaluates the mathematical thinking and strategies of others, and that uses the language of mathematics to express mathematics precisely; and
- engages students in tasks that involve problem solving, reasoning, and communication.

(NCTM, 2007, p. 91)

In Chapter 7, we discussed how "good" mathematics teachers are adept at selecting tasks that generate rich classroom discourse. These tasks are carefully chosen to elicit interaction among students and to promote problem-solving and communication skills. In addition, effective teachers organize the physical and psychological environment in the classroom so that students feel comfortable with being part of the mathematical community and know that their opinions and thinking processes are valued. The assessment of the teacher's ability to select appropriate tasks, to promote a positive classroom climate, and to direct meaningful mathematical conversations in the classroom is a major factor in the observation and improvement of teaching mathematics.

STANDARD 6: ASSESSMENT FOR STUDENT UNDERSTANDING OF MATHEMATICS

Observing the means by which a teacher assesses students' understanding of mathematics should provide evidence that the teacher—

- uses a variety of assessment methods to determine students' understanding of mathematics as well as their ability to apply mathematics in complex and new situations;
- matches assessment methods with the students' developmental level, their mathematical maturity, and other aspects of individual diversity;
- aligns assessment methods with what is taught and how it is taught; and
- uses daily assessment practices to guide instructional practice and to make informed decisions about the learning needs of students.

(NCTM, 2007, p. 100)

If the building principal walks into your classroom and asks to see your syllabus, including a description of how you assess your students and determine final grades, it is important to be able to show how you are using multiple sources of data to fairly and accurately assess student progress. An important consideration in the supervision of mathematics teachers is to determine whether they are valuing performance data beyond paper-and-pencil tests and homework assignments as we discussed in Unit 4.

SPOTlight on Technology

Throughout this book, we have discussed many Web sites that have been created for student use. These sites provide data for analysis, software that can be run on-line, tips for solving problems, and a host of other functions. In the same way, we continue to see an increase in the number of Internet sites that are devoted to the ongoing professional development of teachers. Due in part to the convenience of Internet access, as well as the busy lives that individuals lead in our society, the World Wide Web has rapidly become an excellent source of information for teachers as they explore better ways to run their classrooms.

In 2003, the National Council of Teachers of Mathematics, with the assistance of corporate funding, launched a professional development Web site entitled Reflections (http://nctm.org/resources and click on the Reflections link). At the home page of this site, teachers can select whether to reflect by lesson or by topic, as shown in Figure 13.1.

After selecting a lesson from the next linked page, such as a grade 7 lesson on graphs, teachers can download a lesson plan and read through it, thinking about how that lesson might play out in their own classrooms. Then, they can choose an area to explore in detail. For example, suppose that a teacher is trying to improve the art of asking effective questions in the classroom. There is a link that allows the teacher to explore the discourse that takes place in the lesson and key questions the teacher asks to generate mathematical discussions. Provided within that section are short video clips of the lesson that the teacher can view and reflect on, as well as a list of questions to consider in analyzing the videos. In a similar manner, the teacher can explore the choice of the mathematical task in the lesson, the ways that students learn, decisions the teacher makes, and the underlying mathematics of the problem. Each area involves video clips and even interviews with the teacher in the video reflecting on how students responded to the tasks.

A Web site such as Reflections can be used by teachers as a means of achieving objectives listed in a professional development plan and is particularly convenient because all of the work can be done at a computer in the teacher's home or classroom. As the use of technology continues to expand for students, the same trend continues for the professional development of teachers through CD-ROMs, videos, teleconferencing, distance learning experiences, and Web sites that support the ongoing improvement of classroom teaching.

Figure 13.1   NCTM's Reflections Web Site as a Professional Development Tool

Keep in mind that the six Standards for the Observation, Supervision, and Improvement of Mathematics Teaching represent the ideal process of assessing teaching performance in mathematics. The model recommends an ongoing cycle that includes active involvement by the teacher and the collection of multiple pieces of evidence. The focus of observation and data collection is on those issues that we have identified throughout this text as important in the mathematics classroom—important mathematical content, mathematical processes and practices, the development of a healthy classroom environment, rich classroom discourse, and the use of multiple means of assessment. Just as student assessment should be aligned with what goes on in the classroom and be communicated to the student, the evaluation of teachers also should be an open process with an emphasis on the multiple components of what it takes to be an effective teacher.

If school districts used these six standards to develop their teacher evaluation process, you could be confident that your success was being measured by the degree to which you implement the ideas expressed throughout this text. However, many districts have a "one-size-fits-all" teacher supervision and evaluation process that is used at the elementary, middle, and secondary levels and across content areas. The evaluation tools often include the major components of effective teaching, such as effective lesson planning and teaching, classroom management, and professionalism, but they may not be specific to the mathematics content area. As a result, some of the components mentioned here may not be a part of the assessment process at all. And, in fact, some school districts actually do use one or two classroom observations as the basis of an entire evaluation of the teacher. A sound knowledge of the Standards for the Observation, Supervision, and Improvement of Mathematics Teaching, however, at least gives you a picture of what the National Council of Teachers of Mathematics holds up as an *ideal* in terms of what mathematics teachers should be doing in the classroom and may help you to focus your efforts in your professional development. And if your department has more than one teacher, you can also compare notes with peers (as Standard 2 suggests) to improve your performance in any of the listed areas. In the next section, we discuss how the mathematics teacher can work with others in a department.

Functioning in a Department

In virtually every school or district, secondary and middle school teachers are organized into mathematics departments that are responsible for the teaching and coordination of the mathematics program at that level, which might include some or all of the following activities:

- Organizing and serving on a curriculum-writing team
- Proposing major changes in the curriculum, such as adding or deleting entire courses or changing from a traditional to an integrated sequence of classes
- Selecting textbooks and materials
- Managing a departmental budget for classroom supplies, such as calculators, computer software, or hands-on manipulatives
- Supervising or peer coaching members of the department
- Preparing reports and analyzing results of external assessments such as achievement test scores

Generally, the mathematics department has a chair that is responsible for leading the process, running meetings, and overseeing the implementation of programs. It is extremely important that each member of a department actively contributes to the improvement of the program. You have probably heard the expression "if you're not part of the solution, you're part of the problem," and that is certainly true when it comes to working with other teachers in your school. Part of the responsibility of a mathematics teacher is to identify problems with the program—weaknesses of the curriculum, inappropriate or inadequate content of the texts, or lack of classroom materials—and work toward the improvement of that area. Complaining about the system does not help anyone and, in fact, can spread negativism within the department. Developing a plan of action to improve the program can make a major difference in a school district. It is important to remember that although teachers are responsible for students and accountable to parents and the community, they are also responsible for helping one another enhance the program because every mathematics program can be improved in some way. As we mentioned at the outset of this chapter, the teaching profession *can* be a lonely endeavor, but it certainly doesn't have to be. When we open ourselves up to working with colleagues, a synergy is created—an enthusiasm and energy that is much greater than what teachers can achieve on their own.

In some small school districts, a secondary or middle school mathematics teacher may be the only such teacher at that level. You might find yourself teaching in a small high school with three grade levels in which you teach all of the courses. So much for collegiality? No, not necessarily. As a mathematics teacher, you are one of hundreds of thousands of others around the country who are involved in the same activity. Teachers in small school districts have an even greater need than those in larger districts to connect with mathematics teachers in other locales. Your willingness to share ideas, observe, and work with others around your county, state, or country will greatly enhance your own professional development, as we discuss in the next section.

ngoing Professional Development

Making the Case for Long-Term Development

Throughout this book, we have discussed the importance of capturing teachable moments—those times when students ask just the right question at just the right time—and a teacher can capitalize on the query and turn it into a rich classroom discussion. However, the teaching profession is an art, and the process of making decisions in real time, as the class happens, is a skill that develops gradually. In Chapter 6, we described how sometimes a novice's lesson-planning procedure transforms into a lesson-imaging process for the expert teacher, and we emphasized the role of the teacher in directing classroom discourse in Chapter 7. Fennema and Franke (1992) describe a model for classroom teaching that shows how the teacher's beliefs and knowledge (of content, pedagogy, and learning psychology) interact during a class. Furthermore, Schoenfeld (1998) states that the actions of a teacher and the decisions made while that teacher is leading a lesson are the result of three interacting factors: the teacher's goals, beliefs, and knowledge, as shown in Figure 13.2.

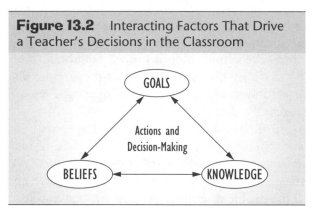

Figure 13.2 Interacting Factors That Drive a Teacher's Decisions in the Classroom

If you think about it, this model makes a great deal of sense. If a teacher firmly believes that mathematics is nothing more than a set of rules to be memorized and skills to be practiced, then a student who presents an alternative strategy for solving a problem is likely to be dismissed because of the *belief* that there is one best way to solve each type of problem—the presentation of another way to look at a problem gets in the way of the procedure that the teacher believes is important to communicate to the class. In a similar way, a lack of content knowledge can drive a teacher's response to a student question. Consider the following classroom situation:

Ms. Bronson's secondary mathematics students have been working on a unit on polynomials, and, without any previous instruction on quadratic equations, she asks them if they can figure out how to solve the equation $x^2 + 6 = 5x$.

> *Ms. Bronson:* Take a few minutes at your table and see if you can come up with a solution. (The students work for 10 minutes, and Sherry raises her hand.) Sherry, what did you and your partner come up with?
>
> *Sherry:* We got an answer of 2.
>
> *Matthew:* So did we. It was easy; you just use guess and check.
>
> *Ms. Bronson:* Is that how you solved it, Sherry?
>
> *Sherry:* No, I solved it like we did linear equations earlier this year. I can show you easier than I can tell you. (Sherry goes up to the board and writes.)
>
> $x^2 + 6 = 5x$, so I wrote it out like this:
>
> $x \cdot x + 6 = 5x$. Now, you just subtract two x's from both sides, so you get $6 = 3x$. If you divide both sides by 3, you get $x = 2$. That's all there is to it.

How would you handle this situation? What was the error in mathematical reasoning? Think about it for a minute and then read on. Let's suppose that Ms. Bronson's content knowledge is fairly weak. If so, she might respond to Sherry's solution by either accepting it as reasonable or, maybe even worse, *telling* Sherry that "you can't do that" and proceeding to show the class how to subtract $5x$ from both sides of the equation and factor. However, if Ms. Bronson is alert and has a solid mathematics background, she will immediately ask herself, "Why did Sherry's method work?" And, with a little thought, she would recognize that subtracting

$x \cdot x$ from one side of the equation and $2x$ from the other side works only when $x = 0$ or $x = 2$ (because $0^2 = 2(0)$ and $2^2 = 2(2)$). In this case, by coincidence, $x \cdot x = 2x$ because $x = 2$, so her method worked. Thinking fast, Ms. Bronson could pose this follow-up equation to the class: $x^2 + 6 = 7x$. If Sherry used the same strategy as she had with the last problem, she would obtain an answer of $x = \frac{6}{5}$ (How?), which does not work. In this case, the actual solutions to the equation are $x = 1$ or $x = 6$, but $1^2 \neq 2(1)$, and $6^2 \neq 2(6)$. By discussing this second example, Sherry and the class recognize that her method does not work for *all* quadratic equations, and this will send the class in search of a third method.

Of course, Ms. Bronson's ability to recognize the error in Sherry's reasoning and to come up with an off-the-cuff counterexample is a result of her firm grasp of the lesson's mathematical content. Furthermore, if it were Ms. Bronson's *goal* to simply *show* the class how to factor to solve a quadratic equation, she never would have posed the problem without previous instruction in the first place. So, the point here is that if we analyze any teaching and learning situation, we will recognize the factors that influence the teacher's behaviors. *Principles and Standards for School Mathematics* (NCTM, 2000) states that "teaching mathematics is a complex endeavor, and there are no easy recipes for helping all students learn or for helping all teachers become effective" (p. 17). Indeed, the power of experience and reflection on practice must not be underestimated. When a teacher seeks out an inservice program, a graduate class, and so forth, those experiences may ultimately affect the teacher's goals, belief system, and knowledge level, thus changing the way the individual runs the classroom. On the contrary, if an undergraduate earns a degree and a teaching license but rarely, if ever, goes back for additional course work, that person may hold the same goals, beliefs, and knowledge for many years. Consequently, that teacher may act almost exactly the same from class to class and from year to year over a long period of time until a program comes along that shakes the system. Professional development activities are designed to press educators into reflecting on what they believe about mathematics education and to provide them with additional content knowledge that may improve their classroom teaching practices. In most states, continuing professional development is required of all teachers, as the states recognize the importance of improving teaching skills over time.

A document calling for the improvement of mathematics and science education entitled *Before It's Too Late* was published in 2000. Former senator and astronaut John Glenn headed the National Commission on Mathematics and Science Teaching for the Twenty-First Century that authored the document. In this booklet, the commission emphasized—as has the National Council of Teachers of Mathematics—the necessity for teachers to receive ongoing professional development. They defined *professional development* as

> a planned, collaborative, educational process of continuous improvement for teachers that helps them to do five things: (1) deepen their knowledge of the subject(s) they are teaching; (2) sharpen their teaching skills in the classroom; (3) keep up with developments in their fields, and in education generally; (4) generate and contribute new knowledge to the profession; and (5) increase their ability to monitor students' work, so they can provide constructive feedback to students and appropriately redirect their own learning. (U.S. Department of Education, 2000, p. 18)

In the next section, we discuss opportunities that are available to teachers for their professional development.

Classroom Dialogues

In a mathematics classroom, the teacher displayed the bar graph shown in Figure 13.3 to the students in the class.

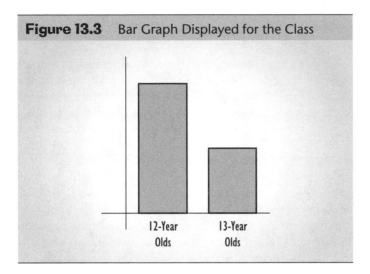

Figure 13.3 Bar Graph Displayed for the Class

Teacher: This bar graph shows the results of a fund-raising activity in a school. Students were asked to sell products from a magazine, and the graph shows the amount of money raised in a class by the 12- and the 13-year-olds in the class. What do we know from looking at the graph?

Student 1: We know that the 12-year-olds brought in more money than the 13-year-olds did.

Student 2: Not only *more* money, but the bar is about twice as high, so we know that the 12-year-olds brought in *twice as much* money as the 13-year-olds did.

Teacher: Can anyone tell me something that the graph does *not* tell us?

Student 1: We don't know the exact dollar amount because the *y*-axis isn't labeled. I mean, the 12-year-olds might have brought in $100, and the 13-year-olds might have brought in $50, or it could be like $500 and $250. We don't know unless the graph is labeled.

Teacher: Good point. Let me show you some labels. (The teacher then places an overlay on the graph that displays the image shown in Figure 13.4.)

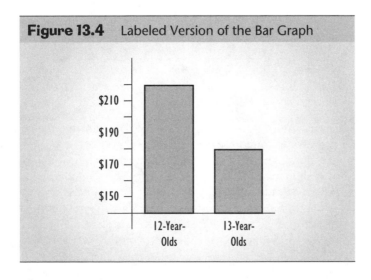

Figure 13.4 Labeled Version of the Bar Graph

Immediately, the students begin to raise their hands.

Student 3: It looks like the 13-year-olds brought in about $180 worth of sales, and the 12-year-olds sold about $220. So, they didn't really outsell the students by twice as much like we originally thought!

Teacher: What about this new version of the graph made you change your mind?

Student 3: I think we all assumed that the *y*-axis started at zero, but it doesn't. When the graph starts at around $140, the height of the stacks can't be compared anymore. I think you tricked us!

The "trick" pulled by the teacher revealed misconceptions about graphing on the part of the students. First, they assumed that the graph's vertical axis started at zero. In seeing the second version of the graph, they learned the importance of providing a scale on a graph and why it is essential to show a "break" along the vertical axis when the first mark skips to a value greater than one unit. Second, the students never brought up the issue of how many students were in each of the age groups. The teacher would need to prompt them again to jump-start this discussion. For example, suppose that the class had seventeen 12-year-olds and five 13-year-olds. Now, the average 12-year-old sold about $13 worth of merchandise, whereas the average 13-year-old sold approximately $36 worth. Therefore, although the bar for 13-year-olds was half as high, the average sale for a student of that age was almost three times as much. These are the types of conversations that should be taking place when students are exploring the topic of data analysis. Are there other issues you might use this example to discuss with your students? What are some other common mistakes that people tend to make when drawing graphs or analyzing the data on a graph? How important are the skills of graphing and analyzing data in our world and, therefore, how much emphasis should the topics receive in a classroom?

Another example of a mistake that students often make is displayed in Figure 13.5.

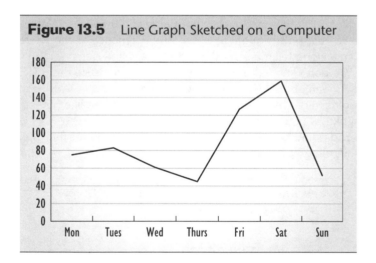

Figure 13.5 Line Graph Sketched on a Computer

In this situation, students were given a table of data showing the number of hot dogs sold at a concession stand for each of the seven days of the week at a ballpark. The students were allowed to use a computer to draw the graph, and the graph shown in Figure 13.5 was submitted by one of the students. Keep in mind that students are expected not only to be able to sketch and analyze a graph but also to know what kind of graph is appropriate in a given situation. Which representations of hot dog sales are appropriate in this case? What is the problem with the graph in this situation? How might the teacher address the misconception?

Opportunities for Professional Development

A professional development specialist conducted a workshop for secondary and middle school mathematics teachers in a local school district. As he was preparing his notes for the presentation, he overheard four comments as the teachers in the room spoke to one another:

- "I really don't want to be here!"
- "Do you know how many mathematics classes I had in college? Just enough to jump through the hoops, and that was enough for me!"
- "I need this workshop like I need a hole in the head."
- "I teach sixth grade. Is there going to be anything in this for me?"

These types of comments are not unusual at professional development workshops, and they might be seen as a sad commentary about the teaching profession. As we analyze these statements closely, however, we realize that the root of this attitude is that teachers want and need something that is relevant to them. After all, students in school sometimes ask, "When are we ever going to have to use this?" so why shouldn't teachers ask the same question? As we discussed in Chapter 3, mathematics needs to be relevant to our students to capture their interest and attention, and adults are no different in this respect. Unfortunately, many teachers have taken classes or workshops that simply were not helpful. So, if you want workshops and courses to be meaningful, you have to be selective about organizations that you join and programs that you attend. And, above all, it is important to attend these types of inservice opportunities with an open mind and to assume that you will always find at least one gem from an inservice presentation. There are many opportunities available to mathematics teachers who want to enhance their ongoing professional development.

First, it is important for mathematics teachers to interact with colleagues. For teachers new to the profession, this might involve having a mentor teacher, under whom the newer teachers apprentice as they gain the critical first years of experience. For more experienced teachers, the mentor may be a peer with whom the seasoned teachers can share their successes and challenges and with whom they can discuss pedagogical and content-related issues. It is very difficult to grow as a professional without conversations with others, just as it is more difficult to learn mathematics without group interaction.

Second, teachers need to take an active role in their own professional development by becoming members of local, state, or national organizations designed to assist their growth process. The National Council of Teachers of Mathematics, for example, has well over 100,000 members and publishes five professional journals throughout the academic year (for information, visit the NCTM on the Web at www.nctm.org). The NCTM also has an affiliate in each state, such as the Colorado Council of Teachers of Mathematics, and most states have affiliates at the local level, such as the Bowling Green State University Council of Teachers of Mathematics. Each organization has its own newsletters and other publications and ordinarily offers inservice programs or meetings that provide teachers with opportunities to connect with others in the profession. Teachers in small school districts can have discussions with professionals in other districts, and those who teach in large districts can get a sense of how other departments and districts function. Membership in professional organizations tends to be relatively inexpensive (a teacher, for example, generally can join the national, state, and local councils for a total of approximately $100 a year) but provides major benefits by allowing you to stay connected with the evolving field of mathematics education.

Third, teachers can attend conferences organized by professional organizations. Each year, the NCTM has a national meeting and several regional conferences, and each state generally has one annual conference as do many of the local affiliates. At a conference, teachers can attend sessions relevant to their grade level and content interest and pick up a great deal of classroom-ready, practical teaching ideas. Between workshops or presentations, teachers also have plenty of time to stand in the hallway and talk to others or to browse displays of the latest texts and materials. Conferences are excellent opportunities to recharge the batteries.

Fourth, mathematics teachers can also benefit from regularly reading such publications as the many self-help and resource books available as well as journals, such as *Mathematics Teacher* or *Mathematics Teaching in the Middle School,* which feature everything from philosophical essays to practical classroom teaching ideas. Just taking an hour a month to browse through a couple of books or journals can provide a practicing teacher with a number of ideas for lesson plans and ways to improve the teaching and learning process. Electronic memberships in professional organizations often allow members to access back issues of journals, with online tools available to search for articles on topics of interest to the teacher.

Similarly, the World Wide Web has become a popular means for finding lessons and ideas. Sites on the Internet feature hundreds of lesson-plan ideas, hands-on activities, and theoretical pieces for reading and discussion. There is much more on the Web than one can deal with in a short period of time, so it is recommended that a teacher take even an hour or two each month simply to surf the Web and look for new sites that may feature ideas for classroom implementation. Browsing on the Internet can be an excellent growth tool as we explore what others are doing and try to rethink some of our own lessons in light of many readily available suggestions. The Appendix contains a listing of suggested Web sites to get you started using the Internet as a professional development tool.

Many universities offer evening, weekend, and summer workshops and graduate courses. It is important for practicing teachers to take part in these workshops and course offerings in order to stay up to date on local, state, and national education issues. One way that practicing teachers get in touch with new standards and trends is by enrolling in university offerings. As soon as one is enrolled and has paid for a class, it becomes a commitment that is difficult to neglect. A commitment such as browsing the Web for an hour a month can easily become a low-priority activity, but class assignments require a commitment of several hours, days, or weeks. In many states, graduate course work is required to maintain certification or licensure, but these graduate programs may be offered free of charge to classroom teachers and are funded by federal or state grants. The best way to find out about the grant-funded programs is to be a member of the professional organizations, which generally advertise programs for professional development through their newsletters and informal networking systems.

Read any good books lately? Another way to improve your knowledge of the teaching profession is to select and read a book on mathematics education. The book might be a practical discussion of classroom projects or a more theoretical book on psychology or cooperative learning, but such a book can help you identify your strengths and challenges as a teacher and set goals for the future. Finally, never underestimate the power of observing another teacher at work within your own school or in another community. Teachers can learn a great deal about themselves simply by walking into another classroom and seeing how another person manages students. For many, student teaching was the only time in their careers that they actually spent some time observing someone else's classroom. Yet, in the business world, people work with other departments, visit other plants and corporate offices, and explore alternate ways of doing business all the time. Some school districts not only *allow* but *require* teachers to visit other classrooms at least once a year—which can be a powerful experience.

In the end, a teacher is simply not "made" in 4 years of undergraduate college preservice experiences. A teacher grows, develops, and becomes a professional over many years. A college degree indicates that the person is ready to enter the profession, but the first 5 to 10 years of teaching are the critical time during which most teachers experience a significant amount of growth. Of course, with the world changing as quickly as it does, much of our current knowledge will be outdated within 5 years, so it becomes important and necessary to explore avenues to continue our development over time and stay current. Selecting any of the suggestions discussed here can be helpful in taking that first step toward long-term growth.

The Professional Development Plan

Some districts and states now require that teachers complete and implement an annual professional development plan or PDP. The PDP is relatively simple; it is a written statement in which a teacher points out personal strengths and challenges as a professional and describes a plan for development in the upcoming academic year.

The PDP is essentially a contract or agreement between the teacher and the school district outlining an intended plan of personal growth for the year. For example, the teacher may decide that a major challenge for the year is to learn to use graphing calculators effectively in the classroom. So, the teacher's plan may include taking a course during the summer at the local university and implementing at least one new unit in the school year that makes effective use of graphing calculators. At the end of the school year, one of the items that the teacher adds to the professional portfolio is the PDP and a written statement about how it was implemented during the academic year. The administrator can sign the PDP and make comments about whether the teacher met the objectives set for the year. The PDP might contain implementation strategies that include visiting other classrooms, joining a professional organization, attending a conference, conducting Internet research, and so on. The PDP is yet another way for teachers to reflect on their practice and formalize a plan to ensure long-term growth.

PROFESSIONAL DEVELOPMENT PLAN

Name: _____

School District/Building: _____

Grade Level(s): _____

Date: _____

Greatest strengths and accomplishments to date as a teacher:

Greatest challenges (needs) as a teacher:

Goals/anticipated outcomes for the academic year:

Activities and resources needed to address goals/outcomes:

Teacher's Signature: _____

Post conference

Administrator's Signature: _____

Comments on the degree to which the plan was implemented:

Conclusion

The world of teaching mathematics can be very exciting as we watch the minds of our students develop and change over time. But we, as teachers, must also be willing to grow as professionals, increasing our knowledge and skills and making each year of teaching better than the previous year. In this chapter, we have looked at the importance of developing a home–school connection, at the process of supervising and improving teaching, and at what it means to be a member of a department and to develop as a professional. In the first edition of *Professional Standards for Teaching Mathematics*, the authors state that "the current reform movement in mathematics education, and in education in general, has as a strong underlying theme—the professionalism of teaching. This view recognizes the teacher as a part of a learning community that continually fosters growth in knowledge, stature, and responsibility" (NCTM, 1991, p. 6). Indeed, the teacher makes all the difference in the classroom—the difference between whether students get excited about mathematics and learn to become problem solvers or whether they develop a fear of and anxiety toward mathematics and are relatively unsuccessful in school.

It has been the intent of this text to encompass the background and underlying theoretical issues of the teaching profession. But, again, a teacher is not made in 4 years of college or even in 5 years of teaching after the initial licensure or certification. Instead, we develop and grow into a style that is all our own after many years of practice, reflection, and refinement. Just as a manuscript is transformed from a rough draft to a published work of art, so is a teacher developed from a naive "rookie" to a seasoned veteran who can eventually serve as a "buddy" to other novice teachers. One mathematics teacher was quoted as saying, "When I reach a point in my career where I feel I have 'arrived' and cannot improve upon what I did last year, I will know that it's time to retire and let someone else take over." The "good teacher" is always open to suggestions and willing to change for the sake of the students—after all, students are what teaching is all about.

> **For bibliographic references and additional resources, see page 420**

Discussion Questions and Activities

1. Make a list of ways to actively involve parents in the teaching and learning of mathematics in addition to the suggestions provided in this chapter. What do you expect of the parents of your students?

2. Review the six Standards for the Observation, Supervision, and Improvement of Mathematics Teaching by the NCTM. If you were a principal and had to weigh the six criteria, similar to the way that we dis-

cussed weighing test scores versus journals and homework in Chapter 11, what relative weight would you assign to each of the criteria?

3. Interview mathematics teachers from three different school districts on how their performance is assessed and evaluated. Compare the teacher evaluation practices of the three school districts to one another and to the six criteria set forth by the NCTM.

4. Interview principals from three different school districts and ask them, "In what ways do you support and encourage ongoing professional development of your mathematics teachers?" Compare the responses. What level of support and encouragement do you expect for ongoing professional development as a teacher?

5. The mathematics department chair often conducts peer evaluations of other mathematics teachers in the school. Discuss some of the advantages and disadvantages of being supervised or evaluated by another teacher as opposed to being supervised by a building-level administrator.

6. Suppose that you are one of five members in the mathematics department at your school. Your department chair would like to adopt a new textbook series for courses that you teach and favors a different series from the one that you selected. How do you deal with the situation in a professional manner, respecting the role of the chair while trying to promote a collaborative decision?

7. Observe a mathematics class or watch a class on video. As you watch the teacher in action, take notes on the teacher's apparent goals in the lesson, beliefs about mathematics and the teacher's role in the classroom, and knowledge of the content area and teaching strategies or pedagogy. Compare your notes to those of a peer who observed the same class or video.

8. Discuss which of the strategies for obtaining ongoing professional development were most appealing to you and why. Which professional experiences do you believe are most valuable for inservice teachers?

9. Comment on the advantages and possible drawbacks to preparing an annual professional development plan that is reviewed and commented on by the principal as described in the chapter.

10. It has been said that it takes 10 years to make a person into a teacher. What does this statement say to you? Do you agree or disagree with this and why?

Recommended Web Sites

Links to these and other sites, updated regularly, can be located by visiting the author's Web site at http://bgmath.org and clicking on the "Links" button.

Professional Organizations

National Council of Teachers of Mathematics (NCTM)

http://www.nctm.org

NCTM is the largest professional organization for improving the teaching of mathematics at the pre-K–12 grade levels. This site includes membership forms, an online store for purchasing books and materials, feature articles for reading, and other general information.

School Science and Mathematics Association (SSMA)

http://www.ssma.org

SSMA is an organization committed to improving mathematics and science education in grades K–12. The site features information about SSMA and its professional journal, access to the SSMA newsletter, special publications, and more.

Common Core State Standards and Assessments

Core Standards

http://www.corestandards.org

This site is the home of the Common Core State Standards. The Standards documents can be downloaded from the site. Also, the latest information about states that have adopted the CCSS and the latest news about implementation of the Standards can be found at this site.

Math Common Core Coalition

http://www.mathccc.org

This site is the home for a coalition of several organizations—from the National Council of Teachers of Mathematics to the Association of Mathematics Teacher Educators—committed to providing resources and advice to states and districts implementing the Common Core State Standards.

Partnership for the Assessment of Readiness for College and Careers (PARCC)

http://www.parcconline.org

This site is the home of the PARCC consortium, consisting of more than 20 states that are collaborating to develop assessments for the Common Core State Standards. The site features information about the assessments and up-to-date progress reports.

SMARTER Balanced Assessment Consortium

http://www.k12.wa.us/smarter

The SMARTER Balance consortium consists of more than 20 states working together to develop assessments for the Common Core State Standards. This site includes the latest news and specific information about the purposes and contents of the assessments.

Curriculum Projects

ARC Center

http://www.comap.com/elementary/projects/arc

The purpose of the ARC Center site is to provide teacher enhancement, leadership development, and public awareness of mathematics education. The site is a great help in rebuilding curriculum for grades K–6 based on the Standards. It also provides resources for professional development. While the ARC Center closed in 2005, the site is still available for research.

COMPASS

http://www.ithaca.edu/compass

Curricular Options in Mathematics Programs for All Secondary Schools (COMPASS) assists schools, teachers, administrators, parent groups, and other community members and constituencies interested in improving secondary school (grades 8–12) mathematics opportunities and experiences for their students. Advice is provided at the site for schools considering selecting standards-based curriculum products.

Show-Me Center

http://showmecenter.missouri.edu

The Show-Me Center, in partnership with the NSF-sponsored middle grades curriculum development satellites and their publishers, provides information and resources needed to support selection and implementation of Standards-based middle grades (grades 5–8) mathematics curricula.

Activities and Lesson Plan Ideas

Coolmath.com

http://www.coolmath.com

Designed "for the pure enjoyment of math," the Coolmath site contains mathematics lesson plans and links, organized by subject area (algebra, geometry, trigonometry, calculus, and so on). It features fractals, puzzles, problems, games, and career information.

Cut-The-Knot

http://cut-the-knot.org

A wealth of applets (mini applications) are available at this site. Teachers can use these applications in the classroom with an interactive whiteboard or can have students use them to explore in a computer lab or at home. It is an excellent resource for those wanting to use visuals and technology in their teaching.

Eisenhower National Clearinghouse

http://www.goenc.com

K–12 mathematics and science lessons plans, activities, a resource finder, reviews of software, and much more are available at the Eisenhower National Clearinghouse site.

Figure This

http://www.figurethis.org

Mathematical challenges for families of middle school students are provided at the Figure This site to motivate students and their caregivers in pursuing mathematical tasks at home.

Illuminations

http://illuminations.nctm.org

Illuminations is a site for teachers that provides lesson plans, Web resources, interactive mathematics tools, and mathematical investigations. NCTM sponsors the site, so all of the lesson plans reflect the spirit of the NCTM Standards.

Mathematics Education Directory—Yahoo!

http://dir.yahoo.com/Science/Mathematics/Education

Links to mathematics Web sites that feature lesson plans, tutoring, research, and so on can be found at the Mathematics Education Directory site.

Mathematics Hotlist

http://sln.fi.edu/tfi/hotlists/math.html

Links to many Web sites featuring games, puzzles, and problems are available at Mathematics Hotlist.

Mathematics WWW Virtual Library

http://www.math.fsu.edu/Virtual/index.php

At this site, a collection of mathematics-related resources is maintained by the Florida State University Department of Mathematics.

Math Archives

http://archives.math.utk.edu

At the Math Archives site, many materials are made available, including topics on mathematics, software, teaching materials, other links, and more.

Mathcounts

http://mathcounts.org

Mathcounts is a competitive problem-solving program for middle school students. The Web site features information about the competition, as well as problems of the week and other helpful resources.

Math Gems

http://www.sciencegems.com/math.html

Mathematics content areas are listed by name, and the Math Gems site is updated regularly with new resources. This is a place to visit if you are looking for information on a particular branch of mathematics.

MegaMath

http://www.c3.lanl.gov/mega-math/menu.html

Each subsection at MegaMath includes activities, vocabulary, background information, big ideas and key concepts, evaluation, for further study, prep and materials, and connections to the NCTM Standards.

National Library of Virtual Manipulatives

http://www.nlvm.usu.edu

With funding from the National Science Foundation, Utah State University features numerous on-line manipulatives that include lesson ideas and hints for users. A grid makes it simple to search by content area and grade level.

PBS Teacher Source

http://pbs.org/teachers

By selecting the grade level of interest, PBS features more than 1,400 lessons and activities across the content areas.

Shodor Interactivate

http://www.shodor.org/interactivate

This site features applets for demonstrations, lesson ideas, activities, and discussions that support the teaching of mathematics. The front page features areas for "Learners" and for "Instructors," as it can be useful to both the teacher and the students.

General Mathematics Education Sites

Annenberg Media Learner.org

http://www.learner.org

The Annenberg Foundation's Web site makes hundreds of hours of streaming video available to teachers. These videos can be used for individual professional development or shown to students within a mathematics lesson from kindergarten through college.

Biographies of Women Mathematicians

http://www.agnesscott.edu/lriddle/women/women.htm

The Biographies of Women Mathematicians project illustrates the numerous achievements of women in the field of mathematics.

The Consortium for Mathematics and Its Applications (COMAP)

http://www.comap.com

COMAP is a nonprofit organization that works with teachers, schools, and the business world to promote the use of mathematics to investigate real-world problems. The site provides membership information, as well as information about products, projects, and contests available to schools.

History Topics Index

http://www-gap.dcs.st-and.ac.uk/~history/Indexes/HistoryTopics.html

Mathematics history may be explored by topic or may be searched by mathematician, year, or location at the History Topics Index site.

Teachers Helping Teachers

http://www.pacificnet.net/~mandel

The Teachers Helping Teachers site contains weekly updated material in many subject areas and is divided into content areas, classroom management, and a topic of the week. There is also a list of other Web sites, a poem of the week, and a stress reduction moment of the week. Users can also contribute lessons and submit questions or problems.

The Math Forum

http://www.mathforum.org

From the home page at Math Forum, you can access what seems to be an endless amount of information on mathematics. Some of the links include the teachers' place, student center, research division, parents and citizens, and Ask Dr. Math where students can seek advice on problem solving. One may also search subject resources, mathematics education, key issues in mathematics, and forum features.

Bibliographic References and Resources

Chapter 1

Beaton, A. E., et al. (1996). *TIMSS: Mathematics achievement in the middle school years*. Chestnut Hill, MA: Center for the Study of Testing, Evaluation, and Educational Policy.

Boston College. (1999). Center for the Study of Testing, Evaluation, and Educational Policy. Retrieved August 20, 1999, from the World Wide Web: http://www.csteep.bc.edu/timss

Brahier, D. J. (Ed.) (2011). *Motivation and disposition: Pathways to learning mathematics. Seventy-third yearbook of the National Council of Teachers of Mathematics*. Reston, VA: NCTM.

Braswell, J., Daane, M., & Grigg, W. (2003). *The nation's report card: Mathematics highlights 2003*. Washington, DC: National Center for Education Statistics.

Braswell, J. S., et al. (2001). *The nation's report card: Mathematics 2000*. Washington, DC: National Center for Education Statistics.

Burrill, G., et al. (2002). *Handheld graphing technology in secondary mathematics: Research findings and implications for classroom practice*. Dallas, TX: Texas Instruments.

Charles, R. I., & Barnett, C. S. (1992). *Problem-solving experiences in pre-algebra*. Menlo Park, CA: Addison-Wesley.

Common Core State Standards Initiative. (2010). *Common core state standards for mathematics*. Washington, DC: National Governors Association Center for Best Practices and Council of Chief State School Officers.

Conference Board of the Mathematical Sciences. (2001). *The mathematical education of teachers*. Providence, RI: American Mathematical Society.

Cuoco, A. A. (Ed.). (2001). *2001 Yearbook of the NCTM: The roles of representation in school mathematics*. Reston, VA: National Council of Teachers of Mathematics.

Dolan, D. T., & Williamson, J. (1983). *Teaching problem-solving strategies*. Menlo Park, CA: Addison-Wesley.

Dossey, J. A., Mullis, I. V., & Jones, C. O. (1993). *Can students do mathematical problem solving?* Washington, DC: U.S. Department of Education.

Dunham, P. H. (2000). Handheld calculators in mathematics education: A research perspective. In E. D. Laughbaum (Ed.), *Handheld technology in mathematics and science education: A collection of papers* (pp. 39–47). Columbus, OH: The Ohio State University.

Elliot, P. C. (Ed.). (1996). *1996 Yearbook of the NCTM: Communication in mathematics and beyond*. Reston, VA: National Council of Teachers of Mathematics.

Fello, S. E., & Paquette, K. R. (2009). Talking and writing in the classroom. *Mathematics Teaching in the Middle School, 14* (7), 410–414.

Fleischman, H. L., et al. (2010). *Highlights from PISA 2009: Performance of U.S. 15-year-old students in reading, mathematics, and science literacy in an international context*. Washington, DC: Center for Education Statistics.

Gonzales, P., et al. (2009). *Highlights from TIMSS 2007: Mathematics and science achievement of U.S. fourth- and eighth-grade students in an international context*. Washington, DC: National Center for Education Statistics.

Gonzales, P., et al. (2000). *Highlights from the Third International Mathematics and Science Study–Repeat (TIMSS–R)*. Washington, DC: National Center for Education Statistics.

Hembree, R., & Dessart, D. J. (1992). Research on calculators in mathematics education. In J. Fey (Ed.), *1992 Yearbook of the NCTM: Calculators in mathematics education* (pp. 23–32). Reston, VA: National Council of Teachers of Mathematics.

Hiebert, J., et al. (2003). *Teaching mathematics in seven countries: Results from the TIMSS 1999 video study*. Washington, DC: National Center for Education Statistics.

House, P. A. (Ed.). (1995). *1995 Yearbook of the NCTM: Connecting mathematics across the curriculum*. Reston, VA: National Council of Teachers of Mathematics.

Illingworth, M. (1996). *Real-life math problem solving*. New York: Scholastic.

International Association for the Evaluation of Educational Achievement. (2007). *Trends in international mathematics and science study (TIMSS), 2007*. Washington, DC: National Center for Education Statistics.

Kenney, P. A., & Silver, E. A. (Eds.). (1997). *Results from the Sixth Mathematics Assessment of the National Assessment of Educational Progress*. Reston, VA: National Council of Teachers of Mathematics.

Kessel, C., Epstein, J., & Keynes, M. (Eds.). (2001). *The mathematical education of teachers*. Washington, DC: American Mathematical Society and Mathematical Association of America.

Kline, M. (1973). *Why Johnny can't add*. New York: St. Martin's.

Krulik, S. (Ed.). (1980). *1980 Yearbook of the NCTM: Problem solving in school mathematics*. Reston, VA: National Council of Teachers of Mathematics.

Leitzel, James R. C. (Ed.). (1991). *A call for change: Recommendations for the mathematical preparation of teachers of mathematics*. Washington, DC: Mathematical Association of America.

Ma, L. (1999). *Knowing and teaching elementary mathematics*. Mahwah, NJ: Erlbaum.

Mathematical Sciences Education Board. (2001). *Knowing and learning mathematics for teaching: Proceedings of a workshop*. Washington, DC: National Academy Press.

Mathematical Sciences Education Board. (1989). *Everybody counts: A report to the nation on the future of mathematics education*. Washington, DC: National Academy Press.

Michigan State University. (1999). Research Center for the International Mathematics and Science Study. Retrieved August 20, 1999, from the World Wide Web: http://ustimss.msu.edu

Mueller, M. F., & Maher, C. A. (2009). Convincing and justifying through reasoning. *Mathematics Teaching in the Middle School, 15* (2), p. 108–116.

National Center for Education Statistics. (2011). *The nation's report card: Mathematics 2009 for grade 12*. Retrieved March 30, 2011, from the World Wide Web: http://nationsreportcard.gov/math_2009

National Center for Education Statistics. (2009). *The nation's report card: Mathematics 2009*. Washington DC: U.S. Department of Education.

National Center for Education Statistics. (2007a). National assessment of educational progress: The nation's report card. Retrieved October 3, 2007, from the World Wide Web: http://nces.ed.gov/nationsreportcard

National Center for Education Statistics. (2007b). TIMSS USA: Trends in international mathematics and science study. Retrieved October 3, 2007, from the World Wide Web: http://nces.ed.gov/timss

National Center for Education Statistics. (2005a). *Highlights from the Trends in International Mathematics and Science Study (TIMSS) 2003*. Washington, DC: U.S. Department of Education.

National Center for Education Statistics. (2005b). *Mathematics concepts and mathematics items: TIMSS 2003*. Washington, DC: U.S. Department of Education.

National Commission on Mathematics and Science Teaching for the Twenty-First Century. (2000). *Before it's too late*. Jessup, MD: U.S. Department of Education.

National Council of Teachers of Mathematics. (2010). *Making it happen: Interpreting and implementing the common core standards for mathematics*. Reston, VA: NCTM.

National Council of Teachers of Mathematics. (2000). *Principles and standards for school mathematics*. Reston, VA: National Council of Teachers of Mathematics.

National Council of Teachers of Mathematics. (1995). *Assessment standards for school mathematics*. Reston, VA: National Council of Teachers of Mathematics.

National Council of Teachers of Mathematics. (1991). *Professional standards for teaching mathematics*. Reston, VA: National Council of Teachers of Mathematics.

National Council of Teachers of Mathematics. (1989). *Curriculum and evaluation standards for school mathematics*. Reston, VA: National Council of Teachers of Mathematics.

National Council of Teachers of Mathematics. (1987). *The developments in school mathematics education around the world: Applications-oriented curricula and technology-supported learning for all students*. Reston, VA: National Council of Teachers of Mathematics.

National Council of Teachers of Mathematics. (1980). *An agenda for action: Recommendations for school mathematics of the 1980s*. Reston, VA: National Council of Teachers of Mathematics.

Ohio Department of Education. (1980). *Becoming a better problem solver: Book 1*. Columbus, OH: Ohio Department of Education.

Ohio Department of Education. (1980). *A resource for problem solving: Book 2*. Columbus, OH: Ohio Department of Education.

Organization for Economic Co-operation and Development. (2011a). *OECD Web site*. Retrieved March 30, 2011, from the World Wide Web: http://www.oecd.org

Organization for Economic Co-operation and Development. (2011b). *Programme for International Student Assessment*. Retrieved March 30, 2011, from the World Wide Web: http://www.pisa.oecd.org

Phillips, E., Gardella, T., Kelly, C., & Stewart, J. (1991). *NCTM 5–8 addenda series: Patterns and functions*. Reston, VA: National Council of Teachers of Mathematics.

Polya, G. (1945). *How to solve it*. Princeton, NJ: Princeton University Press.

Reese, C. M., Miller, K. E., Mazzeo, J., & Dossey, J. A. (1997). *NAEP 1996 mathematics report card for the nation and the states*. Washington, DC: National Center for Education Statistics.

Roberts, S. K. (2010). The important thing about teaching problem solving. *Mathematics Teaching in the Middle School, 16* (2), 104–108.

Schmidt, W. H., McKnight, C. C., Valverde, G. A., Houang, R. T., & Wiley, D. E. (1997). *Many visions, many aims: Volume 1*. The Netherlands: Kluwer Academic.

Schoenfeld, A. H. (Ed.). (1994). *Mathematical thinking and problem solving*. Hillsdale, NJ: Erlbaum.

Schoenfeld, A. H. (1985). *Mathematical problem solving*. Orlando, FL: Academic.

Schoenfeld, A. H. (1983). *Problem solving in the mathematics curriculum: A report, recommendations, and an annotated bibliography*. Washington, DC: Mathematical Association of America.

Secretary's Commission on Achieving Necessary Skills. (1991). *What work requires of schools: A SCANS report for America 2000*. Washington, DC: U.S. Department of Labor.

Sekerak, J. (2010). Competences of mathematical modelling of high school students. *Mathematics Teaching, 220*, 8–12.

Sharp, E. (1964). *A parent's guide to the new mathematics.* New York: E. P. Dutton.

Shufelt, G. (Ed.). (1983). *1983 Yearbook of the NCTM: The agenda in action.* Reston, VA: The National Council of Teachers of Mathematics.

Stiff, L. V. (Ed.). (1999). *1999 Yearbook of the NCTM: Developing mathematical reasoning in grades K–12.* Reston, VA: National Council of Teachers of Mathematics.

Stylianides, G. (2010). Engaging secondary students in reasoning and proving. *Mathematics Teaching, 219*, 39–44.

Tripathi, P. N. (2008). Developing mathematical understanding through multiple representations. *Mathematics Teaching in the Middle School, 13* (8), 438–445.

U.S. Department of Education. (1983). *A nation at risk.* Archived at the Web site of the U.S. Department of Education. Retrieved March 30, 2011, from the World Wide Web: http://www2.ed.gov/pubs/NatAtRisk/risk .html

Chapter 2

Annenberg Media. (2011). *Learner.org.* Retrieved May 24, 2011, from the World Wide Web: http://www.learner.org

Berry III, R. Q. (2004). Spotlight on the principles: The equity principle through the voices of African American male students. *Mathematics Teaching in the Middle School, 10* (2), 100–103.

Brahier, D. J. (2002). Assessment as a lever to reform: Teachers rethinking mathematics education. *Focus on Learning Problems in Mathematics, 24* (3), 61–73.

Eisner, E. (1994). *The educational imagination: On the design and evaluation of school programs* (3rd ed.). New York: Macmillan College Publishing.

Fagan, E. (2005). Spotlight on the principles: Creating an environment for learning with understanding: The learning principle. *Mathematics Teaching in the Middle School, 11* (1), 35–39.

Ferrini-Mundy, J. (2001). Introduction: Perspectives on principles and standards for school mathematics. *School Science and Mathematics, 101* (6), 277–279.

Gilbert, M. C. (2001). Applying the equity principle. *Mathematics Teaching in the Middle School, 7* (1), 18–19, 36.

Graham, K. J., & Fennell, F. (2001). Principles and standards for school mathematics and teacher education: Preparing and empowering teachers. *School Science and Mathematics, 101* (6), 319–327.

Gutstein, E., Middleton, J. A., & Fey, J. T. (2005). Equity in school mathematics education: How can research continue? *Journal for Research in Mathematics Education, 36* (2), 92–100.

Harris, K., Marcus, R., & McLaren, K. (2001). Curriculum materials supporting problem-based teaching. *School Science and Mathematics, 101* (6), 310–318.

Keller, B. A., Hart, E. W., & Martin, W. G. (2001). Illuminating NCTM's principles and standards for school mathematics. *School Science and Mathematics, 101* (6), 292–304.

Kirshner, D. (2002). Untangling teachers' diverse aspirations for student learning: A cross-disciplinary strategy for relating psychological theory to pedagogical practice. *Journal for Research in Mathematics Education, 33* (1), 46–58.

Krehbiel, K. (2008). NCTM's advocacy for mathematics education. *Mathematics Teaching in the Middle School, 14* (1), 18–20.

Lindquist, M. M. (2001). NAEP, TIMSS, and PSSM: Entangled influences. *School Science and Mathematics, 101* (6), 286–291.

McGehee, J., & Griffith, L. K. (2004). Technology enhances student learning across the curriculum. *Mathematics Teaching in the Middle School, 9* (6), 344–349.

Midgett, C. W., & Eddins, S. K. (2001). NCTM's *Principles and standards for school mathematics*: Implications for administrators. *NASSP Bulletin, 85* (623), 35–42.

National Council of Teachers of Mathematics. (2011). *Illuminations.* Retrieved May 24, 2011, from the World Wide Web: http:// illuminations.nctm.org

National Council of Teachers of Mathematics. (2000). *Principles and standards for school mathematics.* Reston, VA: National Council of Teachers of Mathematics.

Olson, M., & Berk, D. (2001). Two mathematicians' perspectives on standards: Interviews with Judith Roitman and Alfred Manaster. *School Science and Mathematics, 101* (6), 305–309.

Reys, B. J., & Bay-Williams, J. M. (2003). Spotlight on the principles: The role of textbooks in implementing the curriculum principle and the learning principle. *Mathematics Teaching in the Middle School, 9* (2), 120–124.

Rubel, L., & Meyer, M. R. (2005). Spotlight on the principles: The pursuit of mathematics for all! *Mathematics Teaching in the Middle School, 10* (9), 479–483.

Soucie, T., Radovic, N., & Svedrec, R. (2010). Making technology work. *Mathematics Teaching in the Middle School, 15* (8), 466–471.

Suh, J. M. (2010). Tech-knowledge and diverse learners. *Mathematics Teaching in the Middle School, 15* (8), 440–447.

Chapter 3

Albrecht, M., Bennett, D., & Block, S. (Eds.). (1997). *Discovering geometry with the Geometer's Sketchpad*. Berkeley, CA: Key Curriculum.

AllPsych Online. (2007). *The virtual psychology classroom*. Retrieved July 13, 2007, from the World Wide Web: http://www.allpsych.com

Archytech. (2003). Improving education through technology. Retrieved July 10, 2003, from the World Wide Web: http://ejad.best.vwh.net

Ball, D. L. (1990). The mathematical understandings that preservice teachers bring to teacher education. *Elementary School Journal, 90,* 449–466.

Beaton, A. E., et al. (1997). *TIMSS: Mathematics achievement in the middle school years*. Chestnut Hill, MA: Boston College.

Ben-Yehuda, M., Lavy, I., Linchevski, L., & Sfard, A. (2005). Doing wrong with words: What bars students' access to arithmetical discourses. *Journal for Research in Mathematics Education, 36* (3), 176–247.

Bieda, K. N. (2010). Enacting proof-related tasks in middle school mathematics: Challenges and opportunities. *Journal for Research in Mathematics Education, 41* (4), 351–382.

Brahier, D. J. (Ed.). (2011). *Motivation and disposition: Pathways to learning mathematics. Seventy-third yearbook of the National Council of Teachers of Mathematics*. Reston, VA: NCTM.

Brooks, J. G., & Brooks, M. G. (1997). *Constructivism: An ASCD professional inquiry kit*. Alexandria, VA: Association for Supervision and Curriculum Development.

Brooks, J. G., & Brooks, M. G. (1993). *In search of understanding: The case for constructivist classrooms*. Alexandria, VA: Association for Supervision and Curriculum Development.

Brown, I., Jr., & Inouye, D. K. (1978). Learned helplessness through modeling: The role of perceived similarity in competence. *Journal of Personality and Social Psychology, 36,* 900–908.

Brualdi, A. C. (1996). Multiple intelligences: Gardner's theory. *ERIC/AE Digest Series*, EDO-TM-96-01, September 1996.

Brumfield, C. (1973). Conventional approaches using synthetic Euclidean geometry. In K. B. Henderson (Ed.), *1973 Yearbook of the NCTM: Geometry in the mathematics curriculum* (pp. 95–115). Reston, VA: National Council of Teachers of Mathematics.

Bruner, J. S. (1973). *Beyond the information given*. New York: W. W. Norton.

Bruner, J. S. (1973). *The relevance of education*. New York: W. W. Norton.

Bruner, J. S. (1966). *Toward a theory of instruction*. New York: W. W. Norton.

Bruner, J. S. (1960). *The process of education*. New York: Vintage.

Cai, J. (1995). *JRME Monograph number 7: A cognitive analysis of U.S. and Chinese students' mathematical performance on tasks involving computation, simple problem solving, and complex problem solving*. Reston, VA: National Council of Teachers of Mathematics.

Cobb, P. (1988). The tension between theories of learning and instruction in mathematics education. *Educational Psychologist, 23* (2), 87–103.

Davis, R. B., Maher, C. A., & Noddings, N. (Eds.). (1990). *JRME Monograph number 4: Constructivist views on the teaching and learning of mathematics*. Reston, VA: National Council of Teachers of Mathematics.

Dickinson, D. J., & Butt, J. A. (1989). The effects of success and failure on high-achieving students. *Education and Treatment of Children, 12,* 243–252.

English, L. D. (Ed.). (2002). *Handbook of international research in mathematics education*. Mahwah, NJ: Erlbaum.

Fennema, E., & Franke, M. L. (1992). Teachers' knowledge and its impact. In D. Grouws (Ed.), *Handbook of research on mathematics teaching and learning* (pp. 147–164). Reston, VA: National Council of Teachers of Mathematics.

Ferrini-Mundy, J., & Schram, T. (1997). *JRME Monograph number 8: The recognizing and recording reform in mathematics education project: Insights, issues, and implications*. Reston, VA: National Council of Teachers of Mathematics.

Ford, M. E. (1992). *Motivating humans: Goals, emotions, and personal agency beliefs*. Newbury Park, CA: Sage.

Fuys, D., Geddes, D., & Tischler, R. (1988). *JRME Monograph number 3: The van Hiele model of thinking in geometry among adolescents*. Reston, VA: National Council of Teachers of Mathematics.

Gardner, H. (1991). *The unschooled mind: How children think and how schools should teach*. New York: Basic Books.

Gardner, H. (1983). *Frames of Mind*. New York: Basic Books.

GeoGebra Web Site. (2011). *GeoGebra software*. Retrieved May 27, 2011, from the World Wide Web: http://www.geogebra.org

Gonzales, P., et al. (2000). *Highlights from the Third International Mathematics and Science Study–Repeat (TIMSS–R)*. Washington, DC: National Center for Education Statistics.

Goos, M. (2004). Learning mathematics in a classroom community of inquiry. *Journal for Research in Mathematics Education, 35* (4), 258–291.

Grouws, D. A. (Ed.). (1992). *Handbook of research on mathematics teaching and learning*. Reston, VA: National Council of Teachers of Mathematics.

Hembree, R. (1990). The nature, effects, and relief of mathematics anxiety. *Journal for Research in Mathematics Education, 21,* 33–46.

Herbst, P. G. (2006). Teaching geometry with problems: Negotiating instructional situations and mathematical tasks. *Journal for Research in Mathematics Education, 37* (4), 313–347.

Hidi, S. (1990). Interest and its contribution as a mental resource for learning. *Review of Educational Research, 6,* 549–571.

Hofstetter, F. (1997). *Cognitive versus behavioral psychology.* Retrieved July 13, 2007, from the World Wide Web: http://www.udel.edu/fth/pbs/webmodel.htm

Knuth, E. J., Stephens, A. C., McNeil, N. M., & Alibali, M. W. (2006). Does understanding the equal sign matter? Evidence from solving equations. *Journal for Research in Mathematics Education, 37* (4), 297–312.

Laborde, C. (1999). Factors of integration of dynamic geometry software in the teaching of mathematics. In A. Gagatsis (Ed.), *A multidimensional approach to learning mathematics and sciences* (pp. 299–312). Nicosia, Cyprus: Intercollege Press.

Lau, P. N.-K., Singh, P., & Hwa, T.-Y. (2009). Constructing mathematics in an interactive classroom context. *Educational Studies in Mathematics, 72* (3), 307–324.

Linchevski, L., & Kutscher, B. (1998). Tell me with whom you're learning, and I'll tell you how much you've learned: Mixed-ability versus same-ability grouping in mathematics. *Journal for Research in Mathematics Education, 29,* 533–554.

Lobato, J., Clarke, D., & Ellis, A. B. (2005). Initiating and eliciting in teaching: A reformulation of telling. *Journal for Research in Mathematics Education, 36* (2), 101–136.

Ma, L. (1999). *Knowing and teaching elementary mathematics.* Mahwah, NJ: Erlbaum.

Malone, T. W., & Lepper, M. R. (1987). Making learning fun: A taxonomy of intrinsic motivations for learning. In R. Snow & M. Farr (Eds.), *Aptitude, learning and instruction volume 3: Cognitive and affective process analyses* (pp. 223–253). Hillsdale, NJ: Erlbaum.

Miller, L. D. (1992). Teacher benefits from using impromptu writing prompts in algebra classes. *Journal for Research in Mathematics Education, 23* (4), 329–340.

Millroy, W. L. (1992). *JRME Monograph number 5: An ethnographic study of the mathematical ideas of a group of carpenters.* Reston, VA: National Council of Teachers of Mathematics.

National Council of Teachers of Mathematics. (1989). *Curriculum and evaluation standards for school mathematics.* Reston, VA: National Council of Teachers of Mathematics.

National Research Council. (2000). *How people learn* (expanded edition). Washington, DC: National Academy.

Nicholls, J. G. (1984). Achievement motivation: Conceptions of ability, subjective experience, task choice, and performance. *Psychological Review, 91* (3), 328–346.

Norton, A., & D'Ambrosio, B. S. (2008). ZPC and ZPD: Zones of teaching and learning. *Journal for Research in Mathematics Education, 39* (3), 220–246.

Ojose, B. (2008). Applying Piaget's theory of cognitive development to mathematics instruction. *Mathematics Educator, 18* (1), 26–30.

Pape, S. J. (2004). Middle school children's problem-solving behavior: A cognitive analysis from a reading comprehension perspective. *Journal for Research in Mathematics Education, 35* (3), 187–219.

Piaget, J. (1969). *The mechanisms of perception.* New York: Basic Books.

Rasmussen, C., & Marrongelle, K. (2006). Pedagogical content tools: Integrated student reasoning and mathematics in instruction. *Journal for Research in Mathematics Education, 37* (5), 388–420.

Riddle, E. M., & Dabbagh, N. (1999). *Lev Vygostky's social development theory.* Retrieved July 13, 2007, from the World Wide Web: http://www.pdxcoopschool.org/Vygotskys.pdf

Rogers, K. B. (1998). Using current research to make "good" decisions about grouping. *NASSP Bulletin, 82,* 38–46.

Santrock, J. W. (2004). *Educational psychology* (2nd ed.). Boston: McGraw-Hill Higher Education.

Senk, S. L. (1985). How well do students write geometry proofs? *Mathematics Teacher, 78,* 448–456.

Serra, M. (2008). *Discovering geometry: An investigative approach* (4th ed.). Berkeley, CA: Key Curriculum.

Serra, M. (1994). *Patty paper geometry.* Berkeley, CA: Key Curriculum.

Shaughnessy, J. M., & Burger, W. F. (1985). Spadework prior to deduction in geometry. *Mathematics Teacher, 78,* 419–428.

Simon, M. A., Tzur, R., Heinz, K., & Kinzel, M. (2004). Explicating a mechanism for conceptual learning: Elaborating the construct of reflective abstraction. *Journal for Research in Mathematics Education, 35* (5), 305–329.

Skemp, R. R. (1979). *Intelligence, learning, and action: A foundation for theory and practice in education.* New York, NY: Wiley.

Skemp, R. R. (1971). *The psychology of learning mathematics.* Middlesex, UK: Pelican.

Skinner, B. F. (1938). *The behavior of organisms: An experimental analysis.* Upper Saddle River, NJ: Prentice Hall.

Slavin, R. E., Madden, N. A., Karweit, N. L., Livermon, B. J., & Donaln, L. (1990). Success for all: First-year outcomes of a comprehensive plan for reforming urban education. *American Educational Research Journal, 27,* 255–278.

Sowder, J., & Schappelle, B. (Eds.). (2002). *Lessons learned from research.* Reston, VA: National Council of Teachers of Mathematics.

Steele, D. F. (2001). Using sociocultural theory to teach mathematics: A Vygotskian perspective. *School Science and Mathematics, 101* (8), 404–416.

Steffe, L. P., & Cobb, P. (1988). *Construction of arithmetical meanings and strategies.* New York: Springer-Verlag.

Stiggins, R. J. (1988). Revitalizing classroom assessment: The highest instructional priority. *Phi Delta Kappan, 69,* 363–372.

Teppo, A. R. (1998). *JRME Monograph number 9: Qualitative research methods in mathematics education.* Reston, VA: National Council of Teachers of Mathematics.

Tymoczko, T. (Ed.). (1998). *New directions in the philosophy of mathematics: An anthology.* Princeton, NJ: Princeton University Press.

Utah State University. (2007). *National library of virtual manipulatives.* Retrieved July 13, 2007, from the World Wide Web: http://nlvm.usu.edu

Vygotsky, L. S. (1978). *Mind in society: The development of higher psychological processes.* Cambridge, MA: Harvard University Press.

Watson, J. M., & Moritz, J. B. (2003). Fairness of dice. *Journal for Research in Mathematics Education, 34* (4), 270–304.

White-Clark, R., et al. (2008). Guide on the side: An instructional approach to meet mathematics standards. *The High School Journal, 91* (4), 40–44.

Whitman, B. S. (1976). Intuitive equation solving skills and the effects on them of formal techniques of equation solving (Doctoral dissertation, Florida State University,

1975). *Dissertation Abstracts International, 36,* 5180A. (University Microfilms No. 76-2720).

Zaslavsky, O., & Shir, K. (2005). Students' conceptions of a mathematical definition. *Journal for Research in Mathematics Education, 36* (4), 317–346.

Zimmerman, B. J., & Blotner, R. (1979). Effects of model persistence and success on children's problem solving. *Journal of Educational Psychology, 71,* 508–513.

Zimmerman, B. J., & Ringle, J. (1981). Effects of model persistence and statements of confidence on children's self-efficacy and problem solving. *Journal of Educational Psychology, 73,* 485–493.

Chapter 4

Achieve. (2011). *Achieve Web site.* Retrieved June 28, 2011, from the World Wide Web: http://www.achieve.org

Alper, L., et al. (1996). Problem-based mathematics—Not just for the college-bound. *Educational Leadership, 53* (8), 18–21.

Anderson, R. D. (1995). Curriculum reform: Dilemmas and promise. *Phi Delta Kappan, 77* (1), 33–36.

Battista, M. T. (1994). Teacher beliefs and the reform movement in mathematics education. *Phi Delta Kappan, 75* (6), 462–463, 466–468, 470.

Beane, J. (1997). *Curriculum integration: Designing the core of democratic education.* New York, NY: Teachers College Press.

Bliss, L. (1996). Six keys to the twenty-second century high school. *School Planning and Management, 36* (5), 22–27.

Chard, D. J., & Kameenui, E. J. (1995). Mathematics instruction for students with diverse learning needs: Heeding the message of the Cheshire cat. *Focus on Learning Problems in Mathematics, 17* (2), 24–38.

College Board. (2006). *College Board standards for college success: Mathematics and statistics.* New York: College Board.

College Board. (2007). *Calculus: Course description.* New York: College Board.

Common Core State Standards Initiative. (2010). *Common core state standards for mathematics.* Washington, DC: National Governors Association Center for Best Practices and Council of Chief State School Officers.

Dossey, J. A. (1991). Discrete mathematics: The math for our time. In M. J. Kenney (Ed.), *1991 yearbook of the NCTM: Discrete mathematics across the curriculum, K–12* (pp. 1–9). Reston, VA: National Council of Teachers of Mathematics.

Eisenhower National Clearinghouse. (2004). *Eisenhower National Clearinghouse Web site.* Retrieved February 14, 2004, from the World Wide Web: http://www.enc.org

Garet, M. S., & Mills, V. L. (1995). Changes in teaching practices: The effects of the curriculum and evaluation standards. *Mathematics Teacher, 88* (5), 380–388.

Goertz, M. E. (2010). National standards: Lessons from the past, directions for the future. In B. J. Reys & R. E. Reys (Eds.), *2010 yearbook of the NCTM: Mathematics curriculum: Issues, trends, and future directions* (pp. 51–63). Reston, VA: National Council of Teachers of Mathematics.

Hart, E. W., & Martin, W. G. (2008). Standards for High School Mathematics: Why, What, How? *Mathematics Teacher, 102* (5), 377–382.

Hershkowitz, R., et al. (2002). Mathematics curriculum development for computerized environments: A designer–research–teacher–learner activity. In L. D. English (Ed.), *Handbook of international research in mathematics education* (pp. 657–694). Mahwah, NJ: Erlbaum.

Hiebert, J. (1999). Relationships between research and the NCTM Standards. *Journal for Research in Mathematics Education, 30* (1), 3–19.

Hirsch, C. R. (Ed.). (1985). *1985 Yearbook of the NCTM: The secondary school mathematics curriculum.* Reston, VA: National Council of Teachers of Mathematics.

Hirschhorn, D. B., et al. (1995). Rethinking the first two years of high school mathematics with the UCSMP. *Mathematics Teacher, 88* (8), 640–647.

Horvath, A., Dietiker, L., Larnell, G., Wang, S., & Smith, J. (2009). Middle-grades mathematics standards: Issues and implications. *Mathematics Teaching in the Middle School, 14* (5), 275–279.

Illinois State Board of Education. (2007). *Mathematics goals and standards (State Goal 9: Geometry).* Chicago: ISBE.

Jones, P. S., & Coxford, A. F. (1970). Abortive reform—Depression and war. In *The thirty-second yearbook of the NCTM: A history of mathematics education* (pp. 46–66). Washington, DC: NCTM.

Kennedy, D. (2003). Getting back to our non-extraneous roots. In S. A. McGraw (Ed.), *Integrated mathematics: Choices and challenges* (pp. 33–41). Reston, VA: National Council of Teachers of Mathematics.

Kilpatrick, J., Martin, W. G., & Schifter, D. (2003). *A research companion to* Principles and standards for school mathematics. Reston, VA: National Council of Teachers of Mathematics.

Konold, C., & Higgins, T. L. (2003). Reasoning about data. In J. Kilpatrick, W. G. Martin, & D. Schifter (Eds.), *A research companion to* Principles and standards for school mathematics (pp. 193–215). Reston, VA: National Council of Teachers of Mathematics.

Lawrenz, C., & Strumpf, L. (2001). *What employers need: A workplace skills analysis.* Kansas City, KS: The Greater Kansas City Chamber of Commerce.

Lott, J. (Ed.). (2001). *Mathematics education dialogues: Integrate to make whole?* Reston, VA: National Council of Teachers of Mathematics.

McGraw, S. A. (2003). *Integrated mathematics: Choices and challenges.* Reston, VA: National Council of Teachers of Mathematics.

Martin, Gary W. (2009). The NCTM High School Curriculum Project: Why it matters to you. *Mathematics Teacher, 103* (3), 164.

Meiring, S. P., Rubenstein, R. N., Schultz, J. E., Lange, J., & Chambers, D. L. (1992). *A core curriculum: Making mathematics count for everyone.* Reston, VA: National Council of Teachers of Mathematics.

National Council of Teachers of Mathematics. (2006). *Curriculum focal points for prekindergarten through grade 8 mathematics: A quest for coherence.* Reston, VA: National Council of Teachers of Mathematics.

National Council of Teachers of Mathematics. (2000). *Principles and standards for school mathematics.* Reston, VA: National Council of Teachers of Mathematics.

National Council of Teachers of Mathematics. (1989). *Curriculum and evaluation standards for school mathematics.* Reston, VA: National Council of Teachers of Mathematics.

National Middle School Association. (2010). *This we believe: Keys to educating young adolescents.* Westerville, OH: National Middle School Association.

National Research Council. (1989). *Everybody counts: A report to the nation on the future of mathematics education.* Washington, DC: National Academy.

Newnan Times-Herald. (2011). Georgia Board of Education OKs math flexibility for its schools. Retrieved June 29, 2011, from the World Wide Web: http://www.times-herald.com/local/Ga-Board-of-Ed-OKs-math-flexibility-75647

Ohio Department of Education. (2004). *Ohio Department of Education Web site.* Retrieved February 24, 2004, from the World Wide Web: http://www.ode.state.oh.us

Parmar, R. S., & Cawley, J. F. (1995). Mathematics curricula frameworks: Goals for general and special education. *Focus on Learning Problems in Mathematics, 17* (2), 50–66.

Paul, F., & Richbart, L. (1985). New York state's new three-year sequence for high school mathematics. In C. R. Hirsch (Ed.), *1985 Yearbook of the NCTM: The secondary school mathematics curriculum* (pp. 200–210). Reston, VA: National Council of Teachers of Mathematics.

Pollack, H. (1987, May). Notes from a talk given at the Mathematical Sciences Education Board. Frameworks Conference, Minneapolis, MN.

Reeve, W. D. (1929). United States. In W. D. Reeve (Ed.), *The fourth yearbook of the NCTM: Significant changes and trends in the teaching of mathematics throughout the world since 1910* (pp. 131–186). New York: Teachers College, Columbia University.

Reys, B. J., & Reys, R. E. (Eds). (2010). *2010 yearbook of the NCTM: Mathematics curriculum: Issues, trends, and future directions* (pp. 25–39). Reston, VA: National Council of Teachers of Mathematics.

Richbart, L. A. (2001). Integrated mathematics after 25 years. In J. Lott (Ed.), *Mathematics dialogues: Integrate to make whole?* (p. 11). Reston, VA: National Council of Teachers of Mathematics.

Robicheaux, R. (1996). Professional development: Caring teachers can realize the vision on the standards. *Mathematics Teaching in the Middle School, 1* (9), 738–742.

Smith, S. Z. et al. (1993). What the NCTM Standards look like in one classroom. *Educational Leadership, 50* (8), 4–7.

Steen, L. A. (Ed.). (1997). *Why numbers count: Quantitative literacy for tomorrow's America.* New York: College Entrance Examination Board.

Steen, L. A. (Ed.). (1990). *On the shoulders of giants: New approaches to numeracy.* Washington, DC: National Academy.

Texas Education Agency. (2011). *The commissioner's draft of the Texas mathematics standards.* Austin, TX: Texas Education Agency, Office of the Commissioner.

Thornton, C. A., & Bley, N. S. (1994). *Windows of opportunity: Mathematics for students with special needs.* Reston, VA: National Council of Teachers of Mathematics.

U.S. Department of Labor. (2007). Speech by U.S. Secretary of Labor Elaine L. Chao. Retrieved July 16, 2007, from the World Wide Web: http://www.dol.gov/_sec/media/speeches/20070622_NASPD.htm

Usiskin, Z. (2010). The current state of the school mathematics curriculum. In B. J. Reys & R. E. Reys (Eds.), *2010 yearbook of the NCTM: Mathematics curriculum: Issues, trends, and future directions* (pp. 25–39). Reston, VA: National Council of Teachers of Mathematics.

Western Michigan University. (2007). Longitudinal study: College mathematics course-taking and performance patterns. Retrieved July 16, 2007, from the World Wide Web: http://www.wmich.edu/cpmp/longitudinalstudysummary.html

Winebrenner, S., & Devlin, B. (2011). Cluster grouping of gifted students: How to provide full-time services on a part-time budget. Retrieved June 28, 2011, from the World Wide Web: http://www.education.com/reference/article/Ref_Cluster_Grouping/

Winebrenner, S., & Brulles, D. (2008). *The cluster grouping handbook: How to challenge gifted students and improve achievement for all.* Minneapolis, MN: Free Spirit Publishing, Inc.

Chapter 5

American Association for the Advancement of Science. (2000). *Middle grades mathematics textbooks: A benchmarks based evaluation.* Annapolis, MD: AAAS Project 2061.

Anderson, L. W. (Ed.), Krathwohl, D. R. (Ed.), Airasian, P. W., Cruikshank, K. A., Mayer, R. E., Pintrich, P. R., Raths, J., & Wittrock, M. C. (2001). *A taxonomy for learning, teaching, and assessing: A revision of Bloom's taxonomy of educational objectives* (Complete edition). New York, NY: Longman.

ARC Center. (2007). *The ARC Center: Alternatives for rebuilding curricula Web site.* Retrieved July 17, 2007, from the World Wide Web: http://www.comap.com/elementary/projects/arc

Ball, D., & Cohen, D. (1996). Reform by the book: What is—or what might be—the role of curriculum materials in teacher learning and instructional reform? *Educational Researcher, 25* (9), 6–8, 14.

Bayfield School District. (2011). Marzano's taxonomy: Useful verbs. Retrieved July 5, 2001, on the World Wide Web: bayfieldsbestpractices.pbworks.com/f/Bprtc.Marzano.taxonomy.verbs.pdf

Bloom, B. S., & Krathwohl, D. R. (1956). *Taxonomy of educational objectives: The classification of educational goals. Handbook I: Cognitive domain.* New York: Longmans, Green.

Choppin, J. M. (2009). Curriculum-context knowledge : Teacher learning from successive enactments of a standards-based mathematics curriculum. *Curriculum Inquiry, 39* (2), 287–320.

Clements, D. H. (2007). Curriculum research: Toward a framework for "research-based curricula." *Journal for Research in Mathematics Education, 38* (1), 35–70.

COMAP. (2004). *COMAP Web site.* Retrieved February 14, 2004, from the World Wide Web: http://www.comap.com

Common Core State Standards Initiative. (2010). *Common core state standards for mathematics.* Washington, DC: National Governors Association Center for Best Practices and Council of Chief State School Officers.

COMPASS. (2004). *Curricular options in mathematics for all secondary students Web site.* Retrieved February 14, 2004, from the World Wide Web: http://www.ithaca.edu/compass

Coxford, A. F., et al. (1998). *Contemporary mathematics in context: A unified approach* (Course 1, Part A). Chicago: Everyday Learning.

Drake, C. (2010). Understanding teachers' strategies for supplementing textbooks. In B. J. Reys & R. E. Reys (Eds.), *2010 yearbook of the NCTM: Mathematics curriculum: Issues, trends, and future directions* (pp. 277–287). Reston, VA: National Council of Teachers of Mathematics.

Educational Resources Information Center. (2004). AskERIC lesson plans. Retrieved February 14, 2004, from the World Wide Web: http://ericir.syr.edu/Virtual/Lessons

Google.com. (2004). *Google search engine Web site.* Retrieved February 14, 2004, from the World Wide Web: http://www.google.com

Hamilton, B. (2011). No reason to fear the common core standards. Retrieved July 1, 2011, from the World Wide Web: http://www.insidetheschool.com/articles/no-reason-to-fear-the-common-core-standards

Hart, E. W., Kenney, M. J., DeBellis, V. A., & Rosenstein, J. G. (2008). *Navigating through discrete mathematics in grades 6–12.* Reston, VA: National Council of Teachers of Mathematics.

Harwell, M. R., et al. (2007). *Standards*-based mathematics curricula and secondary students' performance on standardized achievement tests. *Journal for Research in Mathematics Education, 38* (1), 71–101.

Hudson, R. A., Lahann, P. E., & Lee, J. S. (2010). Considerations in the review and adoption of mathematics textbooks. In B. J. Reys & R. E. Reys (Eds.), *2010 yearbook of the NCTM: Mathematics curriculum: Issues, trends, and future directions* (pp. 213–229). Reston, VA: National Council of Teachers of Mathematics.

Huntley, M. A. (2009). A brief report: Measuring curriculum implementation. *Journal for Research in Mathematics Education, 40* (4), 355–362.

Joyner, J. M., & Bright, G. W. (2001). Implementing and using mathematics standards in North Carolina. *School Science and Mathematics, 101* (6), 280–285.

Kenney, M. J. (Ed.). (1991). *1991 Yearbook of the NCTM: Discrete mathematics across the curriculum, K–12.* Reston, VA: National Council of Teachers of Mathematics.

Krathwohl, D. R. (2002). A revision of Bloom's taxonomy: An overview. *Theory into Practice 41* (4), 212–218.

LiveText Inc. (2007). *Livetext.com.* Retrieved July 17, 2007, from the World Wide Web: https://www.livetext.com

Marzano, R. J. (2001). *Designing a new taxonomy of educational objectives.* Thousand Oaks, CA: Corwin Press.

Math Forum at Drexel. (2004). *The Math Forum Web site.* Retrieved February 14, 2004, from the World Wide Web: http://mathforum.org

National Council of Teachers of Mathematics. (2007). *NCTM Web site.* Retrieved July 17, 2007, from the World Wide Web: http://www.nctm.org

National Council of Teachers of Mathematics. (2000). *Principles and standards for school mathematics.* Reston, VA: National Council of Teachers of Mathematics.

National Council of Teachers of Mathematics. (1989). *Curriculum and evaluation standards for school mathematics.* Reston, VA: National Council of Teachers of Mathematics.

Pennsylvania Department of Education. (2011). Standards aligned system. Retrieved July 1, 2011, from the World Wide Web: http://www.pdesas.org/module/sas/standards/anchors/unpack/#search

Rosenstein, J. G., Franzblau, D. S., & Roberts, F. S. (Eds.). (1998). *Discrete mathematics in the schools*. Reston, VA: National Council of Teachers of Mathematics.

Schwartzman, S. (1996). *The words of mathematics: An etymological dictionary of mathematical terms used in English*. Washington, DC: The Mathematical Association of America.

Show-Me Center. (2007). *The Show-Me Center Web site*. Retrieved July 17, 2007, from the World Wide Web: http://www.showmecenter.missouri.edu

Smith III, J. P., & Star, J. R. (2007). Expanding the notion of impact of K–12 standards-based mathematics and reform calculus programs. *Journal for Research in Mathematics Education, 38* (1), 3–34.

Stiggins, R. J., Rubel, E., & Quellmalz, E. (1988). *Measuring thinking skills in the classroom*. Washington, DC: National Education Association.

Tarr, J. E., Reys, R. E., Reys, B. J., Chávez, Ó., Shih, J., & Osterlind, S. J. (2008). The impact of middle-grades mathematics curricula and the classroom learning environment on student achievement. *Journal for Research in Mathematics Education, 39* (3), 247–280.

Wiggins, G., & McTighe, J. (2006). *Understanding by design: A framework for developing curricular development and assessment*. Alexandria, VA: Association for Supervision and Curriculum Development.

Sample Recommended Resource Books

Bezuszka, S., D'Angelo, L., & Kenney, M. J. (1976). *Applications of finite differences*. Chestnut Hill, MA: Boston College.

Bezuszka, S., D'Angelo, L., & Kenney, M. J. (1976). *Fraction action: Booklet 5*. Chestnut Hill, MA: Boston College.

Bezuszka, S., D'Angelo, L., & Kenney, M. J. (1976). *Fraction action: Booklet 6*. Chestnut Hill, MA: Boston College.

Bezuszka, S., D'Angelo, L., & Kenney, M. J. (1976). *The wonder square*. Chestnut Hill, MA: Boston College.

Bezuszka, S., D'Angelo, L., Kenney, M. J., & Kokoska, S. (1980). *Perfect numbers*. Chestnut Hill, MA: Boston College.

Bezuszka, S., Kenney, M., & Silvery, L. (1977). *Tesselations: The geometry of patterns*. Palo Alto, CA: Creative Publications.

Carlson, R. J., & Winter, M. J. (1993). *Algebra experiments II: Exploring nonlinear functions*. Menlo Park, CA: Addison-Wesley.

Edwards, E. L. (1990). *Algebra for everyone*. Reston, VA: National Council of Teachers of Mathematics.

Farrell, M. A. (1988). *Imaginative ideas for the teacher of mathematics, grades K–12: Ranucci's reservoir*. Reston, VA: National Council of Teachers of Mathematics.

Hirsch, C. R., & Laing, R. A. (Eds.). (1993). *Activities for active learning and teaching: Selections from the "Mathematics Teacher."* Reston, VA: National Council of Teachers of Mathematics.

House, P. (1997). *Mission mathematics: Grades 9–12*. Reston, VA: National Council of Teachers of Mathematics.

Hynes, M. C. (Ed.). (1996). *Ideas: NCTM standards-based instruction, grades 5–8*. Reston, VA: National Council of Teachers of Mathematics.

Kenney, M. J. (1976). *The incredible Pascal's Triangle*. Chestnut Hill, MA: Boston College.

Kenney, M. J. (1976). *The super sum*. Chestnut Hill, MA: Boston College.

O'Connor, V. F., & Hynes, M. C. (1997). *Mission mathematics: Grades 5–8*. Reston, VA: National Council of Teachers of Mathematics.

Saunders, H. (1981). *When are we ever gonna have to use this?* Palo Alto, CA: Dale Seymour.

Souviney, R., Britt, M., Gargiulo, S., & Hughes, P. (1992). *Mathematical investigations: Book three*. Palo Alto, CA: Dale Seymour.

Souviney, R., Britt, M., Gargiulo, S., & Hughes, P. (1992). *Mathematical investigations: Book two*. Palo Alto, CA: Dale Seymour.

Souviney, R., Britt, M., Gargiulo, S., & Hughes, P. (1990). *Mathematical investigations: Book one*. Palo Alto, CA: Dale Seymour.

Willcutt, B. (1995). *Cubes: Building algebraic thinking with progressive patterns*. Pacific Grove, CA: Critical Thinking Press & Software.

Willcutt, B. (1995). *Pattern blocks: Building algebraic thinking with progressive patterns*. Pacific Grove, CA: Critical Thinking Press & Software.

COMAP "Hi-Map" (High School Mathematics) Teaching Modules

Bennett, S., et al. *Module 9: Fair divisions: Getting your fair share*.

Bennett, S., DeTemple, D., Dirks, M., Newell, B., Robertson, J. M., & Tyus, B. *Module 8: The apportionment problem: The search for the perfect democracy*.

Brown, S. I. *Module 7: Student generations*.

Chavey, D. *Module 21: Drawing pictures with one line: Exploring graph theory*.

Cozzens, M., & Porter, R. *Module 2: Recurrence relations— "Counting backwards."*

Cozzens, M. B., & Porter, R. *Module 6: Problem solving using graphs*.

Crowe, D. *Module 4: Symmetry, rigid motions, and patterns*.

Djang, F. C. *Module 11: Applications of geometrical probability*.

Francis, R. L. *Module 10: A mathematical look at the calendar*.

Francis, R. L. *Module 13: The mathematician's coloring book*.

Growney, J. S. *Module 5: Using percent*.

Kumar, G. S. *Module 14: Decision making and math models*.

Lucas, W. F. *Module 19: Fair voting: Weighted votes for unequal constituencies*.

Malkevitch, J., & Froelich, G. *Module 22: Loads of codes*.

Malkevitch, J., & Froelich, G. *Module 1: The mathematical theory of elections*.

Malkevitch, J., Froelich, G., & Froelich, D. *Module 18: Codes galore*.

Martin, W. B. *Module 12: Spheres and satellites.*

Metallo, F. R. *Module 17: The abacus: Its history and applications.*

Meyer, R. W. *Module 16: ExploreSorts.*

Rogers, J. R. *Module 15: A uniform approach to rate and ratio problems: The introduction of the universal rate formula.*

Sriskandarajah, J. *Module 20: Optimality pays: An introduction to linear programming.*

Zagare, F. C. *Module 3: The mathematics of conflict.*

NCTM Navigations Series

The NCTM *Navigations* series began to be released in the Spring of 2001. The following titles comprise the list of books (and their associated CD-ROMs) in the series:

Navigating through Algebra in Grades Pre-K–2, 3–5, 6–8, 9–12 (4 books)

Navigating through Geometry in Grades Pre-K–2, 3–5, 6–8, 9–12 (4 books)

Navigations through Data Analysis and Probability in Grades Pre-K–2, 3–5 (2 books)

Navigating through Data Analysis in Grades 6–8, 9–12 (2 books)

Navigating through Probability in Grades 6–8, 9–12 (2 books)

Navigating through Number and Operations in Grades Pre-K–2, 3–5, 6–8, 9–12 (4 books)

Navigating through Measurement in Grades Pre-K–2, 3–5, 6–8, 9–12 (4 books)

Navigating through Discrete Mathematics in Grades K–5, 6–12 (2 books)

Navigating through Mathematical Connections in Grades 6–8, 9–12 (2 books)

Navigating through Problem Solving and Reasoning in Grades 4, 5, 6, 6–8, 9–12 (5 books)

NCTM Addenda Series Resource Books

Secondary School Addenda Series

Burrill, G., et al. (1992). *Data analysis and statistics across the curriculum.* Reston, VA: National Council of Teachers of Mathematics.

Coxford, A. F., Burks, L., Giamati, C., & Jonik, J. (1991). *Geometry from multiple perspectives.* Reston, VA: National Council of Teachers of Mathematics.

Froelich, G., Bartkovich, K. G., & Foerster, P. A. (1991). *Connecting mathematics.* Reston, VA: National Council of Teachers of Mathematics.

Heid, M. K., Choate, J., Sheets, C., & Zbiek, M. R. (1995). *Algebra in a technological world.* Reston, VA: National Council of Teachers of Mathematics.

Meiring, S. P., Rubenstein, R. N., Schultz, J. E., de Lange, J., & Chambers, D. L. (1992). *A core curriculum: Making mathematics count for everyone.* Reston, VA: National Council of Teachers of Mathematics.

Middle School Addenda Series

Curcio, F. R., et al. (1994). *Understanding rational numbers and proportions.* Reston, VA: National Council of Teachers of Mathematics.

Geddes, D. (1994). *Measurement in the middle grades.* Reston, VA: National Council of Teachers of Mathematics.

Geddes, D., Bove, J., Fortunato, I., Fuys, D. J., Morgenstern, J., & Welschman-Tischler, R. (1991). *Geometry in the middle grades.* Reston, VA: National Council of Teachers of Mathematics.

Phillips, E., Gardella, T., Kelly, C., & Stewart, J. (1991). *Patterns and functions.* Reston, VA: National Council of Teachers of Mathematics.

Reys, B. J., et al. (1991). *Developing number sense in the middle grades.* Reston, VA: National Council of Teachers of Mathematics.

Zawojewski, J. S., et al. (1991). *Dealing with data and chance.* Reston, VA: National Council of Teachers of Mathematics.

NSF-Funded Curricular Materials

Secondary Materials

All Secondary Programs

Visit the COMPASS Web site at http://www.ithaca.edu/compass

Core-Plus Mathematics (CPMP)
Grades: 9–12
Publisher: Glencoe/McGraw-Hill
More information: http://www.glencoe.com/sec/math

SIMMS (Systemic Initiative for Montana Mathematics and Science) Integrated Mathematics
Grades: 9–12
Publisher: Kendall/Hunt Publishing
More information: http://www.simms-im.com

Interactive Mathematics Program (IMP)
Grades: 9–12
Publisher: Key Curriculum Press
More information: http://www.keypress.com

MATH Connections: A Secondary Mathematics Core Curriculum
Grades: 9–11
Publisher: It's About Time, Inc.
More information: http://www.its-about-time.com

Mathematics: Modeling Our World (MMOW)
Grades: 9–12
Publisher: COMAP—The Consortium for Mathematics and Its Applications
More information: http://www.comap.com

Middle School Materials

All Middle School Programs

Visit the Show-Me Center at http://www.showmecenter.missouri.edu

Connected Mathematics Project (CMP)
Grades: 6–8
Publisher: Prentice Hall
More information: http://phschool.com

Mathematics in Context (MiC)
Grades: 5–8

Publisher: Britannica
More information: http://www.mathincontext.eb.com

MathScape: Seeing and Thinking Mathematically
Grades: 6–8
Publisher: Glencoe/McGraw-Hill
More information: http://www2.edc.org/Mathscape

MATH Thematics
Grades: 6–8
Publisher: Holt McDougal
More information: http://www.holtmcdougal.hmhco.com

Chapter 6

The Annenberg/CPB Projects. (2004). The Annenberg/CPB Projects Learner Online. Retrieved February 14, 2004, from the World Wide Web: http://www.learner.org

Austin, J. D., et al. (1992). Coordinating secondary school science and mathematics. *School Science and Mathematics, 92* (2), 64–68.

Ball, D. L., & Schroeder, T. L. (1992). Improving teaching, not standardizing it. *Mathematics Teacher, 85* (1), 67–72.

Bitter, G. (1997). *Understanding teaching: Implementing the NCTM professional standards for teaching mathematics CD-ROM series.* Tempe, AZ: Arizona State University (available through the Association for Supervision and Curriculum Development).

Borich, G. D. (1996). *Effective teaching methods.* New York: Merrill.

Classroom Connect. (1997). *Teaching grades K–12 with the Internet: Internet lesson plans and classroom activities.* Lancaster, PA: Classroom Connect.

Duquette, G. (Ed.). (1997). *Classroom methods and strategies for teaching at the secondary level.* Lewiston, NY: Edwin Mellen.

Gronlund, N. E. (1995). *How to write and use instructional objectives.* Englewood Cliffs, NJ: Merrill.

Gronlund, N. E. (1985). *Stating objectives for classroom instruction.* New York: Macmillan.

Harris, D. E., Carr, J. F., Flynn, T., Petit, M., & Rigney, S. (1996). *How to use standards in the classroom.* Alexandria, VA: Association for Supervision and Curriculum Development.

Henak, R. M. (1984). *Lesson planning for meaningful variety in teaching.* Washington, DC: National Education Association.

Joseph, L. C. (1995). Eisenhower National Clearinghouse—An online bonanza for math and science resources. *Technology Connection, 2* (4), 17.

National Council of Teachers of Mathematics. (2000). *Principles and standards for school mathematics.* Reston, VA: National Council of Teachers of Mathematics.

National Oceanic and Atmospheric Administration. (2011). *National Weather Service Web site.* Retrieved July 13, 2011, from the World Wide Web: http://www.weather.gov

New York City Board of Education. (1986). *How does a lesson plan?* New York: New York City Board of Education.

North Central Regional Educational Laboratory (NCREL). (2002). *Teacher to teacher: Reshaping instruction through lesson study.* Naperville, IL: NCREL.

Ornstein, A. C. (1990). *The systematic design of instruction.* New York: HarperCollins.

Public Broadcasting System. (2004). TeacherLine. Retrieved February 14, 2004, from the World Wide Web: http://www.pbs.org/teachersource/math.htm

Reese, G. C. (2011). The cereal box problem: A lesson in expected value. Retrieved July 13, 2011, from the World Wide Web: http://mste.illinois.edu/reese/cereal/cereal.php

Ridley, L. L. (1995). When a lesson bombs: Hints and suggestions for teachers. *Teaching Exceptional Children, 27* (4), 66–67.

Roberts, P. (1996). *A guide for developing an interdisciplinary thematic unit.* Englewood Cliffs, NJ: Merrill.

Schoaff, E. K. (1993). How to develop a mathematics lesson using technology. *Journal of Computers in Mathematics and Science Teaching, 12* (1), 19–27.

Schoenfeld, A. H. (1998). On theory and models: The case of teaching-in-context. In S. Berenson, K. Dawkins, M. Blanton, W. Coulombe, J. Kolb, K. Norwood, & L. Stiff (Eds.), *Proceedings of the Twentieth Annual Meeting of the North American Chapter of the International Group for the Psychology of Mathematics Education* (pp. 27–38). Columbus, OH: ERIC Clearinghouse for Science, Mathematics, and Environmental Education.

Schroeder, M. L. (1996). Professional development: Lesson design and reflection. *Mathematics Teaching in the Middle School, 1* (8), 648–652.

Stigler, J. W., & Hiebert, J. (1999). *The teaching gap: Best ideas from the world's teachers for improving education in the classroom.* New York: Free Press.

Tyson, P. (1991). Talking about lesson planning: The use of semi-structured interviews in teacher education. *Teacher Education Quarterly, 18* (3), 87–96.

Activities—Selected Lesson Plan Ideas from The Mathematics Teacher

Albrecht, M. (2001). Activities: The volume of a pyramid: Low-tech and high-tech approaches. *Mathematics Teacher, 94* (1), 58–64.

Bergthold, T. (2005). Activities for students: Curve stitching: Linking linear and quadratic functions. *Mathematics Teacher, 98* (5), 348–357.

Beseler, S. (2006). Activities for students: The three-point shoot-out: The logic of hypothesis testing. *Mathematics Teacher, 99* (8), 582–587.

Bezuk, N. S., & Armstrong, B. E. (1993). Activities: Understanding division of fractions. *Mathematics Teacher, 86* (1), 43–46, 56–60.

Biehl, L. C. (2003). Activities: Massive graphs, power laws, and the World Wide Web. *Mathematics Teacher, 96* (6), 434–446.

Biehl, L. C. (1999). Activities: Part 2: Using fractal complexity to analyze mathematical models. *Mathematics Teacher, 92* (2), 128–130, 136–139.

Biehl, L. C. (1998). Activities: Forest fires, oil spills, and fractal geometry, Part 1: Cellular automata and modeling natural phenomena. *Mathematics Teacher, 91* (8), 682–690, 696–698.

Blubaugh, W. L., & Emmons, K. (1999). Activities: Algebra for all: Graphing for all students. *Mathematics Teacher, 92* (4), 323–326, 332–334.

Bremigan, E. G. (2002). Activities: Designing the dynamic domino race. *Mathematics Teacher, 95* (7), 502–508.

Brown, B. (2005). Activities for students: Exponential growth through pattern exploration. *Mathematics Teacher, 98* (6), 434–442.

Brown, S. L., & Rizzardi, M. A. (2005). Activities for students: Averaging rates: Deciding when to use the harmonic or arithmetic mean. *Mathematics Teacher, 98* (9), 626–636.

Caglayan, G. (2006). Activities for students: Visualizing summation formulas. *Mathematics Teacher, 100* (1), 70–74.

Calzada, M. E., & Scariano, S. M. (2006). Activities for students: A natural bridge from algebra and geometry to trigonometry. *Mathematics Teacher, 99* (6), 450–458.

Carlton, M. A., & Mortlock, M. V. (2005). Activities for students: Teaching probability and statistics through game shows. *Mathematics Teacher, 98* (8), 564–570.

Coes, L. (1994). Activities: The functions of a toy balloon. *Mathematics Teacher, 87* (8), 619–622, 628–629.

Craine, T. V. (1996). Activities: A graphical approach to the quadratic formula. *Mathematics Teacher, 89* (1), 34–38, 44–46.

DeTemple, D. W., & Walker, D. A. (1996). Activities: Some colorful mathematics. *Mathematics Teacher, 89* (4), 307–312, 318–320.

Disher, F. (1995). Activities: Graphing art. *Mathematics Teacher, 88* (2), 124–128, 134–136.

Ebert, D. (2006). Activities for students: Using statistical testing to approximate π. *Mathematics Teacher, 100* (3), 216–219.

Edwards, M. T. (2005). Activities for students: Using overhead projectors to explore size change transformations. *Mathematics Teacher, 98* (7), 498–507.

Erich, D. J. (2002). Activities: Authentic assessment in the geometry classroom: Calculating the classroom air-exchange rate. *Mathematics Teacher, 95* (6), 422–428.

Ford, R. (2004). Activities for students: Discovering and exploring Mandelbrot set points with a graphing calculator. *Mathematics Teacher, 98* (1), 38–46.

Fox, T. B. (2005). Activities for students: Transformations on data sets and their effects on descriptive statistics. *Mathematics Teacher, 99* (3), 208–217.

Froelich, G. (2000). Activities: Modeling soft-drink packaging. *Mathematics Teacher, 93* (6), 478–482, 485–487.

Gates, J., Stuart, J. A., Bonawi-tan, W., & Loehr, S. (2004). Activities for students: Managing returns in a catalog distribution center. *Mathematics Teacher, 98* (2), 118–128.

Herman, M. (2006). Activities for students: Introducing parametric equations through graphing calculator explorations. *Mathematics Teacher, 99* (9), 637–643.

Herman, M., Milou, E., & Schiffman, J. (2004). Activities for students: Unit fractions and their "basimal" representations: Exploring patterns. *Mathematics Teacher, 98* (4), 274–284.

Hill, C. (2002). Activities: Print-shop paper cutting: Ratios in algebra. *Mathematics Teacher, 95* (4), 260–268.

Holliday, B. W., & Duf, L. R. (2004). Activities: Using graphing calculators to model real-world data. *Mathematics Teacher, 97* (5), 328–342.

Horak, V. M. (2005a). Activities for students: Biology as a source for algebra equations: Insects. *Mathematics Teacher, 99* (1), 55–59.

Horak, V. M. (2005b). Activities for students: Biology as a source for algebra equations: The heart. *Mathematics Teacher, 99* (4), 296–301.

Jung, I., & Kim, Y. (2004). Activities: Using geometry software to revisit the ellipse. *Mathematics Teacher, 97* (3), 184–191.

Kasprzak, E. M. (2002). Activities: Designing a window. *Mathematics Teacher, 95* (5), 346–359.

Kelly, G., Ewers, T., & Proctor, L. (2002). Activities: Developing spatial sense: Comparing appearance with reality. *Mathematics Teacher, 95* (9), 702–712.

Kennedy, J. B. (1996). Activities: An interest in radioactivity. *Mathematics Teacher, 89* (3), 209–214, 228–230.

Lanier, S., & Barrs, S. (2003). Activities: Let's play plinko: A lesson in simulations and experimental probabilities. *Mathematics Teacher, 96* (9), 626–633.

Mack, C. W. (1995). Activities: Exploring three- and four-dimensional space. *Mathematics Teacher, 88* (7), 572–578, 588–590.

Magnus, T. D. (2000). Activities: Will the best candidate win? *Mathematics Teacher, 93* (1), 18–23, 27–28.

McElhaney, K. W. (2004). Activities: Demonstrating Boolean logic using simple electrical circuits. *Mathematics Teacher, 97* (2), 126–134.

Nelson, C. Q., & Williams, N. L. (2007). Activities for students: Sprinklers and amusement parks: What do they have to do with geometry? *Mathematics Teacher, 100* (6), 440–445.

Nelson, J. E., Coffey, M., & Huffman, E. (2003). Activities: Stop this runaway truck, please. *Mathematics Teacher, 96* (8), 548–561.

Perdew, P. R. (2002). Activities: Sports and distance-rate–time. *Mathematics Teacher, 95* (3), 192–199.

Rauff, J. V. (2003). Activities: A millennium prize problem for students. *Mathematics Teacher, 96* (1), 26–39.

Reinstein, D., Sally, P., & Camp, D. R. (1997). Activities: Generating fractals through self-replication. *Mathematics Teacher, 90* (1), 34–38, 43–45.

Richardson, M., & Gabrosek, J. (2004). Activities: A-B-C, 1-2-3. *Mathematics Teacher, 97* (4), 270–282.

Schabel, C. (2006). Activities for students: Using statistics to check on Elvis. *Mathematics Teacher, 99* (5), 372–377.

Schultz, H., & Bonsangue, M. V. (1995). Activities: Time for trigonometry. *Mathematics Teacher, 88* (5), 393–396, 405–410.

Utley, J., & Wolfe, J. (2004). Activities: Geoboard areas: Students' remarkable ideas. *Mathematics Teacher, 97* (1), 18–26.

Van Dyke, F. (2003). Activities: Using graphs to introduce functions. *Mathematics Teacher, 96* (2), 126–137.

Van Dyke, F. (1996). Activities: The inverse of a function. *Mathematics Teacher, 89* (2), 121–126, 132–133.

Westegaard, S. A. (1998). Activities: Stitching quilts into coordinate geometry. *Mathematics Teacher, 91* (7), 587–592, 598–600.

Wilkins, J. L. M., & Hicks, D. (2001). Activities: A s(t)imulating study of map projections: An exploration integrating mathematics and social studies. *Mathematics Teacher, 94* (8), 660–671.

Wood, E. (1995). Activities: Gas-bill mathematics. *Mathematics Teacher, 88* (3), 214–218, 224–227.

Young, V. (2002). Activities: A matter of "survival." *Mathematics Teacher, 95* (2), 100–112.

Chapter 7

Allen, J. (2004). *Tools for teaching content literacy.* Portland, ME: Stenhouse Publishers.

Alper, L., et al. (1995). Implementing the professional standards for teaching mathematics: What is it worth? *Mathematics Teacher, 88* (7), 598–602.

Andrini, B. (1991). *Cooperative learning and mathematics: A multi-structural approach.* San Juan Capistrano, CA: Resources for Teachers, Inc.

Artzt, A. F., & Newman, C. M. (1997). *How to use cooperative learning in the mathematics class* (2nd ed.). Reston, VA: National Council of Teachers of Mathematics.

Arvold, B., et al. (1996). Implementing the professional standards for teaching mathematics: Analyzing teaching and learning: The art of listening. *Mathematics Teacher, 89* (4), 326–329.

Barton, M. L., & Heidema, C. (2002). *Teaching reading in mathematics: A supplement to* Teaching reading in the content areas: If not me, then who? 2nd edition (2nd ed.). Alexandria, VA: Association for Supervision and Curriculum Development.

Becker, J. P., & Shimada, S. (1997). *The open-ended approach: A new proposal for teaching mathematics.* Reston, VA: National Council of Teachers of Mathematics.

Bennett, C. A. (2010). "It's Hard Getting Kids to Talk About Math": Helping New Teachers Improve Mathematical Discourse. *Action in Teacher Education, 32* (3), 79–89.

Cauley, K. M., & Seyfarth, J. T. (1995). Curriculum reform in middle level and high school mathematics. *NASSP Bulletin, 79* (567), 22–30.

Chuska, K. R. (1995). *Improving classroom questions: A teacher's guide to increasing student motivation, participation, and higher-level thinking.* Bloomington, IN: Phi Delta Kappa Educational Foundation.

Coates, G. D. (2009). Cooperative learning. *Mathematics Teaching in the Middle School, 15* (4), 244–245.

Cook, C. J., & Rasmussen, C. M. (1991). *Cues for effective questioning.* Evanston, IL: Self-Published.

Cooney, T. J. (Ed.). (1990). *1990 Yearbook of the NCTM: Teaching and learning mathematics in the 1990s.* Reston, VA: National Council of Teachers of Mathematics.

Curriculum Research and Development Group. (1997). *Geometry learning project, version 7.1.* Honolulu, HI: University of Hawaii.

D'Ambrosio, B. S. (1995). Implementing the professional standards for teaching mathematics: Highlighting the humanistic dimensions of mathematics activity through classroom discourse. *Mathematics Teacher, 88* (9), 770–772.

Davis, R. B., & Maher, C. A. (Ed.). (1993). *Schools, mathematics, and the world of reality.* Boston: Allyn & Bacon.

Dockterman, D. A. (1994). *Cooperative learning and technology.* Watertown, MA: Tom Snyder Productions, Inc.

Edwards, M. T. (2003). Calculator-based computer algebra systems: Tools for meaningful algebraic understanding. In J. T. Fey, A. Cuoco, C. Kieran, L. McMullin, & R. M. Zbiek (Eds.), *Computer algebra systems in secondary school mathematics education* (pp. 117–134). Reston, VA: National Council of Teachers of Mathematics.

Erickson, T. (1989). *Getting it together: Math problems for groups, grades 4–12.* Berkeley, CA: Lawrence Hall of Science.

Feldt, C. C. (1993). Becoming a teacher of mathematics: A constructive, interactive process. *Mathematics Teacher, 86* (5), 400–403.

Fey, J. T., Cuoco, C., Kieran, L., McMullin, L., & Zbiek, R. M. (Eds.). (2003). *Computer algebra systems in secondary school mathematics education.* Reston, VA: National Council of Teachers of Mathematics.

Fisher, D., & Frey, N. (2012). *Improving adolescent literacy: Content area strategies at work.* (3rd ed.) Boston, MA: Allyn & Bacon.

Gillies, R. (2004). The effects of cooperative learning on junior high school students during small group learning. *Learning and Instruction, 14* (2), 197–213.

Ginsburg-Block, M. D., Rohrbeck, C. A., & Fantuzzo, J. W. (2006). A meta-analytic review of social, self-concept, and behavioral outcomes of peer-assisted learning. *Journal of Educational Psychology, 98*, 732–749.

Glasser, W. (1986). *Control theory in the classroom.* New York: Harper & Row.

Godwin, G. (1974). *The odd woman.* New York: Berkley.

Goldenberg, E. P. (2003). Algebra and computer algebra. In J. T. Fey, A. Cuoco, C. Kieran, L. McMullin, & R. M. Zbiek (Eds.), *Computer algebra systems in secondary school mathematics education* (pp. 9–30). Reston, VA: National Council of Teachers of Mathematics.

Goodlad, J. (1984). *A place called school: Prospects for the future.* New York: McGraw-Hill.

Guyton, E. (1991). Cooperative learning and elementary social studies. *Social Education, 55* (5), 313–315.

Heid, M. K., Blume, G. W., Hollebrands, K., & Piez, C. (2002). Computer algebra systems in mathematics instruction: Implications from research. *Mathematics Teacher, 95* (8), 586–591.

Hiebert, J., & Wearne, D. (1986). Procedures over concepts: The acquisition of decimal number knowledge. In J. Hiebert (Ed.), *Conceptual and procedural knowledge: The case of mathematics* (pp. 199–223). Hillsdale, NJ: Erlbaum.

Holubec, E. J. (1992). How do you get there from here? Getting started with cooperative learning. *Contemporary Education, 63* (3), 181–184.

Jakucyn, N., & Kerr, K. E. (2002). Getting started with CAS: Our story. *Mathematics Teacher, 95* (8), 628–632.

Johnson, D. W., & Johnson, R. T. (1984). *Circles of learning: Cooperation in the classroom.* Alexandria, VA: Association for Supervision and Curriculum Development.

Johnson, D. W., Johnson, R. T., & Holubec, H. J. (1987). *Structuring cooperative learning: Lesson plans for teachers.* Edina, MN: Interaction.

Kagan Online. (2007). *Kagan Publishing and Professional Development.* Retrieved July 19, 2007, from the World Wide Web: http://www.kaganonline.com

Kagan, S. (1994). *Cooperative learning.* San Clemente, CA: Kagan Cooperative Learning.

Lantz-Andersson, A., Linderoth, J., & Säljö, R. (2009). What's the problem? Meaning making and learning to do mathematical word problems in the context of digital tools. *Instructional Science, 37* (4), 325–343.

Leiva, M. A. (1995). Implementing the professional standards for teaching mathematics: Empowering teaching through the evaluation process. *Mathematics Teacher, 88* (1), 44–47.

Li, Q., & Ma, X. (2010). A meta-analysis of the effects of computer technology on school students' mathematics learning. *Educational Psychology Review, 22* (3), 215–243.

Lindquist, M. M. (1993). Tides of change: Teachers at the helm. *Arithmetic Teacher, 41* (1), 64–68.

Mahoney, J. F. (2002). Computer algebra systems in our schools: Some axioms and some examples. *Mathematics Teacher, 95* (8), 598–605.

Math Forum at Drexel. (2004). *The Math Forum Web site.* Retrieved February 21, 2004, from the World Wide Web: http://mathforum.org

Middleton, J. A., & Goepfert, P. (1996). *Inventive strategies for teaching mathematics: Implementing standards for reform.* Washington, DC: American Psychological Association.

Mousley, J., & Sullivan, P. (1996). *Learning about teaching.* Reston, VA: National Council of Teachers of Mathematics (distributor).

National Council of Teachers of Mathematics. (2007). *Mathematics teaching today: Improving practice, improving student learning* (2nd ed.; T. Martin, Ed.). Reston, VA: National Council of Teachers of Mathematics.

National Council of Teachers of Mathematics. (2000). *Principles and standards for school mathematics.* Reston, VA: National Council of Teachers of Mathematics.

National Council of Teachers of Mathematics. (1991). *Professional standards for teaching mathematics.* Reston, VA: National Council of Teachers of Mathematics.

National Council of Teachers of Mathematics. (1989). *Curriculum and evaluation standards for school mathematics.* Reston, VA: National Council of Teachers of Mathematics.

Nebesniak, A. L., & Heaton, R. M. (2010). Student confidence and student involvement. *Mathematics Teaching in the Middle School, 16* (2), 96.

Pierce, R. U., & Stacey, K. C. (2002). Algebraic insight: The algebra needed to use computer algebra systems. *Mathematics Teacher, 95* (8), 622–627.

Prevost, F. J. (1993). Implementing the professional standards for teaching mathematics: Rethinking how we teach: Learning mathematical pedagogy. *Mathematics Teacher, 86* (1), 75–79.

Rubenstein, R. N. (2007). Focused strategies for middle-grades mathematics vocabulary development. *Mathematics teaching in the middle school, 13* (4), 200.

Ruthven, K., Deaney, R., & Hennessy, S. (2009). Using graphing software to teach about algebraic forms: A study of technology-supported practice in secondary-school mathematics. *Educational Studies in Mathematics, 71* (3), 279–297.

Schifter, D. (Ed.). (1996). *What's happening in math class? Envisioning new practices through teacher narratives.* New York, NY: Teachers College Columbia University.

Schulman, L. (1986). Those who understand: Knowledge growth in teaching. *Educational Researcher, 15* (2), 4–14.

Shotsberger, P. G. (1999). INSTRUCT: Standards for teaching mathematics. Retrieved August 20, 1999, from the World Wide Web: http://instruct.cms.uncwil.edu/standard.html

Slavin, R. E. (1988). Cooperative learning and student achievement. *Educational Leadership, 45,* 31–33.

Smith, M. S., & Stein, M. K. (2011). *5 practices for orchestrating productive mathematics discussions.* Reston, VA: National Council of Teachers of Mathematics.

Stephen F. Austin State University Web Site. (2011). *Glossary of NCATE terms.* Retrieved July 19, 2011, from the World Wide Web: http://www.sfasu.edu/education/about/accreditations/ncate/about/glossary.asp#N

Wiggins, G., & McTighe, J. (1998). *Understanding by design.* Alexandria, VA: Association for Supervision and Curriculum Development.

Chapter 8

Barbeau, E., & Brown, S. (Eds.). (1997). Algebra focus issue. *Mathematics Teacher, 90* (2).

Battista, M. T. (2009). Highlights of research on learning school geometry. In T. Craine & R. Rubenstein (Eds.), *2010 Yearbook of the NCTM: Understanding geometry for a changing world* (pp. 91–108).

Bright, G., Brewer, W., McClain, K., & Mooney, E. S. (2003). *Navigating through data analysis in grades 6–8.* Reston, VA: National Council of Teachers of Mathematics.

Burke, M., Erickson, D., Lott, J. W., & Obert, M. (2001). *Navigating through algebra in grades 9–12.* Reston, VA: National Council of Teachers of Mathematics.

Chapin, S., Koziol, A., MacPherson, J., & Rezba, C. (2002). *Navigating through data analysis and probability in grades 3–5.* Reston, VA: National Council of Teachers of Mathematics.

Clarke, D. (1994). Ten key principles from research for the professional development of mathematics teachers. In D. B. Aichele (Ed.), *1994 Yearbook of the NCTM: Professional development for teachers of mathematics* (pp. 37–48). Reston, VA: National Council of Teachers of Mathematics.

Clements, D. H. (Ed.). (2003). *2003 Yearbook of the NCTM: Learning and teaching measurement.* Reston, VA: National Council of Teachers of Mathematics.

Common Core State Standards Initiative. (2010). *Common core state standards for mathematics.* Washington, DC: National Governors Association Center for Best Practices and Council of Chief State School Officers.

Cook, W. (2007). The traveling salesman problem. Retrieved July 23, 2007, from the World Wide Web: http://www.tsp.gatech.edu

Coxford, A. F. (Ed.). (1988). *1988 Yearbook of the NCTM: The ideas of algebra, K–12.* Reston, VA: National Council of Teachers of Mathematics.

Cuevas, G. J., & Yeatts, K. (2001). *Navigating through algebra in grades 3–5.* Reston, VA: National Council of Teachers of Mathematics.

Friel, S., Rachlin, S., & Doyle, D. (2001). *Navigating through algebra in grades 6–8.* Reston, VA: National Council of Teachers of Mathematics.

Gavin, M. K., Belkin, L. P., Spinelli, A. M., & St. Marie, J. (2001). *Navigating through geometry in grades 3–5.* Reston, VA: National Council of Teachers of Mathematics.

Graham, K., Cuoco, A., & Zimmermann, G. (2010). *Focus in high school mathematics: Reasoning and sense making in algebra.* Reston, VA: National Council of Teachers of Mathematics.

Hollenbrands, K. P., & Smith, R. C. (2009). Using interactive geometry software to teach secondary school geometry: Implications from research. In T. Craine & R. Rubenstein (Eds.), *2010 Yearbook of the NCTM: Understanding geometry for a changing world* (pp. 221–232).

Huff, D. (1954). *How to lie with statistics.* New York: W. W. Norton.

Jones, D. (2010). Recommendations for statistics and probability in school mathematics over the past century. In B. Reys, R. Reys, & R. Rubenstein (Eds.), *2010 Yearbook of the NCTM: Mathematics curriculum: Issues, trends, and future direction* (pp. 65–75).

Kaput, J. J. (1997). Transforming algebra from an engine of inequity to an engine of mathematical power by "algebrafying" the K–12 curriculum. A paper from *The Nature and Role of Algebra in the K–14 Curriculum.* Arlington, VA: National Science Foundation.

Kenney, M. J. (Ed.). (1991). *1991 Yearbook of the NCTM: Discrete mathematics across the curriculum, K–12.* Reston, VA: National Council of Teachers of Mathematics.

Konold, C., & Higgins, T. L. (2003). Reasoning about data. In J. Kilpatrick, W. G. Martin, & D. Schifter (Eds.), *A research companion to* Principles and standards for school mathematics (pp. 193–215). Reston, VA: National Council of Teachers of Mathematics.

Lappan, G., Fey, J. T., Fitzgerald, W. M., Friel, S. N., & Phillips, E. D. (2004). *What do you expect? Probability and expected value.* Upper Saddle River, NJ: Pearson Prentice Hall.

Lindquist, M. M. (Ed.). (1987). *1987 Yearbook of the NCTM: Learning and teaching geometry, K–12.* Reston, VA: National Council of Teachers of Mathematics.

Litwiller, B. (Ed.). (2002). *2002 Yearbook of the NCTM: Making sense of fractions, ratios, and proportions.* Reston, VA: National Council of Teachers of Mathematics.

Lott, J. W. (Ed.). (2000, April). Algebra? A gate! A barrier! A mystery! *Mathematics Education Dialogues.*

Martin, W. G., Carter, J., Forster, S., Howe, R., Kader, G., Kepner, H., Quander, J. R., McCallum, W., Robinson, E., Snipes, V., & Valdez, P. (2009). *Focus in high school mathematics: Reasoning and sense making.* Reston, VA: National Council of Teachers of Mathematics.

Mathematical Sciences Education Board. (1998). *The nature and role of algebra in the K–14 curriculum: Proceedings of a national symposium.* Washington, DC: National Academy Press.

McCrone, S. M., King, J., Orihuela, Y., & Robinson, E. (2010). *Focus in high school mathematics: Reasoning and sense making in geometry.* Reston, VA: National Council of Teachers of Mathematics.

Moore-Harris, B. (1997). Algebra focus issue. *Mathematics Teaching in the Middle School,* (2) 4.

Morrow, L. J. (Ed.). (1998). *1998 Yearbook of the NCTM: The teaching and learning of algorithms in school mathematics.* Reston, VA: National Council of Teachers of Mathematics.

Moses, B. (Ed.). (1997). Algebra focus issue. *Teaching Children Mathematics,* (3) 6.

Museum of Harmony and Golden Section. (2011). *Golden Section in Greek's Art.* Retrieved August 26, 2011, from the World Wide Web: http://www.goldenmuseum.com

National Council of Teachers of Mathematics. (2011). *Illuminations.* Retrieved May 24, 2011, from the World Wide Web: http://illuminations.nctm.org

National Council of Teachers of Mathematics. (2009). *Focus on high school mathematics: Reasoning and sense making.* Reston, VA: National Council of Teachers of Mathematics.

National Council of Teachers of Mathematics. (2006). *Curriculum focal points for prekindergarten through grade 8 mathematics: A quest for coherence.* Reston, VA: National Council of Teachers of Mathematics.

National Council of Teachers of Mathematics. (2000). *Principles and standards for school mathematics.* Reston, VA: National Council of Teachers of Mathematics.

Owens, D. T. (Ed.). (1993). *Research ideas for the classroom: Middle grades mathematics.* Reston, VA: National Council of Teachers of Mathematics.

Phi: The Golden Number. (2011). *History (of Phi).* Retrieved August 26, 2011, from the World Wide Web: http://www.GoldenNumber.net

Pugalee, D. K., Frykholm, J., Johnson, A., Slovin, H., Malloy, C., & Preston, R. (2002). *Navigating through geometry in grades 6–8.* Reston, VA: National Council of Teachers of Mathematics.

Scan My Essay Web Site. (2011). *Viper software.* Retrieved August 29, 2011, from the World Wide Web: http://www.scanmyessay.com

Shaughnessy, J. M., Chance, B., & Kranendonk, H. (2009). *Focus in high school mathematics: Reasoning and sense making in statistics and probability.* Reston, VA: National Council of Teachers of Mathematics.

Turnitin Web Site. (2011). *Turn It In software.* Retrieved August 29, 2011, from the World Wide Web: http://www.geogebra.org

Usiskin, Z. (1997). Doing algebra in grades K–4. *Teaching Children Mathematics, 3* (6), 346–356.

Wilson, P. S. (Ed.). (1993). *Research ideas for the classroom: High school mathematics.* Reston, VA: National Council of Teachers of Mathematics.

Zbiek, R. M., & Heid, M. K. (2008). Digging deeply into intermediate algebra: Using symbols to reason and technology to connect symbols and graphs. In C. Greenes & R. Rubenstein (Eds.), *2008 Yearbook of the NCTM: Algebra and algebraic thinking in school mathematics* (pp. 247–259).

Chapter 9

American Statistical Association. (1997). Report from the American Statistical Association's advisory review group. Retrieved September 11, 2003, from the World Wide Web: http://www.stat.ncsu.edu/stated/standards.html

Brams, S. J., et al. (2003). *For all practical purposes* (6th ed.). New York: W. H. Freeman.

Bressoud, D. M. (2007). The changing face of calculus: First-semester calculus as a high school course. *MAA Online.* Retrieved July 23, 2007, from the World Wide Web: http://www.maa.org/features/faceofcalculus.html

College Board. (2011a). *AP Calculus AB: Student score distributions.* Retrieved February 2, 2012, from the World Wide Web: http://apcentral.collegeboard.com/apc/public/repository/2011_Calculus_AB_Score_Dist.pdf

College Board. (2011b). *AP Calculus BC: Student score distributions.* Retrieved February 2, 2012, from the World Wide Web: http://apcentral.collegeboard.com/apc/public/repository/2011_Calculus_BC_Score_Dist.pdf

College Board. (2010). *Calculus: Course description.* New York: College Board.

College Board. (2006). *College Board standards for college success: Mathematics and statistics.* New York: College Board.

Common Core State Standards Initiative. (2010). *Common core state standards for mathematics.* Washington, DC: National Governors Association Center for Best Practices and Council of Chief State School Officers.

Cozzens, M. B., & Porter, R. (1987). *Problem solving using graphs.* Arlington, MA: COMAP, Inc.

Crisler, N., Fisher, P., & Froelich, G. (2000). *Discrete mathematics through applications* (2nd ed.). New York: W. H. Freeman.

Day, R., Kelley, P., Krussel, L., Lott, J. W., & Hirstein, J. (2001). *Navigating through geometry in grades 9–12.* Reston, VA: National Council of Teachers of Mathematics.

DeNavas-Walt, C., & Cleveland, R. (2002). *Money income in the United States: 2001.* Washington, DC: U.S. Government Printing Office.

Dossey, J. A. (1991). Discrete mathematics: The math for our time. In M. J. Kenney (Ed.), *1991 Yearbook of the NCTM: Discrete mathematics across the curriculum K–12* (pp. 1–9). Reston, VA: National Council of Teachers of Mathematics.

Foerster, P. (2007). *Precalculus with trigonometry: Concepts and applications* (2nd ed.). Emeryville, CA: Key Curriculum Press.

Godino, J., Cañizares, M. J., & Díaz, C. (2003). Teaching probability to pre-service primary school teachers through simulation. *Proceedings of the 54th Session of the International Statistical Institute,* Bulletin of ISI. Berlin: ISI.

Grunbaum, B., & Shephard, G. C. (1993). Pick's theorem. *The American Mathematical Monthly, 88,* 150–161.

Hart, E. W. (1998). Algorithmic problem solving in discrete mathematics. In L. J. Morrow (Ed.), *1998 Yearbook of the NCTM: The teaching and learning of algorithms in school mathematics* (pp. 251–267). Reston, VA: National Council of Teachers of Mathematics.

Hersberger, J. R., Frederick, W. G., & Lipman, M. L. (1991). Discrete mathematics in the traditional middle school curriculum. In M. J. Kenney (Ed.), *1991 Yearbook of the NCTM: Discrete mathematics across the curriculum, K–12* (pp. 51–54). Reston, VA: National Council of Teachers of Mathematics.

Konold, C., Pollatsek, A., Well, A., Lohmeier, J., & Lipson, A. (1993). Inconsistencies in students' reasoning about probability. *Journal for Research in Mathematics Education, 24* (5), 392–414.

Leake, L. (1998). The traveling salesperson: Some algorithms are different. In L. J. Morrow (Ed.), *1998 Yearbook of the NCTM: The teaching and learning of algorithms in school mathematics* (pp. 268–273). Reston, VA: National Council of Teachers of Mathematics.

Lindsay, B., Kettenring, J., & Siegmund, D. (Eds.). (2003). *Statistics: Challenges and opportunities for the twenty-first century.* Retrieved September 11, 2003, from the World Wide Web: http://www.stat.psu.edu/%7Ebgl/nsf_report.pdf

Michigan Section of MAA. (2001). Position statement on the fourth year of high school mathematics. Retrieved July 23, 2007, from the World Wide Web: http://sections.maa.org/michigan/newsletters/Spr01Newsletter/hsCalc.html

National Council of Teachers of Mathematics. (2000). *Principles and standards for school mathematics.* Reston, VA: National Council of Teachers of Mathematics.

National Council of Teachers of Mathematics. (1989). *Curriculum and evaluation standards for school mathematics.* Reston, VA: National Council of Teachers of Mathematics.

National Science Board. (2006). *Science and engineering indicators 2006.* Arlington, VA: National Science Board.

Peitgen, H. O., Jurgens, H., Saupe, D., Maletsky, E., Perciante, T., & Yunker, L. (1992). *Fractals for the classroom, volume one.* New York: Springer-Verlag.

Rosenstein, J. G., Franzblau, D. S., & Roberts, F. S. (Eds.). (1997). *Discrete mathematics in the schools.* Providence, RI: American Mathematical Society.

Shaughnessy, J. M. (2003). Research on students' understandings of probability. In J. Kilpatrick, W. G. Martin, & D. Schifter (Eds.), *A research companion to Principles and standards for school mathematics* (pp. 216–226). Reston, VA: National Council of Teachers of Mathematics.

Chapter 10

Barton, J., & Collins, A. (1997). *Portfolio assessment: A handbook for educators.* Menlo Park, CA: Addison-Wesley.

Becker, J. P., & Shimada, S. (1997). *The open-ended approach: A new proposal for teaching mathematics.* Reston, VA: National Council of Teachers of Mathematics.

Brahier, D. J. (2001). *Assessment in middle and high school mathematics: A teacher's guide.* Larchmont, NY: Eye on Education.

Bryant, D., & Driscoll, M. (1998). *Exploring classroom assessment in mathematics.* Reston, VA: National Council of Teachers of Mathematics.

California Assessment Program. (1989). *A question of thinking: A first look at students' performance on open-ended questions in mathematics.* Sacramento, CA: California State Department of Education.

Clarke, D. (1997). *Constructive assessment in mathematics.* Berkeley, CA: Key Curriculum.

College Board. (2011). *Calculator policy (on the SAT).* Retrieved July 21, 2011, from the World Wide Web: http://sat.collegeboard.org/register/sat-test-day-checklist

Cross, M. (1995). *How to's in getting started with assessment and evaluation using portfolios.* Barrie, Ontario: Exclusive Educational Products.

Crowley, Mary L. (1997). Aligning assessment with classroom practices: A promising testing format. *Mathematics Teacher, 90* (9), 706–711.

Danielson, C. (1997). *A collection of performance tasks and rubrics: Middle school mathematics.* Larchmont, NY: Eye on Education.

De Fina, A. A. (1992). *Portfolio assessment: Getting started.* New York: Scholastic.

Dossey, J. A., Mullis, I. V., & Jones, C. O. (1993). *Can students do mathematical problem solving?* Washington, DC: U.S. Department of Education.

Driscoll, M. (1995). Implementing the professional standards for teaching mathematics: "The farther out you go . . .": Assessment in the classroom. *Mathematics Teacher, 88* (5), 420–425.

Educational Testing Service. (1993). *Performance Assessment Sampler.* Princeton, NJ: Educational Testing Service.

Freedman, R. L. (1994). *Open-ended questioning: A handbook for educators.* Menlo Park, CA: Addison-Wesley.

Fukawa-Connelly, T., & Buck, S. (2010). Using portfolio assignments to assess students' mathematical thinking. *Mathematics Teacher, 103* (9), 649–654.

Graue, M. E., & Smith, S. Z. (1996). Shaping assessment through instructional innovation. *Journal of Mathematical Behavior, 15* (2), 113–136.

Haines, C., & Izard, J. (1994). Assessing mathematical communications about projects and investigations. *Educational Studies in Mathematics, 27* (4), 373–386.

Hart, D. (1994). *Authentic assessment: A handbook for educators.* Menlo Park, CA: Addison-Wesley.

Hunting, R. P., & Doig, B. A. (1997). Clinical assessment in mathematics: Learning the craft. *Focus on Learning Problems in Mathematics, 19* (3), 29–48.

Jasmine, J. (1994). *Middle school assessment.* Huntington Beach, CA: Teacher Created Materials.

Kuhs, T. (1992). *Mathematics assessment: Alternative approaches* (video program). Reston, VA: National Council of Teachers of Mathematics.

Kulm, G. (1990). *Assessing higher order thinking in mathematics.* Washington, DC: American Association for the Advancement of Science.

Lambdin, D. V. (1993). The NCTM's 1989 evaluation standards: Recycled ideas whose time has come? In N. L. Webb (Ed.), *1993 Yearbook of the NCTM: Assessment in the mathematics classroom* (pp. 7–16). Reston, VA: National Council of Teachers of Mathematics.

Lesh, R., & Lamon, S. J. (1992). *Assessment of authentic performance in school mathematics.* Washington, DC: American Association for the Advancement of Science.

Mathematical Sciences Education Board National Research Council. (1993). *Measuring counts: A conceptual guide for mathematics assessment.* Washington, DC: National Academy.

Mathematical Sciences Education Board National Research Council. (1993). *Measuring up: Prototypes for mathematics assessment.* Washington, DC: National Academy Press.

McGatha, M. B., & Darcy, P. (2010). Rubrics at play. *Mathematics Teaching in the Middle School, 15* (6), 328–36.

McIntosh, M. E. (1997). Formative assessment in mathematics. *The Clearing House, 71,* 92–96.

National Council of Teachers of Mathematics. (2005). *Grades 6–8: Mathematics assessment sampler.* Reston, VA: National Council of Teachers of Mathematics.

National Council of Teachers of Mathematics. (2005). *Grades 9–12: Mathematics assessment sampler.* Reston, VA: National Council of Teachers of Mathematics.

National Council of Teachers of Mathematics. (2000). *Principles and standards for school mathematics.* Reston, VA: National Council of Teachers of Mathematics.

National Council of Teachers of Mathematics. (1996). *Emphasis on assessment: Readings from NCTM's school-based journals.* Reston, VA: National Council of Teachers of Mathematics.

National Council of Teachers of Mathematics. (1995). *Assessment standards for school mathematics.* Reston, VA: National Council of Teachers of Mathematics.

National Council of Teachers of Mathematics. (1989). *Curriculum and evaluation standards for school mathematics.* Reston, VA: National Council of Teachers of Mathematics.

Ohlsen, M. T. (2007). Classroom Assessment Practices of Secondary School Members of NCTM. *American Secondary Education, 36* (1), 4–14.

PARCC. (2012). *Partnership for assessment of college and careers.* Retrieved February 6, 2012, from the World Wide Web: http://parcconline.org

Panizzon, D., & Pegg, J. (2008). Assessment practices: Empowering mathematics and science teachers in rural secondary schools to enhance student learning. *International Journal of Science and Mathematics Education, 6* (2), 417–436.

Romberg, T. A. (1992). *Mathematics assessment and evaluation.* Albany, NY: State University of New York Press.

Ross, J. A., Hogaboam-Gray, A., & Rolheiser, C. (2002). Student self-evaluation in grade 5–6 mathematics effects on problem-solving achievement. *Educational Assessment, 8* (1), 43–58.

Ryan, C. D. (1994). *Authentic assessment.* Westminster, CA: Teacher Created Materials.

SBAC. (2012). *SMARTER Balanced Assessment Consortium.* Retrieved February 10, 2012, from the World Wide Web: http://k12.wa.us/smarter

Seeley, A. E. (1994). *Portfolio assessment.* Westminster, CA: Teacher Created Materials.

Sharma, M. C. (1996). Assessment of mathematics learning. *Math Notebook, 10* (1–2), 1–52.

Spitzer, H. S. (1951). Testing instruments and practices in relation to present concepts of teaching arithmetic. In N. B. Henry (Ed.), *The teaching of arithmetic, Fiftieth Yearbook for the National Society for the Study of Education, Pt. 2* (pp. 186–202). Chicago: University of Chicago Press.

Stenmark, J. K. (1991). *Mathematics assessment: Myths, models, good questions, and practical suggestions.* Reston, VA: National Council of Teachers of Mathematics.

Stenmark, J. K. (Ed.). (1989). *Assessment alternatives in mathematics.* Berkeley, CA: Regents, University of California.

Stewart, C., & Chance, L. (1995). Making connections: Journal writing and the professional teaching standards. *Mathematics Teacher, 88* (2), 92–95.

Sueltz, A. (1961). The role of evaluation in the classroom. In D. A. Johnson (Ed.), *Evaluation in mathematics, Twenty-Sixth Yearbook of the National Council of Teachers of Mathematics* (pp. 7–20). Washington, DC: National Council of Teachers of Mathematics.

Sueltz, A., Boyton, H., & Sauble, I. (1946). The measurement of understanding in elementary school mathematics. In W. A. Brownell (Ed.), *The measurement of understanding, Forty-Fifth Yearbook of the National Society for the Study of Education, Pt. 1.* Chicago: University of Chicago Press.

Texas Instruments. (1997). *Getting started with CBR including 5 student activities.* Dallas, TX: Texas Instruments, Inc.

Weaver, J. F. (1970). Evaluation and the classroom teachers. In E. C. Begle (Ed.), *Mathematics education, Sixty-Ninth Yearbook of the National Society for the Study of Education, Pt. 1.* Chicago: University of Chicago Press.

Webb, N. (Ed.). (1993). *1993 Yearbook of the NCTM: Assessment in the mathematics classroom.* Reston, VA: National Council of Teachers of Mathematics.

Chapter 11

Beaton, A. E., et al. (1996). *TIMSS: Mathematics achievement in the middle school years.* Chestnut Hill, MA: Center for the Study of Testing, Evaluation, and Educational Policy.

Belcher, T., Coates, G. D., Franco, J., & Mayfield-Ingram, K. (1997). Assessment and equity. In J. Trentacosta (Ed.), *1997 Yearbook of the NCTM: Multicultural and gender equity in the mathematics classroom: The gift of diversity* (pp. 195–200). Reston, VA: National Council of Teachers of Mathematics.

Black, P., & Wiliam, D. (1998). Inside the black box: Raising standards through classroom assessment. *Phi Delta Kappan, 80* (2), 139–148.

Bolte, L. A. (1999). Using concept maps and interpretive essays for assessment in mathematics. *School Science and Mathematics, 99* (1), 19–30.

Brahier, D. J. (2001). *Assessment in middle and high school mathematics: A teacher's guide.* Larchmont, NY: Eye on Education.

Braswell, J. S., et al. (2001). *The nation's report card: Mathematics 2000.* Washington, DC: National Center for Education Statistics.

Bush, W. S., & Leinwand, S. (Eds.) (2000). *Mathematics assessment: A practical handbook for grades 6–8.* Reston, VA: National Council of Teachers of Mathematics.

Bush, W. S., & Greer, A. S. (Eds.) (1999). *Mathematics assessment: A practical handbook for grades 9–12.* Reston, VA: National Council of Teachers of Mathematics.

Cooney, T. J., Badger, E., & Wilson, M. R. (1993). Assessment, understanding mathematics, and distinguishing visions from mirages. In N. L. Webb (Ed.), *1993 Yearbook of the NCTM: Assessment in the mathematics classroom* (pp. 239–247). Reston, VA: National Council of Teachers of Mathematics.

Croom, L. (1997). Mathematics for all students: Access, excellence, and equity. In J. Trentacosta (Ed.), *1997 NCTM Yearbook: Multicultural and gender equity in the mathematics classroom: The gift of diversity* (pp. 1–9). Reston, VA: National Council of Teachers of Mathematics.

Dettmers, S., Trautwein, U., Luedtke, O., Kunter, M., & Baumert, J. (2010). Homework works if homework quality is high: Using multilevel modeling to predict the development of achievement in mathematics. *Journal of Educational Psychology, 102* (2), 467–482.

Eisenhower National Clearinghouse. (1998). *Making schools work for every child* (CD-ROM). Columbus, OH: Eisenhower National Clearinghouse.

Garet, M. S., & Mills, V. L. (1995). Changes in teaching practices: The effects of the curriculum and evaluation standards. *Mathematics Teacher, 88,* 380–389.

Heritage, M., Kim, J., Vendlinski, T., & Herman, J. (2009). From evidence to action: A seamless process in formative assessment? *Educational Measurement, 28* (3), 24–31.

Lambdin, D. V. (1995). Implementing the assessment standards for school mathematics: An open-and-shut case? Openness in the assessment process. *Mathematics Teacher, 88* (8), 680–684.

Mayer, J., & Hillman, S. (1996). Implementing the assessment standards for school mathematics: Assessing students' thinking through writing. *Mathematics Teacher, 89* (5), 428–432.

McLean, E. (1993). Tips for beginners: Steps for better homework. *Mathematics Teacher, 86* (3), 212.

National Council of Teachers of Mathematics. (2000). *Principles and standards for school mathematics.* Reston, VA: National Council of Teachers of Mathematics.

National Council of Teachers of Mathematics. (1995). *Assessment standards for school mathematics.* Reston, VA: National Council of Teachers of Mathematics.

Orbis Software, Inc. (2010). *Easy Grade Pro 4.1* [computer software]. Puyallup, WA: Orbis.

Perie, M., Moran, R., & Lutkus, A. D. (2005). *NAEP 2004 trends in academic progress: Three decades of student performance in reading and mathematics* (NCES 2005–464). Washington, D.C.: U.S. Department of Education, Institute of Education.

Senk, S. L., Beckmann, C. E., & Thompson, D. R. (1997). Assessment and grading in high school mathematics classes. *Journal for Research in Mathematics Education, 28,* 187–215.

Stenmark, J. K., & Bush, W. S. (Eds.) (2001). *Mathematics assessment: A practical handbook for grades 3–5.* Reston, VA: National Council of Teachers of Mathematics.

Trentacosta, J. (Ed.). (1997). *1997 Yearbook of the NCTM: Multicultural and gender equity in the mathematics classroom: The gift of diversity.* Reston, VA: National Council of Teachers of Mathematics.

U.S. Department of Eduction. (2011). *No Child Left Behind Act of 2001.* Retrieved July 22, 2011, from the World Wide Web: http://www2.ed.gov/policy/elsec/leg/esea02/index.html

Vincent, M. L., & Wilson, L. (1996). Implementing the assessment standards for school mathematics: Informal assessment: A story from the classroom. *Mathematics Teacher, 89* (3), 248–250.

Chapter 12

Access Center (2011). *Differentiated instruction for math.* Retrieved August 31, 2011, from the World Wide Web: http://www.k8accesscenter.org/training_resources/math differentiation.asp

American Association of University Women (AAUW). (1992). *How schools shortchange girls.* Washington, DC: AAUW Education Foundation.

Baxter, J., Woodward, J., Voorhies, J., & Wong, J. (2002). We talk about it, but do they get it? *Learning Disabilities Research and Practice, 17* (3), 173–185.

Becker, J. R., & Jacobs, J. E. (2001). Introduction. In J. E. Jacobs, J. R. Becker, & G. F. Gilmer (Eds.), *Changing the faces of mathematics: Perspectives on gender* (pp. 1–8). Reston, VA: National Council of Teachers of Mathematics.

Belcher, T., Coates, G. D., Franco, J., & Mayfield-Ingram, K. (1997). Assessment and equity. In J. Trentacosta (Ed.), *1997 Yearbook of the NCTM: Multicultural and gender equity in the mathematics classroom: The gift of diversity* (pp. 195–200). Reston, VA: National Council of Teachers of Mathematics.

Bley, N. (1994). Accommodating special needs. In C. Thornton & N. S. Bley (Eds.), *Windows of opportunity: Mathematics for students with special needs* (pp. 137–164). Reston, VA: National Council of Teachers of Mathematics.

Braswell, J. S., et al. (2001). *The nation's report card: Mathematics 2000.* Washington, DC: National Center for Education Statistics.

Brown University. (2011). *Education alliance Web site.* Retrieved August 31, 2011, from the World Wide Web: http://www.lab.brown.edu/tdl

Cawley, J. (2002). Mathematics interventions and students with high incidence disabilities. *Remedial and Special Education, 23* (1), 2–6.

Chval, K. B., & Davis, J. A. (2008). The gifted student. *Mathematics Teaching in the Middle School, 14* (5), 267–274.

Colorado Springs School District 11. (2011). *Eight components of sheltered instruction.* Retrieved August 31, 2011, from the World Wide Web: http://d11.org

Concord Special Education Parents Advisory Committee (SPED PAC). (2003). *What is an IEP?* Retrieved September 21, 2003, from the World Wide Web: http://www.concordspedpac.org

Croom, L. (1997). Mathematics for all students: Access, excellence, and equity. In J. Trentacosta (Ed.), *1997 NCTM Yearbook: Multicultural and gender equity in the mathematics classroom: The gift of diversity* (pp. 1–9). Reston, VA: National Council of Teachers of Mathematics.

Cuevas, G., & Driscoll, M. (Eds.). (1993). *Reaching all students with mathematics.* Reston, VA: National Council of Teachers of Mathematics.

Deal, L. J., & Wismer, M. G. (2010). NCTM Principles and Standards for mathematically talented students. *Gifted Child Today, 33,* 55–65.

Echevaria, J., Vogt, M., & Short, D. J. (2010). *The SIOP model for teaching mathematics to English learners.* Boston, MA: Allyn & Bacon.

Echevaria, J., Vogt, M., & Short, D. J. (2007). *Making content comprehensible for English learners: The SIOP model, third edition.* Boston, MA: Allyn & Bacon.

Edwards, C. A. (Ed.). (1999). *Changing the faces of mathematics: Perspectives on Asian Americans and Pacific Islanders.* Reston, VA: National Council of Teachers of Mathematics.

Eisenhower National Clearinghouse. (2003). Mathematics and science for students with special needs. *ENC Focus, 10* (2).

Eisenhower National Clearinghouse. (1998a). *Making schools work for every child* (CD-ROM). Columbus, OH: Eisenhower National Clearinghouse.

Eisenhower National Clearinghouse. (1998b). Multicultural approaches in math and science. *ENC Focus, 5* (1).

ELD Strategies. (2011). The SIOP model. Retrieved August 31, 2011, from the World Wide Web: http://eldstrategies.com/siopmodel.html

Ellis, M., & Malloy, C. (2008). *Mathematics for every student: Responding to diversity, grades 6–8.* Reston, VA: National Council of Teachers of Mathematics.

Ernst-Slavit, G., & Slavit, D. (2007). Educational reform, mathematics, & diverse learners: Meeting the needs of all students. *Multicultural Education, 14* (4), 20–27.

Fennema, E. (1994). Gender and mathematics education research. *NCRMSE Research Review: The Teaching and Learning of Mathematics, 3,* 6–7.

Frankenstein, M. (1997). In addition to the mathematics: Including equity issues in the curriculum. In J. Trentacosta (Ed.), *1997 Yearbook of the NCTM: Multicultural and gender equity in the mathematics classroom: The gift of diversity.* Reston, VA: National Council of Teachers of Mathematics.

Greenes, C., Garfunkel, F., & DeBussey, M. (1994). Planning for instruction: The individualized education plan and the mathematics individualized learning plan. In C. Thornton and N. S. Bley (Eds.), *Windows of opportunity: Mathematics for students with special needs* (pp. 115–135). Reston, VA: National Council of Teachers of Mathematics.

Hankes, J. E., & Fast, G. R. (2002a). Investigating the correspondence between Native American pedagogy and constructivist-based instruction. In J. E. Hankes & G. R. Fast (Eds.), *Changing the faces of mathematics: Perspectives on indigenous people of North America* (pp. 37–48). Reston, VA: National Council of Teachers of Mathematics.

Hankes, J. E., & Fast, G. R. (Eds.). (2002b). *Changing the faces of mathematics: Perspectives on indigenous people of North America.* Reston, VA: National Council of Teachers of Mathematics.

Jacobs, J. E., & Becker, J. R. (1997). Creating a gender-equitable multicultural classroom using feminist pedagogy. In J. Trentacosta (Ed.), *1997 Yearbook of the NCTM: Multicultural and gender equity in the mathematics classroom: The gift of diversity* (pp. 107–114). Reston, VA: National Council of Teachers of Mathematics.

Jacobs, J. E., Becker, J. R., & Gilmer, G. F. (Eds.). (2001). *Changing the faces of mathematics: Perspectives on gender.* Reston, VA: National Council of Teachers of Mathematics.

Learning Disabilities Association of America. (2007). *LDEA Web site.* Retrieved July 25, 2007, from the World Wide Web: http://www.ldaamerica.org/aboutld/teachers/index.asp

Learning Disabilities Association of America. (2004). *Differentiated instruction*. Retrieved July 25, 2007, from the World Wide Web: http://www.ldaamerica.org/news/print_DIFFERENTIATED_INSTRUCTION.asp

Leder, G. C. (1992). Mathematics and gender: Changing perspectives. In D. A. Grouws (Ed.), *Handbook of research on mathematics teaching and learning* (pp. 597–622). Reston, VA: National Council of Teachers of Mathematics.

Little, C. A., Hauser, S., & Corbishley, J. (2009). Constructing complexity for differentiated learning. *Mathematics Teaching in the Middle School, 15* (1), 34–42.

Lock, R. H. (1996). Adapting mathematics instruction in the general education classroom for students with mathematics disabilities. *LD Forum*. Retrieved September 24, 2003, from the World Wide Web: http://www.Ldonline.org/ld_indepth/ math_skills/adapt_cld.html

Lott, J. W. (Ed.). (2000, April). Algebra: A gate! A barrier! A mystery! *Mathematics Education Dialogues*.

Maccini, P., & Gagnon, J. (2007). Math graphic organizers for students with disabilities. Retrieved July 25, 2007, from the World Wide Web: http://www.k8accesscenter.org/training_resources/mathgraphicorganizers.asp

Malloy, C. (2009). *Mathematics for every student: Responding to diversity, grades 9–12*. Reston, VA: National Council of Teachers of Mathematics.

Malloy, C. E. (1997). Including African American students in the mathematics community. In J. Trentacosta (Ed.), *1997 Yearbook of the NCTM: Multicultural and gender equity in the mathematics classroom: The gift of diversity* (pp. 23–33). Reston, VA: National Council of Teachers of Mathematics.

Malloy, C. E., & Brader-Araje, L. (1998). *Challenges in the mathematics education of African American children: Proceedings of the Benjamin Banneker association leadership conference*. Reston, VA: National Council of Teachers of Mathematics.

Menendez, R. (Director), & Musca, T. (Producer). (1988). *Stand and deliver* [motion picture]. USA: Warner Studios.

Meyen, E., & Greer, D. (2009). The role of instructional planning in math instruction for students with learning disabilities. *Focus on Exceptional Children, 41* (5), 1–12.

Michigan Department of Education and the NCREL. (1999). *Connecting with the learner: An equity toolkit*. Oak Brook, IL: North Central Regional Educational Laboratory.

Milner, H. R. (2010). What does teacher education have to do with teaching? Implications for diversity studies. *Journal of Teacher Education, 61* (1–2), pp. 118–131.

Montague, M., Applegate, B., & Marquard, K. (1993). Cognitive strategy instruction and mathematical problem-solving performance of students with learning disabilities. *Learning Disabilities Research and Practice, 8* (4), 223–232.

Morris, C. (1995). Female and male differences in attributional explanations for leisure success and failure. *The 1995 leisure research symposium*. Retrieved October 9, 2003, from the World Wide Web: http://www.indiana.edu/~lrs/ lrs95/cmorris95.html

Mullis, I. V. S., Martin, M. O., Fierros, E. G., Goldberg, A. L., & Stemler, S. E. (2000). *Gender differences in achievement: IEA's Third International Mathematics and Science Study (TIMMS)*. Chestnut Hill, MA: TIMSS International Study Center.

National Center for Education Statistics. (2009). National assessment of educational progress: The nation's report card, 2009. Retrieved August 30, 2011, from the World Wide Web: http://nces.ed.gov/nationsreportcard

National Council of Teachers of Mathematics. (2000). *Principles and standards for school mathematics*. Reston, VA: National Council of Teachers of Mathematics.

National Council of Teachers of mathematics. (2007). *Mathematics teaching today: Improving practice, improving student learning* (2nd ed.; T. Martin, Ed.). Reston, VA: National Council of Teachers of Mathematics.

National Science Board. (2006). *Science and engineering indicators 2006*. Arlington, VA: National Science Board.

National Science Foundation. (1996). *Women, minorities, and persons with disabilities in science and engineering: 1996*. Arlington, VA: National Science Foundation.

National Science Foundation. (1994). *Women, minorities, and persons with disabilities in science and engineering: 1994*. Arlington, VA: National Science Foundation.

Nation's Report Card. (2011). Mathematics results, 2009. Retrieved August 30, 2011, from the World Wide Web: http://nationsreportcard.gov/math_2009

Nelson, D., Joseph, G. C., & Williams, J. (1993). *Multicultural mathematics: Teaching mathematics from a global perspective*. New York: Oxford University Press.

Ortiz-Franco, L., Hernandez, N. G., & De La Cruz, Y. (Eds.). (1999). *Changing the faces of mathematics: Perspectives on Latinos*. Reston, VA: National Council of Teachers of Mathematics.

Pew Research Center. (2011). *Hispanic media: Faring better than mainstream media*. Retrieved August 31, 2011, from the World Wide Web: http://pewresearch.org/pubs/2093/spanish-language-media-hispanic-newspapers-television-radio-magazines-di

Potrikus, A. S. (2003, September 20). Girls surging past boys academically, new study says. *The Seattle Times*. Retrieved September 24, 2003, from the World Wide Web: http://seattletimes.nwsource.com/html/nationalworld/ 2001737939_read20.html

Salend, S. J. (1994). *Effective mainstreaming: Creating inclusive classrooms* (2nd ed.). New York: Macmillan.

Secada, W. G. (Ed.). (2000). *Changing the faces of mathematics: Perspectives on multiculturalism and gender equity*. Reston, VA: National Council of Teachers of Mathematics.

Secada, W. G., Fennema, E., & Adajian, L. B. (1994). *New directions for equity in mathematics education*. Reston, VA: National Council of Teachers of Mathematics.

Secada, W. G., Strutchens, M. E., Johnson, M. L., & Tate, W. F. (Eds.). (2000). *Changing the faces of mathematics: Perspectives on African Americans*. Reston, VA: National Council of Teachers of Mathematics.

Small, M. (2009). *Good questions: Great ways to differentiate mathematics instruction.* New York: Teachers College Press.

Strong, D. S., & Cobb, N. B. (2000). Algebra for all: It's a matter of equity, expectations, and effectiveness. In J. W. Lott (Ed.), Algebra? A gate! A barrier! A mystery!, *Mathematics Education Dialogues.*

Strutchens, M. E. (2000). Confronting beliefs and stereotypes that impede the mathematical empowerment of African American students. In M. E. Strutchens, M. L. Johnson, & W. F. Tate (Eds.), *Changing the faces of mathematics: Perspectives on African Americans* (pp. 1–14). Reston, VA: National Council of Teachers of Mathematics.

Strutchens, M. E., Johnson, M. L., & Tate, W. F. (Eds.). (2000). *Changing the faces of mathematics: Perspectives on African Americans.* Reston, VA: National Council of Teachers of Mathematics.

Tomlinson, C. A. (2005). Traveling the road to differentiation in staff development. *Journal of Staff Development, 26* (4).

Tomlinson, C. A. (1999). *The differentiated classroom: Responding to the needs of all learners.* Alexandria, VA: Association for Supervision and Curriculum Development.

Tomlinson, C. A. (1995). Differentiating instruction for advanced learners in the mixed-ability middle school classroom. Retrieved July 25, 2007, from the World Wide Web: http://www.kidsource.com/kidsource/content/diff_instruction.html

Thornton, C. A., & Bley, N. S. (Eds.). (1994). *Windows of opportunity: Mathematics for students with special needs.* Reston, VA: National Council of Teachers of Mathematics.

Thurlow, M. (2002). Accommodations for students with disabilities in high school. *National Center on Secondary Education and Transition Issue Brief, 1* (1), 1–7.

Trentacosta, J. (Ed.). (1997). *1997 Yearbook of the NCTM: Multicultural and gender equity in the mathematics classroom: The gift of diversity.* Reston, VA: National Council of Teachers of Mathematics.

Trumbull, E., Nelson-Barber, S., & Mitchell, J. (2002). Enhancing mathematics instruction for indigenous American students. In J. E. Hankes & G. R. Fast (Eds.), *Changing the faces of mathematics: Perspectives on indigenous people of North America* (pp. 1–18). Reston, VA: National Council of Teachers of Mathematics.

U.S. Department of Education. (2010). *Digest of education statistics, 2010.* Washington, DC: U.S. Department of Education, National Center for Education Statistics.

U.S. Department of Education. (2009). *Assisting students struggling with mathematics: Response to intervention (RtI) for elementary and middle schools.* Washington, DC: Institute of Education Sciences.

U.S. Department of Education. (2001). *Twenty-third annual report to Congress on the implementation of the Individuals with Disabilities Education Act.* Jessup, MD: Education Publications Center.

Vogt, M., & Echevarria, J. (2007). *99 ideas and activities for teaching English learners with the SIOP model.* Boston, MA: Allyn & Bacon.

Vogt, M., & Echevarria, J. (2006). *Teaching ideas for implementing the SIOP model.* Santa Monica, CA: Pearson Achievement Solutions.

Wagner, M., Newman, L., Cameto, R., Levine, P., & Marder, C. (2003). *Going to school: Instructional contexts, programs, and participation of secondary school students with disabilities.* Menlo Park, CA: U.S. Office of Special Education Programs.

Wright, C. C. (1996). *Learning disabilities in mathematics.* Retrieved September 24, 2003, from the World Wide Web: http://www.Ldonline.org/ld_indepth/math_skills/math-1.html

You, Z. (2010). Gender differences in mathematics learning. *School Science and Mathematics, 110* (3), 115–117.

Chapter 13

Aichele, D. B. (Ed.). (1994). *1994 Yearbook of the NCTM: Professional development for teachers of mathematics.* Reston, VA: National Council of Teachers of Mathematics.

American Association of Colleges of Teacher Education. (2011). *Experts anticipate national Teacher Performanced Assessment.* Retrieved August 29, 2011, from the World Wide Web: http://aacte.org/index.php?/Media-Center/AACTE-in-the-News/experts-anticipate-national-teacher-performance-assessment.html

Ball, D. L. (1993). With an eye on the mathematical horizon: Dilemmas of teaching elementary school mathematics. *Elementary School Journal, 93* (4), 373–397.

Bell, C. A., Wilson, S., Higgins, T., & McCoach, D. B. (2010). Measuring the effects of professional development on teacher knowledge: The case of developing mathematical ideas. *Journal for Research in Mathematics Education, 41* (5), 479–512.

Chambers, D. L., & Hankes, J. E. (1994). Using knowledge of children's thinking to change teaching. In D. B. Aichele (Ed.), *1994 Yearbook of the NCTM: Professional development for teachers of mathematics* (pp. 286–295). Reston, VA: National Council of Teachers of Mathematics.

Clark, J. (1996). Involving parents in the middle school. *Teaching PreK–8, 27* (3), 52–53.

College Board. (2003). *SAT verbal and math scores up significantly as a record-breaking number of students take the test: Average math score at highest level in more than 35 years.* Retrieved August 26, 2003, from the World Wide Web: http://www.collegeboard.com/press

Driscoll, M., & Lord, B. (1990). Professionals in a changing profession. In T. J. Cooney (Ed.), *1990 Yearbook of the NCTM: Teaching and learning mathematics in the 1990s* (pp. 237–245). Reston, VA: National Council of Teachers of Mathematics.

Dwyer, C. A. (1998). Psychometrics of Praxis III: Classroom performance assessments. *Journal of Personnel Evaluation in Education, 12* (2), 163–187.

Eckmier, J., & Bunyan, R. (1995). Mentor teachers: Key to educational renewal. *Educational Horizons, 73* (3), 124–129.

Educational Testing Service (ETS). (2003). *Praxis III: Classroom performance assessments.* Retrieved August 28, 2003, from the World Wide Web: http://www.ets.org/praxis/prxaboutIII.html

Eisenhower National Clearinghouse. (1998). Family involvement in education. *ENC Focus, 5* (3).

Epstein, J. L., & Hollifield, J. H. (1996). Title I and school–family–community partnerships: Using research to realize the potential. *Journal of Education for Students Placed at Risk, 1* (3), 263–278.

Fennema, E., & Franke, M. L. (1992). Teachers' knowledge and its impact. In D. A. Grouws (Ed.), *Handbook of research on mathematics teaching and learning* (pp. 147–164). Reston, VA: National Council of Teachers of Mathematics.

Ganser, T. (1996). Mentor roles: Views of participants in a state-mandated program. *Midwestern Educational Research, 9* (2), 15–20.

Heck, D. J., Banilower, E. R., Weiss, I. R., & Rosenberg, S. L. (2008). Studying the effects of professional development: The case of the NSF's local systemic change through teacher enhancement initiative. *Journal for Research in Mathematics Education, 39* (2), 113–152.

Kanter, P. F. (1992). *Helping your child learn math.* Washington, DC: U.S. Department of Education (Office of Educational Research and Improvement).

Licklinder, B. L., et al. (1996). Cooperative learning: Staff development for teacher preparation. *Schools in the Middle, 6* (1), 33–36.

Lord, W. J. (1996). Professional preparation: Implications for teachers and principals. *Schools in the Middle, 6* (1), 37–39.

Lovitt, C., Stephens, M., Clarke, D., & Romberg, T. A. (1990). Mathematics teachers reconceptualizing their roles. In T. J. Cooney (Ed.), *1990 Yearbook of the NCTM: Teaching and learning mathematics in the 1990s* (pp. 229–236). Reston, VA: National Council of Teachers of Mathematics.

Miller, L. D., & Hunt, N. P. (1994). Professional development through action research. In D. B. Aichele (Ed.), *1994 Yearbook of the NCTM: Professional development for teachers of mathematics* (pp. 296–303). Reston, VA: National Council of Teachers of Mathematics.

Moss, P. A., Schutz, A. M., & Collins, K. M. (1998). An integrative approach to portfolio evaluations for teacher licensure. *Journal of Personnel Evaluation in Education, 12* (2), 139–161.

Nassau, C. D. (1995). The seventh-year stretch. *American School Board Journal, 182* (11), 30–32.

National Clearinghouse for Comprehensive School Reform. (2003). *Step by step: Creating a professional development plan.* Retrieved August 29, 2003, from the World Wide Web: http://www.goodschools.gwu.edu/sbs/CPDP.html

National Council of Teachers of Mathematics. (2007). *Mathematics teaching today: Improving practice, improving student learning* (2nd ed.; T. Martin, Ed.). Reston, VA: National Council of Teachers of Mathematics.

National Council of Teachers of Mathematics. (2003a). *Illuminations Web site.* Retrieved August 29, 2003, from the World Wide Web: http://illuminations.nctm.org

National Council of Teachers of Mathematics. (2003b). *Reflections Web site.* Retrieved August 29, 2003, from the World Wide Web: http://www.nctm.org/eresources/reflections/index.htm

National Council of Teachers of Mathematics. (2000). *Principles and standards for school mathematics.* Reston, VA: National Council of Teachers of Mathematics.

National Council of Teachers of Mathematics. (1995). *Assessment standards for school mathematics.* Reston, VA: National Council of Teachers of Mathematics.

National Council of Teachers of Mathematics. (1991). *Professional standards for teaching mathematics.* Reston, VA: National Council of Teachers of Mathematics.

National Council of Teachers of Mathematics. (1989). *Curriculum and evaluation standards for school mathematics.* Reston, VA: National Council of Teachers of Mathematics.

Nolder, R., & Johnson, D. (1995). Professional development. Bringing teachers to the centre of the stage. *Mathematics in School, 24* (1), 32–36.

North Carolina Public Schools. (2003). The INTASC Standards. Retrieved August 28, 2003, from the World Wide Web: http://licensurepublic.dpi.state.nc.us/.../Form%20IS-C%20INTASC%20Standards

Patall, E. A., Cooper, H., & Robinson, J. C. (2008). Parent involvement in homework: A research synthesis. *Review of Educational Research, 78* (4), 1039–1101.

Price, J. (1995). Selling and buying reform: If we build it, will they come? *Mathematics Teacher, 88* (6), 532–534.

Roschelle, J., Shechtman, N., Tatar, D., Hegedus, S., Hopkins, B., Empson, S., Knudsen, J., & Gallagher, L. (2010). Integration of technology, curriculum, and professional development for advancing middle school mathematics: Three large-scale studies. *American Educational Research Journal, 47* (4), 833–878.

Schoenfeld, A. H. (1998). On theory and models: The case of teaching-in-context. In S. Berenson, K. Dawkins, M. Blanton, W. Coulombe, J. Kolb, K. Norwood, & L. Stiff (Eds.), *Proceedings of the Twentieth Annual Meeting of the North American Chapter of the International Group for the Psychology of Mathematics Education* (pp. 27–38). Columbus, OH: ERIC Clearinghouse for Science, Mathematics, and Environmental Education.

Sherman, H. J., & Jaeger, T. (1995). Professional development: Teachers' communication and collaboration—Keys to student achievement. *Mathematics Teaching in the Middle School, 1* (6), 454–458.

Silver, E. A., & Kilpatrick, J. (1994). E Pluribus Unum: Challenges of diversity in the future of mathematics education research. *Journal for Research in Mathematics Education, 25* (6), 734–754.

Sirvani, H. (2007). The effect of teacher communication with parents on students' mathematics achievement. *American Secondary Education, 36* (1), 31–46.

Stenmark, J. K., Thompson, V., & Cossey, R. (1986). *Family math.* Berkeley, CA: Lawrence Hall of Science.

Tanner, B., et al. (1995). Scheduling time to maximize staff development opportunities. *Journal of Staff Development, 16* (4), 14–19.

Taylor, R. (Ed.). (1986). *Professional development for teachers of mathematics: A handbook.* Reston, VA: National Council of Teachers of Mathematics: National Council of Supervisors of Mathematics.

Texley, J. (1996). Mentor roles: Views of participants in a state-mandated program. *Midwestern Educational Researcher, 9* (2), 15–20.

U.S. Department of Education. (2000). *Before it's too late: A report to the nation from the National Commission on Mathematics and Science Teaching for the Twenty-First Century.* Washington, DC: U.S. Department of Education.

Index